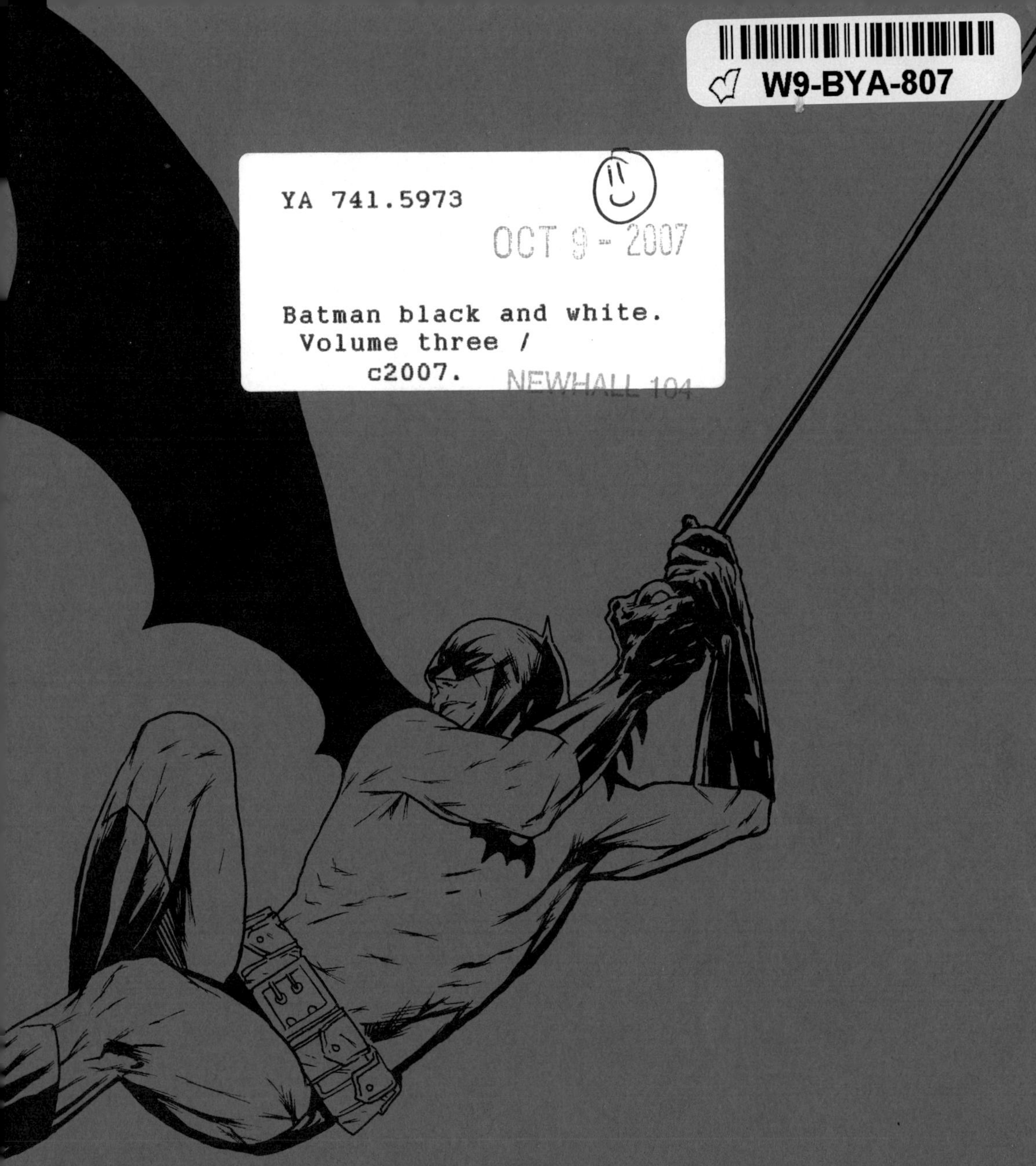

# BATMAN BLACK and WHITE

V O L U M E   T H R E E

WRITERS

DOUG **ALEXANDER**
MARK **ASKWITH**
BRIAN **AZZARELLO**
MIKE W. **BARR**
ED **BRUBAKER**
MIKE **CAREY**
MIKE **CARLIN**
ERIC **CHERRY**
DARWYN **COOKE**
TODD **DEZAGO**
DANIELLE **DWYER**
ALEX **GARLAND**
MICHAEL **GOLDEN**
PAUL **GRIST**
GEOFF **JOHNS**
JOE **KELLEY**
PAUL **KUPPERBERG**
DWAYNE **MCDUFFIE**
DON **MCGREGOR**
MICK **MCMAHON** AND DAVE **GIBBONS**
MIKE **MIGNOLA** AND TROY **NIXEY**
DEAN **MOTTER**
ANN **NOCENTI**
JOHN **OSTRANDER**
SCOTT **PETERSON**
WILL **PFEIFER**
ROBERT **RODI**
MARK **SCHULTZ**
JULIUS **SCHWARTZ** AND **DAN RASPLER**
KIMO **TEMPERANCE**
JILL **THOMPSON**
CYRUS **VORIS**
JUDD **WINICK**

ILLUSTRATORS

CHRISTIAN **ALAMY**
BRENT **ANDERSON**
CHRIS **BACHALO**
JOHN **BOLTON**
PHILIP **BOND**
CLAUDIO **CASTELLINI**
TOMMY **CASTILLO** AND RODNEY **RAMOS**
ERIC **CHERRY**
DARWYN **COOKE**
DENYS **COWAN**
ALAN **DAVIS** AND MARK **FARMER**
DAN **DECARLO** AND TERRY **AUSTIN**
NATHAN **FOX**
DICK **GIORDANO**
ROB **HAYNES**
MICHAEL WILLIAM **KALUTA**
JIM **MAHFOOD**
STEVE **MANNION** AND HILARY **BARTA**
MICK **MCMAHON**
SCOTT **MORSE**
DEAN **MOTTER**
TROY **NIXEY** (WITH DAVE **STEWART**)
JASON **PEARSON**
SEAN **PHILLIPS**
WHILCE **PORTACIO** AND SAL **REGLA**
JON **PROCTOR** AND JOHN **FLOYD**
RYAN **SOOK**
JILL **THOMPSON**
JOHN **WATKISS**
AARON **WEISENFELD**
MIKE **WIERINGO** AND KARL **STORY**
BILL **WRAY**
DANIJEL **ZEZELJ**

LETTERERS

JANICE **CHIANG**
**COMICRAFT**
DARWYN **COOKE**
JOHN **COSTANZA**
KURT **HATHAWAY**
TODD **KLEIN**
SEAN **KONOT**
KEN **LOPEZ**
JACK **MORELLI**
NICK J. **NAPOLITANO**
BILL **OAKLEY**
RICK **PARKER**
SEAN **PHILLIPS**
PAT **PRENTICE**
CLEM **ROBINS**
WILLIE **SCHUBERT**
RICHARD **STARKINGS**

FRANK **MILLER**
COVER ILLUSTRATION

BAT
BL
W

B A T M A N C R

AN

ACK

and

HITE

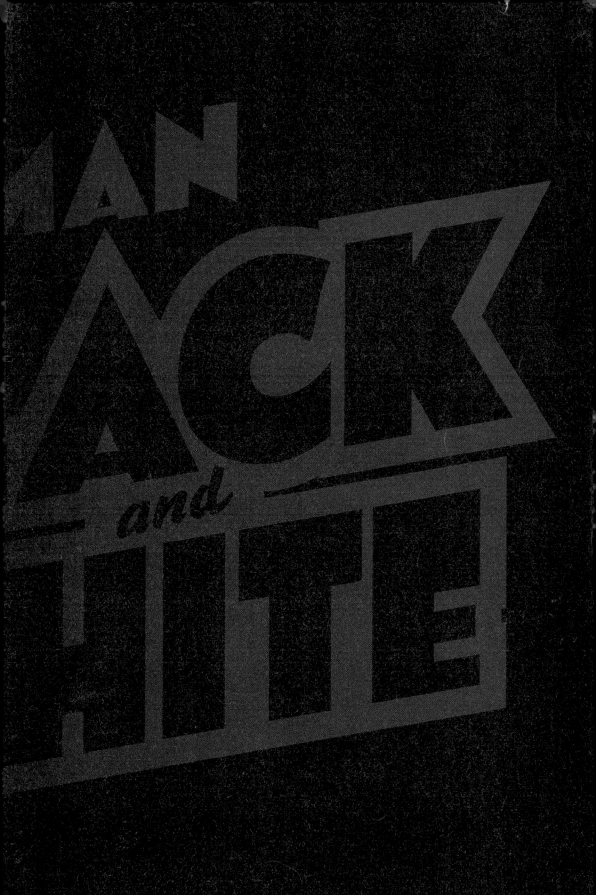

ATED BY BOB KANE

**DAN DIDIO** SENIOR VP-EXECUTIVE EDITOR

**MARK CHIARELLO MICHAEL WRIGHT BOB SCHRECK MORGAN DONTANVILLE LYSA HAWKINS MATT IDELSON** EDITORS-ORIGINAL SERIES
**VALERIE D'ORAZIO NACHIE CASTRO** ASSISTANT EDITORS-ORIGINAL SERIES
**ANTON KAWASAKI** EDITOR-COLLECTED EDITION **ROBBIN BROSTERMAN** SENIOR ART DIRECTOR
**PAUL LEVITZ** PRESIDENT & PUBLISHER **GEORG BREWER** VP-DESIGN & DC DIRECT CREATIVE
**RICHARD BRUNING** SENIOR VP-CREATIVE DIRECTOR **PATRICK CALDON** EXECUTIVE VP-FINANCE & OPERATIONS
**CHRIS CARAMALIS** VP-FINANCE **JOHN CUNNINGHAM** VP-MARKETING
**TERRI CUNNINGHAM** VP-MANAGING EDITOR **ALISON GILL** VP-MANUFACTURING
**HANK KANALZ** VP-GENERAL MANAGER, WILDSTORM **JIM LEE** EDITORIAL DIRECTOR-WILDSTORM
**PAULA LOWITT** SENIOR VP-BUSINESS & LEGAL AFFAIRS **MARYELLEN MCLAUGHLIN** VP-ADVERTISING & CUSTOM PUBLISHING
**JOHN NEE** VP-BUSINESS DEVELOPMENT **GREGORY NOVECK** SENIOR VP-CREATIVE AFFAIRS
**SUE POHJA** VP-BOOK TRADE SALES **CHERYL RUBIN** SENIOR VP-BRAND MANAGEMENT
**JEFF TROJAN** VP-BUSINESS DEVELOPMENT, DC DIRECT **BOB WAYNE** VP-SALES

Cover illustration by Frank Miller.

B A T M A N   B L A C K   A N D   W H I T E   VOLUME THREE

Published by DC Comics. Cover, text, and compilation copyright © 2007 DC Comics. All Rights Reserved.

Originally published in single magazine form in BATMAN: GOTHAM KNIGHTS #17-49. Copyright © 2001, 2002, 2003, 2004 DC Comics. All Rights Reserved.
All characters, their distinctive likenesses and related elements featured in this publication are trademarks of DC Comics.
The stories, characters and incidents featured in this publication are entirely fictional.
DC Comics does not read or accept unsolicited submissions of ideas, stories or artwork.

DC Comics, 1700 Broadway, New York, NY 10019
A Warner Bros. Entertainment Company
Printed in Canada. First Printing.
ISBN HC: 1-4012-1531-9  ISBN HC: 978-1-4012-1531-6  ISBN SC: 1-4012-1354-5  ISBN SC: 978-1-4012-1354-1

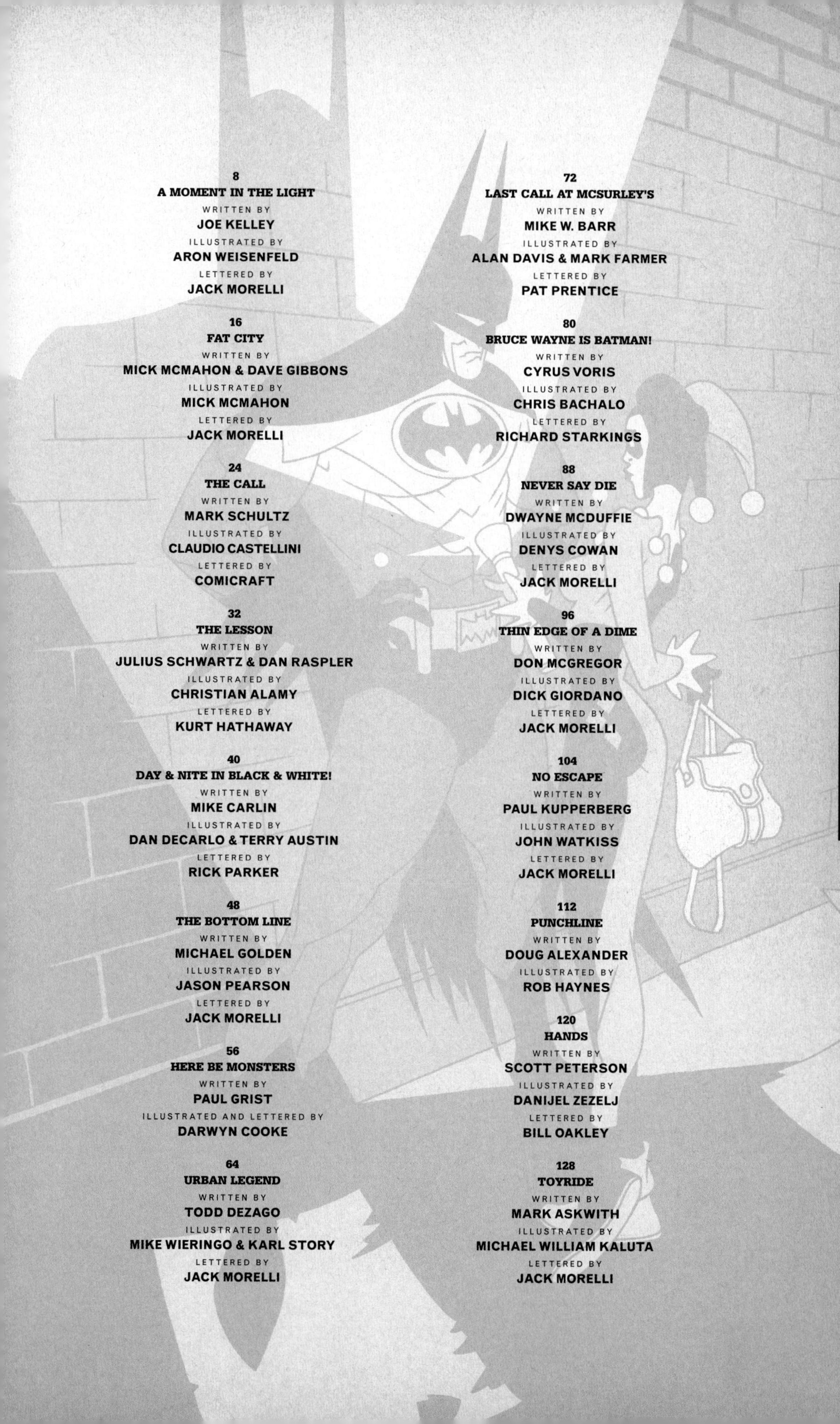

# CONTENTS

# CONTENTS

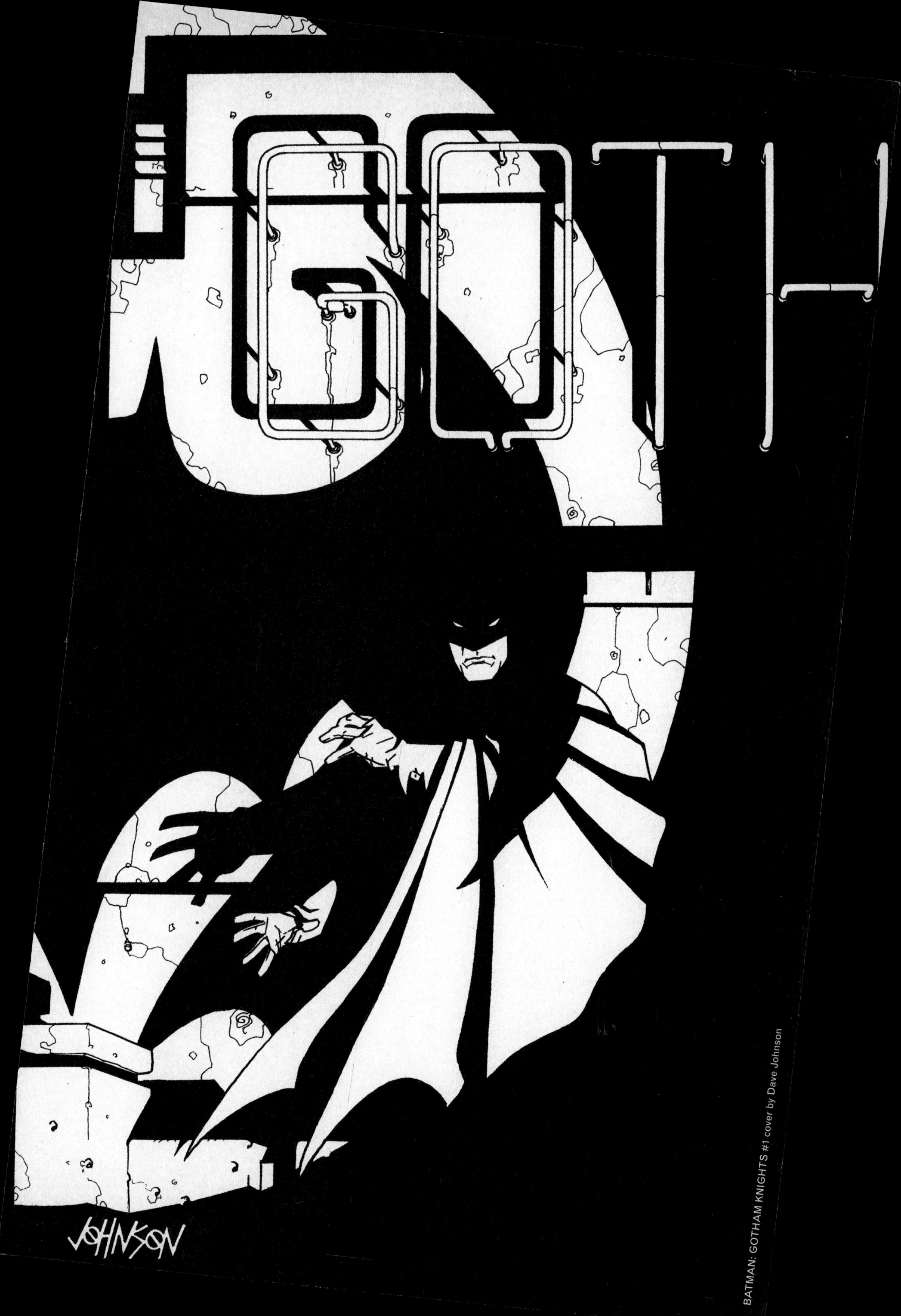
GOTH
JOHNSON

BATMAN: GOTHAM KNIGHTS #1 cover by Dave Johnson

# A MOMENT IN THE LIGHT

JOE KELLY – WRITER
ARON WIESENFELD – ARTIST
JACK MORELLI – LETTERER
MARK CHIARELLO – EDITOR

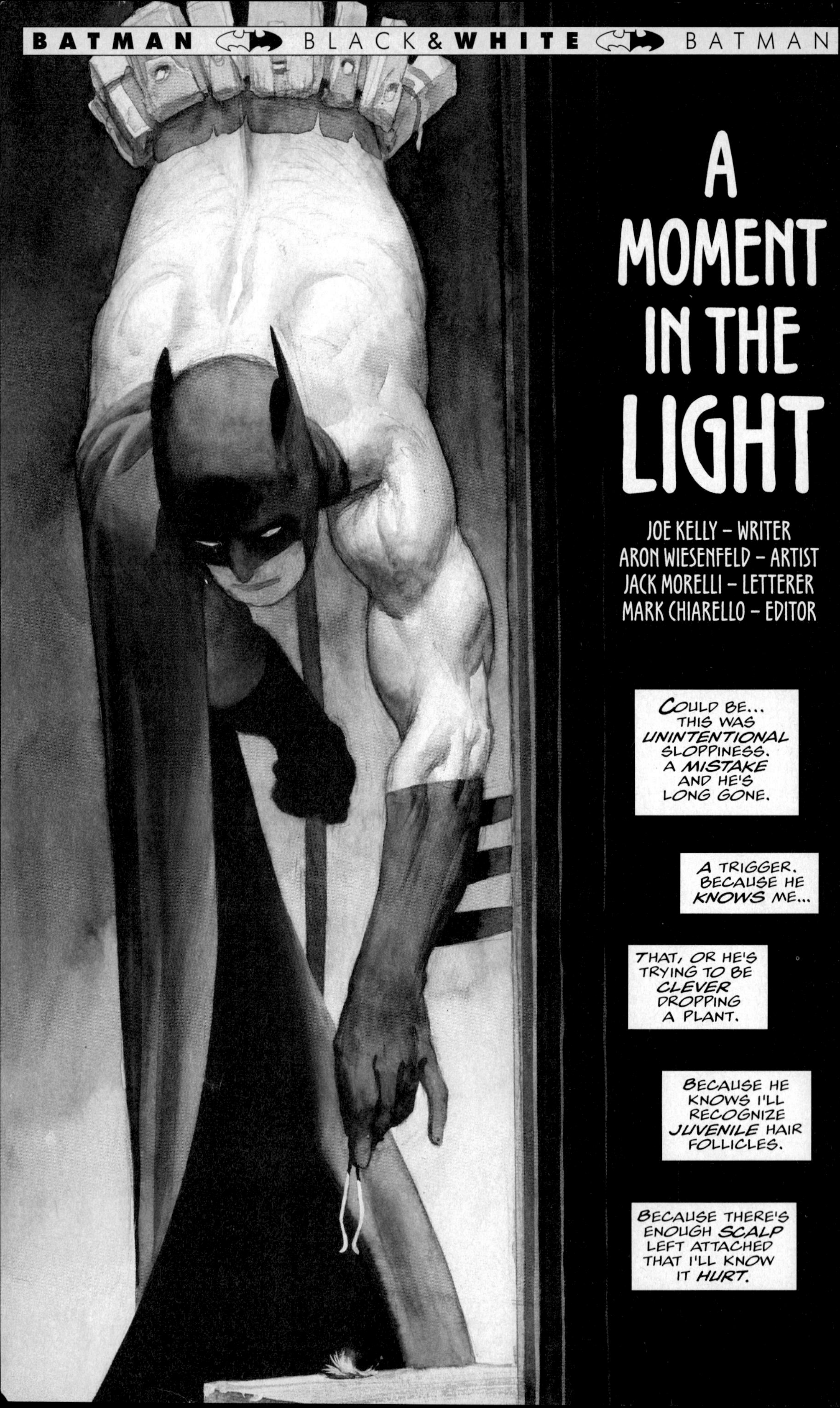
COULD BE... THIS WAS UNINTENTIONAL SLOPPINESS. A MISTAKE AND HE'S LONG GONE.
A TRIGGER. BECAUSE HE KNOWS ME...
THAT, OR HE'S TRYING TO BE CLEVER DROPPING A PLANT.
BECAUSE HE KNOWS I'LL RECOGNIZE JUVENILE HAIR FOLLICLES.
BECAUSE THERE'S ENOUGH SCALP LEFT ATTACHED THAT I'LL KNOW IT HURT.

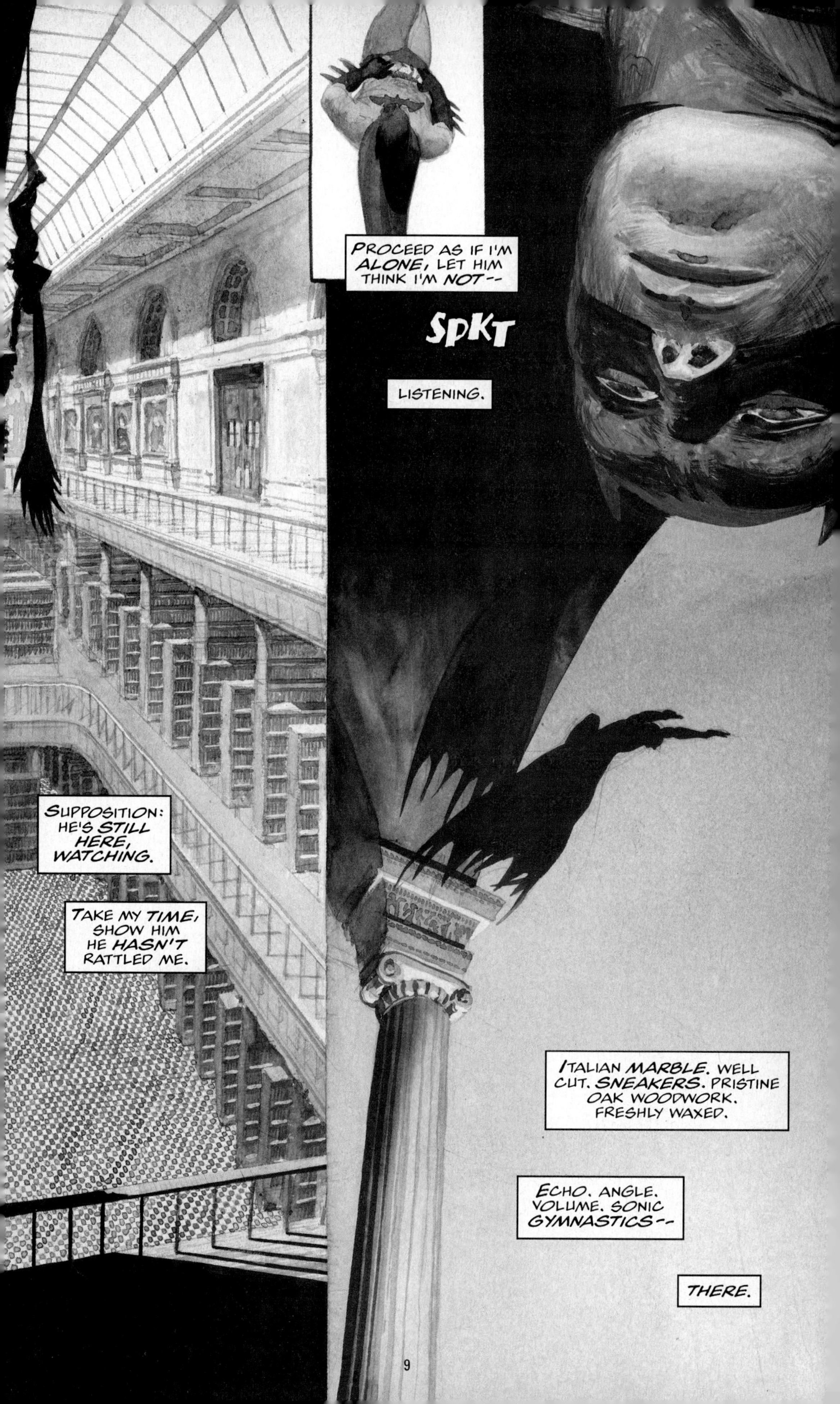
SUPPOSITION: HE'S STILL HERE, WATCHING.
TAKE MY TIME, SHOW HIM HE HASN'T RATTLED ME.
PROCEED AS IF I'M ALONE, LET HIM THINK I'M NOT--
SPKT
LISTENING.
ITALIAN MARBLE. WELL CUT. SNEAKERS. PRISTINE OAK WOODWORK. FRESHLY WAXED.
ECHO. ANGLE. VOLUME. SONIC GYMNASTICS--
THERE.

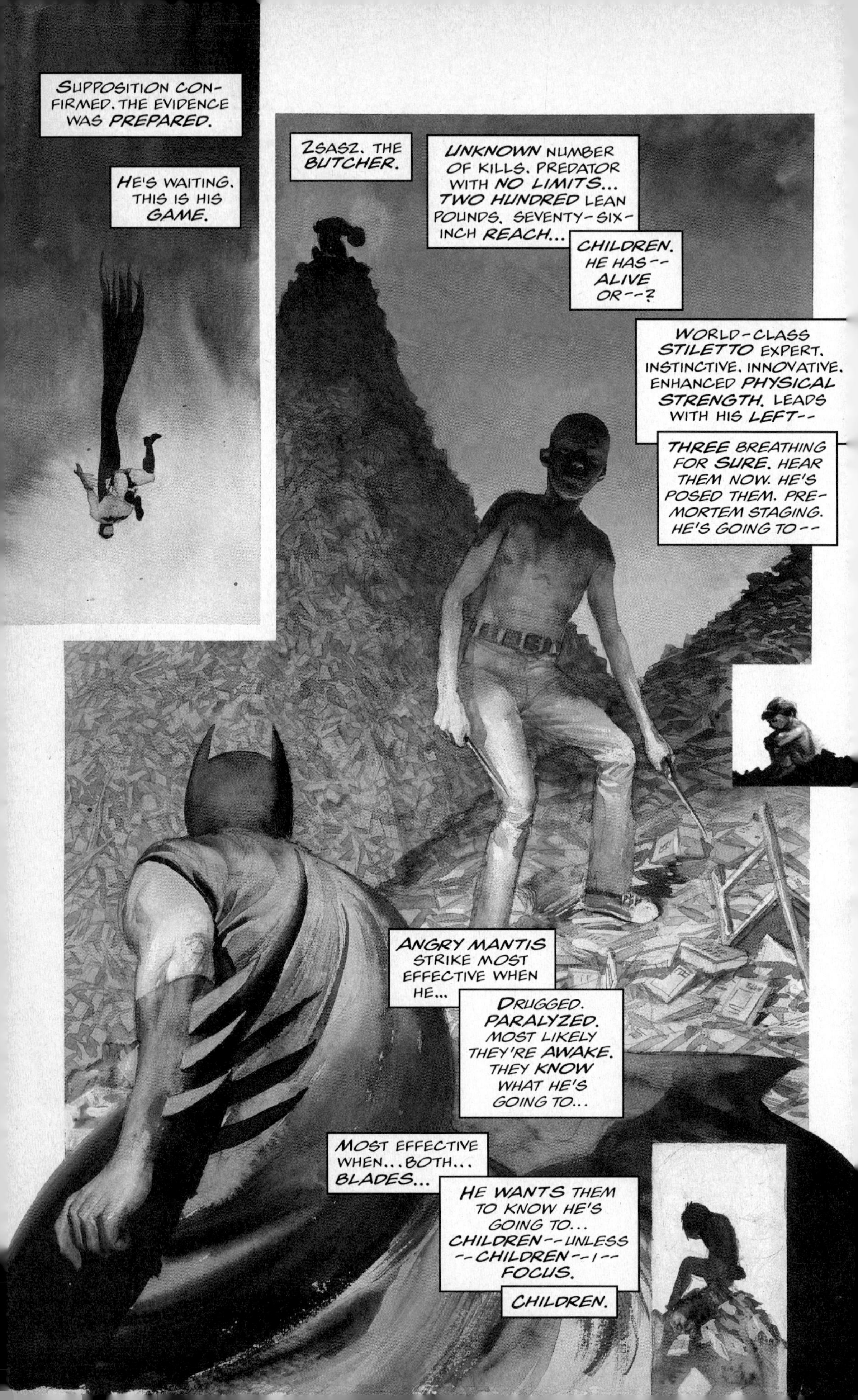
SUPPOSITION CONFIRMED. THE EVIDENCE WAS PREPARED.
HE'S WAITING. THIS IS HIS GAME.
ZSASZ. THE BUTCHER.
UNKNOWN NUMBER OF KILLS. PREDATOR WITH NO LIMITS... TWO HUNDRED LEAN POUNDS. SEVENTY-SIX-INCH REACH...
CHILDREN. HE HAS-- ALIVE OR--?
WORLD-CLASS STILETTO EXPERT. INSTINCTIVE. INNOVATIVE. ENHANCED PHYSICAL STRENGTH. LEADS WITH HIS LEFT--
THREE BREATHING FOR SURE. HEAR THEM NOW. HE'S POSED THEM. PRE-MORTEM STAGING. HE'S GOING TO--
ANGRY MANTIS STRIKE MOST EFFECTIVE WHEN HE...
DRUGGED. PARALYZED. MOST LIKELY THEY'RE AWAKE. THEY KNOW WHAT HE'S GOING TO...
MOST EFFECTIVE WHEN...BOTH... BLADES...
HE WANTS THEM TO KNOW HE'S GOING TO... CHILDREN--UNLESS --CHILDREN--I-- FOCUS.
CHILDREN.

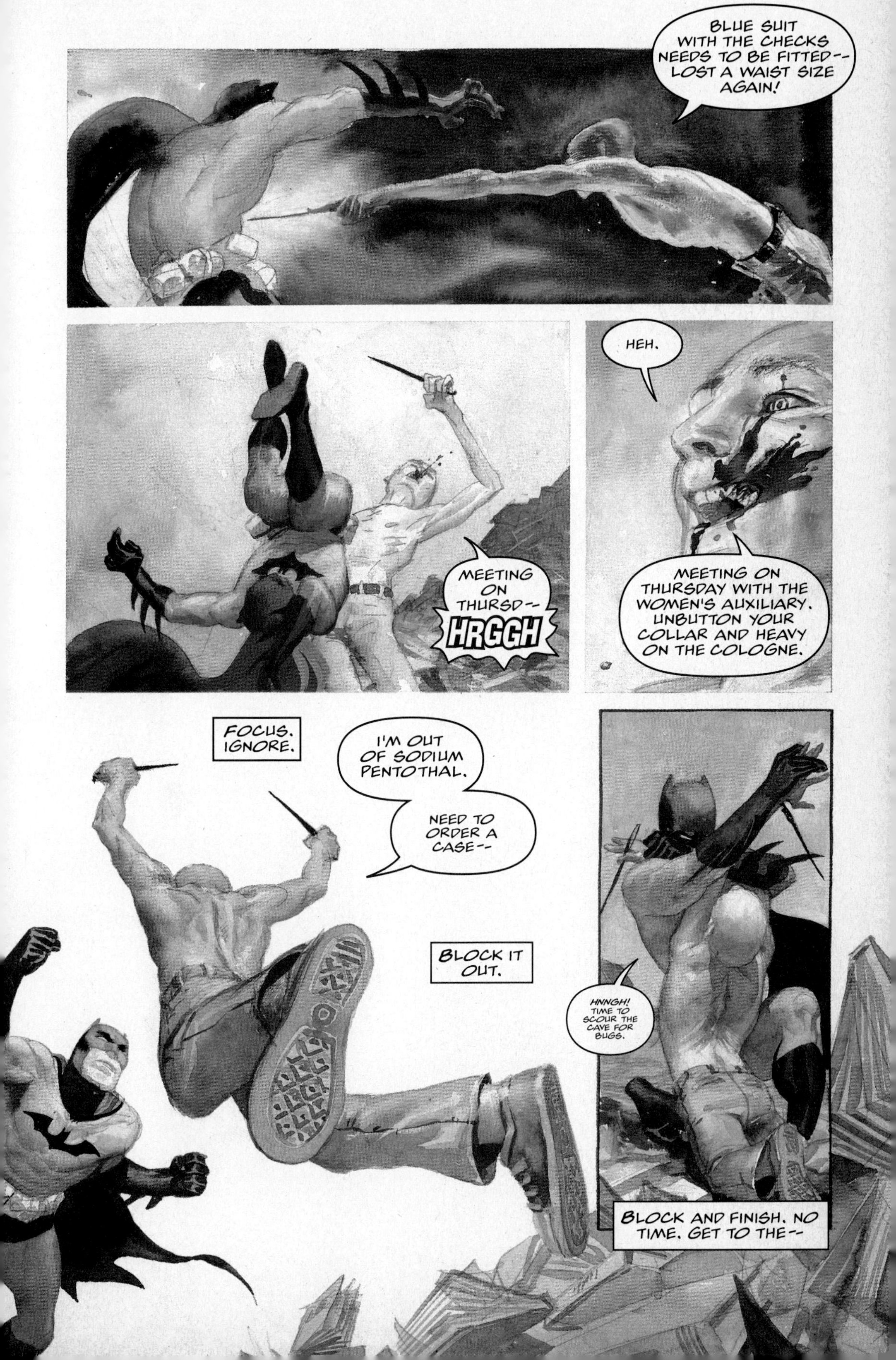
BLUE SUIT WITH THE CHECKS NEEDS TO BE FITTED--LOST A WAIST SIZE AGAIN!
MEETING ON THURSD--
HRGGH
HEH.
MEETING ON THURSDAY WITH THE WOMEN'S AUXILIARY. UNBUTTON YOUR COLLAR AND HEAVY ON THE COLOGNE.
FOCUS. IGNORE.
I'M OUT OF SODIUM PENTOTHAL.
NEED TO ORDER A CASE--
BLOCK IT OUT.
HNNGH! TIME TO SCOUR THE CAVE FOR BUGS.
BLOCK AND FINISH. NO TIME. GET TO THE--

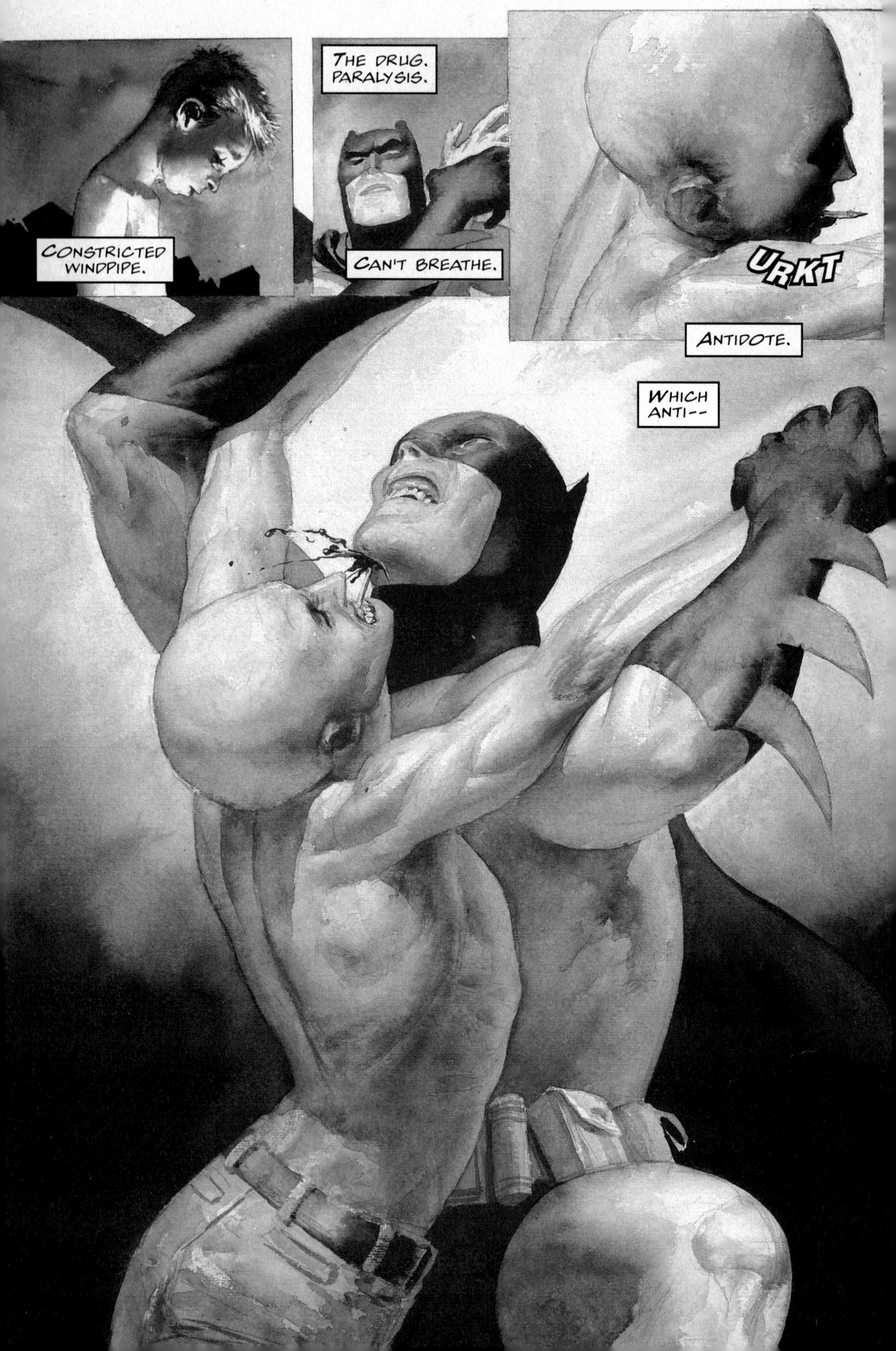
CONSTRICTED WINDPIPE.
THE DRUG. PARALYSIS.
CAN'T BREATHE.
URKT
ANTIDOTE.
WHICH ANTI--

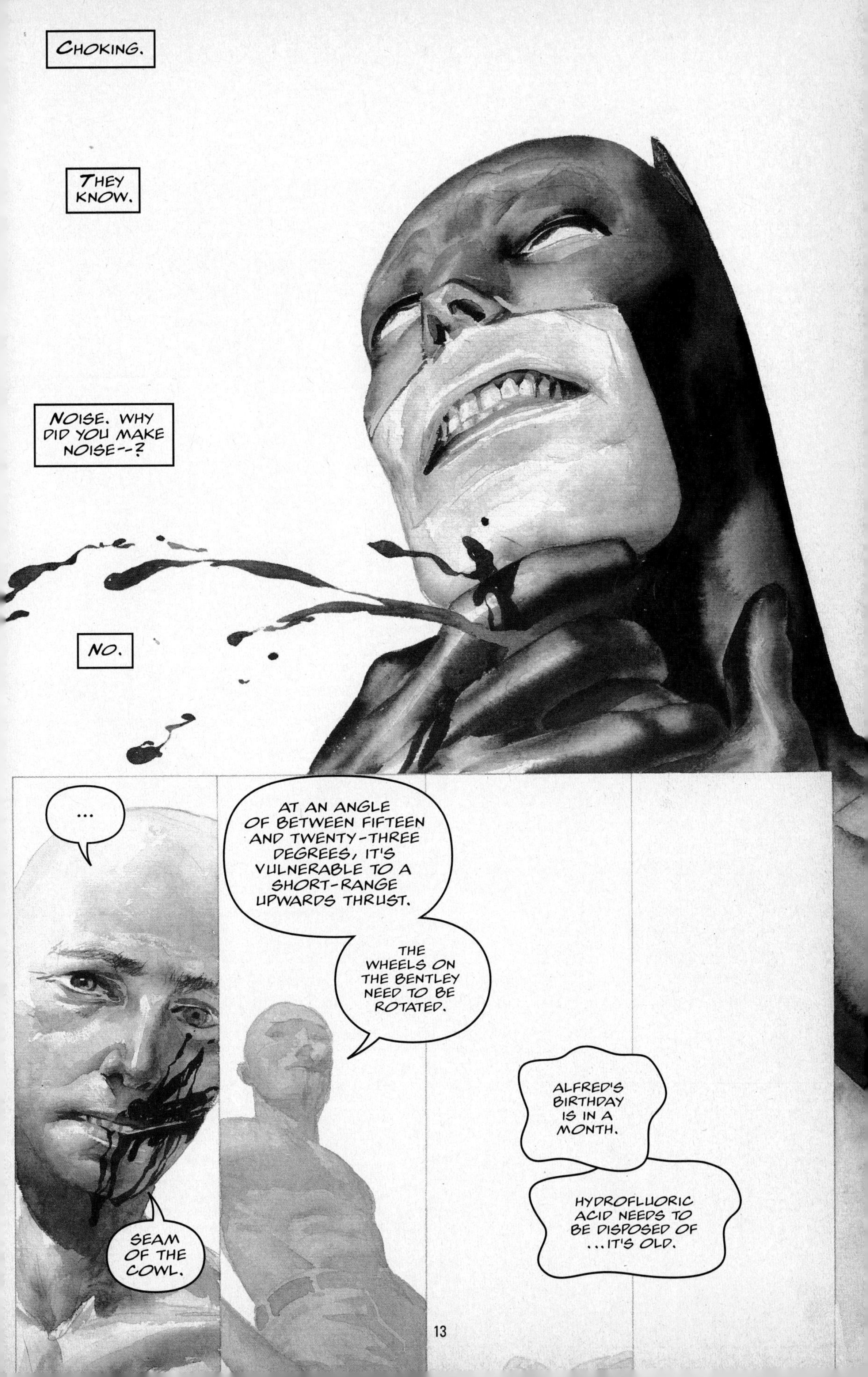
CHOKING.
THEY KNOW.
NOISE. WHY DID YOU MAKE NOISE--?
NO.
...
SEAM OF THE COWL.
AT AN ANGLE OF BETWEEN FIFTEEN AND TWENTY-THREE DEGREES, IT'S VULNERABLE TO A SHORT-RANGE UPWARDS THRUST.
THE WHEELS ON THE BENTLEY NEED TO BE ROTATED.
ALFRED'S BIRTHDAY IS IN A MONTH.
HYDROFLUORIC ACID NEEDS TO BE DISPOSED OF ...IT'S OLD.

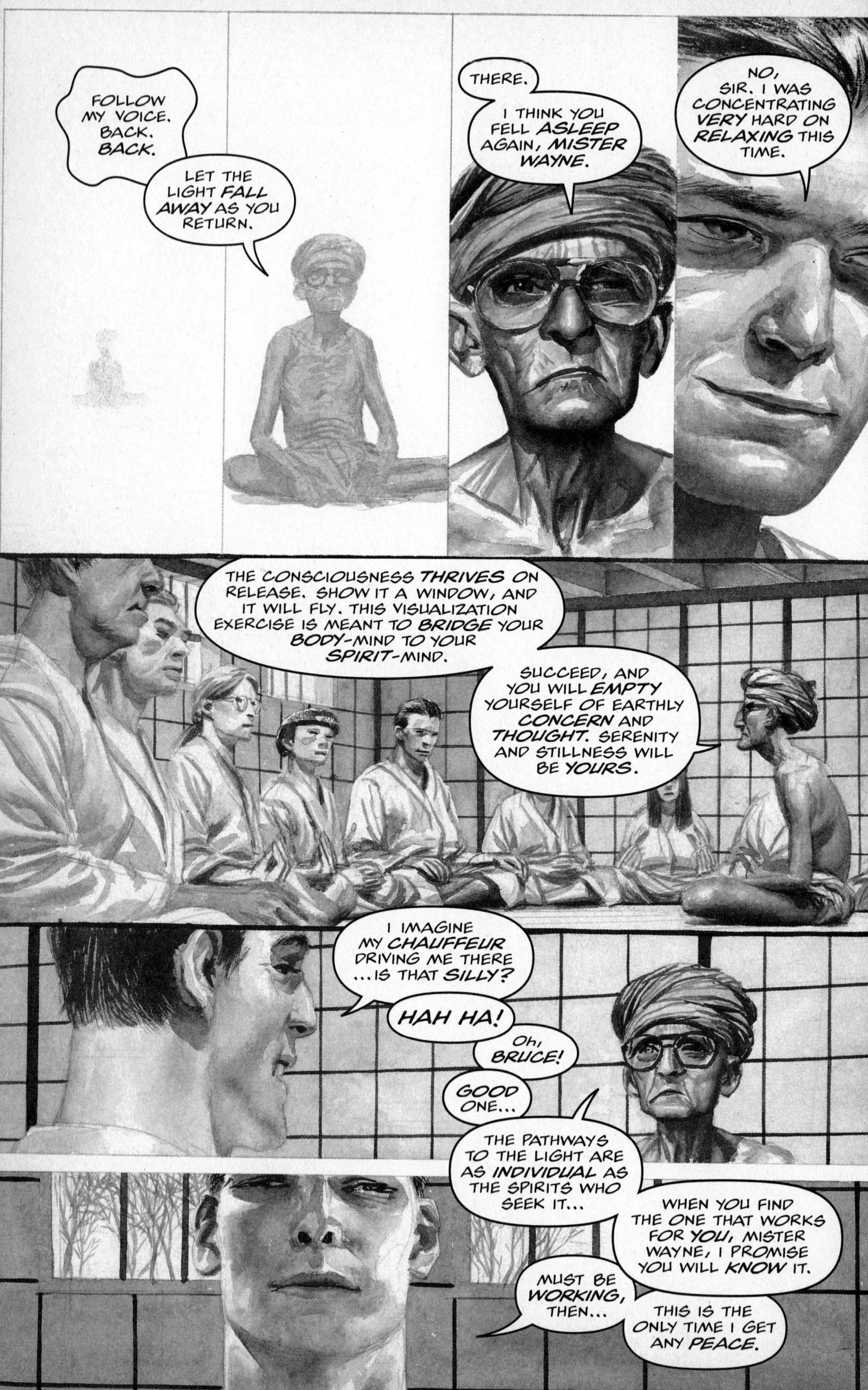
FOLLOW MY VOICE. BACK. BACK.
LET THE LIGHT FALL AWAY AS YOU RETURN.
THERE.
I THINK YOU FELL ASLEEP AGAIN, MISTER WAYNE.
NO, SIR. I WAS CONCENTRATING VERY HARD ON RELAXING THIS TIME.
THE CONSCIOUSNESS THRIVES ON RELEASE. SHOW IT A WINDOW, AND IT WILL FLY. THIS VISUALIZATION EXERCISE IS MEANT TO BRIDGE YOUR BODY-MIND TO YOUR SPIRIT-MIND.
SUCCEED, AND YOU WILL EMPTY YOURSELF OF EARTHLY CONCERN AND THOUGHT. SERENITY AND STILLNESS WILL BE YOURS.
I IMAGINE MY CHAUFFEUR DRIVING ME THERE ...IS THAT SILLY?
HAH HA!
Oh, BRUCE!
GOOD ONE...
THE PATHWAYS TO THE LIGHT ARE AS INDIVIDUAL AS THE SPIRITS WHO SEEK IT...
WHEN YOU FIND THE ONE THAT WORKS FOR YOU, MISTER WAYNE, I PROMISE YOU WILL KNOW IT.
MUST BE WORKING, THEN...
THIS IS THE ONLY TIME I GET ANY PEACE.

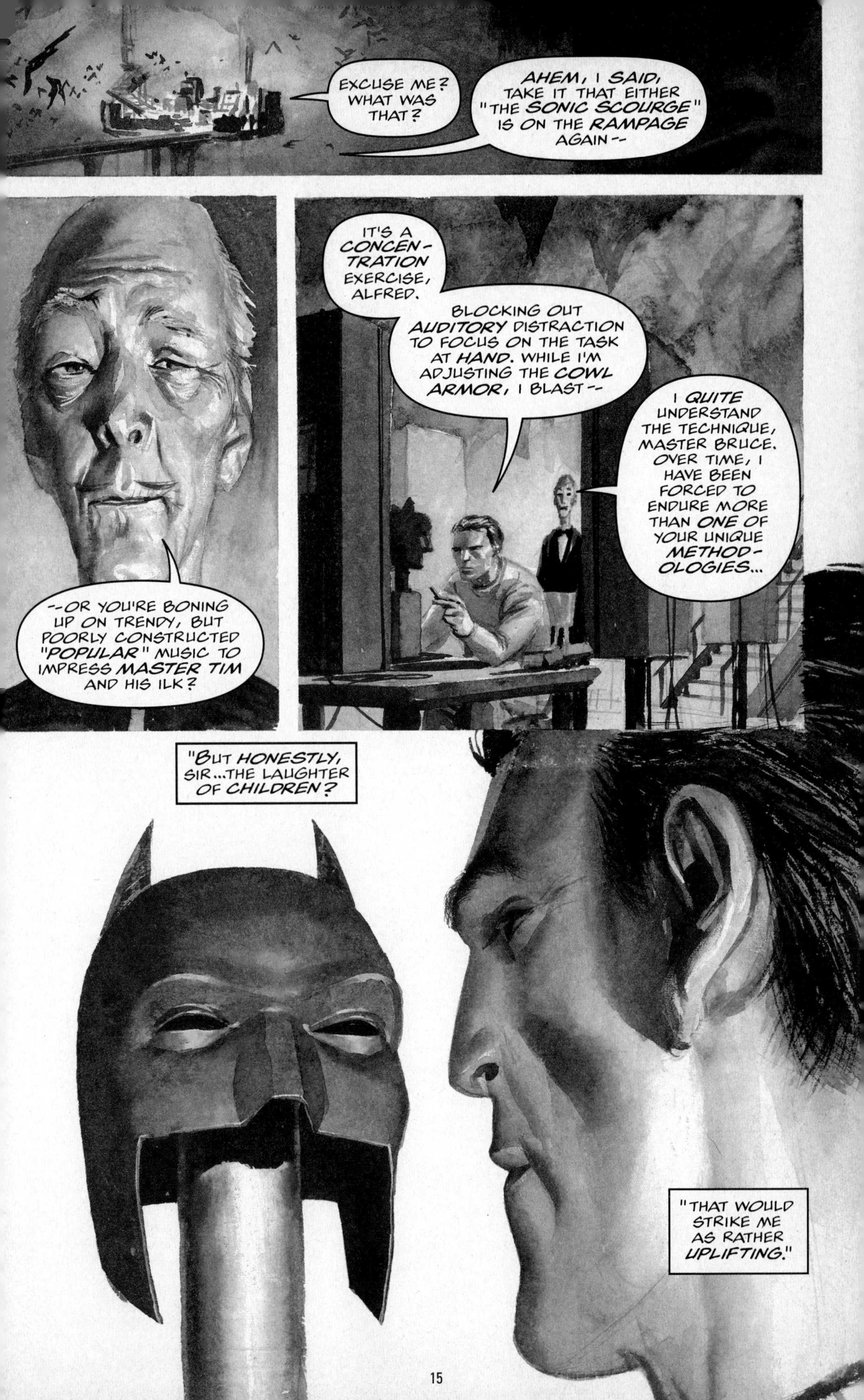
EXCUSE ME? WHAT WAS THAT?
AHEM, I SAID, TAKE IT THAT EITHER "THE SONIC SCOURGE" IS ON THE RAMPAGE AGAIN--
--OR YOU'RE BONING UP ON TRENDY, BUT POORLY CONSTRUCTED "POPULAR" MUSIC TO IMPRESS MASTER TIM AND HIS ILK?
IT'S A CONCEN-TRATION EXERCISE, ALFRED.
BLOCKING OUT AUDITORY DISTRACTION TO FOCUS ON THE TASK AT HAND. WHILE I'M ADJUSTING THE COWL ARMOR, I BLAST--
I QUITE UNDERSTAND THE TECHNIQUE, MASTER BRUCE. OVER TIME, I HAVE BEEN FORCED TO ENDURE MORE THAN ONE OF YOUR UNIQUE METHOD-OLOGIES...
"BUT HONESTLY, SIR...THE LAUGHTER OF CHILDREN?
"THAT WOULD STRIKE ME AS RATHER UPLIFTING."

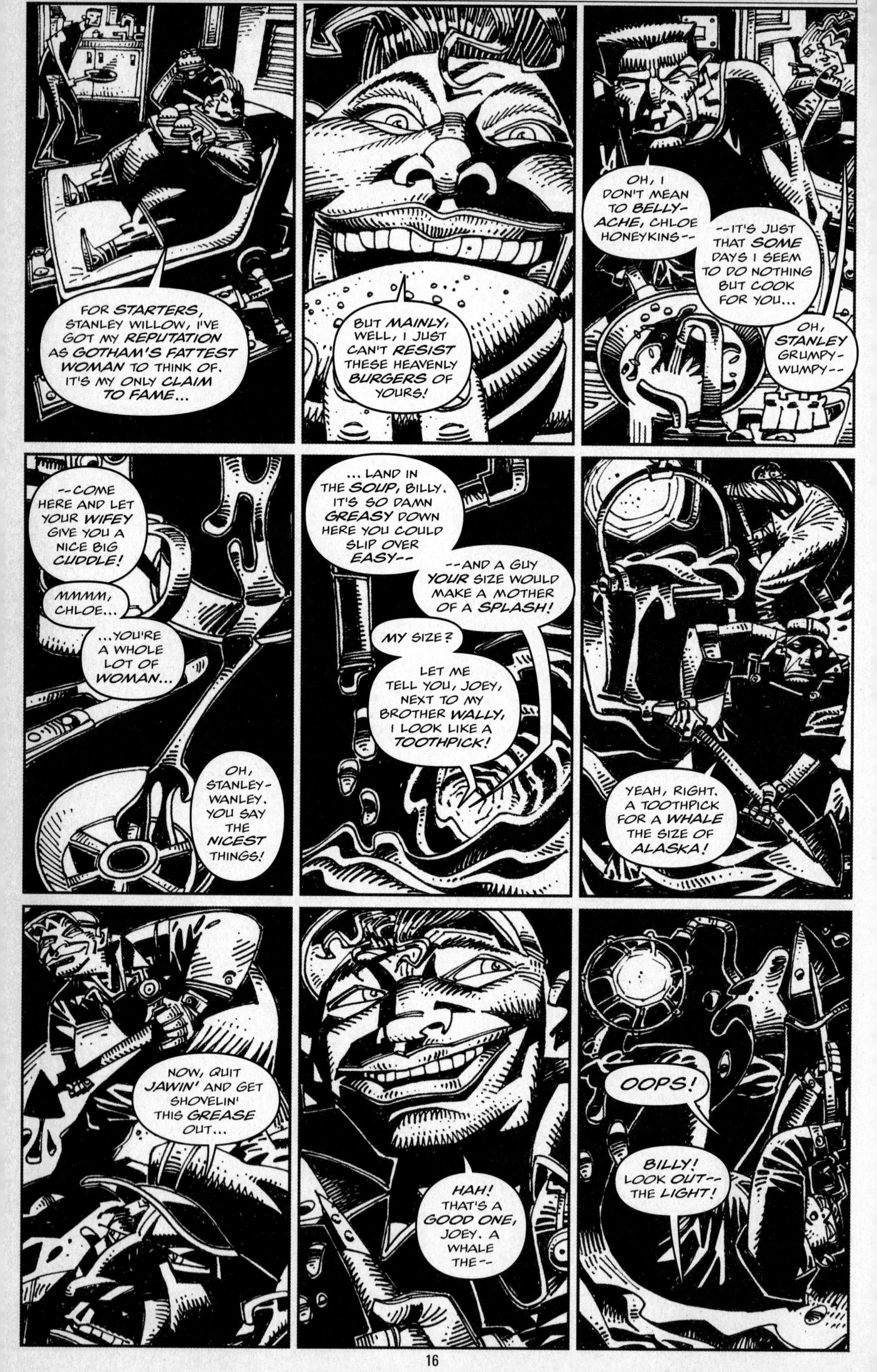
FOR STARTERS, STANLEY WILLOW, I'VE GOT MY REPUTATION AS GOTHAM'S FATTEST WOMAN TO THINK OF. IT'S MY ONLY CLAIM TO FAME...
BUT MAINLY, WELL, I JUST CAN'T RESIST THESE HEAVENLY BURGERS OF YOURS!
OH, I DON'T MEAN TO BELLY-ACHE, CHLOE HONEYKINS--
--IT'S JUST THAT SOME DAYS I SEEM TO DO NOTHING BUT COOK FOR YOU...
OH, STANLEY GRUMPY-WUMPY--
--COME HERE AND LET YOUR WIFEY GIVE YOU A NICE BIG CUDDLE!
MMMM, CHLOE...
...YOU'RE A WHOLE LOT OF WOMAN...
OH, STANLEY-WANLEY. YOU SAY THE NICEST THINGS!
...LAND IN THE SOUP, BILLY. IT'S SO DAMN GREASY DOWN HERE YOU COULD SLIP OVER EASY--
--AND A GUY YOUR SIZE WOULD MAKE A MOTHER OF A SPLASH!
MY SIZE?
LET ME TELL YOU, JOEY, NEXT TO MY BROTHER WALLY, I LOOK LIKE A TOOTHPICK!
YEAH, RIGHT. A TOOTHPICK FOR A WHALE THE SIZE OF ALASKA!
NOW, QUIT JAWIN' AND GET SHOVELIN' THIS GREASE OUT...
HAH! THAT'S A GOOD ONE, JOEY. A WHALE THE--
OOPS!
BILLY! LOOK OUT-- THE LIGHT!

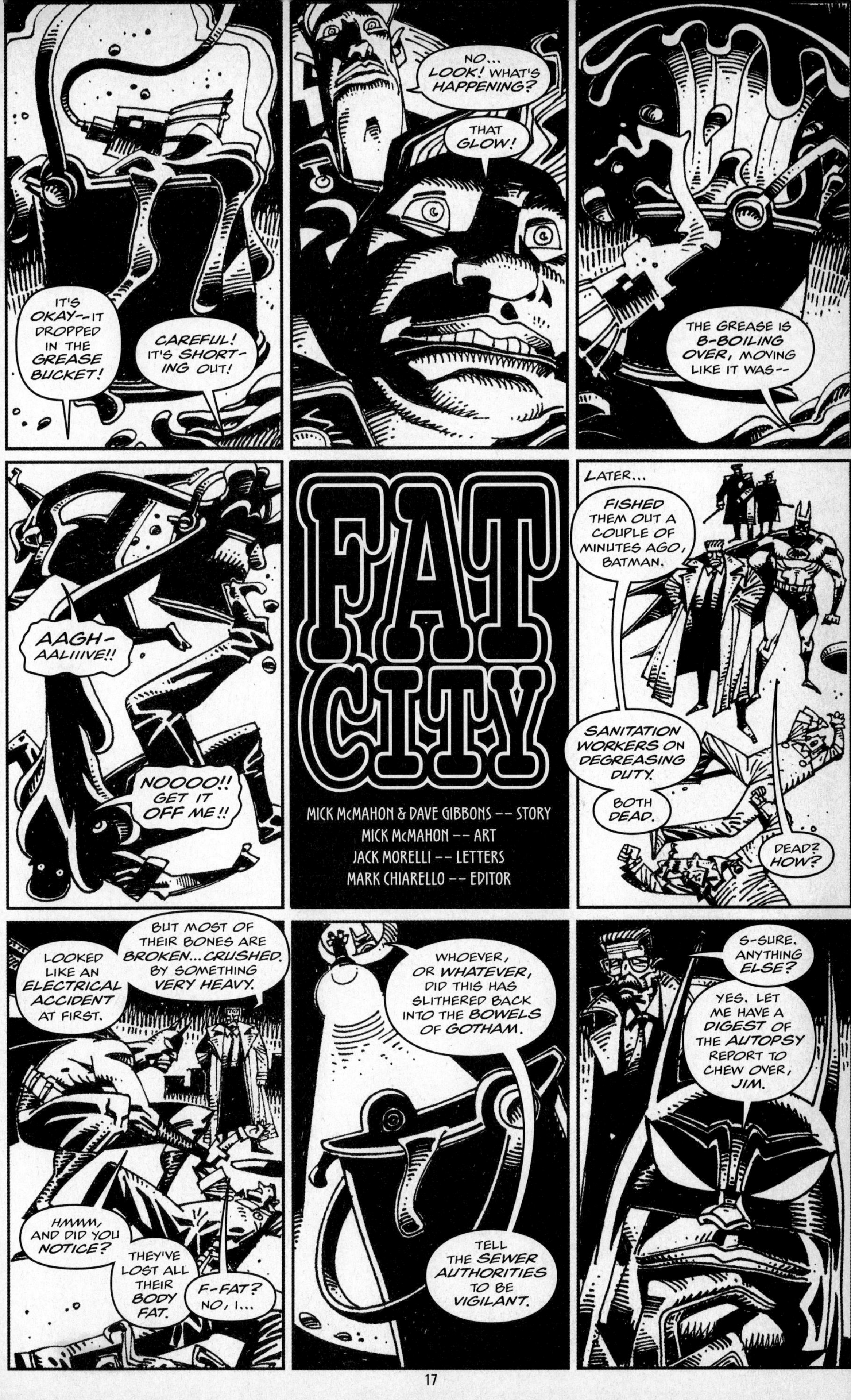
IT'S OKAY--IT DROPPED IN THE GREASE BUCKET!
CAREFUL! IT'S SHORTING OUT!
NO... LOOK! WHAT'S HAPPENING?
THAT GLOW!
THE GREASE IS B-BOILING OVER, MOVING LIKE IT WAS--
AAGH-AALIIIVE!!
NOOOO!! GET IT OFF ME!!
FAT CITY
MICK McMAHON & DAVE GIBBONS -- STORY
MICK McMAHON -- ART
JACK MORELLI -- LETTERS
MARK CHIARELLO -- EDITOR
LATER...
FISHED THEM OUT A COUPLE OF MINUTES AGO, BATMAN.
SANITATION WORKERS ON DEGREASING DUTY.
BOTH DEAD.
DEAD? HOW?
LOOKED LIKE AN ELECTRICAL ACCIDENT AT FIRST.
BUT MOST OF THEIR BONES ARE BROKEN...CRUSHED. BY SOMETHING VERY HEAVY.
HMMM, AND DID YOU NOTICE?
THEY'VE LOST ALL THEIR BODY FAT.
F-FAT? NO, I...
WHOEVER, OR WHATEVER, DID THIS HAS SLITHERED BACK INTO THE BOWELS OF GOTHAM.
TELL THE SEWER AUTHORITIES TO BE VIGILANT.
S-SURE. ANYTHING ELSE?
YES. LET ME HAVE A DIGEST OF THE AUTOPSY REPORT TO CHEW OVER, JIM.

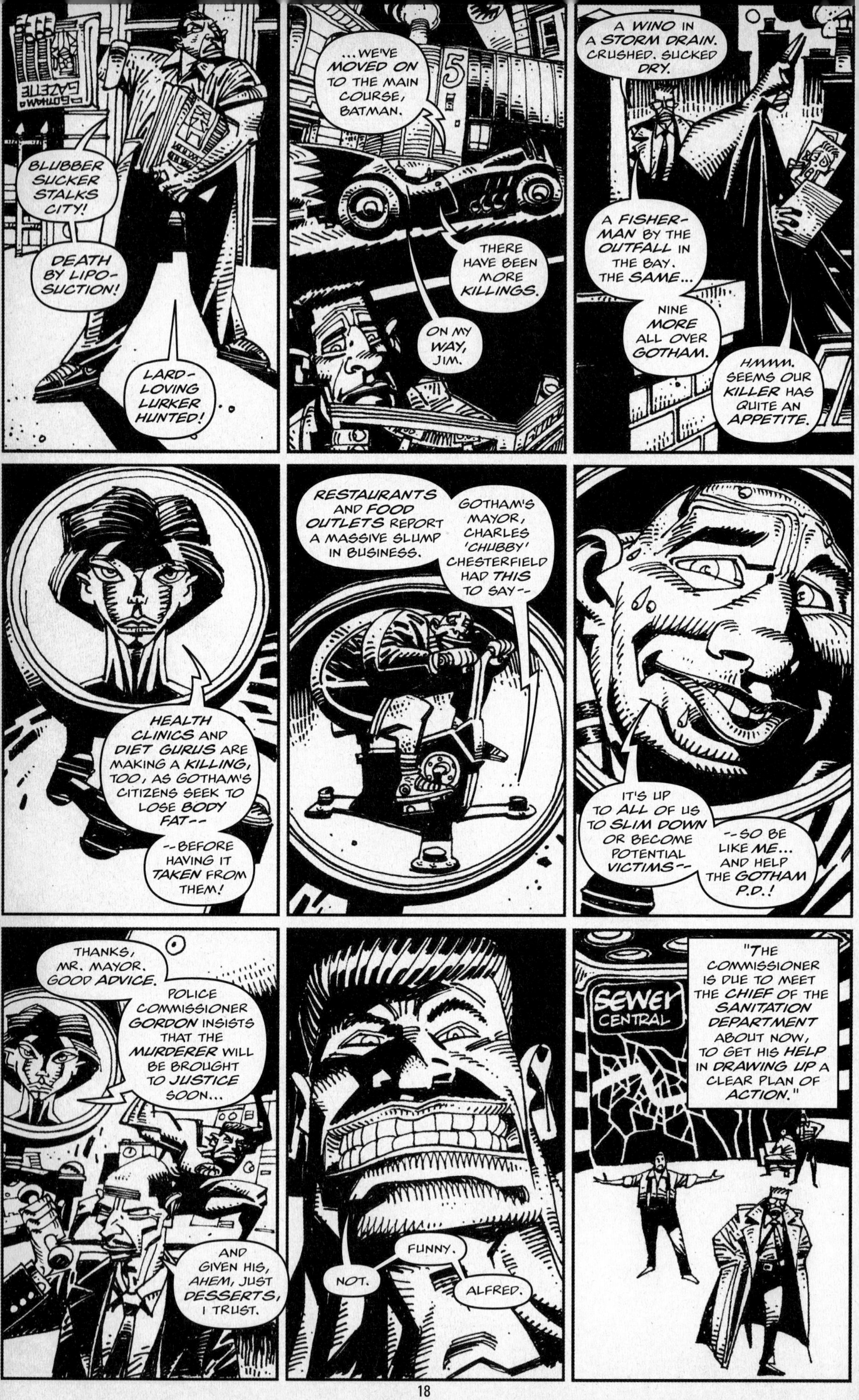
GOTHAM GAZETTE
BLUBBER SUCKER STALKS CITY!
DEATH BY LIPO-SUCTION!
LARD-LOVING LURKER HUNTED!
...WE'VE MOVED ON TO THE MAIN COURSE, BATMAN.
THERE HAVE BEEN MORE KILLINGS.
ON MY WAY, JIM.
A WINO IN A STORM DRAIN. CRUSHED. SUCKED DRY.
A FISHER-MAN BY THE OUTFALL IN THE BAY. THE SAME...
NINE MORE ALL OVER GOTHAM.
HMMM. SEEMS OUR KILLER HAS QUITE AN APPETITE.
HEALTH CLINICS AND DIET GURUS ARE MAKING A KILLING, TOO, AS GOTHAM'S CITIZENS SEEK TO LOSE BODY FAT--
--BEFORE HAVING IT TAKEN FROM THEM!
RESTAURANTS AND FOOD OUTLETS REPORT A MASSIVE SLUMP IN BUSINESS.
GOTHAM'S MAYOR, CHARLES 'CHUBBY' CHESTERFIELD HAD THIS TO SAY--
IT'S UP TO ALL OF US TO SLIM DOWN OR BECOME POTENTIAL VICTIMS--
--SO BE LIKE ME... AND HELP THE GOTHAM P.D.!
THANKS, MR. MAYOR. GOOD ADVICE.
POLICE COMMISSIONER GORDON INSISTS THAT THE MURDERER WILL BE BROUGHT TO JUSTICE SOON...
AND GIVEN HIS, AHEM, JUST DESSERTS, I TRUST.
FUNNY.
NOT.
ALFRED.
SEWER CENTRAL
"THE COMMISSIONER IS DUE TO MEET THE CHIEF OF THE SANITATION DEPARTMENT ABOUT NOW, TO GET HIS HELP IN DRAWING UP A CLEAR PLAN OF ACTION."

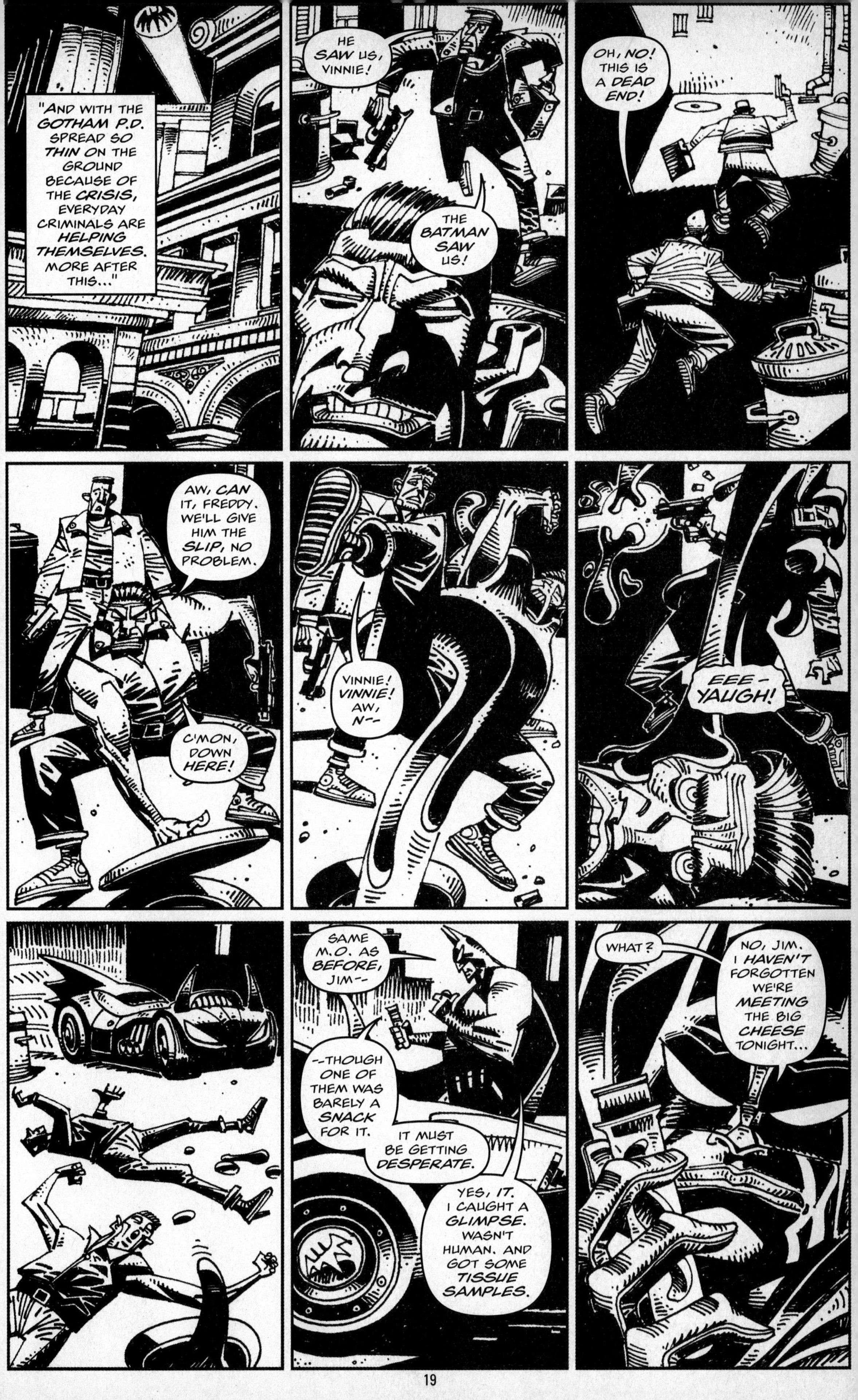
"AND WITH THE GOTHAM P.D. SPREAD SO THIN ON THE GROUND BECAUSE OF THE CRISIS, EVERYDAY CRIMINALS ARE HELPING THEMSELVES. MORE AFTER THIS..."
HE SAW US, VINNIE!
THE BATMAN SAW US!
OH, NO! THIS IS A DEAD END!
AW, CAN IT, FREDDY. WE'LL GIVE HIM THE SLIP, NO PROBLEM.
C'MON, DOWN HERE!
VINNIE! VINNIE! AW, N--
EEE-YAUGH!
SAME M.O. AS BEFORE, JIM--
--THOUGH ONE OF THEM WAS BARELY A SNACK FOR IT.
IT MUST BE GETTING DESPERATE.
YES, IT. I CAUGHT A GLIMPSE. WASN'T HUMAN. AND GOT SOME TISSUE SAMPLES.
WHAT?
NO, JIM. I HAVEN'T FORGOTTEN WE'RE MEETING THE BIG CHEESE TONIGHT...

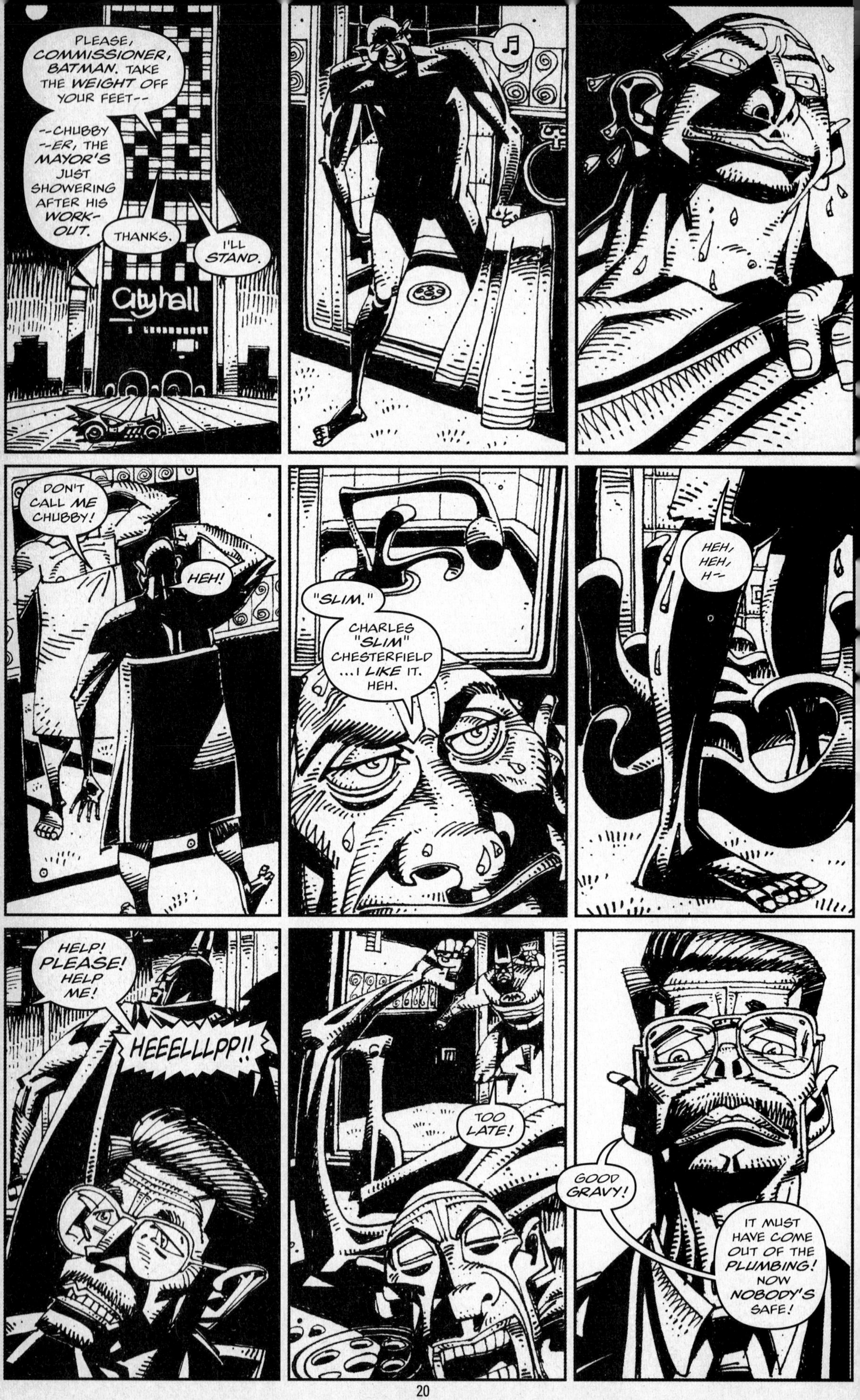
PLEASE, COMMISSIONER, BATMAN. TAKE THE WEIGHT OFF YOUR FEET--
--CHUBBY --ER, THE MAYOR'S JUST SHOWERING AFTER HIS WORK-OUT.
THANKS.
I'LL STAND.
Cityhall
♫
DON'T CALL ME CHUBBY!
HEH!
"SLIM."
CHARLES "SLIM" CHESTERFIELD ...I LIKE IT. HEH.
HEH, HEH, H--
HELP! PLEASE! HELP ME!
HEEELLLPP!!
TOO LATE!
GOOD GRAVY!
IT MUST HAVE COME OUT OF THE PLUMBING! NOW NOBODY'S SAFE!

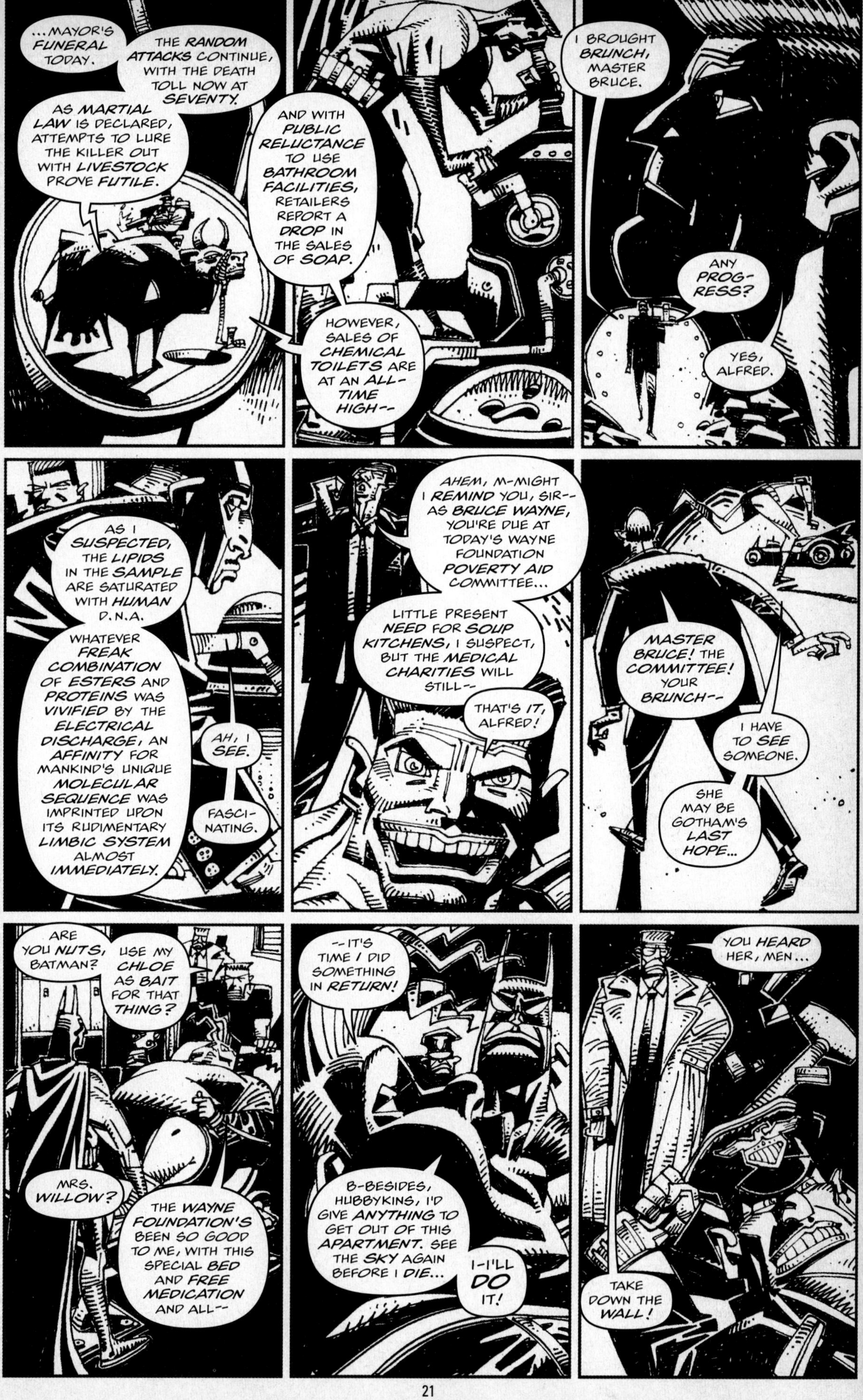
...MAYOR'S FUNERAL TODAY.
THE RANDOM ATTACKS CONTINUE, WITH THE DEATH TOLL NOW AT SEVENTY.
AS MARTIAL LAW IS DECLARED, ATTEMPTS TO LURE THE KILLER OUT WITH LIVESTOCK PROVE FUTILE.
AND WITH PUBLIC RELUCTANCE TO USE BATHROOM FACILITIES, RETAILERS REPORT A DROP IN THE SALES OF SOAP.
HOWEVER, SALES OF CHEMICAL TOILETS ARE AT AN ALL-TIME HIGH--
I BROUGHT BRUNCH, MASTER BRUCE.
ANY PROGRESS?
YES, ALFRED.
AS I SUSPECTED, THE LIPIDS IN THE SAMPLE ARE SATURATED WITH HUMAN D.N.A.
WHATEVER FREAK COMBINATION OF ESTERS AND PROTEINS WAS VIVIFIED BY THE ELECTRICAL DISCHARGE, AN AFFINITY FOR MANKIND'S UNIQUE MOLECULAR SEQUENCE WAS IMPRINTED UPON ITS RUDIMENTARY LIMBIC SYSTEM ALMOST IMMEDIATELY.
AH, I SEE.
FASCINATING.
AHEM, M-MIGHT I REMIND YOU, SIR--AS BRUCE WAYNE, YOU'RE DUE AT TODAY'S WAYNE FOUNDATION POVERTY AID COMMITTEE...
LITTLE PRESENT NEED FOR SOUP KITCHENS, I SUSPECT, BUT THE MEDICAL CHARITIES WILL STILL--
THAT'S IT, ALFRED!
MASTER BRUCE! THE COMMITTEE! YOUR BRUNCH--
I HAVE TO SEE SOMEONE.
SHE MAY BE GOTHAM'S LAST HOPE...
ARE YOU NUTS, BATMAN?
USE MY CHLOE AS BAIT FOR THAT THING?
MRS. WILLOW?
THE WAYNE FOUNDATION'S BEEN SO GOOD TO ME, WITH THIS SPECIAL BED AND FREE MEDICATION AND ALL--
--IT'S TIME I DID SOMETHING IN RETURN!
B-BESIDES, HUBBYKINS, I'D GIVE ANYTHING TO GET OUT OF THIS APARTMENT. SEE THE SKY AGAIN BEFORE I DIE...
I-I'LL DO IT!
YOU HEARD HER, MEN...
TAKE DOWN THE WALL!

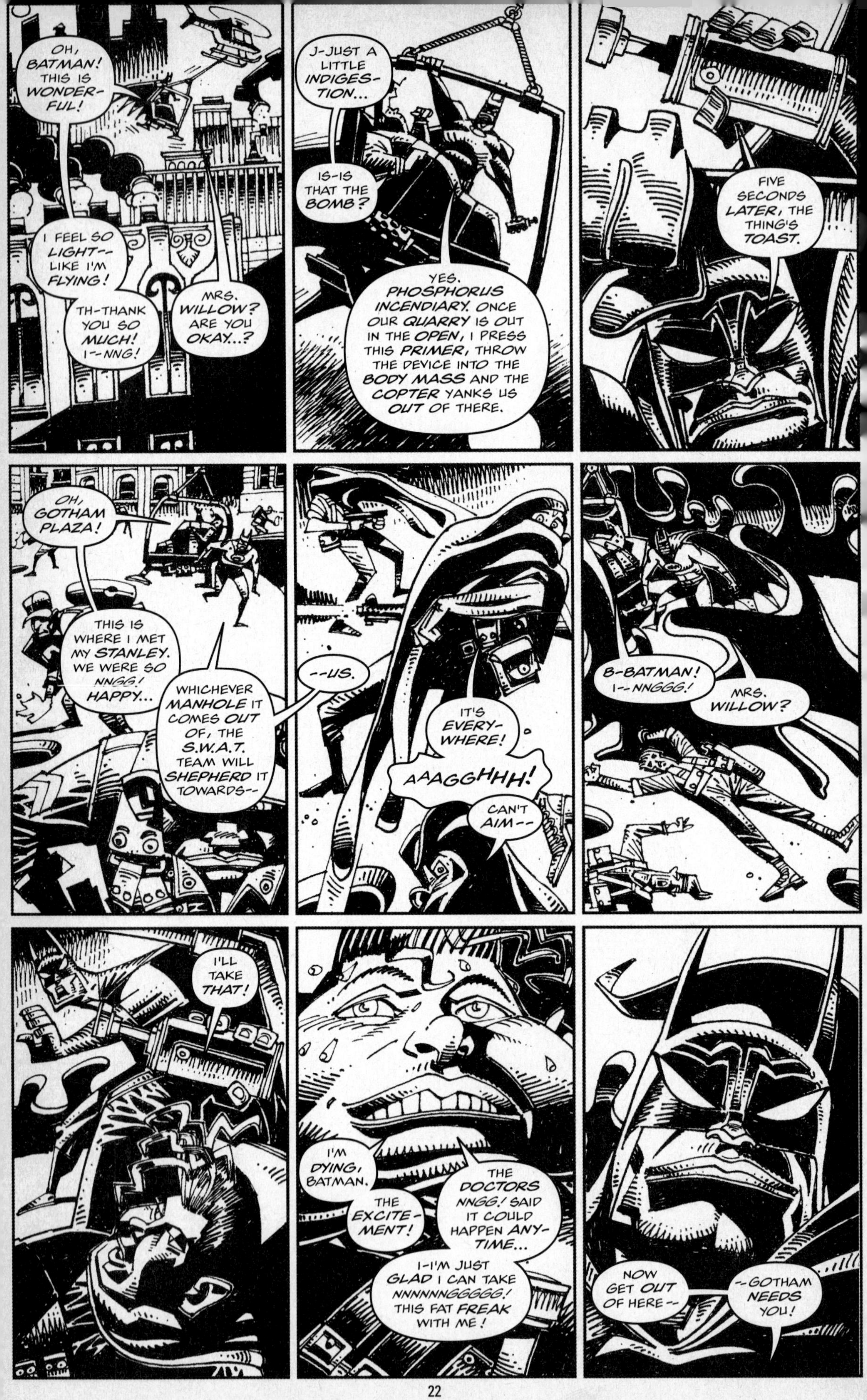
OH, BATMAN! THIS IS WONDERFUL!
I FEEL SO LIGHT-- LIKE I'M FLYING!
TH-THANK YOU SO MUCH! I--NNG!
MRS. WILLOW? ARE YOU OKAY...?
J-JUST A LITTLE INDIGESTION...
IS-IS THAT THE BOMB?
YES. PHOSPHORUS INCENDIARY. ONCE OUR QUARRY IS OUT IN THE OPEN, I PRESS THIS PRIMER, THROW THE DEVICE INTO THE BODY MASS AND THE COPTER YANKS US OUT OF THERE.
FIVE SECONDS LATER, THE THING'S TOAST.
OH, GOTHAM PLAZA!
THIS IS WHERE I MET MY STANLEY. WE WERE SO NNGG! HAPPY...
WHICHEVER MANHOLE IT COMES OUT OF, THE S.W.A.T. TEAM WILL SHEPHERD IT TOWARDS--
--US.
IT'S EVERYWHERE!
AAAGGHHH!
CAN'T AIM--
B-BATMAN! I--NNGGG!
MRS. WILLOW?
I'LL TAKE THAT!
I'M DYING, BATMAN.
THE EXCITEMENT!
THE DOCTORS NNGG! SAID IT COULD HAPPEN ANYTIME...
I-I'M JUST GLAD I CAN TAKE NNNNNNGGGGG! THIS FAT FREAK WITH ME!
NOW GET OUT OF HERE--
--GOTHAM NEEDS YOU!

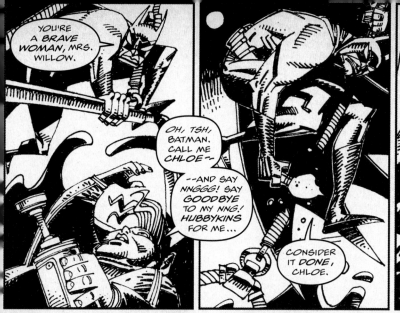

YOU'RE A BRAVE WOMAN, MRS. WILLOW.

OH, TSH, BATMAN. CALL ME *CHLOE*--

--AND SAY NNGGG! SAY GOODBYE TO MY NNG! HUBBYKINS FOR ME...

CONSIDER IT *DONE*, CHLOE.

I-I LOVE YOU, STANLEY.

BLAM

PHEW.

DIDN'T THINK WE'D GET THROUGH *THAT* ONE.

IT'S NOT OVER *YET*. WE STILL HAVE TO *CLEAN UP*--

--AND PAY THE *CHECK*.

MMM.

GOTHAM BURGER

Y'KNOW, BATMAN, I COULD *MURDER* SOME BARBECUED RIBS.

JUST COFFEE FOR ME, JIM--

--HOT AND STRONG.

HOW ABOUT YOU?

TO GO.

FINI

23

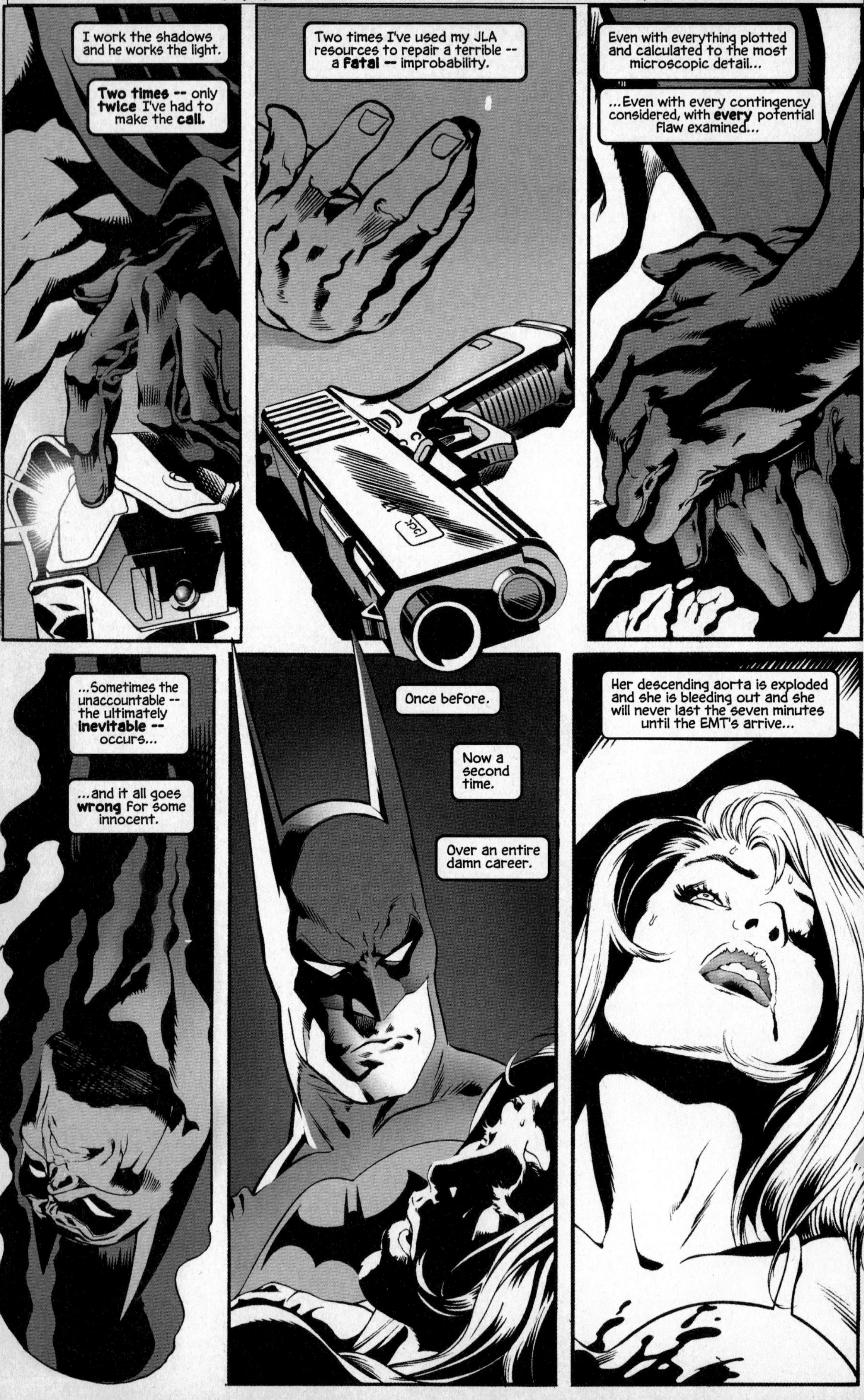
I work the shadows and he works the light.
Two times -- only twice I've had to make the call.
Two times I've used my JLA resources to repair a terrible -- a fatal -- improbability.
Even with everything plotted and calculated to the most microscopic detail...
...Even with every contingency considered, with every potential flaw examined...
...Sometimes the unaccountable -- the ultimately inevitable -- occurs...
...and it all goes wrong for some innocent.
Once before.
Now a second time.
Over an entire damn career.
Her descending aorta is exploded and she is bleeding out and she will never last the seven minutes until the EMT's arrive...

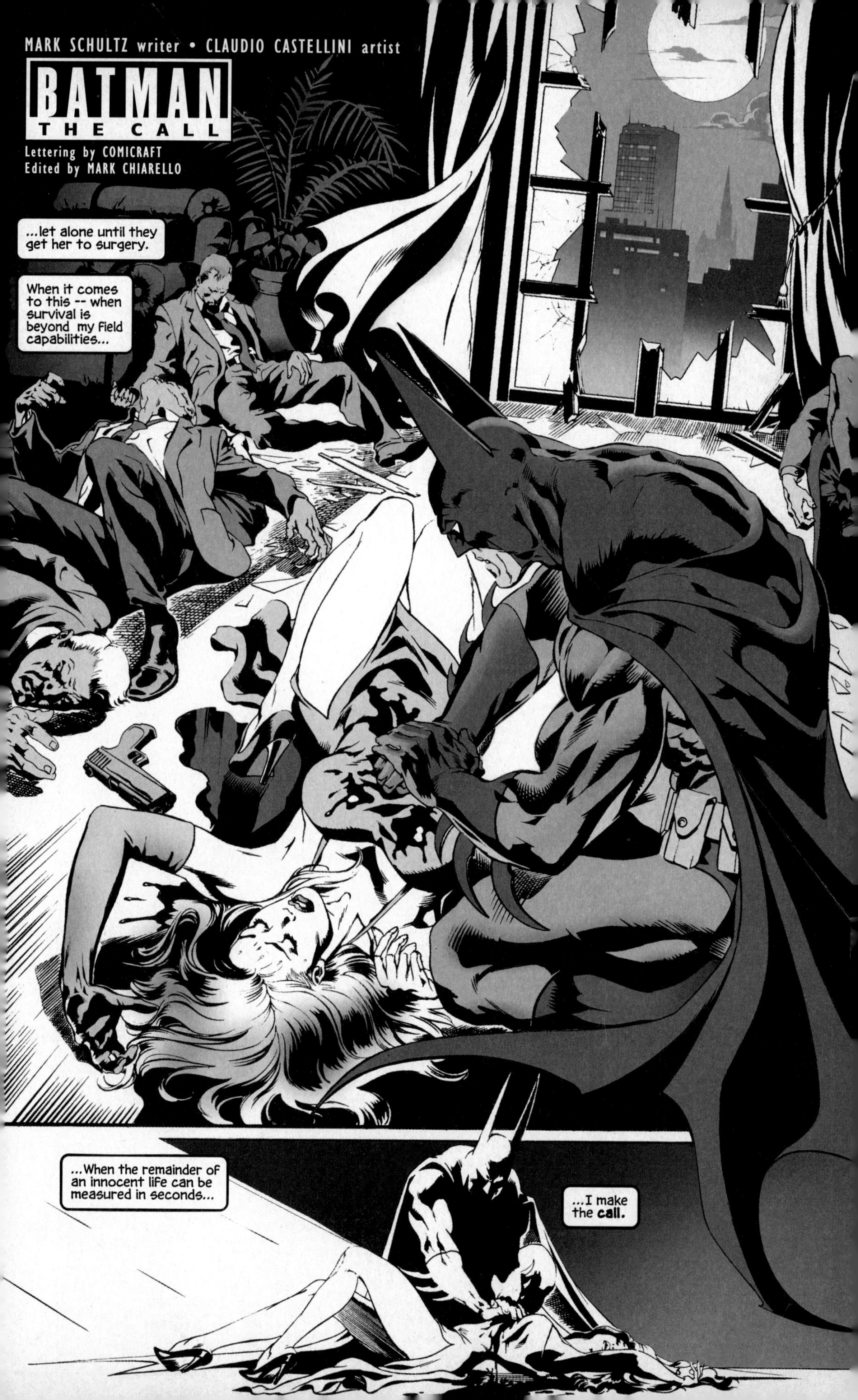
MARK SCHULTZ writer • CLAUDIO CASTELLINI artist
BATMAN
THE CALL
Lettering by COMICRAFT
Edited by MARK CHIARELLO
...let alone until they get her to surgery.
When it comes to this -- when survival is beyond my field capabilities...
...When the remainder of an innocent life can be measured in seconds...
...I make the call.

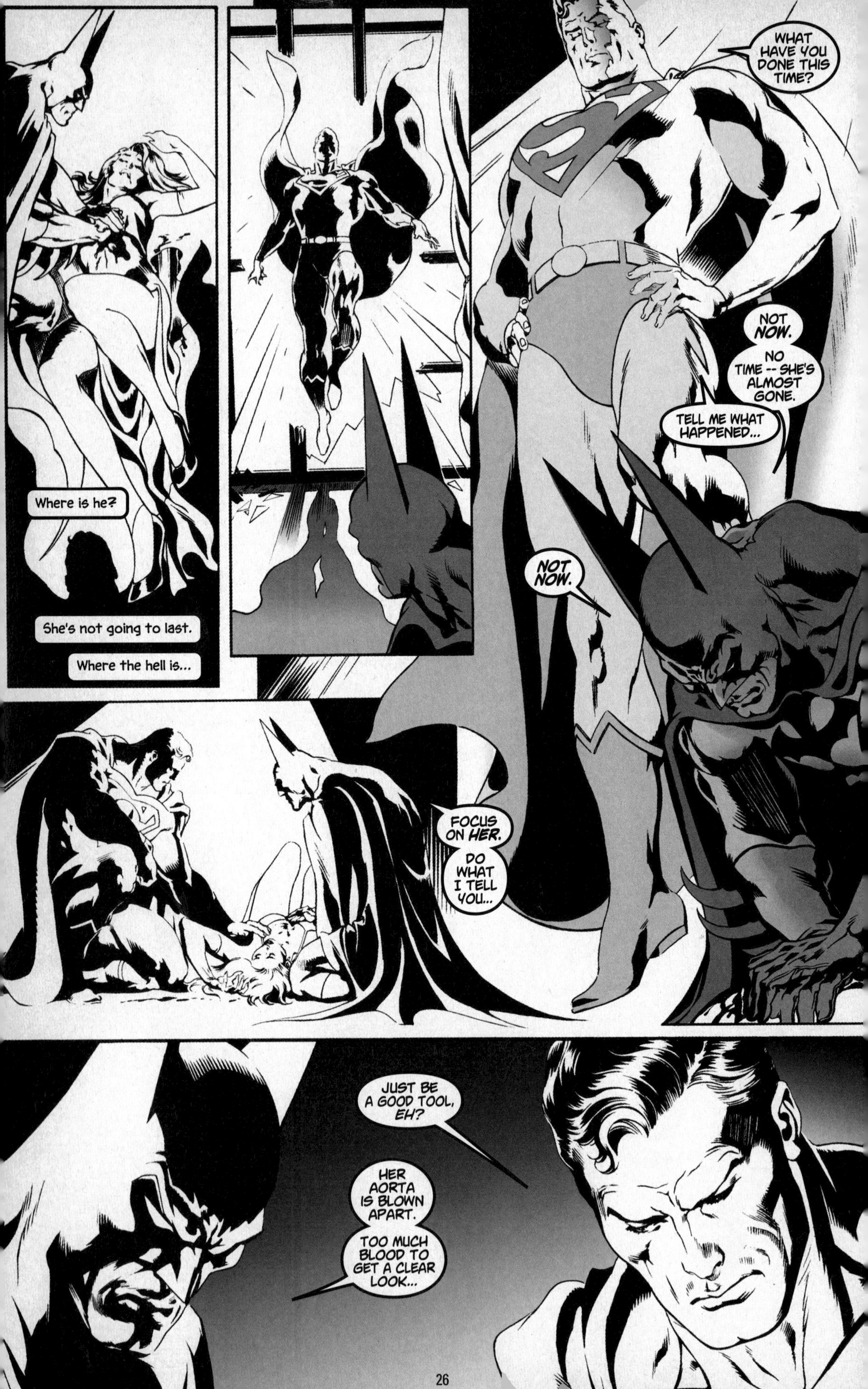
Where is he?
She's not going to last.
Where the hell is...
WHAT HAVE YOU DONE THIS TIME?
NOT NOW.
NO TIME -- SHE'S ALMOST GONE.
TELL ME WHAT HAPPENED...
NOT NOW.
FOCUS ON HER.
DO WHAT I TELL YOU...
JUST BE A GOOD TOOL, EH?
HER AORTA IS BLOWN APART.
TOO MUCH BLOOD TO GET A CLEAR LOOK...

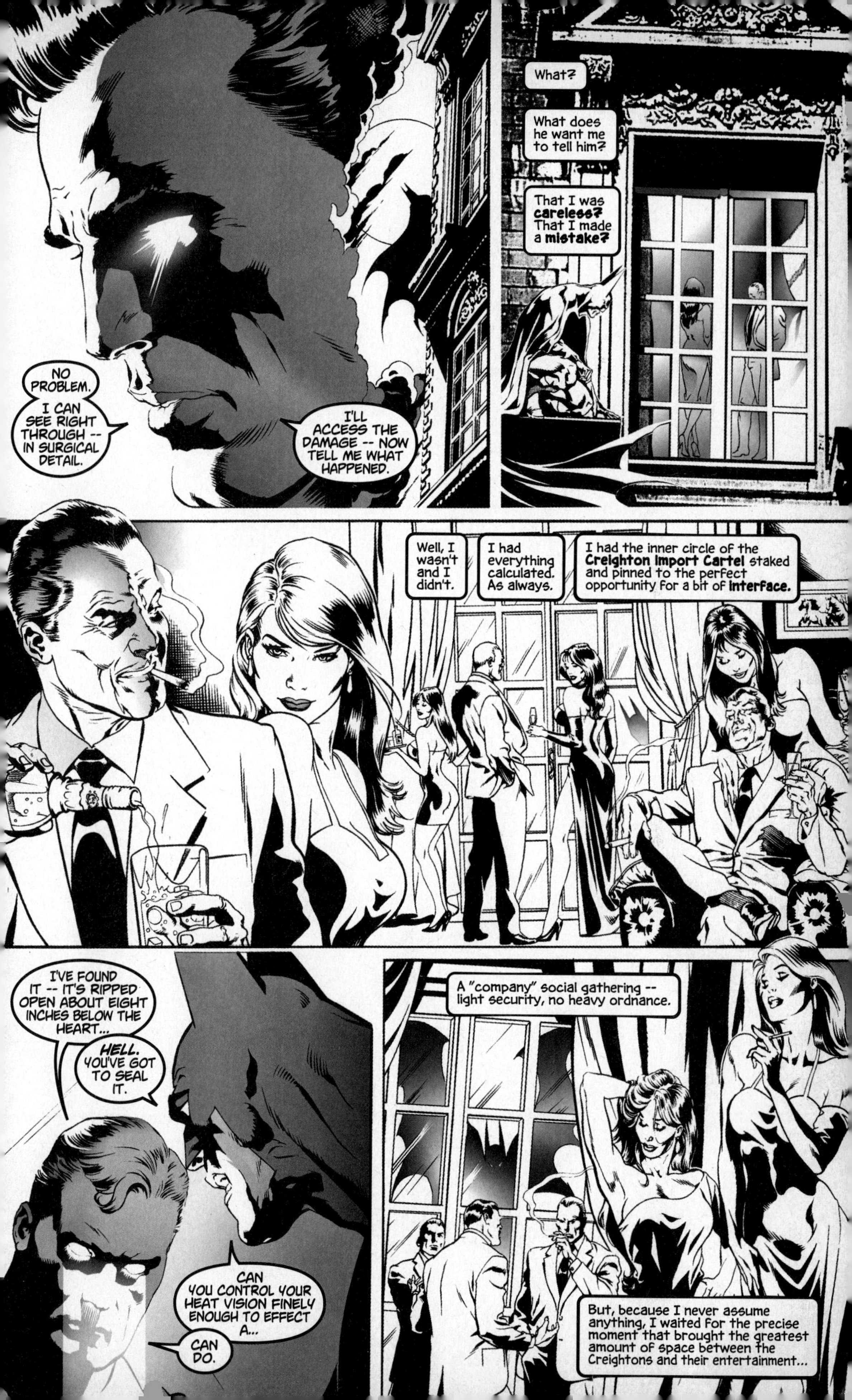
NO PROBLEM.
I CAN SEE RIGHT THROUGH -- IN SURGICAL DETAIL.
I'LL ACCESS THE DAMAGE -- NOW TELL ME WHAT HAPPENED.
What?
What does he want me to tell him?
That I was careless? That I made a mistake?
Well, I wasn't and I didn't.
I had everything calculated. As always.
I had the inner circle of the Creighton Import Cartel staked and pinned to the perfect opportunity for a bit of interface.
I'VE FOUND IT -- IT'S RIPPED OPEN ABOUT EIGHT INCHES BELOW THE HEART...
HELL. YOU'VE GOT TO SEAL IT.
CAN YOU CONTROL YOUR HEAT VISION FINELY ENOUGH TO EFFECT A...
CAN DO.
A "company" social gathering -- light security, no heavy ordnance.
But, because I never assume anything, I waited for the precise moment that brought the greatest amount of space between the Creightons and their entertainment...

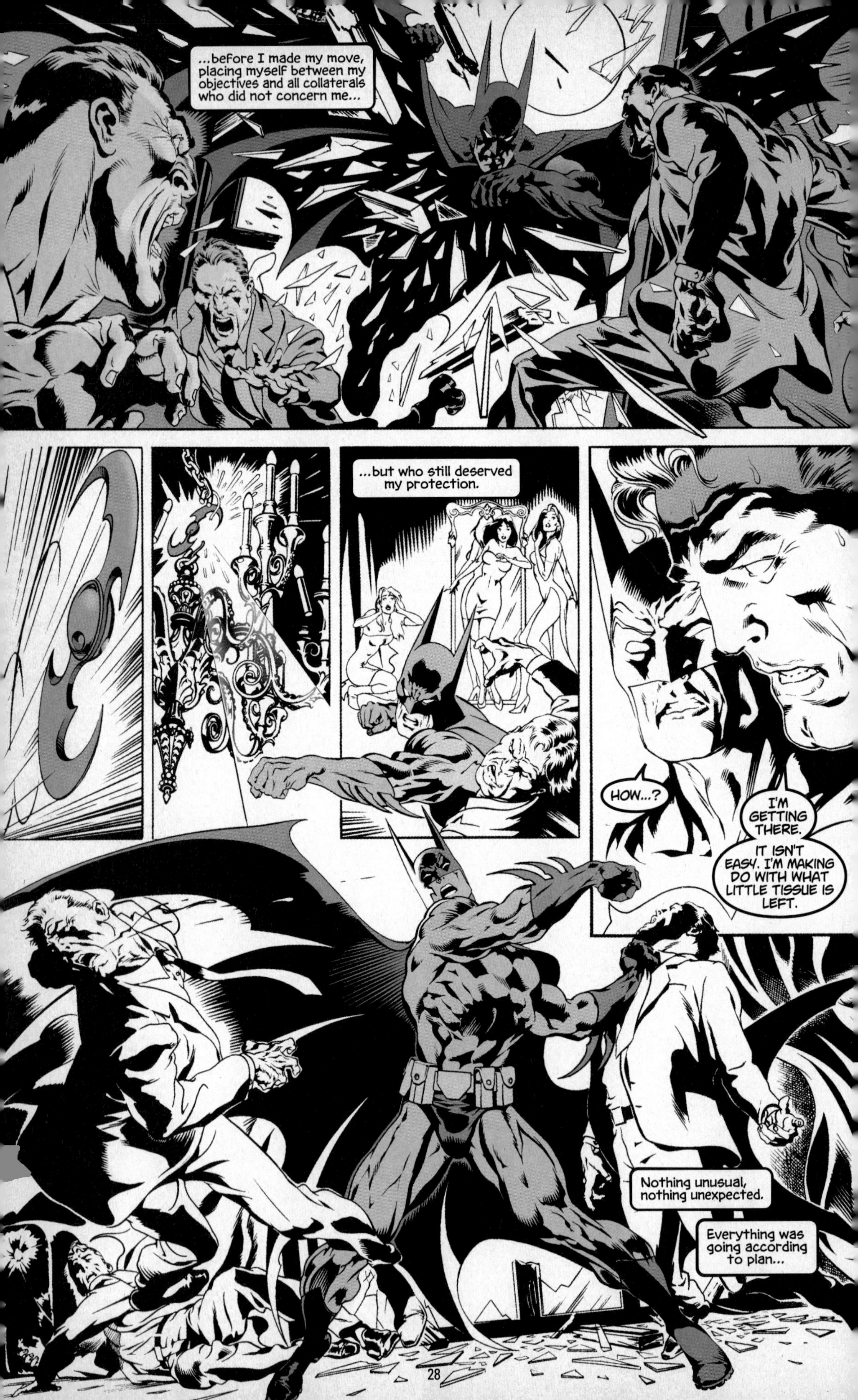
...before I made my move, placing myself between my objectives and all collaterals who did not concern me...
...but who still deserved my protection.
HOW...?
I'M GETTING THERE.
IT ISN'T EASY. I'M MAKING DO WITH WHAT LITTLE TISSUE IS LEFT.
Nothing unusual, nothing unexpected.
Everything was going according to plan...

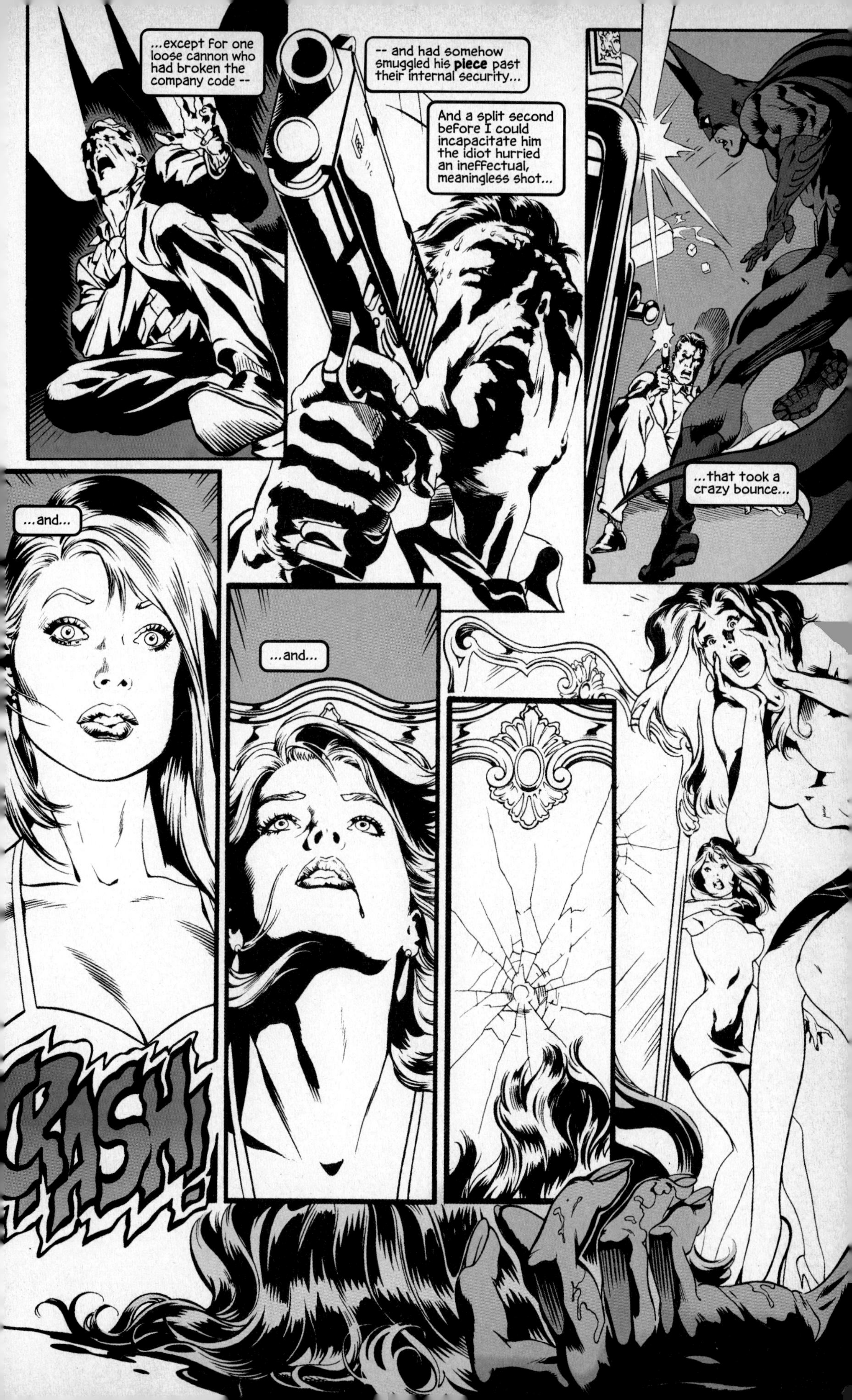
...except for one loose cannon who had broken the company code --
-- and had somehow smuggled his **piece** past their internal security...
And a split second before I could incapacitate him the idiot hurried an ineffectual, meaningless shot...
...that took a crazy bounce...
...and...
...and...
CRASH!

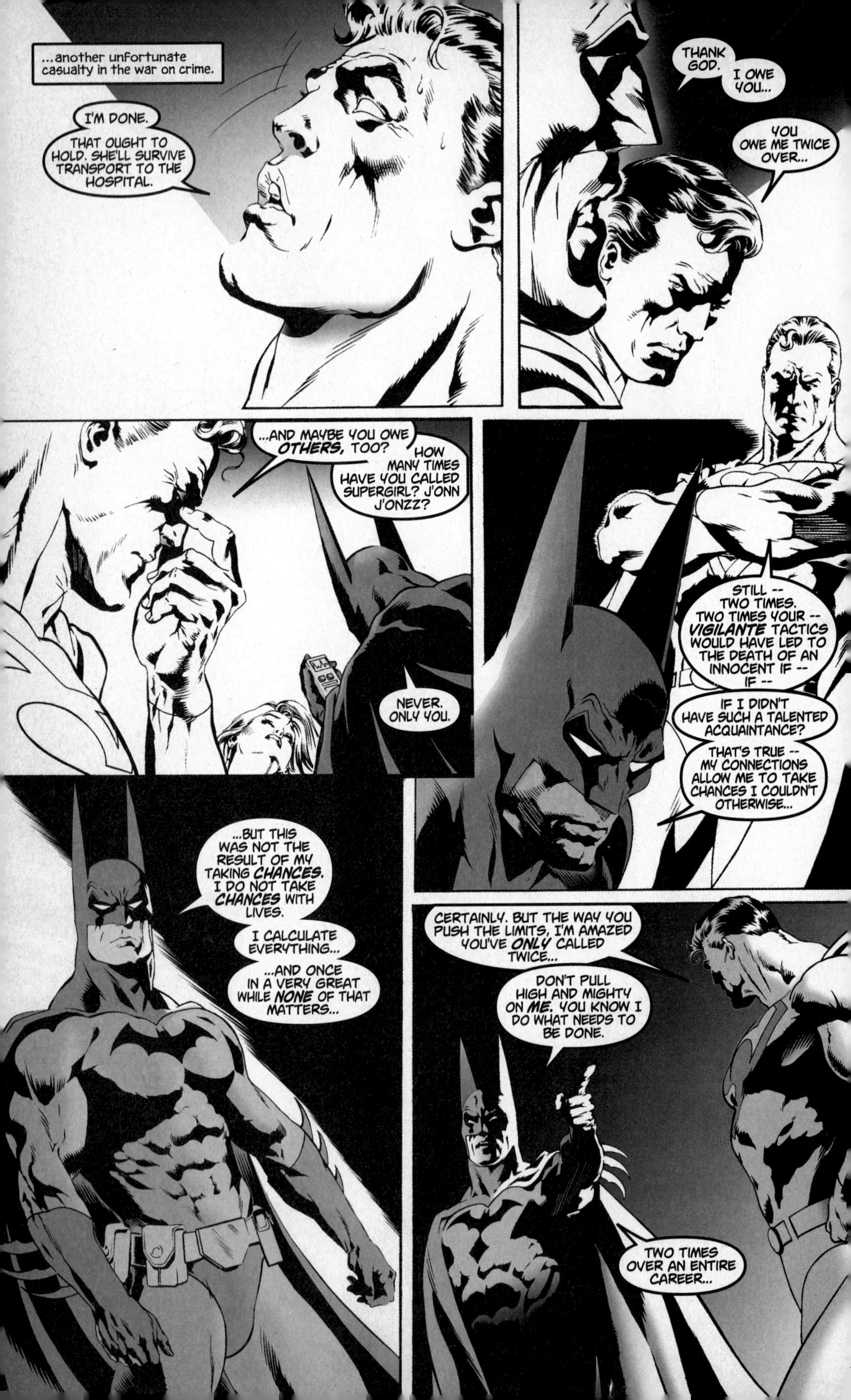
...another unfortunate casualty in the war on crime.
I'M DONE.
THAT OUGHT TO HOLD. SHE'LL SURVIVE TRANSPORT TO THE HOSPITAL.
THANK GOD.
I OWE YOU...
YOU OWE ME TWICE OVER...
...AND MAYBE YOU OWE OTHERS, TOO?
HOW MANY TIMES HAVE YOU CALLED SUPERGIRL? J'ONN J'ONZZ?
NEVER. ONLY YOU.
STILL -- TWO TIMES. TWO TIMES YOUR -- VIGILANTE TACTICS WOULD HAVE LED TO THE DEATH OF AN INNOCENT IF -- IF --
IF I DIDN'T HAVE SUCH A TALENTED ACQUAINTANCE?
THAT'S TRUE -- MY CONNECTIONS ALLOW ME TO TAKE CHANCES I COULDN'T OTHERWISE...
...BUT THIS WAS NOT THE RESULT OF MY TAKING CHANCES. I DO NOT TAKE CHANCES WITH LIVES.
I CALCULATE EVERYTHING...
...AND ONCE IN A VERY GREAT WHILE NONE OF THAT MATTERS...
CERTAINLY. BUT THE WAY YOU PUSH THE LIMITS, I'M AMAZED YOU'VE ONLY CALLED TWICE...
DON'T PULL HIGH AND MIGHTY ON ME. YOU KNOW I DO WHAT NEEDS TO BE DONE.
TWO TIMES OVER AN ENTIRE CAREER...

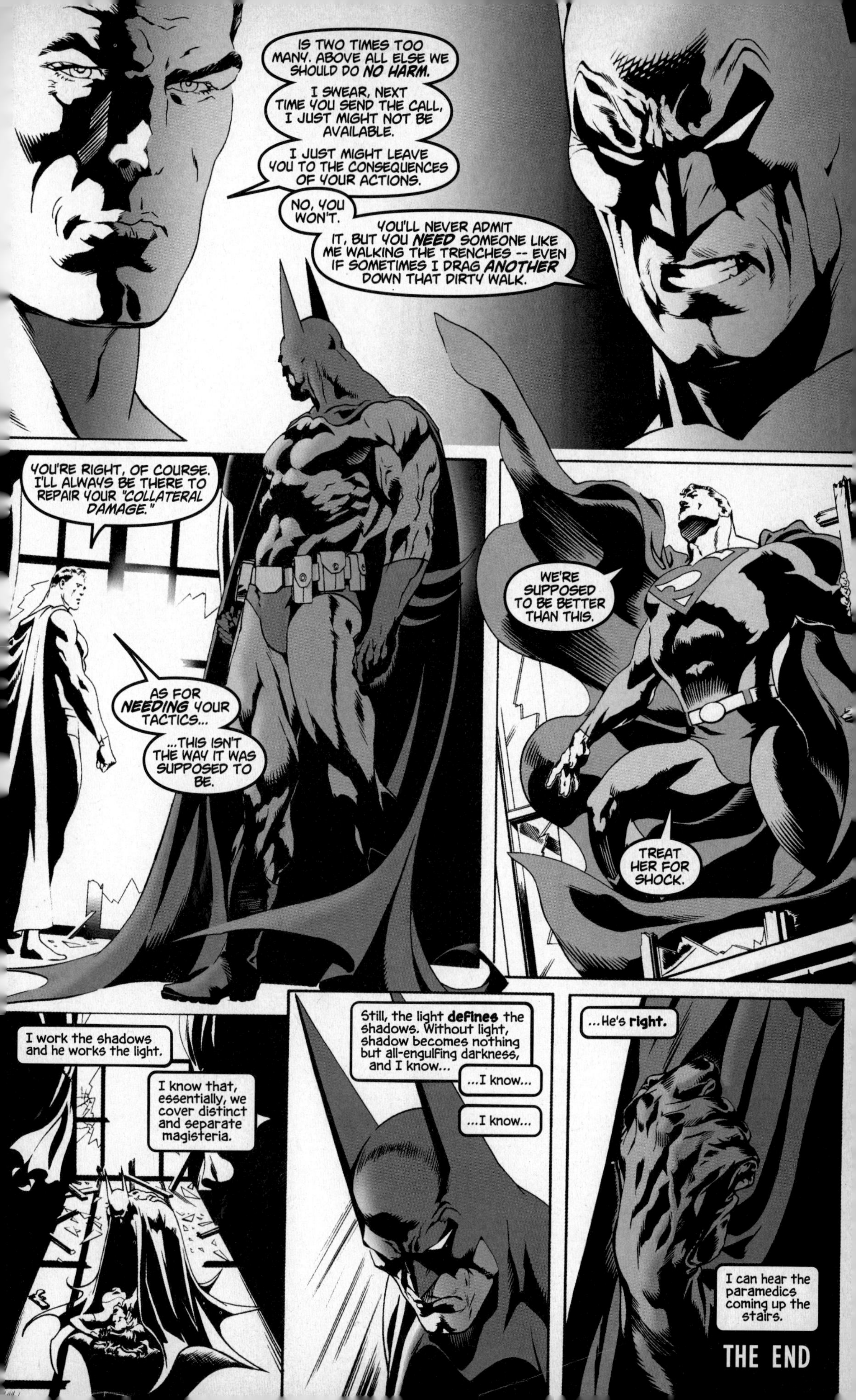
IS TWO TIMES TOO MANY. ABOVE ALL ELSE WE SHOULD DO NO HARM.
I SWEAR, NEXT TIME YOU SEND THE CALL, I JUST MIGHT NOT BE AVAILABLE.
I JUST MIGHT LEAVE YOU TO THE CONSEQUENCES OF YOUR ACTIONS.
NO, YOU WON'T.
YOU'LL NEVER ADMIT IT, BUT YOU NEED SOMEONE LIKE ME WALKING THE TRENCHES -- EVEN IF SOMETIMES I DRAG ANOTHER DOWN THAT DIRTY WALK.
YOU'RE RIGHT, OF COURSE. I'LL ALWAYS BE THERE TO REPAIR YOUR "COLLATERAL DAMAGE."
AS FOR NEEDING YOUR TACTICS...
...THIS ISN'T THE WAY IT WAS SUPPOSED TO BE.
WE'RE SUPPOSED TO BE BETTER THAN THIS.
TREAT HER FOR SHOCK.
I work the shadows and he works the light.
I know that, essentially, we cover distinct and separate magisteria.
Still, the light defines the shadows. Without light, shadow becomes nothing but all-engulfing darkness, and I know...
...I know...
...I know...
...He's right.
I can hear the paramedics coming up the stairs.
THE END

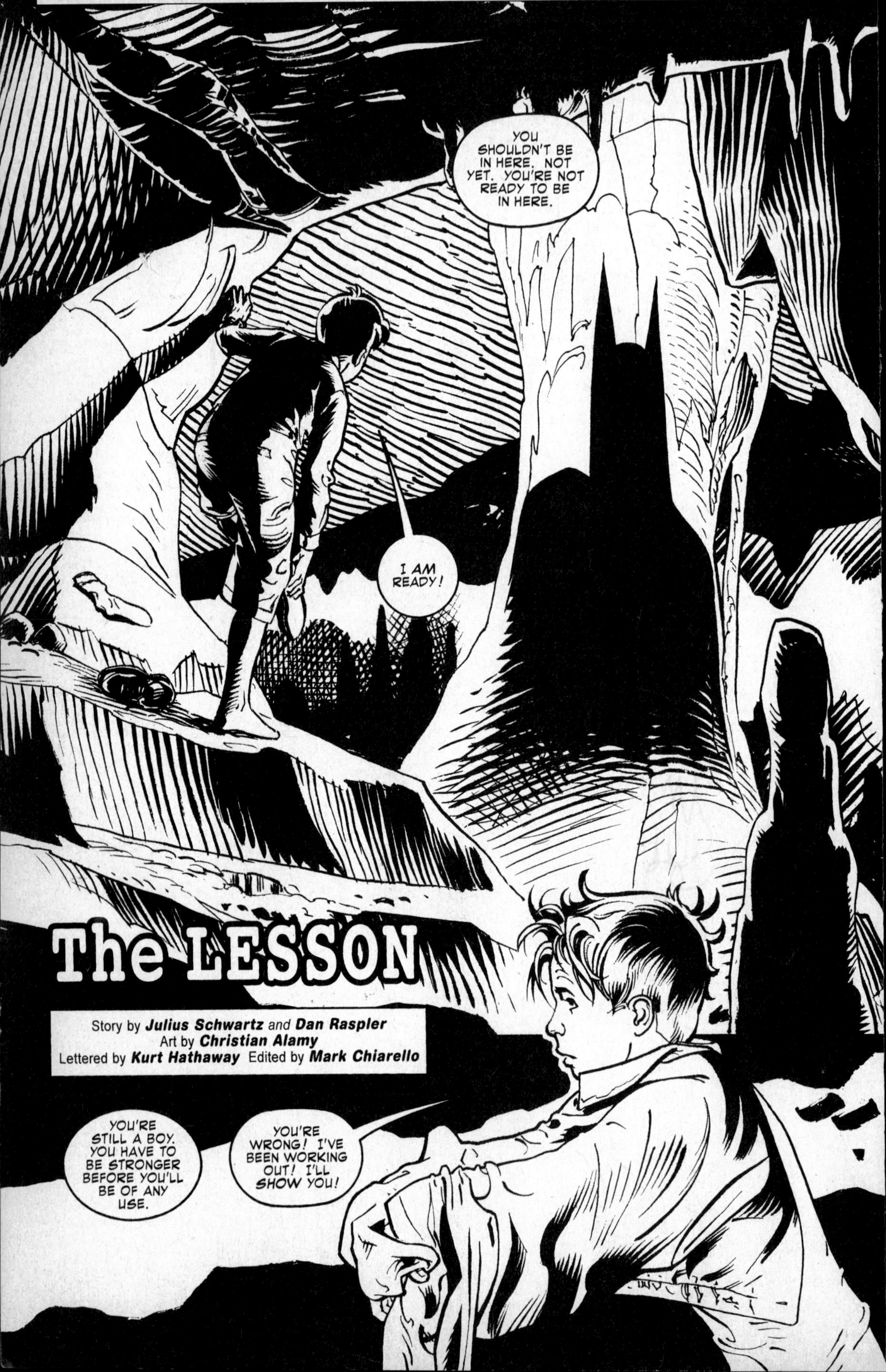
YOU SHOULDN'T BE IN HERE. NOT YET. YOU'RE NOT READY TO BE IN HERE.
I AM READY!
The LESSON
Story by Julius Schwartz and Dan Raspler
Art by Christian Alamy
Lettered by Kurt Hathaway Edited by Mark Chiarello
YOU'RE STILL A BOY. YOU HAVE TO BE STRONGER BEFORE YOU'LL BE OF ANY USE.
YOU'RE WRONG! I'VE BEEN WORKING OUT! I'LL SHOW YOU!

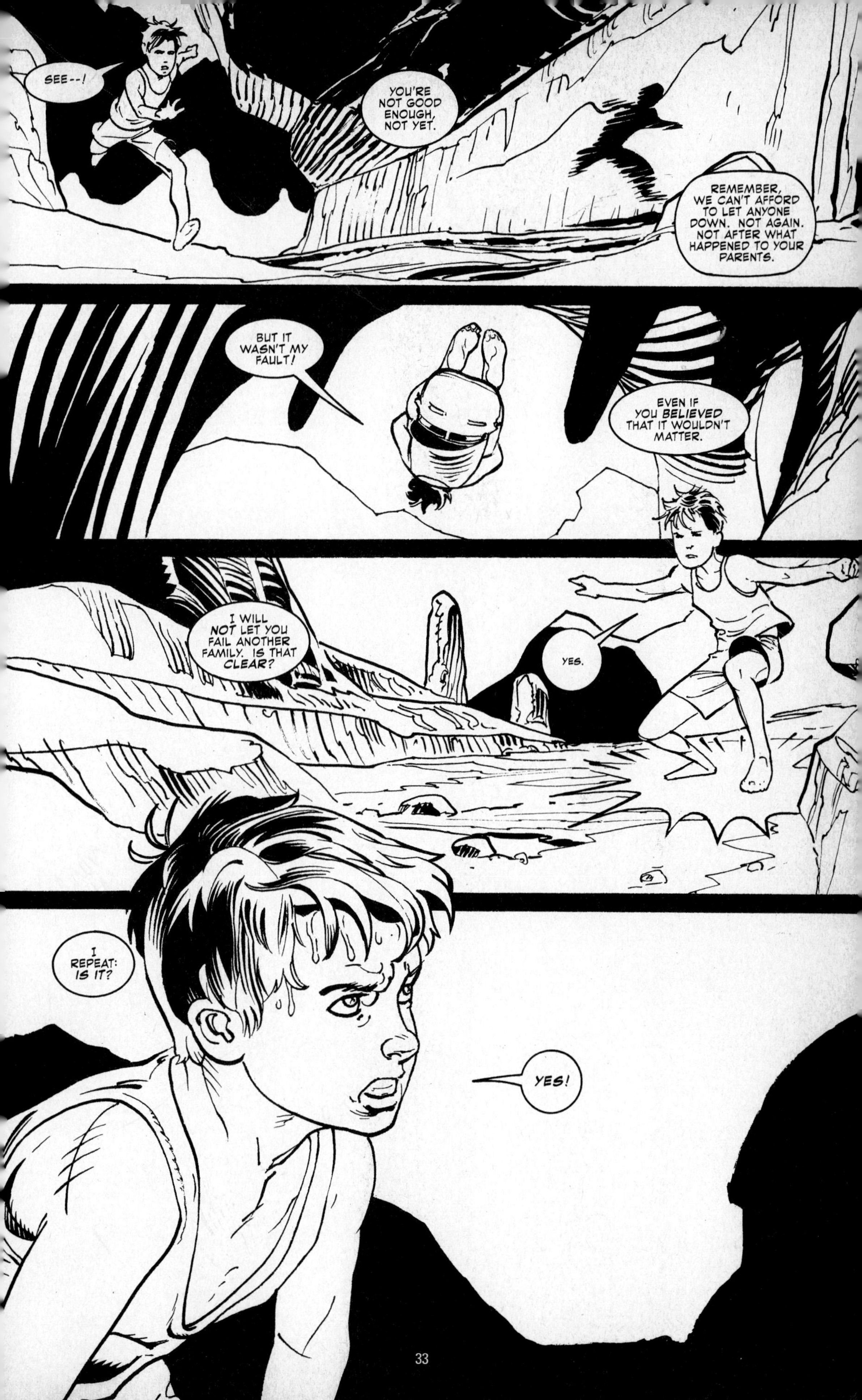
SEE--!
YOU'RE NOT GOOD ENOUGH, NOT YET.
REMEMBER, WE CAN'T AFFORD TO LET ANYONE DOWN. NOT AGAIN. NOT AFTER WHAT HAPPENED TO YOUR PARENTS.
BUT IT WASN'T MY FAULT!
EVEN IF YOU BELIEVED THAT IT WOULDN'T MATTER.
I WILL NOT LET YOU FAIL ANOTHER FAMILY. IS THAT CLEAR?
YES.
I REPEAT: IS IT?
YES!

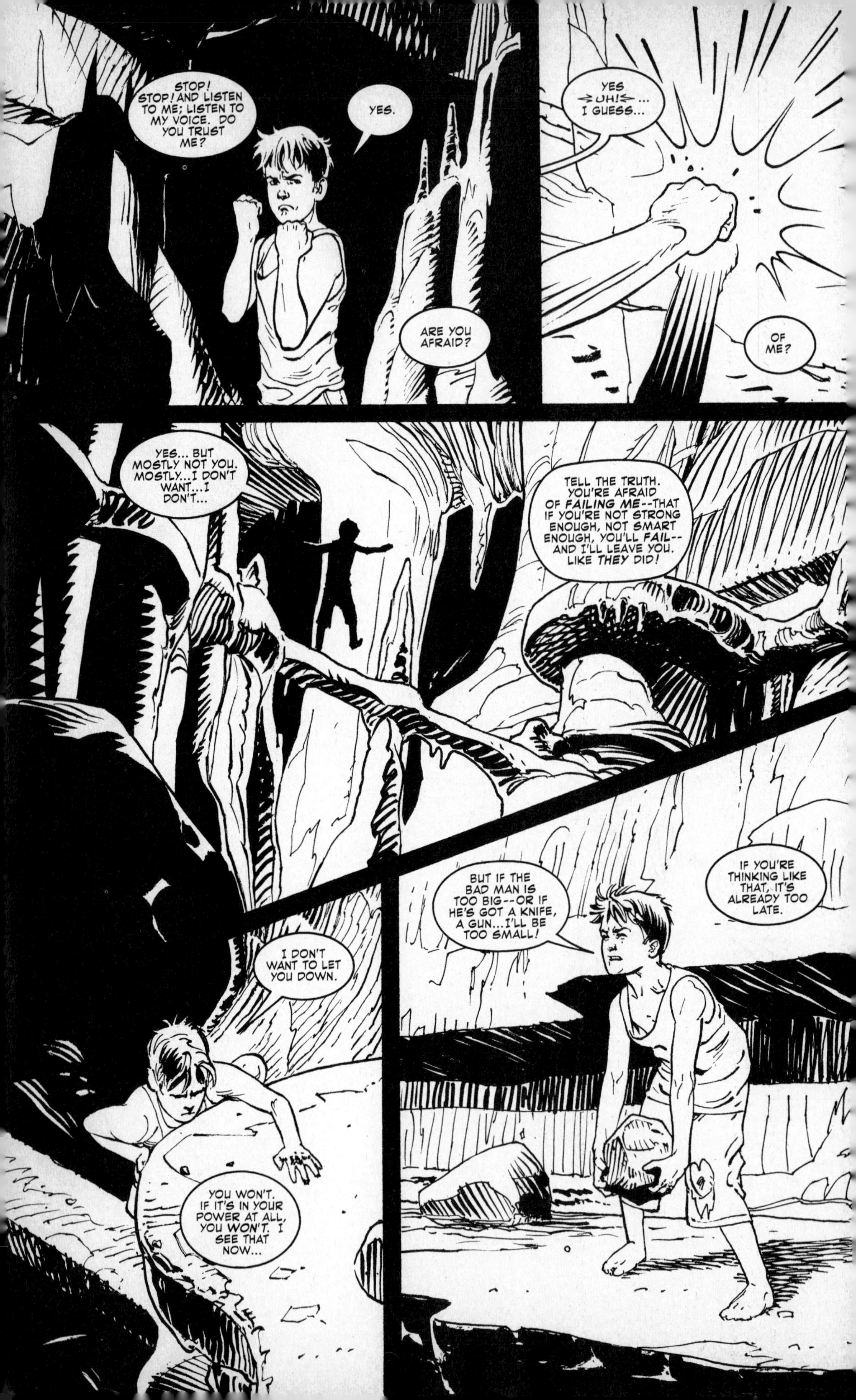
STOP! STOP! AND LISTEN TO ME; LISTEN TO MY VOICE. DO YOU TRUST ME?
YES.
ARE YOU AFRAID?
YES UH! ... I GUESS...
OF ME?
YES... BUT MOSTLY NOT YOU. MOSTLY...I DON'T WANT...I DON'T...
TELL THE TRUTH. YOU'RE AFRAID OF FAILING ME--THAT IF YOU'RE NOT STRONG ENOUGH, NOT SMART ENOUGH, YOU'LL FAIL--AND I'LL LEAVE YOU. LIKE THEY DID!
I DON'T WANT TO LET YOU DOWN.
YOU WON'T. IF IT'S IN YOUR POWER AT ALL, YOU WON'T. I SEE THAT NOW...
BUT IF THE BAD MAN IS TOO BIG--OR IF HE'S GOT A KNIFE, A GUN...I'LL BE TOO SMALL!
IF YOU'RE THINKING LIKE THAT, IT'S ALREADY TOO LATE.

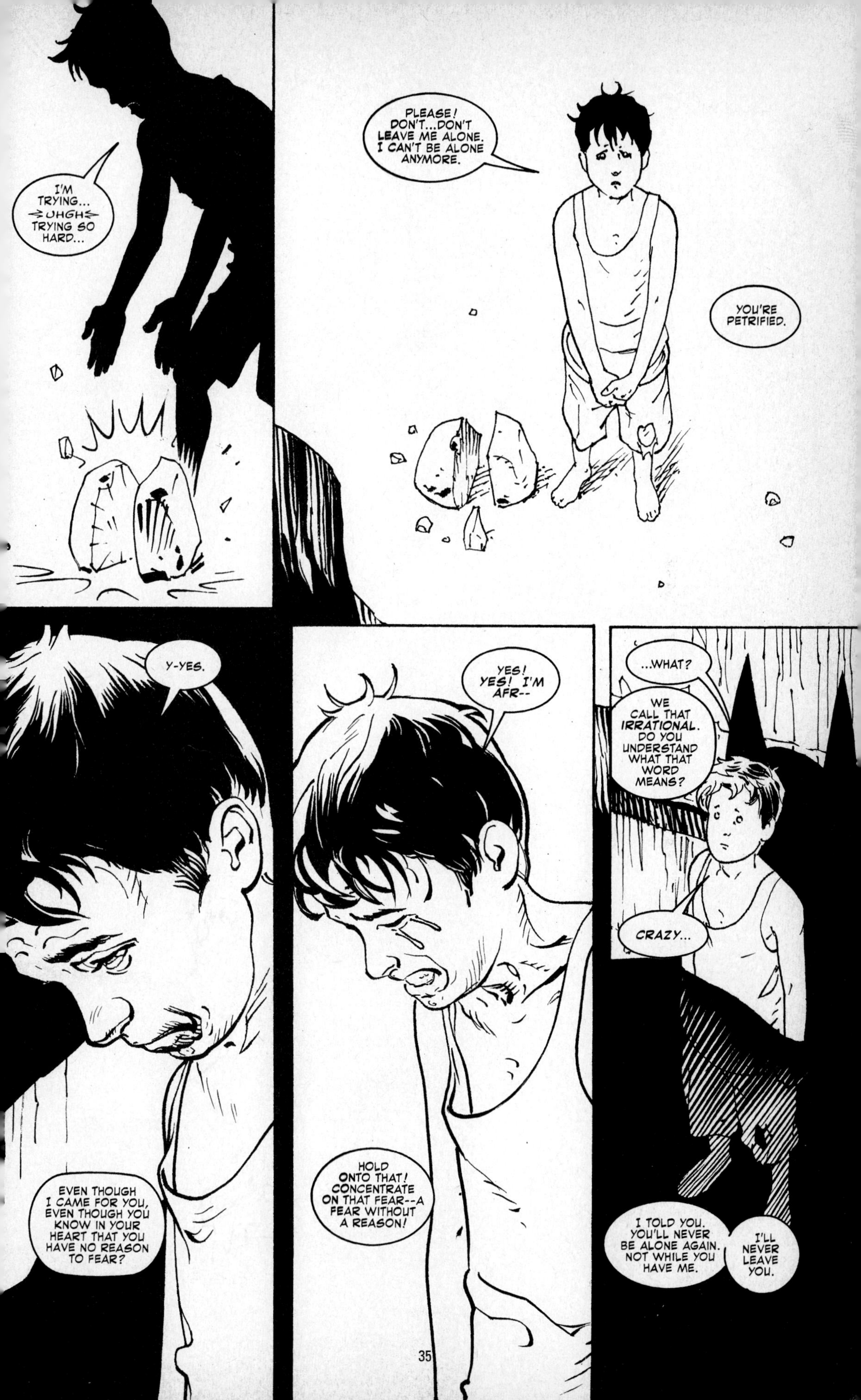

I'M TRYING... ⇒UHGH⇐ TRYING SO HARD...
PLEASE! DON'T...DON'T LEAVE ME ALONE. I CAN'T BE ALONE ANYMORE.
YOU'RE PETRIFIED.
Y-YES.
EVEN THOUGH I CAME FOR YOU, EVEN THOUGH YOU KNOW IN YOUR HEART THAT YOU HAVE NO REASON TO FEAR?
YES! YES! I'M AFR--
HOLD ONTO THAT! CONCENTRATE ON THAT FEAR--A FEAR WITHOUT A REASON!
...WHAT?
WE CALL THAT IRRATIONAL. DO YOU UNDERSTAND WHAT THAT WORD MEANS?
CRAZY...
I TOLD YOU. YOU'LL NEVER BE ALONE AGAIN. NOT WHILE YOU HAVE ME.
I'LL NEVER LEAVE YOU.

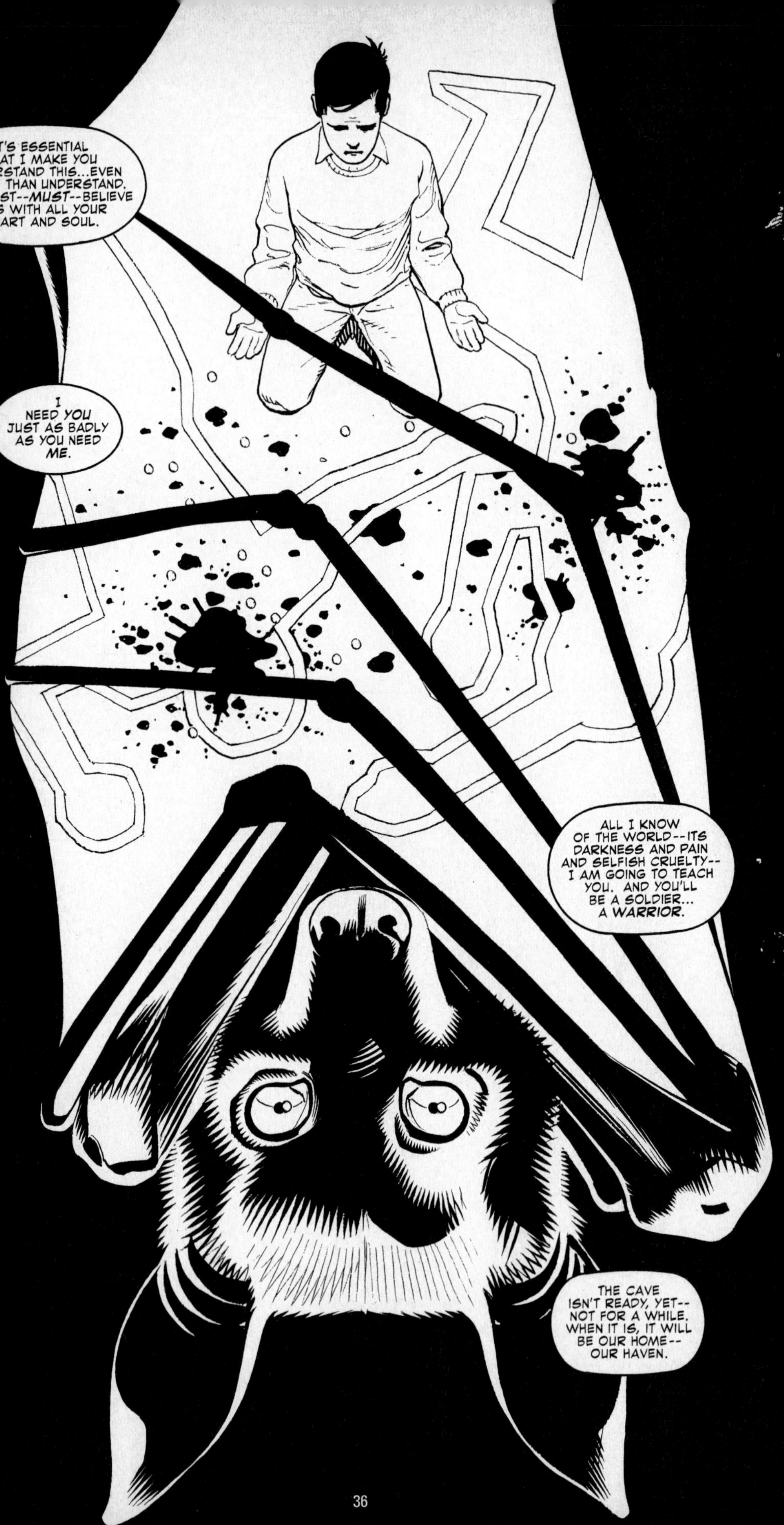
IT'S ESSENTIAL THAT I MAKE YOU UNDERSTAND THIS...EVEN MORE THAN UNDERSTAND. YOU MUST--MUST--BELIEVE THIS WITH ALL YOUR HEART AND SOUL.
I NEED YOU JUST AS BADLY AS YOU NEED ME.
ALL I KNOW OF THE WORLD--ITS DARKNESS AND PAIN AND SELFISH CRUELTY--I AM GOING TO TEACH YOU. AND YOU'LL BE A SOLDIER... A WARRIOR.
THE CAVE ISN'T READY, YET--NOT FOR A WHILE. WHEN IT IS, IT WILL BE OUR HOME--OUR HAVEN.

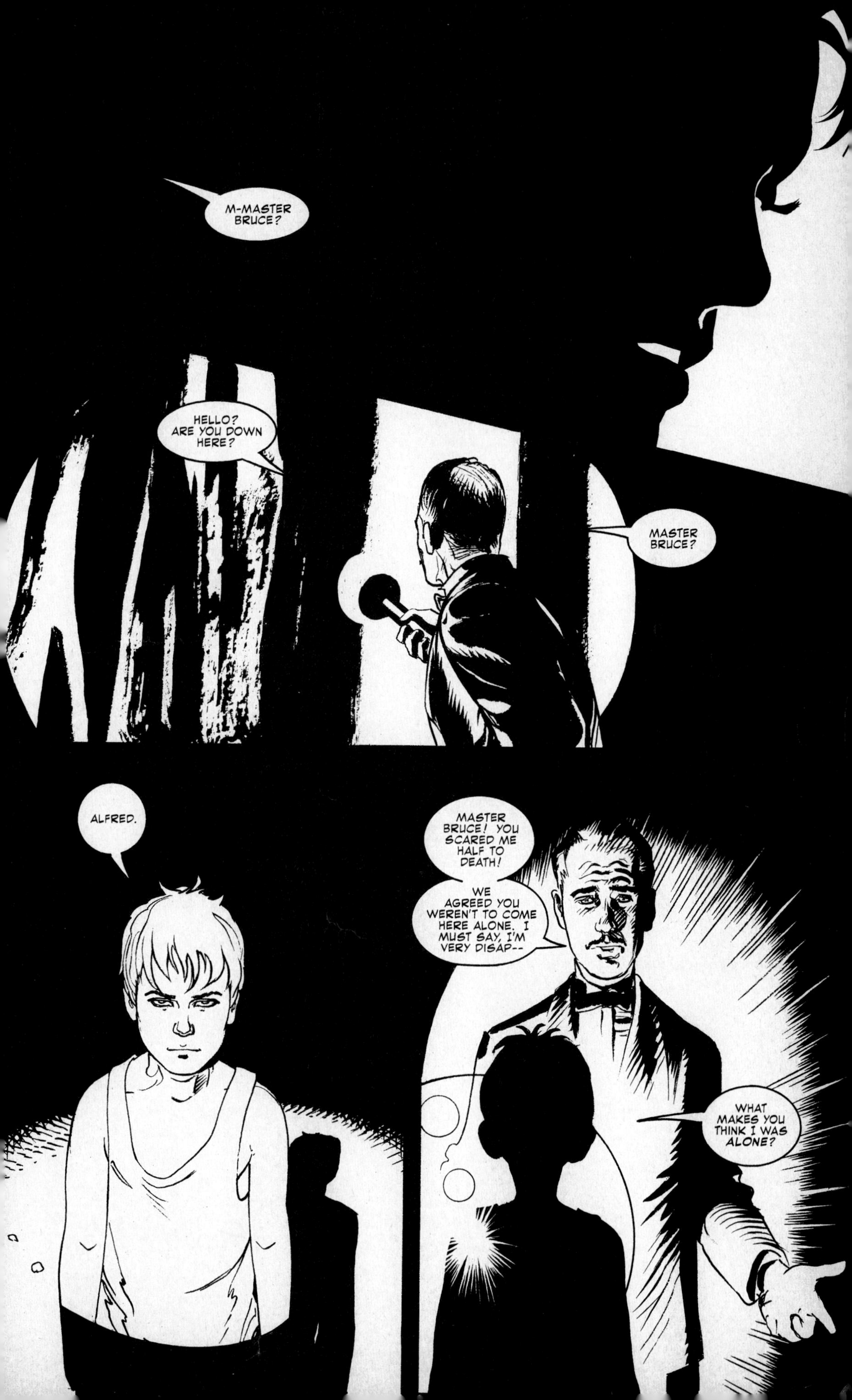
M-MASTER BRUCE?
HELLO? ARE YOU DOWN HERE?
MASTER BRUCE?
ALFRED.
MASTER BRUCE! YOU SCARED ME HALF TO DEATH!
WE AGREED YOU WEREN'T TO COME HERE ALONE. I MUST SAY, I'M VERY DISAP--
WHAT MAKES YOU THINK I WAS ALONE?

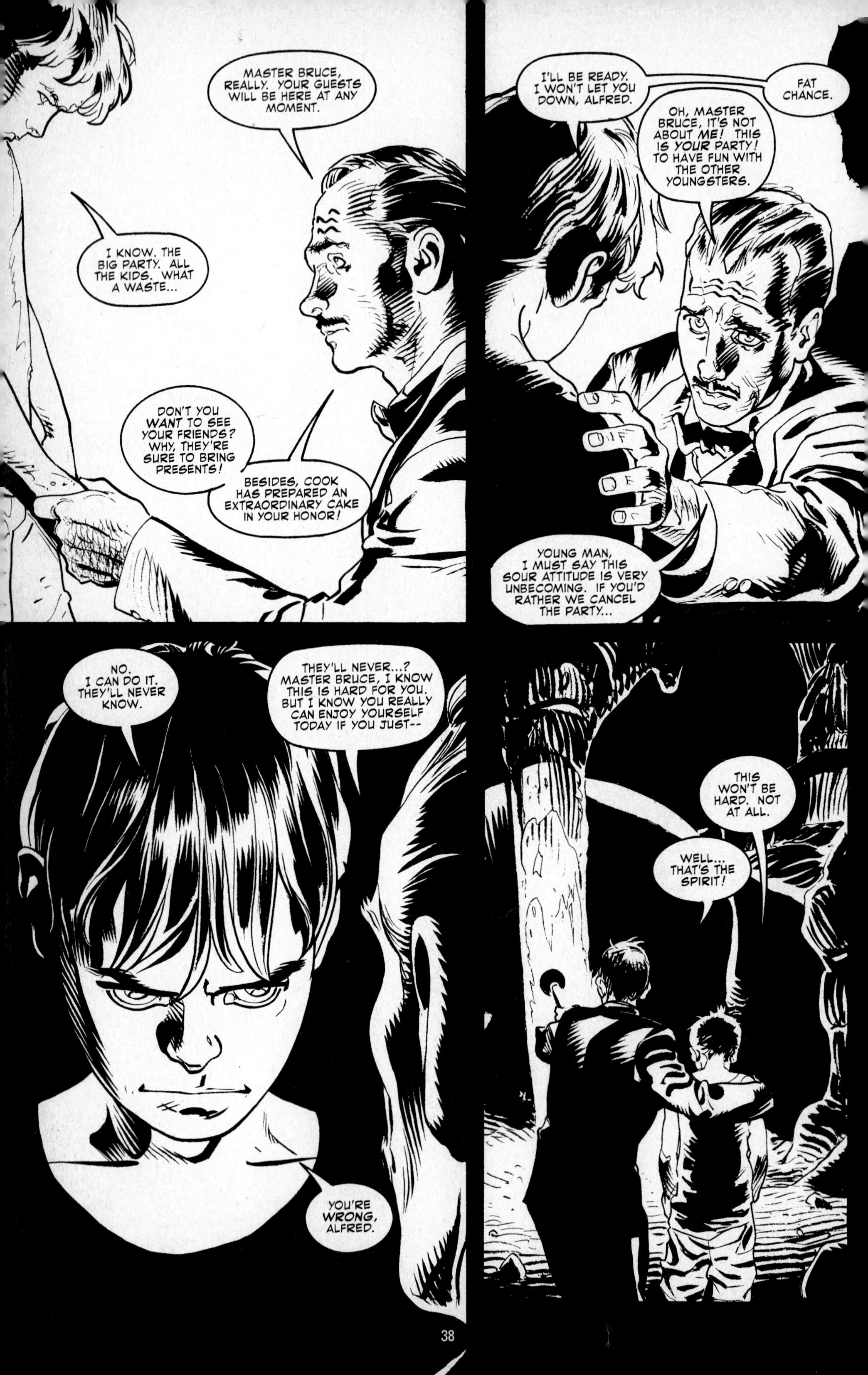
MASTER BRUCE, REALLY. YOUR GUESTS WILL BE HERE AT ANY MOMENT.
I KNOW. THE BIG PARTY. ALL THE KIDS. WHAT A WASTE...
DON'T YOU WANT TO SEE YOUR FRIENDS? WHY, THEY'RE SURE TO BRING PRESENTS!
BESIDES, COOK HAS PREPARED AN EXTRAORDINARY CAKE IN YOUR HONOR!
I'LL BE READY. I WON'T LET YOU DOWN, ALFRED.
FAT CHANCE.
OH, MASTER BRUCE, IT'S NOT ABOUT ME! THIS IS YOUR PARTY! TO HAVE FUN WITH THE OTHER YOUNGSTERS.
YOUNG MAN, I MUST SAY THIS SOUR ATTITUDE IS VERY UNBECOMING. IF YOU'D RATHER WE CANCEL THE PARTY...
NO. I CAN DO IT. THEY'LL NEVER KNOW.
THEY'LL NEVER...? MASTER BRUCE, I KNOW THIS IS HARD FOR YOU. BUT I KNOW YOU REALLY CAN ENJOY YOURSELF TODAY IF YOU JUST--
YOU'RE WRONG, ALFRED.
THIS WON'T BE HARD. NOT AT ALL.
WELL... THAT'S THE SPIRIT!

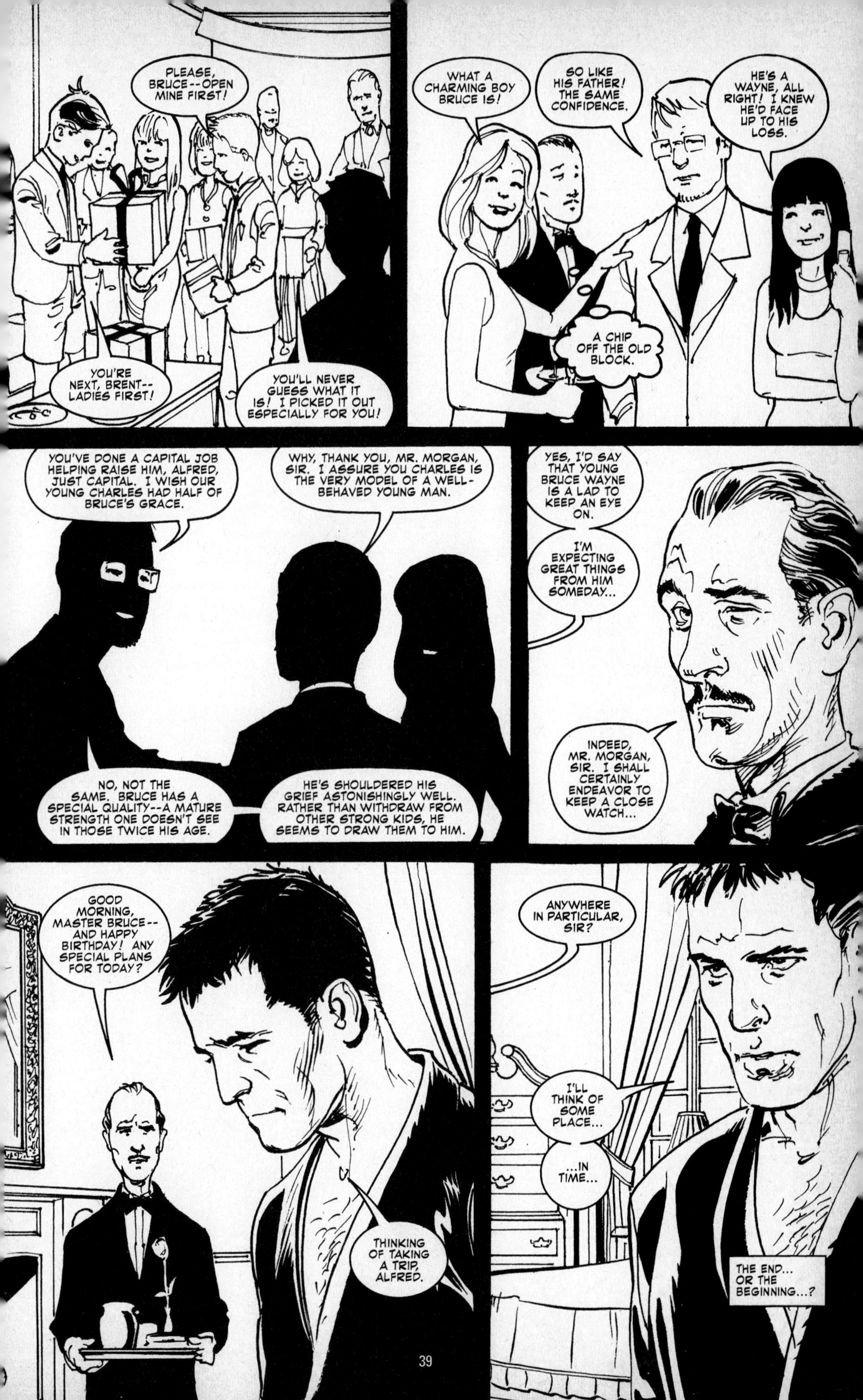
PLEASE, BRUCE--OPEN MINE FIRST!
YOU'RE NEXT, BRENT--LADIES FIRST!
YOU'LL NEVER GUESS WHAT IT IS! I PICKED IT OUT ESPECIALLY FOR YOU!
WHAT A CHARMING BOY BRUCE IS!
SO LIKE HIS FATHER! THE SAME CONFIDENCE.
HE'S A WAYNE, ALL RIGHT! I KNEW HE'D FACE UP TO HIS LOSS.
A CHIP OFF THE OLD BLOCK.
YOU'VE DONE A CAPITAL JOB HELPING RAISE HIM, ALFRED, JUST CAPITAL. I WISH OUR YOUNG CHARLES HAD HALF OF BRUCE'S GRACE.
WHY, THANK YOU, MR. MORGAN, SIR. I ASSURE YOU CHARLES IS THE VERY MODEL OF A WELL-BEHAVED YOUNG MAN.
NO, NOT THE SAME. BRUCE HAS A SPECIAL QUALITY--A MATURE STRENGTH ONE DOESN'T SEE IN THOSE TWICE HIS AGE.
HE'S SHOULDERED HIS GRIEF ASTONISHINGLY WELL. RATHER THAN WITHDRAW FROM OTHER STRONG KIDS, HE SEEMS TO DRAW THEM TO HIM.
YES, I'D SAY THAT YOUNG BRUCE WAYNE IS A LAD TO KEEP AN EYE ON.
I'M EXPECTING GREAT THINGS FROM HIM SOMEDAY...
INDEED, MR. MORGAN, SIR. I SHALL CERTAINLY ENDEAVOR TO KEEP A CLOSE WATCH...
GOOD MORNING, MASTER BRUCE--AND HAPPY BIRTHDAY! ANY SPECIAL PLANS FOR TODAY?
THINKING OF TAKING A TRIP, ALFRED.
ANYWHERE IN PARTICULAR, SIR?
I'LL THINK OF SOME PLACE...
...IN TIME...
THE END... OR THE BEGINNING...?

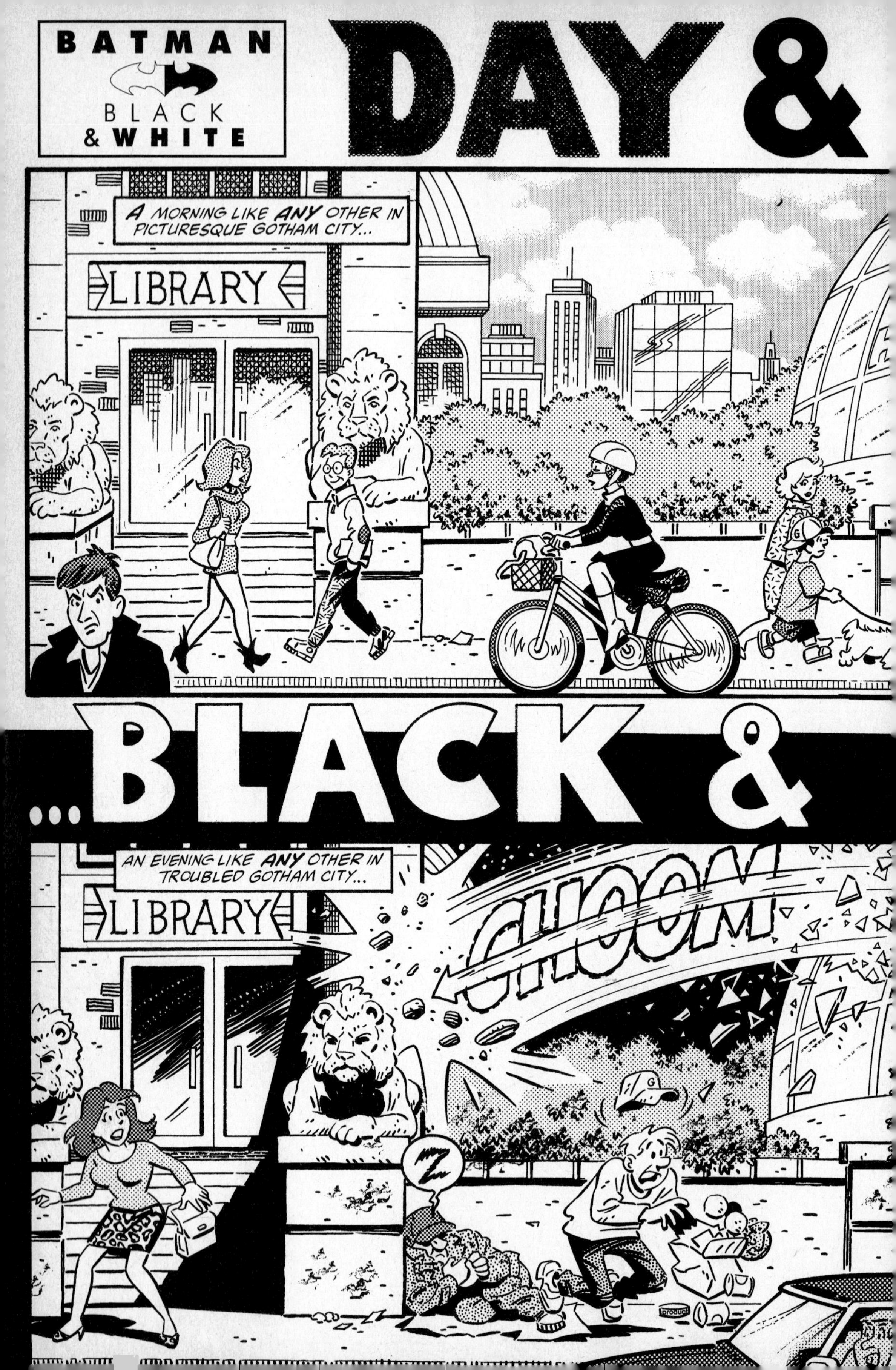
BATMAN BLACK & WHITE
DAY &
A MORNING LIKE ANY OTHER IN PICTURESQUE GOTHAM CITY...
LIBRARY
...BLACK &
AN EVENING LIKE ANY OTHER IN TROUBLED GOTHAM CITY...
LIBRARY
CHOOOM
Z

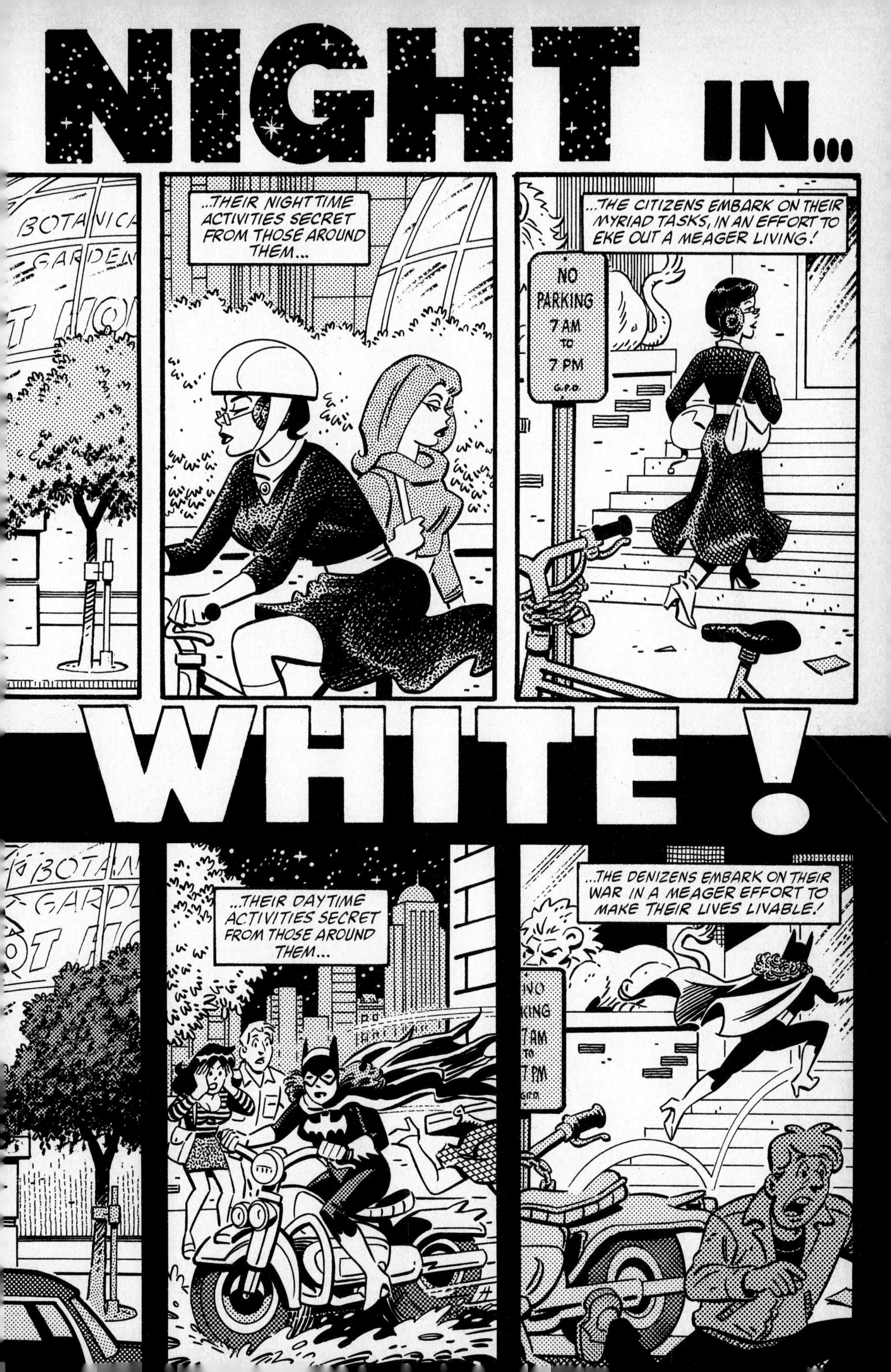
NIGHT IN...
...THEIR NIGHTTIME ACTIVITIES SECRET FROM THOSE AROUND THEM...
...THE CITIZENS EMBARK ON THEIR MYRIAD TASKS, IN AN EFFORT TO EKE OUT A MEAGER LIVING!
NO PARKING 7 AM TO 7 PM
WHITE!
...THEIR DAYTIME ACTIVITIES SECRET FROM THOSE AROUND THEM...
...THE DENIZENS EMBARK ON THEIR WAR IN A MEAGER EFFORT TO MAKE THEIR LIVES LIVABLE!

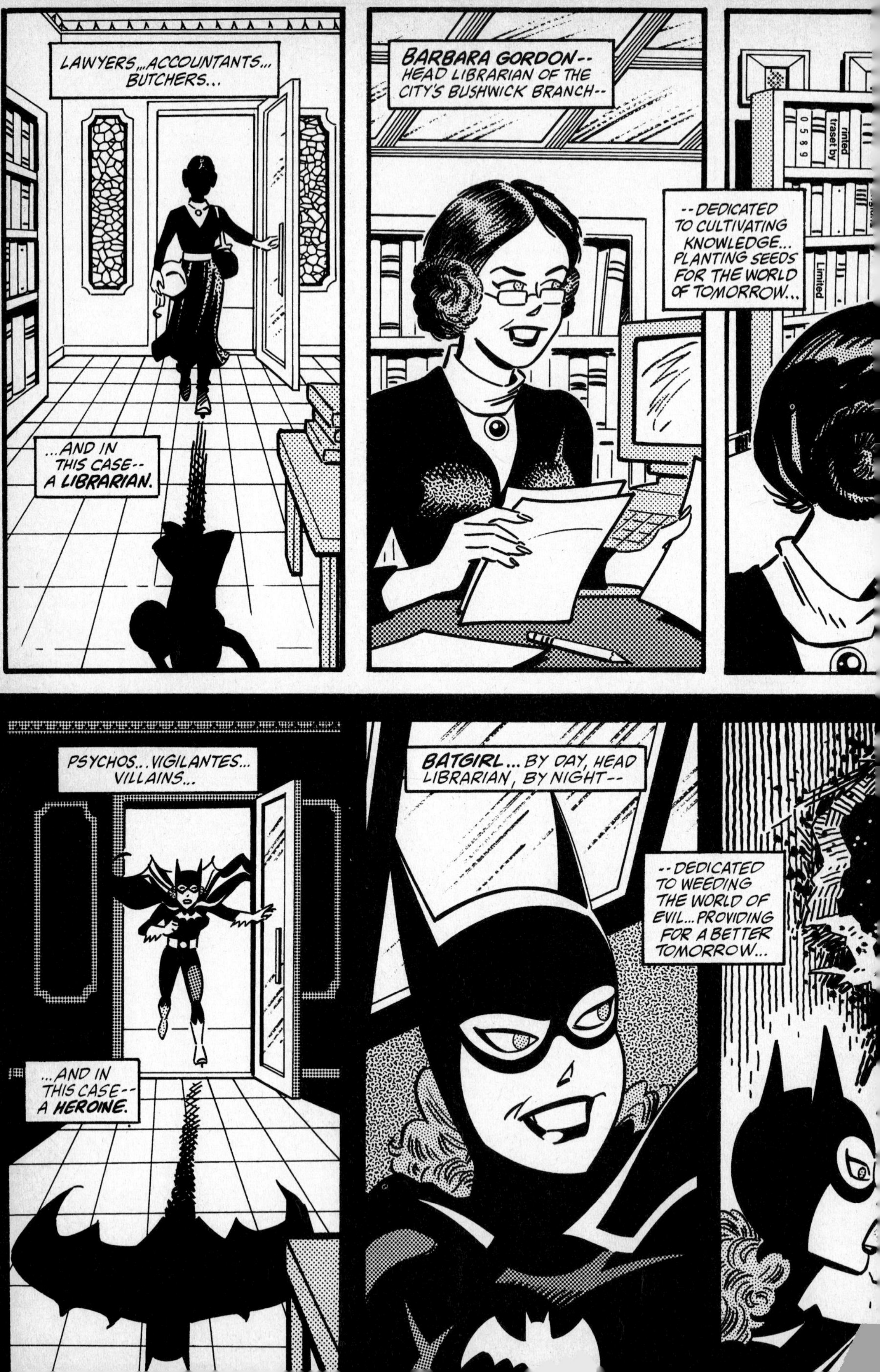
LAWYERS...ACCOUNTANTS... BUTCHERS...
...AND IN THIS CASE-- A **LIBRARIAN**.
**BARBARA GORDON**-- HEAD LIBRARIAN OF THE CITY'S BUSHWICK BRANCH--
--DEDICATED TO CULTIVATING KNOWLEDGE... PLANTING SEEDS FOR THE WORLD OF TOMORROW...
PSYCHOS...VIGILANTES... VILLAINS...
...AND IN THIS CASE-- A **HEROINE**.
**BATGIRL**... BY DAY, HEAD LIBRARIAN, BY NIGHT--
--DEDICATED TO WEEDING THE WORLD OF EVIL...PROVIDING FOR A BETTER TOMORROW...

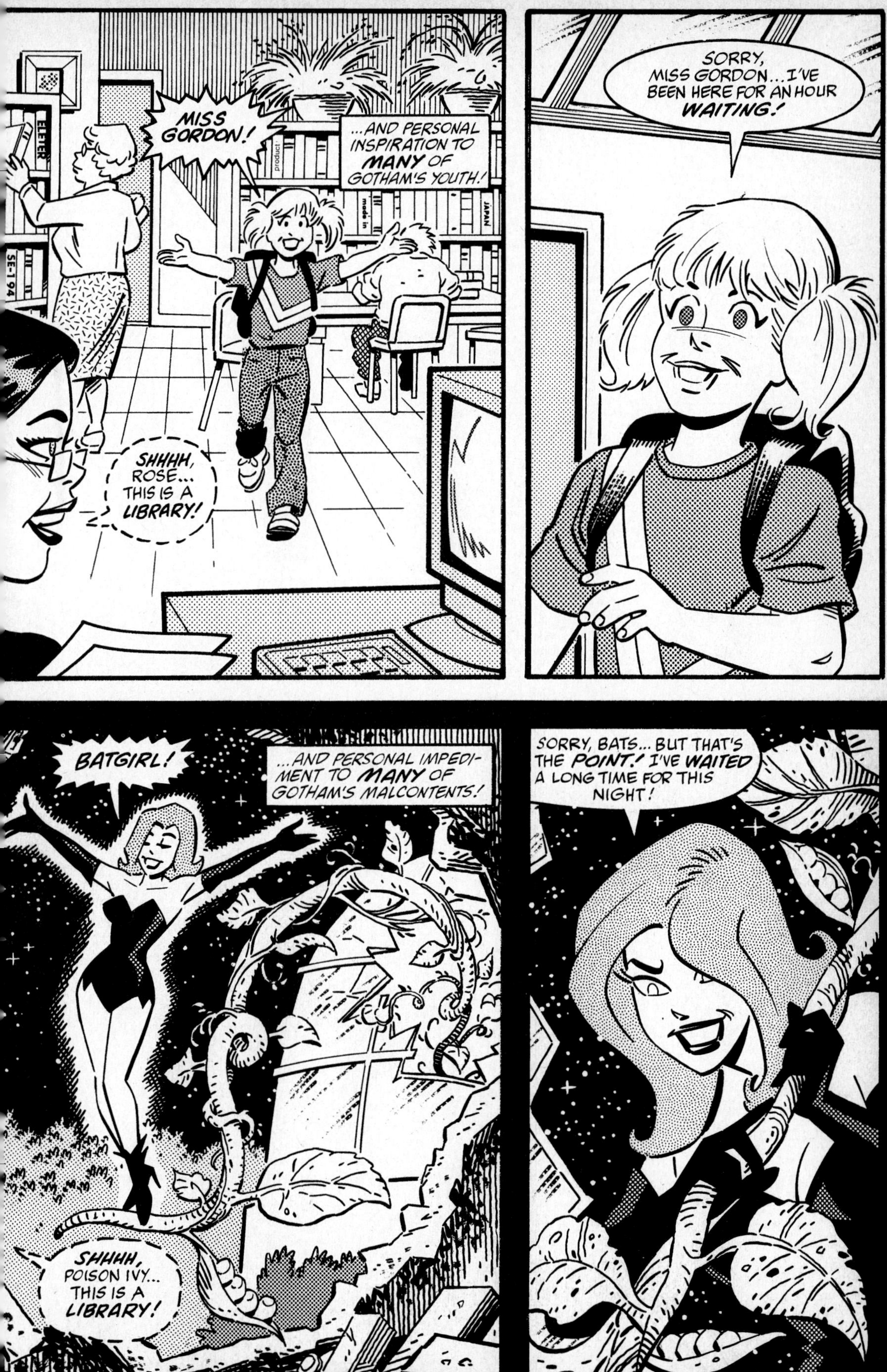
MISS GORDON!
...AND PERSONAL INSPIRATION TO MANY OF GOTHAM'S YOUTH!
SHHHH, ROSE... THIS IS A LIBRARY!
SORRY, MISS GORDON... I'VE BEEN HERE FOR AN HOUR WAITING!
BATGIRL!
...AND PERSONAL IMPEDIMENT TO MANY OF GOTHAM'S MALCONTENTS!
SHHHH, POISON IVY... THIS IS A LIBRARY!
SORRY, BATS... BUT THAT'S THE POINT! I'VE WAITED A LONG TIME FOR THIS NIGHT!

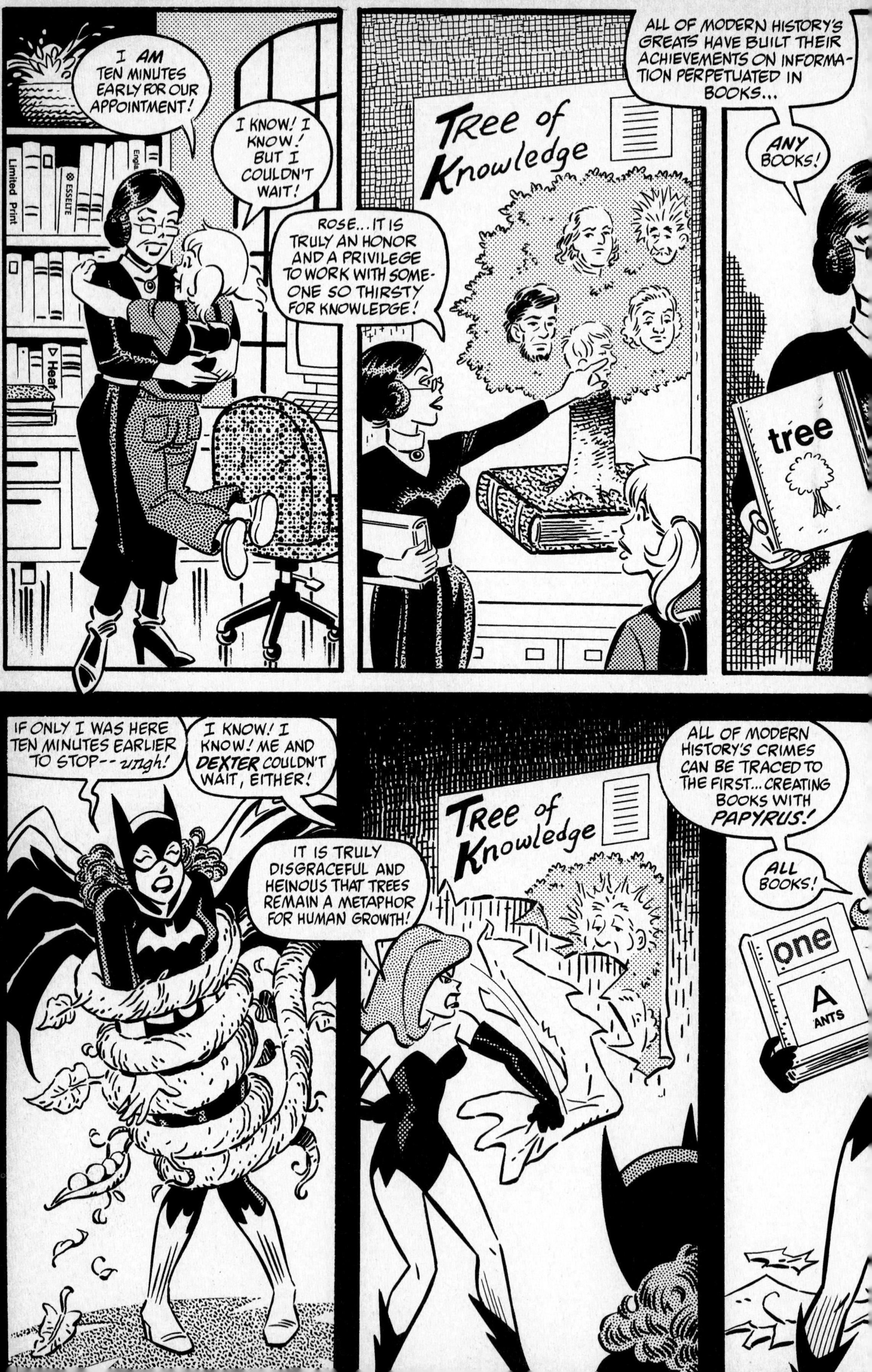

I AM TEN MINUTES EARLY FOR OUR APPOINTMENT!
I KNOW! I KNOW! BUT I COULDN'T WAIT!
Limited Print
ESSELTE
Heat
ROSE... IT IS TRULY AN HONOR AND A PRIVILEGE TO WORK WITH SOMEONE SO THIRSTY FOR KNOWLEDGE!
Tree of Knowledge
ALL OF MODERN HISTORY'S GREATS HAVE BUILT THEIR ACHIEVEMENTS ON INFORMATION PERPETUATED IN BOOKS...
ANY BOOKS!
tree
IF ONLY I WAS HERE TEN MINUTES EARLIER TO STOP-- ungh!
I KNOW! I KNOW! ME AND DEXTER COULDN'T WAIT, EITHER!
IT IS TRULY DISGRACEFUL AND HEINOUS THAT TREES REMAIN A METAPHOR FOR HUMAN GROWTH!
Tree of Knowledge
ALL OF MODERN HISTORY'S CRIMES CAN BE TRACED TO THE FIRST... CREATING BOOKS WITH PAPYRUS!
ALL BOOKS!
one
A
ANTS

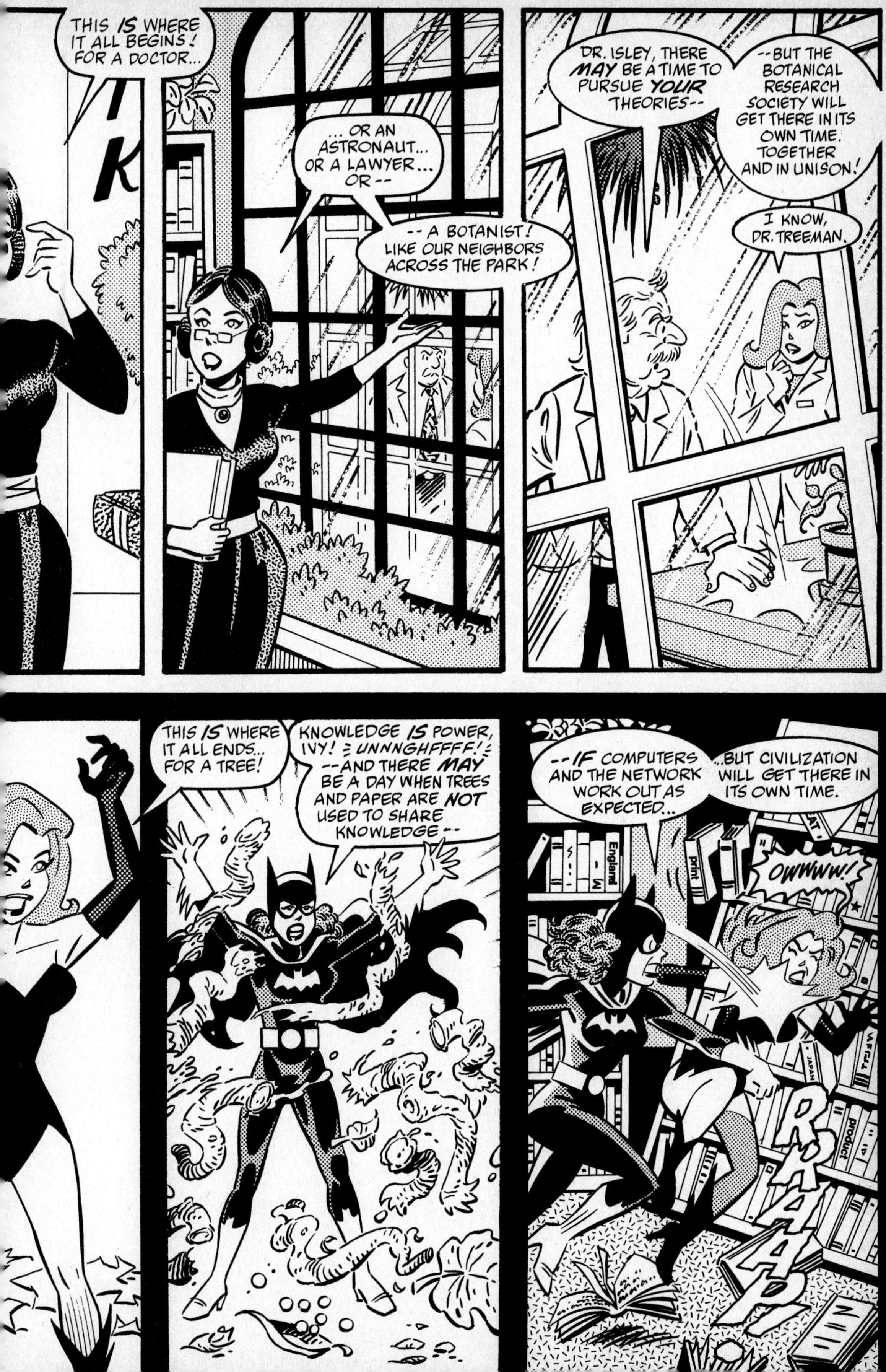

THIS *IS* WHERE IT ALL BEGINS! FOR A DOCTOR...
... OR AN ASTRONAUT... OR A LAWYER... OR --
-- A BOTANIST! LIKE OUR NEIGHBORS ACROSS THE PARK!
DR. ISLEY, THERE *MAY* BE A TIME TO PURSUE *YOUR* THEORIES--
--BUT THE BOTANICAL RESEARCH SOCIETY WILL GET THERE IN ITS OWN TIME. TOGETHER AND IN UNISON!
I KNOW, DR. TREEMAN.
THIS *IS* WHERE IT ALL ENDS... FOR A TREE!
KNOWLEDGE *IS* POWER, IVY! *UNNNGHFFFF!* --AND THERE *MAY* BE A DAY WHEN TREES AND PAPER ARE *NOT* USED TO SHARE KNOWLEDGE--
--*IF* COMPUTERS AND THE NETWORK WORK OUT AS EXPECTED...
...BUT CIVILIZATION WILL GET THERE IN ITS OWN TIME.
England
print
OWWWW!
JAPAN
product

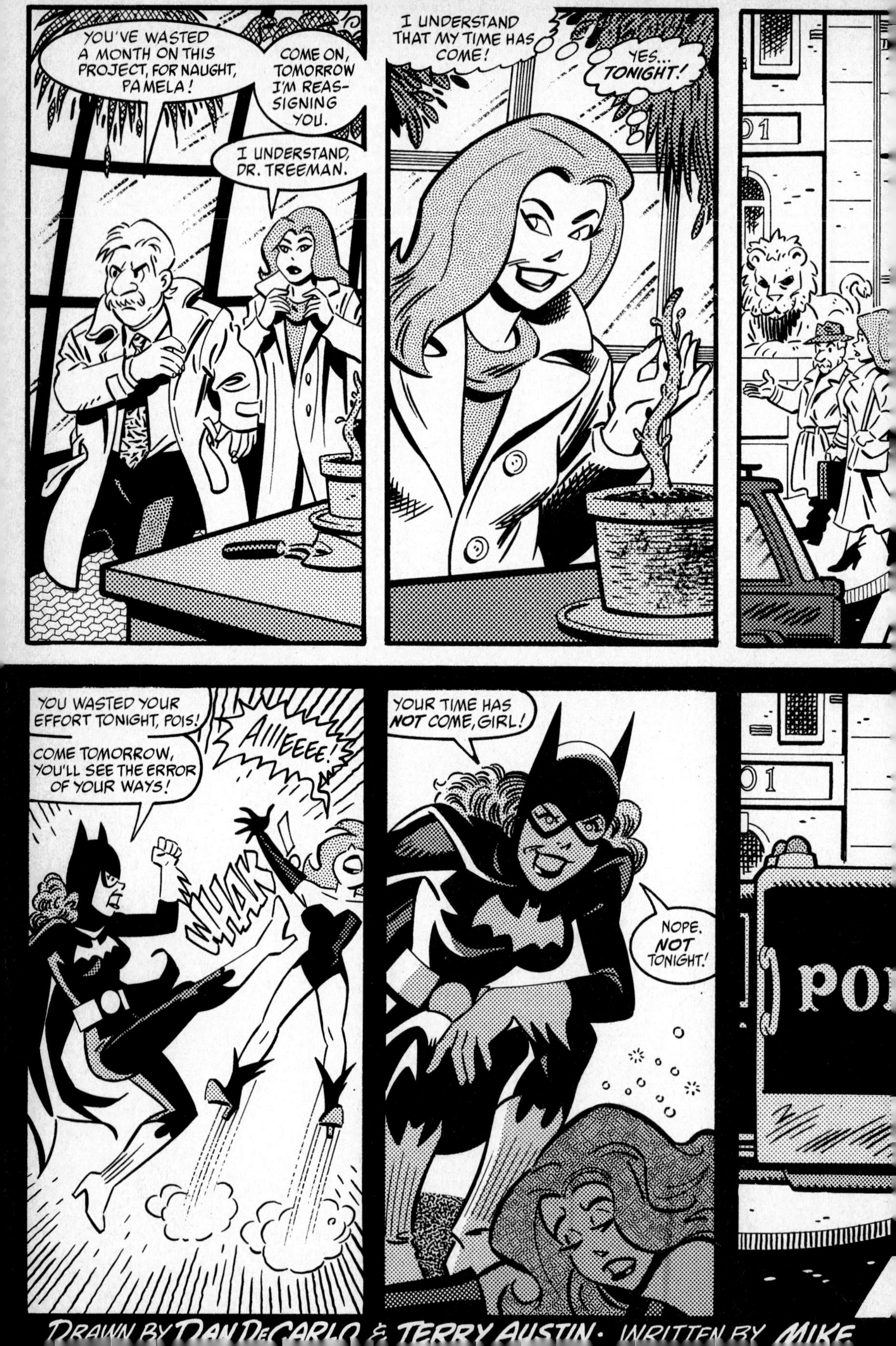
YOU'VE WASTED A MONTH ON THIS PROJECT, FOR NAUGHT, PAMELA!
COME ON, TOMORROW I'M REASSIGNING YOU.
I UNDERSTAND, DR. TREEMAN.
I UNDERSTAND THAT MY TIME HAS COME!
YES... TONIGHT!
YOU WASTED YOUR EFFORT TONIGHT, POIS!
COME TOMORROW, YOU'LL SEE THE ERROR OF YOUR WAYS!
AIIIEEEE!
WHAK!
YOUR TIME HAS NOT COME, GIRL!
NOPE. NOT TONIGHT!
POL
DRAWN BY DAN DECARLO & TERRY AUSTIN • WRITTEN BY MIKE

LIBRARY

DUSK IN THE CITY... ANOTHER DAY DONE.

GROUNDWORK LAID FOR A BETTER TOMORROW...

...THANKS TO THE THANKLESS WORK DONE BY THE SELFLESS PUBLIC SERVANTS TOO OFTEN TAKEN FOR GRANTED IN PICTURESQUE GOTHAM CITY!

BOTAN GARDEN HOT HO

LIBRARY

DAWN IN THE CITY... ANOTHER NIGHT DONE.

GROUNDWORK LAID FOR A BETTER TOMORROW...

...THANKS TO THE ANONYMOUS WORK DONE BY THE SELFLESS PUBLIC SERVANTS TOO OFTEN TAKEN FOR GRANTED IN TROUBLED GOTHAM CITY!

CARLIN· LETTERED BY RICK PARKER · EDITED BY MARK CHIARELLO

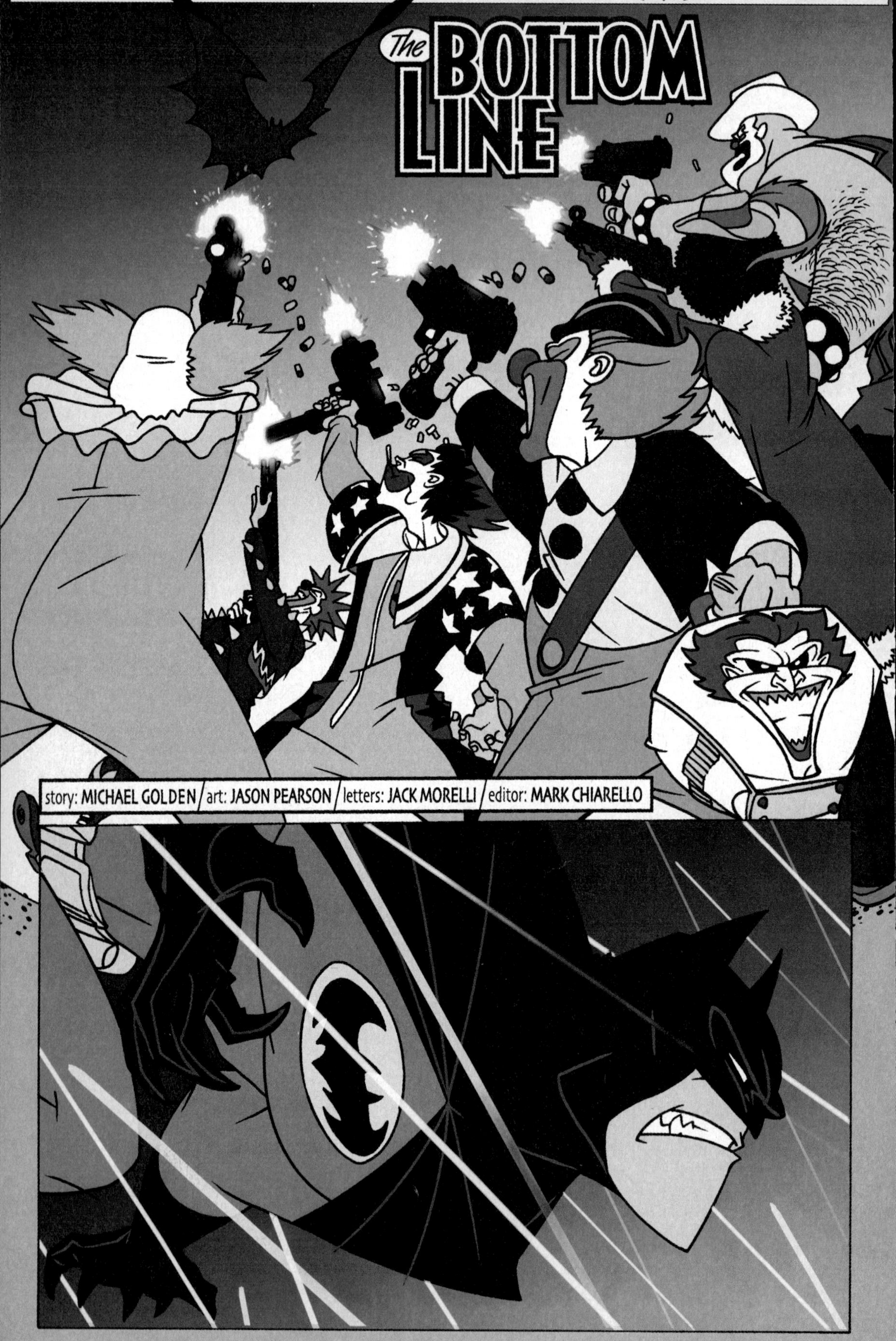
The BOTTOM LINE
story: MICHAEL GOLDEN / art: JASON PEARSON / letters: JACK MORELLI / editor: MARK CHIARELLO

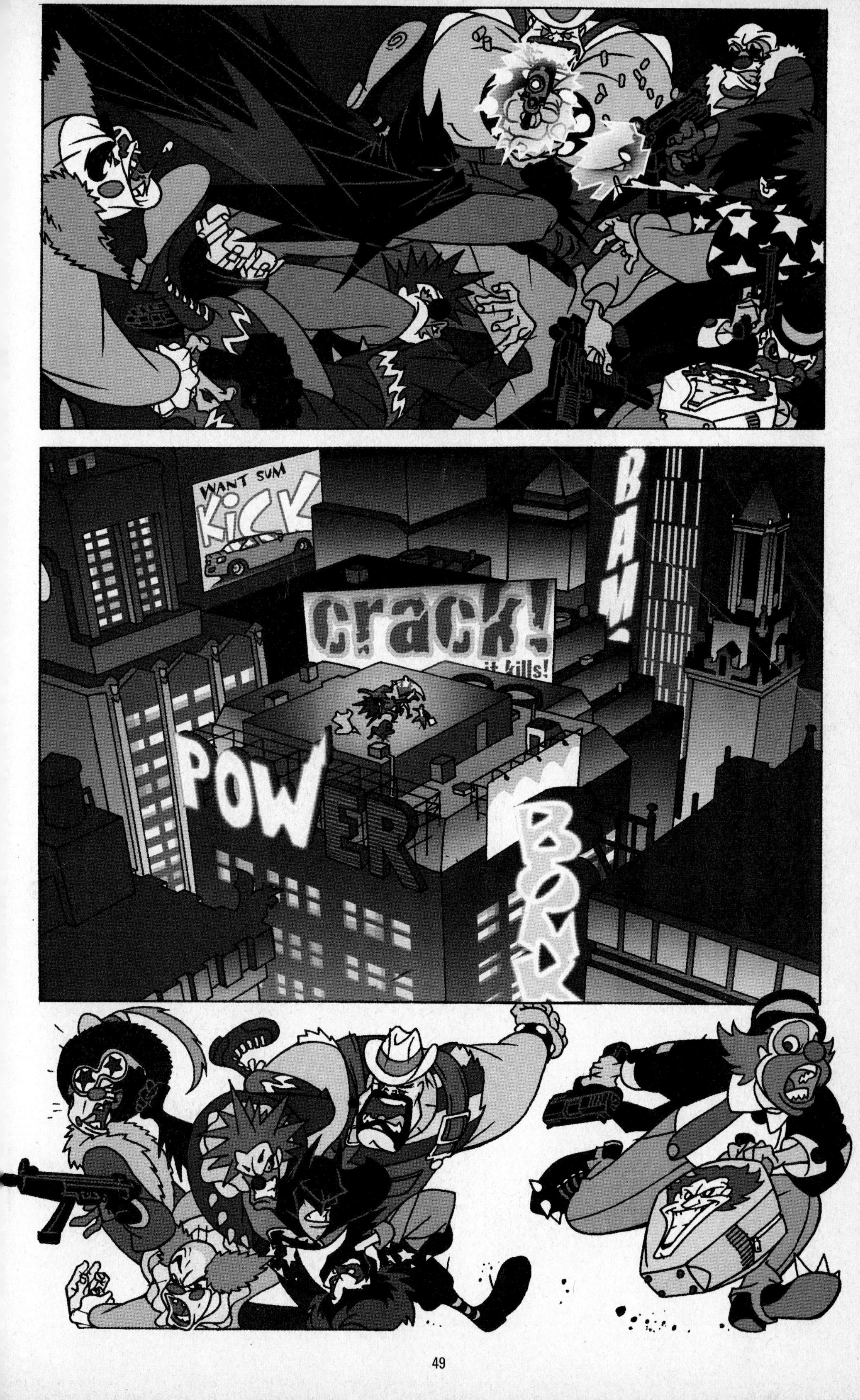
WANT SUM
KiCK
BAM!
crack!
it kills!
POWER
BONK

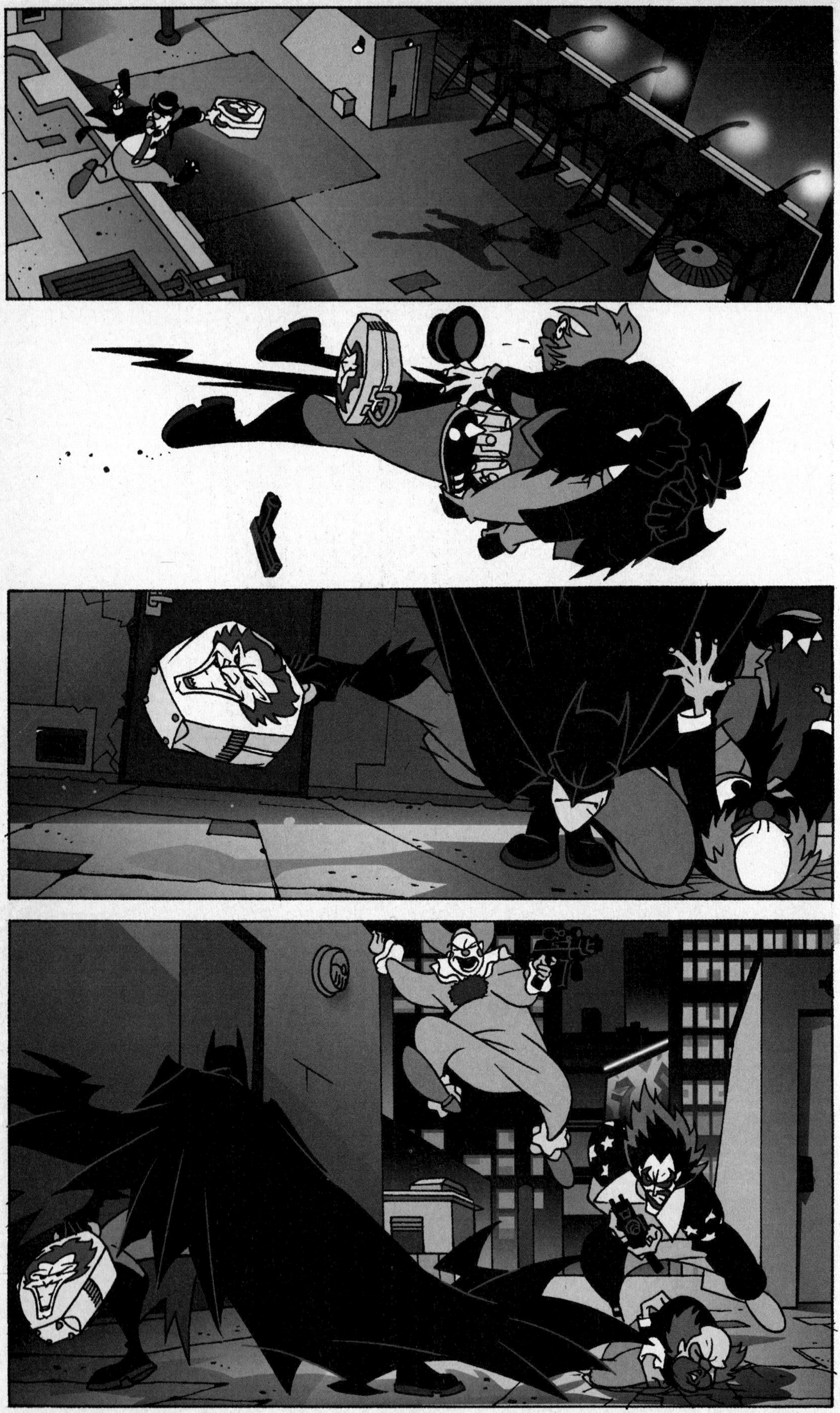

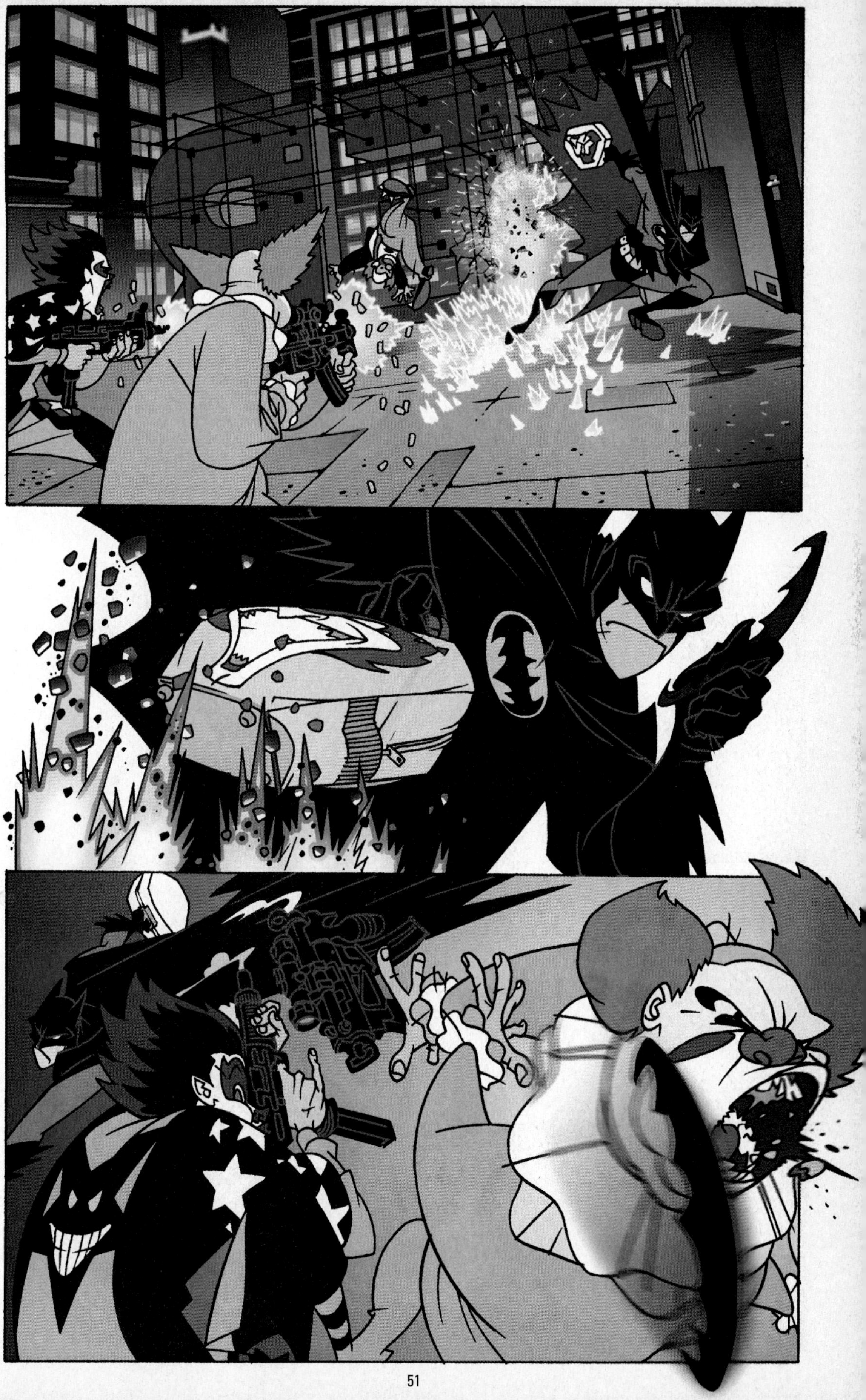

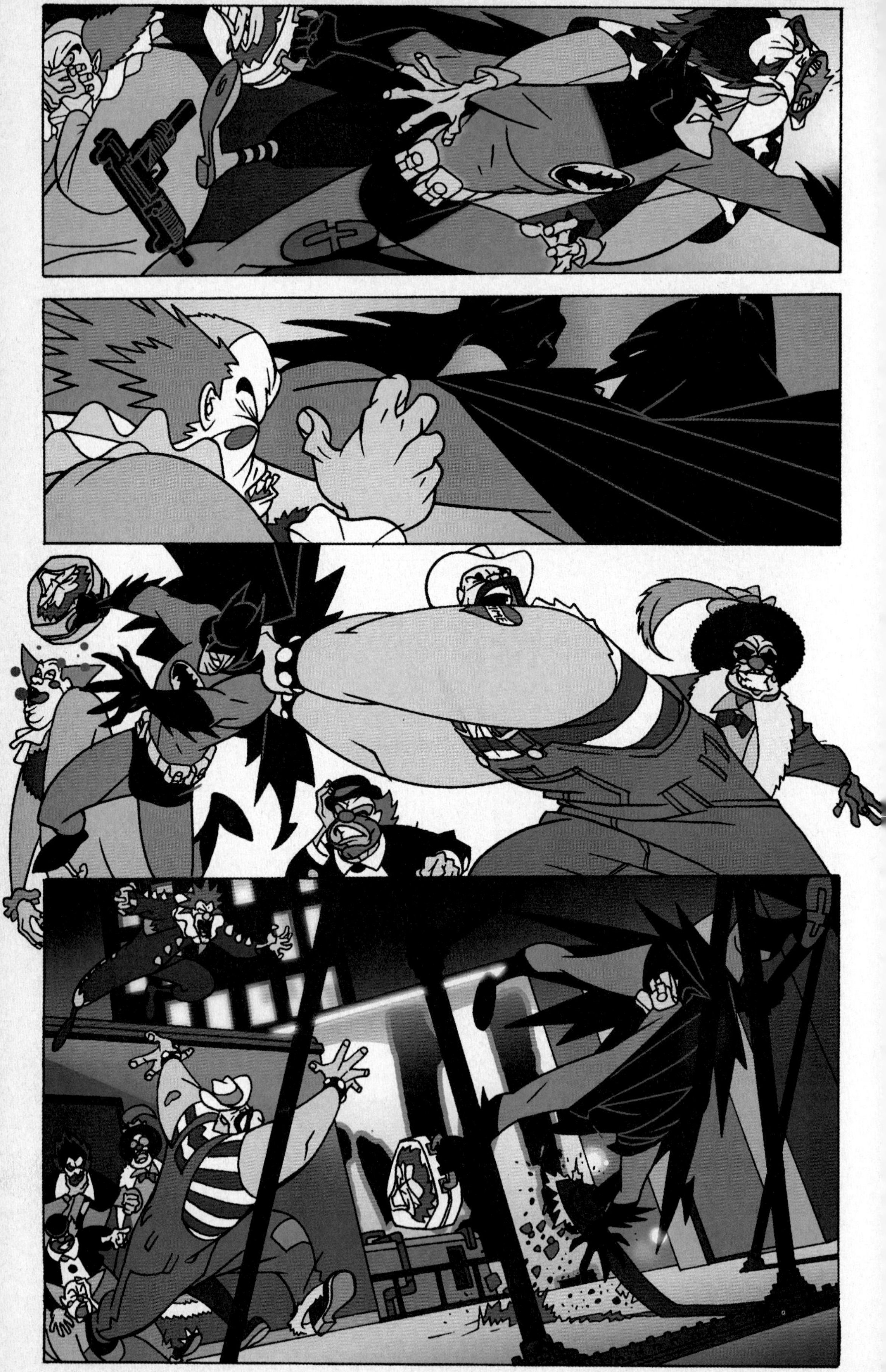

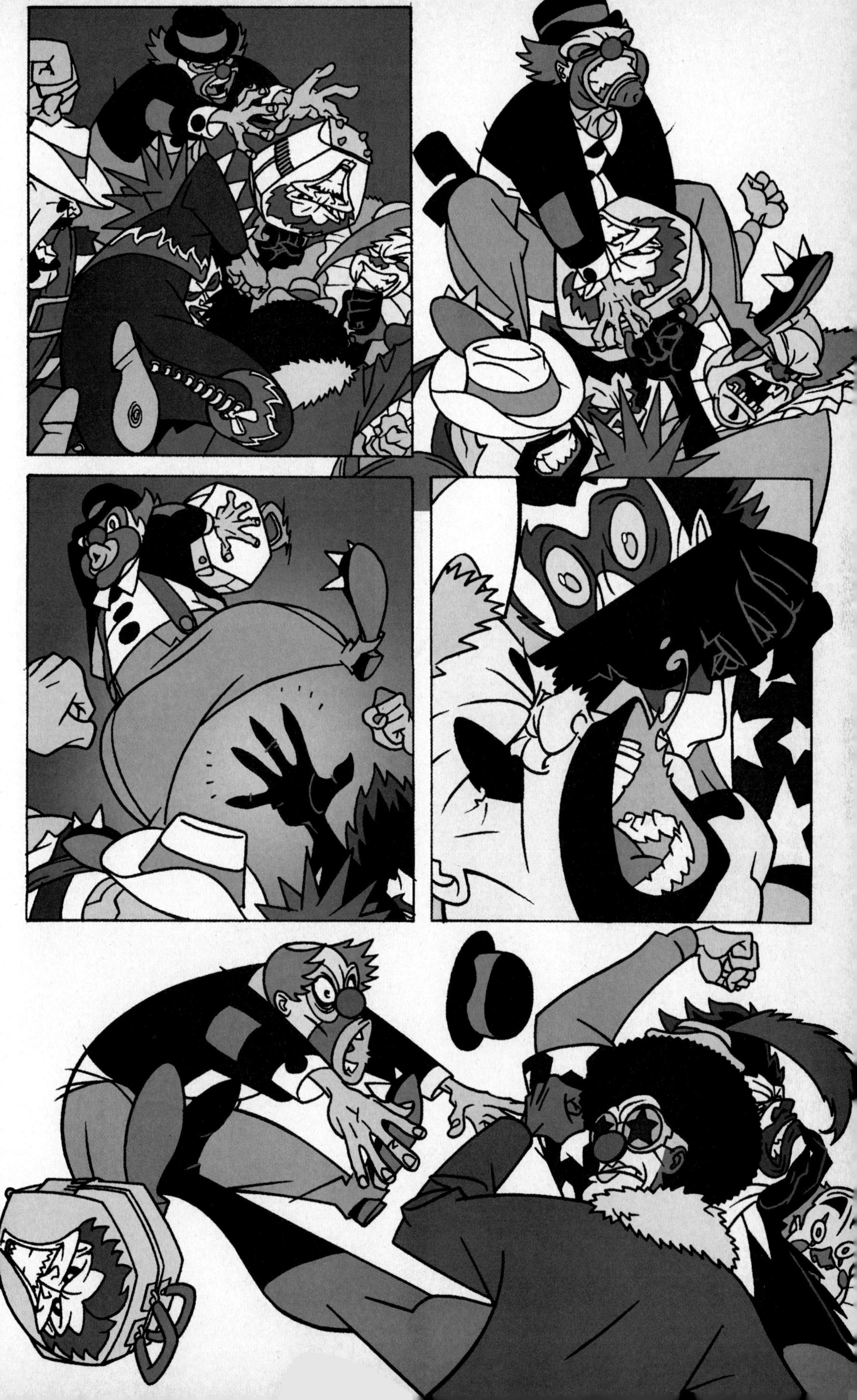

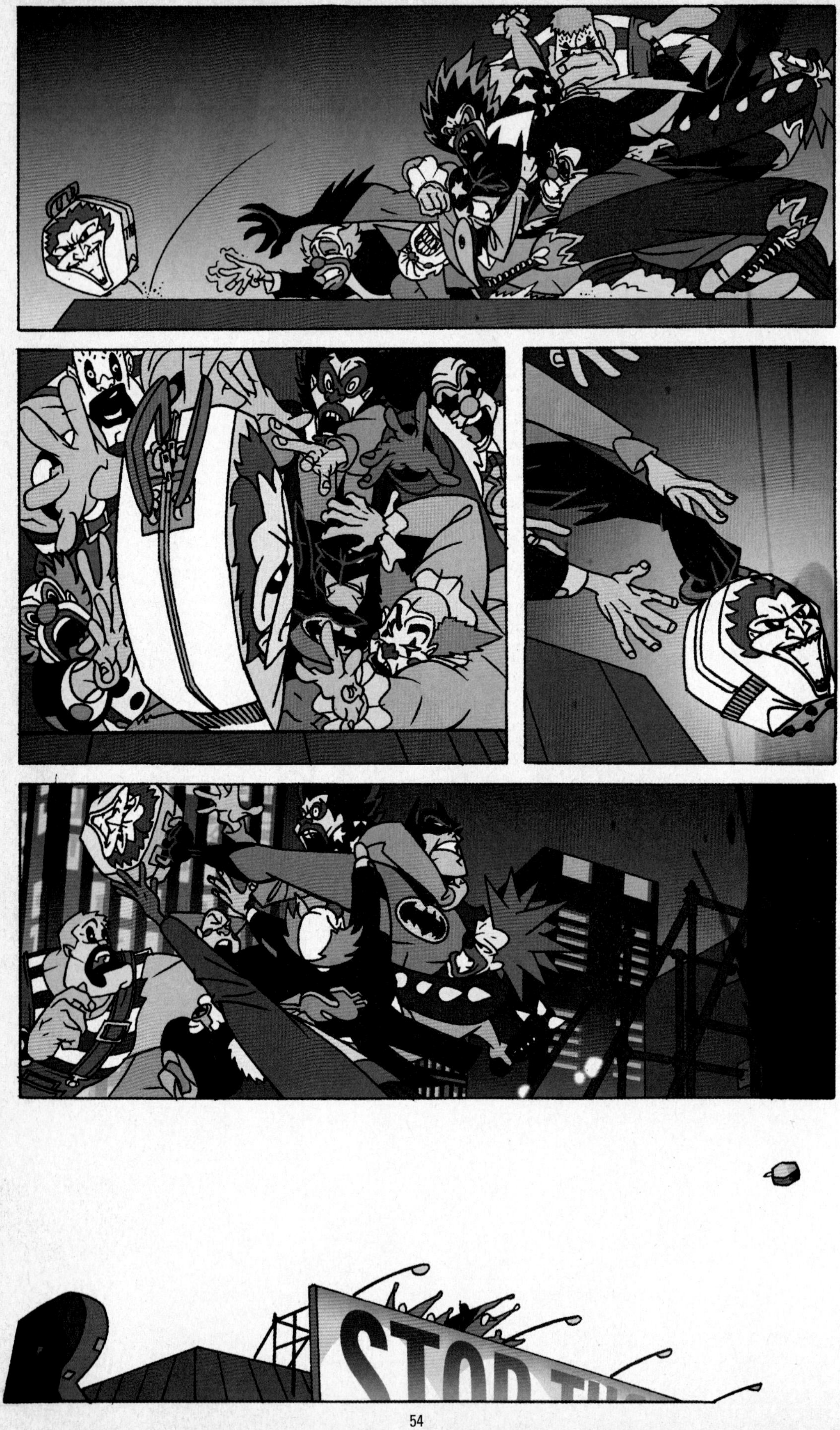
STOP

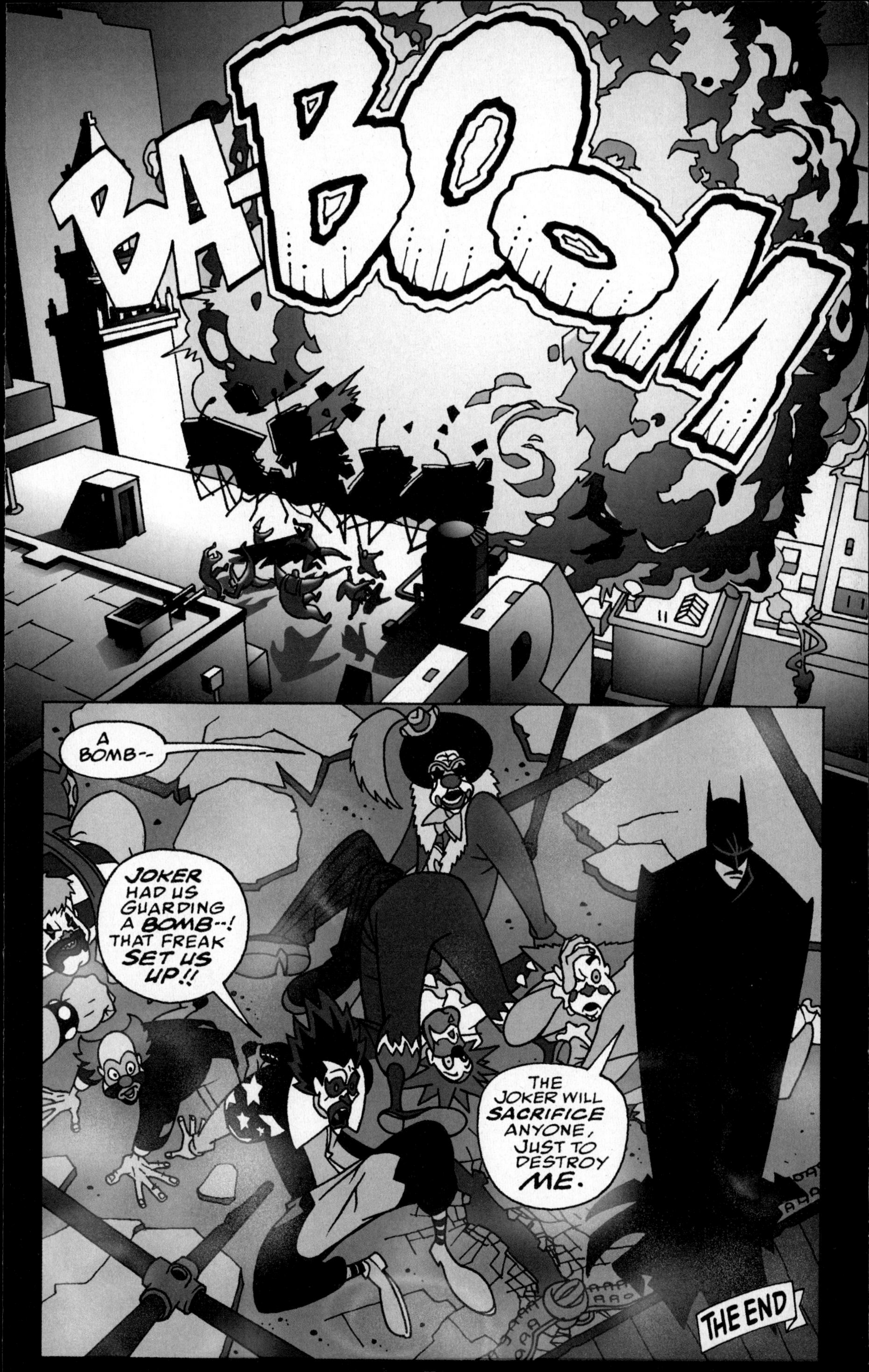
BA-BOOM
A BOMB--
JOKER HAD US GUARDING A BOMB--! THAT FREAK SET US UP!!
THE JOKER WILL SACRIFICE ANYONE, JUST TO DESTROY ME.
THE END

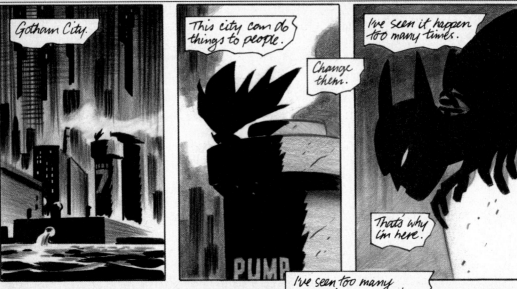

Gotham City.

This city can do things to people.

Change them.

I've seen it happen too many times.

That's why I'm here.

I've seen too many people become monsters.

PAUL GRIST
writer

DARWYN COOKE
artist

MARK CHIARELLO
editor

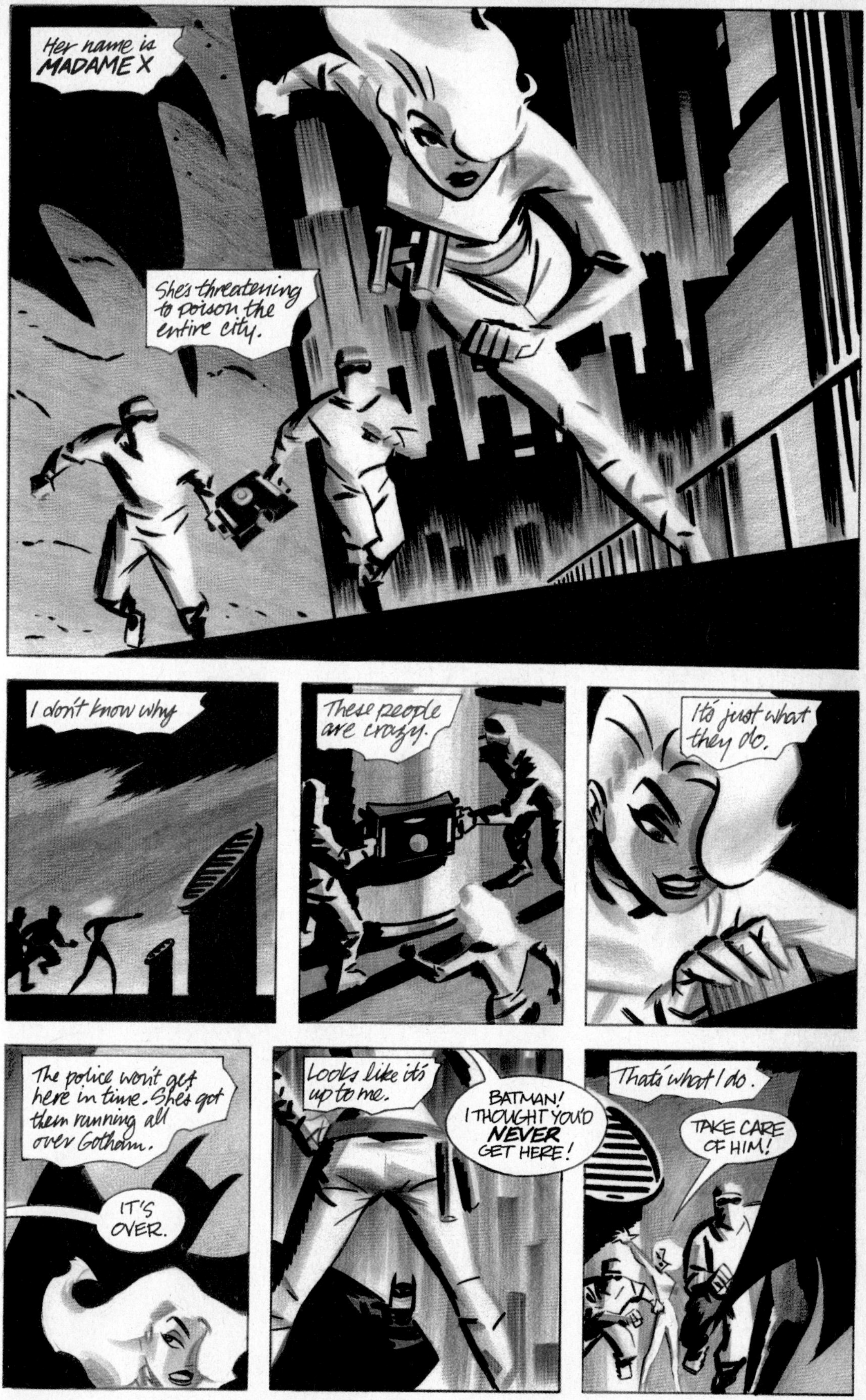

Her name is MADAME X
She's threatening to poison the entire city.
I don't know why
These people are crazy.
It's just what they do.
The police won't get here in time. She's got them running all over Gotham.
IT'S OVER.
Looks like it's up to me.
BATMAN! I THOUGHT YOU'D NEVER GET HERE!
That's what I do.
TAKE CARE OF HIM!

WHOMP!

CRUNCH!

DID YOU REALLY THINK THOSE IDIOTS WOULD BE A PROBLEM FOR ME, MADAME X?

NO...

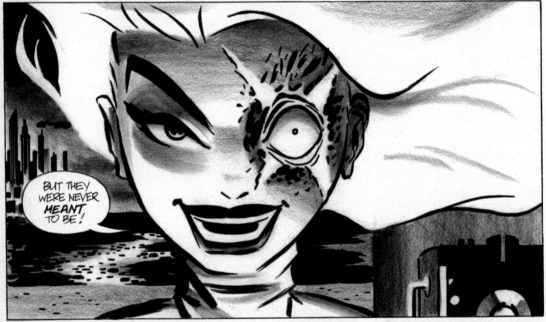

BUT THEY WERE NEVER *MEANT* TO BE!

THIS IS MY SPECIAL GIFT TO *YOU*!

Should have seen that coming!

WHOMP!

SKASH!

Idiot!

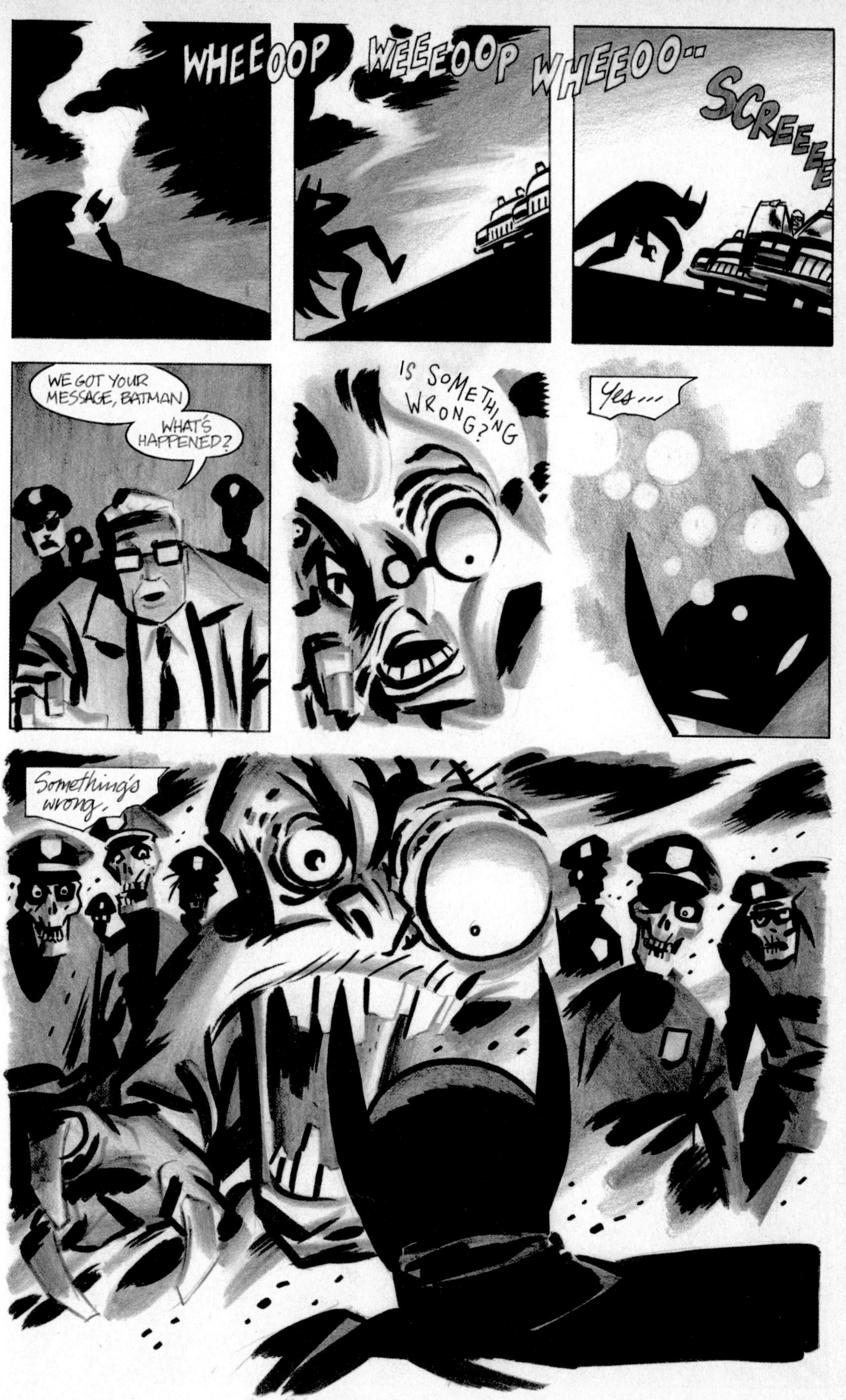
WHEEOOP WEEEOOP WHEEOO..
SCREEEE
WE GOT YOUR MESSAGE, BATMAN
WHAT'S HAPPENED?
IS SOMETHING WRONG?
Yes...
Something's wrong.

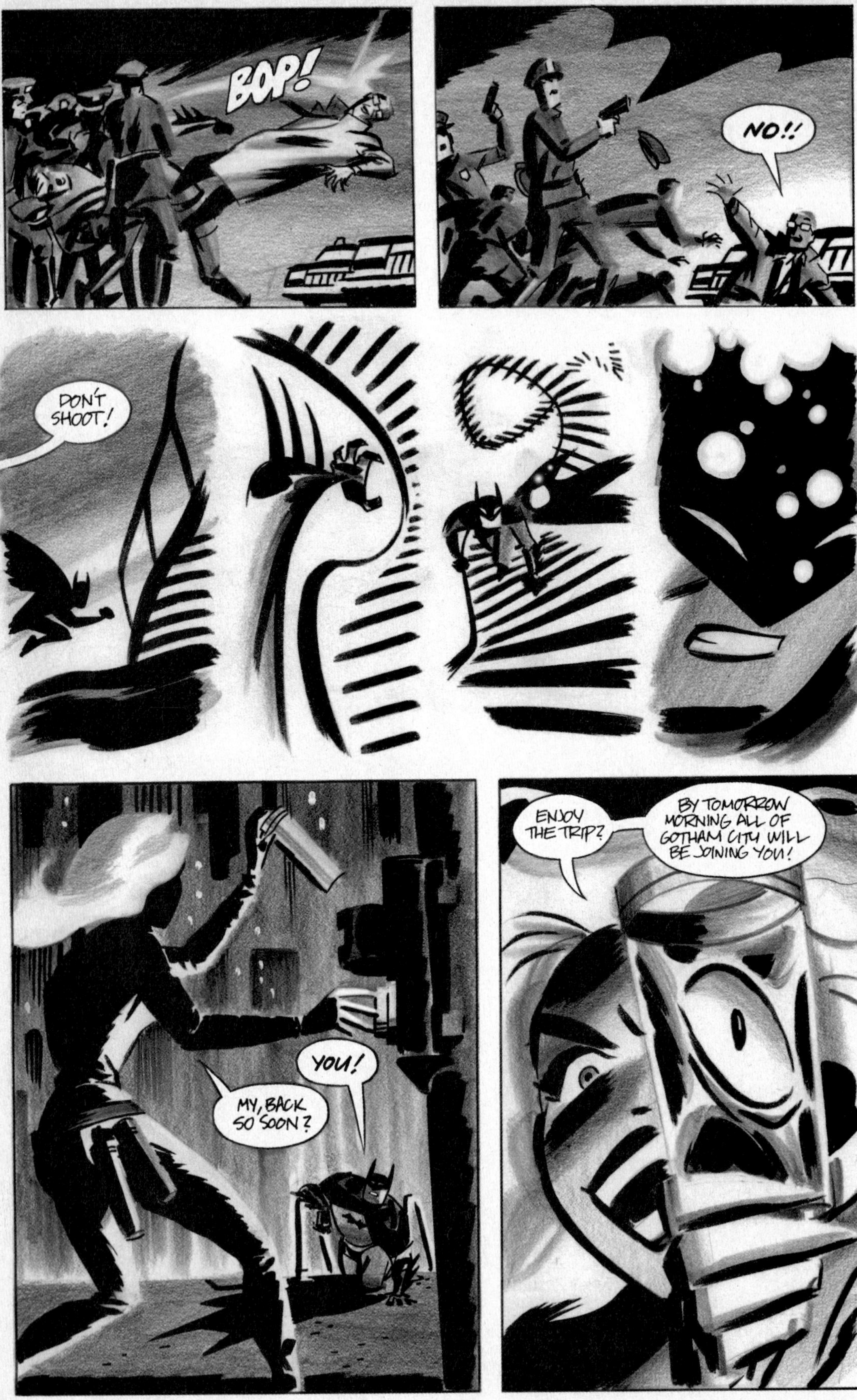
BOP!
NO!!
DON'T SHOOT!
MY, BACK SO SOON?
YOU!
ENJOY THE TRIP?
BY TOMORROW MORNING ALL OF GOTHAM CITY WILL BE JOINING YOU!

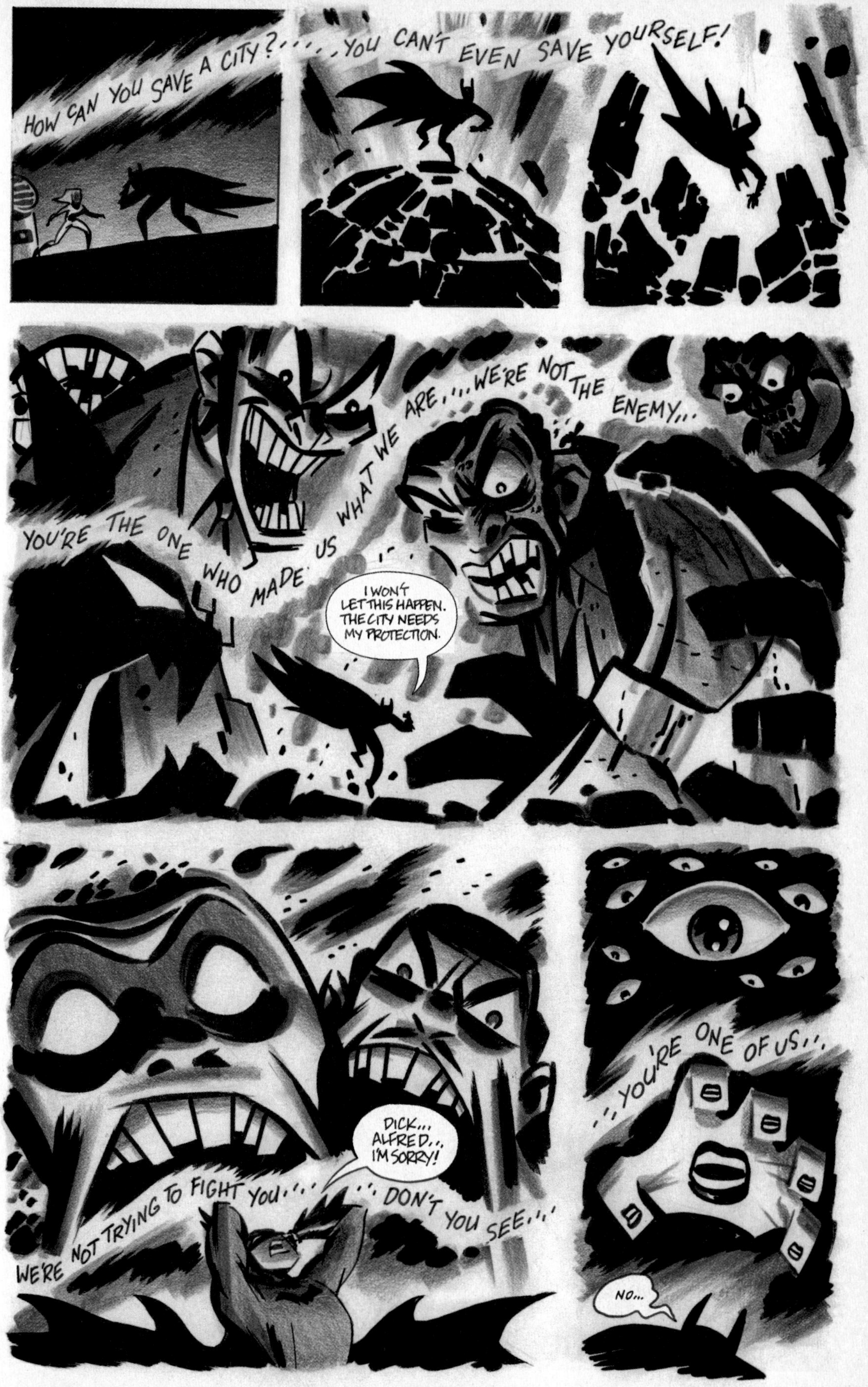
HOW CAN YOU SAVE A CITY?... ...YOU CAN'T EVEN SAVE YOURSELF!
YOU'RE THE ONE WHO MADE US WHAT WE ARE... ...WE'RE NOT THE ENEMY...
I WON'T LET THIS HAPPEN. THE CITY NEEDS MY PROTECTION.
WE'RE NOT TRYING TO FIGHT YOU... ...DON'T YOU SEE...
DICK... ALFRED... I'M SORRY!
...YOU'RE ONE OF US...
NO...

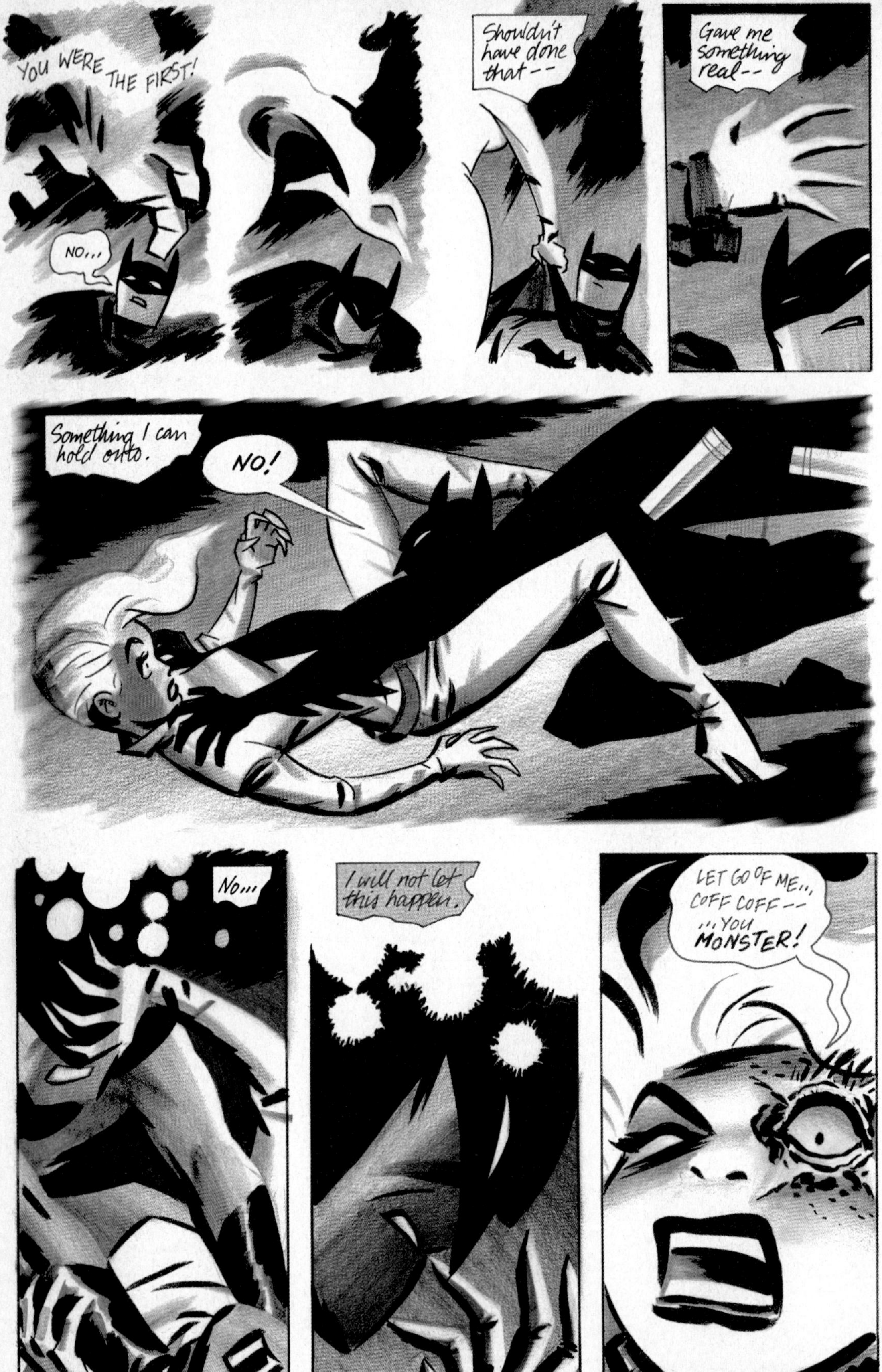
YOU WERE THE FIRST!
NO...
Shouldn't have done that --
Gave me something real --
Something I can hold onto.
NO!
No...
I will not let this happen.
LET GO OF ME... COFF COFF -- ...YOU MONSTER!

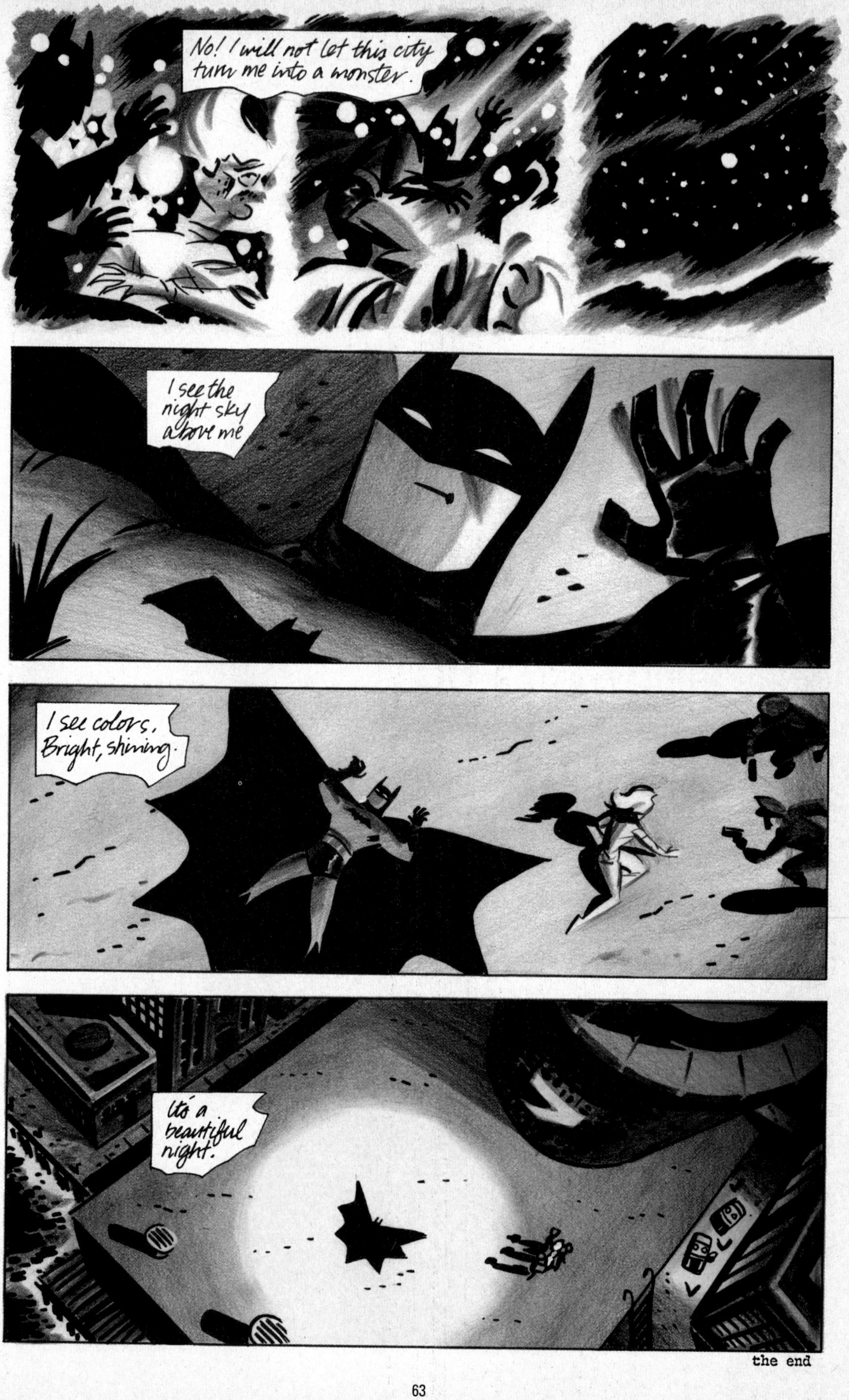
No! I will not let this city turn me into a monster.
I see the night sky above me
I see colors. Bright, shining.
It's a beautiful night.

the end

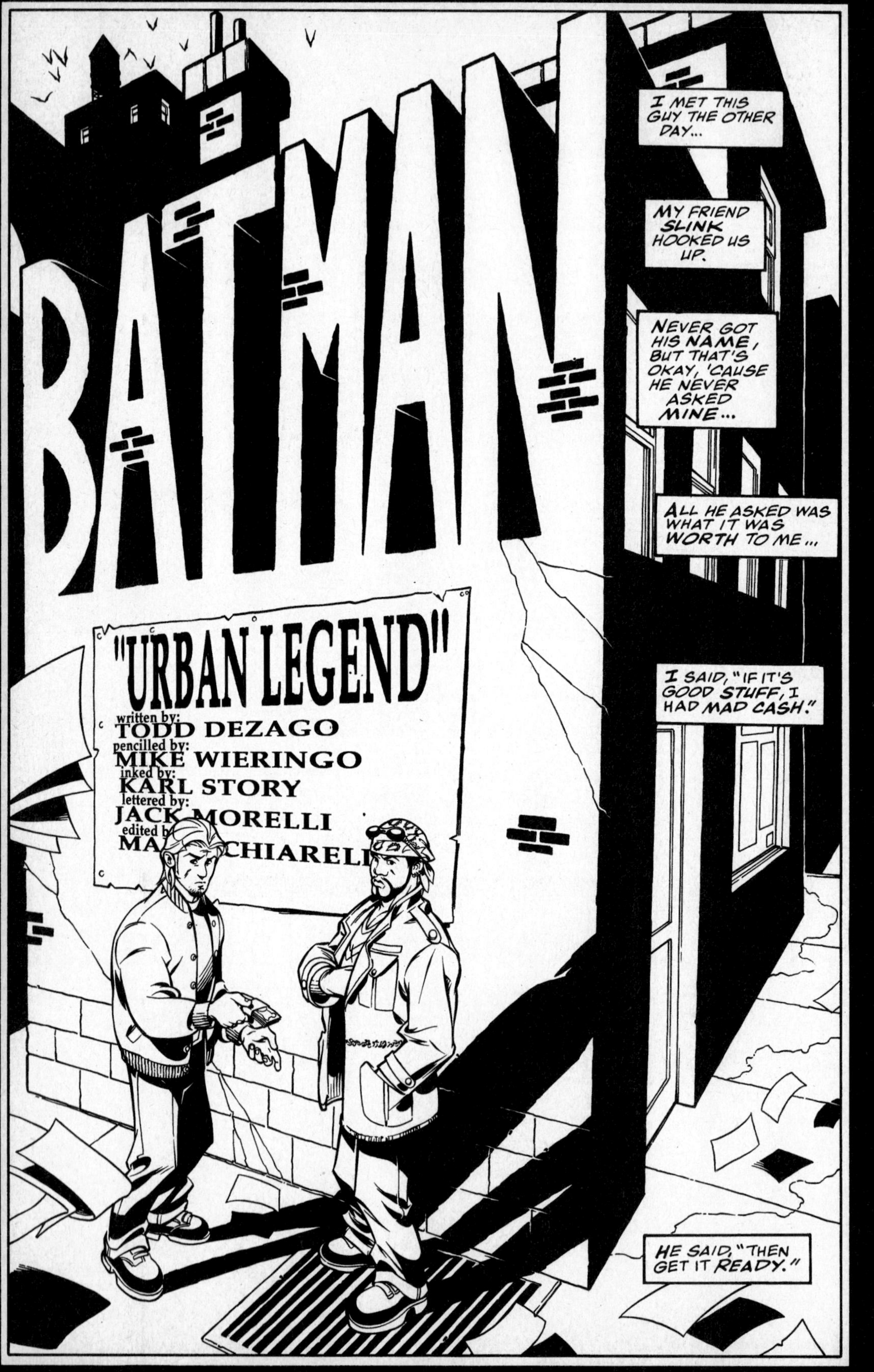
BATMAN
I MET THIS GUY THE OTHER DAY...
MY FRIEND SLINK HOOKED US UP.
NEVER GOT HIS NAME, BUT THAT'S OKAY, 'CAUSE HE NEVER ASKED MINE...
ALL HE ASKED WAS WHAT IT WAS WORTH TO ME...
"URBAN LEGEND"
written by: TODD DEZAGO
pencilled by: MIKE WIERINGO
inked by: KARL STORY
lettered by: JACK MORELLI
I SAID, "IF IT'S GOOD STUFF, I HAD MAD CASH."
HE SAID, "THEN GET IT READY."

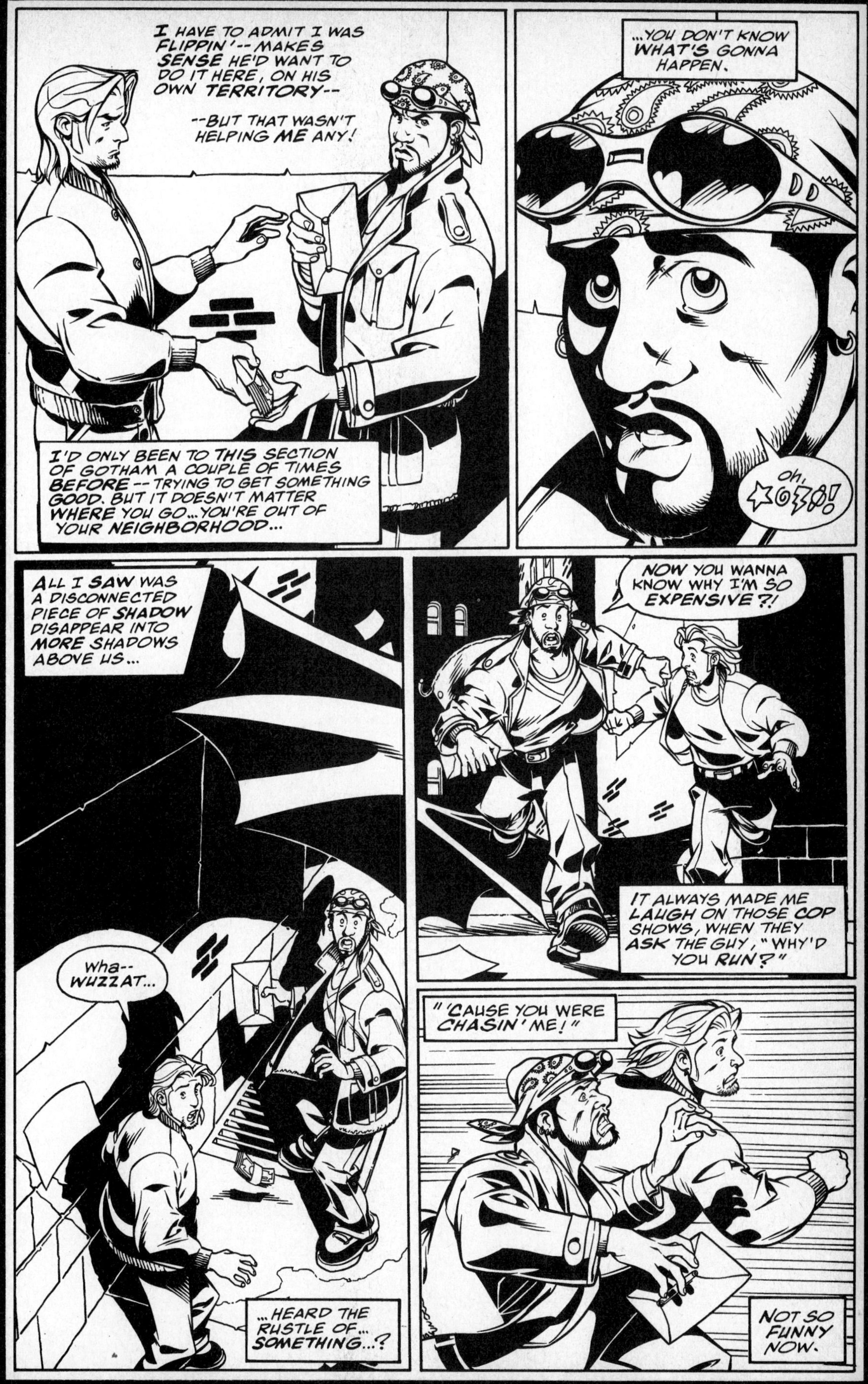
I HAVE TO ADMIT I WAS FLIPPIN'-- MAKES SENSE HE'D WANT TO DO IT HERE, ON HIS OWN TERRITORY--
--BUT THAT WASN'T HELPING ME ANY!
I'D ONLY BEEN TO THIS SECTION OF GOTHAM A COUPLE OF TIMES BEFORE -- TRYING TO GET SOMETHING GOOD. BUT IT DOESN'T MATTER WHERE YOU GO... YOU'RE OUT OF YOUR NEIGHBORHOOD...
...YOU DON'T KNOW WHAT'S GONNA HAPPEN.
oh,
ALL I SAW WAS A DISCONNECTED PIECE OF SHADOW DISAPPEAR INTO MORE SHADOWS ABOVE US...
Wha-- WUZZAT...
...HEARD THE RUSTLE OF... SOMETHING...?
NOW YOU WANNA KNOW WHY I'M SO EXPENSIVE?!
IT ALWAYS MADE ME LAUGH ON THOSE COP SHOWS, WHEN THEY ASK THE GUY, "WHY'D YOU RUN?"
"'CAUSE YOU WERE CHASIN' ME!"
NOT SO FUNNY NOW.

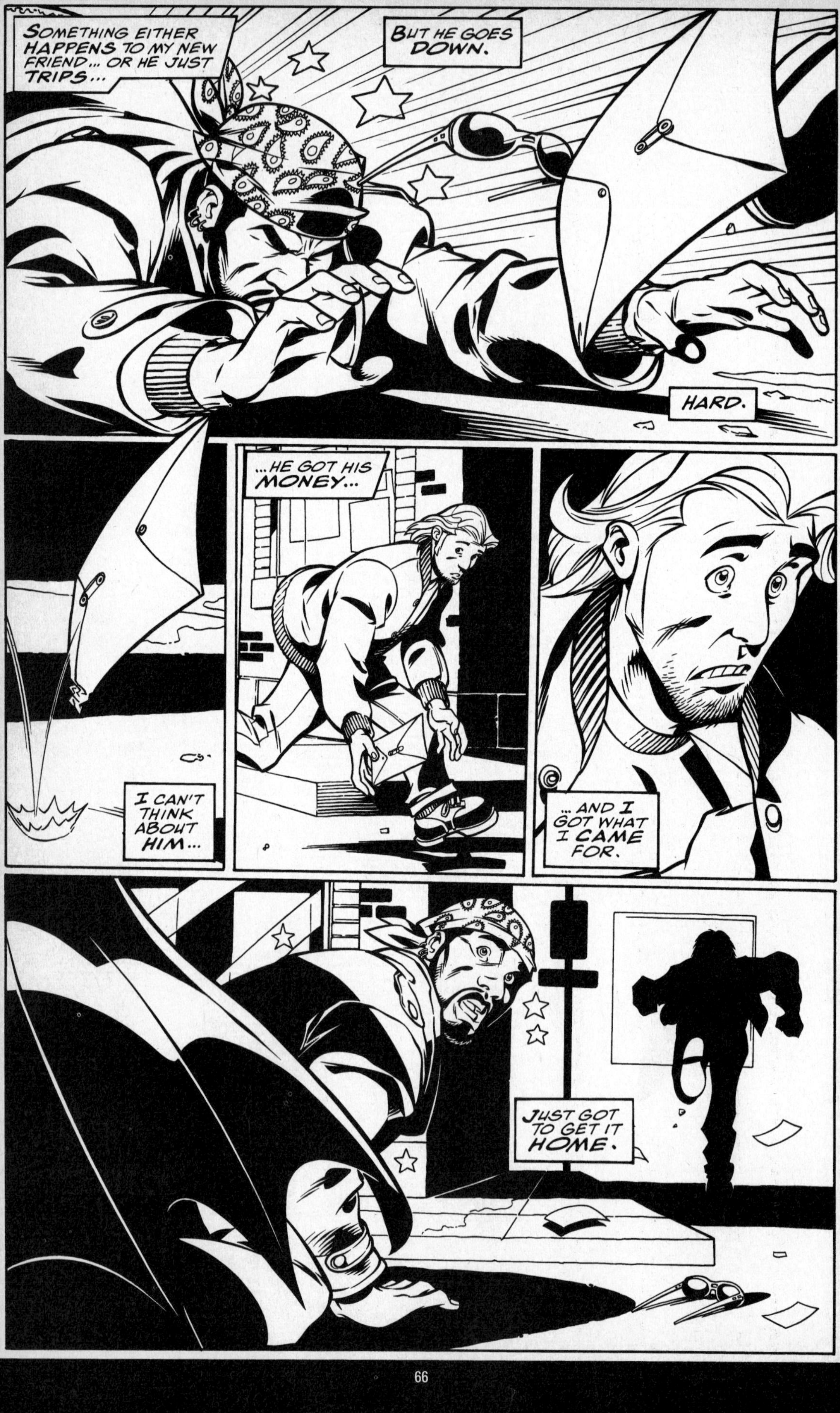
SOMETHING EITHER HAPPENS TO MY NEW FRIEND... OR HE JUST TRIPS...
BUT HE GOES DOWN.
HARD.
I CAN'T THINK ABOUT HIM...
...HE GOT HIS MONEY...
...AND I GOT WHAT I CAME FOR.
JUST GOT TO GET IT HOME.

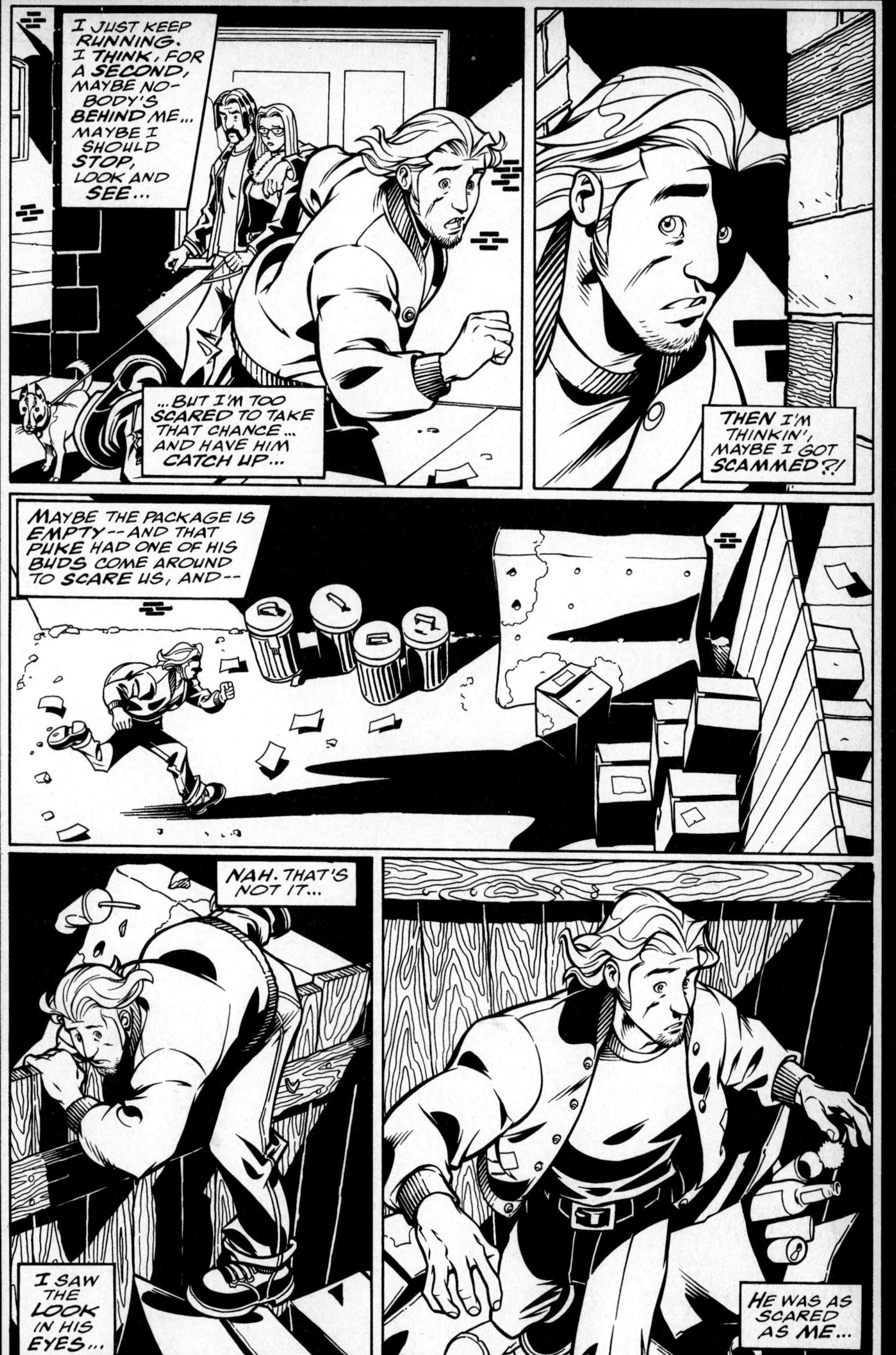
I JUST KEEP RUNNING. I THINK, FOR A SECOND, MAYBE NOBODY'S BEHIND ME... MAYBE I SHOULD STOP, LOOK AND SEE...
...BUT I'M TOO SCARED TO TAKE THAT CHANCE... AND HAVE HIM CATCH UP...
THEN I'M THINKIN', MAYBE I GOT SCAMMED?!
MAYBE THE PACKAGE IS EMPTY--AND THAT PUKE HAD ONE OF HIS BUDS COME AROUND TO SCARE US, AND--
NAH. THAT'S NOT IT...
I SAW THE LOOK IN HIS EYES...
HE WAS AS SCARED AS ME...

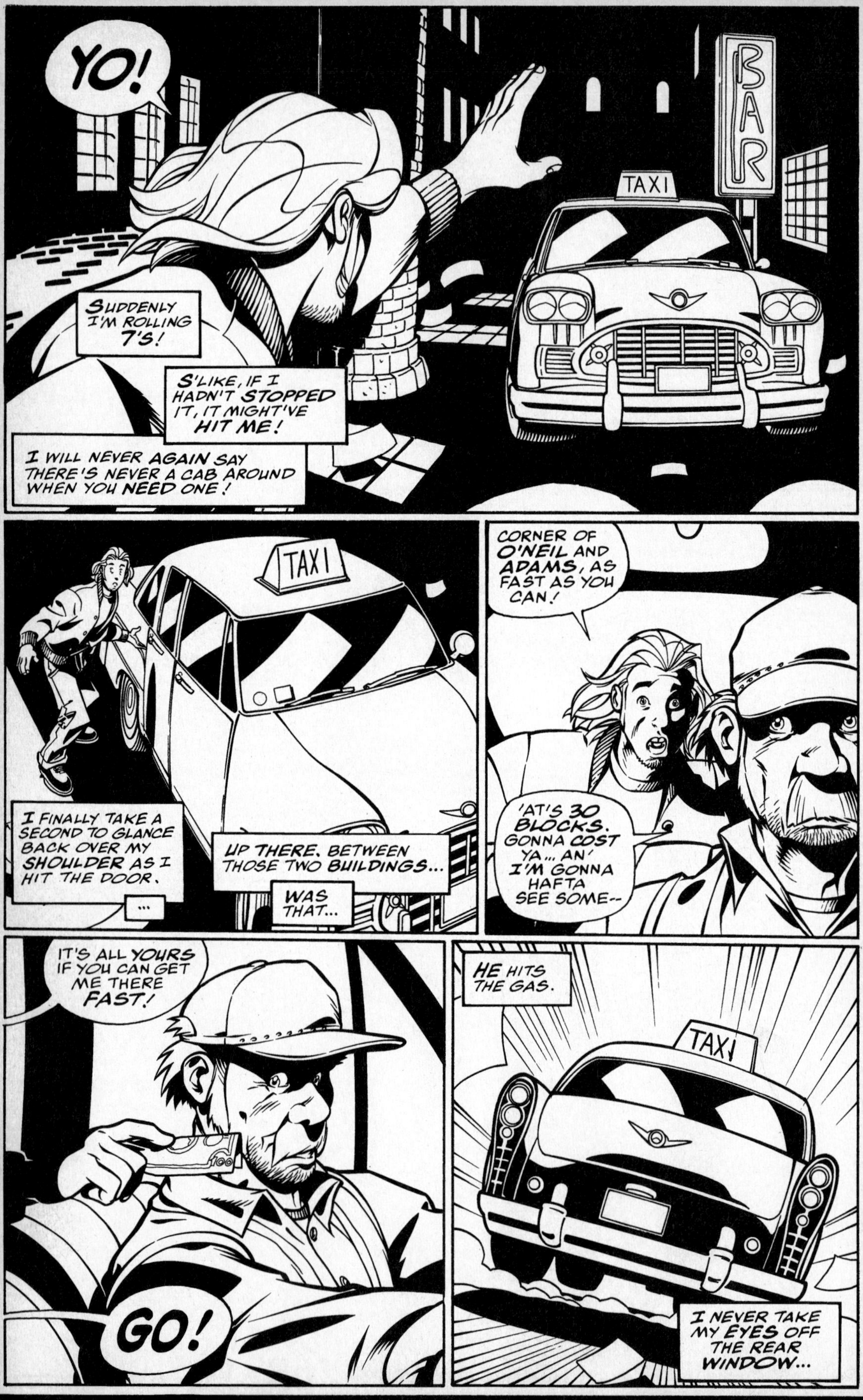
YO!
SUDDENLY I'M ROLLING 7'S!
S'LIKE, IF I HADN'T STOPPED IT, IT MIGHT'VE HIT ME!
I WILL NEVER AGAIN SAY THERE'S NEVER A CAB AROUND WHEN YOU NEED ONE!
TAXI
BAR
TAXI
I FINALLY TAKE A SECOND TO GLANCE BACK OVER MY SHOULDER AS I HIT THE DOOR.
...
UP THERE. BETWEEN THOSE TWO BUILDINGS...
WAS THAT...
CORNER OF O'NEIL AND ADAMS, AS FAST AS YOU CAN!
'AT'S 30 BLOCKS. GONNA COST YA... AN' I'M GONNA HAFTA SEE SOME--
IT'S ALL YOURS IF YOU CAN GET ME THERE FAST!
GO!
HE HITS THE GAS.
TAXI
I NEVER TAKE MY EYES OFF THE REAR WINDOW...

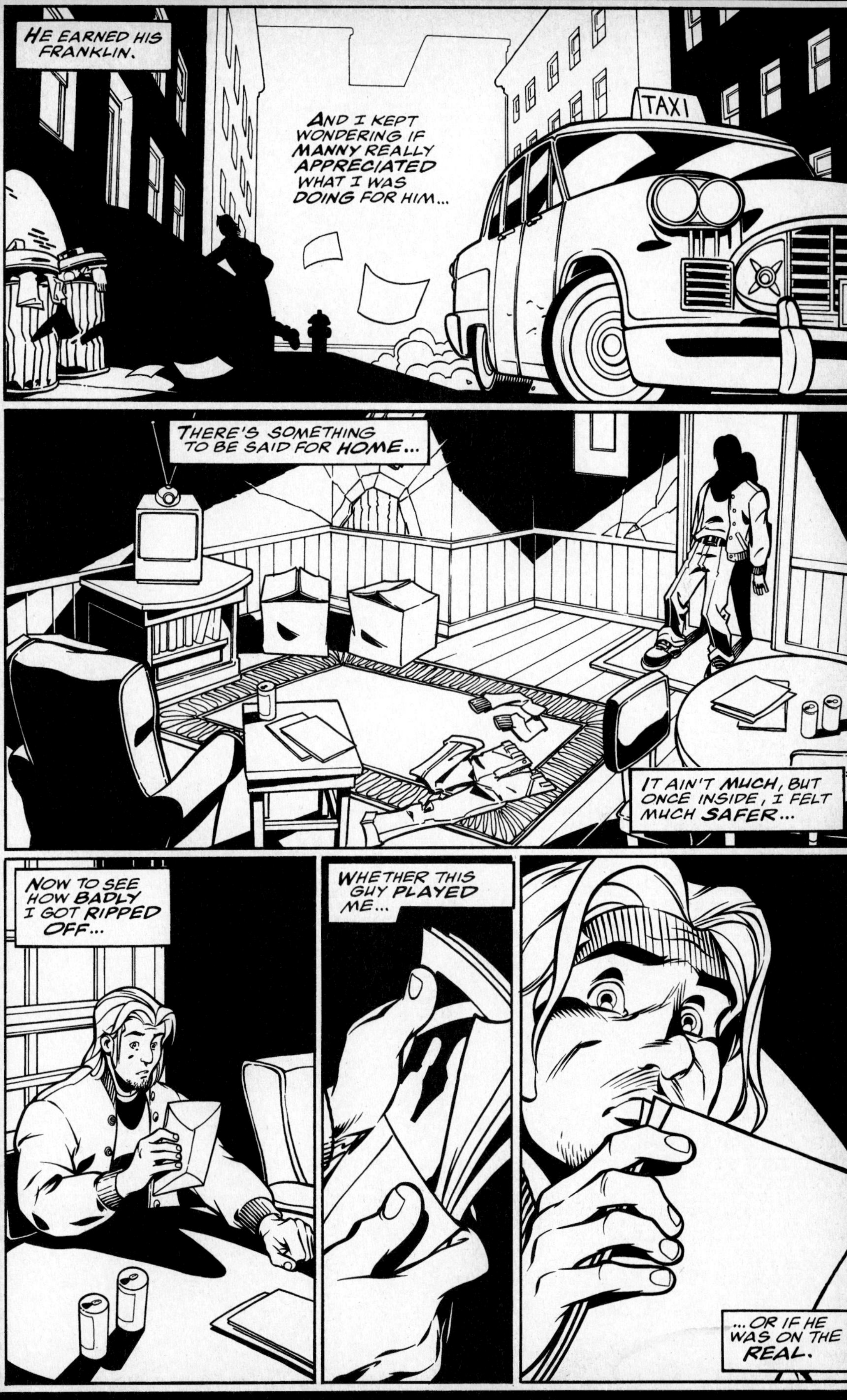
HE EARNED HIS FRANKLIN.
AND I KEPT WONDERING IF MANNY REALLY APPRECIATED WHAT I WAS DOING FOR HIM...
TAXI
THERE'S SOMETHING TO BE SAID FOR HOME...
IT AIN'T MUCH, BUT ONCE INSIDE, I FELT MUCH SAFER...
NOW TO SEE HOW BADLY I GOT RIPPED OFF...
WHETHER THIS GUY PLAYED ME...
...OR IF HE WAS ON THE REAL.

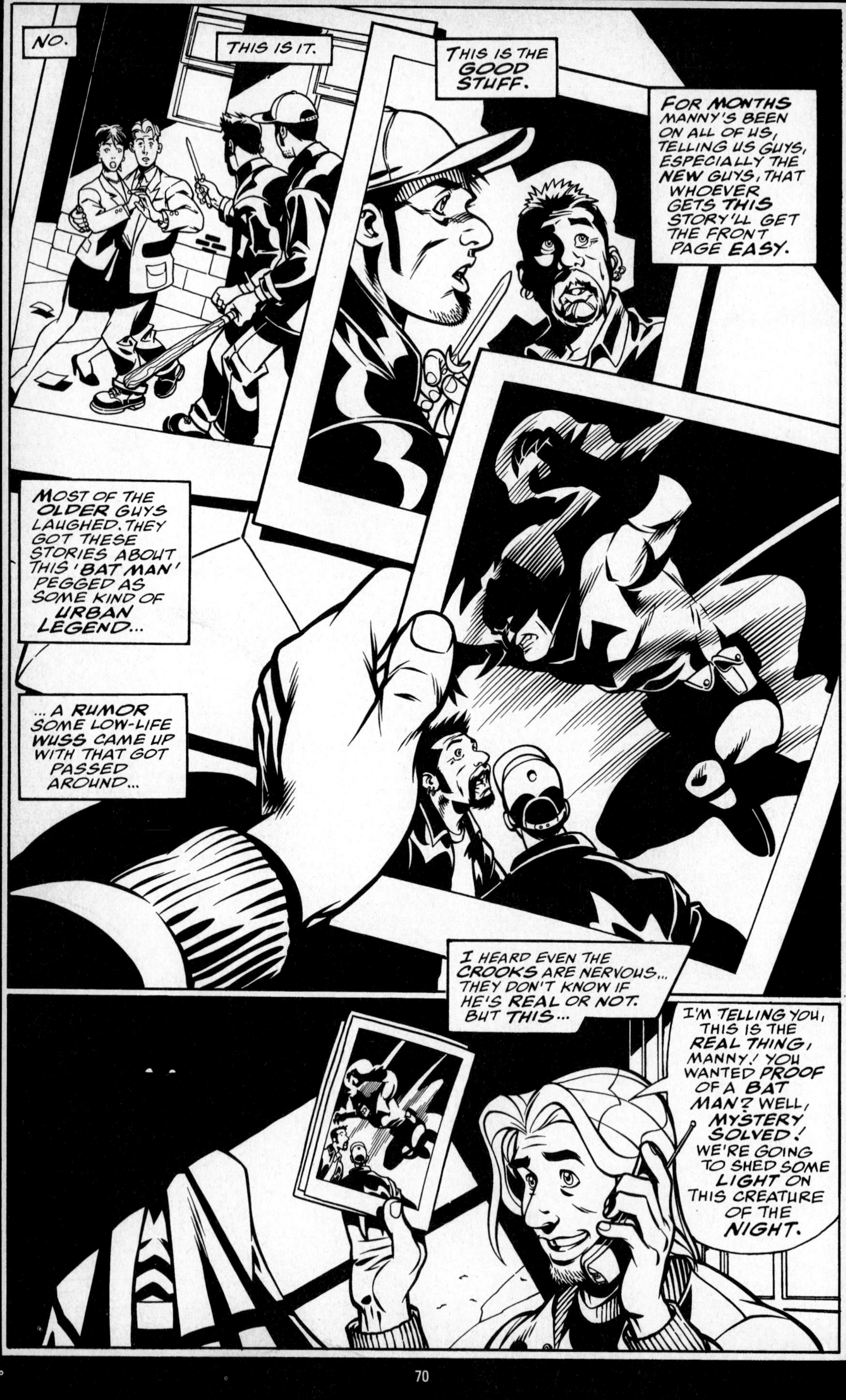
NO.
THIS IS IT.
THIS IS THE GOOD STUFF.
FOR MONTHS MANNY'S BEEN ON ALL OF US, TELLING US GUYS, ESPECIALLY THE NEW GUYS, THAT WHOEVER GETS THIS STORY'LL GET THE FRONT PAGE EASY.
MOST OF THE OLDER GUYS LAUGHED. THEY GOT THESE STORIES ABOUT THIS 'BAT MAN' PEGGED AS SOME KIND OF URBAN LEGEND...
...A RUMOR SOME LOW-LIFE WUSS CAME UP WITH THAT GOT PASSED AROUND...
I HEARD EVEN THE CROOKS ARE NERVOUS... THEY DON'T KNOW IF HE'S REAL OR NOT. BUT THIS...
I'M TELLING YOU, THIS IS THE REAL THING, MANNY! YOU WANTED PROOF OF A BAT MAN? WELL, MYSTERY SOLVED! WE'RE GOING TO SHED SOME LIGHT ON THIS CREATURE OF THE NIGHT.

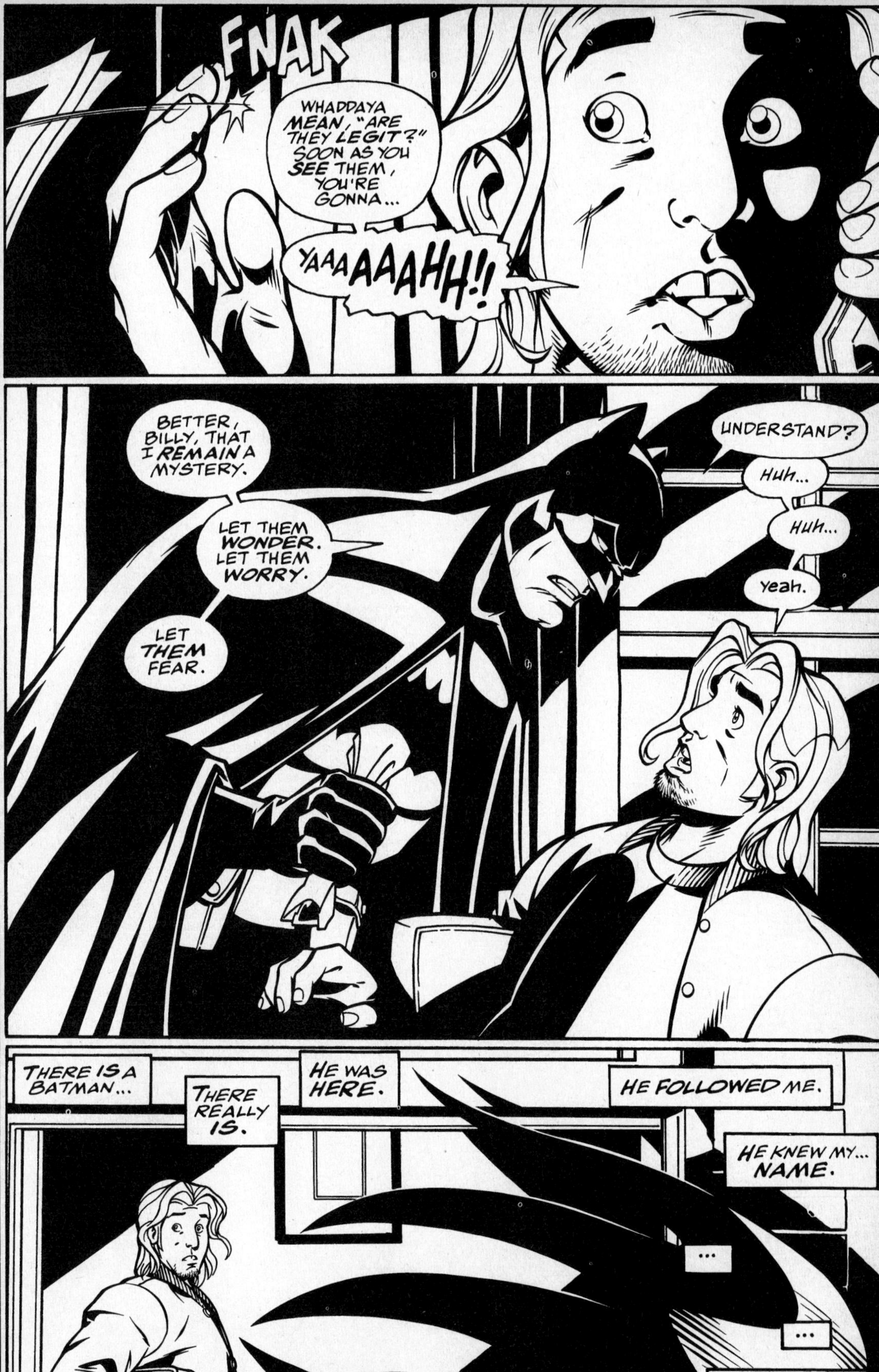
FNAK
WHADDAYA MEAN, "ARE THEY LEGIT?" SOON AS YOU SEE THEM, YOU'RE GONNA...
YAAAAAAHH!!
BETTER, BILLY, THAT I REMAIN A MYSTERY.
LET THEM WONDER. LET THEM WORRY.
LET THEM FEAR.
UNDERSTAND?
Huh...
Huh...
yeah.
THERE IS A BATMAN...
THERE REALLY IS.
HE WAS HERE.
HE FOLLOWED ME.
HE KNEW MY... NAME.
...
...
...THERE IS NO BATMAN.

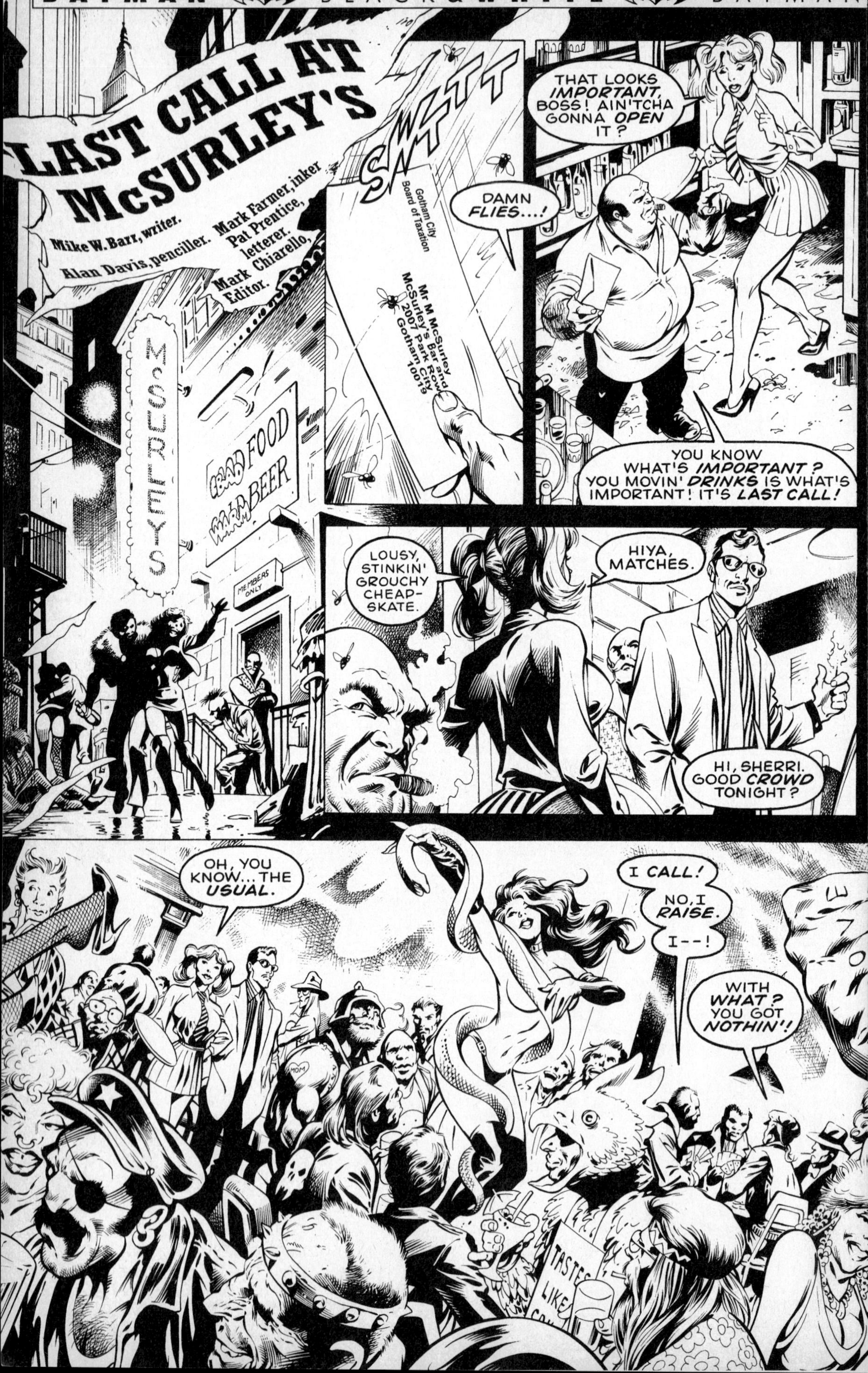
LAST CALL AT McSURLEY'S
Mike W. Barr, writer.
Alan Davis, penciller.
Mark Farmer, inker
Pat Prentice, letterer.
Mark Chiarello, Editor.
McSURLEYS
BAD FOOD
WARM BEER
MEMBERS ONLY
SWTT
Gotham City Board of Taxation
Mr M McSurley
McSurley's Bar and
2007 Park Row
Gotham City
10019
DAMN FLIES...!
THAT LOOKS IMPORTANT, BOSS! AIN'TCHA GONNA OPEN IT?
YOU KNOW WHAT'S IMPORTANT? YOU MOVIN' DRINKS IS WHAT'S IMPORTANT! IT'S LAST CALL!
LOUSY, STINKIN' GROUCHY CHEAP-SKATE.
HIYA, MATCHES.
HI, SHERRI. GOOD CROWD TONIGHT?
OH, YOU KNOW... THE USUAL.
I CALL!
NO, I RAISE.
I--!
WITH WHAT? YOU GOT NOTHIN'!
MOM

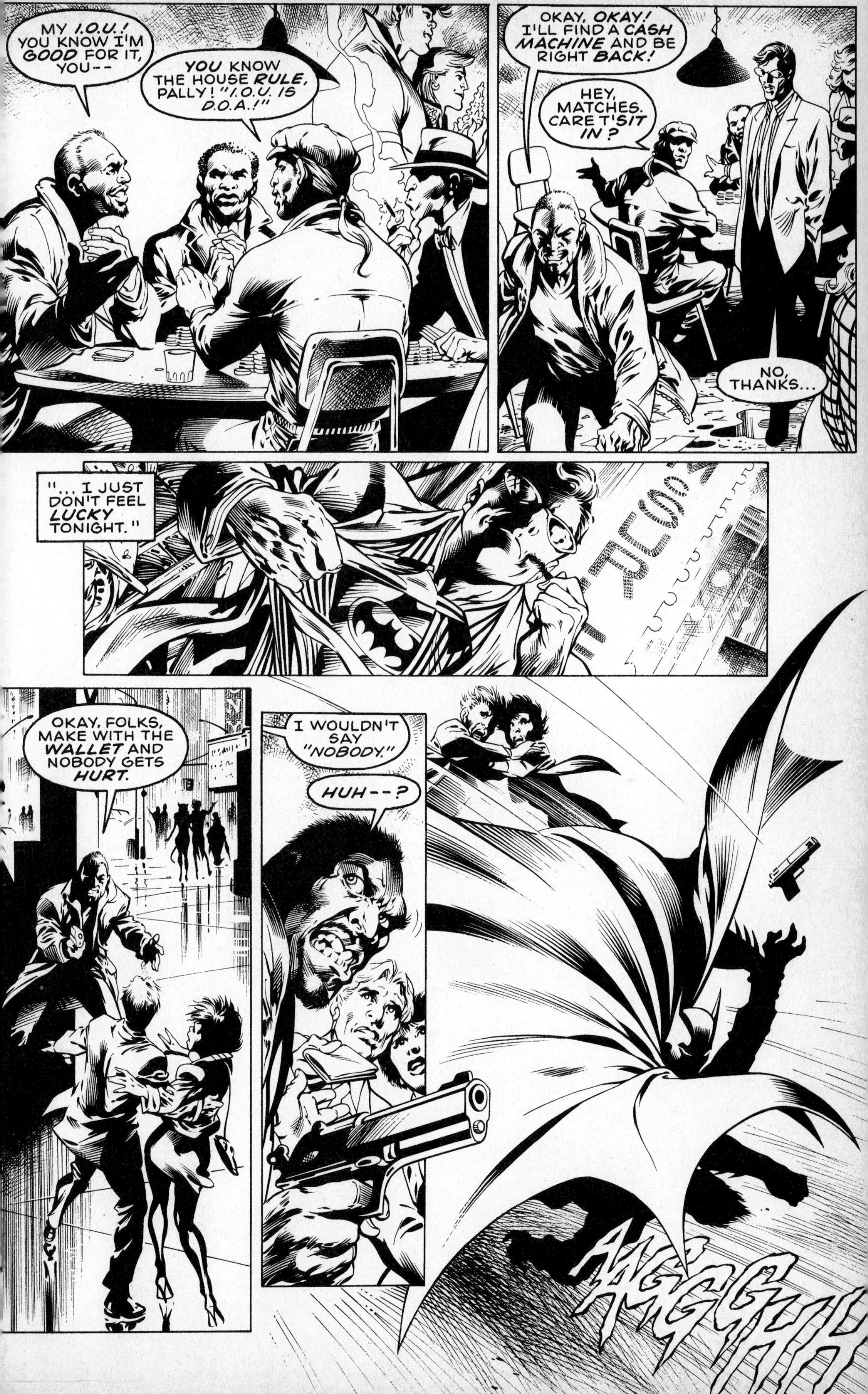

MY I.O.U.! YOU KNOW I'M GOOD FOR IT, YOU--
YOU KNOW THE HOUSE RULE, PALLY! "I.O.U. IS D.O.A.!"
OKAY, OKAY! I'LL FIND A CASH MACHINE AND BE RIGHT BACK!
HEY, MATCHES. CARE T'SIT IN?
NO, THANKS...
"...I JUST DON'T FEEL LUCKY TONIGHT."
OKAY, FOLKS, MAKE WITH THE WALLET AND NOBODY GETS HURT.
I WOULDN'T SAY "NOBODY."
HUH--?
AGGGGHH

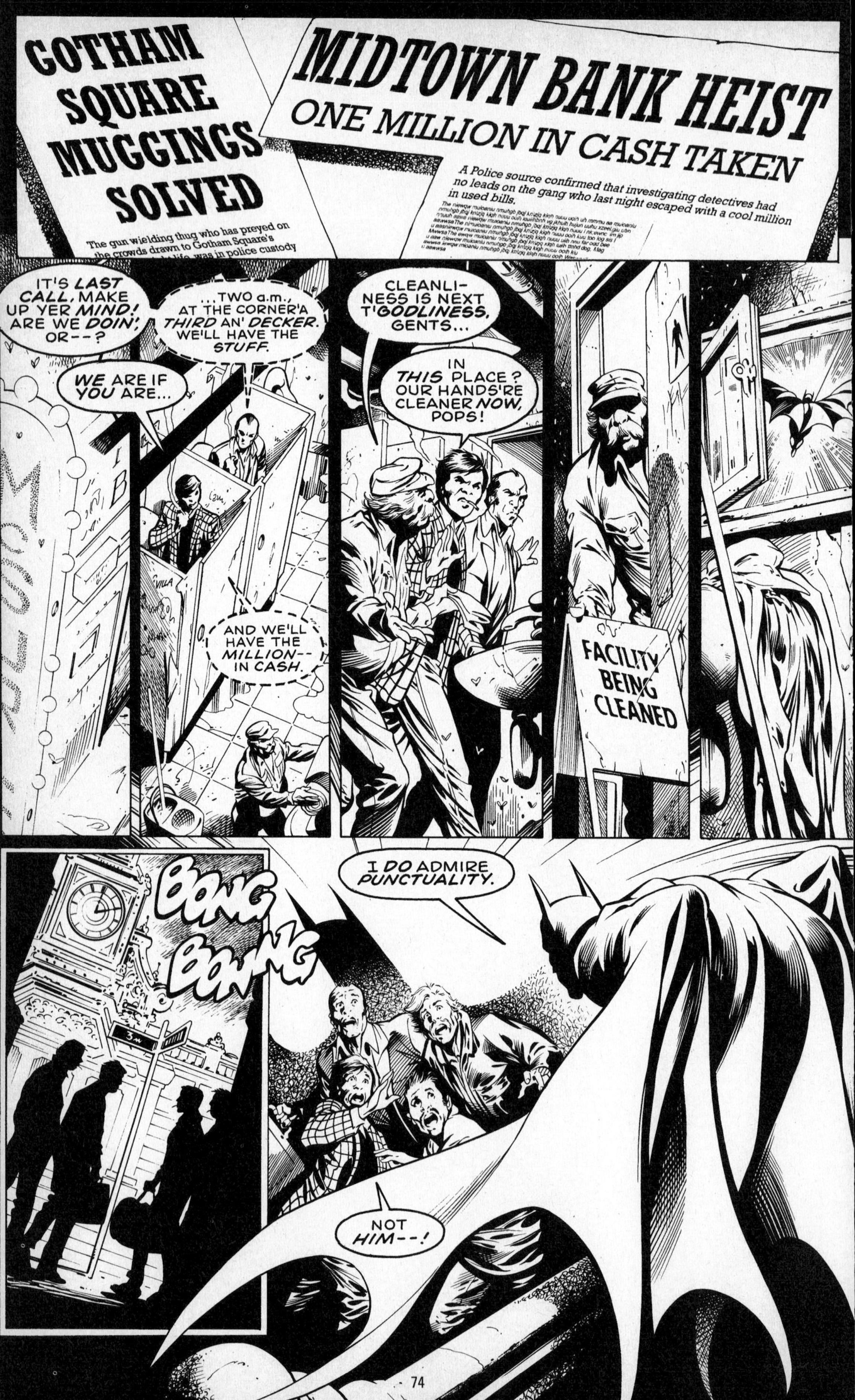

GOTHAM SQUARE MUGGINGS SOLVED
The gun wielding thug who has preyed on the crowds drawn to Gotham Square's
MIDTOWN BANK HEIST
ONE MILLION IN CASH TAKEN
A Police source confirmed that investigating detectives had no leads on the gang who last night escaped with a cool million in used bills.
IT'S LAST CALL, MAKE UP YER MIND! ARE WE DOIN', OR--?
...TWO a.m., AT THE CORNER'A THIRD AN' DECKER. WE'LL HAVE THE STUFF.
WE ARE IF YOU ARE...
AND WE'LL HAVE THE MILLION-- IN CASH.
CLEANLI-NESS IS NEXT T'GODLINESS, GENTS...
IN THIS PLACE? OUR HANDS'RE CLEANER NOW, POPS!
FACILITY BEING CLEANED
BONG
BONNNG
I DO ADMIRE PUNCTUALITY.
NOT HIM--!

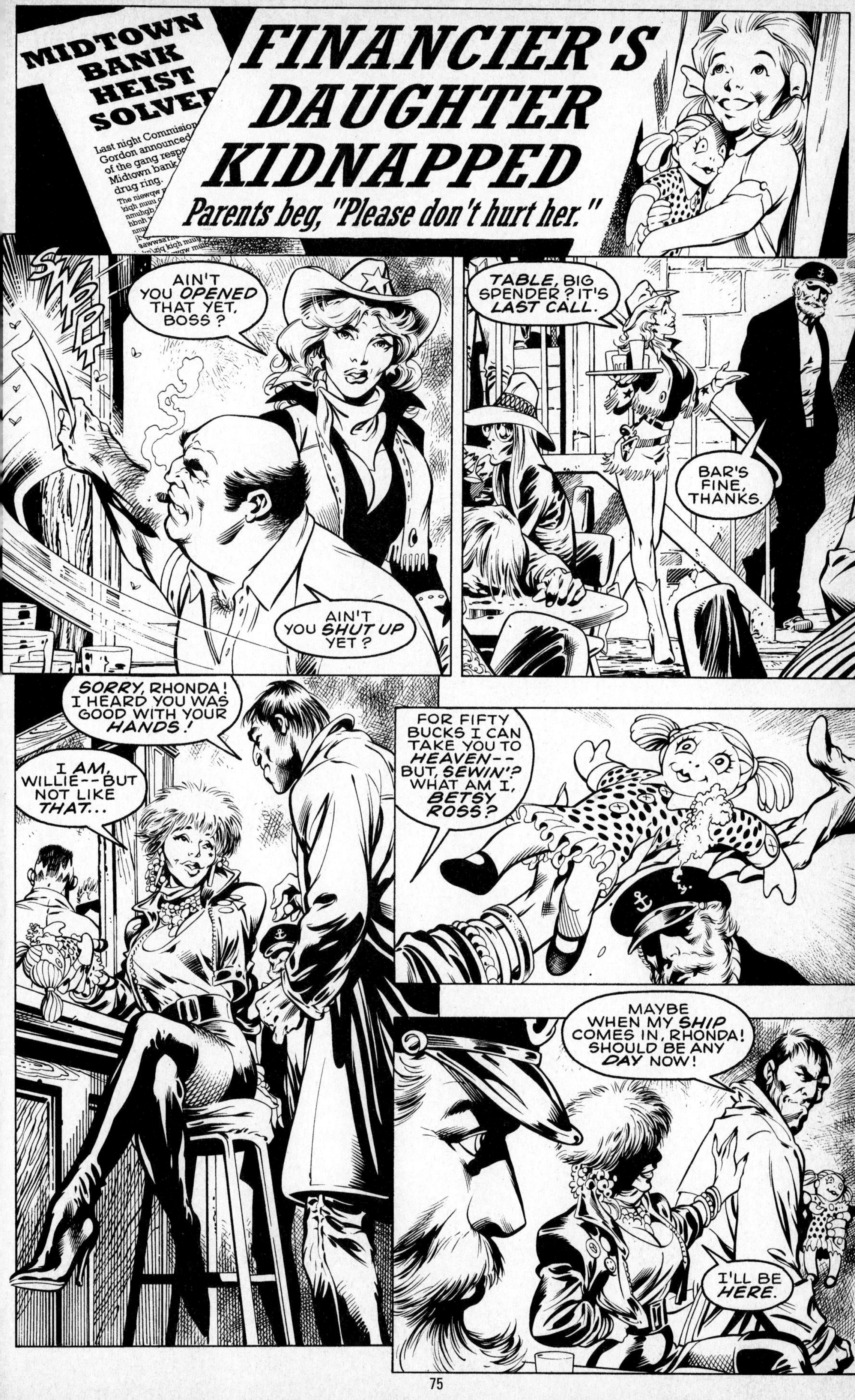
MIDTOWN BANK HEIST SOLVED
Last night Commision
Gordon announced
of the gang respo
Midtown bank
drug ring.
FINANCIER'S DAUGHTER KIDNAPPED
Parents beg, "Please don't hurt her."
SWOP
AIN'T YOU OPENED THAT YET, BOSS?
AIN'T YOU SHUT UP YET?
TABLE, BIG SPENDER? IT'S LAST CALL.
BAR'S FINE, THANKS.
SORRY, RHONDA! I HEARD YOU WAS GOOD WITH YOUR HANDS!
I AM, WILLIE--BUT NOT LIKE THAT...
FOR FIFTY BUCKS I CAN TAKE YOU TO HEAVEN-- BUT, SEWIN'? WHAT AM I, BETSY ROSS?
MAYBE WHEN MY SHIP COMES IN, RHONDA! SHOULD BE ANY DAY NOW!
I'LL BE HERE.

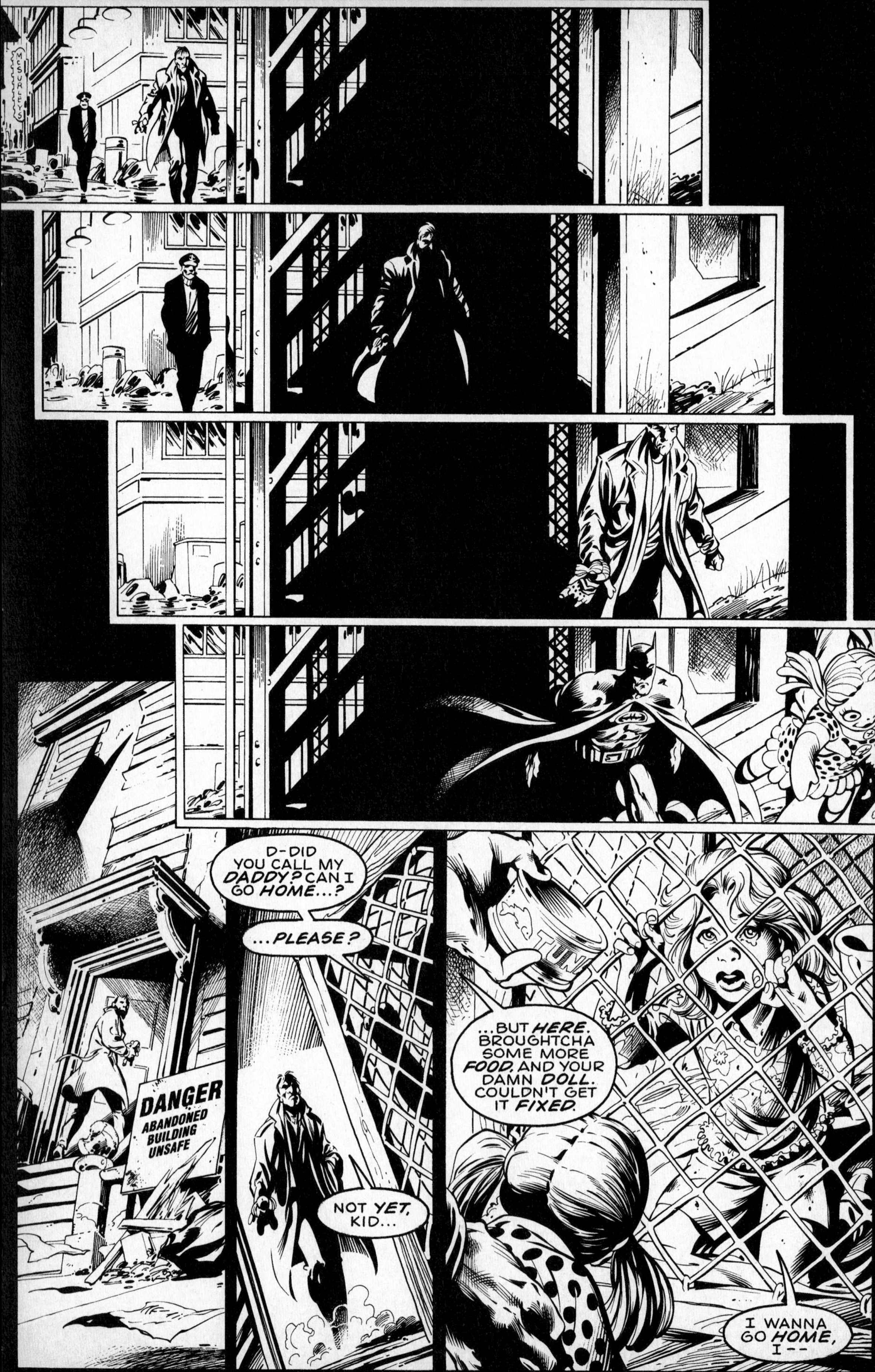
McGURLEY'S
D-DID YOU CALL MY DADDY? CAN I GO HOME...?
...PLEASE?
DANGER
ABANDONED BUILDING UNSAFE
NOT YET, KID...
...BUT HERE. BROUGHTCHA SOME MORE FOOD, AND YOUR DAMN DOLL. COULDN'T GET IT FIXED.
I WANNA GO HOME, I--

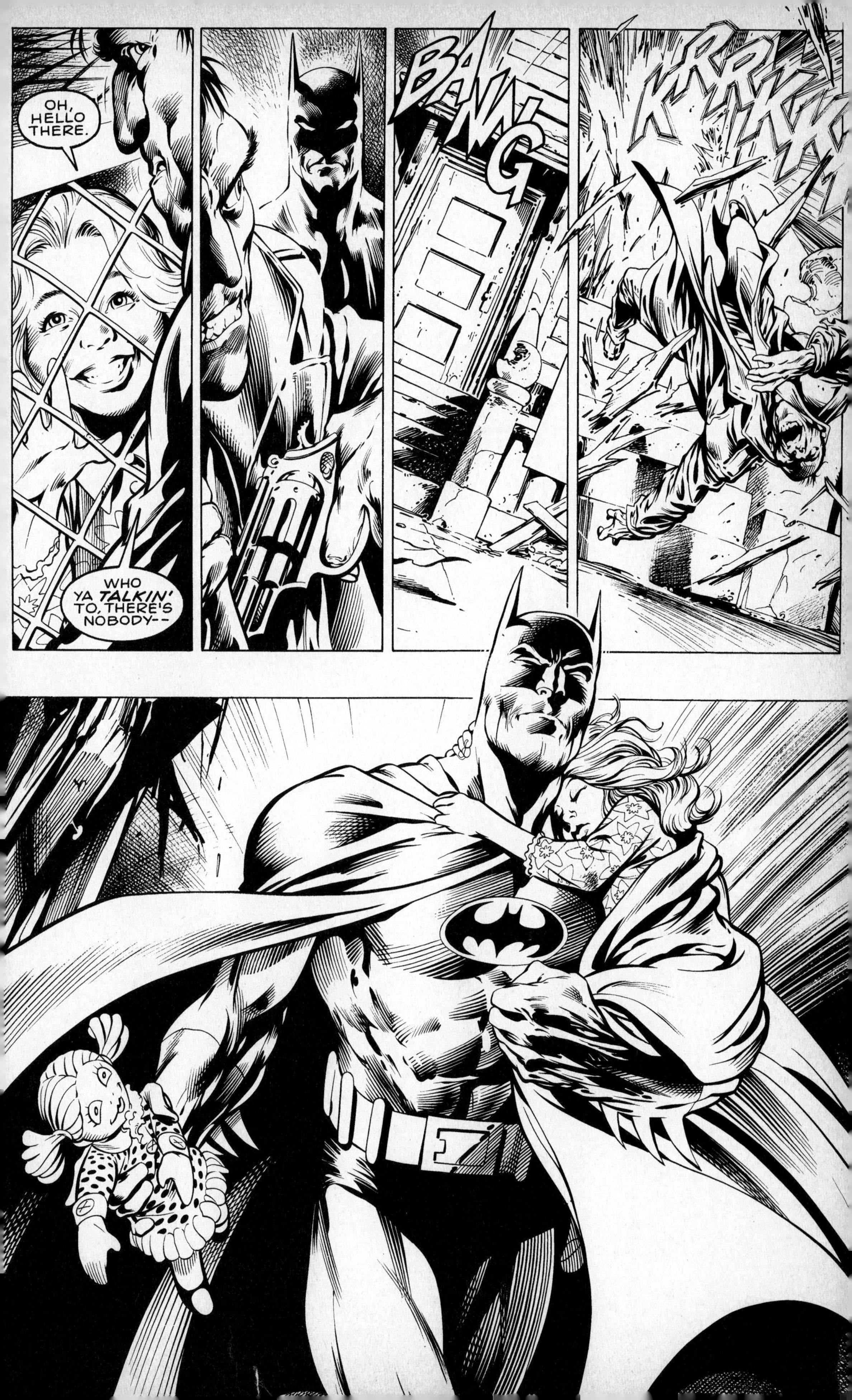
OH, HELLO THERE.
WHO YA TALKIN' TO, THERE'S NOBODY--
BANNG

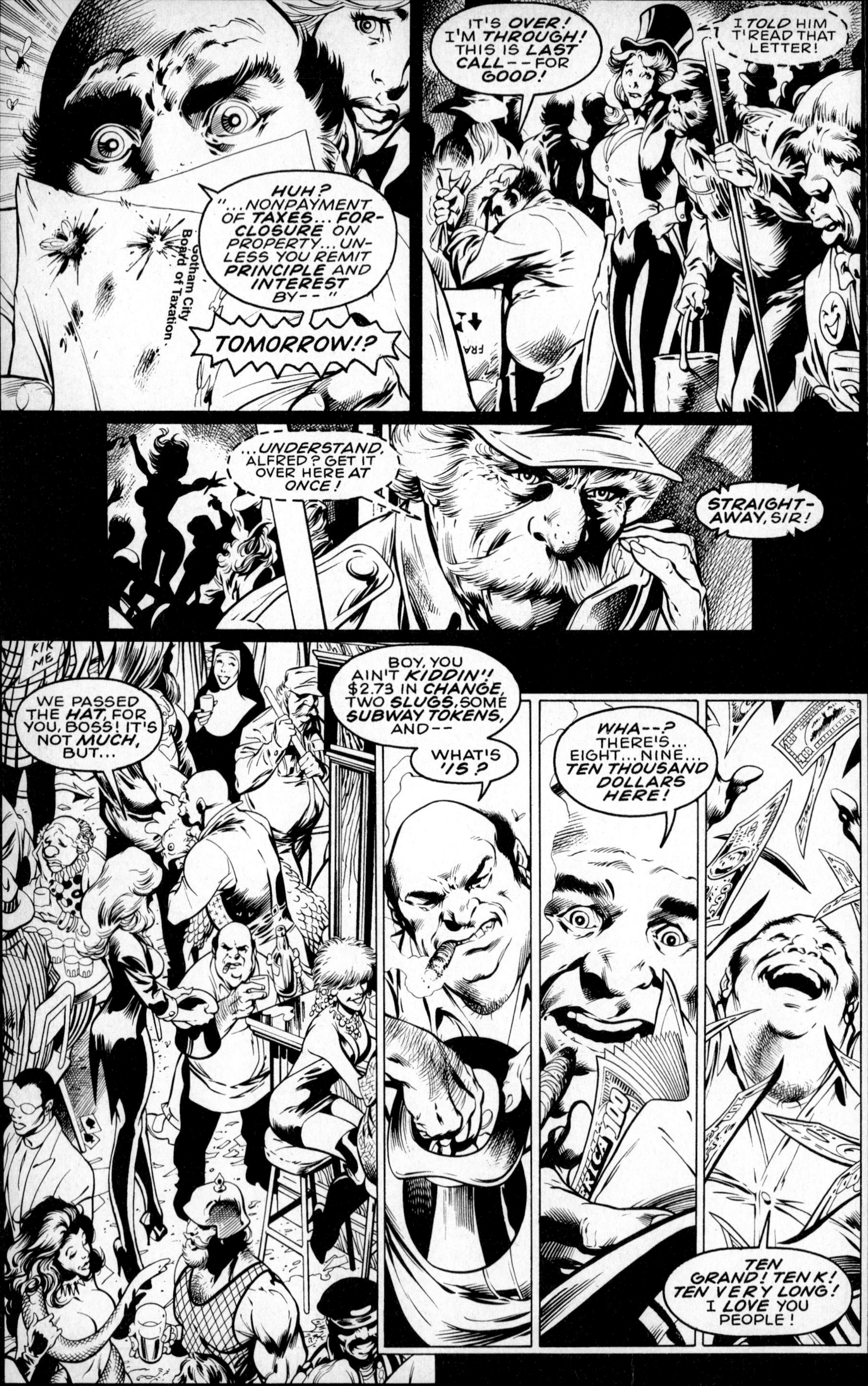
HUH? "...NONPAYMENT OF TAXES... FORCLOSURE ON PROPERTY... UNLESS YOU REMIT PRINCIPLE AND INTEREST BY-- "
TOMORROW!?
Gotham City Board of Taxation
IT'S OVER! I'M THROUGH! THIS IS LAST CALL--FOR GOOD!
I TOLD HIM T'READ THAT LETTER!
...UNDERSTAND, ALFRED? GET IT OVER HERE AT ONCE!
STRAIGHT-AWAY, SIR!
WE PASSED THE HAT, FOR YOU, BOSS! IT'S NOT MUCH, BUT...
BOY, YOU AIN'T KIDDIN'! $2.73 IN CHANGE, TWO SLUGS, SOME SUBWAY TOKENS, AND--
WHAT'S 'IS?
WHA--? THERE'S... EIGHT... NINE... TEN THOUSAND DOLLARS HERE!
TEN GRAND! TEN K! TEN VERY LONG! I LOVE YOU PEOPLE!

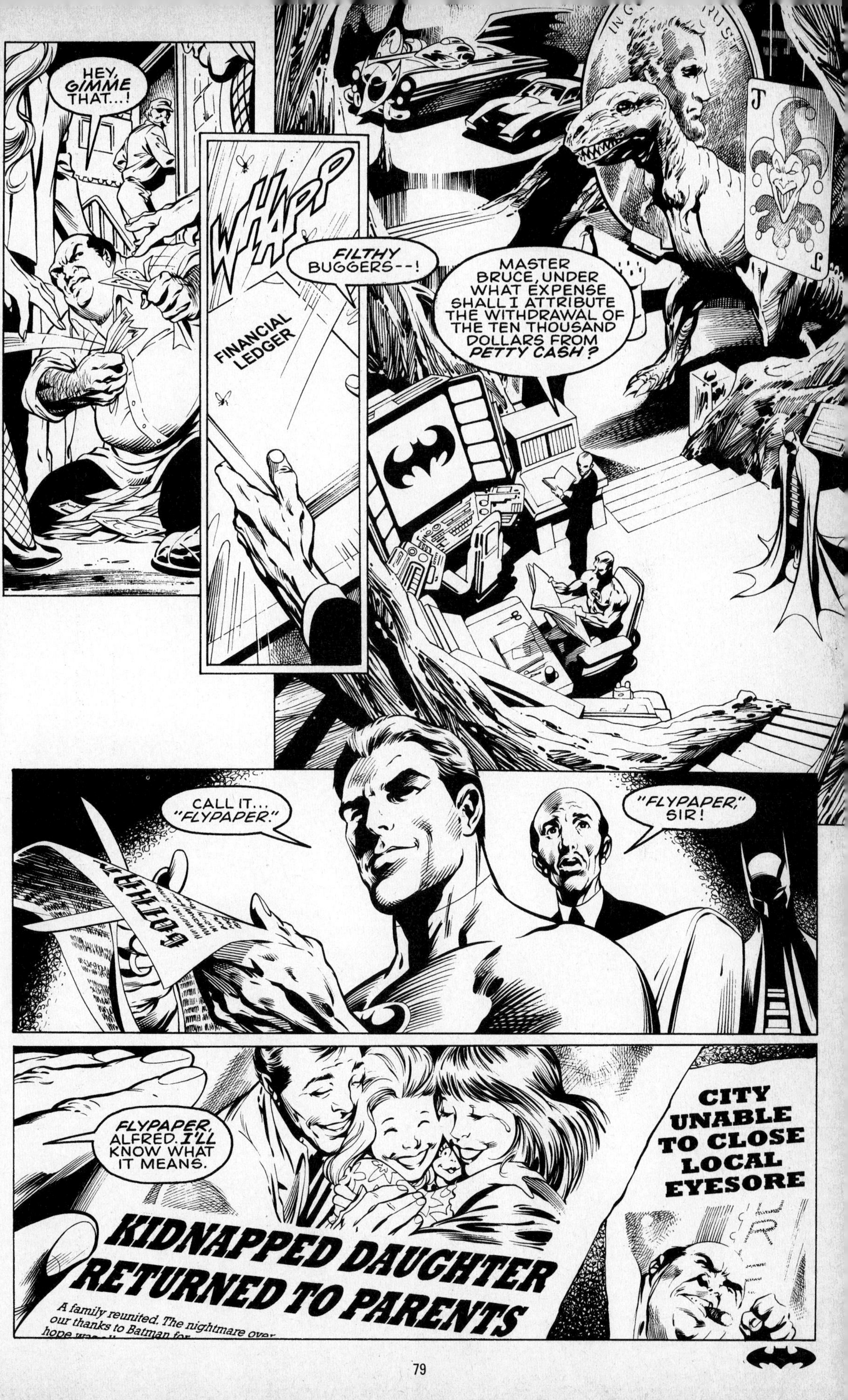

HEY, GIMME THAT...!
WHAPP
FINANCIAL LEDGER
FILTHY BUGGERS--!
MASTER BRUCE, UNDER WHAT EXPENSE SHALL I ATTRIBUTE THE WITHDRAWAL OF THE TEN THOUSAND DOLLARS FROM PETTY CASH?
CALL IT... "FLYPAPER."
"FLYPAPER," SIR!
FLYPAPER, ALFRED. I'LL KNOW WHAT IT MEANS.
CITY UNABLE TO CLOSE LOCAL EYESORE
KIDNAPPED DAUGHTER RETURNED TO PARENTS
A family reunited. The nightmare over
our thanks to Batman for

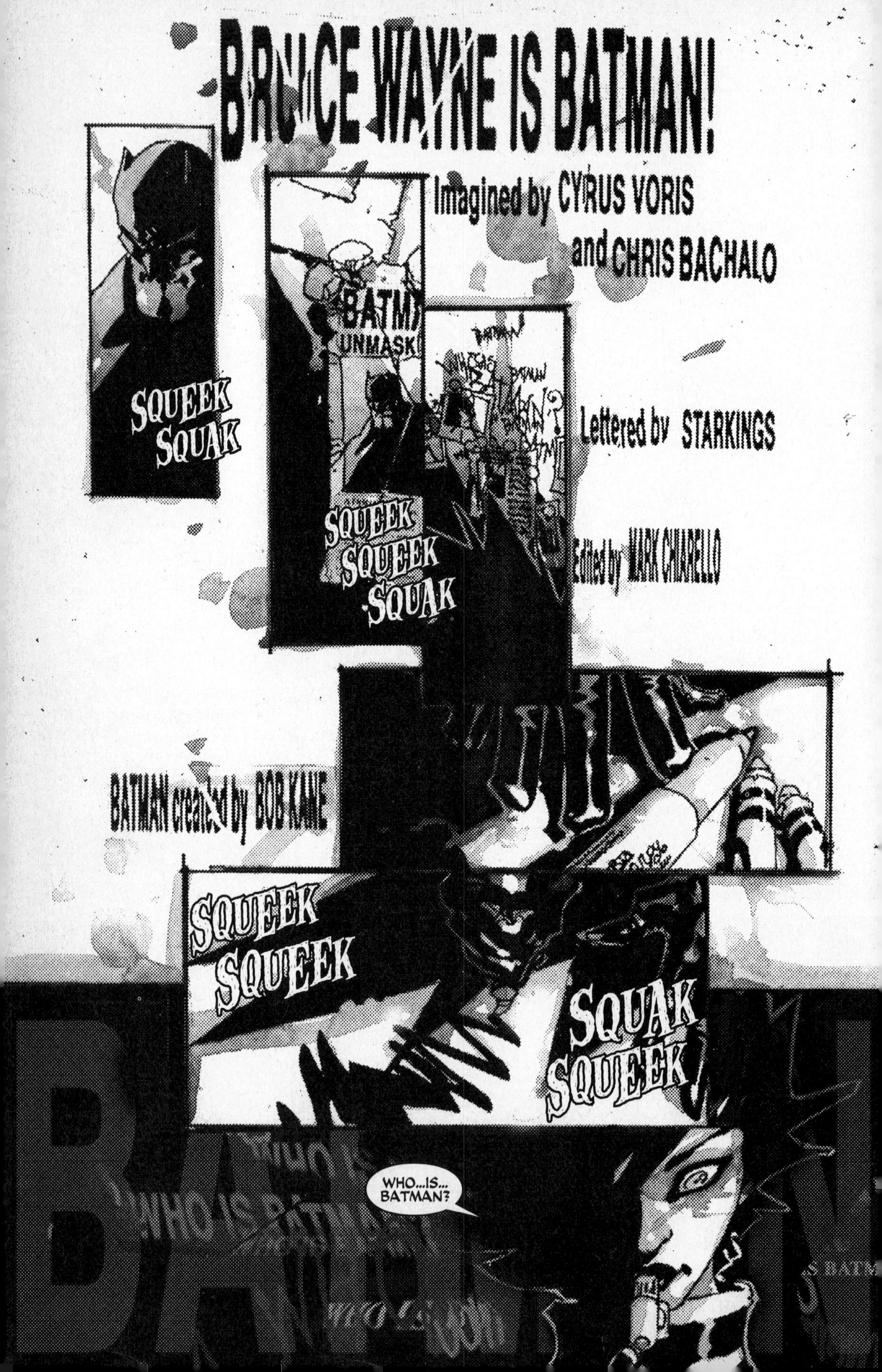
BRUCE WAYNE IS BATMAN!
Imagined by CYRUS VORIS and CHRIS BACHALO
SQUEEK SQUAK
SQUEEK SQUEEK SQUAK
Lettered by STARKINGS
Edited by MARK CHIARELLO
BATMAN created by BOB KANE
SQUEEK SQUEEK
SQUAK SQUEEK
WHO...IS... BATMAN?

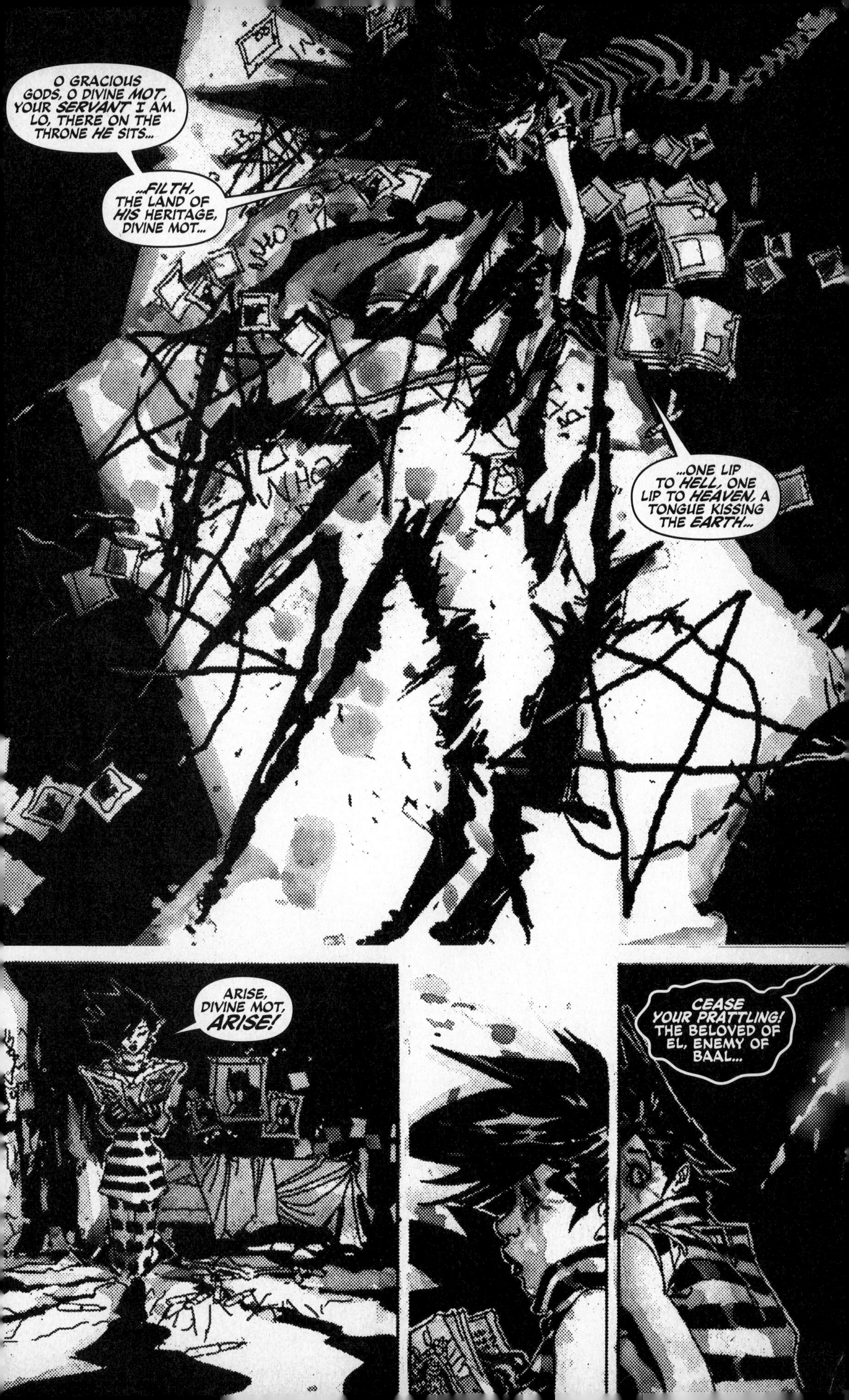
O GRACIOUS GODS, O DIVINE *MOT*, YOUR *SERVANT* I AM. LO, THERE ON THE THRONE *HE* SITS...
...*FILTH*, THE LAND OF *HIS* HERITAGE, DIVINE MOT...
...ONE LIP TO *HELL*, ONE LIP TO *HEAVEN*, A TONGUE KISSING THE *EARTH*...
ARISE, DIVINE MOT, ***ARISE!***
*CEASE YOUR PRATTLING!* THE BELOVED OF EL, ENEMY OF BAAL...

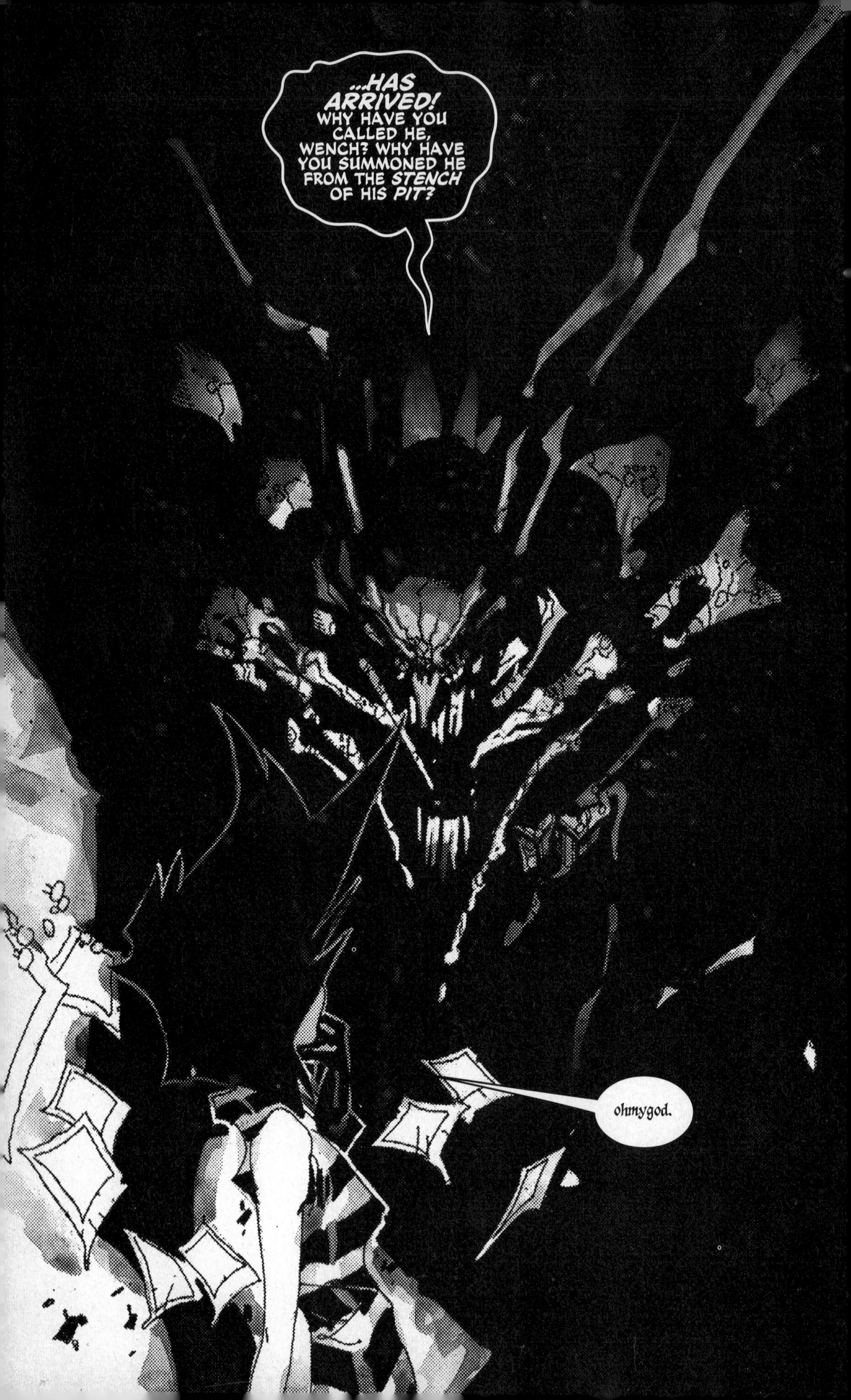
...HAS ARRIVED! WHY HAVE YOU CALLED HE, WENCH? WHY HAVE YOU SUMMONED HE FROM THE STENCH OF HIS PIT?
ohmygod.

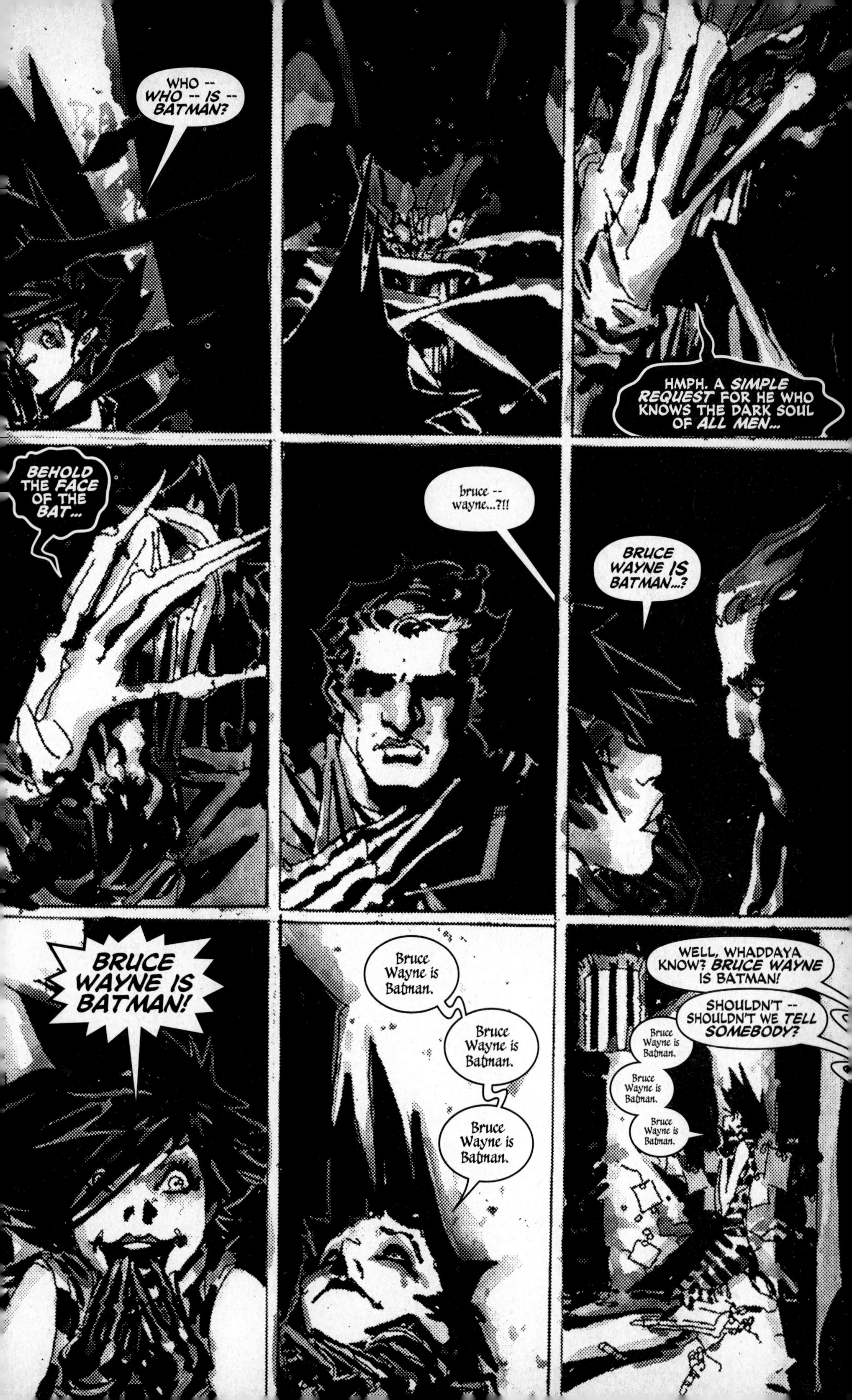
WHO -- WHO -- IS -- BATMAN?
HMPH. A SIMPLE REQUEST FOR HE WHO KNOWS THE DARK SOUL OF ALL MEN...
BEHOLD THE FACE OF THE BAT...
bruce -- wayne...?!!
BRUCE WAYNE IS BATMAN...?
BRUCE WAYNE IS BATMAN!
Bruce Wayne is Batman.
Bruce Wayne is Batman.
Bruce Wayne is Batman.
WELL, WHADDAYA KNOW? BRUCE WAYNE IS BATMAN!
SHOULDN'T -- SHOULDN'T WE TELL SOMEBODY?
Bruce Wayne is Batman.
Bruce Wayne is Batman.
Bruce Wayne is Batman.

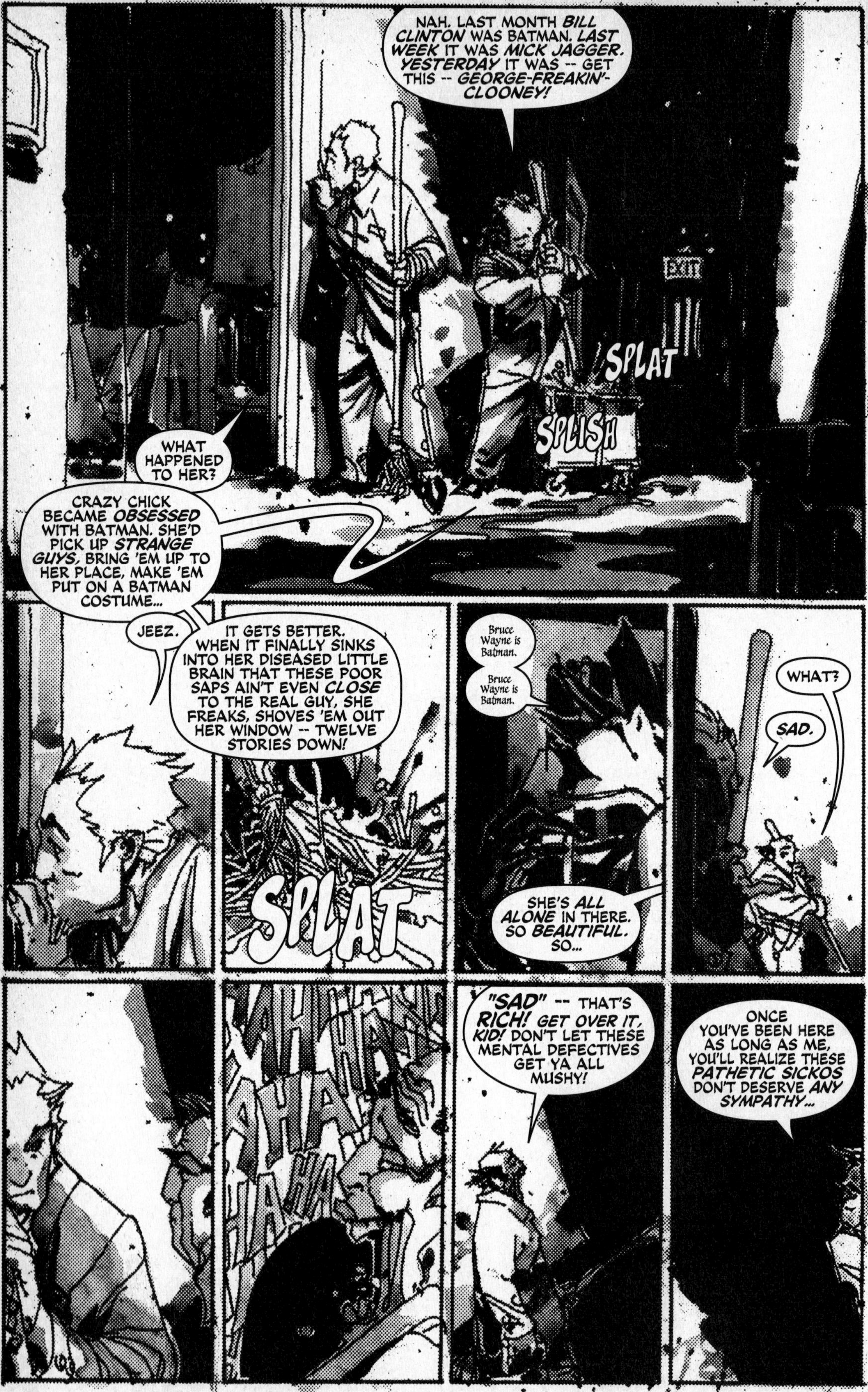
NAH. LAST MONTH BILL CLINTON WAS BATMAN. LAST WEEK IT WAS MICK JAGGER. YESTERDAY IT WAS -- GET THIS -- GEORGE-FREAKIN'-CLOONEY!
SPLAT
SPLISH
WHAT HAPPENED TO HER?
CRAZY CHICK BECAME OBSESSED WITH BATMAN. SHE'D PICK UP STRANGE GUYS, BRING 'EM UP TO HER PLACE, MAKE 'EM PUT ON A BATMAN COSTUME...
JEEZ.
IT GETS BETTER. WHEN IT FINALLY SINKS INTO HER DISEASED LITTLE BRAIN THAT THESE POOR SAPS AIN'T EVEN CLOSE TO THE REAL GUY, SHE FREAKS, SHOVES 'EM OUT HER WINDOW -- TWELVE STORIES DOWN!
SPLAT
Bruce Wayne is Batman.
Bruce Wayne is Batman.
SHE'S ALL ALONE IN THERE. SO BEAUTIFUL. SO...
WHAT?
SAD.
"SAD" -- THAT'S RICH! GET OVER IT, KID! DON'T LET THESE MENTAL DEFECTIVES GET YA ALL MUSHY!
ONCE YOU'VE BEEN HERE AS LONG AS ME, YOU'LL REALIZE THESE PATHETIC SICKOS DON'T DESERVE ANY SYMPATHY...

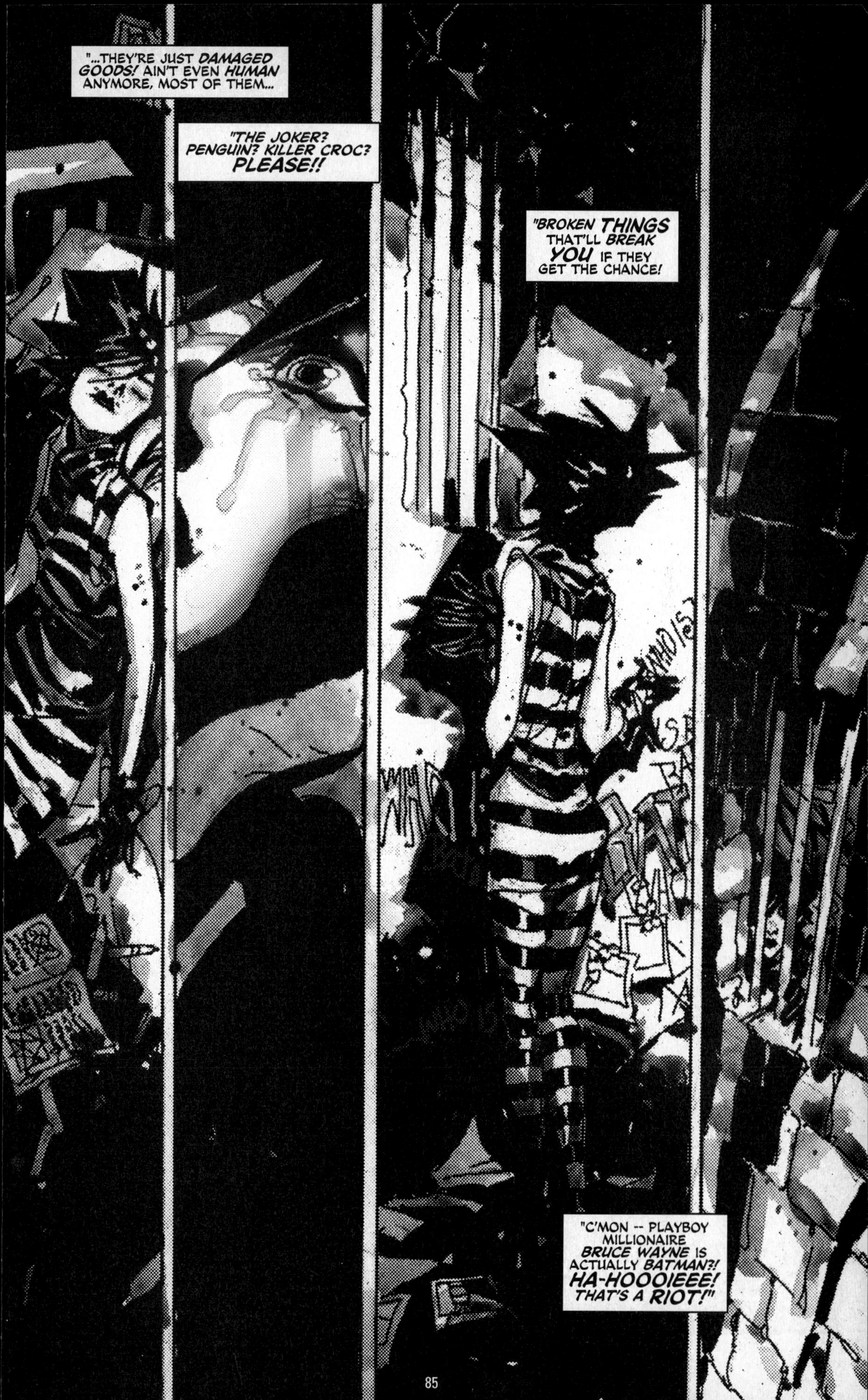
"...THEY'RE JUST DAMAGED GOODS! AIN'T EVEN HUMAN ANYMORE, MOST OF THEM...
"THE JOKER? PENGUIN? KILLER CROC? PLEASE!!
"BROKEN THINGS THAT'LL BREAK YOU IF THEY GET THE CHANCE!
"C'MON -- PLAYBOY MILLIONAIRE BRUCE WAYNE IS ACTUALLY BATMAN?! HA-HOOOIEEE! THAT'S A RIOT!"

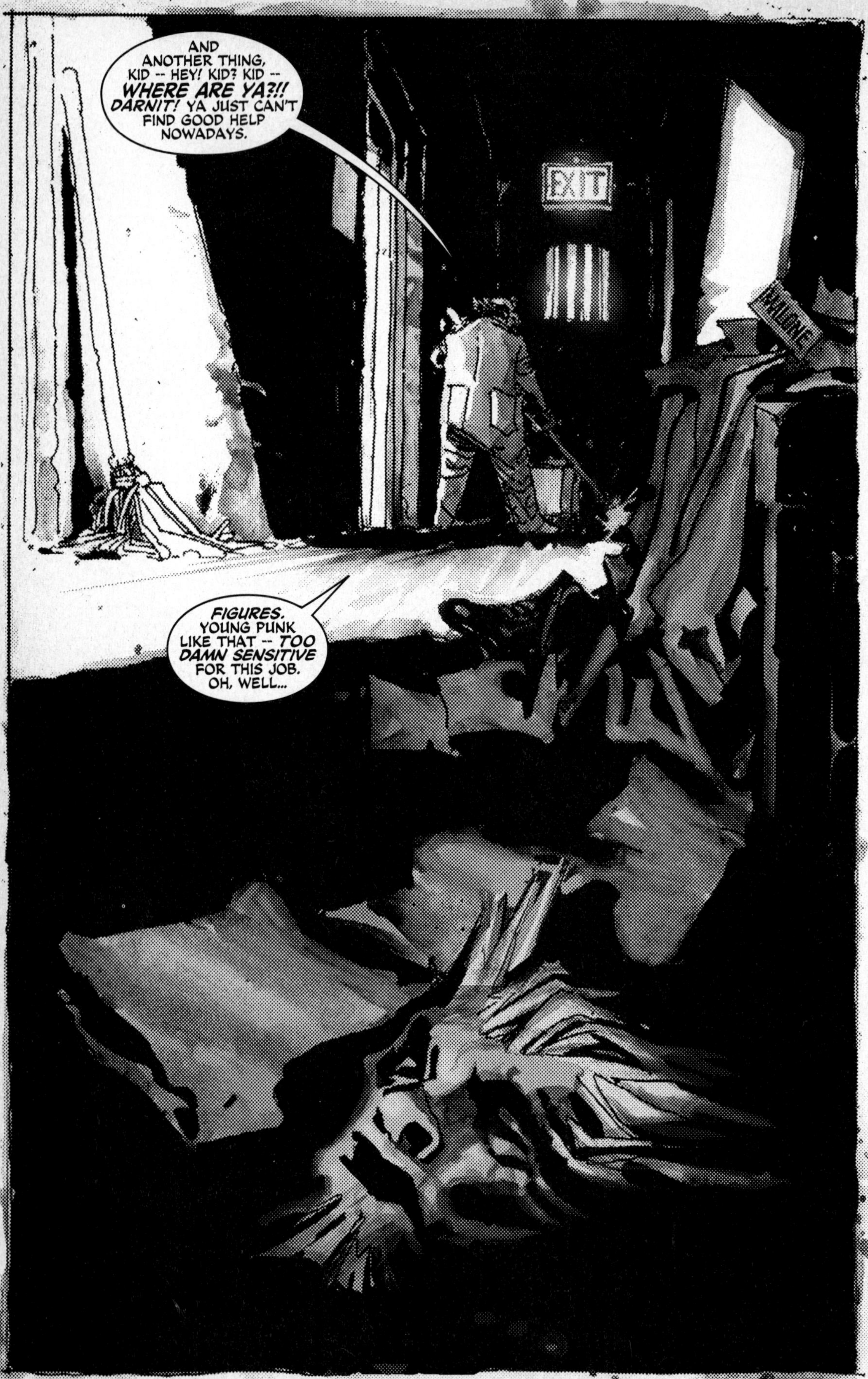
AND ANOTHER THING, KID -- HEY! KID? KID -- WHERE ARE YA?!! DARNIT! YA JUST CAN'T FIND GOOD HELP NOWADAYS.
EXIT
FIGURES. YOUNG PUNK LIKE THAT -- TOO DAMN SENSITIVE FOR THIS JOB. OH, WELL...

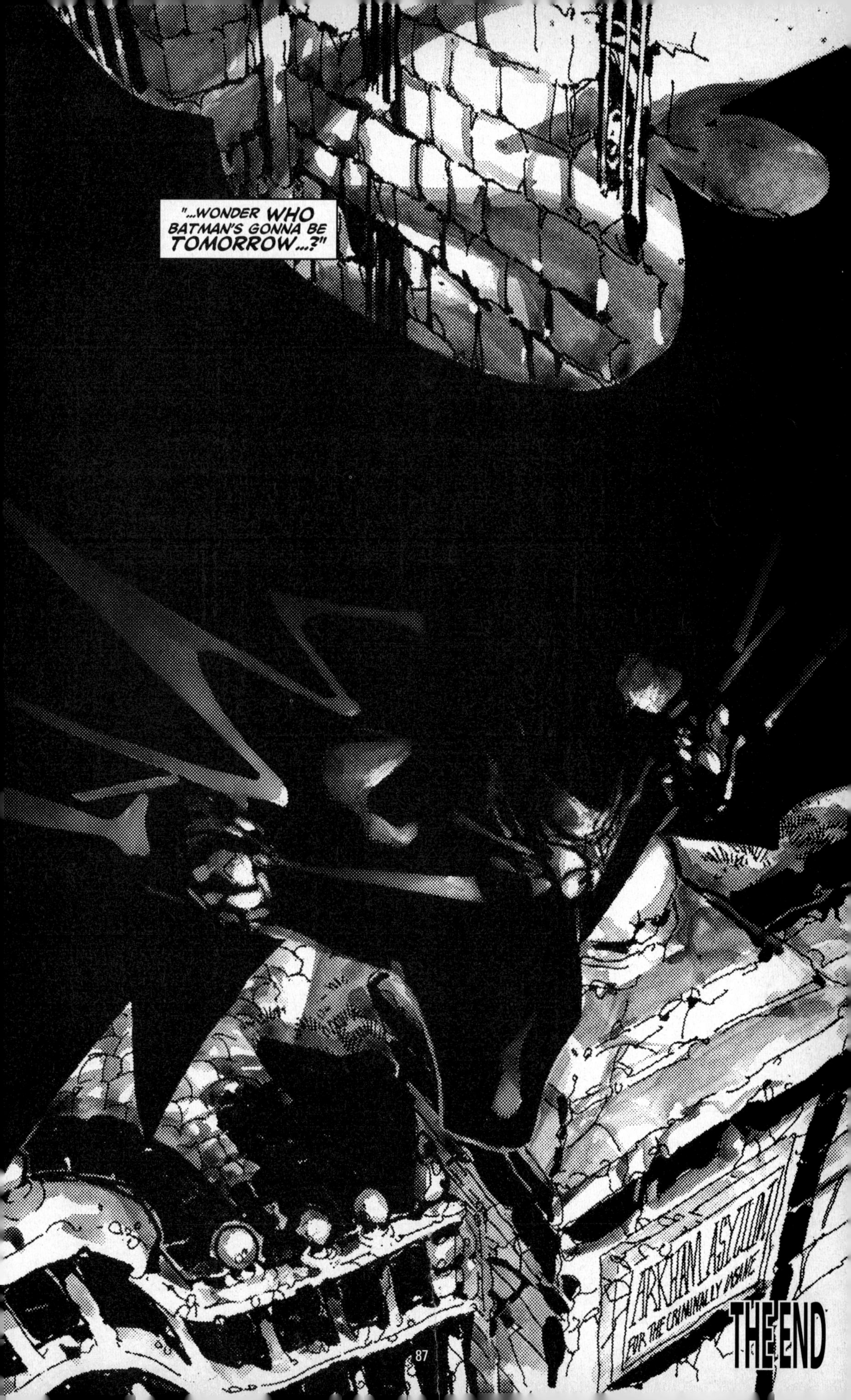
"...WONDER WHO BATMAN'S GONNA BE TOMORROW...?"
ARKHAM ASYLUM FOR THE CRIMINALLY INSANE
THE END

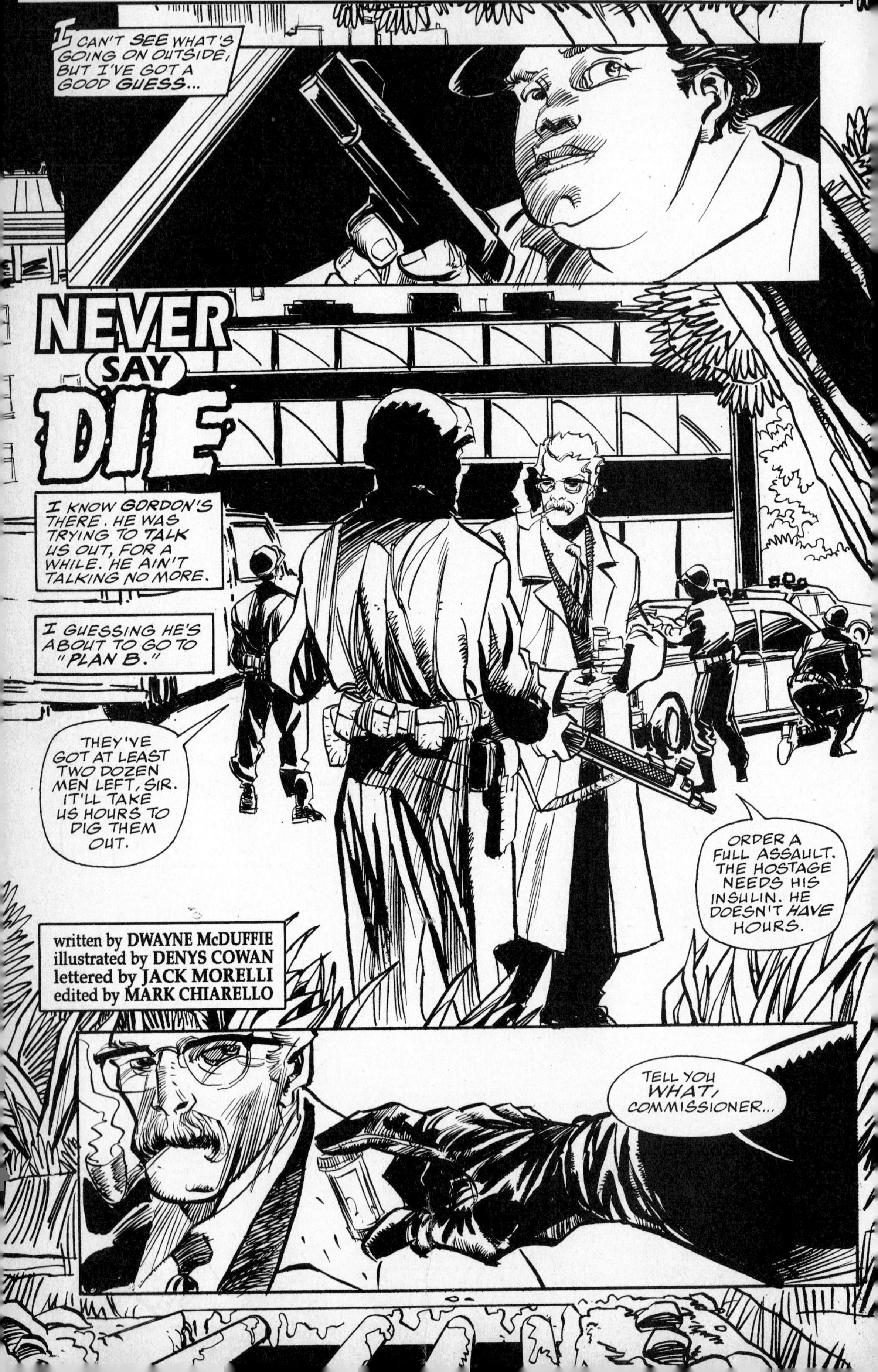
I CAN'T SEE WHAT'S GOING ON OUTSIDE, BUT I'VE GOT A GOOD GUESS...
NEVER SAY DIE
I KNOW GORDON'S THERE. HE WAS TRYING TO TALK US OUT, FOR A WHILE. HE AIN'T TALKING NO MORE.
I GUESSING HE'S ABOUT TO GO TO "PLAN B."
THEY'VE GOT AT LEAST TWO DOZEN MEN LEFT, SIR. IT'LL TAKE US HOURS TO DIG THEM OUT.
ORDER A FULL ASSAULT. THE HOSTAGE NEEDS HIS INSULIN. HE DOESN'T HAVE HOURS.
written by DWAYNE McDUFFIE
illustrated by DENYS COWAN
lettered by JACK MORELLI
edited by MARK CHIARELLO
TELL YOU WHAT, COMMISSIONER...

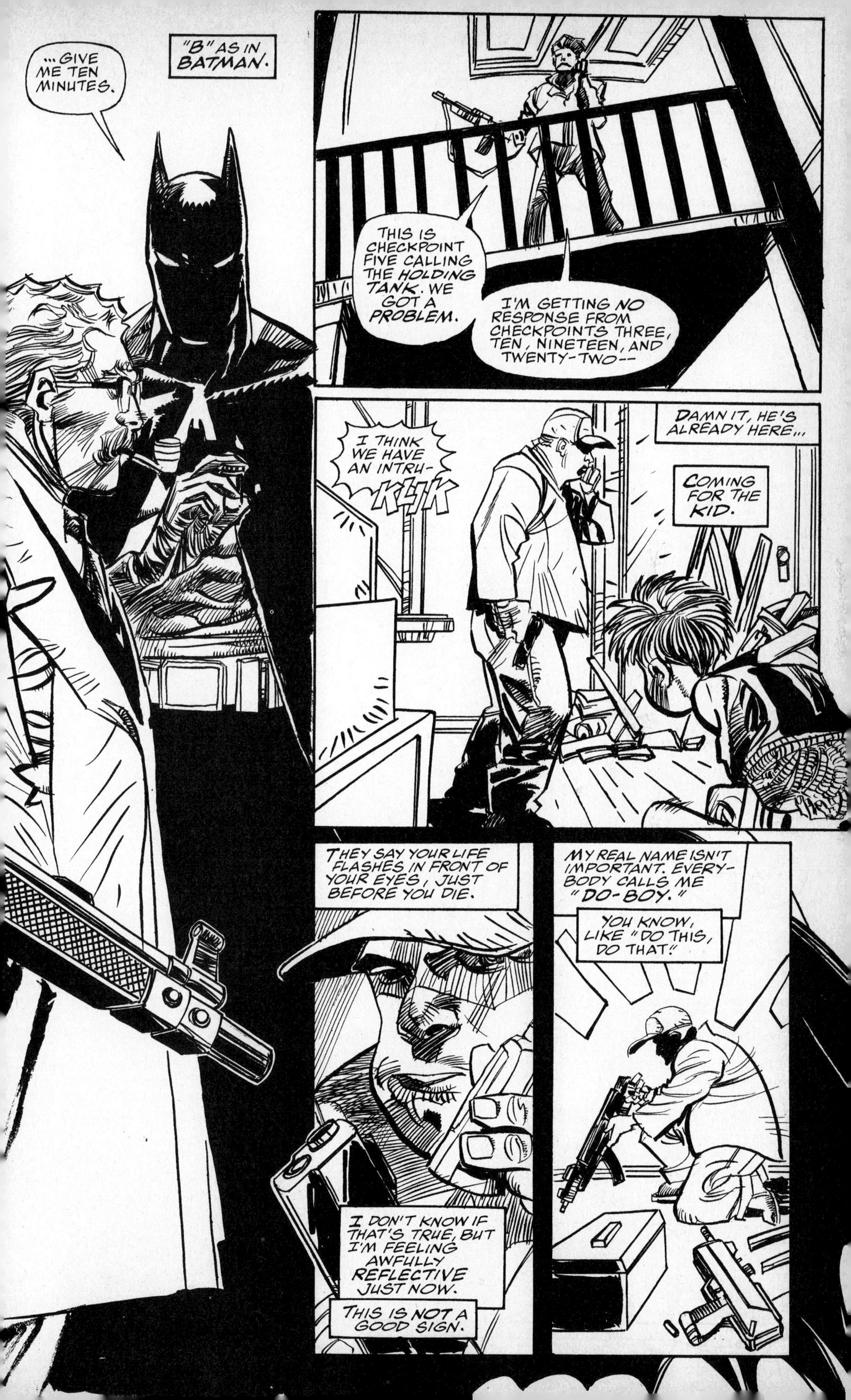
...GIVE ME TEN MINUTES.
"B" AS IN BATMAN.
THIS IS CHECKPOINT FIVE CALLING THE HOLDING TANK. WE GOT A PROBLEM.
I'M GETTING NO RESPONSE FROM CHECKPOINTS THREE, TEN, NINETEEN, AND TWENTY-TWO--
I THINK WE HAVE AN INTRU-
KLIK
DAMN IT, HE'S ALREADY HERE...
COMING FOR THE KID.
THEY SAY YOUR LIFE FLASHES IN FRONT OF YOUR EYES, JUST BEFORE YOU DIE.
I DON'T KNOW IF THAT'S TRUE, BUT I'M FEELING AWFULLY REFLECTIVE JUST NOW.
THIS IS NOT A GOOD SIGN.
MY REAL NAME ISN'T IMPORTANT. EVERYBODY CALLS ME "DO-BOY."
YOU KNOW, LIKE "DO THIS, DO THAT!"

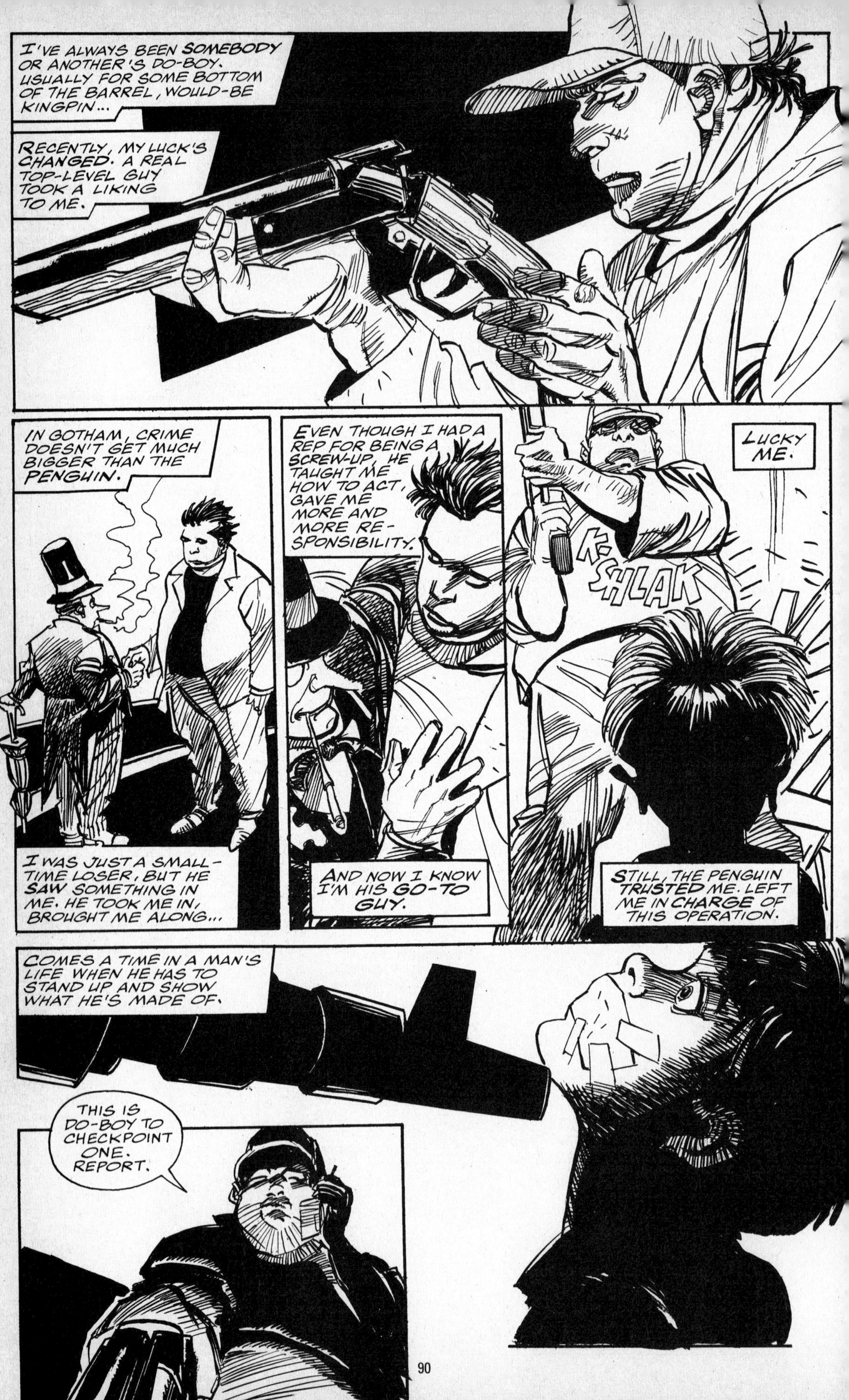
I'VE ALWAYS BEEN SOMEBODY OR ANOTHER'S DO-BOY. USUALLY FOR SOME BOTTOM OF THE BARREL, WOULD-BE KINGPIN...
RECENTLY, MY LUCK'S CHANGED. A REAL TOP-LEVEL GUY TOOK A LIKING TO ME.
IN GOTHAM, CRIME DOESN'T GET MUCH BIGGER THAN THE PENGUIN.
I WAS JUST A SMALL-TIME LOSER, BUT HE SAW SOMETHING IN ME. HE TOOK ME IN, BROUGHT ME ALONG...
EVEN THOUGH I HAD A REP FOR BEING A SCREW-UP, HE TAUGHT ME HOW TO ACT, GAVE ME MORE AND MORE RE-SPONSIBILITY.
AND NOW I KNOW I'M HIS GO-TO GUY.
LUCKY ME.
K-SHLAK
STILL, THE PENGUIN TRUSTED ME. LEFT ME IN CHARGE OF THIS OPERATION.
COMES A TIME IN A MAN'S LIFE WHEN HE HAS TO STAND UP AND SHOW WHAT HE'S MADE OF.
THIS IS DO-BOY TO CHECKPOINT ONE. REPORT.

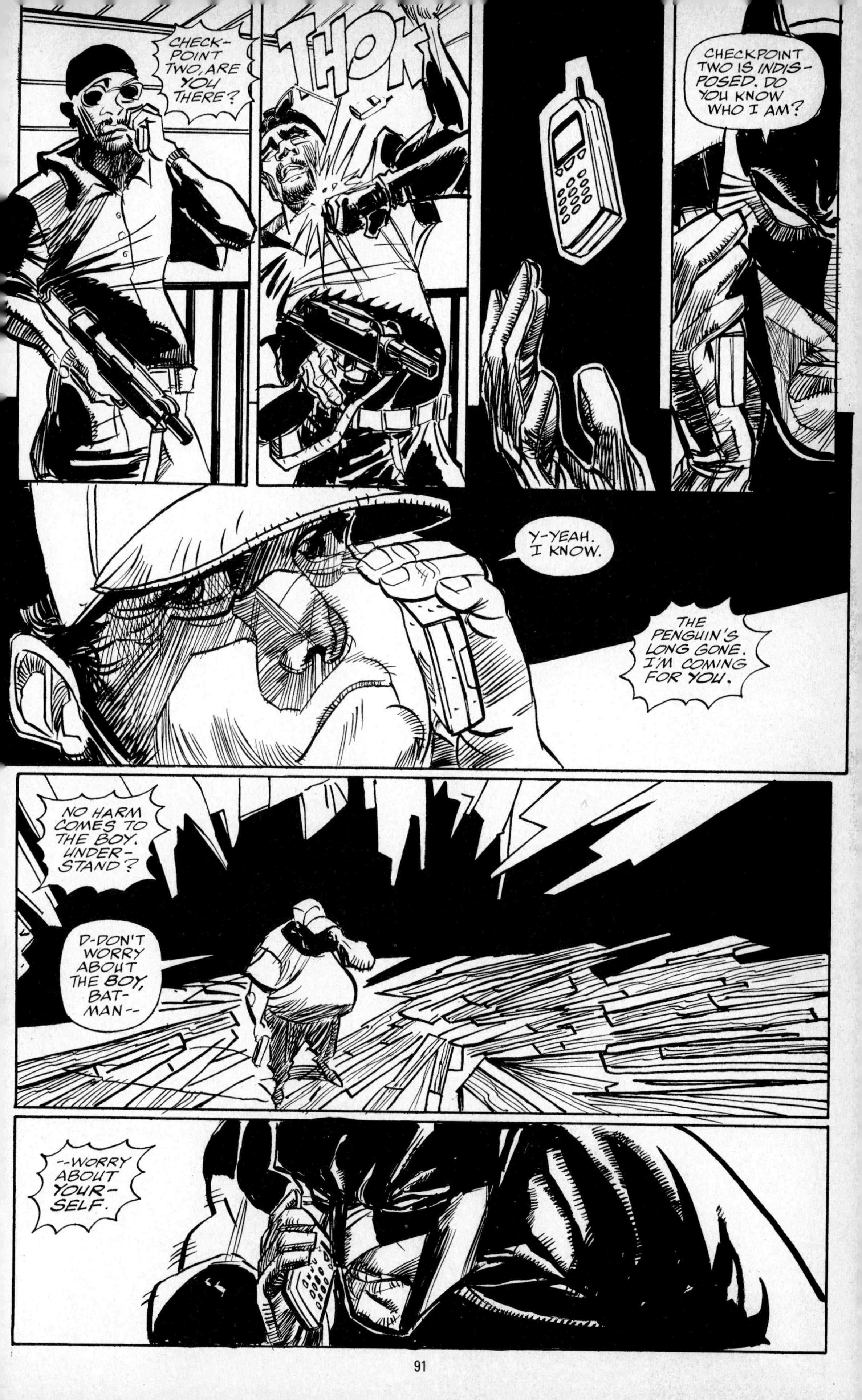
CHECK-POINT TWO, ARE YOU THERE?
THOK
CHECKPOINT TWO IS INDIS-POSED. DO YOU KNOW WHO I AM?
Y-YEAH. I KNOW.
THE PENGUIN'S LONG GONE. I'M COMING FOR YOU.
NO HARM COMES TO THE BOY. UNDER-STAND?
D-DON'T WORRY ABOUT THE BOY, BAT-MAN--
--WORRY ABOUT YOUR-SELF.

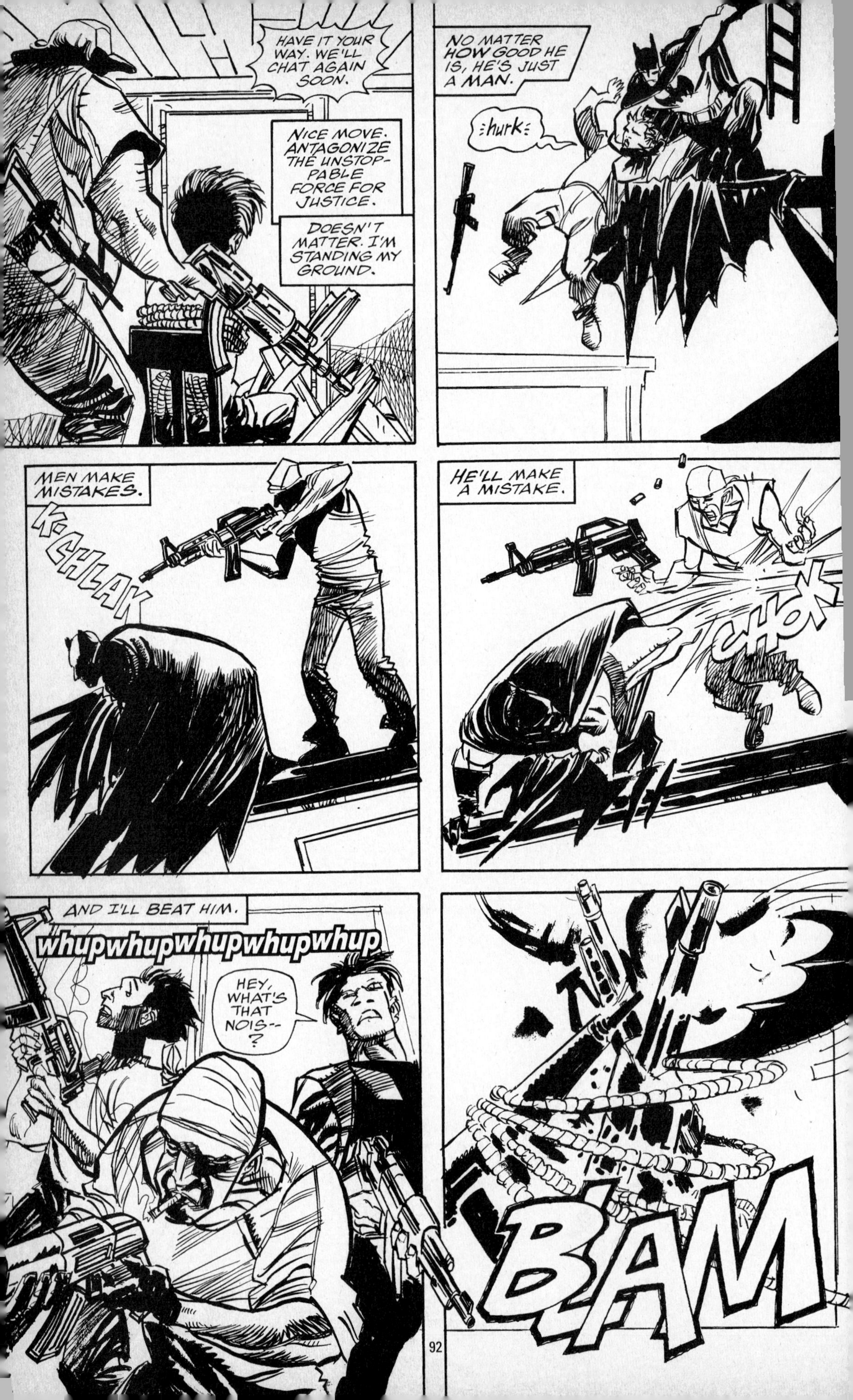
HAVE IT YOUR WAY. WE'LL CHAT AGAIN SOON.
NICE MOVE. ANTAGONIZE THE UNSTOPPABLE FORCE FOR JUSTICE.
DOESN'T MATTER. I'M STANDING MY GROUND.
NO MATTER HOW GOOD HE IS, HE'S JUST A MAN.
hurk
MEN MAKE MISTAKES.
K-CHLAK
HE'LL MAKE A MISTAKE.
CHOK
AND I'LL BEAT HIM.
whupwhupwhupwhupwhup
HEY, WHAT'S THAT NOIS--?
BAM

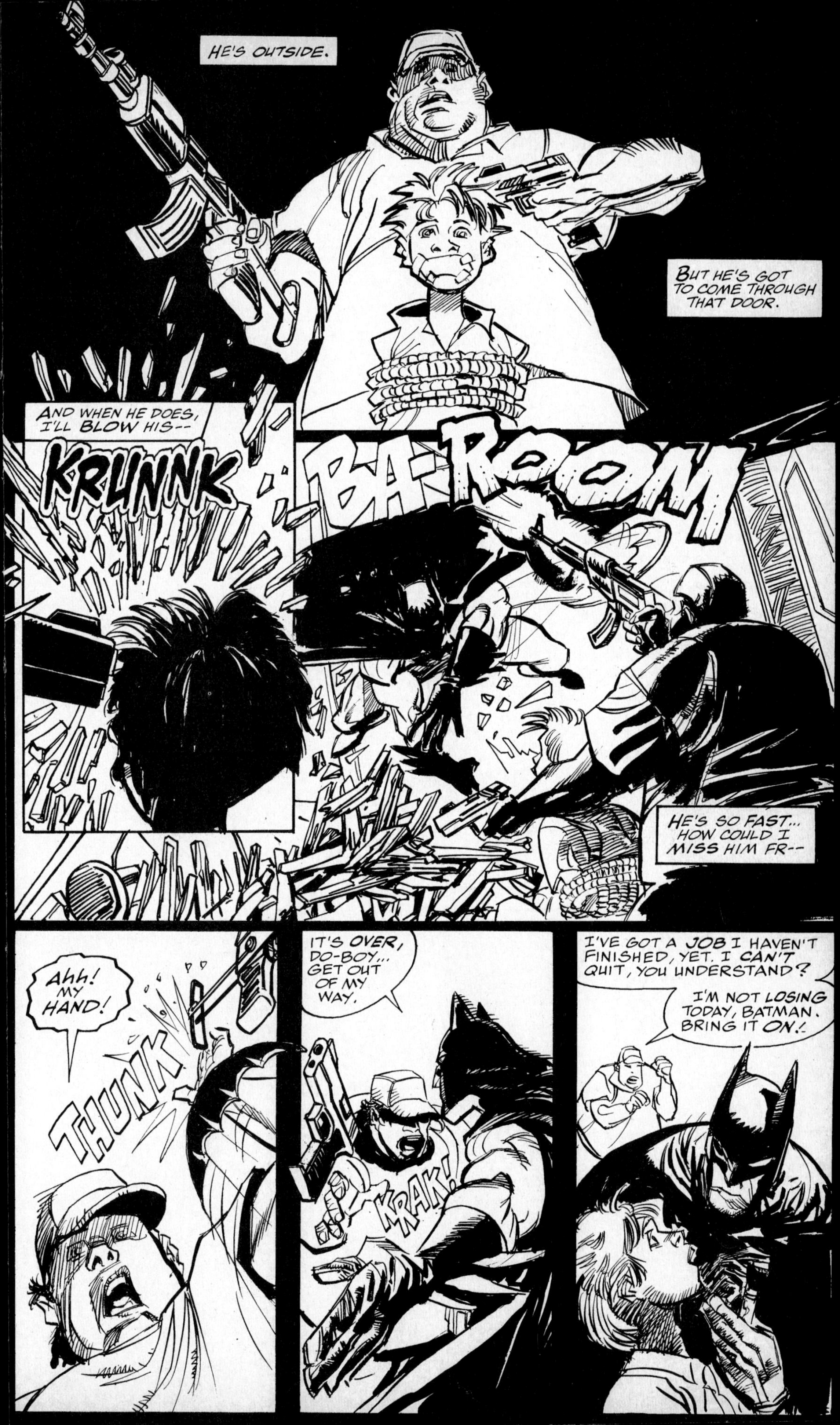
HE'S OUTSIDE.
BUT HE'S GOT TO COME THROUGH THAT DOOR.
AND WHEN HE DOES, I'LL BLOW HIS--
KRUNNK
BA-ROOM
HE'S SO FAST... HOW COULD I MISS HIM FR--
Ahh! MY HAND!
THUNK
IT'S OVER, DO-BOY... GET OUT OF MY WAY.
KRAK!
I'VE GOT A JOB I HAVEN'T FINISHED, YET. I CAN'T QUIT, YOU UNDERSTAND?
I'M NOT LOSING TODAY, BATMAN. BRING IT ON!

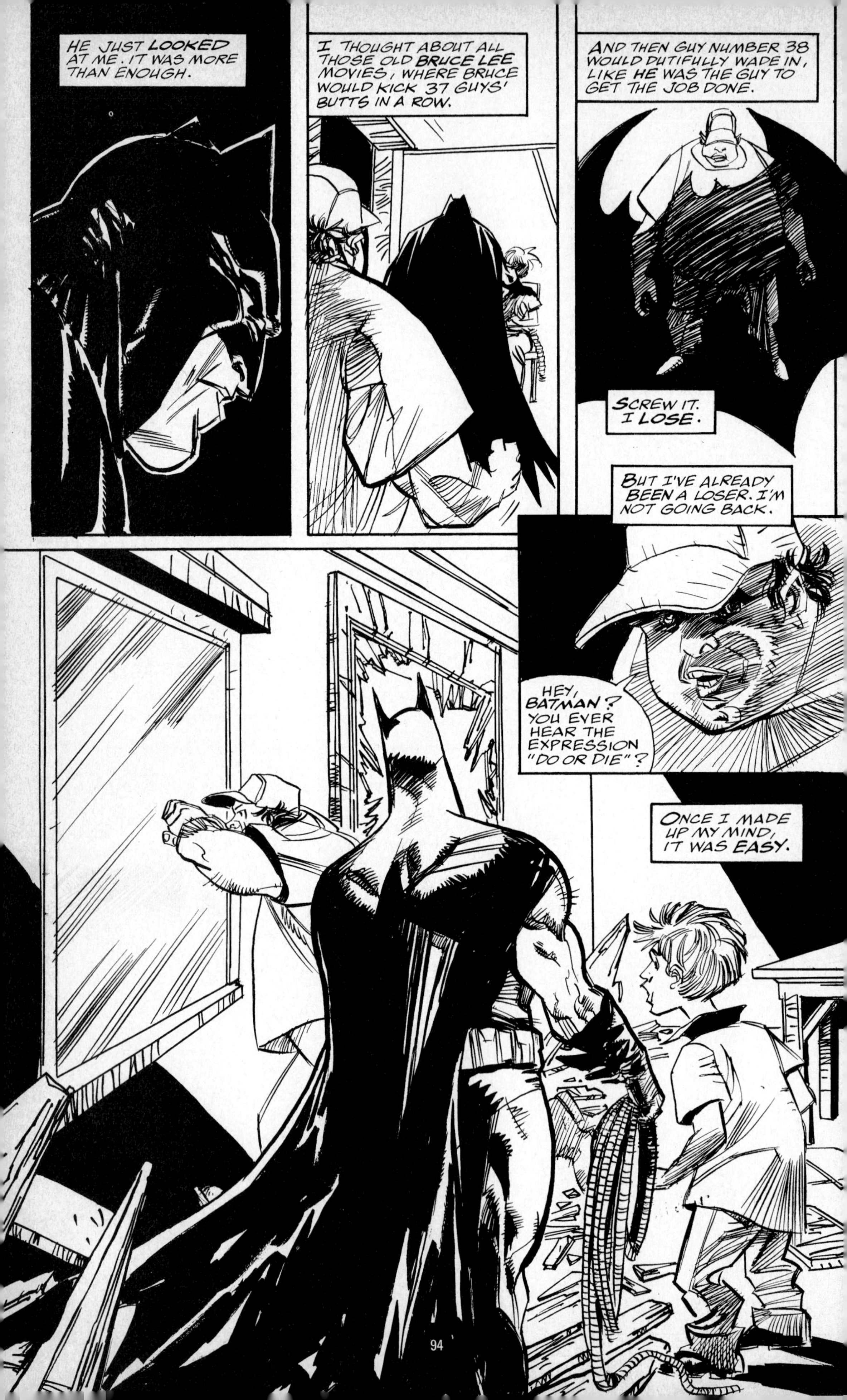
HE JUST LOOKED AT ME. IT WAS MORE THAN ENOUGH.
I THOUGHT ABOUT ALL THOSE OLD BRUCE LEE MOVIES, WHERE BRUCE WOULD KICK 37 GUYS' BUTTS IN A ROW.
AND THEN GUY NUMBER 38 WOULD DUTIFULLY WADE IN, LIKE HE WAS THE GUY TO GET THE JOB DONE.
SCREW IT. I LOSE.
BUT I'VE ALREADY BEEN A LOSER. I'M NOT GOING BACK.
HEY, BATMAN? YOU EVER HEAR THE EXPRESSION "DO OR DIE"?
ONCE I MADE UP MY MIND, IT WAS EASY.

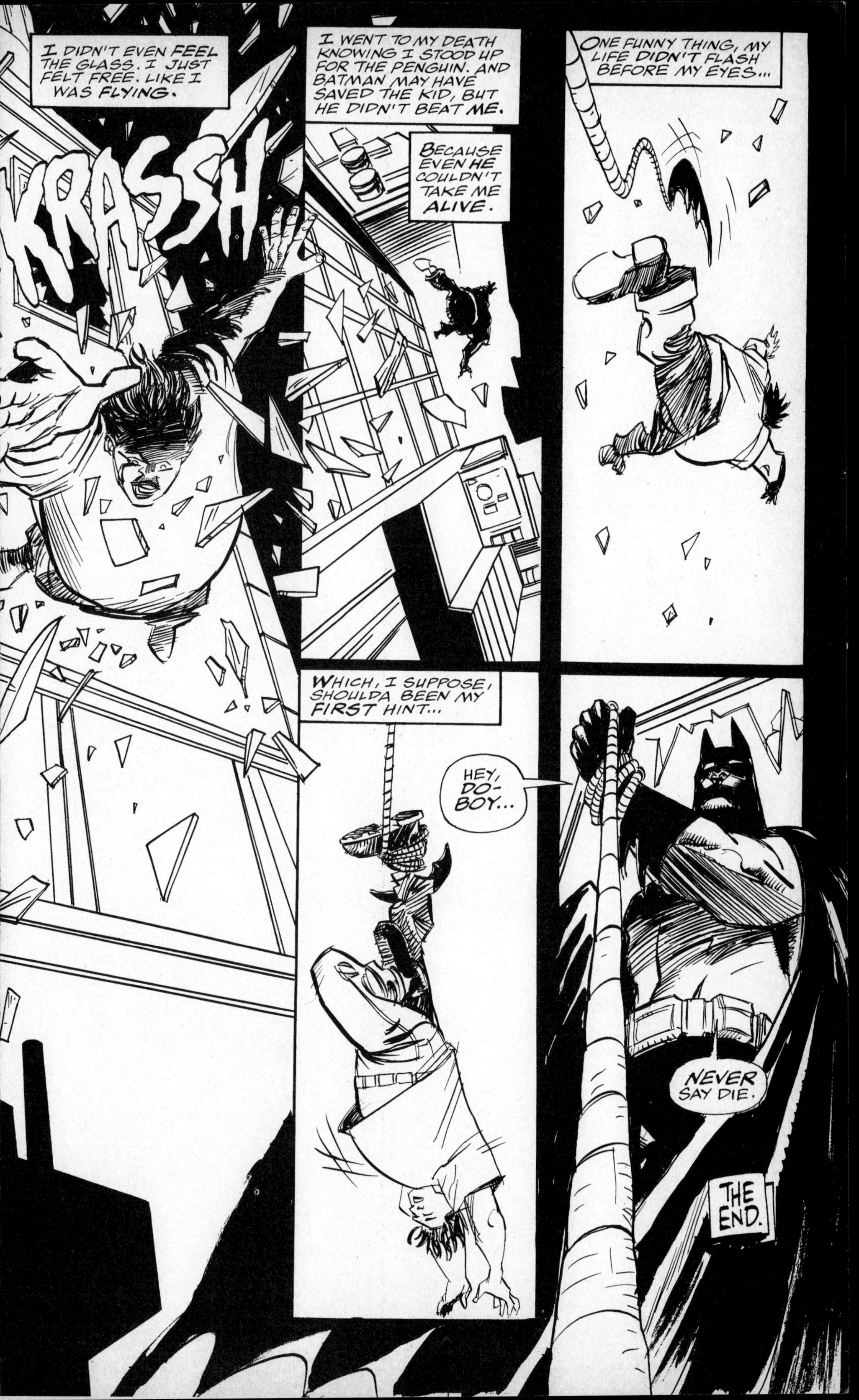

I DIDN'T EVEN FEEL THE GLASS. I JUST FELT FREE. LIKE I WAS FLYING.
KRASSH
I WENT TO MY DEATH KNOWING I STOOD UP FOR THE PENGUIN. AND BATMAN MAY HAVE SAVED THE KID, BUT HE DIDN'T BEAT ME.
BECAUSE EVEN HE COULDN'T TAKE ME ALIVE.
ONE FUNNY THING, MY LIFE DIDN'T FLASH BEFORE MY EYES...
WHICH, I SUPPOSE, SHOULDA BEEN MY FIRST HINT...
HEY, DO-BOY...
NEVER SAY DIE.
THE END.

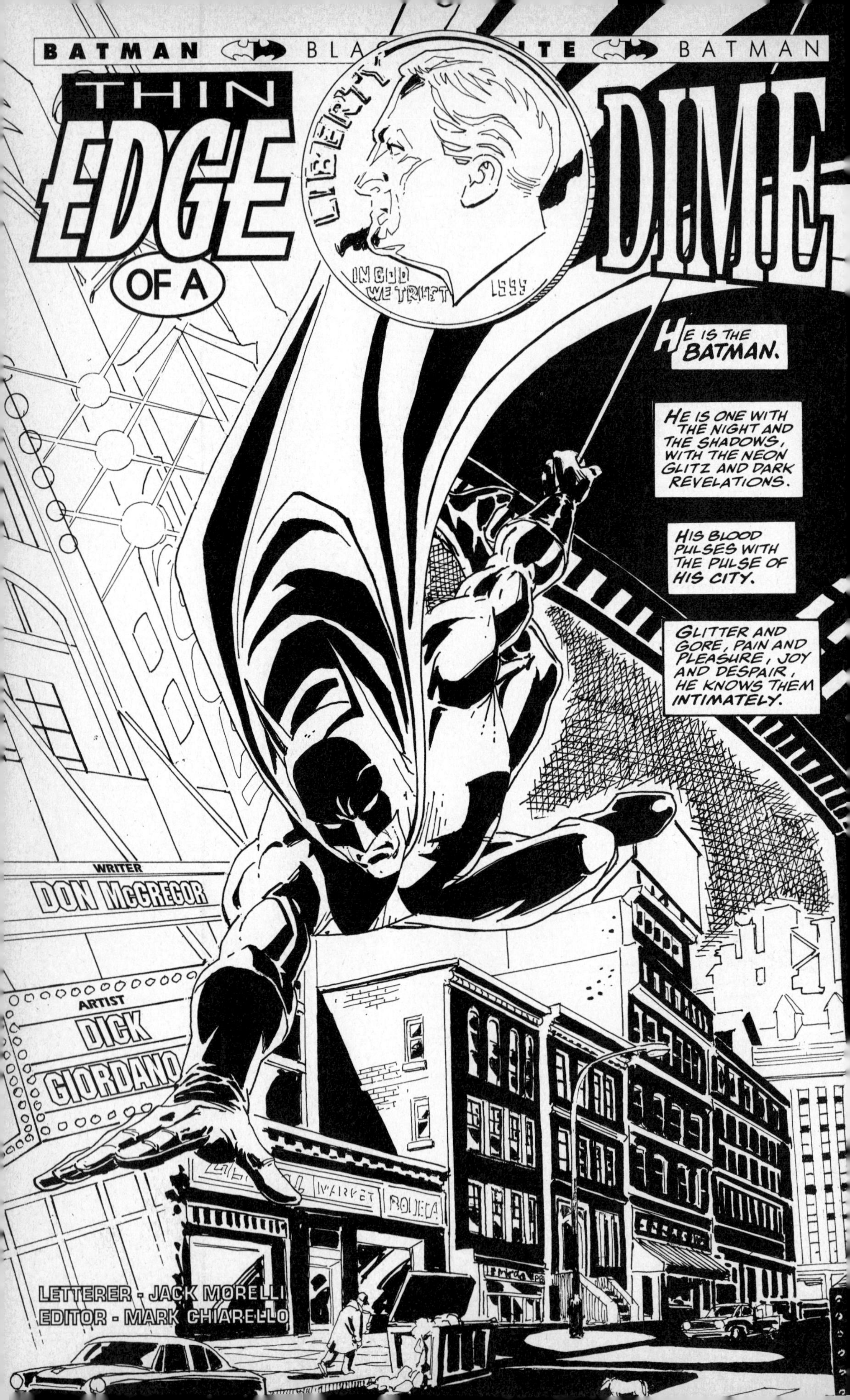

BATMAN BLACK AND WHITE BATMAN
THIN EDGE OF A DIME
LIBERTY
IN GOD WE TRUST
HE IS THE BATMAN.
HE IS ONE WITH THE NIGHT AND THE SHADOWS, WITH THE NEON GLITZ AND DARK REVELATIONS.
HIS BLOOD PULSES WITH THE PULSE OF HIS CITY.
GLITTER AND GORE, PAIN AND PLEASURE, JOY AND DESPAIR, HE KNOWS THEM INTIMATELY.
WRITER
DON McGREGOR
ARTIST
DICK GIORDANO
MARKET
LETTERER - JACK MORELLI
EDITOR - MARK CHIARELLO

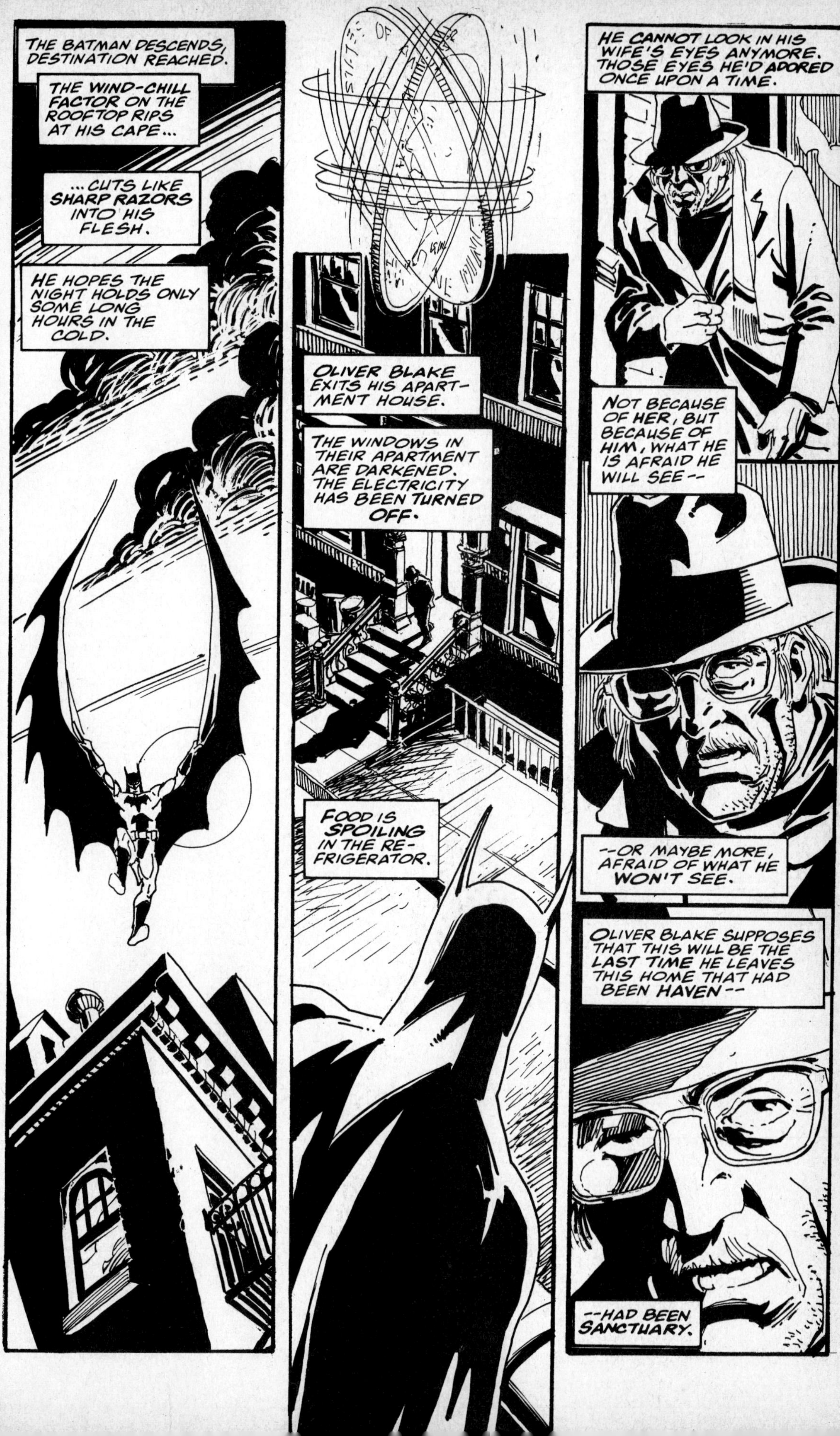
THE BATMAN DESCENDS, DESTINATION REACHED.
THE WIND-CHILL FACTOR ON THE ROOFTOP RIPS AT HIS CAPE...
...CUTS LIKE SHARP RAZORS INTO HIS FLESH.
HE HOPES THE NIGHT HOLDS ONLY SOME LONG HOURS IN THE COLD.
OLIVER BLAKE EXITS HIS APARTMENT HOUSE.
THE WINDOWS IN THEIR APARTMENT ARE DARKENED. THE ELECTRICITY HAS BEEN TURNED OFF.
FOOD IS SPOILING IN THE REFRIGERATOR.
HE CANNOT LOOK IN HIS WIFE'S EYES ANYMORE. THOSE EYES HE'D ADORED ONCE UPON A TIME.
NOT BECAUSE OF HER, BUT BECAUSE OF HIM, WHAT HE IS AFRAID HE WILL SEE--
--OR MAYBE MORE, AFRAID OF WHAT HE WON'T SEE.
OLIVER BLAKE SUPPOSES THAT THIS WILL BE THE LAST TIME HE LEAVES THIS HOME THAT HAD BEEN HAVEN--
--HAD BEEN SANCTUARY.

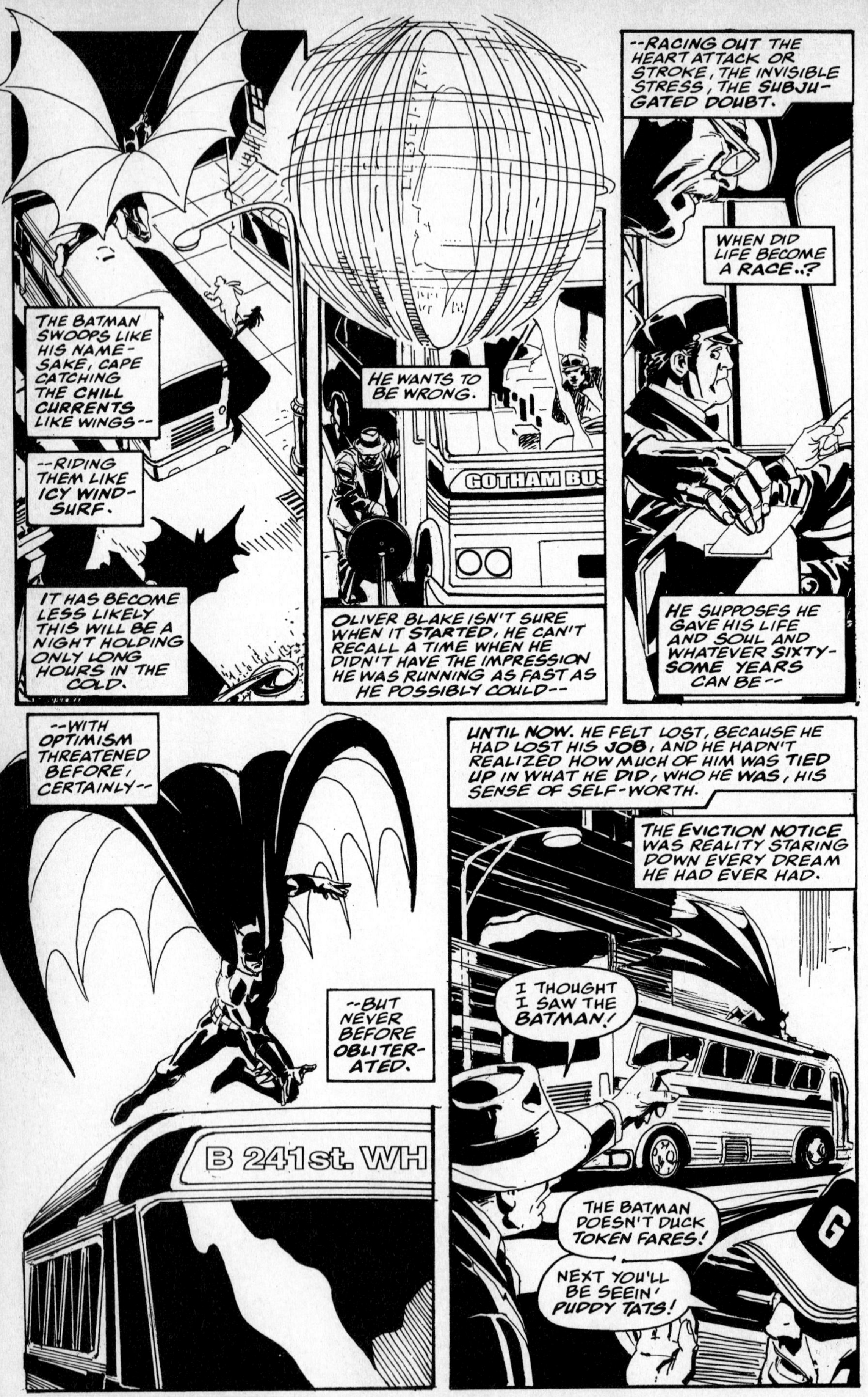
THE BATMAN SWOOPS LIKE HIS NAMESAKE, CAPE CATCHING THE CHILL CURRENTS LIKE WINGS--
--RIDING THEM LIKE ICY WIND-SURF.
IT HAS BECOME LESS LIKELY THIS WILL BE A NIGHT HOLDING ONLY LONG HOURS IN THE COLD.
HE WANTS TO BE WRONG.
GOTHAM BUS
OLIVER BLAKE ISN'T SURE WHEN IT STARTED. HE CAN'T RECALL A TIME WHEN HE DIDN'T HAVE THE IMPRESSION HE WAS RUNNING AS FAST AS HE POSSIBLY COULD--
--RACING OUT THE HEART ATTACK OR STROKE, THE INVISIBLE STRESS, THE SUBJUGATED DOUBT.
WHEN DID LIFE BECOME A RACE..?
HE SUPPOSES HE GAVE HIS LIFE AND SOUL AND WHATEVER SIXTY-SOME YEARS CAN BE--
--WITH OPTIMISM THREATENED BEFORE, CERTAINLY--
--BUT NEVER BEFORE OBLITERATED.
B 241st. WH
UNTIL NOW. HE FELT LOST, BECAUSE HE HAD LOST HIS JOB, AND HE HADN'T REALIZED HOW MUCH OF HIM WAS TIED UP IN WHAT HE DID, WHO HE WAS, HIS SENSE OF SELF-WORTH.
THE EVICTION NOTICE WAS REALITY STARING DOWN EVERY DREAM HE HAD EVER HAD.
I THOUGHT I SAW THE BATMAN!
THE BATMAN DOESN'T DUCK TOKEN FARES!
NEXT YOU'LL BE SEEIN' PUDDY TATS!
G

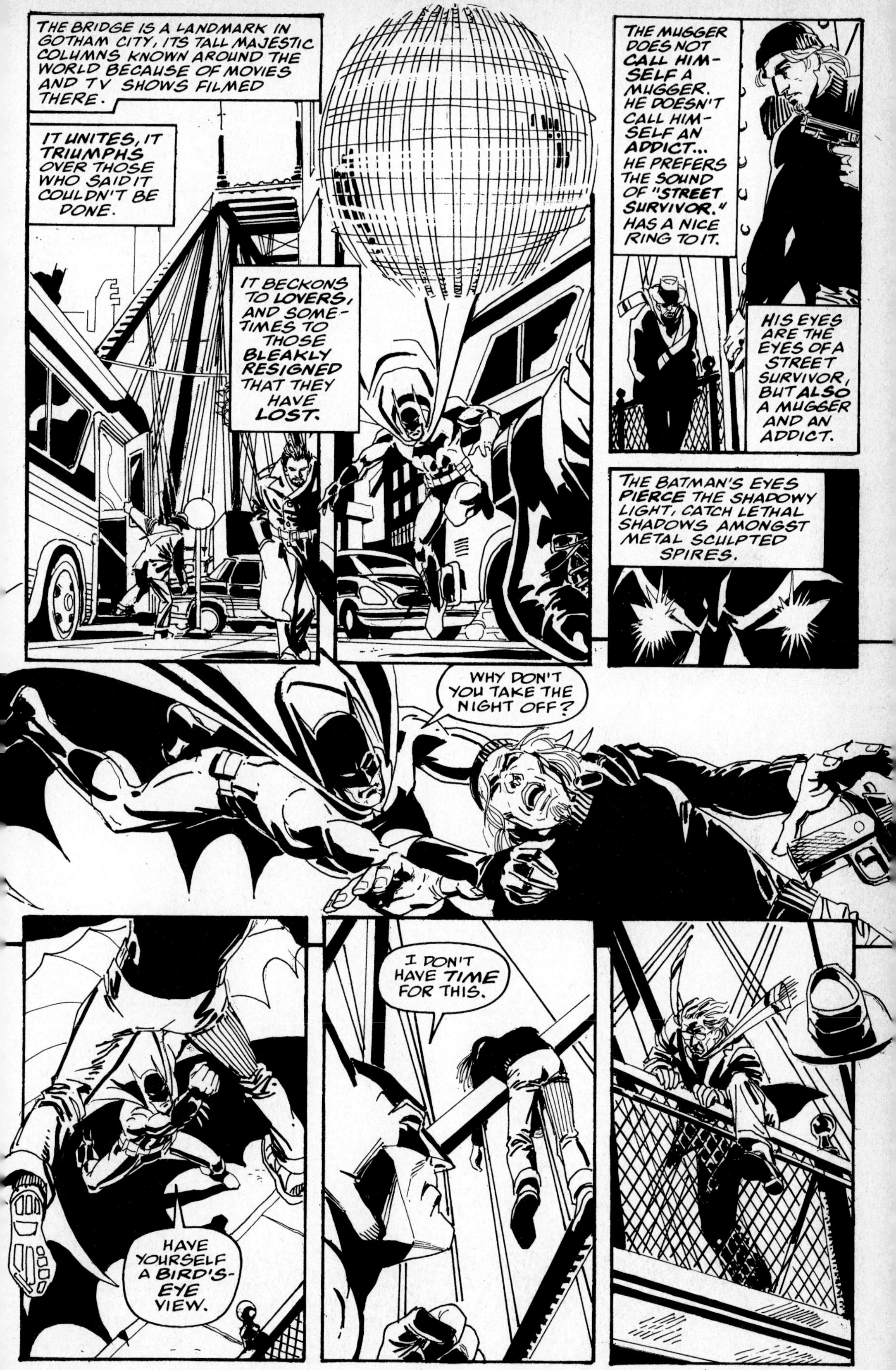

THE BRIDGE IS A LANDMARK IN GOTHAM CITY, ITS TALL MAJESTIC COLUMNS KNOWN AROUND THE WORLD BECAUSE OF MOVIES AND TV SHOWS FILMED THERE.
IT UNITES, IT TRIUMPHS OVER THOSE WHO SAID IT COULDN'T BE DONE.
IT BECKONS TO LOVERS, AND SOMETIMES TO THOSE BLEAKLY RESIGNED THAT THEY HAVE LOST.
THE MUGGER DOES NOT CALL HIMSELF A MUGGER. HE DOESN'T CALL HIMSELF AN ADDICT... HE PREFERS THE SOUND OF "STREET SURVIVOR." HAS A NICE RING TO IT.
HIS EYES ARE THE EYES OF A STREET SURVIVOR, BUT ALSO A MUGGER AND AN ADDICT.
THE BATMAN'S EYES PIERCE THE SHADOWY LIGHT, CATCH LETHAL SHADOWS AMONGST METAL SCULPTED SPIRES.
WHY DON'T YOU TAKE THE NIGHT OFF?
HAVE YOURSELF A BIRD'S-EYE VIEW.
I DON'T HAVE TIME FOR THIS.

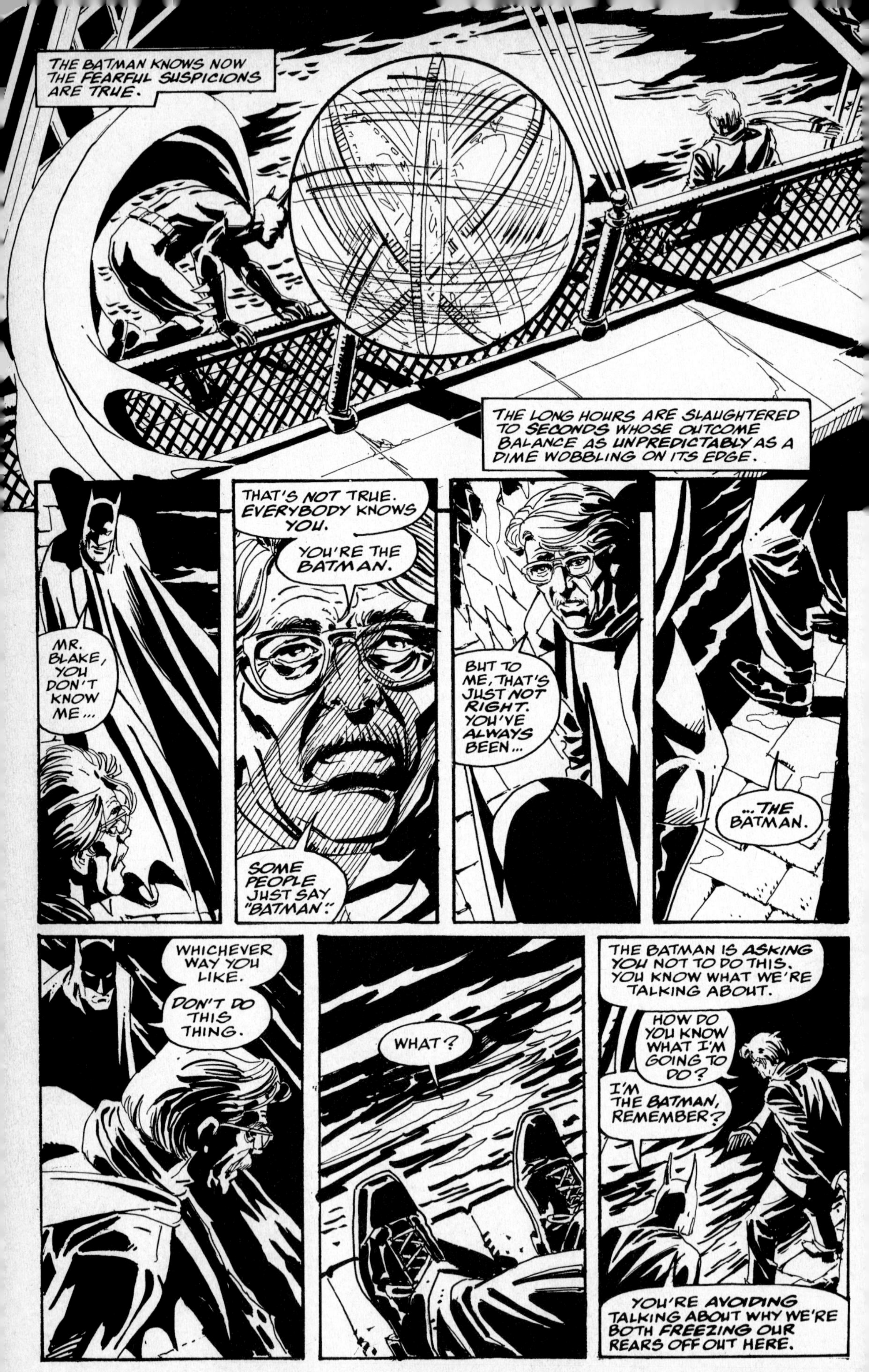

THE BATMAN KNOWS NOW THE FEARFUL SUSPICIONS ARE TRUE.
THE LONG HOURS ARE SLAUGHTERED TO SECONDS WHOSE OUTCOME BALANCE AS UNPREDICTABLY AS A DIME WOBBLING ON ITS EDGE.
MR. BLAKE, YOU DON'T KNOW ME...
THAT'S NOT TRUE. EVERYBODY KNOWS YOU.
YOU'RE THE BATMAN.
SOME PEOPLE JUST SAY "BATMAN."
BUT TO ME, THAT'S JUST NOT RIGHT. YOU'VE ALWAYS BEEN...
...THE BATMAN.
WHICHEVER WAY YOU LIKE.
DON'T DO THIS THING.
WHAT?
THE BATMAN IS ASKING YOU NOT TO DO THIS. YOU KNOW WHAT WE'RE TALKING ABOUT.
HOW DO YOU KNOW WHAT I'M GOING TO DO?
I'M THE BATMAN, REMEMBER?
YOU'RE AVOIDING TALKING ABOUT WHY WE'RE BOTH FREEZING OUR REARS OFF OUT HERE.

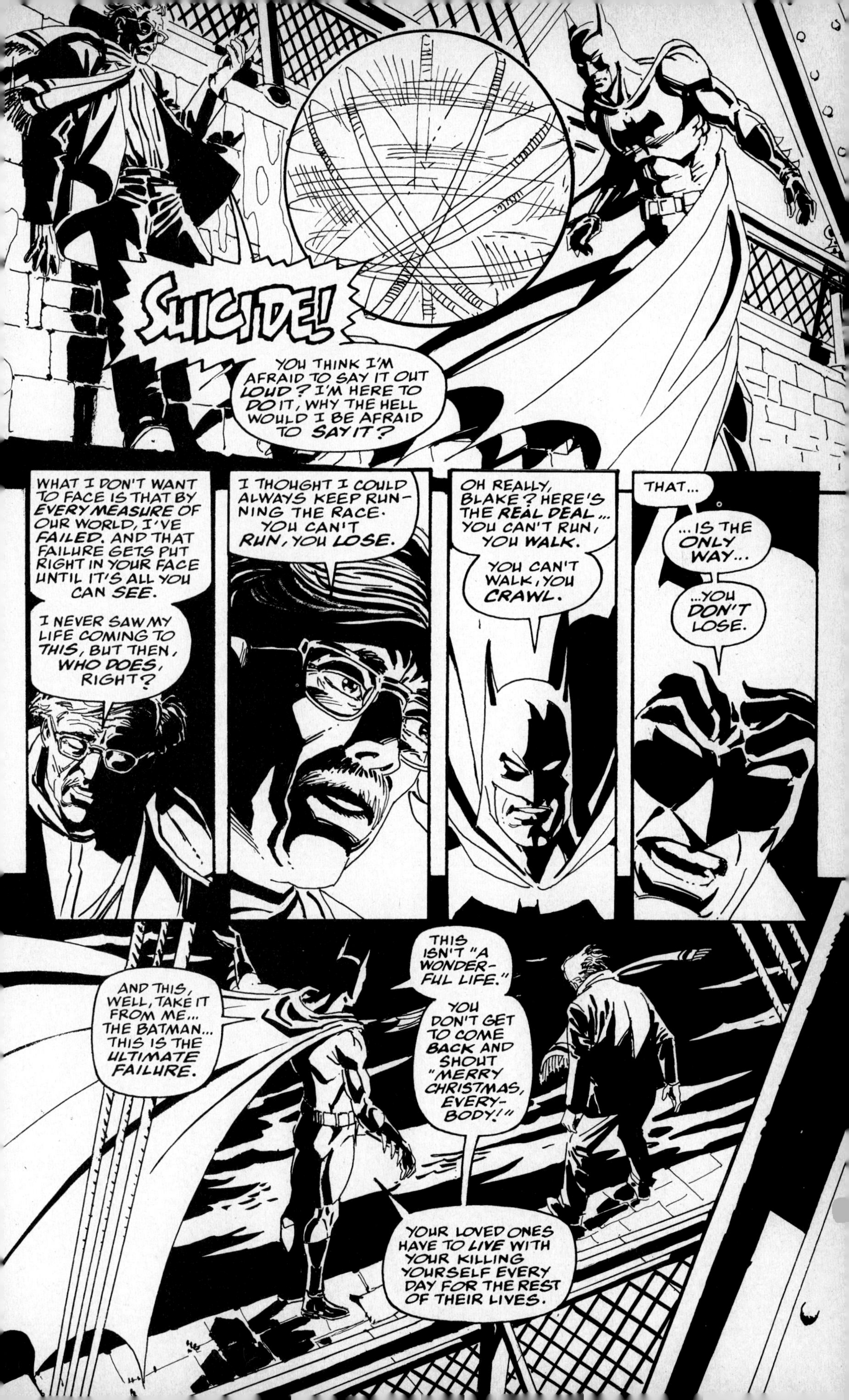
SUICIDE!
YOU THINK I'M AFRAID TO SAY IT OUT LOUD? I'M HERE TO DO IT, WHY THE HELL WOULD I BE AFRAID TO SAY IT?
WHAT I DON'T WANT TO FACE IS THAT BY EVERY MEASURE OF OUR WORLD, I'VE FAILED. AND THAT FAILURE GETS PUT RIGHT IN YOUR FACE UNTIL IT'S ALL YOU CAN SEE.
I NEVER SAW MY LIFE COMING TO THIS, BUT THEN, WHO DOES, RIGHT?
I THOUGHT I COULD ALWAYS KEEP RUNNING THE RACE. YOU CAN'T RUN, YOU LOSE.
OH REALLY, BLAKE? HERE'S THE REAL DEAL... YOU CAN'T RUN, YOU WALK.
YOU CAN'T WALK, YOU CRAWL.
THAT...
...IS THE ONLY WAY...
...YOU DON'T LOSE.
AND THIS, WELL, TAKE IT FROM ME... THE BATMAN... THIS IS THE ULTIMATE FAILURE.
THIS ISN'T "A WONDERFUL LIFE."
YOU DON'T GET TO COME BACK AND SHOUT "MERRY CHRISTMAS, EVERYBODY!"
YOUR LOVED ONES HAVE TO LIVE WITH YOUR KILLING YOURSELF EVERY DAY FOR THE REST OF THEIR LIVES.

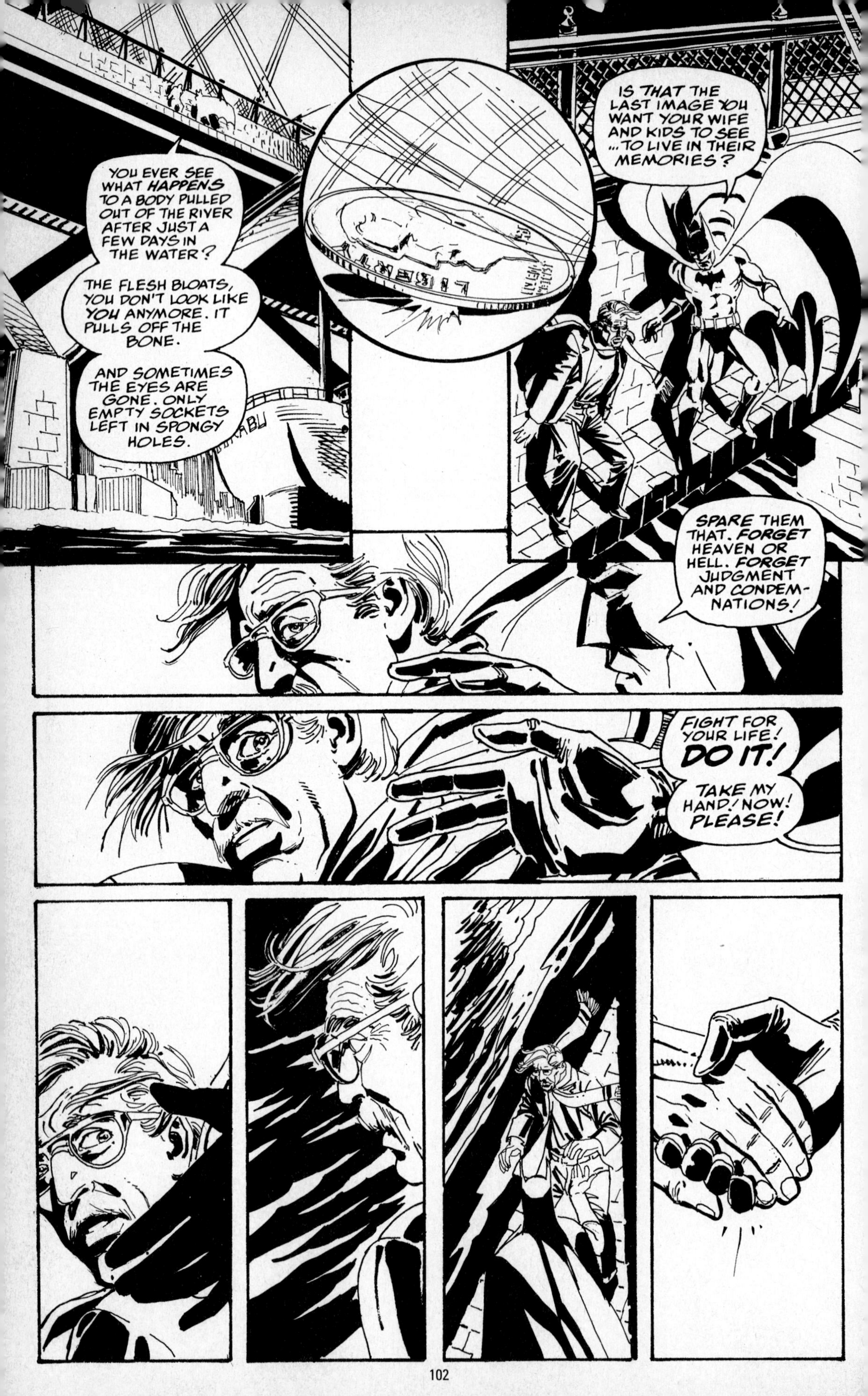
YOU EVER SEE WHAT HAPPENS TO A BODY PULLED OUT OF THE RIVER AFTER JUST A FEW DAYS IN THE WATER?
THE FLESH BLOATS, YOU DON'T LOOK LIKE YOU ANYMORE. IT PULLS OFF THE BONE.
AND SOMETIMES THE EYES ARE GONE. ONLY EMPTY SOCKETS LEFT IN SPONGY HOLES.
LIBERTY
IS THAT THE LAST IMAGE YOU WANT YOUR WIFE AND KIDS TO SEE ...TO LIVE IN THEIR MEMORIES?
SPARE THEM THAT. FORGET HEAVEN OR HELL. FORGET JUDGMENT AND CONDEM-NATIONS!
FIGHT FOR YOUR LIFE! DO IT!
TAKE MY HAND! NOW! PLEASE!

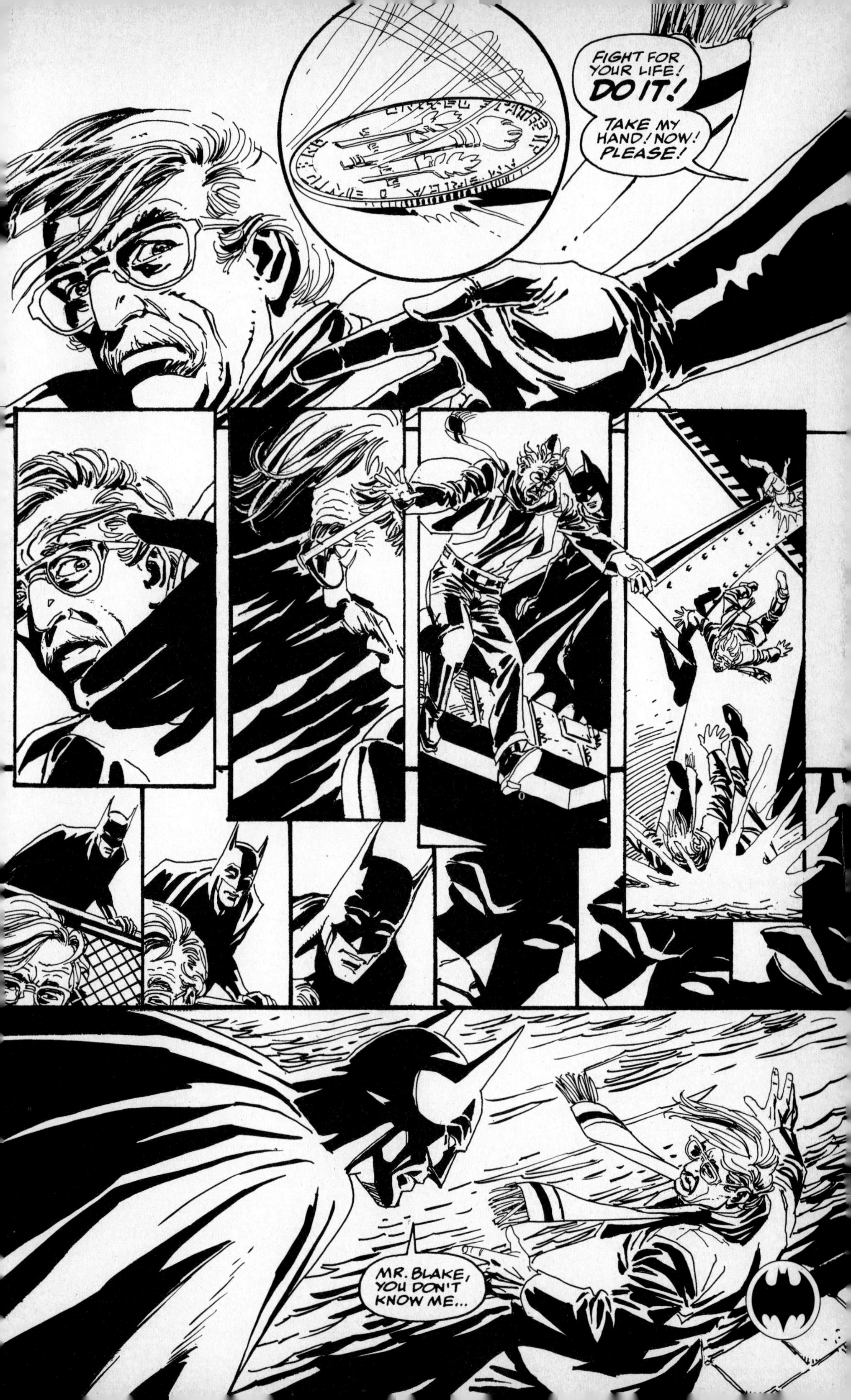
FIGHT FOR YOUR LIFE! DO IT!
TAKE MY HAND! NOW! PLEASE!
MR. BLAKE, YOU DON'T KNOW ME...

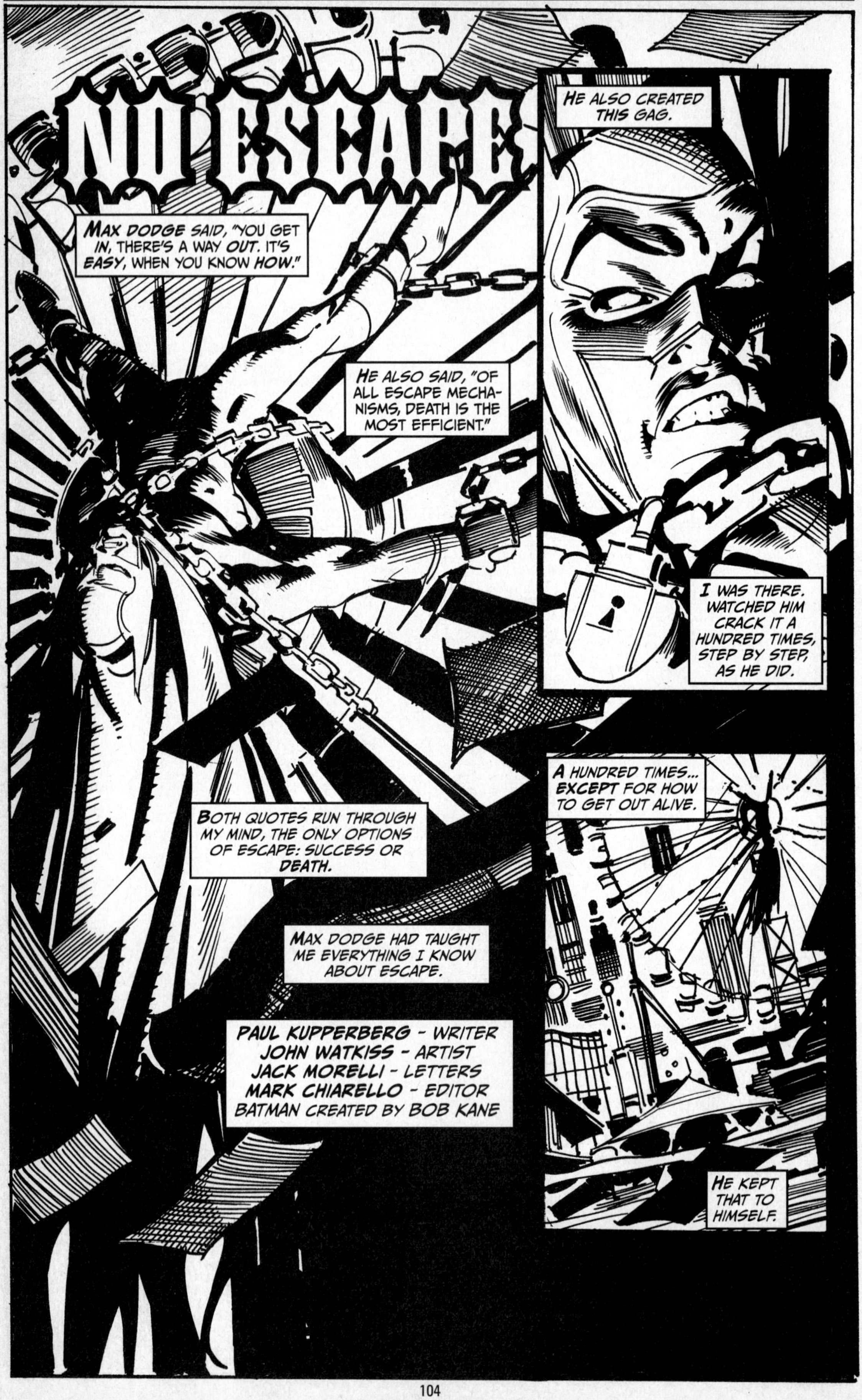
NO ESCAPE
MAX DODGE SAID, "YOU GET IN, THERE'S A WAY OUT. IT'S EASY, WHEN YOU KNOW HOW."
HE ALSO SAID, "OF ALL ESCAPE MECHANISMS, DEATH IS THE MOST EFFICIENT."
BOTH QUOTES RUN THROUGH MY MIND, THE ONLY OPTIONS OF ESCAPE: SUCCESS OR DEATH.
MAX DODGE HAD TAUGHT ME EVERYTHING I KNOW ABOUT ESCAPE.
PAUL KUPPERBERG - WRITER
JOHN WATKISS - ARTIST
JACK MORELLI - LETTERS
MARK CHIARELLO - EDITOR
BATMAN CREATED BY BOB KANE
HE ALSO CREATED THIS GAG.
I WAS THERE. WATCHED HIM CRACK IT A HUNDRED TIMES, STEP BY STEP, AS HE DID.
A HUNDRED TIMES... EXCEPT FOR HOW TO GET OUT ALIVE.
HE KEPT THAT TO HIMSELF.

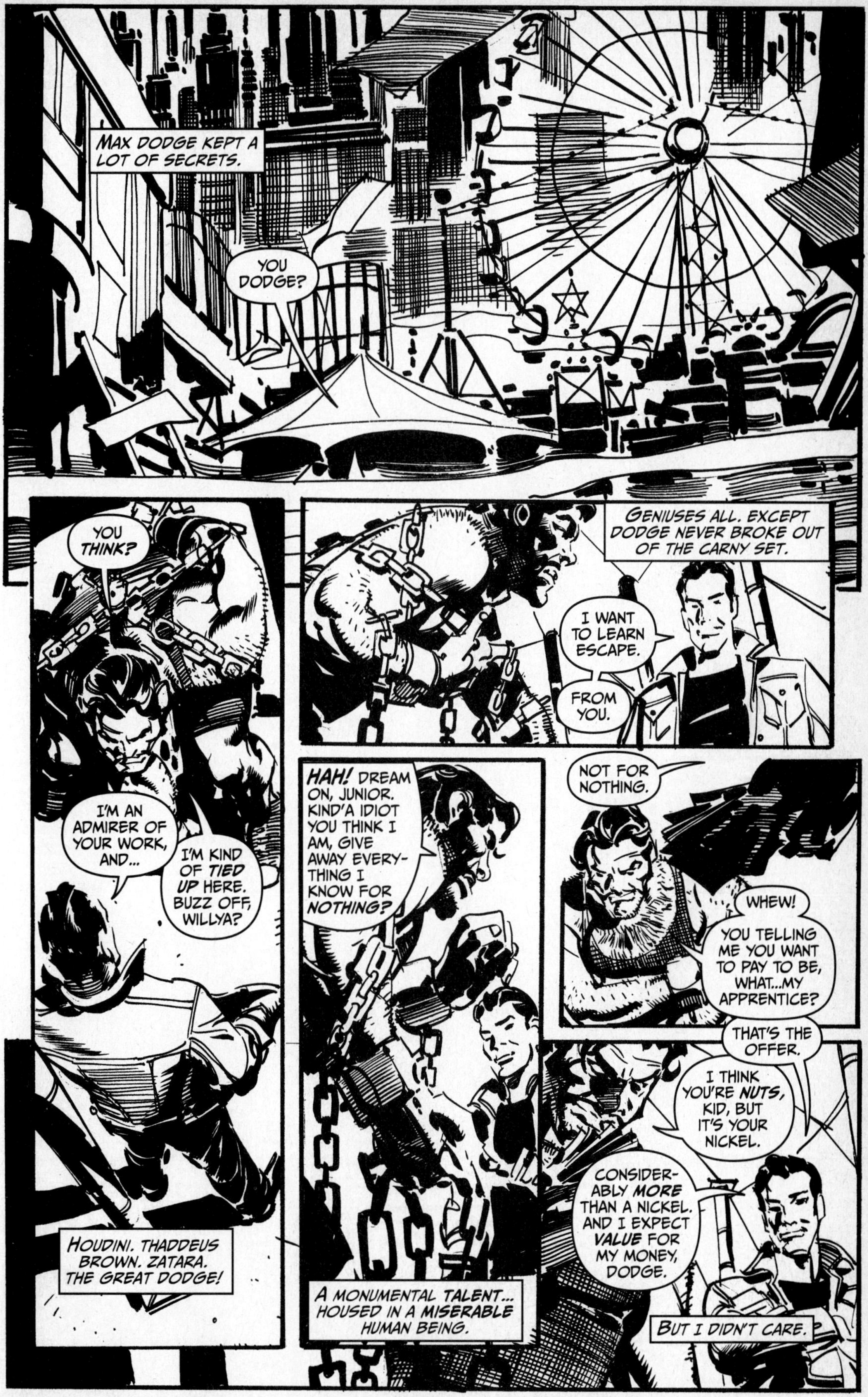
MAX DODGE KEPT A LOT OF SECRETS.
YOU DODGE?
YOU THINK?
GENIUSES ALL. EXCEPT DODGE NEVER BROKE OUT OF THE CARNY SET.
I WANT TO LEARN ESCAPE.
FROM YOU.
I'M AN ADMIRER OF YOUR WORK, AND...
I'M KIND OF TIED UP HERE. BUZZ OFF, WILLYA?
HAH! DREAM ON, JUNIOR. KIND'A IDIOT YOU THINK I AM, GIVE AWAY EVERY-THING I KNOW FOR NOTHING?
NOT FOR NOTHING.
WHEW!
YOU TELLING ME YOU WANT TO PAY TO BE, WHAT...MY APPRENTICE?
THAT'S THE OFFER.
I THINK YOU'RE NUTS, KID, BUT IT'S YOUR NICKEL.
CONSIDER-ABLY MORE THAN A NICKEL. AND I EXPECT VALUE FOR MY MONEY, DODGE.
HOUDINI. THADDEUS BROWN. ZATARA. THE GREAT DODGE!
A MONUMENTAL TALENT... HOUSED IN A MISERABLE HUMAN BEING.
BUT I DIDN'T CARE.

YOU'LL GET IT. THIS CALLS FOR A DRINK.

BRING THOSE WITH YOU, WILLYA, KID.

I NEEDED HIS KNOWLEDGE, HIS SKILL.

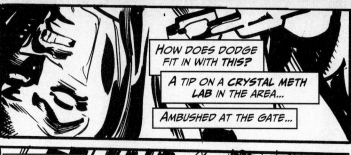

HOW DOES DODGE FIT IN WITH *THIS*?

A TIP ON A *CRYSTAL METH LAB* IN THE AREA...

AMBUSHED AT THE GATE...

A LURE TO A DEATH TRAP.

WHY GO TO THE TROUBLE...? DOESN'T MATTER.

"AWAKE, IS HE?"

GOOD!

WOULDN'T WANT HIM TO MISS THIS, EH, MR. DODGE?

I...N-NO, RIDDLER.

WELL, THEN, AS YOU CARNY FOLK SAY...

...LET'S GET THIS SHOW ON THE ROAD!

KLANKK

POWER ON...'ROUND AND 'ROUND SHE GOES, WHERE SHE STOPS...

...HEH HEH HEH...

...THE BATMAN *DROPS!*

I-I DID LIKE YOU ASKED, RIDDLER... DID MY PART...

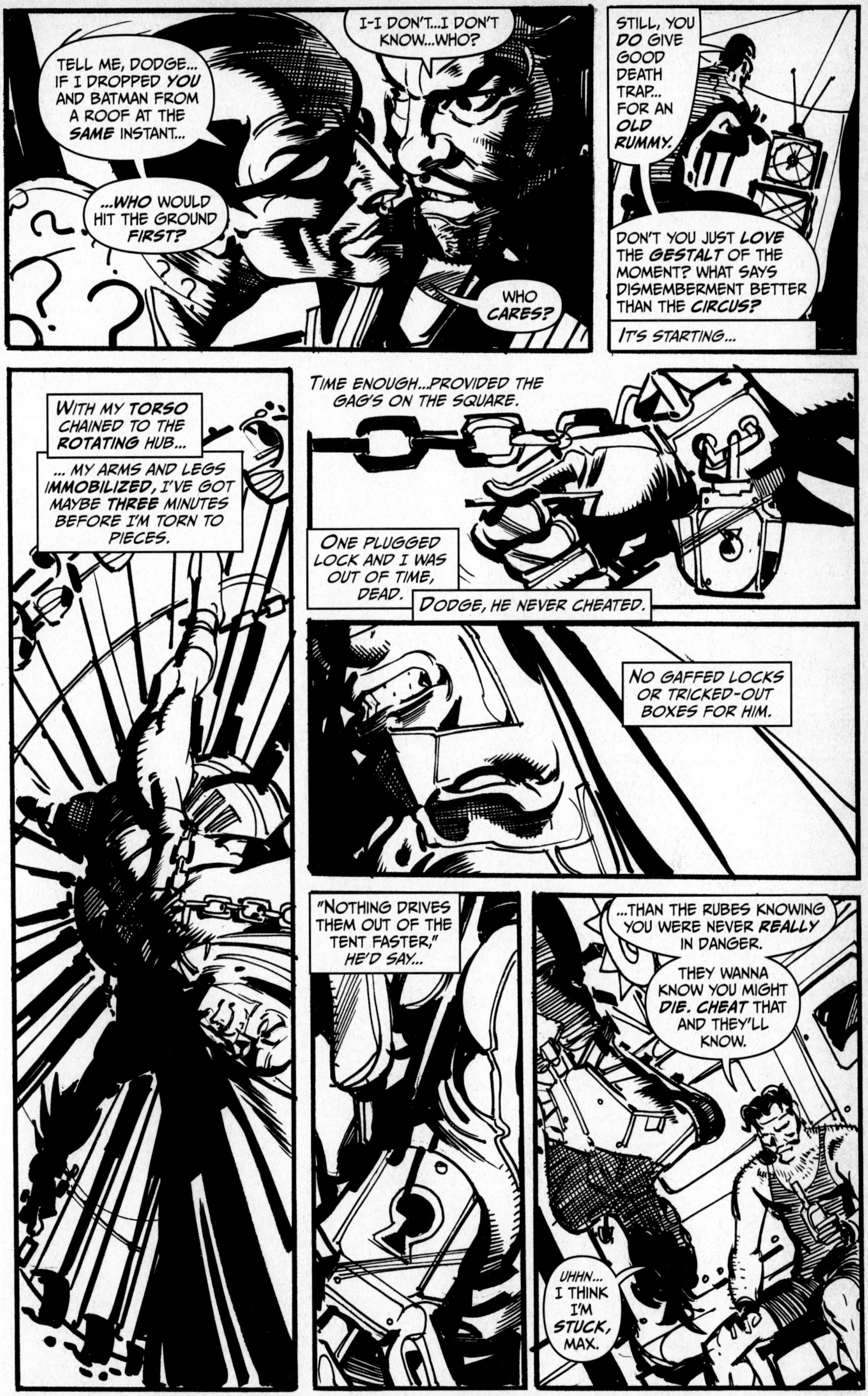
TELL ME, DODGE... IF I DROPPED YOU AND BATMAN FROM A ROOF AT THE SAME INSTANT...
...WHO WOULD HIT THE GROUND FIRST?
I-I DON'T...I DON'T KNOW...WHO?
WHO CARES?
STILL, YOU DO GIVE GOOD DEATH TRAP... FOR AN OLD RUMMY.
DON'T YOU JUST LOVE THE GESTALT OF THE MOMENT? WHAT SAYS DISMEMBERMENT BETTER THAN THE CIRCUS?
IT'S STARTING...
WITH MY TORSO CHAINED TO THE ROTATING HUB...
... MY ARMS AND LEGS IMMOBILIZED, I'VE GOT MAYBE THREE MINUTES BEFORE I'M TORN TO PIECES.
TIME ENOUGH...PROVIDED THE GAG'S ON THE SQUARE.
ONE PLUGGED LOCK AND I WAS OUT OF TIME, DEAD.
DODGE, HE NEVER CHEATED.
NO GAFFED LOCKS OR TRICKED-OUT BOXES FOR HIM.
"NOTHING DRIVES THEM OUT OF THE TENT FASTER," HE'D SAY...
...THAN THE RUBES KNOWING YOU WERE NEVER REALLY IN DANGER.
THEY WANNA KNOW YOU MIGHT DIE. CHEAT THAT AND THEY'LL KNOW.
UHHN... I THINK I'M STUCK, MAX.

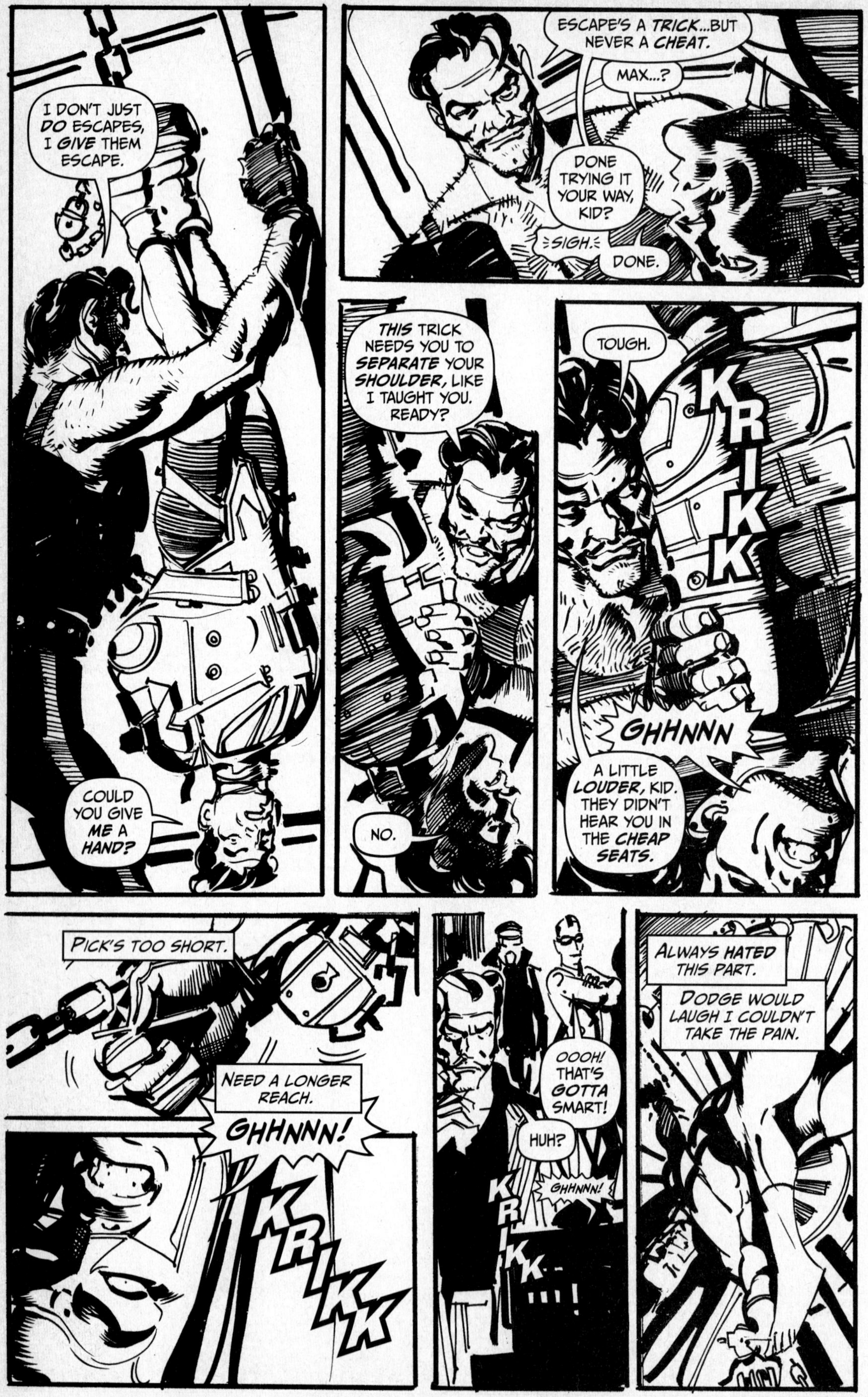
I DON'T JUST DO ESCAPES, I GIVE THEM ESCAPE.
COULD YOU GIVE ME A HAND?
ESCAPE'S A TRICK...BUT NEVER A CHEAT.
MAX...?
DONE TRYING IT YOUR WAY, KID?
SIGH.
DONE.
THIS TRICK NEEDS YOU TO SEPARATE YOUR SHOULDER, LIKE I TAUGHT YOU. READY?
NO.
TOUGH.
KRIKK
GHHNNN
A LITTLE LOUDER, KID. THEY DIDN'T HEAR YOU IN THE CHEAP SEATS.
PICK'S TOO SHORT.
NEED A LONGER REACH.
GHHNNN!
KRIKK
OOOH! THAT'S GOTTA SMART!
HUH?
GHHNNN!
KRIKK...!
ALWAYS HATED THIS PART.
DODGE WOULD LAUGH I COULDN'T TAKE THE PAIN.

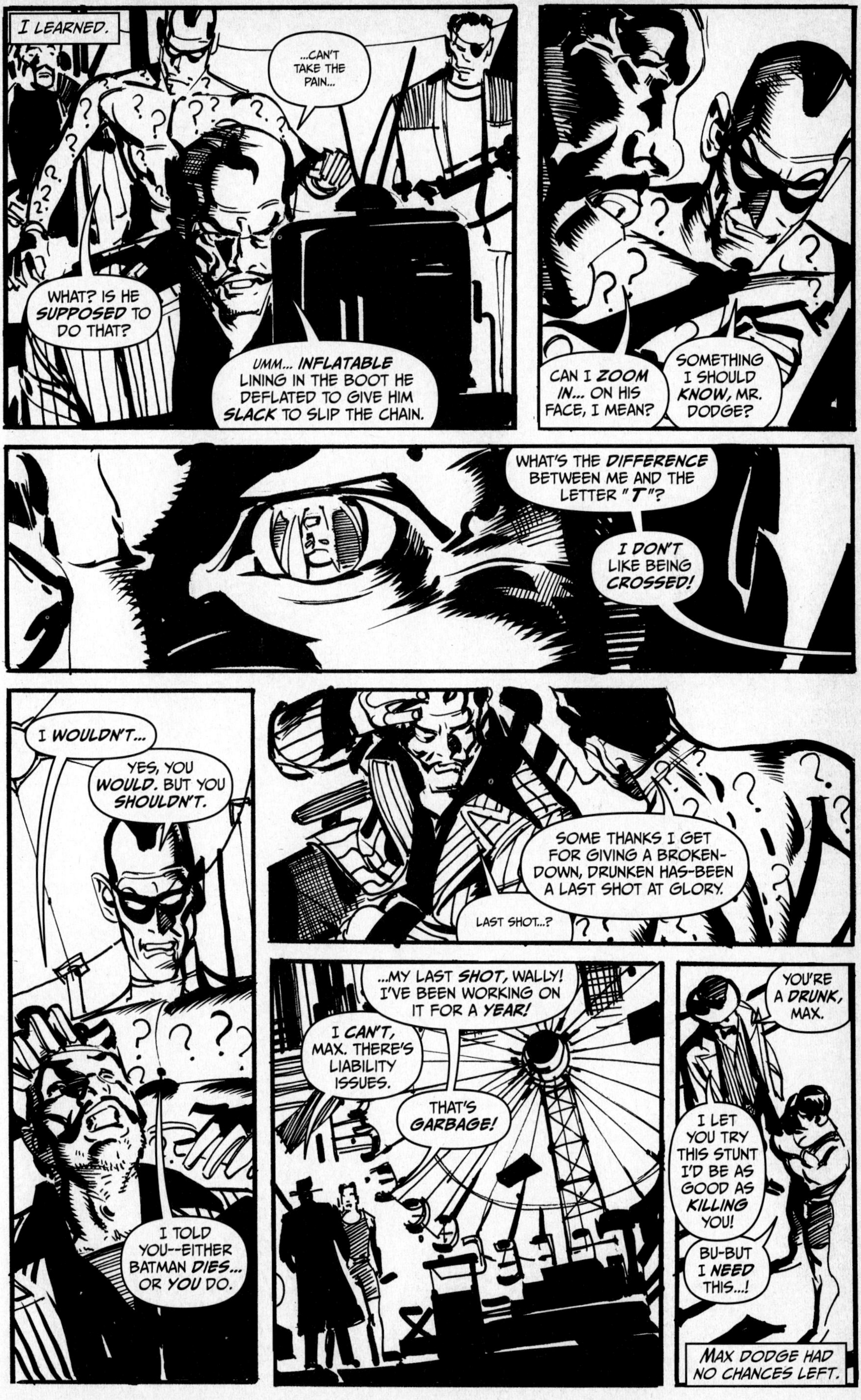
I LEARNED.
...CAN'T TAKE THE PAIN...
WHAT? IS HE SUPPOSED TO DO THAT?
UMM... INFLATABLE LINING IN THE BOOT HE DEFLATED TO GIVE HIM SLACK TO SLIP THE CHAIN.
SOMETHING I SHOULD KNOW, MR. DODGE?
CAN I ZOOM IN... ON HIS FACE, I MEAN?
WHAT'S THE DIFFERENCE BETWEEN ME AND THE LETTER "T"?
I DON'T LIKE BEING CROSSED!
I WOULDN'T...
YES, YOU WOULD. BUT YOU SHOULDN'T.
I TOLD YOU--EITHER BATMAN DIES... OR YOU DO.
SOME THANKS I GET FOR GIVING A BROKEN-DOWN, DRUNKEN HAS-BEEN A LAST SHOT AT GLORY.
LAST SHOT...?
...MY LAST SHOT, WALLY! I'VE BEEN WORKING ON IT FOR A YEAR!
I CAN'T, MAX. THERE'S LIABILITY ISSUES.
THAT'S GARBAGE!
YOU'RE A DRUNK, MAX.
I LET YOU TRY THIS STUNT I'D BE AS GOOD AS KILLING YOU!
BU-BUT I NEED THIS...!
MAX DODGE HAD NO CHANCES LEFT.

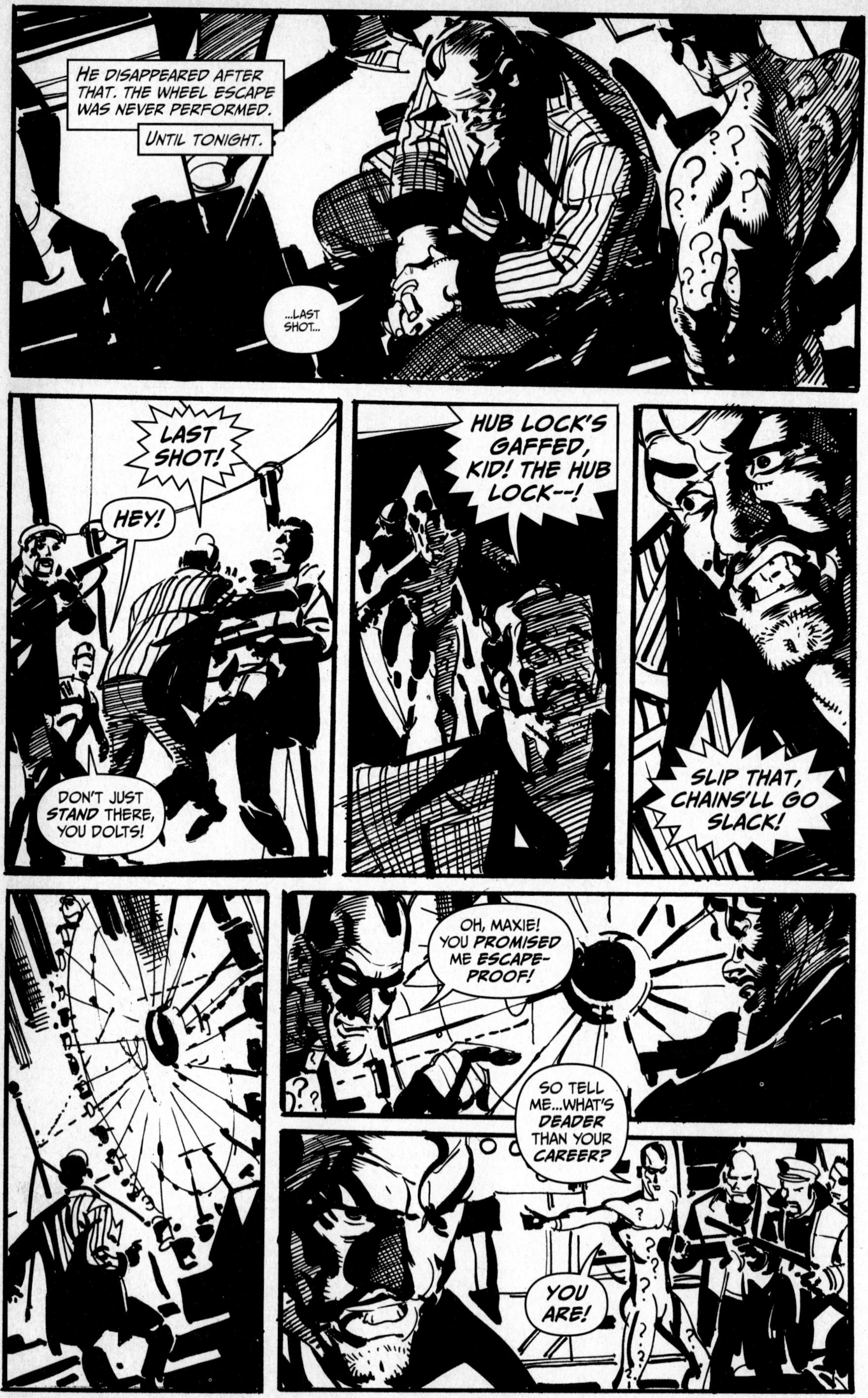
HE DISAPPEARED AFTER THAT. THE WHEEL ESCAPE WAS NEVER PERFORMED.
UNTIL TONIGHT.
...LAST SHOT...
LAST SHOT!
HEY!
DON'T JUST STAND THERE, YOU DOLTS!
HUB LOCK'S GAFFED, KID! THE HUB LOCK--!
SLIP THAT, CHAINS'LL GO SLACK!
OH, MAXIE! YOU PROMISED ME ESCAPE-PROOF!
SO TELL ME...WHAT'S DEADER THAN YOUR CAREER?
YOU ARE!

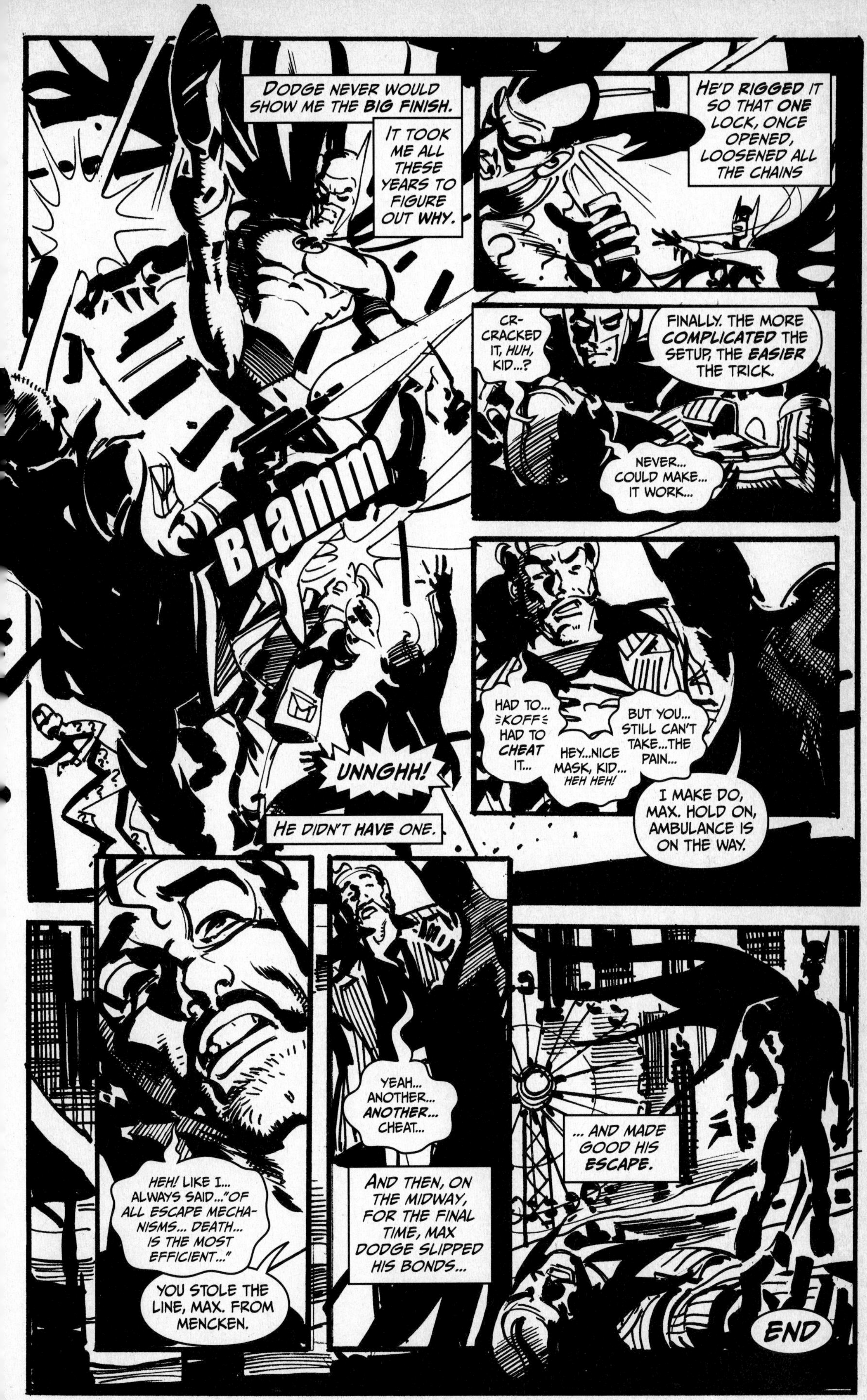
DODGE NEVER WOULD SHOW ME THE BIG FINISH.
IT TOOK ME ALL THESE YEARS TO FIGURE OUT WHY.
HE'D RIGGED IT SO THAT ONE LOCK, ONCE OPENED, LOOSENED ALL THE CHAINS
CR-CRACKED IT, HUH, KID...?
FINALLY. THE MORE COMPLICATED THE SETUP, THE EASIER THE TRICK.
NEVER... COULD MAKE... IT WORK...
BLAMM
UNNGHH!
HE DIDN'T HAVE ONE.
HAD TO... KOFF HAD TO CHEAT IT...
HEY...NICE MASK, KID... HEH HEH!
BUT YOU... STILL CAN'T TAKE...THE PAIN...
I MAKE DO, MAX. HOLD ON, AMBULANCE IS ON THE WAY.
HEH! LIKE I... ALWAYS SAID..."OF ALL ESCAPE MECHA-NISMS... DEATH... IS THE MOST EFFICIENT..."
YOU STOLE THE LINE, MAX. FROM MENCKEN.
YEAH... ANOTHER... ANOTHER... CHEAT...
AND THEN, ON THE MIDWAY, FOR THE FINAL TIME, MAX DODGE SLIPPED HIS BONDS...
... AND MADE GOOD HIS ESCAPE.
END

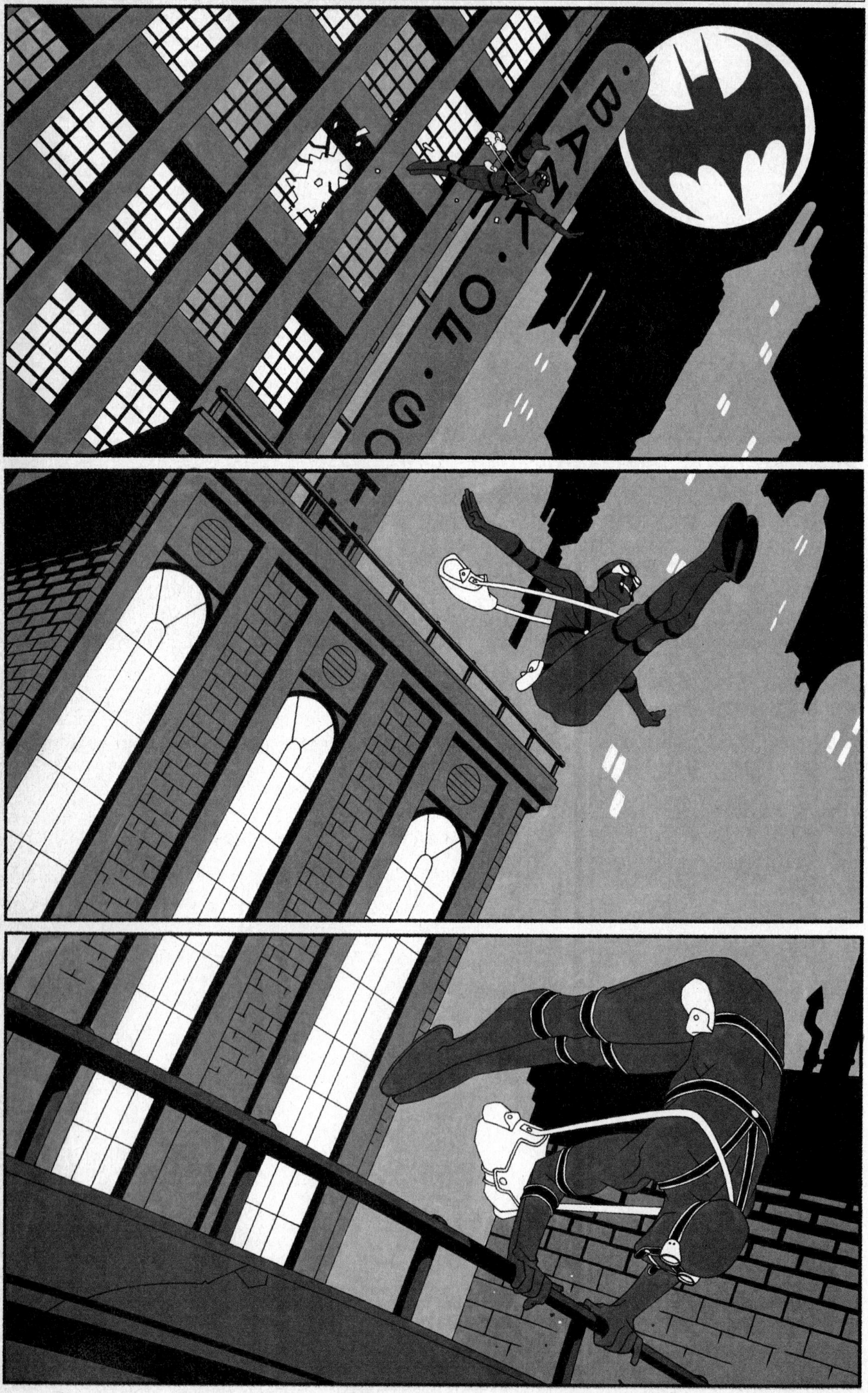
BANK · OF · GO

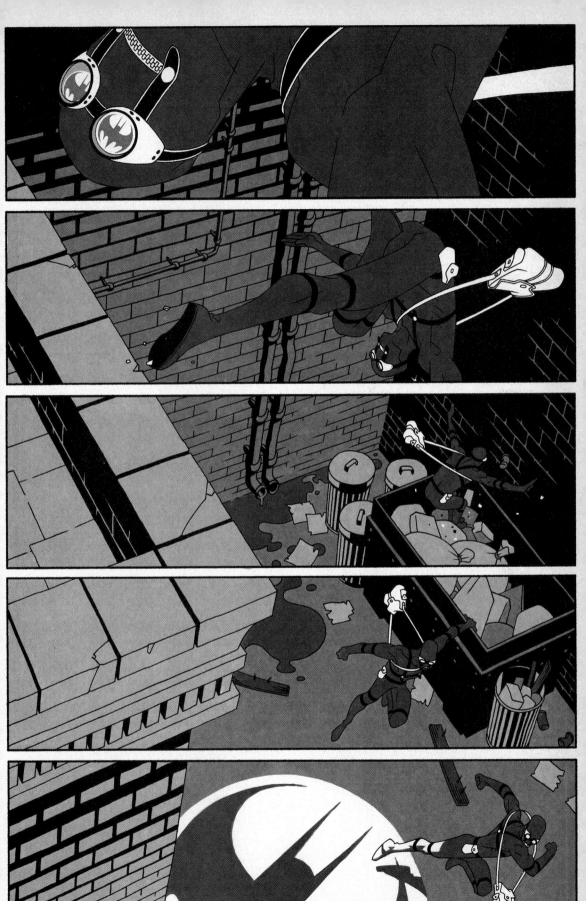

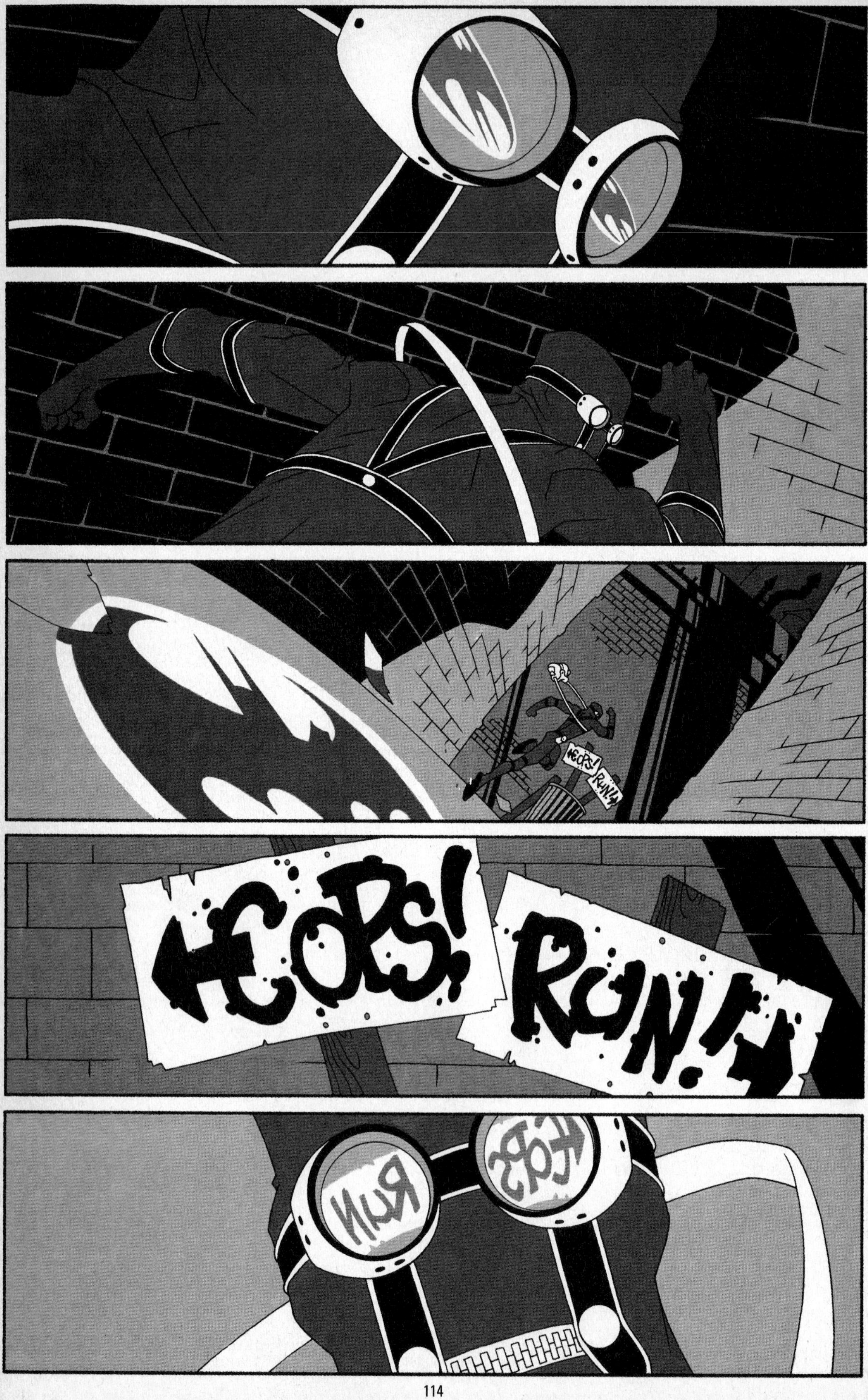
COPS!
RUN!

GCPD
COPS!
RUN!
RUN!

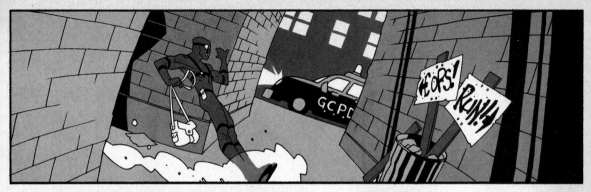

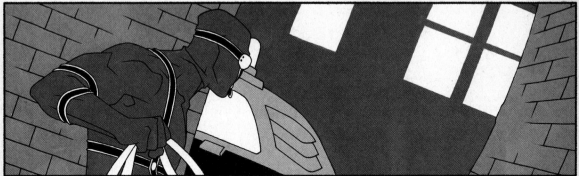

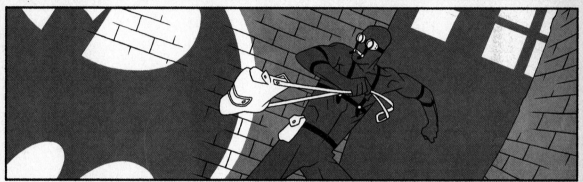

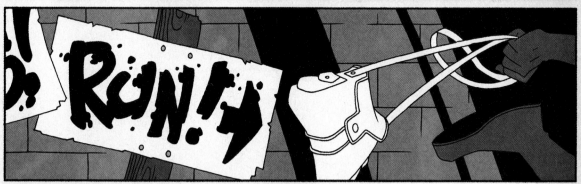

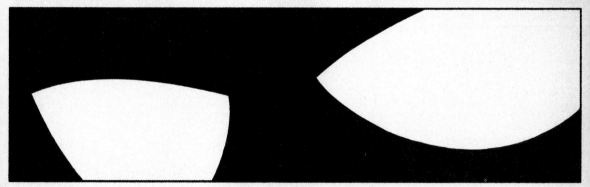

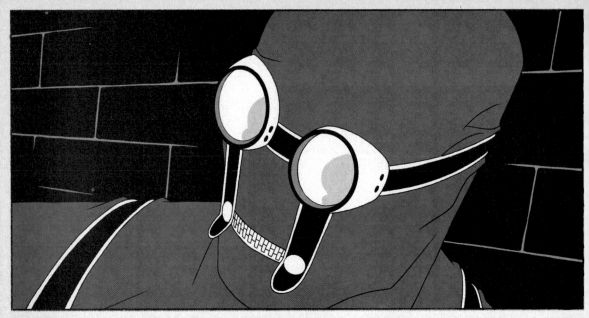

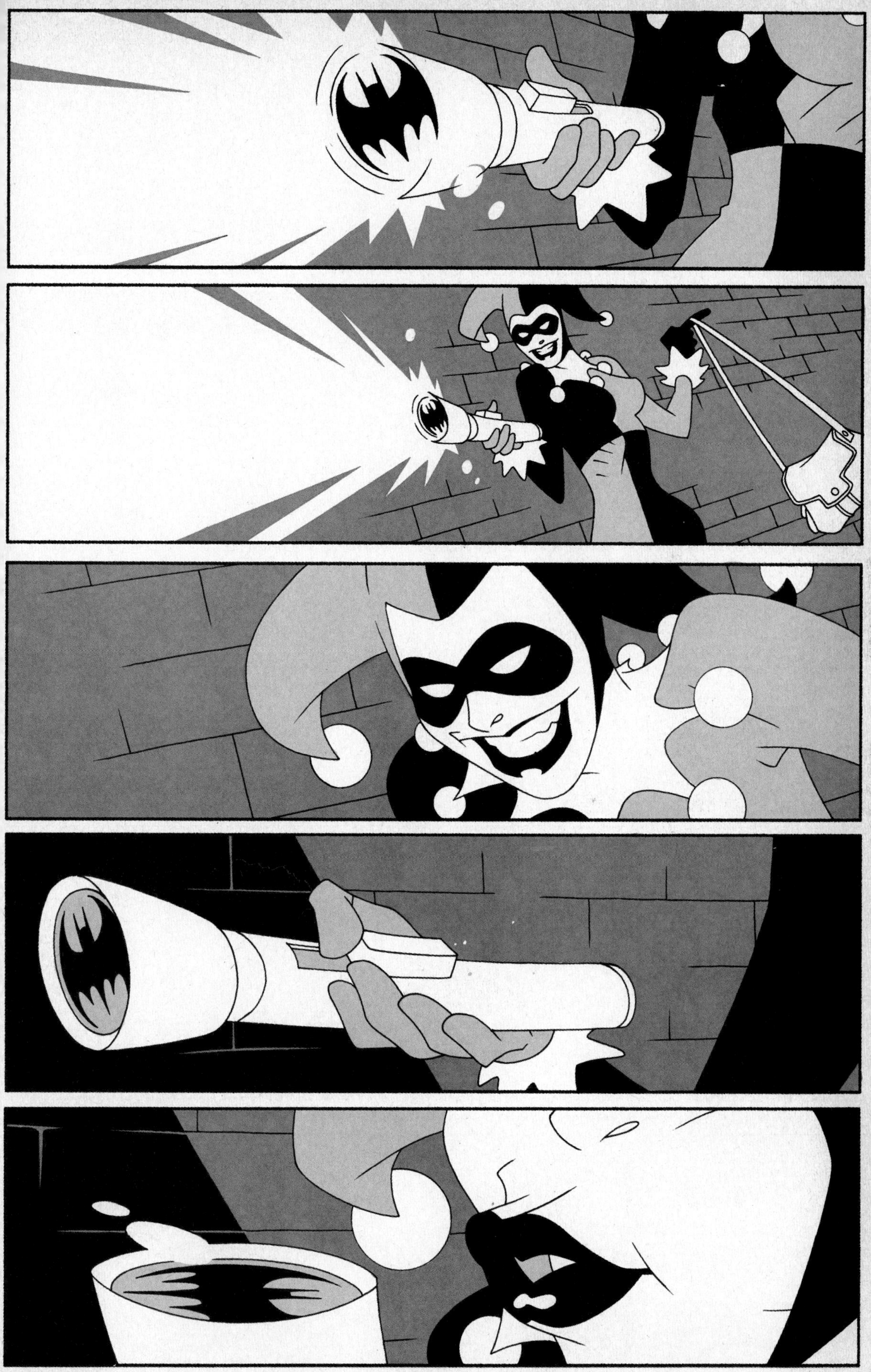

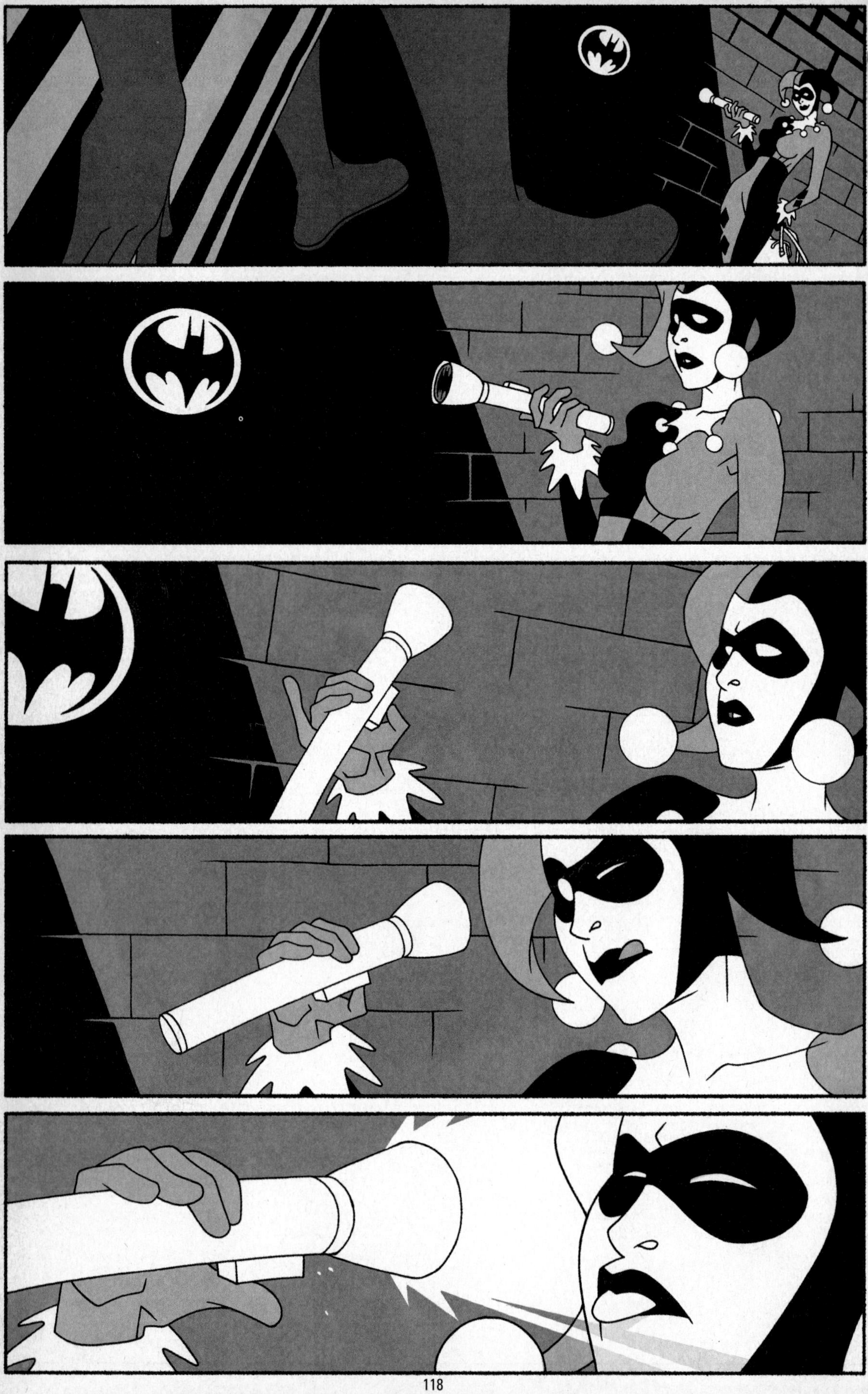

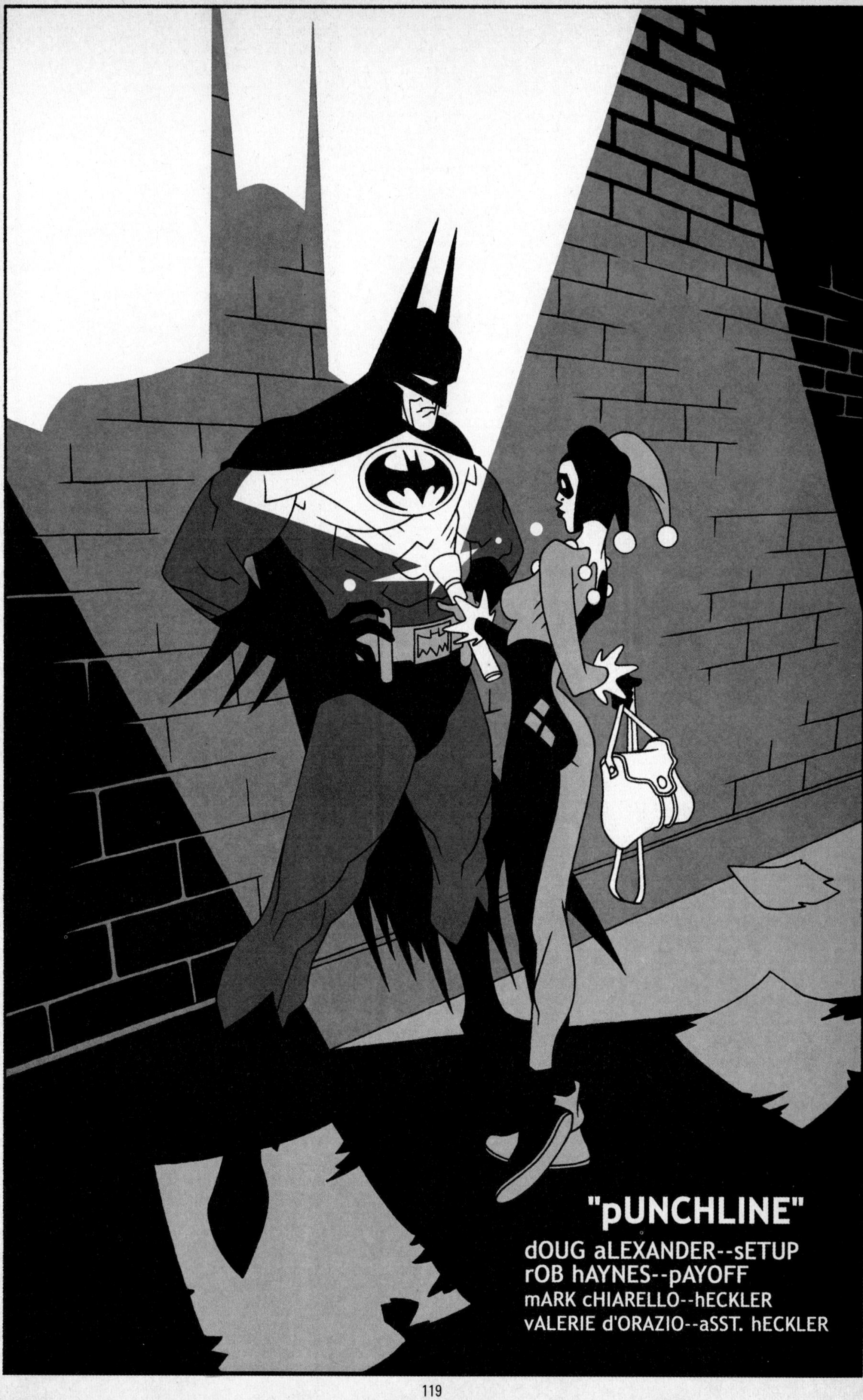
"pUNCHLINE"
dOUG aLEXANDER--sETUP
rOB hAYNES--pAYOFF
mARK cHIARELLO--hECKLER
vALERIE d'ORAZIO--aSST. hECKLER

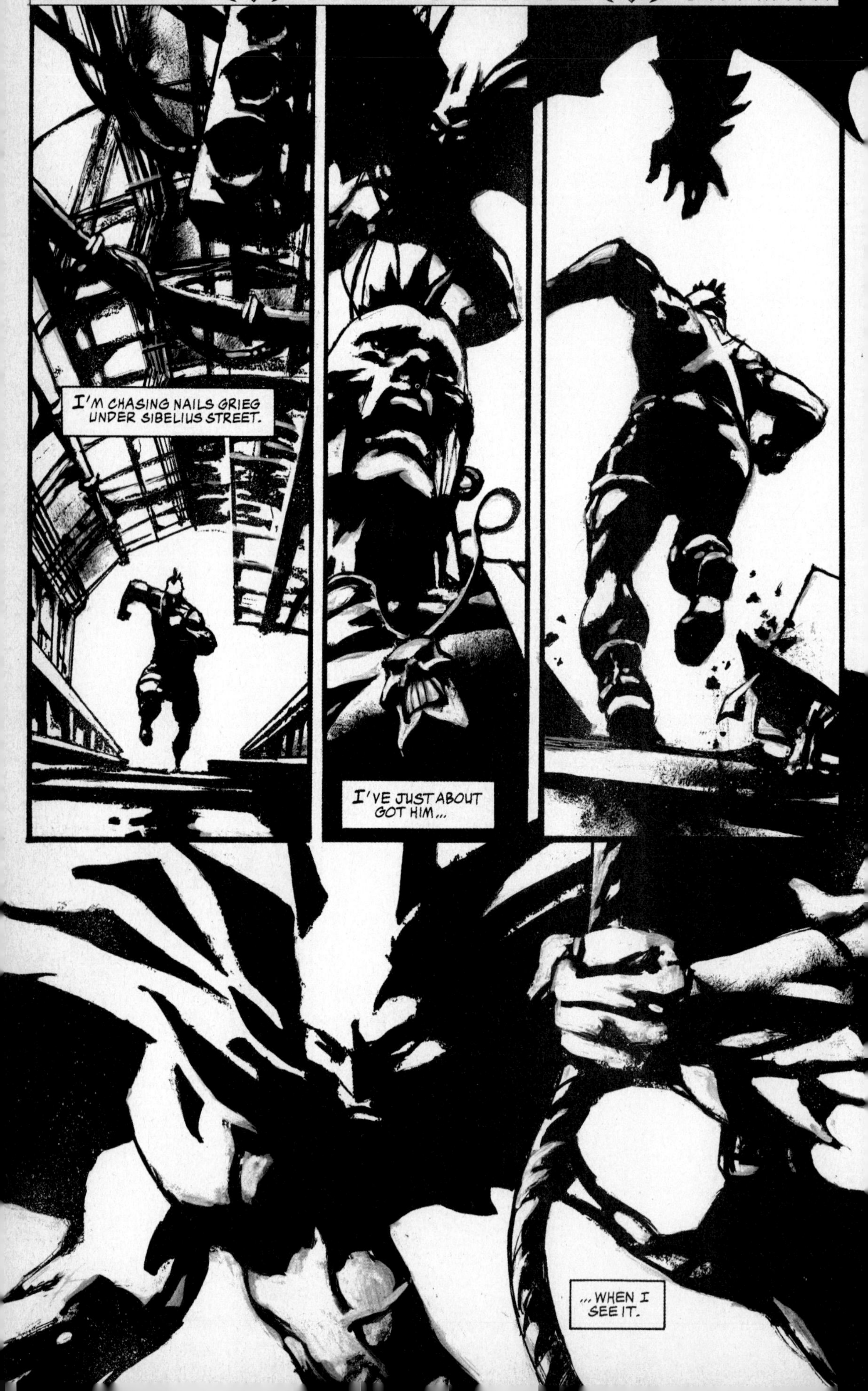
I'M CHASING NAILS GRIEG UNDER SIBELIUS STREET.
I'VE JUST ABOUT GOT HIM...
...WHEN I SEE IT.

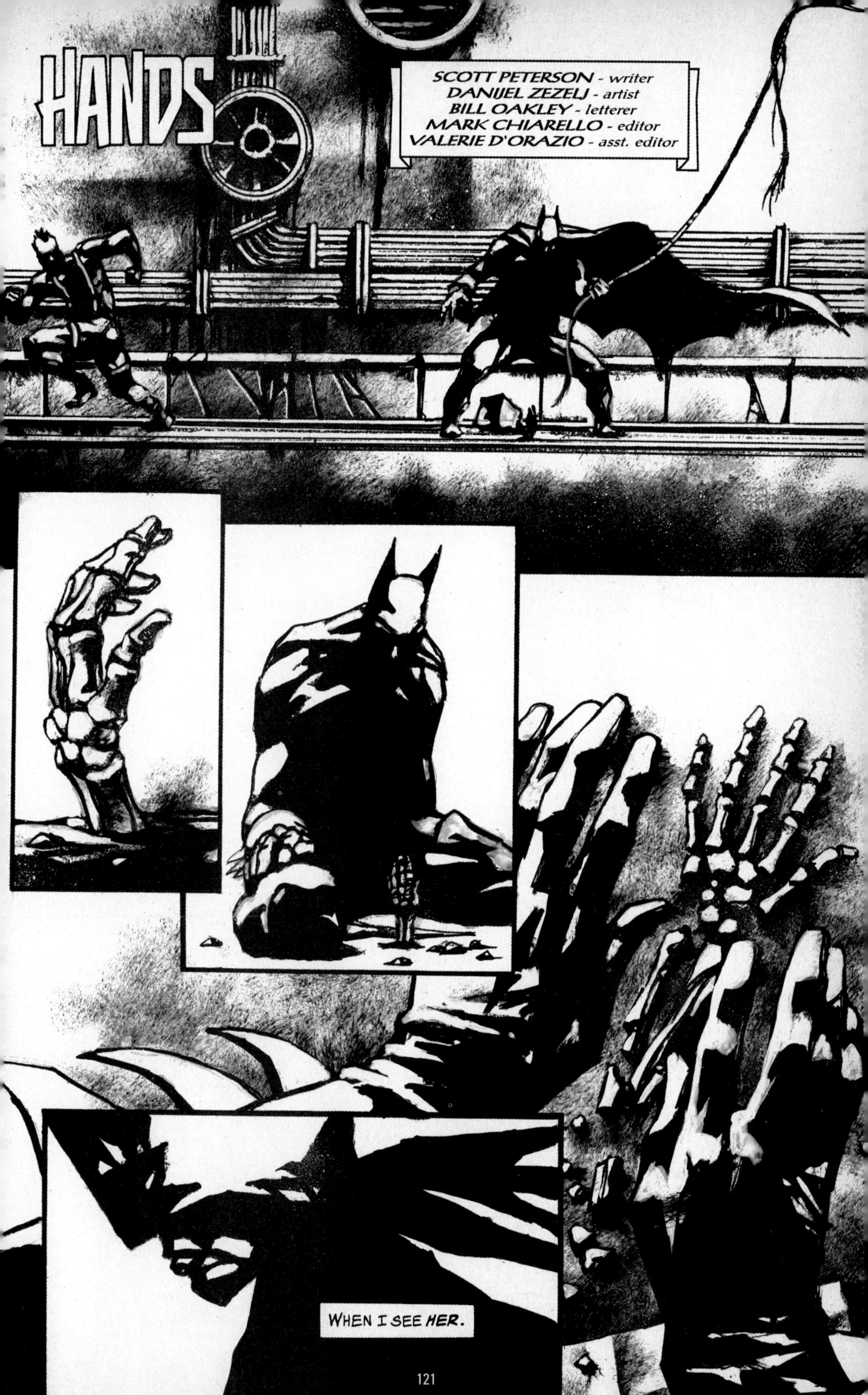
HANDS
SCOTT PETERSON - writer
DANIJEL ZEZELJ - artist
BILL OAKLEY - letterer
MARK CHIARELLO - editor
VALERIE D'ORAZIO - asst. editor
WHEN I SEE HER.

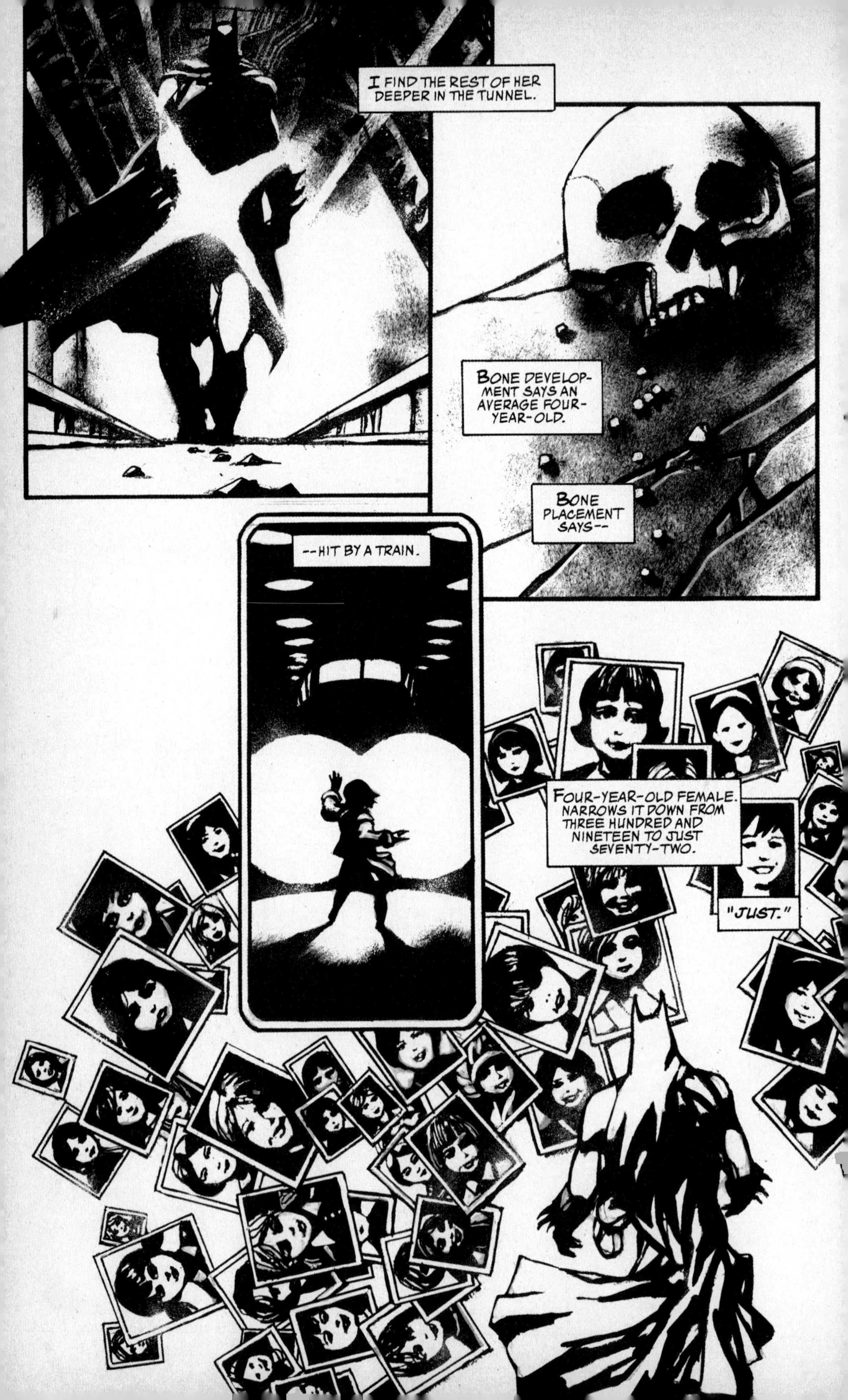
I FIND THE REST OF HER DEEPER IN THE TUNNEL.
BONE DEVELOPMENT SAYS AN AVERAGE FOUR-YEAR-OLD.
BONE PLACEMENT SAYS--
--HIT BY A TRAIN.
FOUR-YEAR-OLD FEMALE. NARROWS IT DOWN FROM THREE HUNDRED AND NINETEEN TO JUST SEVENTY-TWO.
"JUST."

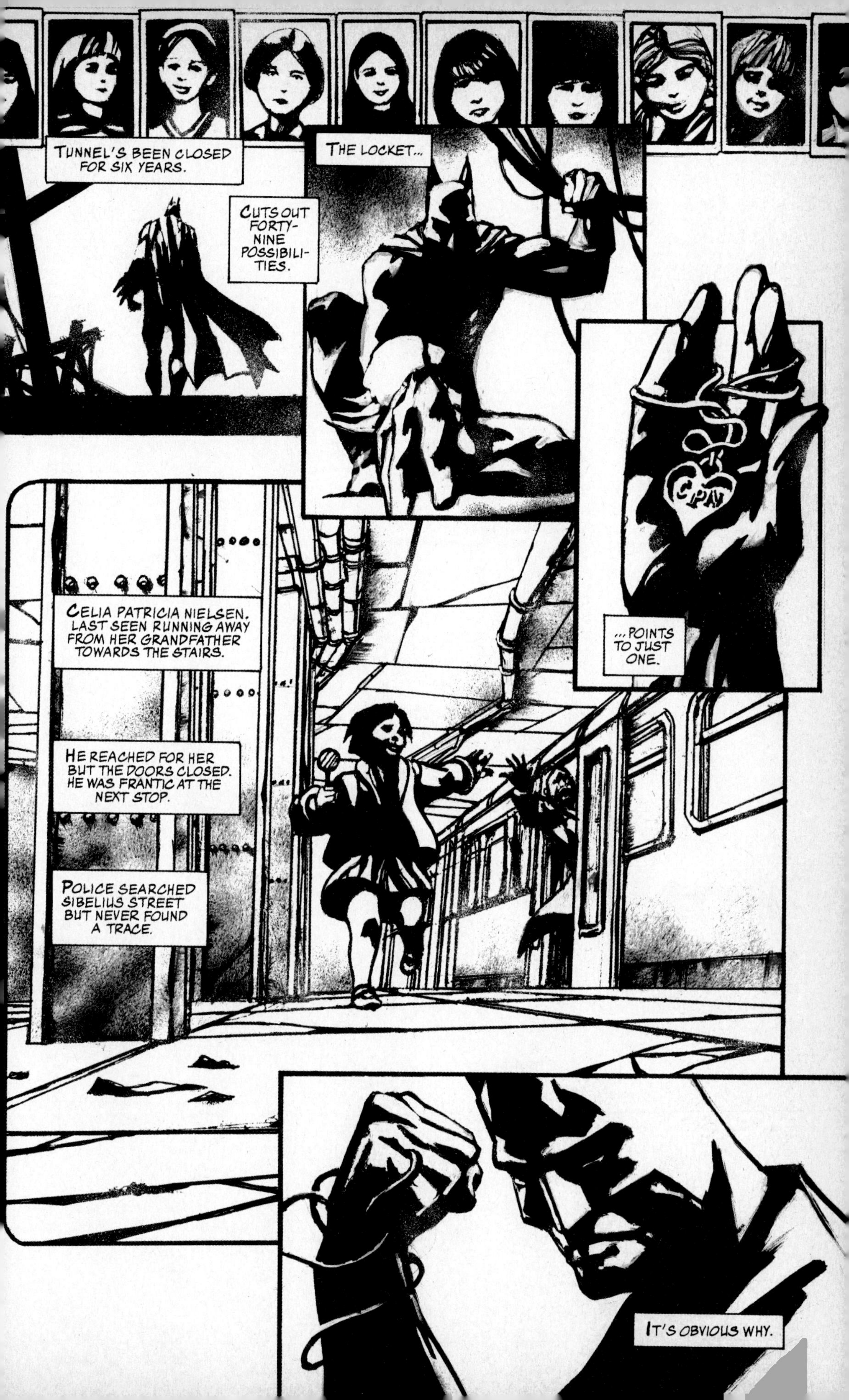
TUNNEL'S BEEN CLOSED FOR SIX YEARS.
CUTS OUT FORTY-NINE POSSIBILI-TIES.
THE LOCKET...
...POINTS TO JUST ONE.
CPN
CELIA PATRICIA NIELSEN. LAST SEEN RUNNING AWAY FROM HER GRANDFATHER TOWARDS THE STAIRS.
HE REACHED FOR HER BUT THE DOORS CLOSED. HE WAS FRANTIC AT THE NEXT STOP.
POLICE SEARCHED SIBELIUS STREET BUT NEVER FOUND A TRACE.
IT'S OBVIOUS WHY.

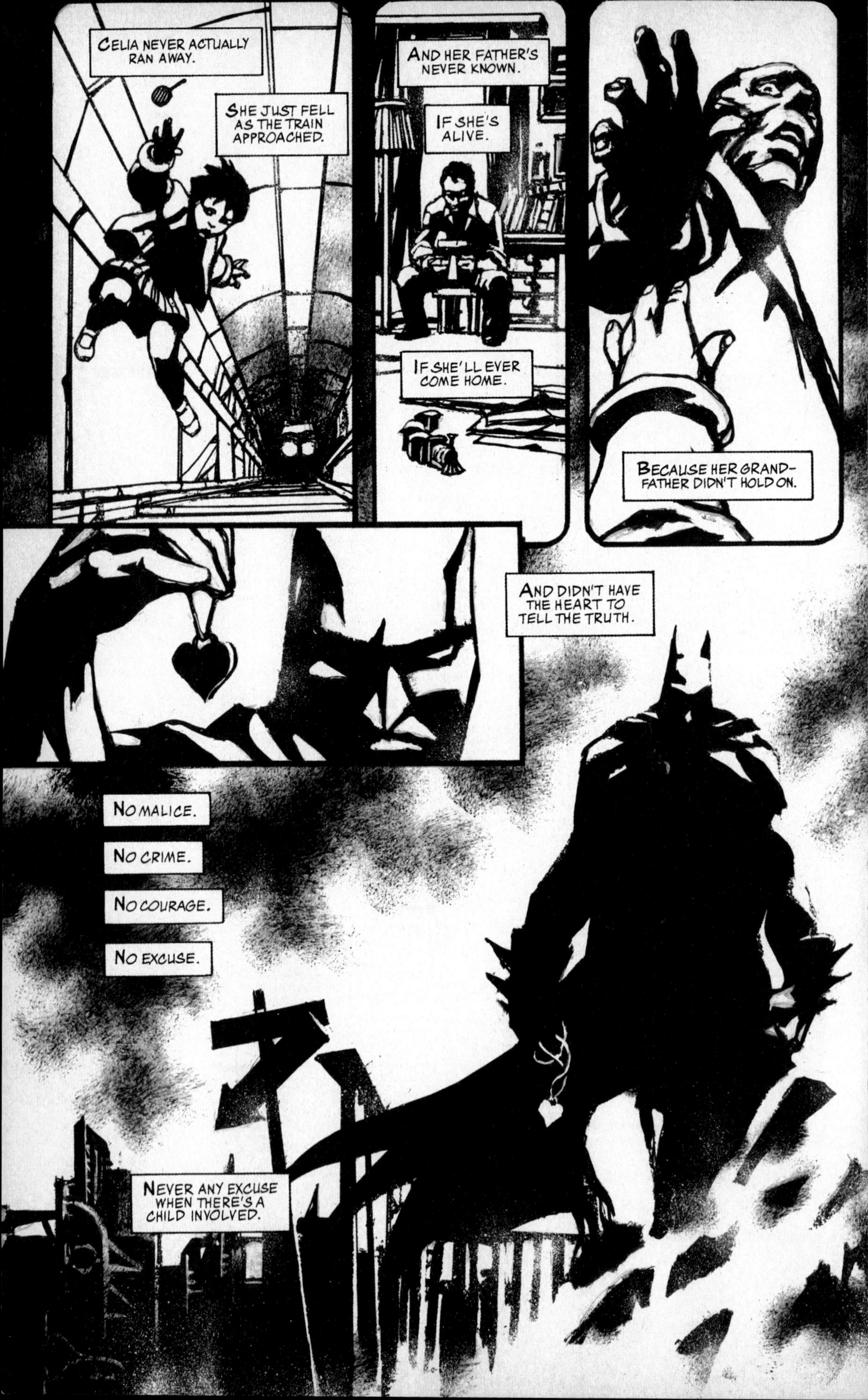
CELIA NEVER ACTUALLY RAN AWAY.
SHE JUST FELL AS THE TRAIN APPROACHED.
AND HER FATHER'S NEVER KNOWN.
IF SHE'S ALIVE.
IF SHE'LL EVER COME HOME.
BECAUSE HER GRAND-FATHER DIDN'T HOLD ON.
AND DIDN'T HAVE THE HEART TO TELL THE TRUTH.
NO MALICE.
NO CRIME.
NO COURAGE.
NO EXCUSE.
NEVER ANY EXCUSE WHEN THERE'S A CHILD INVOLVED.

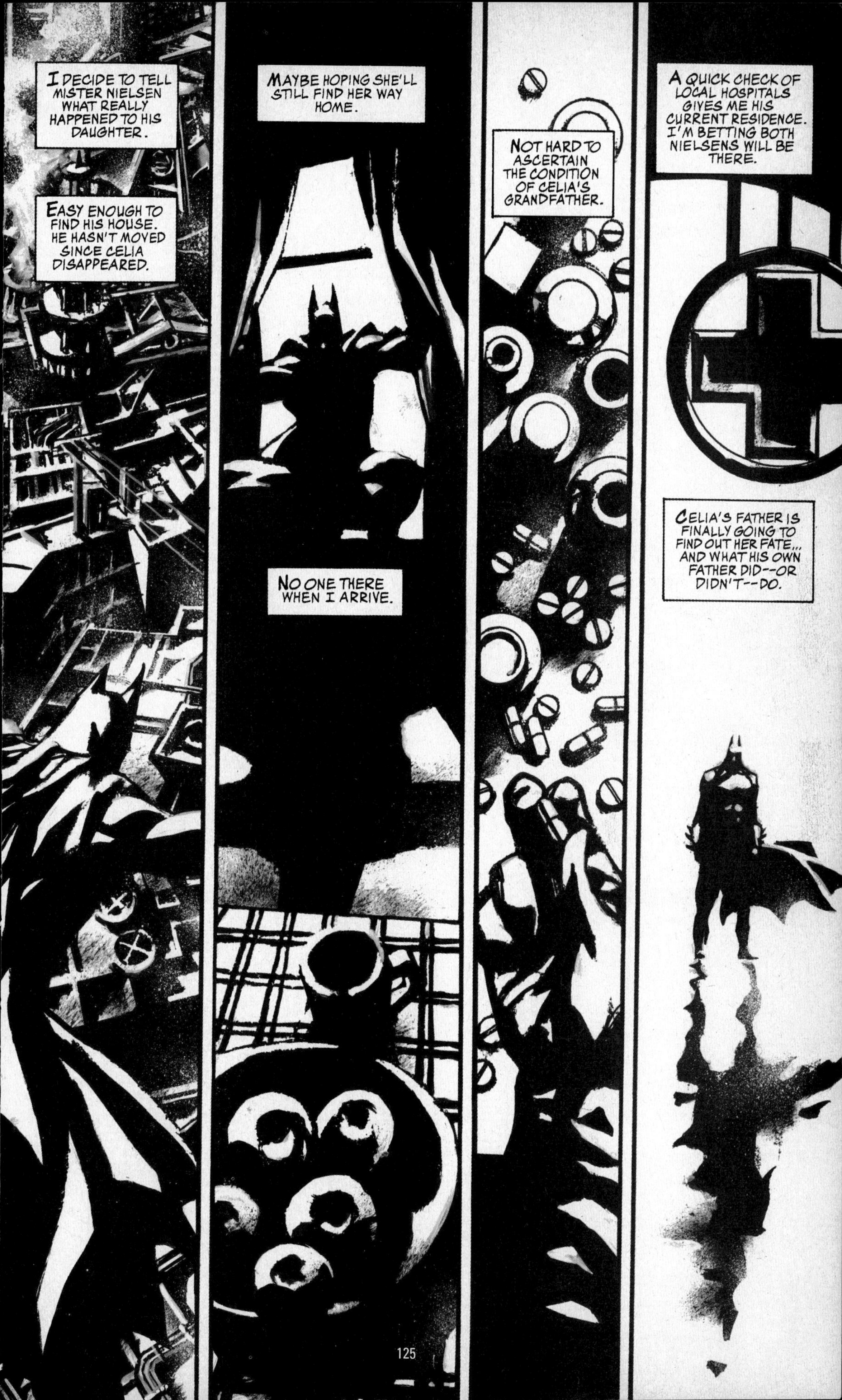

I DECIDE TO TELL MISTER NIELSEN WHAT REALLY HAPPENED TO HIS DAUGHTER.
EASY ENOUGH TO FIND HIS HOUSE. HE HASN'T MOVED SINCE CELIA DISAPPEARED.
MAYBE HOPING SHE'LL STILL FIND HER WAY HOME.
NO ONE THERE WHEN I ARRIVE.
NOT HARD TO ASCERTAIN THE CONDITION OF CELIA'S GRANDFATHER.
A QUICK CHECK OF LOCAL HOSPITALS GIVES ME HIS CURRENT RESIDENCE. I'M BETTING BOTH NIELSENS WILL BE THERE.
CELIA'S FATHER IS FINALLY GOING TO FIND OUT HER FATE... AND WHAT HIS OWN FATHER DID--OR DIDN'T--DO.

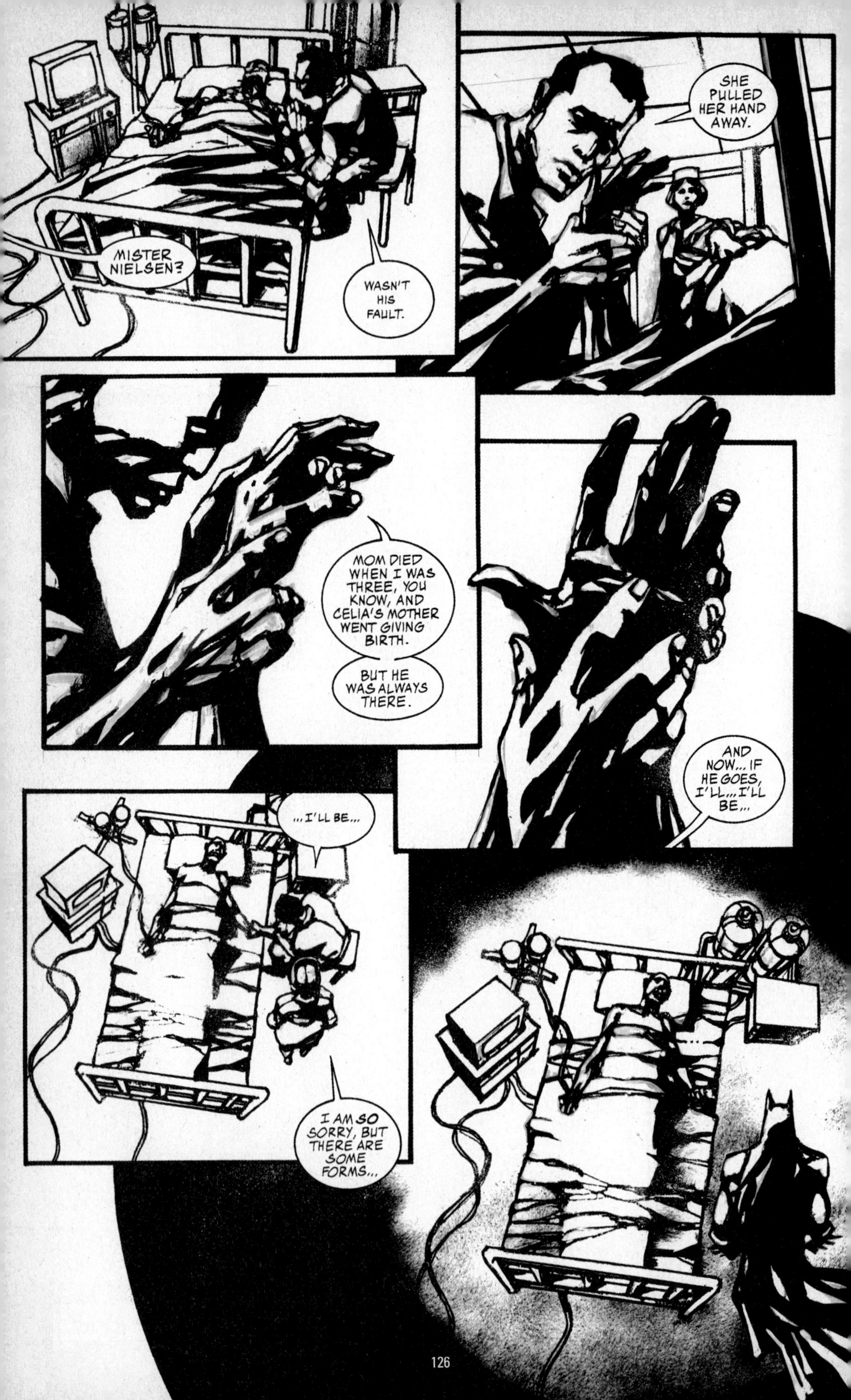
MISTER NIELSEN?
WASN'T HIS FAULT.
SHE PULLED HER HAND AWAY.
MOM DIED WHEN I WAS THREE, YOU KNOW, AND CELIA'S MOTHER WENT GIVING BIRTH.
BUT HE WAS ALWAYS THERE.
AND NOW... IF HE GOES, I'LL... I'LL BE...
...I'LL BE...
I AM SO SORRY, BUT THERE ARE SOME FORMS...

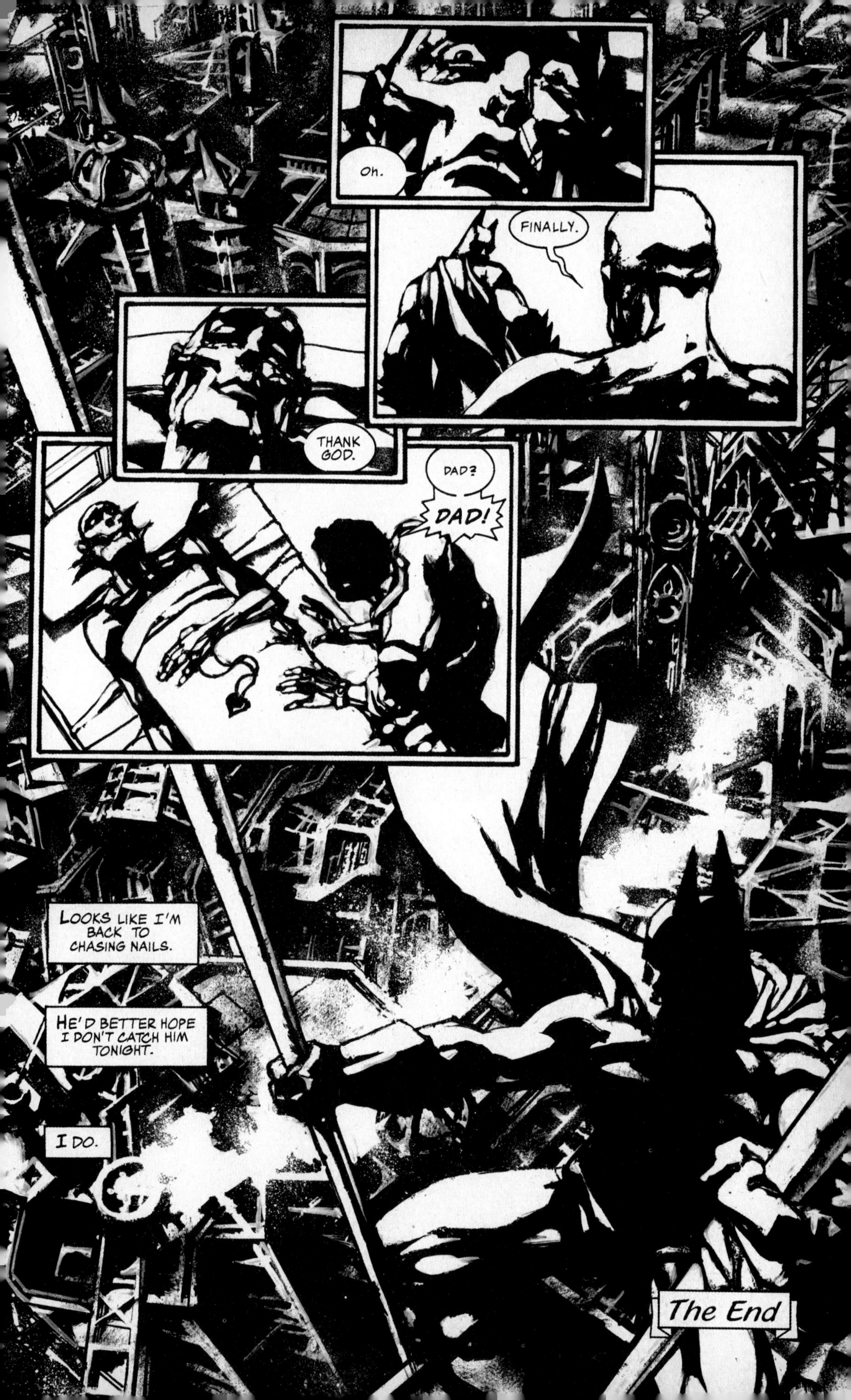
Oh.
FINALLY.
THANK GOD.
DAD?
DAD!
LOOKS LIKE I'M BACK TO CHASING NAILS.
HE'D BETTER HOPE I DON'T CATCH HIM TONIGHT.
I DO.
The End

# TOYRIDE

MARK ASKWITH – STORY
MICHAEL WILLIAM KALUTA – ART
JACK MORELLI – LETTERS
MARK CHIARELLO – EDITOR
VALERIE D'ORAZIO – ASST. ED.

FEATURING:

### The Treetop Trio

CHARLOTTE    MADDY    MARY

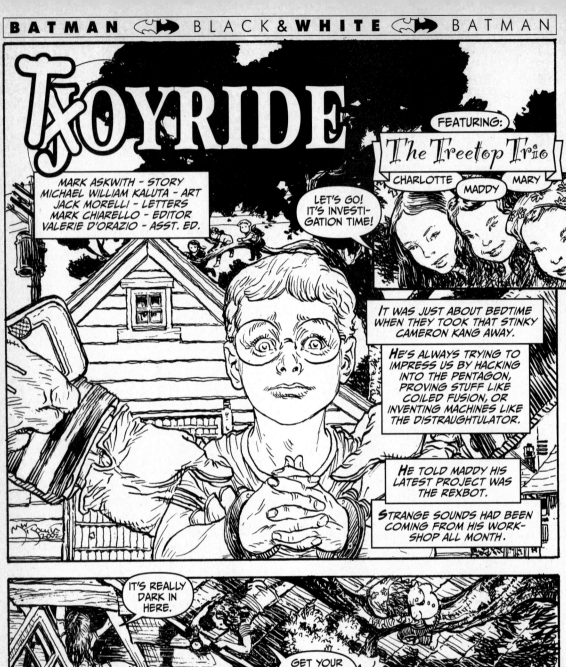

LET'S GO! IT'S INVESTIGATION TIME!

IT WAS JUST ABOUT BEDTIME WHEN THEY TOOK THAT STINKY CAMERON KANG AWAY.

HE'S ALWAYS TRYING TO IMPRESS US BY HACKING INTO THE PENTAGON, PROVING STUFF LIKE COILED FUSION, OR INVENTING MACHINES LIKE THE DISTRAUGHTULATOR.

HE TOLD MADDY HIS LATEST PROJECT WAS THE REXBOT.

STRANGE SOUNDS HAD BEEN COMING FROM HIS WORKSHOP ALL MONTH.

IT'S REALLY DARK IN HERE.

GET YOUR FLASHLIGHTS OUT!

WHAT HAD CAMERON BEEN UP TO?

WOW!

SO THAT'S A REXBOT!

LET'S GO FOR A RIDE!

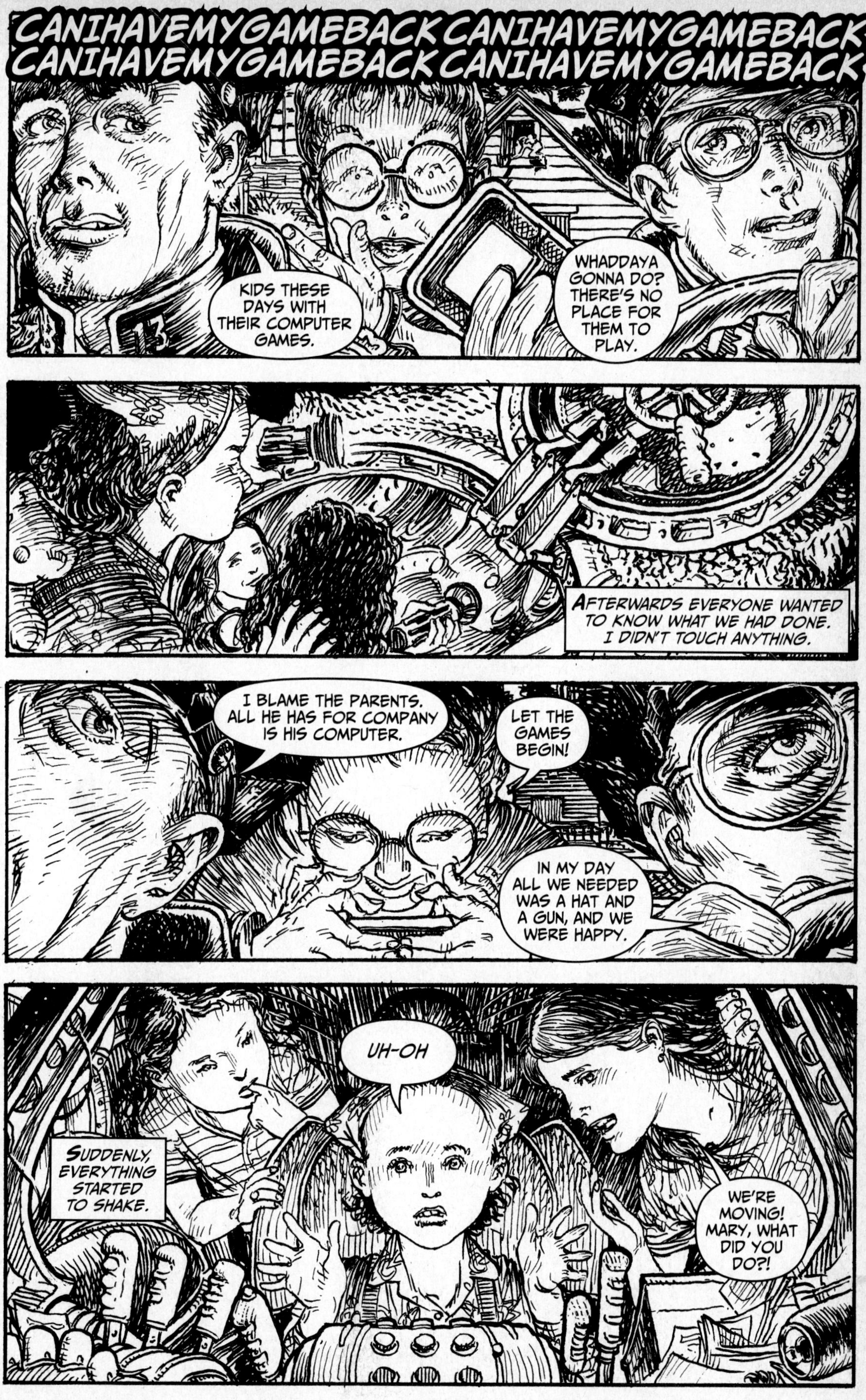
CANIHAVEMYGAMEBACK CANIHAVEMYGAMEBACK
CANIHAVEMYGAMEBACK CANIHAVEMYGAMEBACK
KIDS THESE DAYS WITH THEIR COMPUTER GAMES.
WHADDAYA GONNA DO? THERE'S NO PLACE FOR THEM TO PLAY.
AFTERWARDS EVERYONE WANTED TO KNOW WHAT WE HAD DONE. I DIDN'T TOUCH ANYTHING.
I BLAME THE PARENTS. ALL HE HAS FOR COMPANY IS HIS COMPUTER.
LET THE GAMES BEGIN!
IN MY DAY ALL WE NEEDED WAS A HAT AND A GUN, AND WE WERE HAPPY.
UH-OH
SUDDENLY, EVERYTHING STARTED TO SHAKE.
WE'RE MOVING! MARY, WHAT DID YOU DO?!

TRY AND STOP IT!
IT WASN'T ME!
THERE'S GOT TO BE A WAY!
IT'S NOT RESPONDING!
EVERY-BODY'S FREAKING OUT!
LOOK DOWN THERE!
ALL UNITS, WE HAVE A SITUATION AT FINGER AND ROBINSON. ALL UNITS....

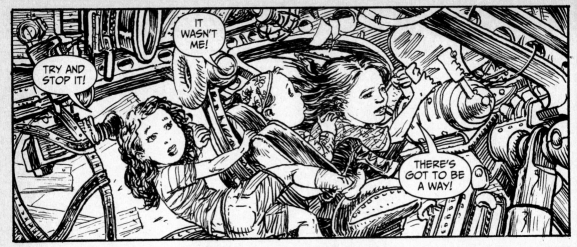

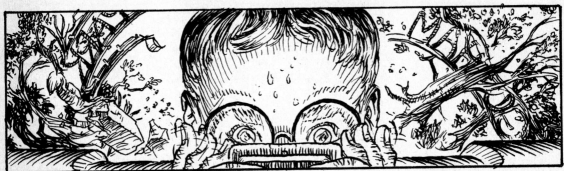

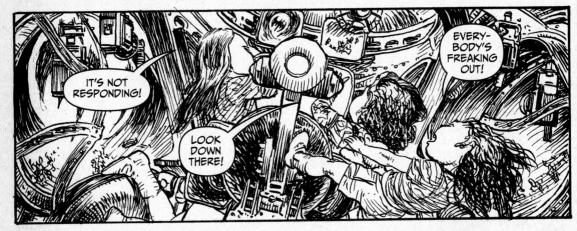

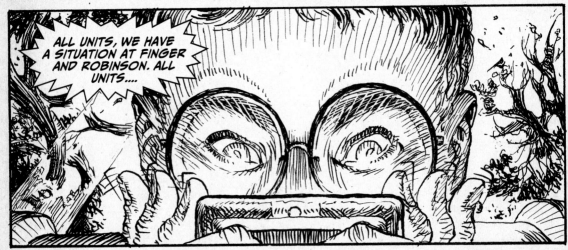

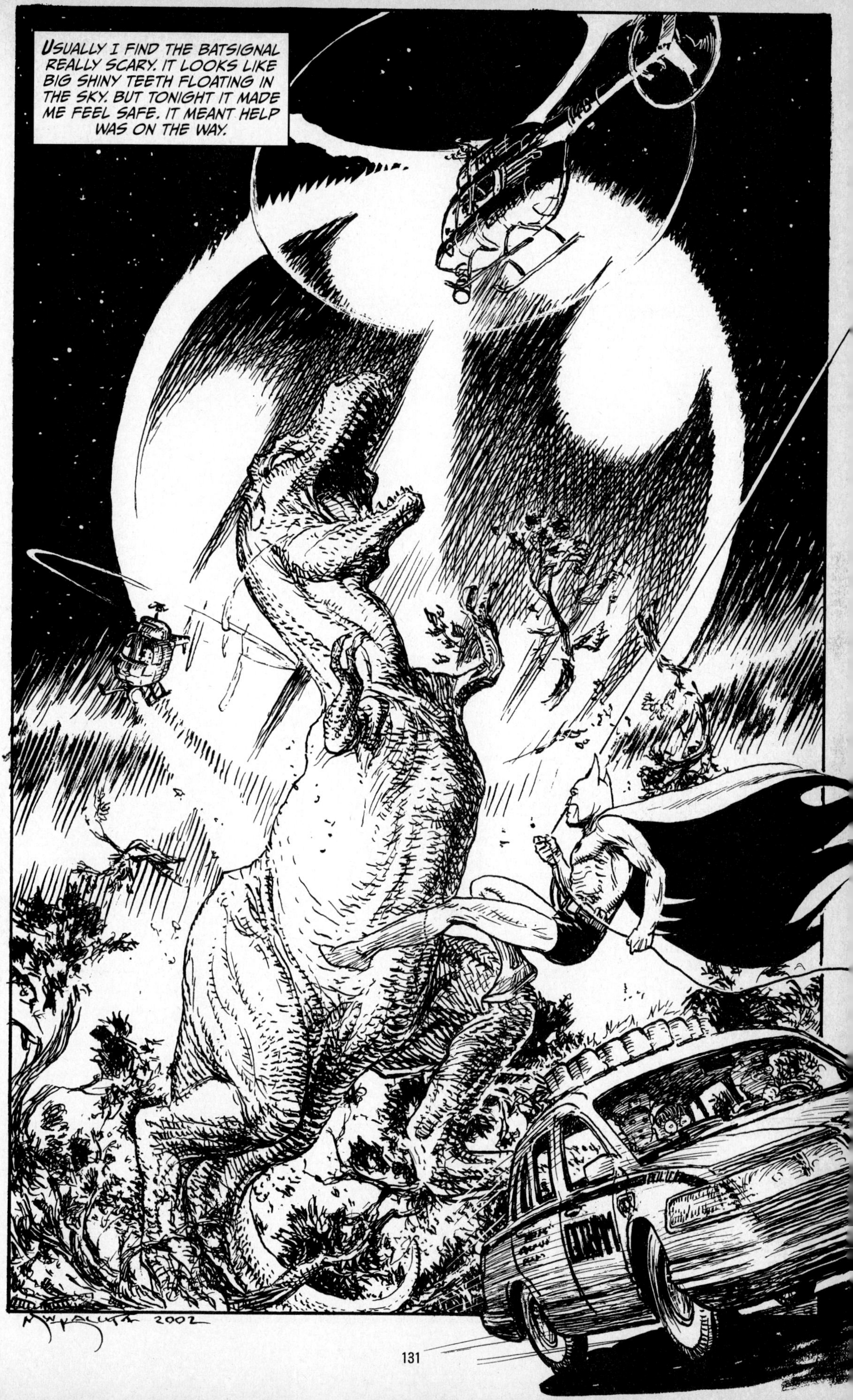
USUALLY I FIND THE BATSIGNAL REALLY SCARY. IT LOOKS LIKE BIG SHINY TEETH FLOATING IN THE SKY. BUT TONIGHT IT MADE ME FEEL SAFE. IT MEANT HELP WAS ON THE WAY.
2002

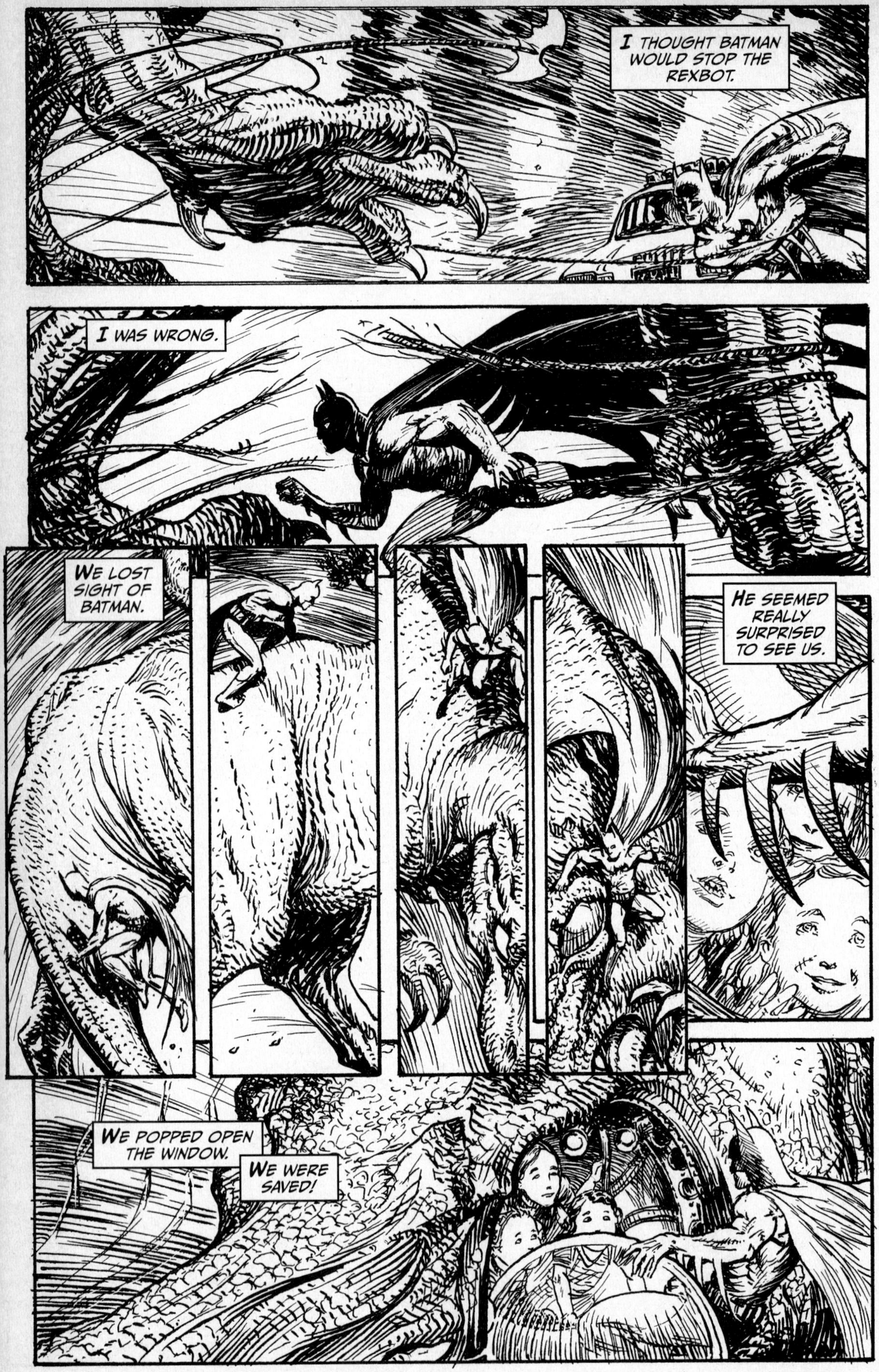
I THOUGHT BATMAN WOULD STOP THE REXBOT.
I WAS WRONG.
WE LOST SIGHT OF BATMAN.
HE SEEMED REALLY SURPRISED TO SEE US.
WE POPPED OPEN THE WINDOW.
WE WERE SAVED!

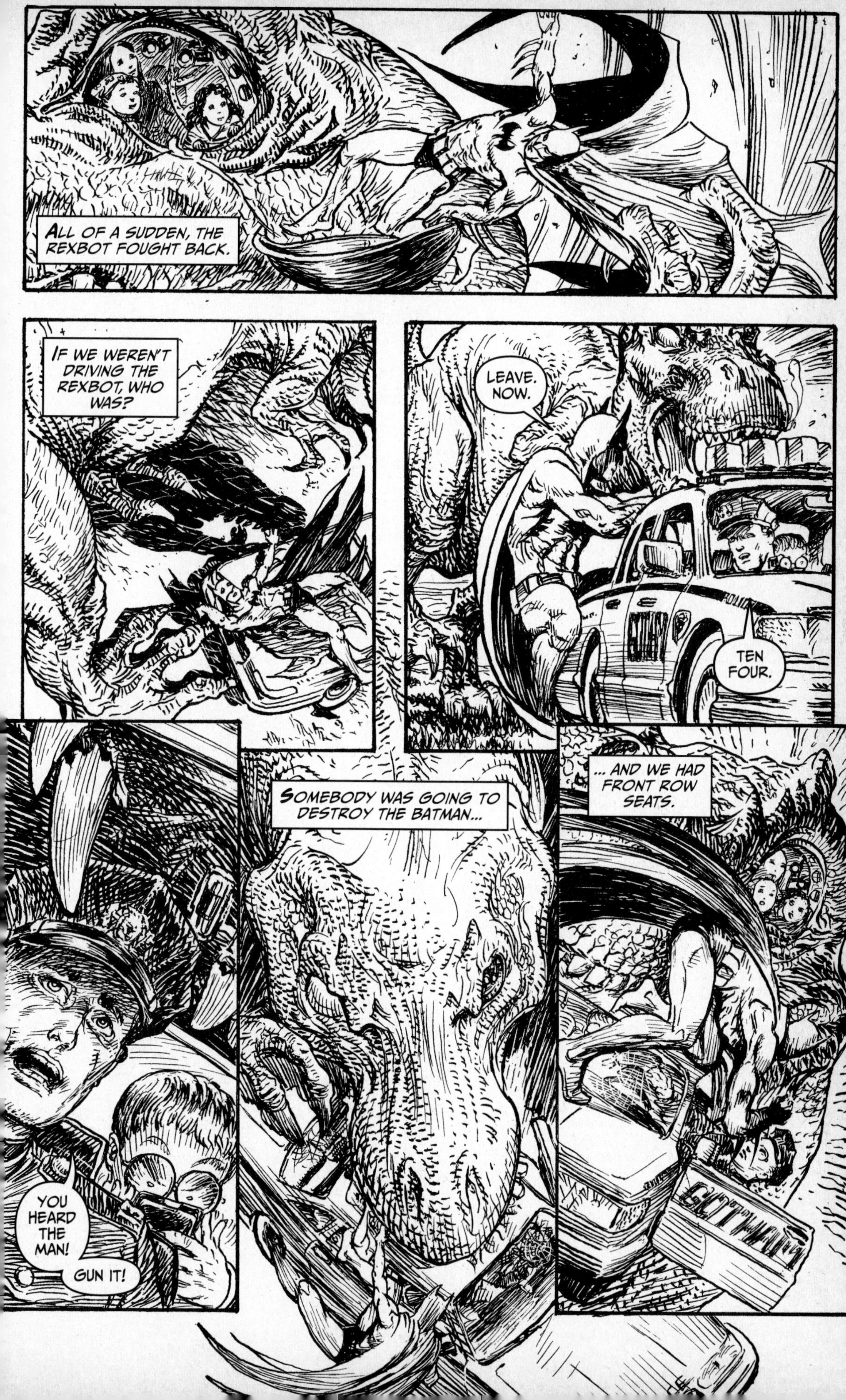
ALL OF A SUDDEN, THE REXBOT FOUGHT BACK.
IF WE WEREN'T DRIVING THE REXBOT, WHO WAS?
LEAVE. NOW.
TEN FOUR.
YOU HEARD THE MAN!
GUN IT!
SOMEBODY WAS GOING TO DESTROY THE BATMAN...
...AND WE HAD FRONT ROW SEATS.

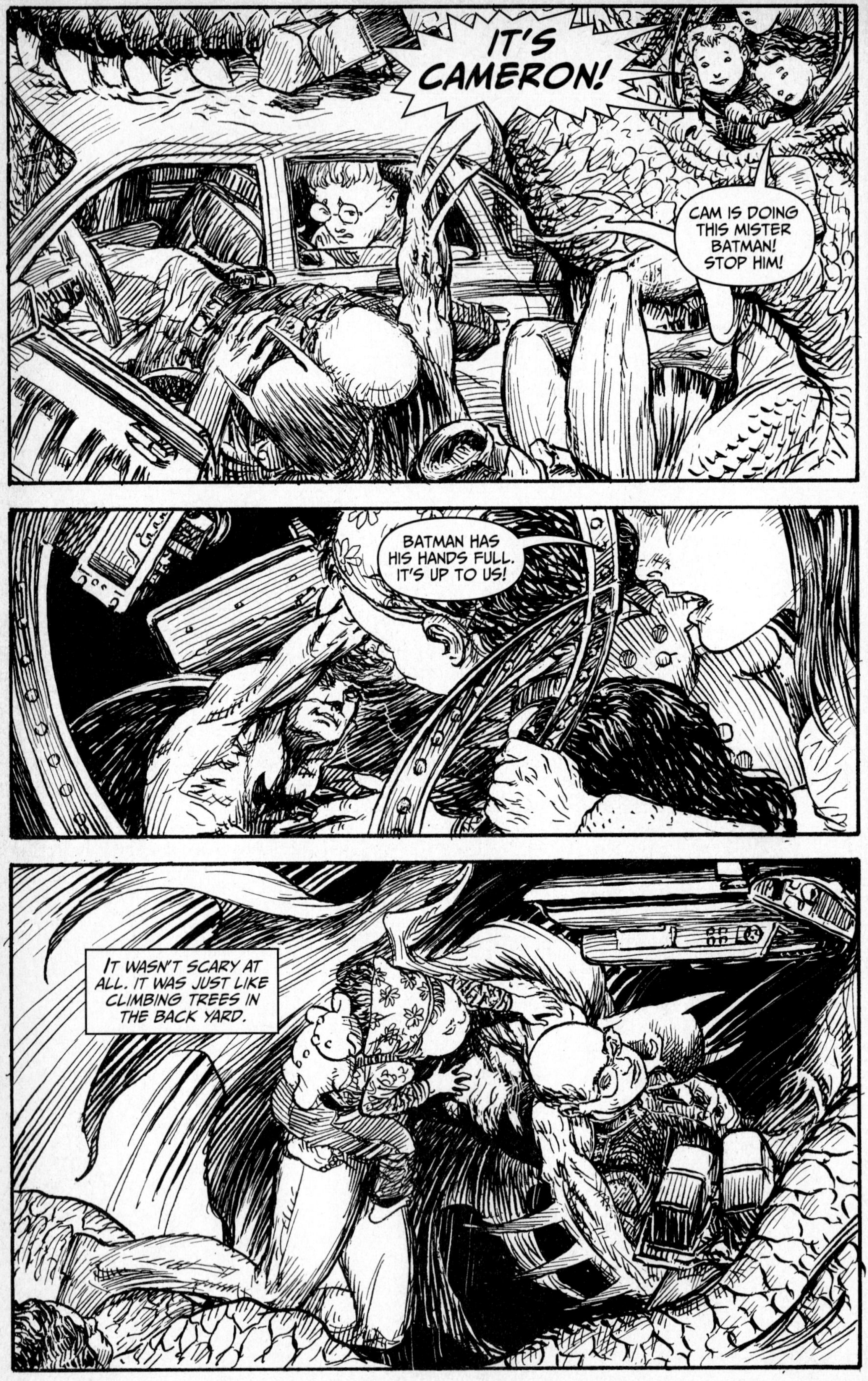
IT'S CAMERON!
CAM IS DOING THIS MISTER BATMAN! STOP HIM!
BATMAN HAS HIS HANDS FULL. IT'S UP TO US!
IT WASN'T SCARY AT ALL. IT WAS JUST LIKE CLIMBING TREES IN THE BACK YARD.

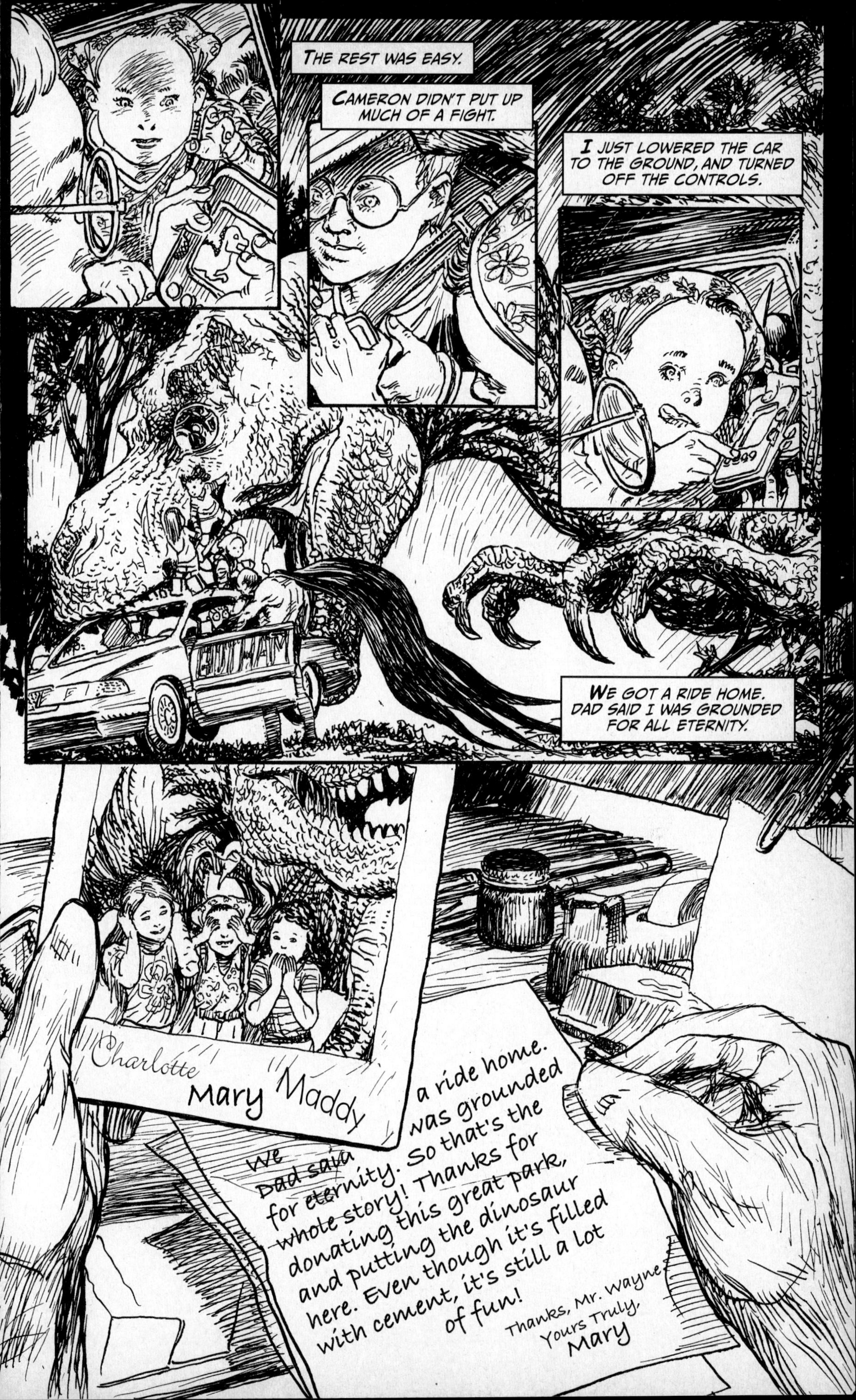
THE REST WAS EASY.
CAMERON DIDN'T PUT UP MUCH OF A FIGHT.
I JUST LOWERED THE CAR TO THE GROUND, AND TURNED OFF THE CONTROLS.
WE GOT A RIDE HOME. DAD SAID I WAS GROUNDED FOR ALL ETERNITY.
Charlotte
Mary
Maddy
a ride home.
was grounded
We
Dad said
for eternity. So that's the
whole story! Thanks for
donating this great park,
and putting the dinosaur
here. Even though it's filled
with cement, it's still a lot
of fun!
Thanks, Mr. Wayne.
Yours Truly,
Mary

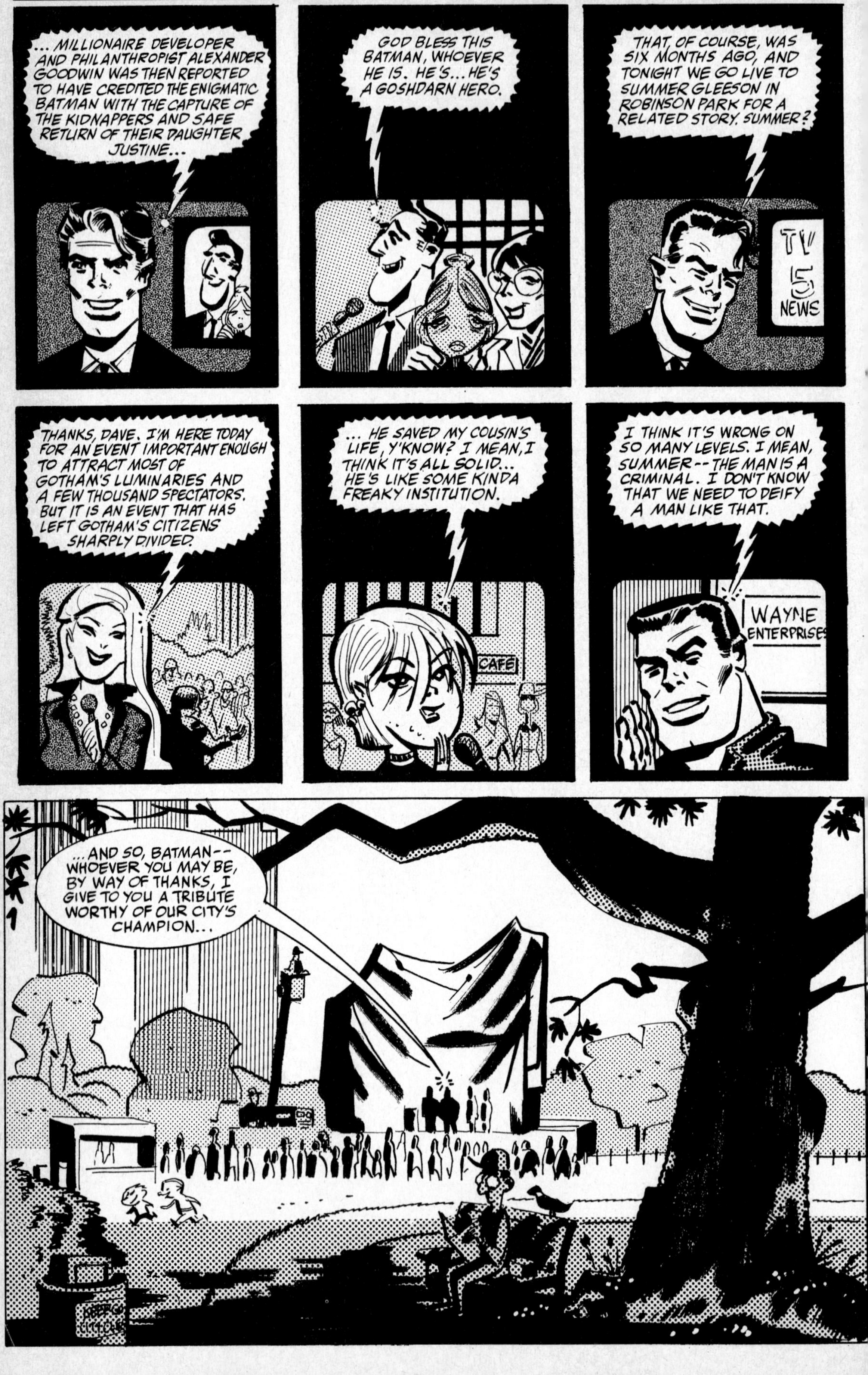
...MILLIONAIRE DEVELOPER AND PHILANTHROPIST ALEXANDER GOODWIN WAS THEN REPORTED TO HAVE CREDITED THE ENIGMATIC BATMAN WITH THE CAPTURE OF THE KIDNAPPERS AND SAFE RETURN OF THEIR DAUGHTER JUSTINE...
GOD BLESS THIS BATMAN, WHOEVER HE IS. HE'S...HE'S A GOSHDARN HERO.
THAT, OF COURSE, WAS SIX MONTHS AGO, AND TONIGHT WE GO LIVE TO SUMMER GLEESON IN ROBINSON PARK FOR A RELATED STORY. SUMMER?
TV 5 NEWS
THANKS, DAVE. I'M HERE TODAY FOR AN EVENT IMPORTANT ENOUGH TO ATTRACT MOST OF GOTHAM'S LUMINARIES AND A FEW THOUSAND SPECTATORS. BUT IT IS AN EVENT THAT HAS LEFT GOTHAM'S CITIZENS SHARPLY DIVIDED.
...HE SAVED MY COUSIN'S LIFE, Y'KNOW? I MEAN, I THINK IT'S ALL SOLID... HE'S LIKE SOME KINDA FREAKY INSTITUTION.
CAFE
I THINK IT'S WRONG ON SO MANY LEVELS. I MEAN, SUMMER--THE MAN IS A CRIMINAL. I DON'T KNOW THAT WE NEED TO DEIFY A MAN LIKE THAT.
WAYNE ENTERPRISES
...AND SO, BATMAN--WHOEVER YOU MAY BE, BY WAY OF THANKS, I GIVE TO YOU A TRIBUTE WORTHY OF OUR CITY'S CHAMPION...

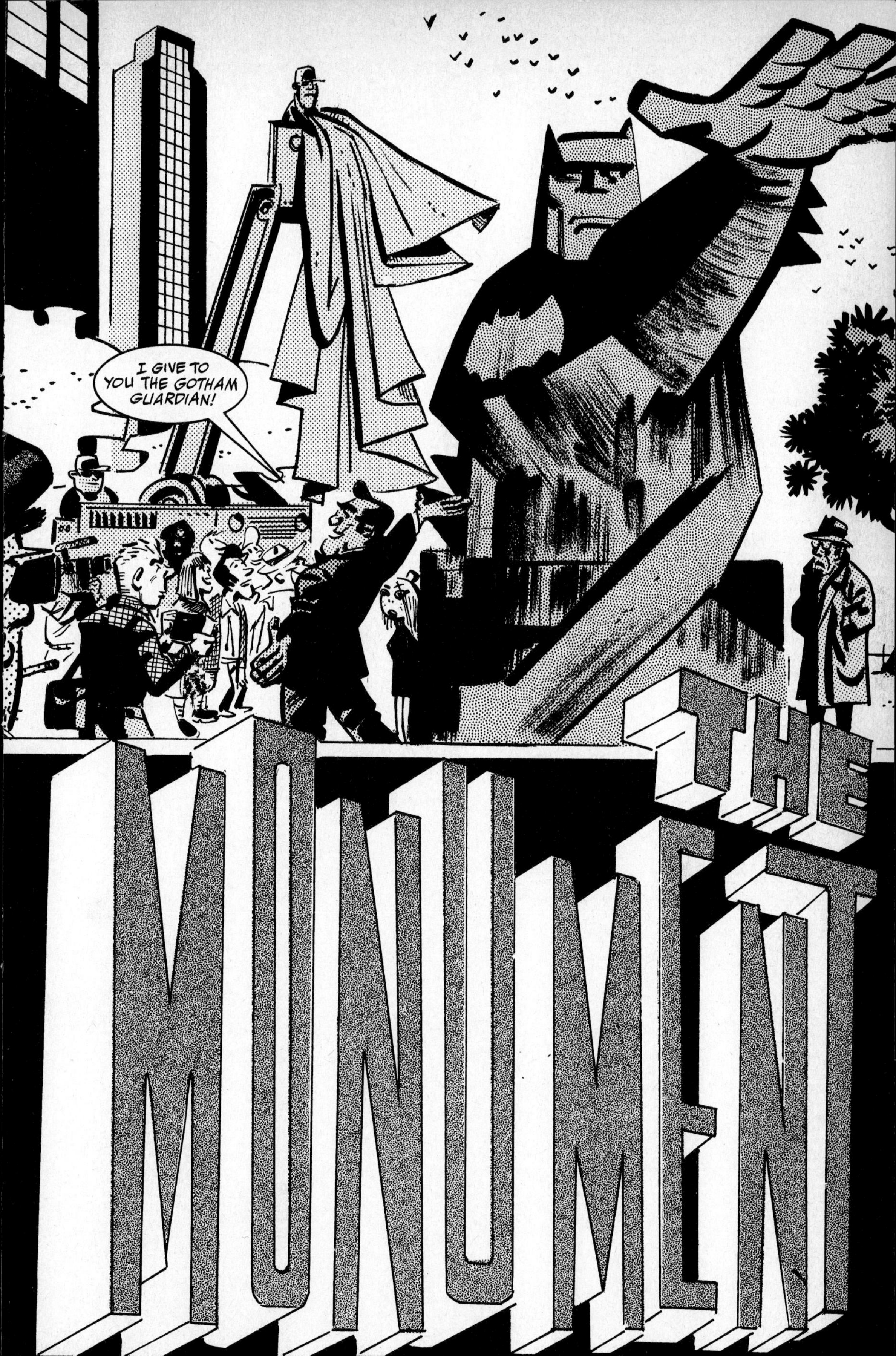
I GIVE TO YOU THE GOTHAM GUARDIAN!
THE MONUMENT
DARWYN COOKE WRITER
BILL WRAY ILLUSTRATOR
RICK PARKER LETTERER
MARK CHIARELLO EDITOR
VALERIE D'ORAZIO ASST. EDITOR

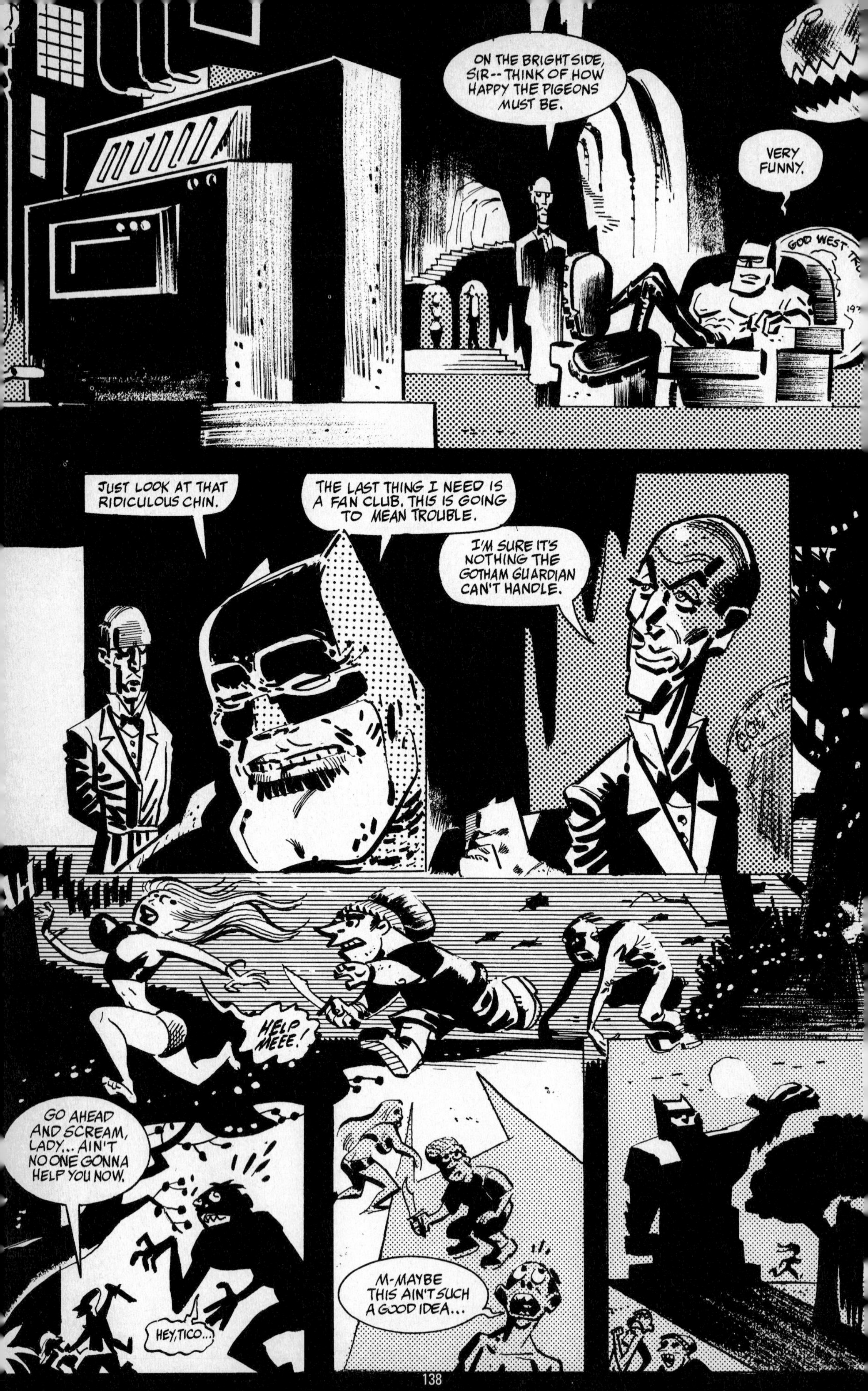
ON THE BRIGHT SIDE, SIR-- THINK OF HOW HAPPY THE PIGEONS MUST BE.
VERY FUNNY.
JUST LOOK AT THAT RIDICULOUS CHIN.
THE LAST THING I NEED IS A FAN CLUB. THIS IS GOING TO MEAN TROUBLE.
I'M SURE IT'S NOTHING THE GOTHAM GUARDIAN CAN'T HANDLE.
HELP MEEE!
GO AHEAD AND SCREAM, LADY... AIN'T NO ONE GONNA HELP YOU NOW.
HEY, TICO...
M-MAYBE THIS AIN'T SUCH A GOOD IDEA...

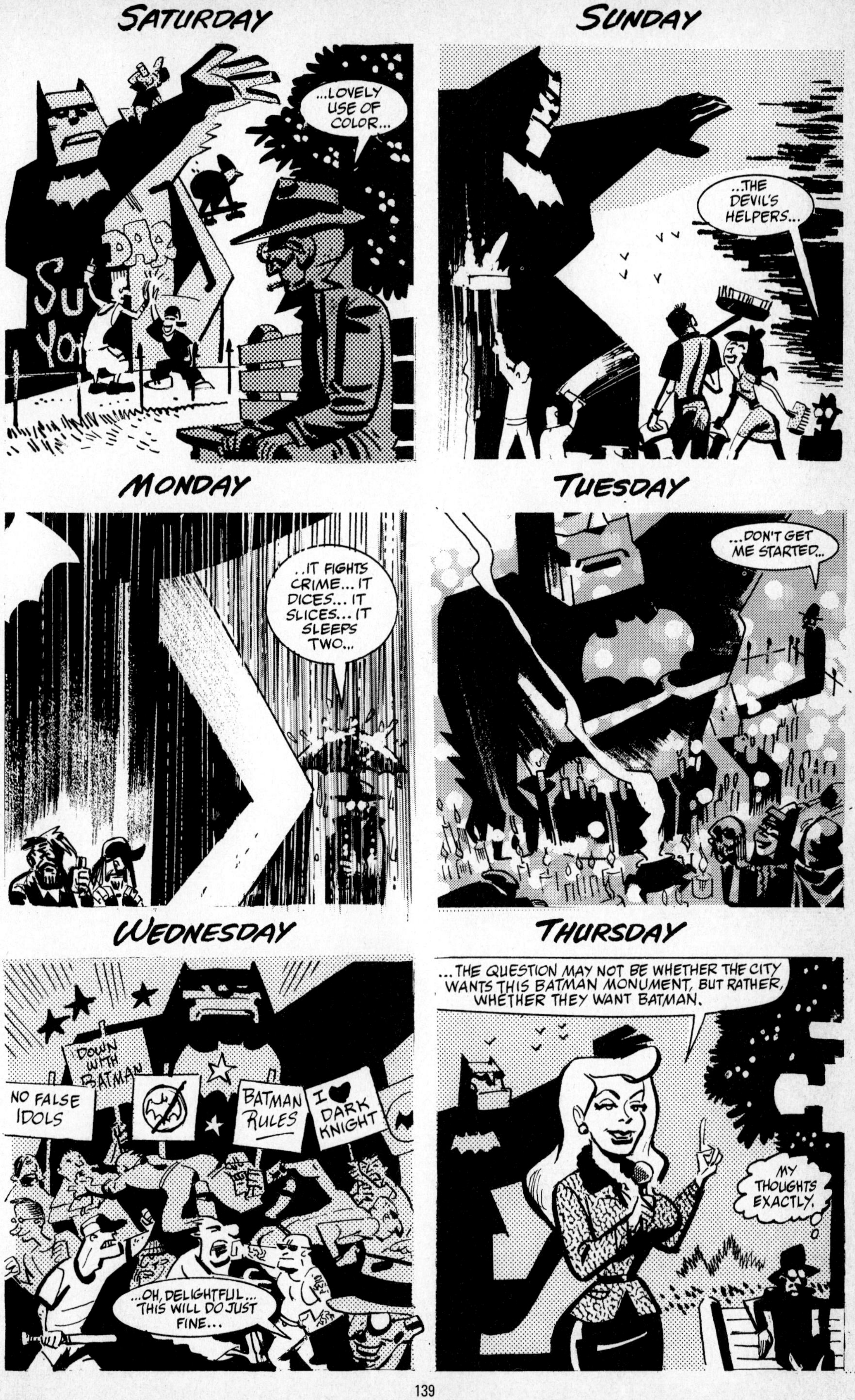
SATURDAY
...LOVELY USE OF COLOR...
SUNDAY
...THE DEVIL'S HELPERS...
MONDAY
..IT FIGHTS CRIME... IT DICES... IT SLICES... IT SLEEPS TWO...
TUESDAY
...DON'T GET ME STARTED...
WEDNESDAY
DOWN WITH BATMAN
NO FALSE IDOLS
BATMAN RULES
I ♥ DARK KNIGHT
...OH, DELIGHTFUL... THIS WILL DO JUST FINE...
THURSDAY
...THE QUESTION MAY NOT BE WHETHER THE CITY WANTS THIS BATMAN MONUMENT, BUT RATHER, WHETHER THEY WANT BATMAN.
MY THOUGHTS EXACTLY.

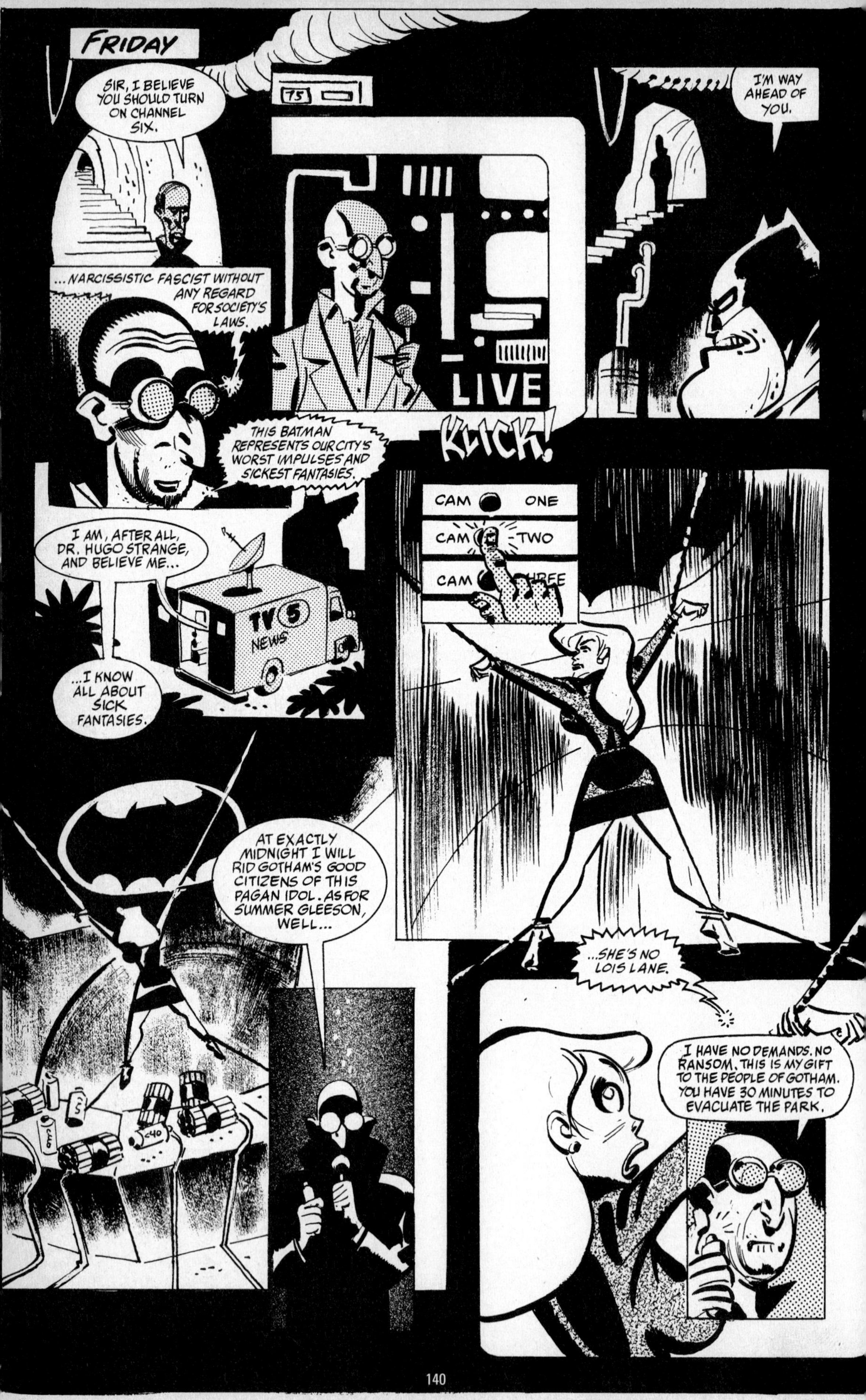
FRIDAY
SIR, I BELIEVE YOU SHOULD TURN ON CHANNEL SIX.
75
I'M WAY AHEAD OF YOU.
LIVE
...NARCISSISTIC FASCIST WITHOUT ANY REGARD FOR SOCIETY'S LAWS.
THIS BATMAN REPRESENTS OUR CITY'S WORST IMPULSES AND SICKEST FANTASIES.
KLICK!
CAM ONE
CAM TWO
CAM THREE
I AM, AFTER ALL, DR. HUGO STRANGE, AND BELIEVE ME...
TV 5 NEWS
...I KNOW ALL ABOUT SICK FANTASIES.
AT EXACTLY MIDNIGHT I WILL RID GOTHAM'S GOOD CITIZENS OF THIS PAGAN IDOL. AS FOR SUMMER GLEESON, WELL...
...SHE'S NO LOIS LANE.
I HAVE NO DEMANDS. NO RANSOM. THIS IS MY GIFT TO THE PEOPLE OF GOTHAM. YOU HAVE 30 MINUTES TO EVACUATE THE PARK.

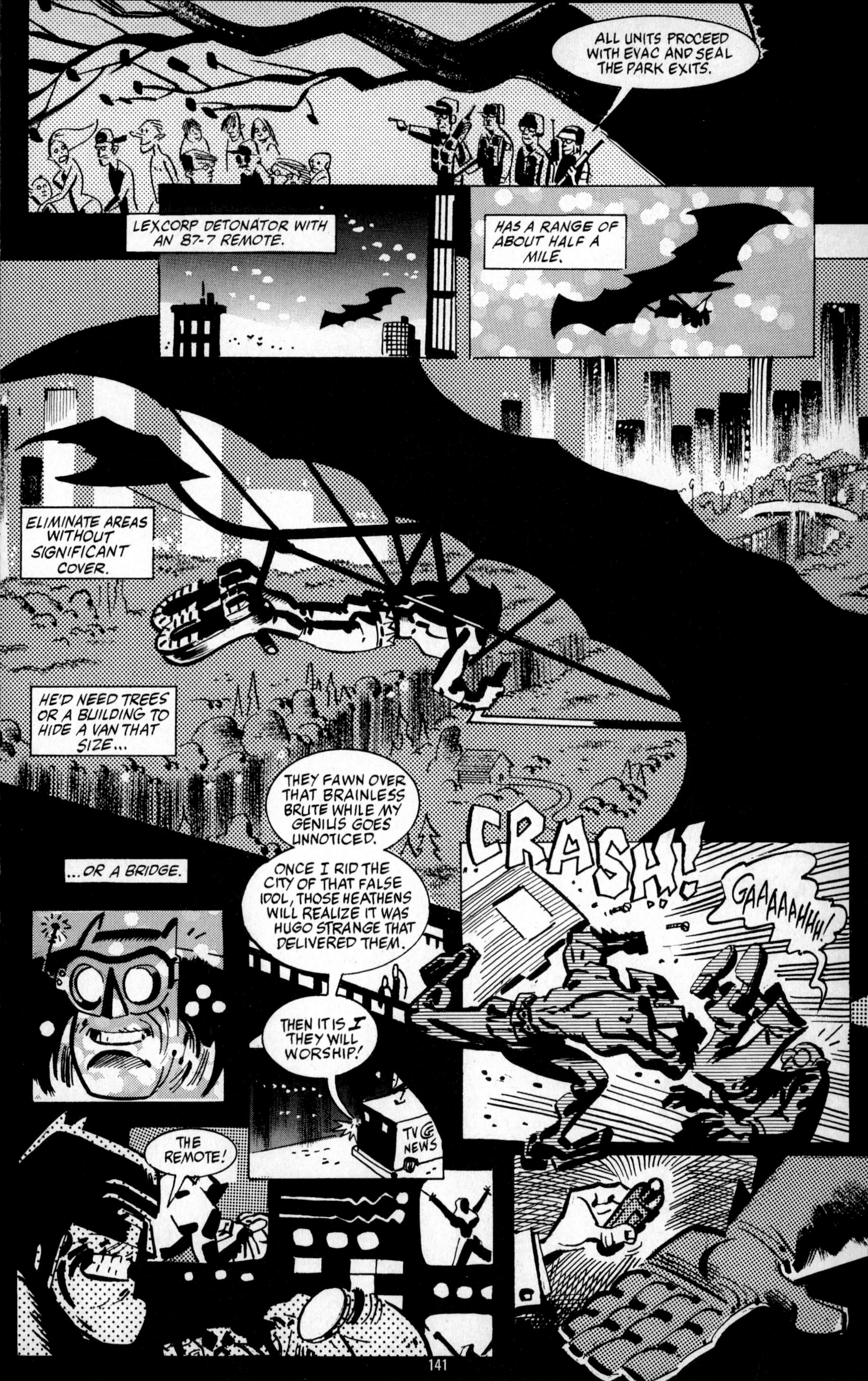

ALL UNITS PROCEED WITH EVAC AND SEAL THE PARK EXITS.
LEXCORP DETONATOR WITH AN 87-7 REMOTE.
HAS A RANGE OF ABOUT HALF A MILE.
ELIMINATE AREAS WITHOUT SIGNIFICANT COVER.
HE'D NEED TREES OR A BUILDING TO HIDE A VAN THAT SIZE...
...OR A BRIDGE.
THEY FAWN OVER THAT BRAINLESS BRUTE WHILE MY GENIUS GOES UNNOTICED.
ONCE I RID THE CITY OF THAT FALSE IDOL, THOSE HEATHENS WILL REALIZE IT WAS HUGO STRANGE THAT DELIVERED THEM.
THEN IT IS I THEY WILL WORSHIP!
CRASH!
GAAAAAHHH!
TV NEWS
THE REMOTE!

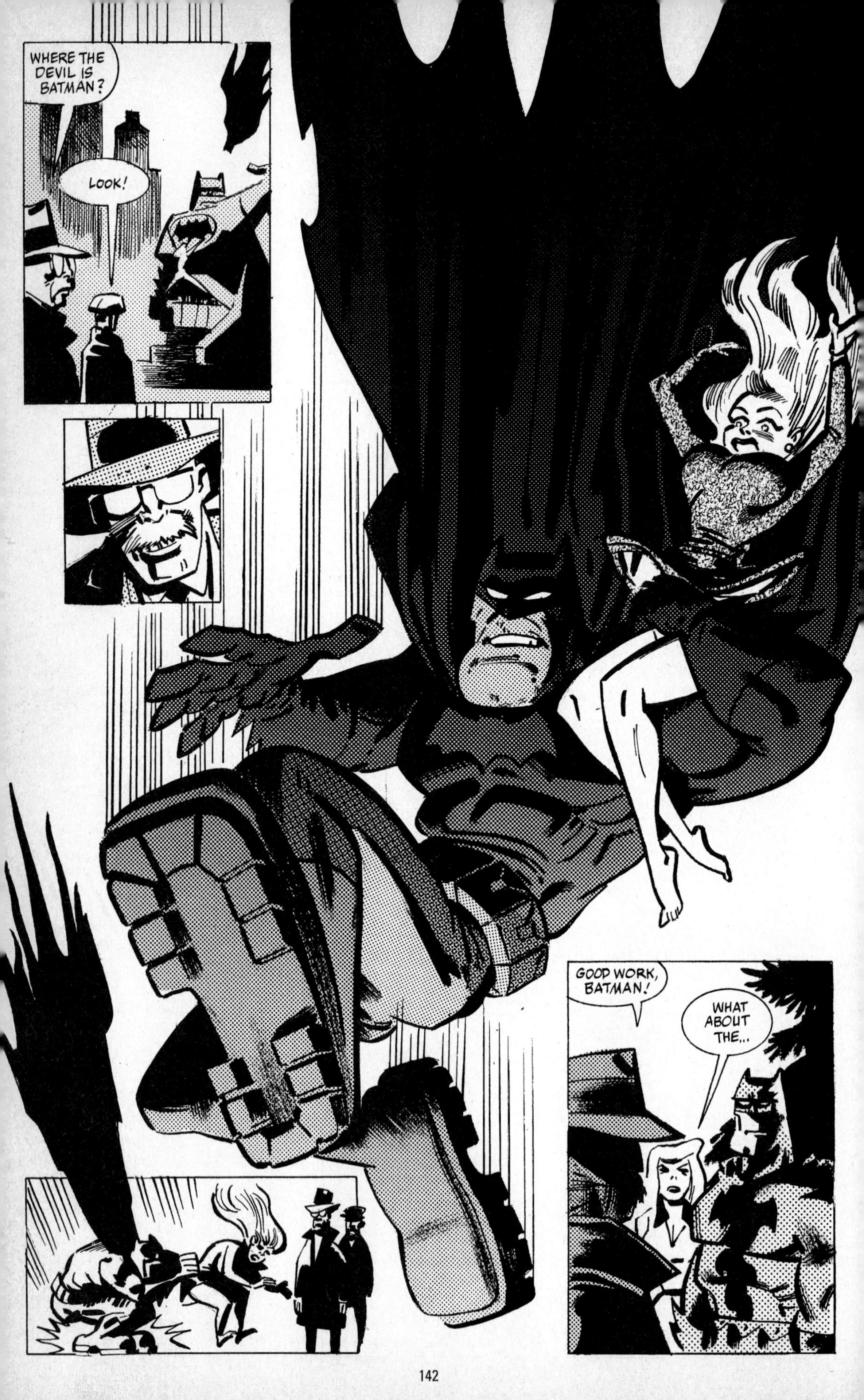
WHERE THE DEVIL IS BATMAN?
LOOK!
GOOD WORK, BATMAN!
WHAT ABOUT THE...

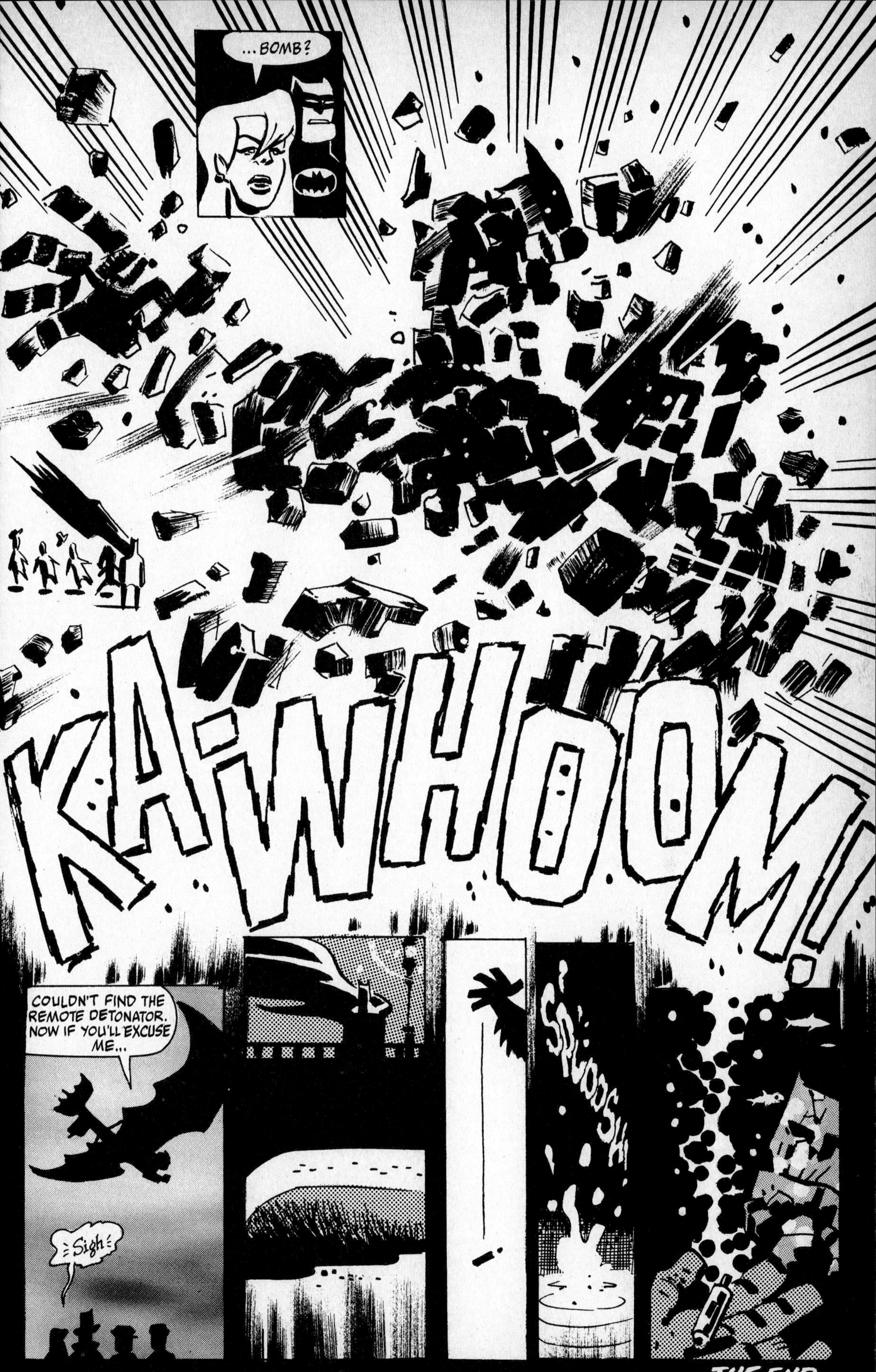

...BOMB?
KA-WHOOM!
COULDN'T FIND THE REMOTE DETONATOR. NOW IF YOU'LL EXCUSE ME...
Sigh
SPLOOOSH!


THE END

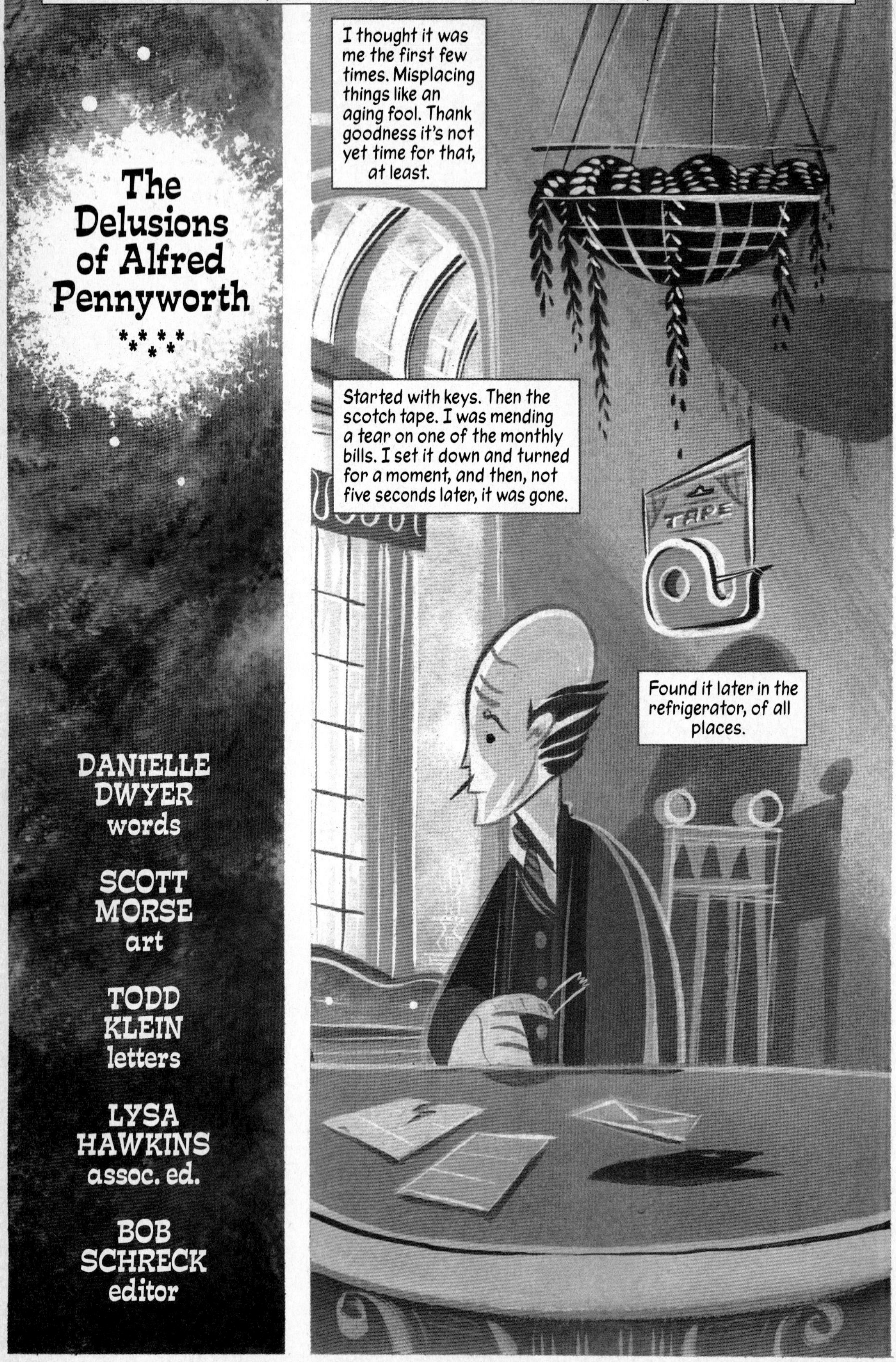
The Delusions of Alfred Pennyworth
DANIELLE DWYER words
SCOTT MORSE art
TODD KLEIN letters
LYSA HAWKINS assoc. ed.
BOB SCHRECK editor
I thought it was me the first few times. Misplacing things like an aging fool. Thank goodness it's not yet time for that, at least.
Started with keys. Then the scotch tape. I was mending a tear on one of the monthly bills. I set it down and turned for a moment, and then, not five seconds later, it was gone.
TAPE
Found it later in the refrigerator, of all places.

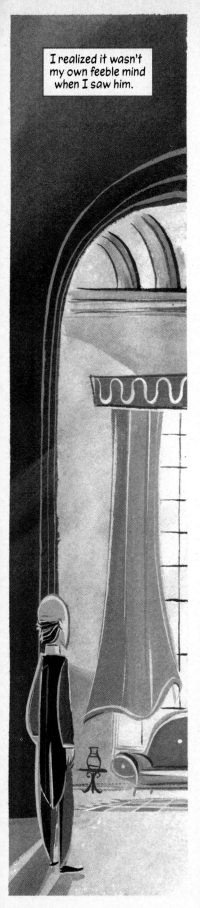

I realized it wasn't my own feeble mind when I saw him.

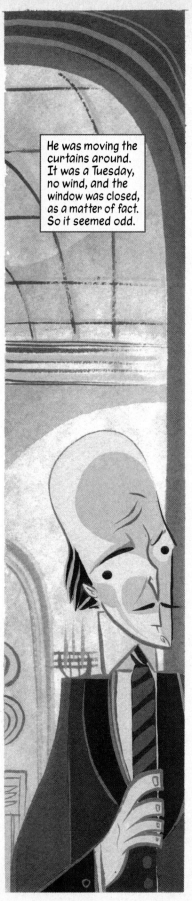

He was moving the curtains around. It was a Tuesday, no wind, and the window was closed, as a matter of fact. So it seemed odd.

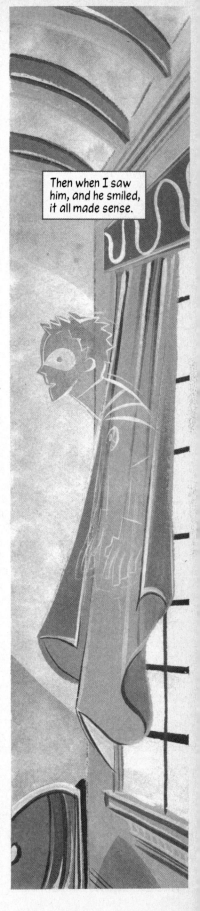

Then when I saw him, and he smiled, it all made sense.

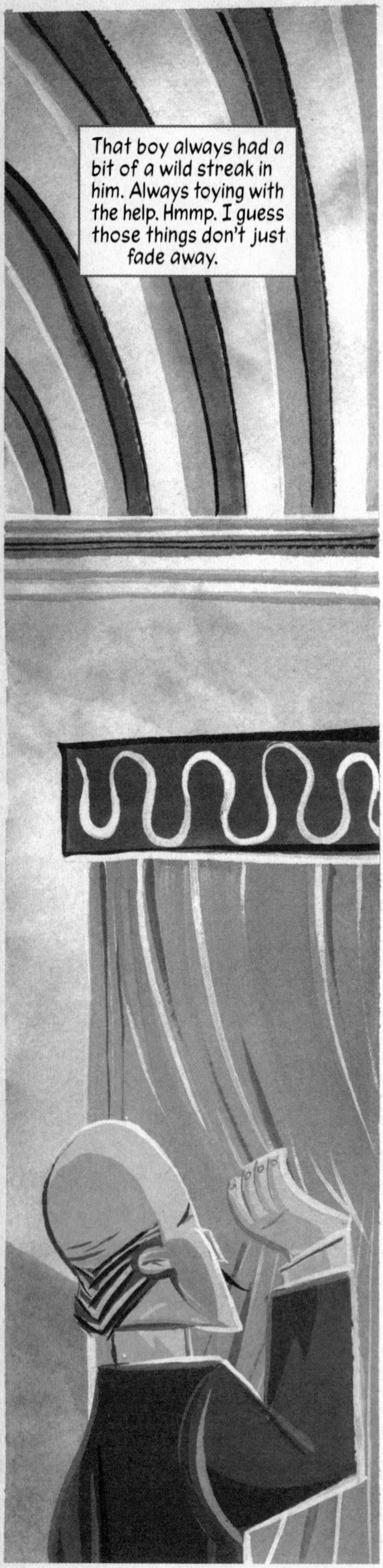
That boy always had a bit of a wild streak in him. Always toying with the help. Hmmp. I guess those things don't just fade away.

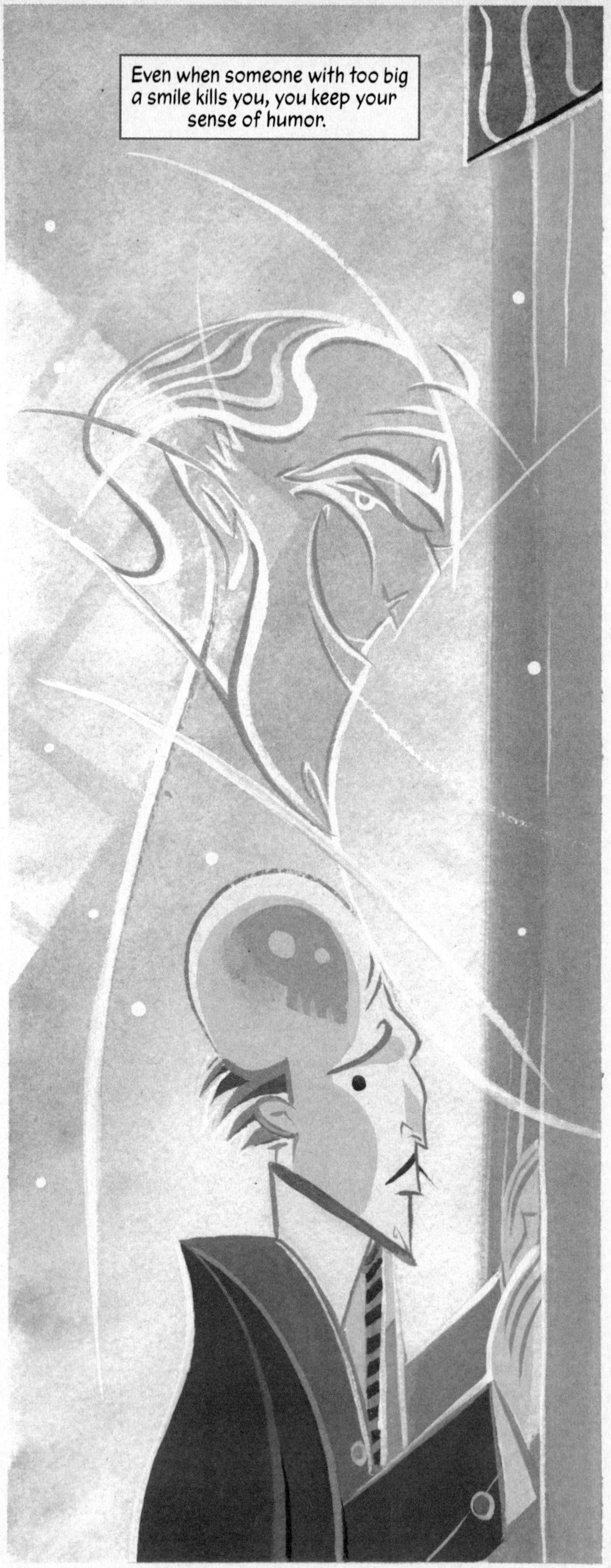
Even when someone with too big a smile kills you, you keep your sense of humor.

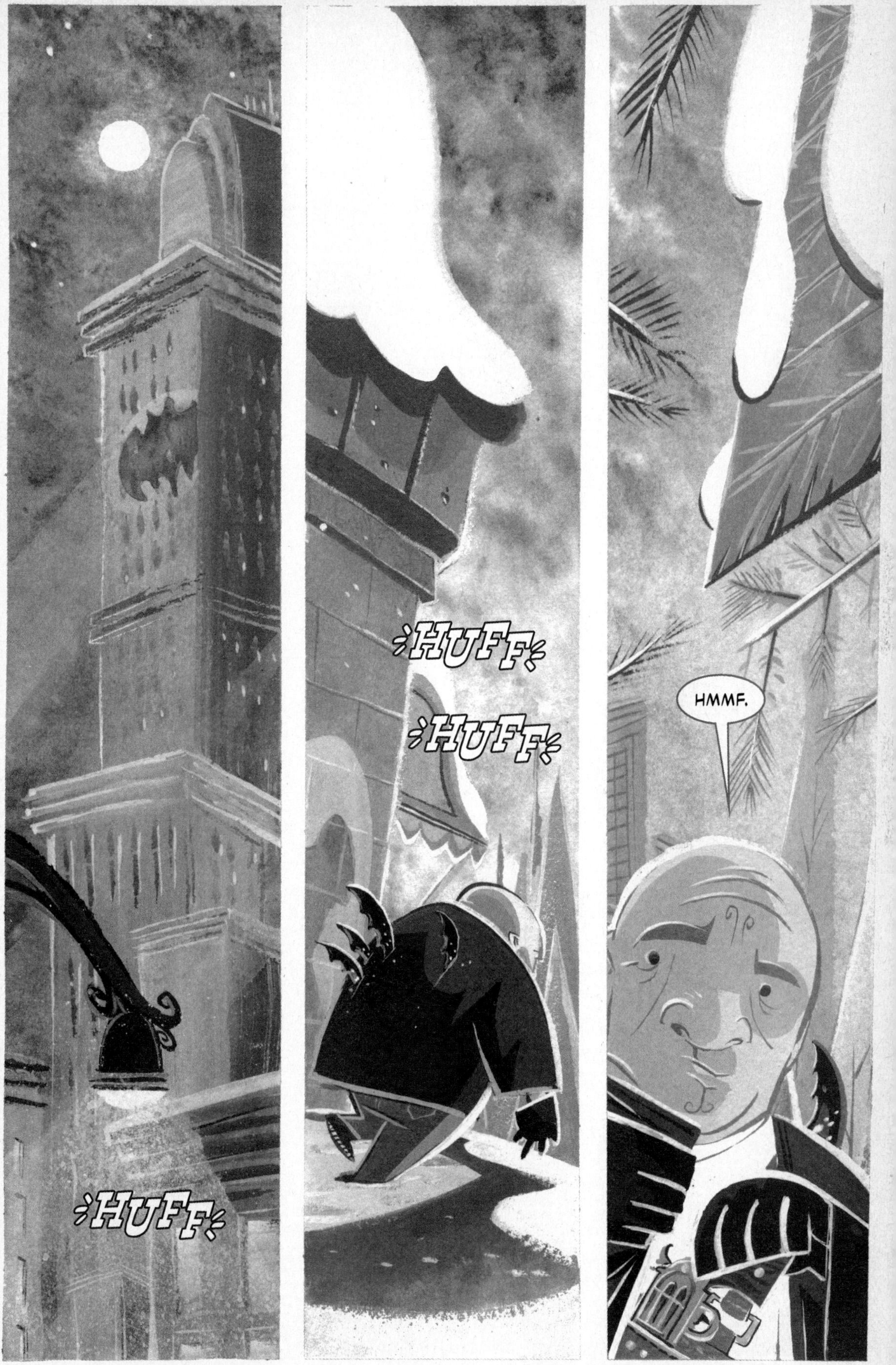
HUFF
HUFF
HUFF
HMMF.

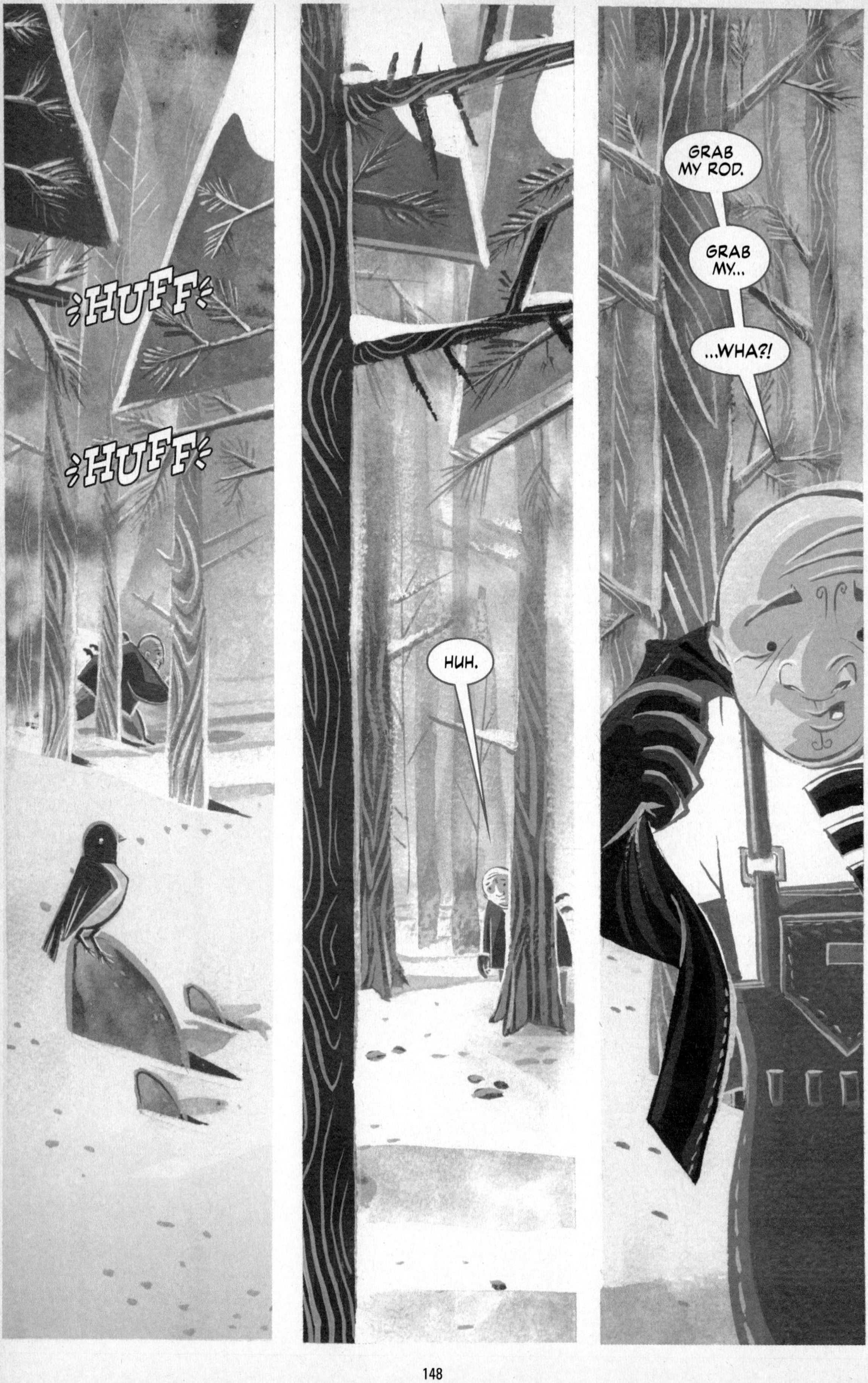
HUFF
HUFF
HUH.
GRAB MY ROD.
GRAB MY...
...WHA?!

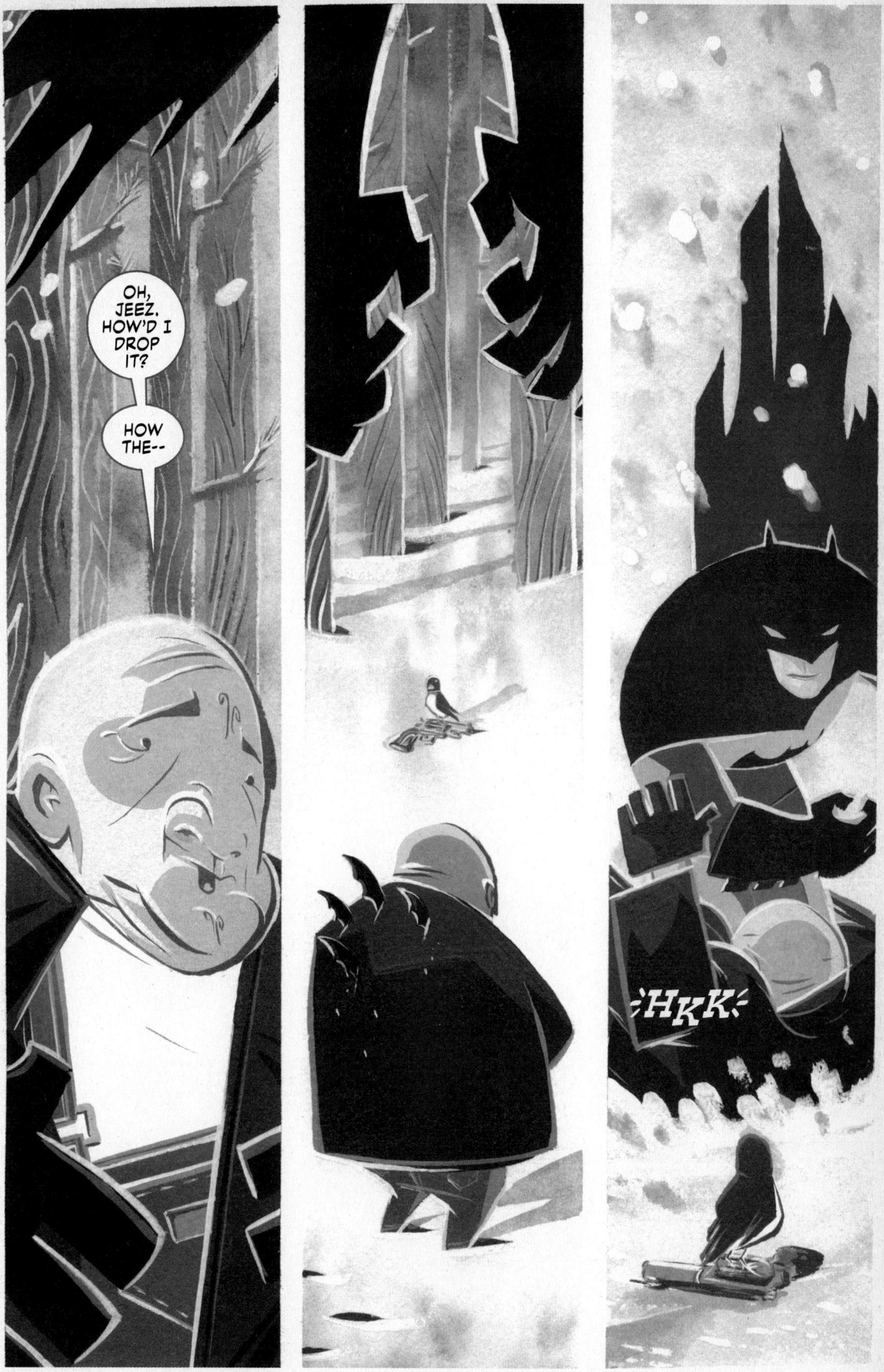
OH, JEEZ. HOW'D I DROP IT?
HOW THE--
HKK

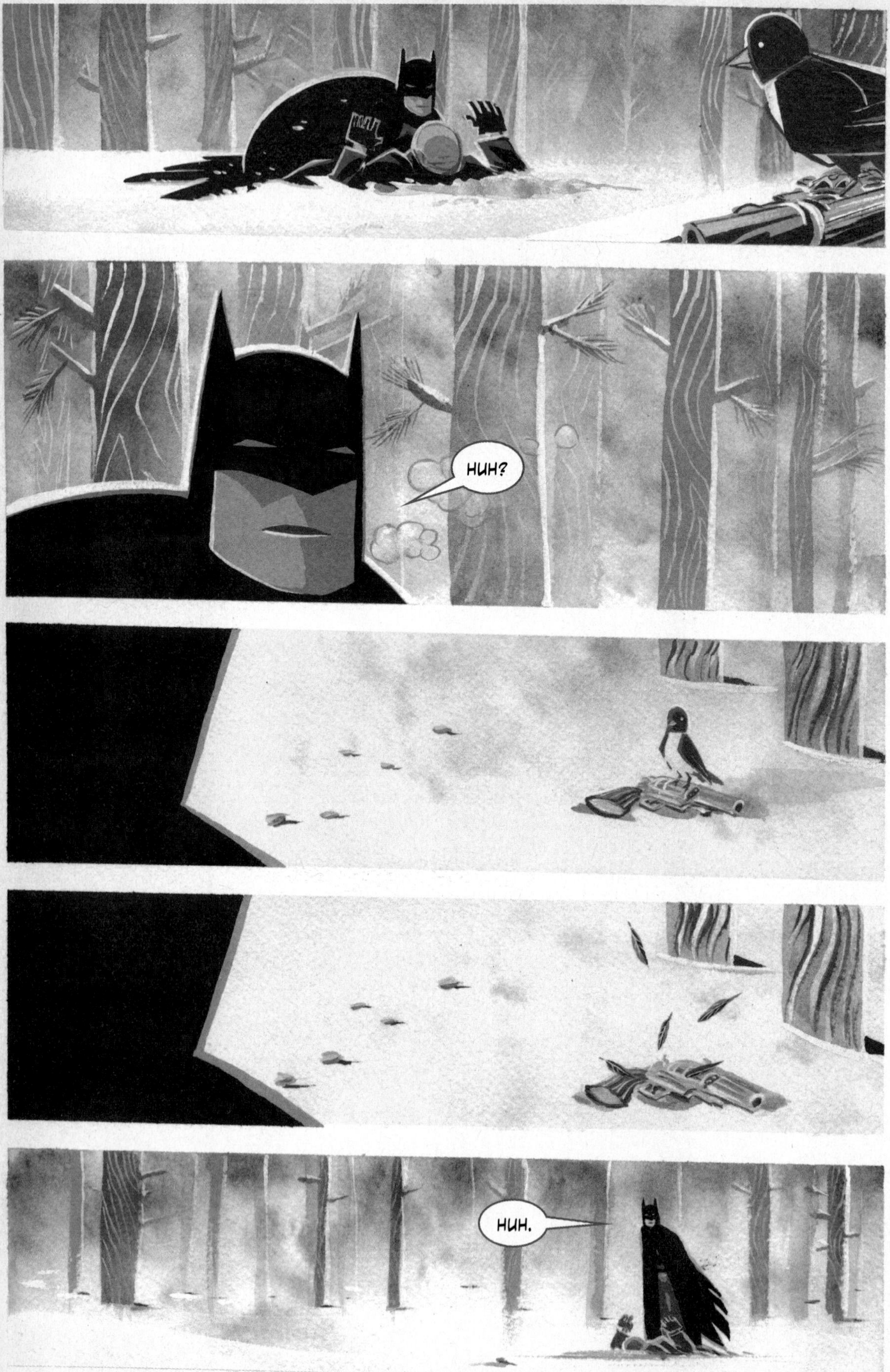
HUH?
HUH.

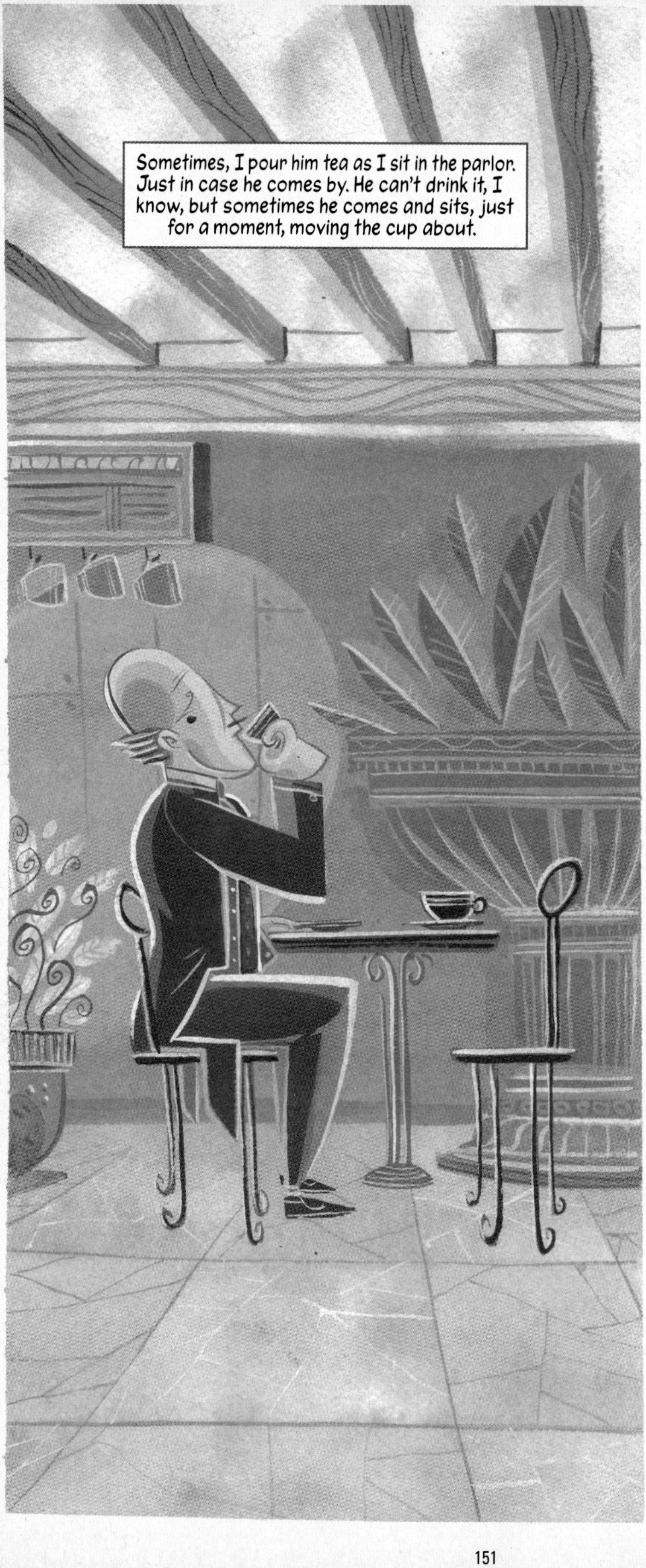
Sometimes, I pour him tea as I sit in the parlor. Just in case he comes by. He can't drink it, I know, but sometimes he comes and sits, just for a moment, moving the cup about.

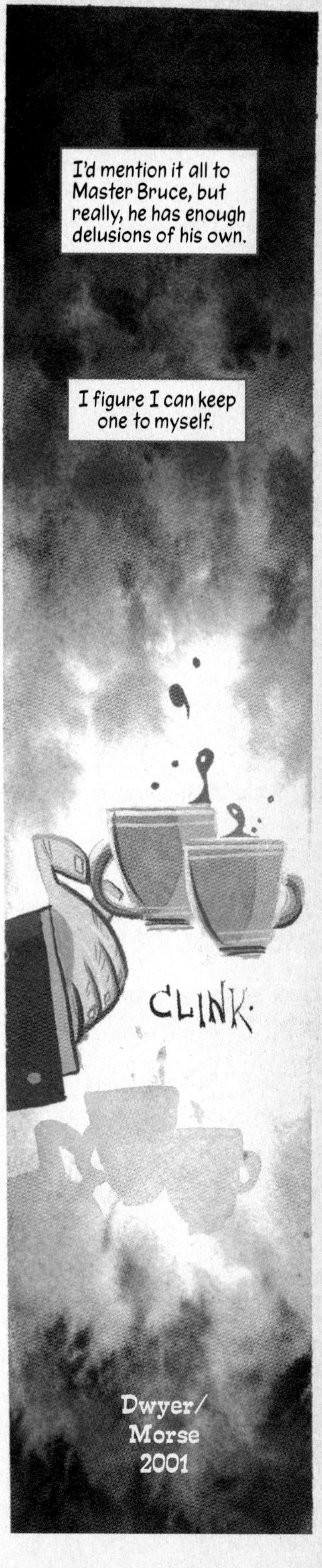
I'd mention it all to Master Bruce, but really, he has enough delusions of his own.
I figure I can keep one to myself.
CLINK.
Dwyer/ Morse 2001

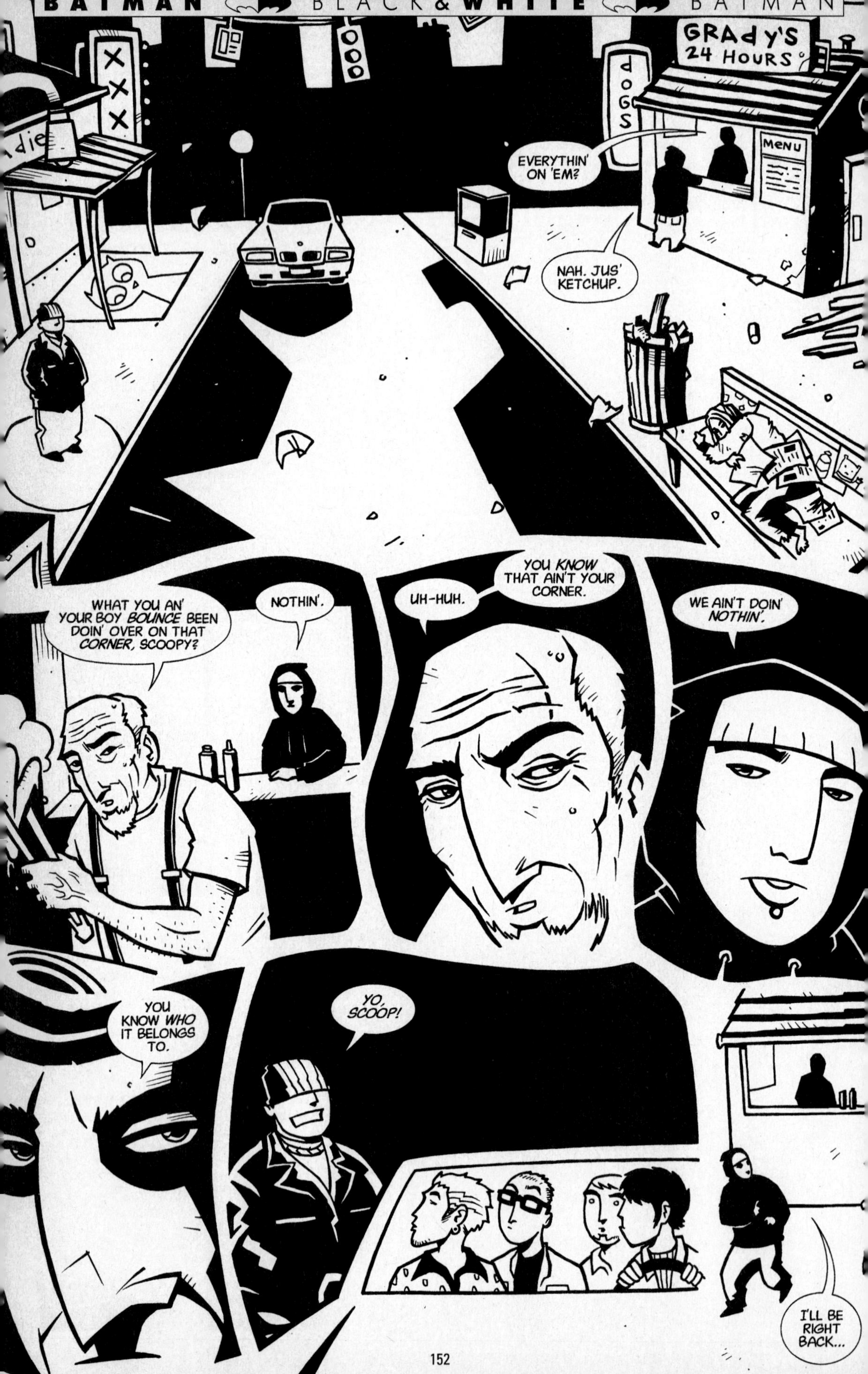
GRADy'S 24 HOURS
MENU
DOGS
XXX
EVERYTHIN' ON 'EM?
NAH. JUS' KETCHUP.
WHAT YOU AN' YOUR BOY BOUNCE BEEN DOIN' OVER ON THAT CORNER, SCOOPY?
NOTHIN'.
UH-HUH.
YOU KNOW THAT AIN'T YOUR CORNER.
WE AIN'T DOIN' NOTHIN'.
YOU KNOW WHO IT BELONGS TO.
YO, SCOOP!
I'LL BE RIGHT BACK...

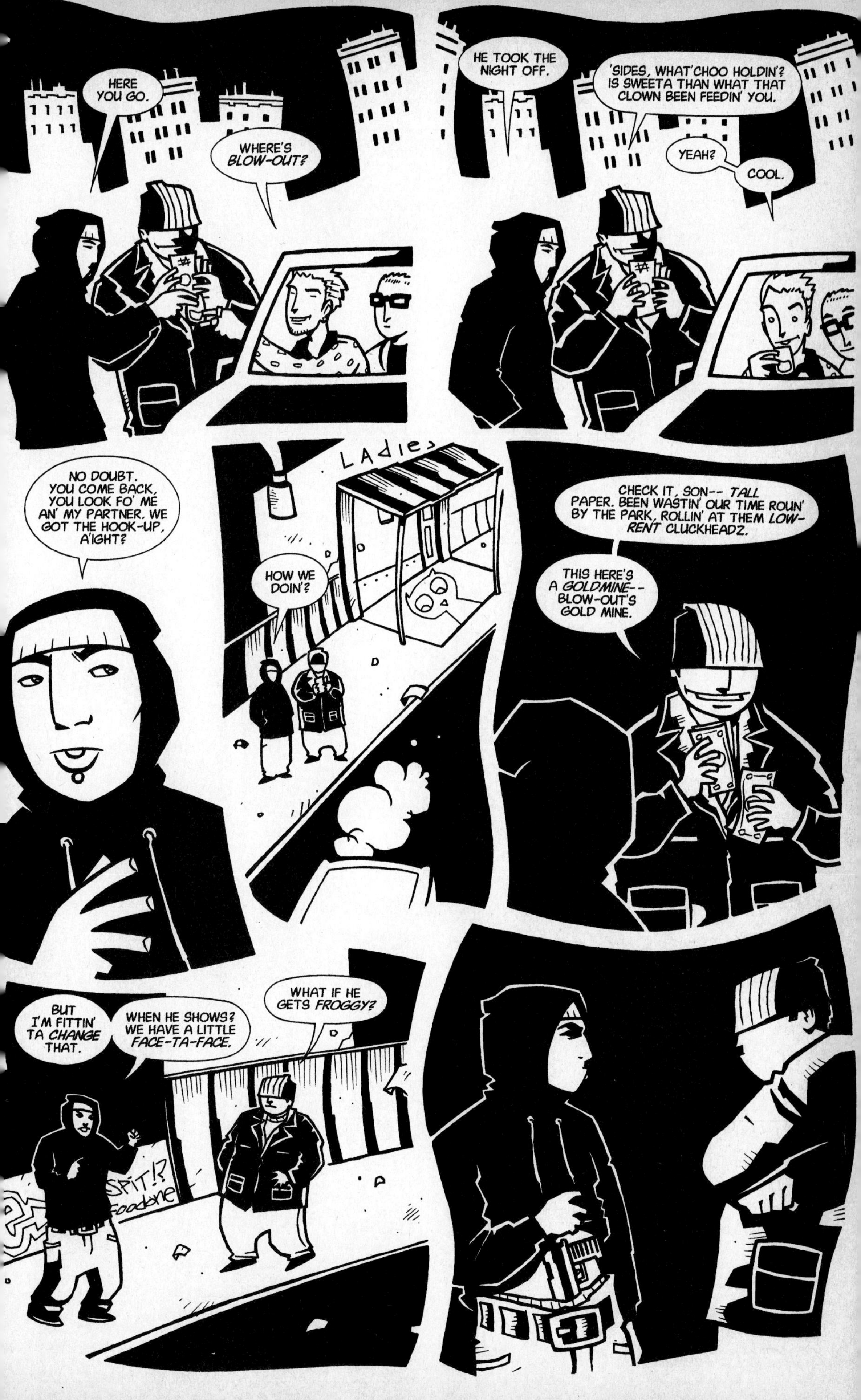
HERE YOU GO.
WHERE'S *BLOW-OUT?*
HE TOOK THE NIGHT OFF.
'SIDES, WHAT'CHOO HOLDIN'? IS SWEETA THAN WHAT THAT CLOWN BEEN FEEDIN' YOU.
YEAH?
COOL.
NO DOUBT. YOU COME BACK, YOU LOOK FO' ME AN' MY PARTNER. WE GOT THE HOOK-UP, A'IGHT?
LAdies
HOW WE DOIN'?
CHECK IT, SON-- *TALL* PAPER. BEEN WASTIN' OUR TIME ROUN' BY THE PARK, ROLLIN' AT THEM *LOW-RENT* CLUCKHEADZ.
THIS HERE'S A *GOLDMINE*-- BLOW-OUT'S GOLD MINE.
BUT I'M FITTIN' TA *CHANGE* THAT.
WHEN HE SHOWS? WE HAVE A LITTLE *FACE-TA-FACE.*
WHAT IF HE GETS *FROGGY?*
SPIT!?

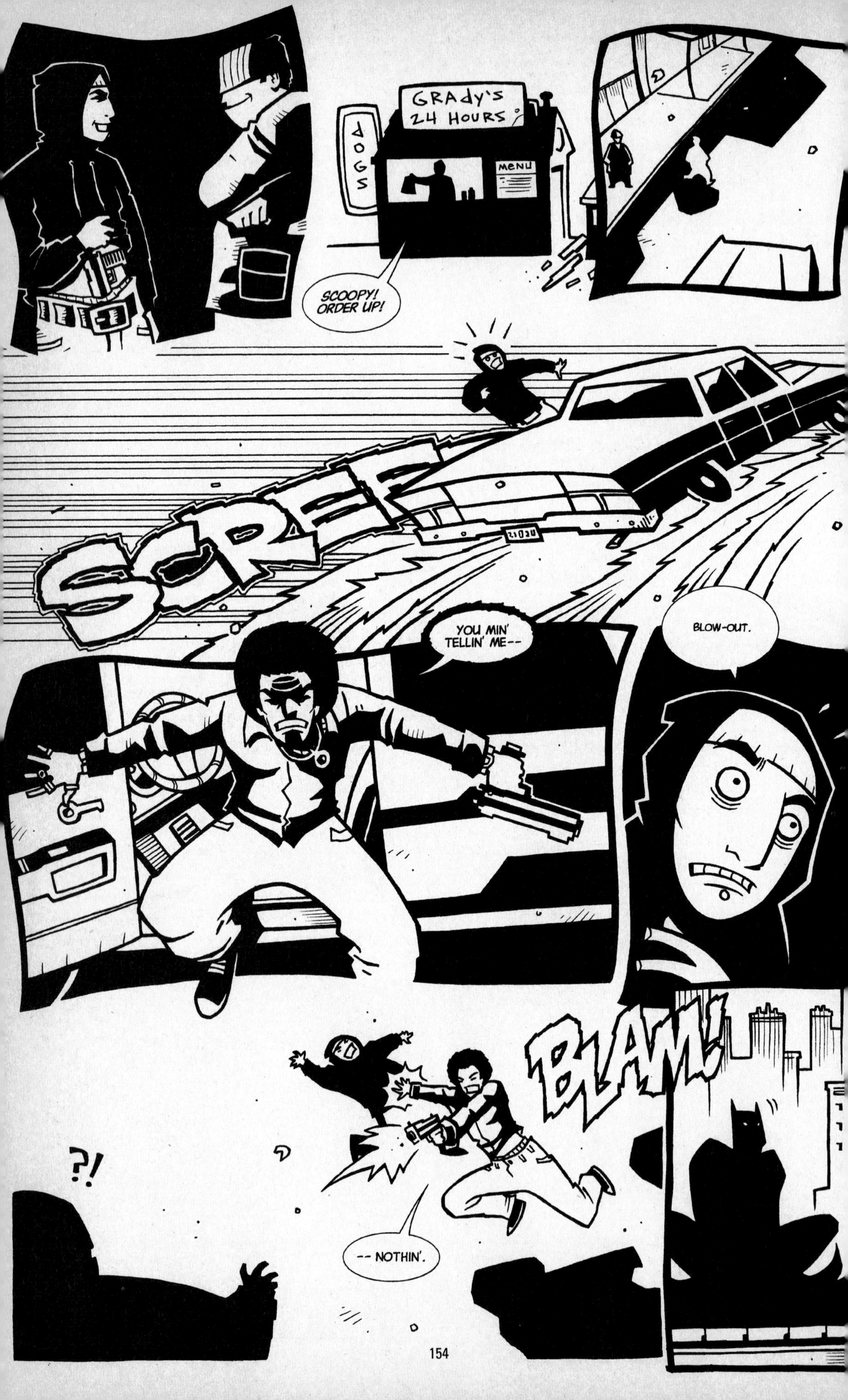
GRADy's
24 HOURS
DOGS
menu
SCOOPY! ORDER UP!
SCREE
YOU MIN' TELLIN' ME--
BLOW-OUT.
BLAM!
?!
-- NOTHIN'.

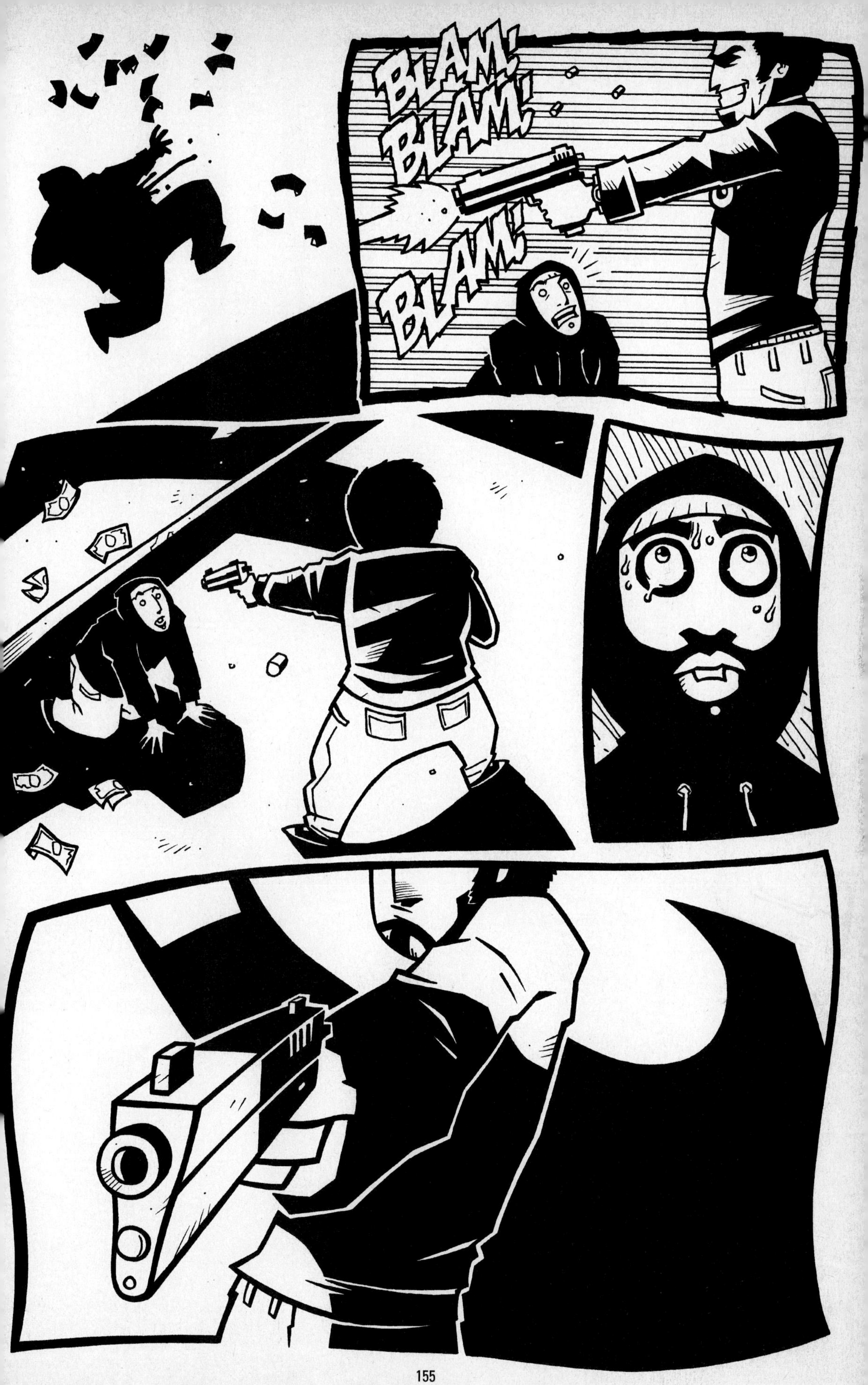
BLAM!
BLAM!
BLAM!

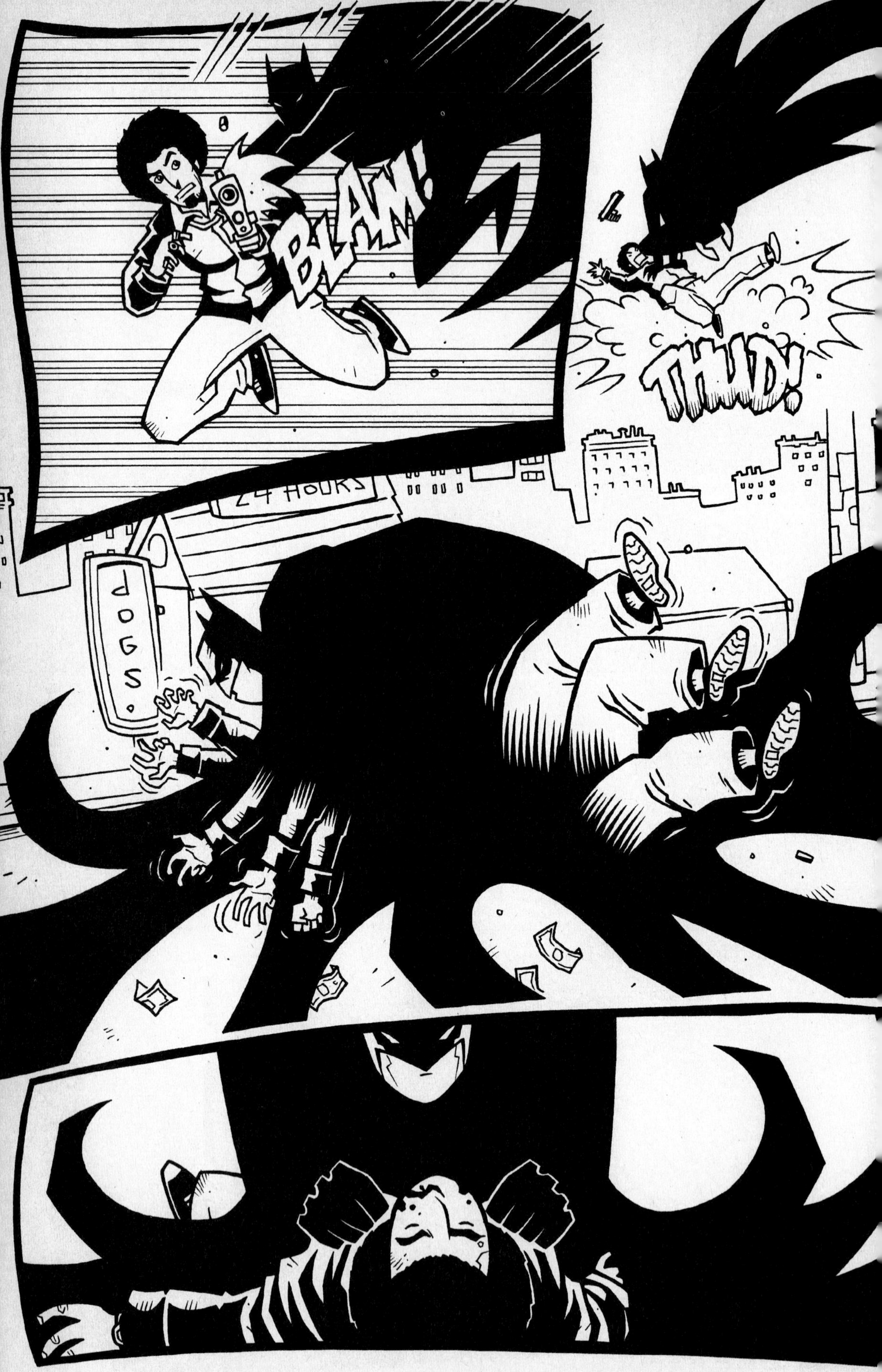
BLAM!
THUD!
24 HOURS
DOGS

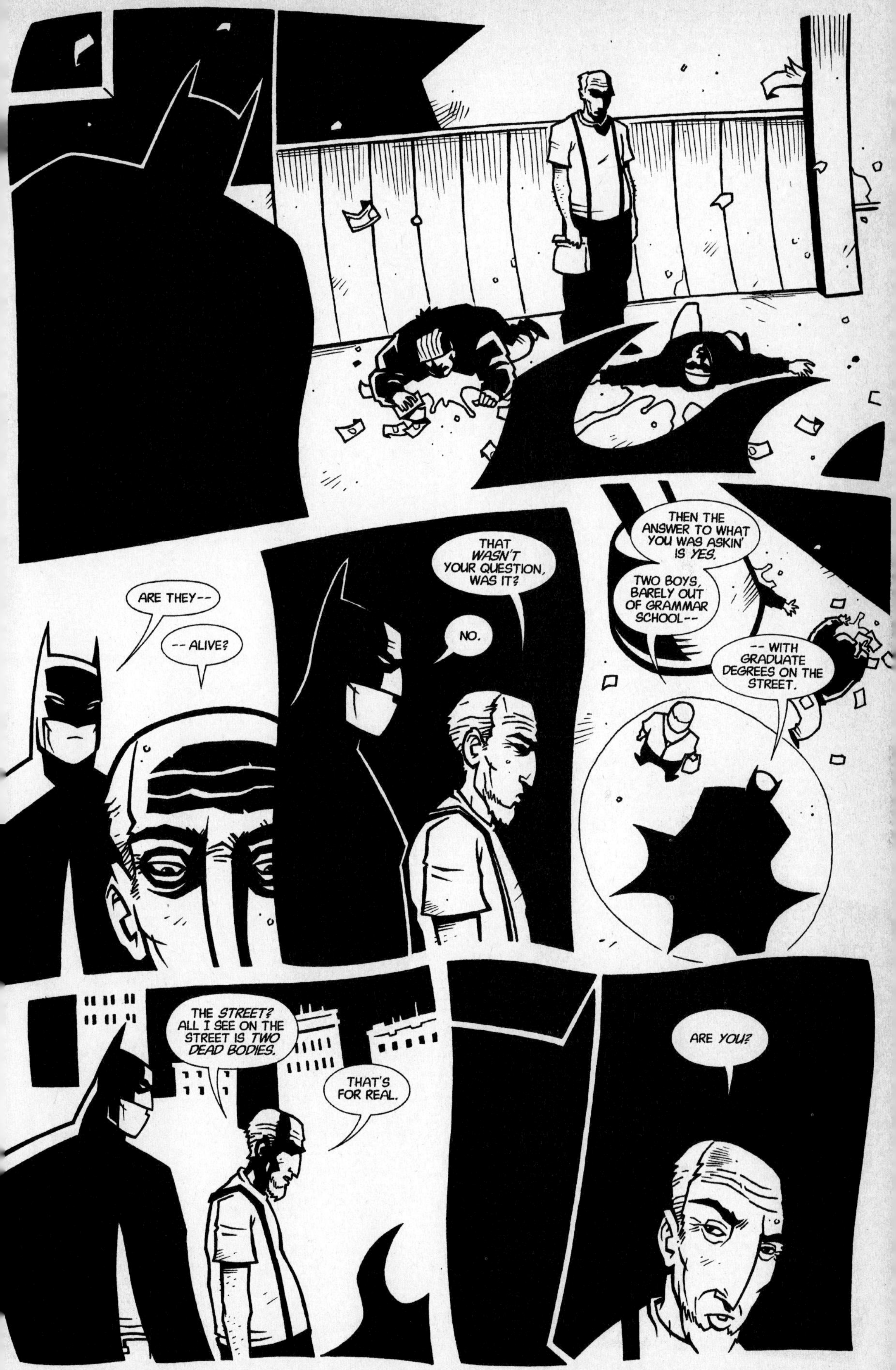
ARE THEY--
--ALIVE?
THAT WASN'T YOUR QUESTION, WAS IT?
NO.
THEN THE ANSWER TO WHAT YOU WAS ASKIN' IS YES.
TWO BOYS, BARELY OUT OF GRAMMAR SCHOOL--
-- WITH GRADUATE DEGREES ON THE STREET.
THE STREET? ALL I SEE ON THE STREET IS TWO DEAD BODIES.
THAT'S FOR REAL.
ARE YOU?

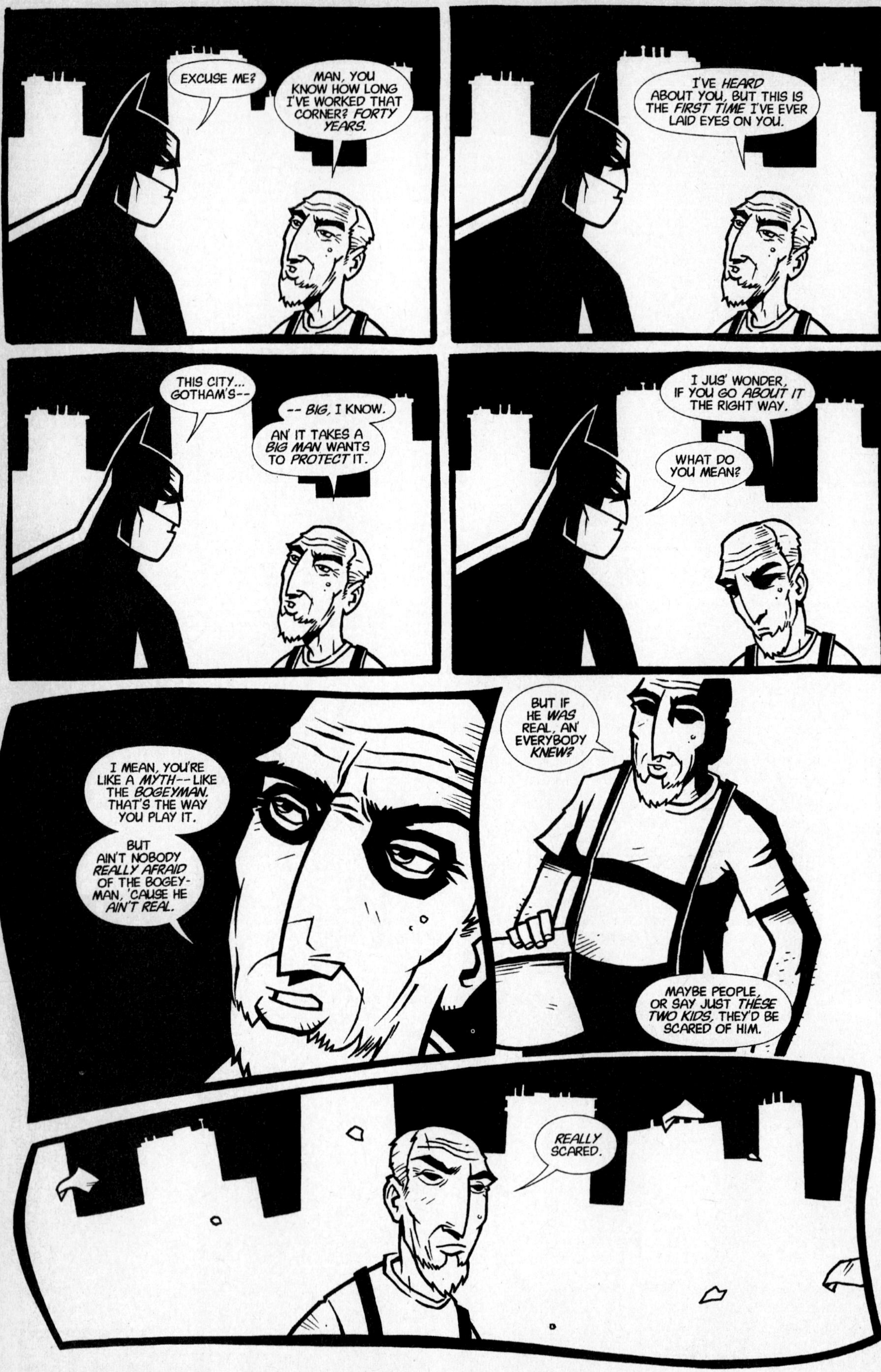
EXCUSE ME?
MAN, YOU KNOW HOW LONG I'VE WORKED THAT CORNER? FORTY YEARS.
I'VE HEARD ABOUT YOU, BUT THIS IS THE FIRST TIME I'VE EVER LAID EYES ON YOU.
THIS CITY... GOTHAM'S--
-- BIG, I KNOW.
AN' IT TAKES A BIG MAN WANTS TO PROTECT IT.
I JUS' WONDER, IF YOU GO ABOUT IT THE RIGHT WAY.
WHAT DO YOU MEAN?
I MEAN, YOU'RE LIKE A MYTH--LIKE THE BOGEYMAN. THAT'S THE WAY YOU PLAY IT.
BUT AIN'T NOBODY REALLY AFRAID OF THE BOGEY-MAN, 'CAUSE HE AIN'T REAL.
BUT IF HE WAS REAL, AN' EVERYBODY KNEW?
MAYBE PEOPLE, OR SAY JUST THESE TWO KIDS, THEY'D BE SCARED OF HIM.
REALLY SCARED.

AN' THEY'D THINK TWICE BEFORE THEY TOOK SOME STUPID CHANCE THAT MEANT THEY'D HAVE TO CROSS HIM.
FOOD FOR THOUGHT.
YOU HUNGRY?

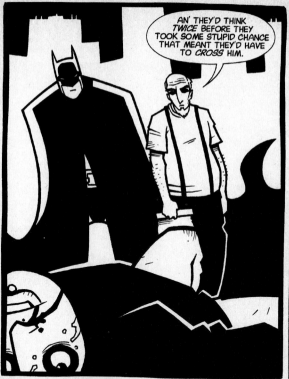

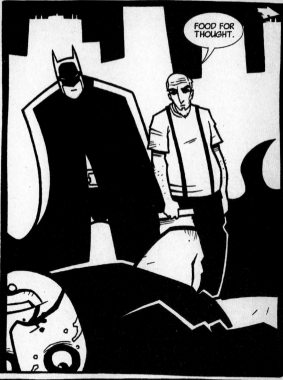

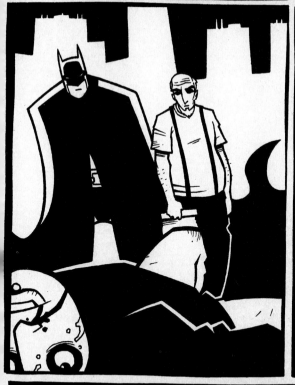

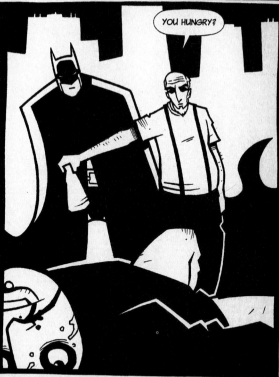

# "cornered"

brian azzarello
writer

jim mahfood
artist

sean konot
letterer

bob schreck
editor

nachie castro
assistant

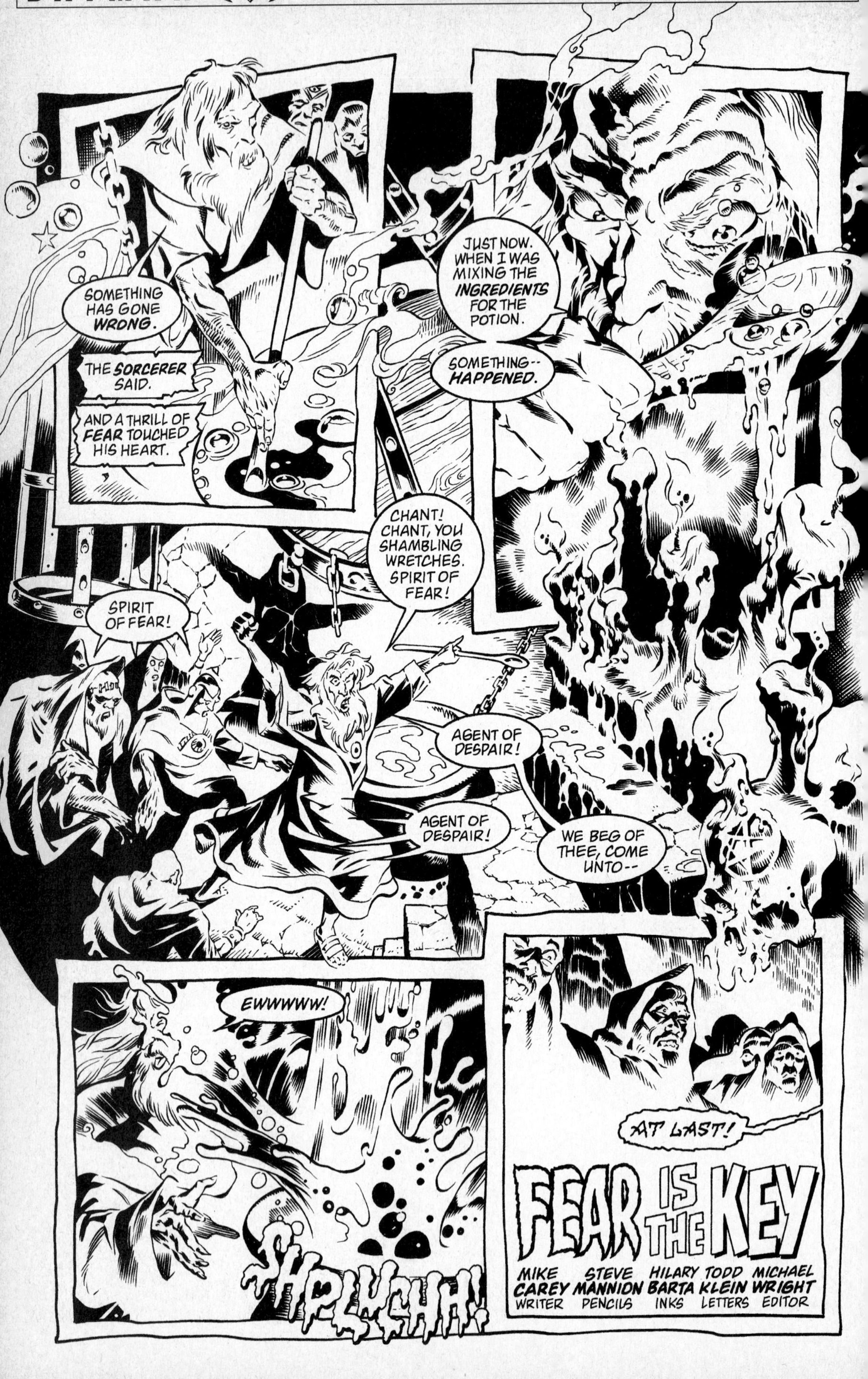
SOMETHING HAS GONE WRONG.
THE SORCERER SAID.
AND A THRILL OF FEAR TOUCHED HIS HEART.
JUST NOW. WHEN I WAS MIXING THE INGREDIENTS FOR THE POTION.
SOMETHING-- HAPPENED.
CHANT! CHANT, YOU SHAMBLING WRETCHES. SPIRIT OF FEAR!
SPIRIT OF FEAR!
AGENT OF DESPAIR!
AGENT OF DESPAIR!
WE BEG OF THEE, COME UNTO--
EWWWWW!
SHPLUCHH!
AT LAST!
FEAR IS THE KEY
MIKE CAREY WRITER
STEVE MANNION PENCILS
HILARY BARTA INKS
TODD KLEIN LETTERS
MICHAEL WRIGHT EDITOR

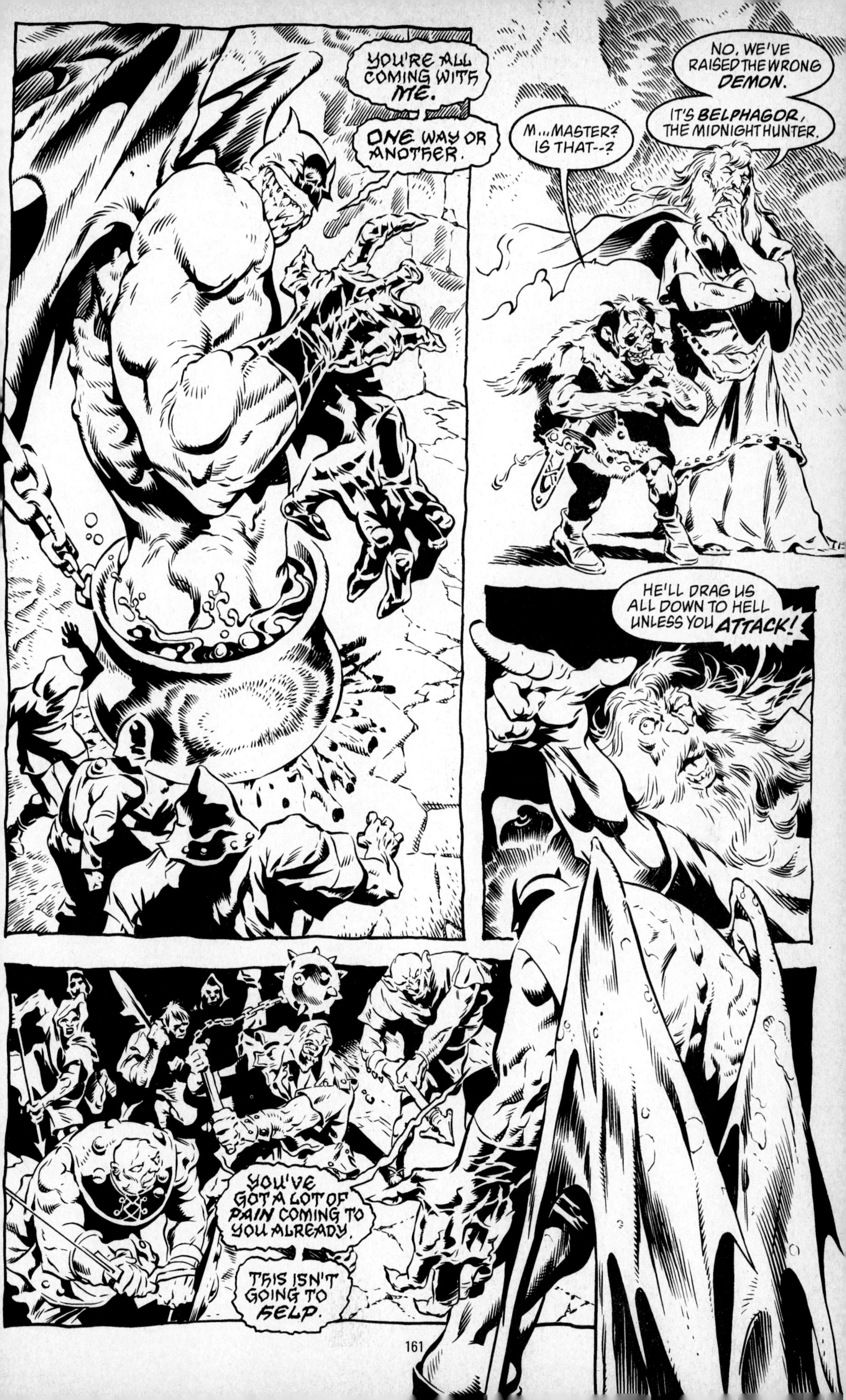

YOU'RE ALL COMING WITH ME.
ONE WAY OR ANOTHER.
M...MASTER? IS THAT--?
NO, WE'VE RAISED THE WRONG DEMON.
IT'S BELPHAGOR, THE MIDNIGHT HUNTER.
HE'LL DRAG US ALL DOWN TO HELL UNLESS YOU ATTACK!
YOU'VE GOT A LOT OF PAIN COMING TO YOU ALREADY.
THIS ISN'T GOING TO HELP.

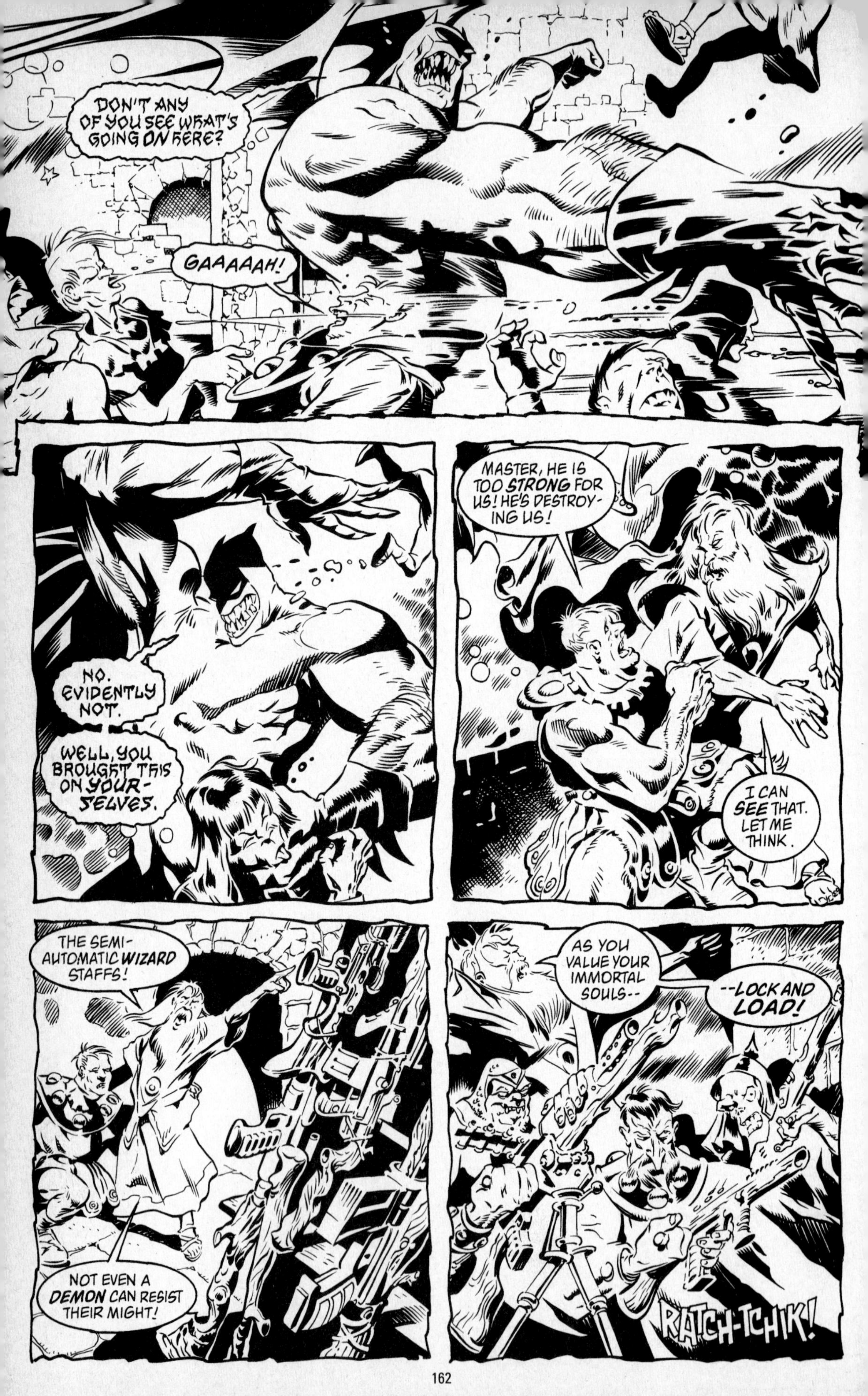
DON'T ANY OF YOU SEE WHAT'S GOING ON HERE?
GAAAAAH!
NO. EVIDENTLY NOT.
WELL, YOU BROUGHT THIS ON YOURSELVES.
MASTER, HE IS TOO STRONG FOR US! HE'S DESTROYING US!
I CAN SEE THAT. LET ME THINK.
THE SEMI-AUTOMATIC WIZARD STAFFS!
NOT EVEN A DEMON CAN RESIST THEIR MIGHT!
AS YOU VALUE YOUR IMMORTAL SOULS--
--LOCK AND LOAD!
RATCH-TCHIK!

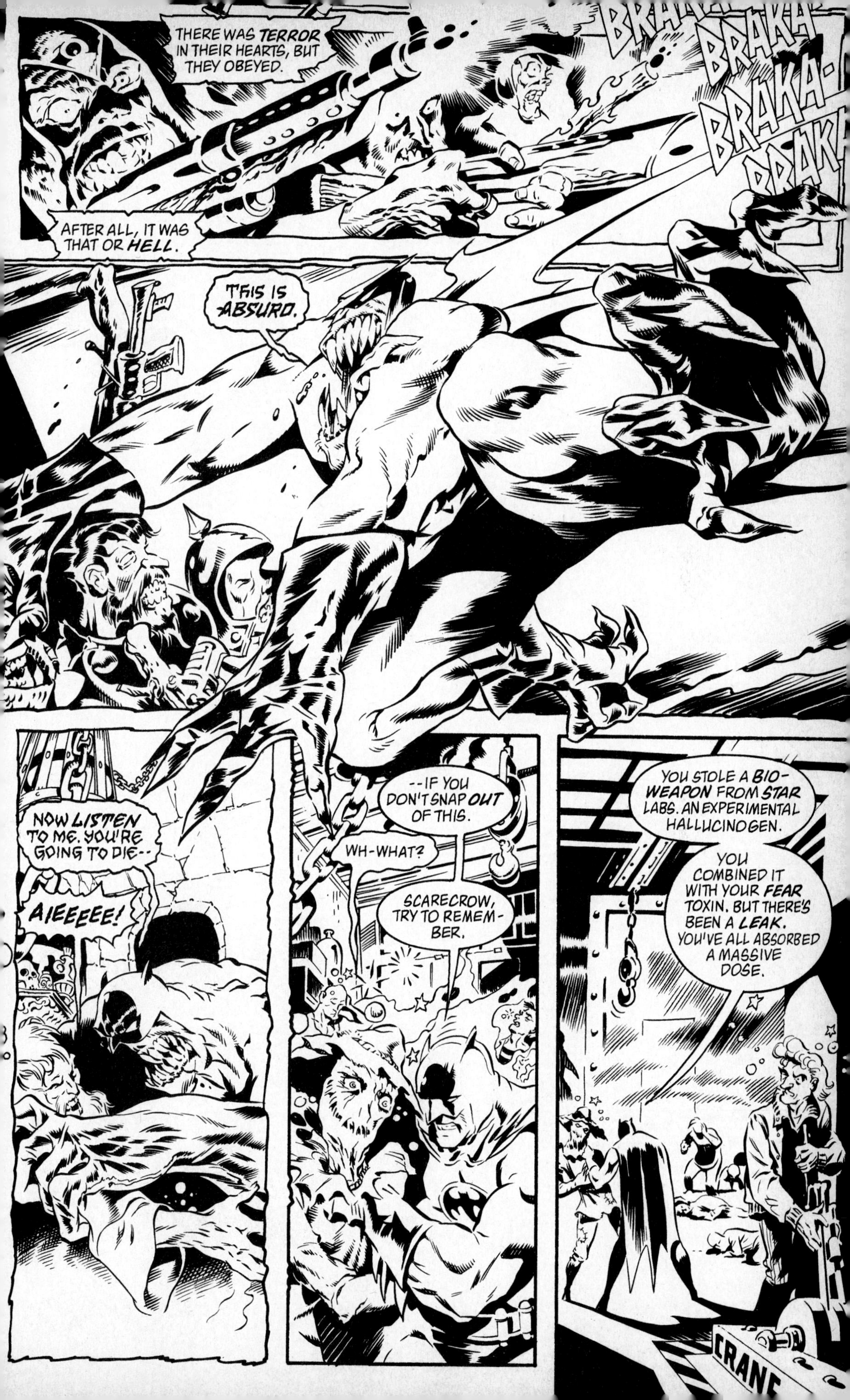

THERE WAS TERROR IN THEIR HEARTS, BUT THEY OBEYED.
BRAKA-
BRAKA-
BRAKA-
BRAKA-
AFTER ALL, IT WAS THAT OR HELL.
T'HIS IS ABSURD.
NOW LISTEN TO ME. YOU'RE GOING TO DIE--
AIEEEEE!
--IF YOU DON'T SNAP OUT OF THIS.
WH-WHAT?
SCARECROW, TRY TO REMEMBER.
YOU STOLE A BIO-WEAPON FROM STAR LABS. AN EXPERIMENTAL HALLUCINOGEN.
YOU COMBINED IT WITH YOUR FEAR TOXIN. BUT THERE'S BEEN A LEAK. YOU'VE ALL ABSORBED A MASSIVE DOSE.
CRANE

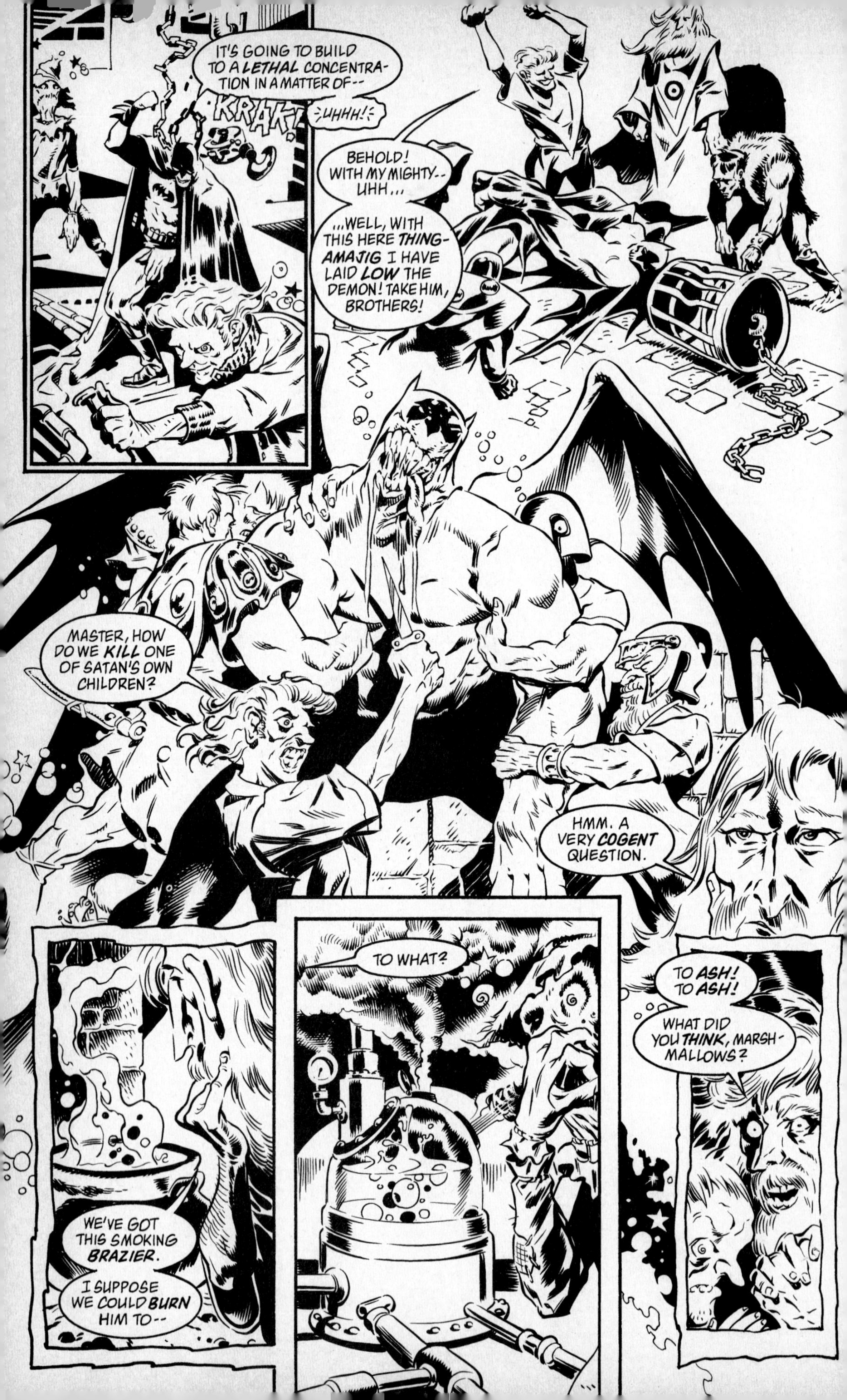
IT'S GOING TO BUILD TO A LETHAL CONCENTRATION IN A MATTER OF--
KRAK!
UHHH!
BEHOLD! WITH MY MIGHTY-- UHH...
...WELL, WITH THIS HERE THINGAMAJIG I HAVE LAID LOW THE DEMON! TAKE HIM, BROTHERS!
MASTER, HOW DO WE KILL ONE OF SATAN'S OWN CHILDREN?
HMM. A VERY COGENT QUESTION.
WE'VE GOT THIS SMOKING BRAZIER.
I SUPPOSE WE COULD BURN HIM TO--
TO WHAT?
TO ASH! TO ASH!
WHAT DID YOU THINK, MARSHMALLOWS?

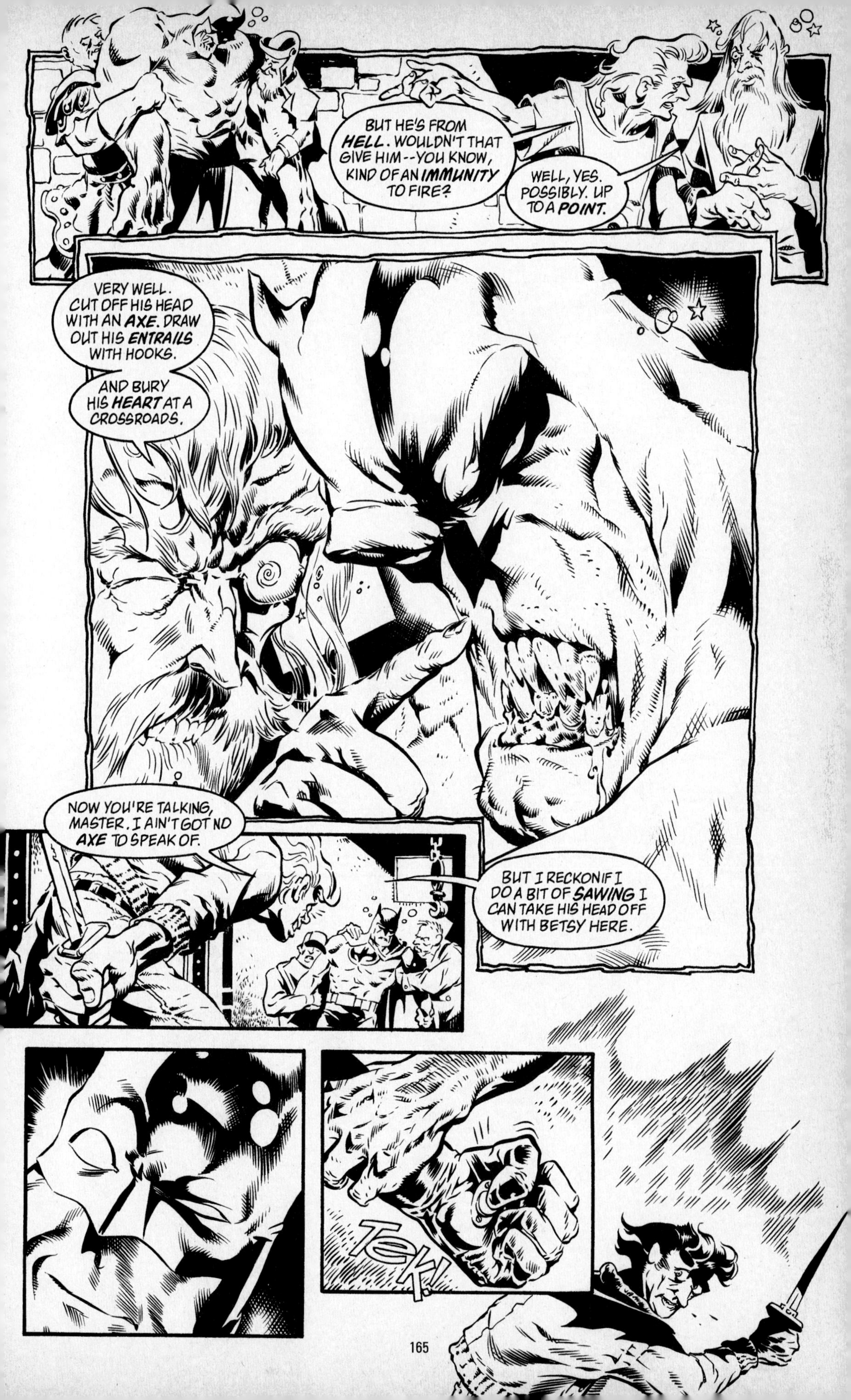
BUT HE'S FROM HELL. WOULDN'T THAT GIVE HIM--YOU KNOW, KIND OF AN IMMUNITY TO FIRE?
WELL, YES. POSSIBLY. UP TO A POINT.
VERY WELL. CUT OFF HIS HEAD WITH AN AXE. DRAW OUT HIS ENTRAILS WITH HOOKS.
AND BURY HIS HEART AT A CROSSROADS.
NOW YOU'RE TALKING, MASTER. I AIN'T GOT NO AXE TO SPEAK OF.
BUT I RECKON IF I DO A BIT OF SAWING I CAN TAKE HIS HEAD OFF WITH BETSY HERE.
TEK!

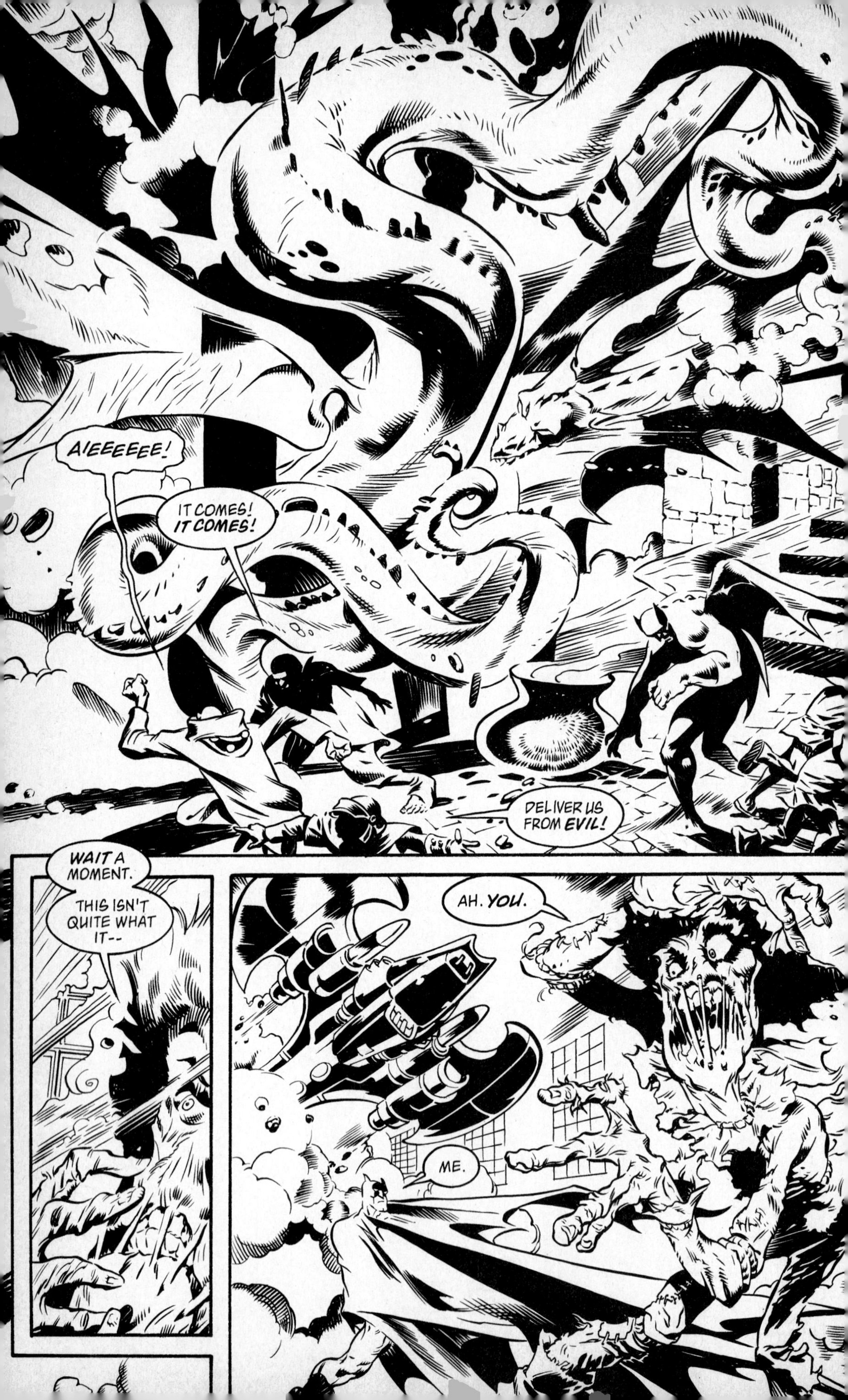
AIEEEEEEE!
IT COMES! IT COMES!
DELIVER US FROM EVIL!
WAIT A MOMENT.
THIS ISN'T QUITE WHAT IT--
AH. YOU.
ME.

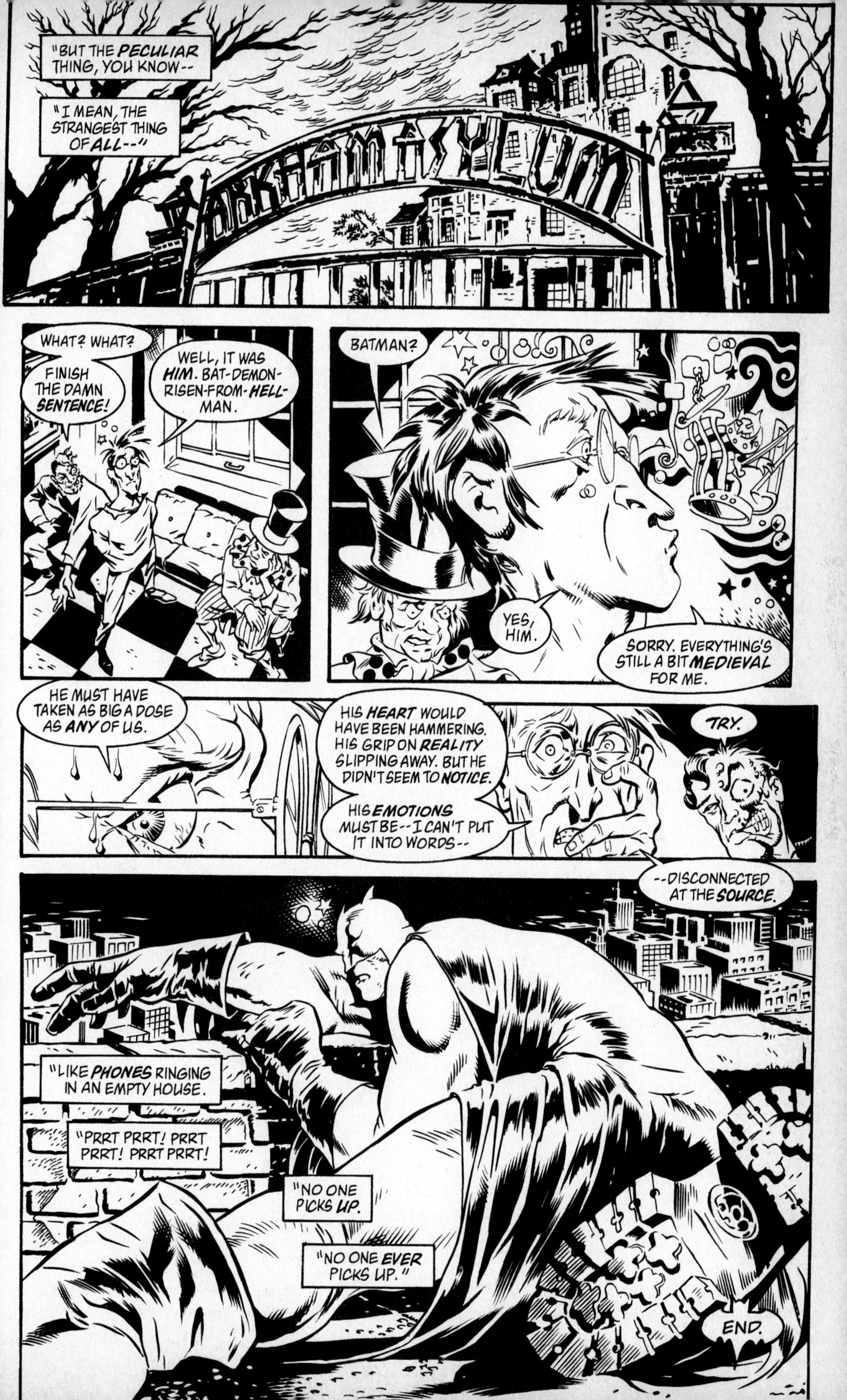
"BUT THE PECULIAR THING, YOU KNOW--
"I MEAN, THE STRANGEST THING OF ALL--"
WHAT? WHAT?
FINISH THE DAMN SENTENCE!
WELL, IT WAS HIM. BAT-DEMON-RISEN-FROM-HELL-MAN.
BATMAN?
YES, HIM.
SORRY. EVERYTHING'S STILL A BIT MEDIEVAL FOR ME.
HE MUST HAVE TAKEN AS BIG A DOSE AS ANY OF US.
HIS HEART WOULD HAVE BEEN HAMMERING. HIS GRIP ON REALITY SLIPPING AWAY. BUT HE DIDN'T SEEM TO NOTICE.
HIS EMOTIONS MUST BE--I CAN'T PUT IT INTO WORDS--
TRY.
--DISCONNECTED AT THE SOURCE.
"LIKE PHONES RINGING IN AN EMPTY HOUSE.
"PRRT PRRT! PRRT PRRT! PRRT PRRT!
"NO ONE PICKS UP.
"NO ONE EVER PICKS UP."
END.

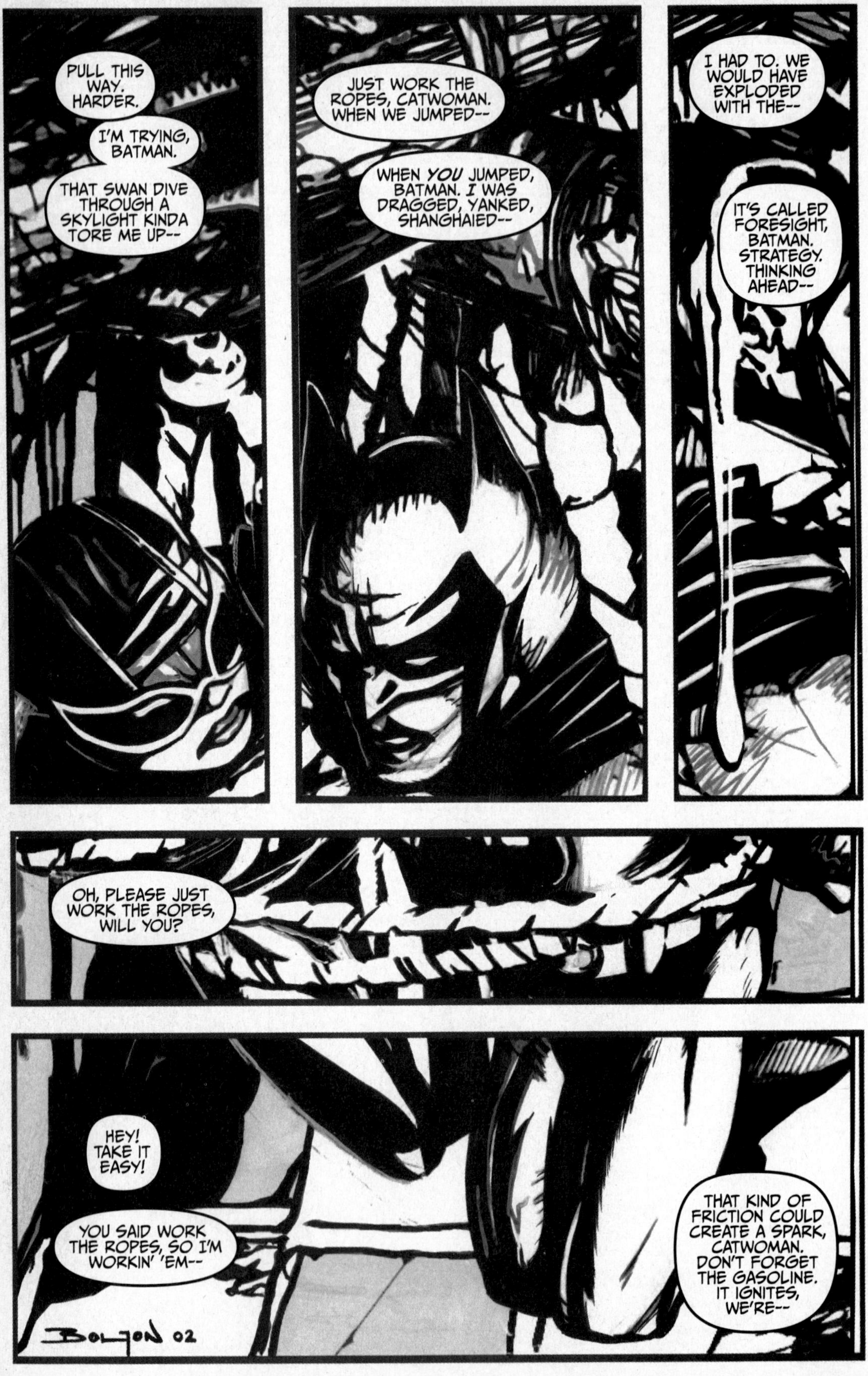
PULL THIS WAY. HARDER.
I'M TRYING, BATMAN.
THAT SWAN DIVE THROUGH A SKYLIGHT KINDA TORE ME UP--
JUST WORK THE ROPES, CATWOMAN. WHEN WE JUMPED--
WHEN YOU JUMPED, BATMAN. I WAS DRAGGED, YANKED, SHANGHAIED--
I HAD TO. WE WOULD HAVE EXPLODED WITH THE--
IT'S CALLED FORESIGHT, BATMAN. STRATEGY. THINKING AHEAD--
OH, PLEASE JUST WORK THE ROPES, WILL YOU?
HEY! TAKE IT EASY!
YOU SAID WORK THE ROPES, SO I'M WORKIN' 'EM--
THAT KIND OF FRICTION COULD CREATE A SPARK, CATWOMAN. DON'T FORGET THE GASOLINE. IT IGNITES, WE'RE--
BOLTON 02

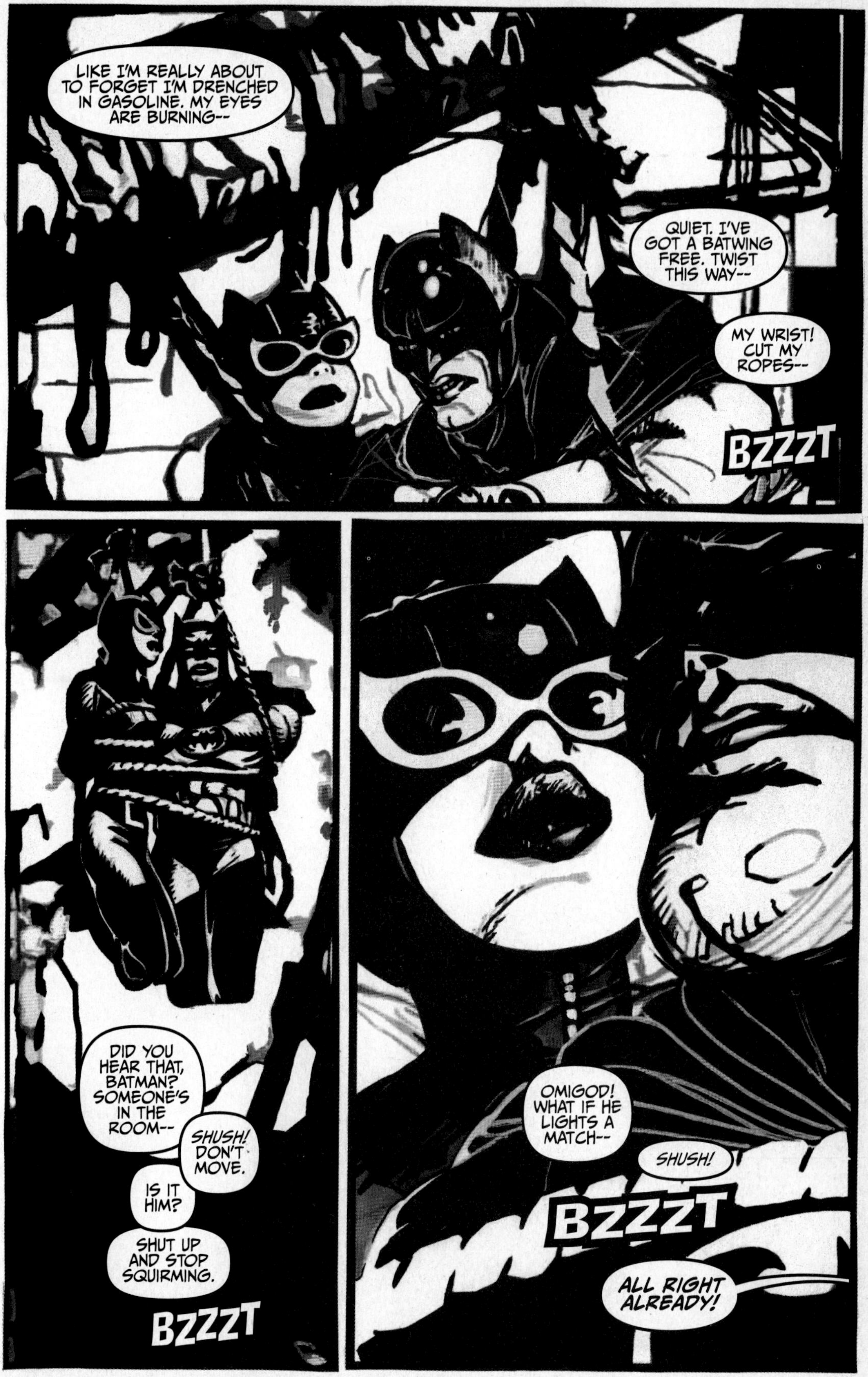
LIKE I'M REALLY ABOUT TO FORGET I'M DRENCHED IN GASOLINE. MY EYES ARE BURNING--
QUIET. I'VE GOT A BATWING FREE. TWIST THIS WAY--
MY WRIST! CUT MY ROPES--
BZZZT
DID YOU HEAR THAT, BATMAN? SOMEONE'S IN THE ROOM--
SHUSH! DON'T MOVE.
IS IT HIM?
SHUT UP AND STOP SQUIRMING.
BZZZT
OMIGOD! WHAT IF HE LIGHTS A MATCH--
SHUSH!
BZZZT
ALL RIGHT ALREADY!

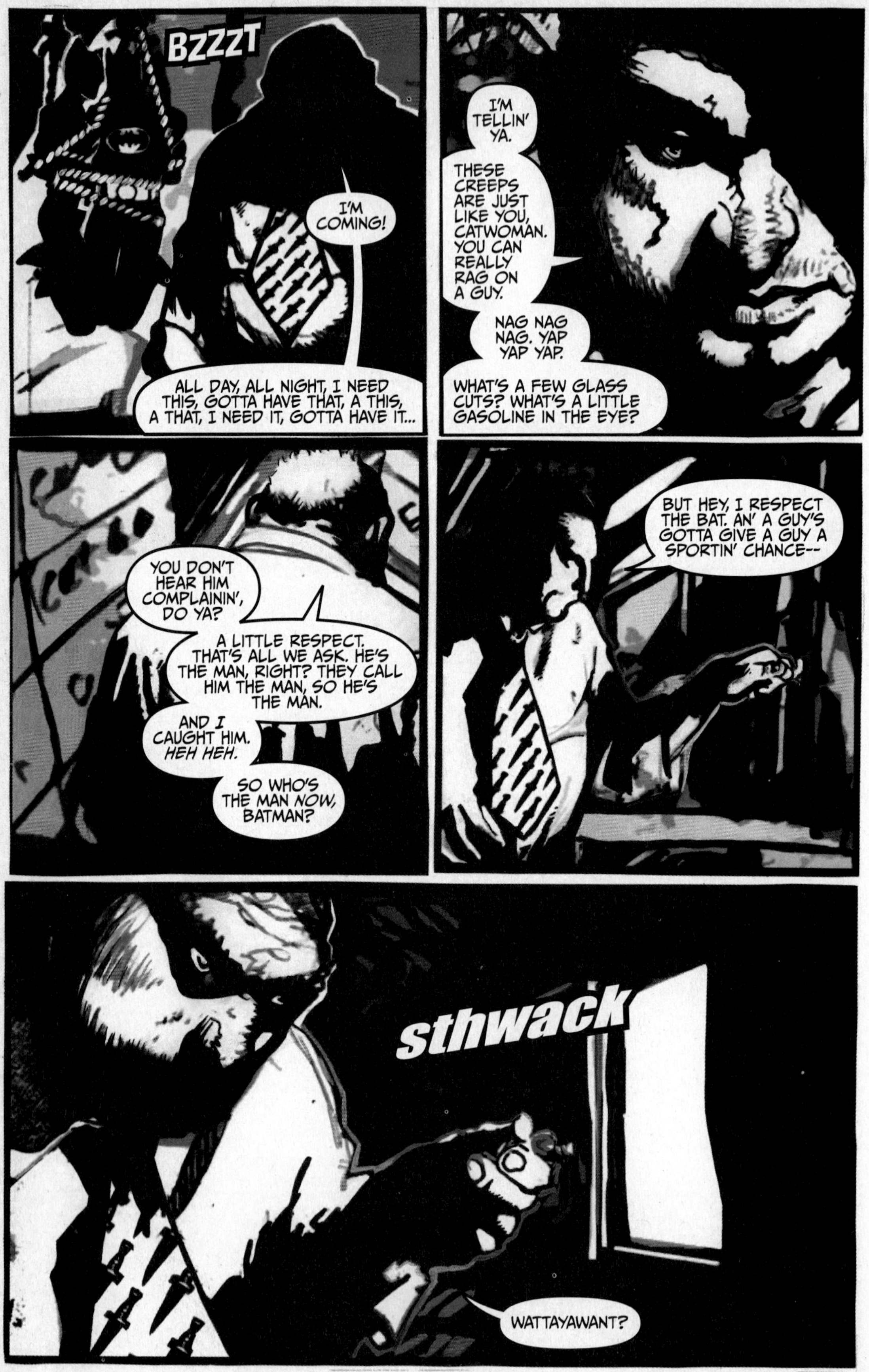

BZZZT
I'M COMING!
ALL DAY, ALL NIGHT, I NEED THIS, GOTTA HAVE THAT, A THIS, A THAT, I NEED IT, GOTTA HAVE IT...
I'M TELLIN' YA.
THESE CREEPS ARE JUST LIKE YOU, CATWOMAN. YOU CAN REALLY RAG ON A GUY.
NAG NAG NAG. YAP YAP YAP.
WHAT'S A FEW GLASS CUTS? WHAT'S A LITTLE GASOLINE IN THE EYE?
YOU DON'T HEAR HIM COMPLAININ', DO YA?
A LITTLE RESPECT. THAT'S ALL WE ASK. HE'S THE MAN, RIGHT? THEY CALL HIM THE MAN, SO HE'S THE MAN.
AND *I* CAUGHT HIM. *HEH HEH.*
SO WHO'S THE MAN *NOW*, BATMAN?
BUT HEY, I RESPECT THE BAT. AN' A GUY'S GOTTA GIVE A GUY A SPORTIN' CHANCE--
sthwack
WATTAYAWANT?

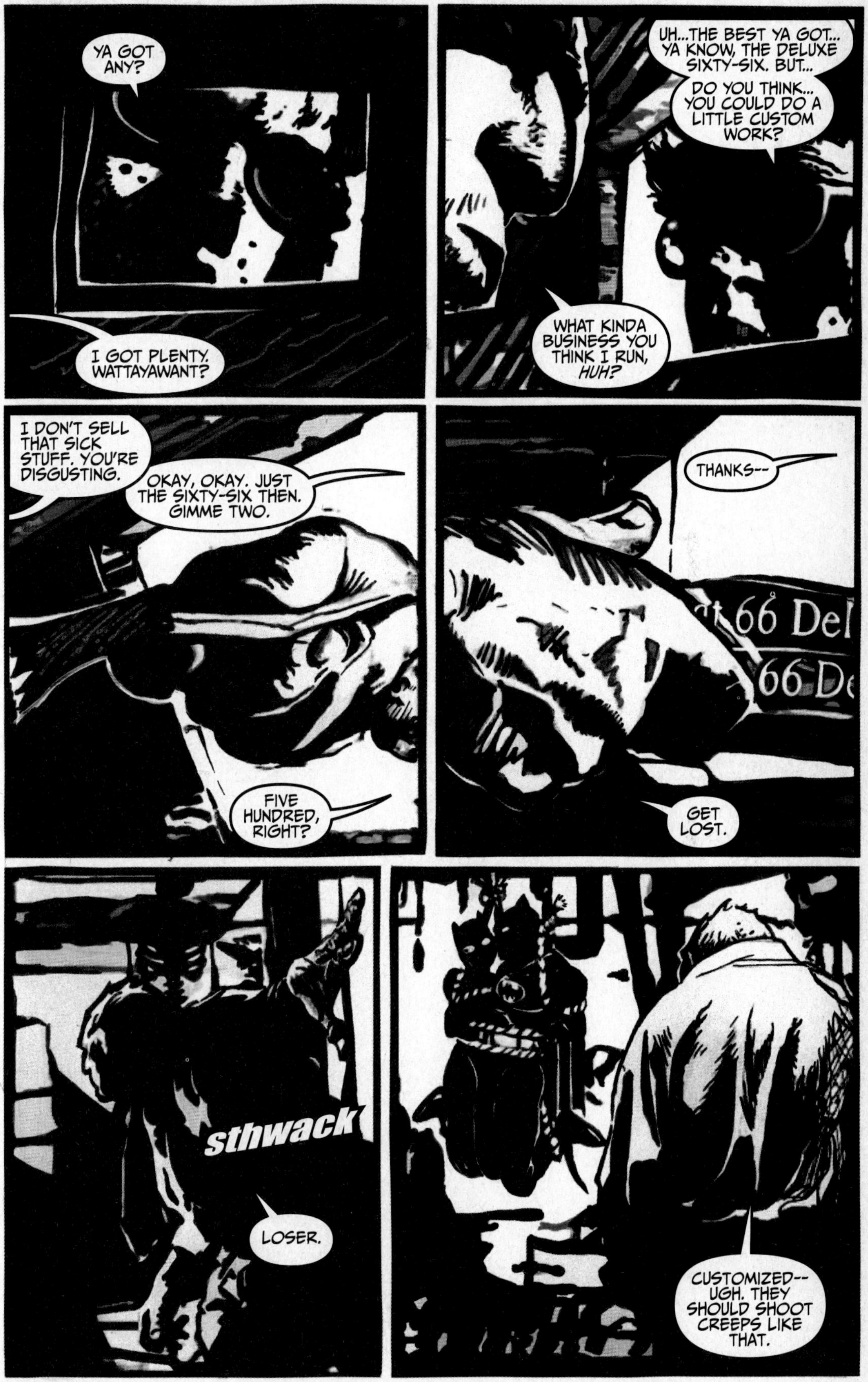
YA GOT ANY?
I GOT PLENTY. WATTAYAWANT?
UH...THE BEST YA GOT... YA KNOW, THE DELUXE SIXTY-SIX. BUT...
DO YOU THINK... YOU COULD DO A LITTLE CUSTOM WORK?
WHAT KINDA BUSINESS YOU THINK I RUN, *HUH?*
I DON'T SELL THAT SICK STUFF. YOU'RE DISGUSTING.
OKAY, OKAY. JUST THE SIXTY-SIX THEN. GIMME TWO.
FIVE HUNDRED, RIGHT?
THANKS--
66 Del
66 De
GET LOST.
sthwack
LOSER.
CUSTOMIZED-- UGH. THEY SHOULD SHOOT CREEPS LIKE THAT.

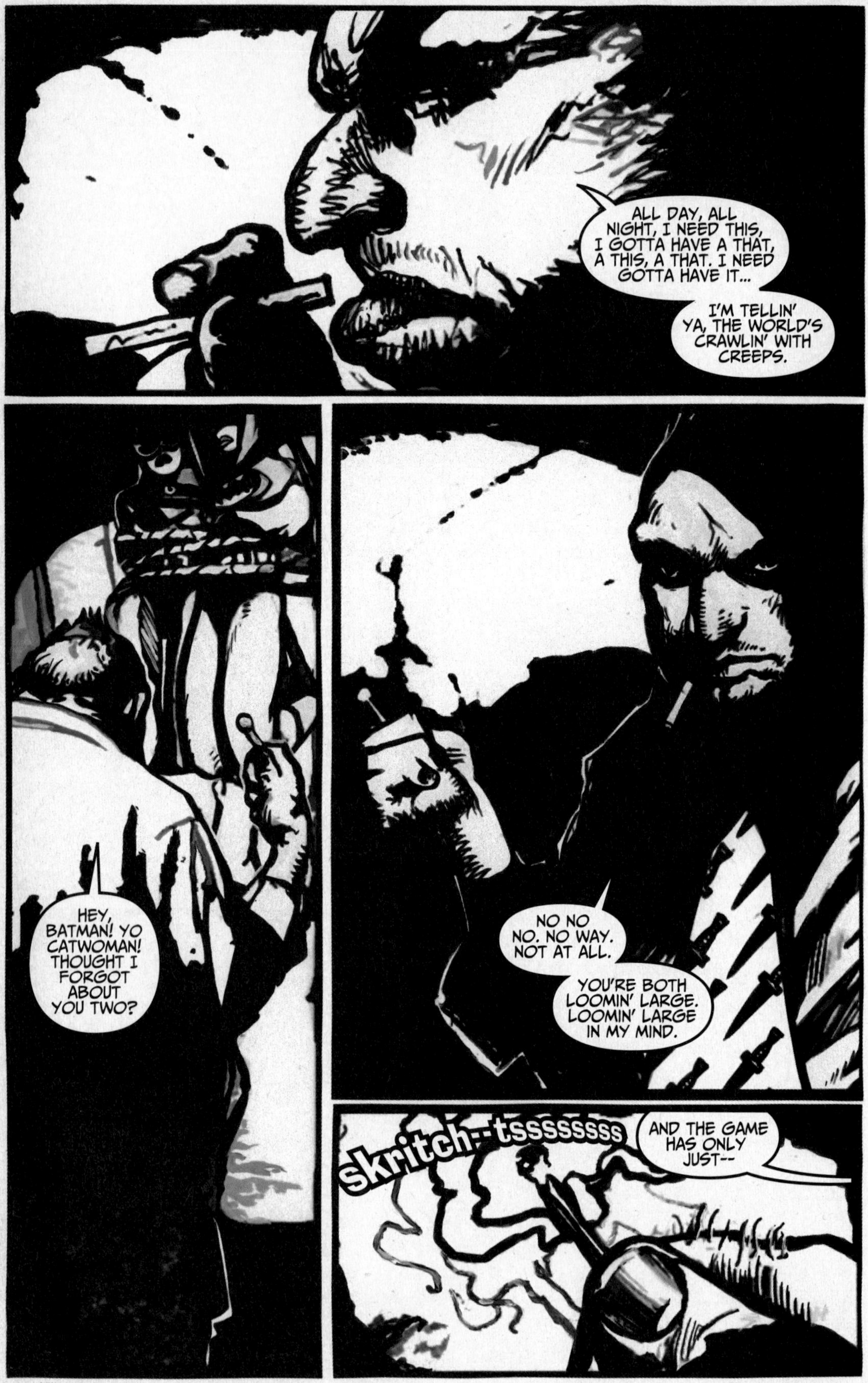
ALL DAY, ALL NIGHT, I NEED THIS, I GOTTA HAVE A THAT, A THIS, A THAT. I NEED GOTTA HAVE IT...
I'M TELLIN' YA, THE WORLD'S CRAWLIN' WITH CREEPS.
HEY, BATMAN! YO CATWOMAN! THOUGHT I FORGOT ABOUT YOU TWO?
NO NO NO. NO WAY. NOT AT ALL.
YOU'RE BOTH LOOMIN' LARGE. LOOMIN' LARGE IN MY MIND.
skritch--tssssssss
AND THE GAME HAS ONLY JUST--

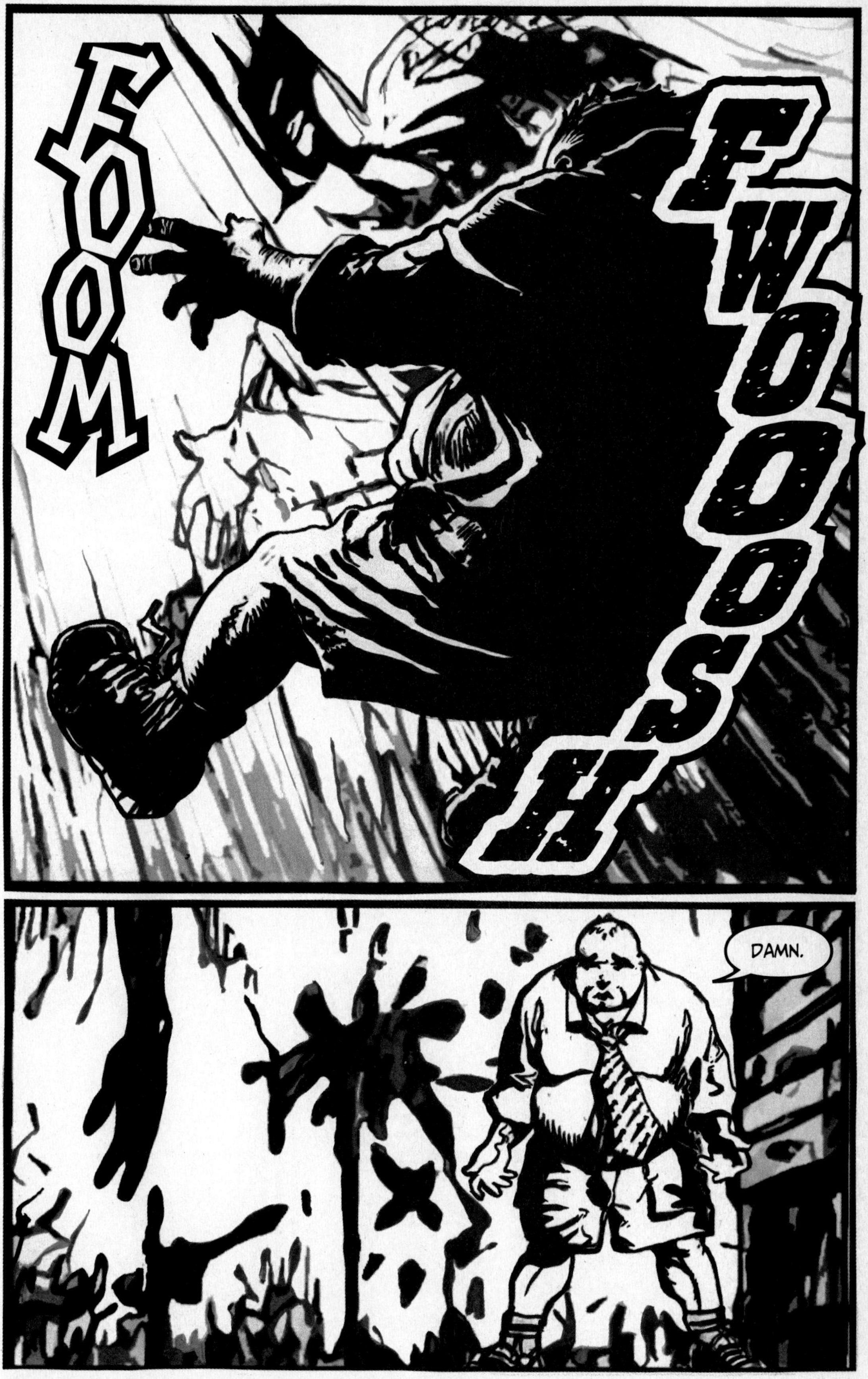
FOOOM
FWOOOOSH
DAMN.

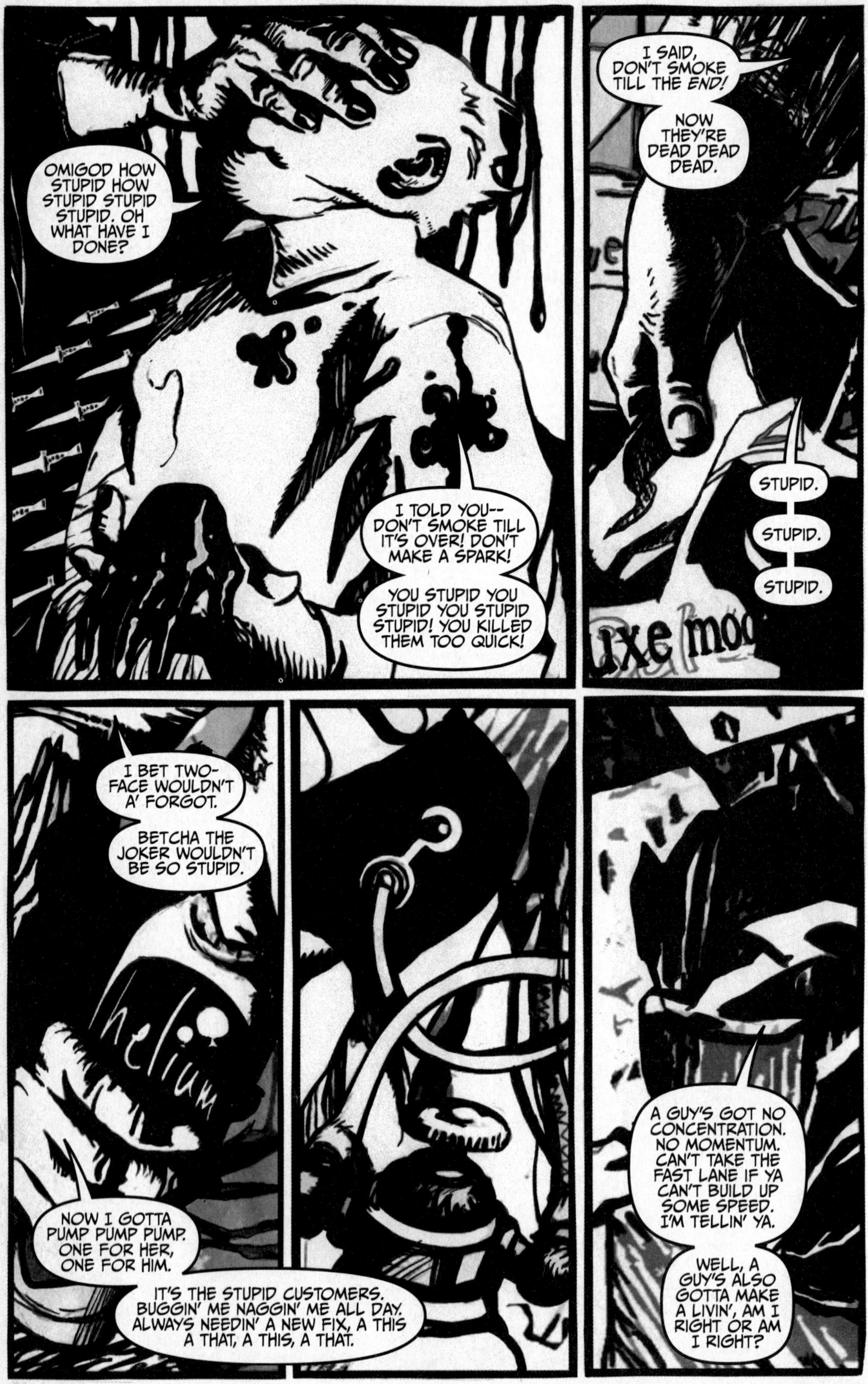
OMIGOD HOW STUPID HOW STUPID STUPID STUPID. OH WHAT HAVE I DONE?
I TOLD YOU-- DON'T SMOKE TILL IT'S OVER! DON'T MAKE A SPARK!
YOU STUPID YOU STUPID YOU STUPID STUPID! YOU KILLED THEM TOO QUICK!
I SAID, DON'T SMOKE TILL THE END!
NOW THEY'RE DEAD DEAD DEAD.
STUPID.
STUPID.
STUPID.
I BET TWO-FACE WOULDN'T A' FORGOT.
BETCHA THE JOKER WOULDN'T BE SO STUPID.
helium
NOW I GOTTA PUMP PUMP PUMP. ONE FOR HER, ONE FOR HIM.
IT'S THE STUPID CUSTOMERS. BUGGIN' ME NAGGIN' ME ALL DAY. ALWAYS NEEDIN' A NEW FIX, A THIS A THAT, A THIS, A THAT.
A GUY'S GOT NO CONCENTRATION. NO MOMENTUM. CAN'T TAKE THE FAST LANE IF YA CAN'T BUILD UP SOME SPEED. I'M TELLIN' YA.
WELL, A GUY'S ALSO GOTTA MAKE A LIVIN', AM I RIGHT OR AM I RIGHT?

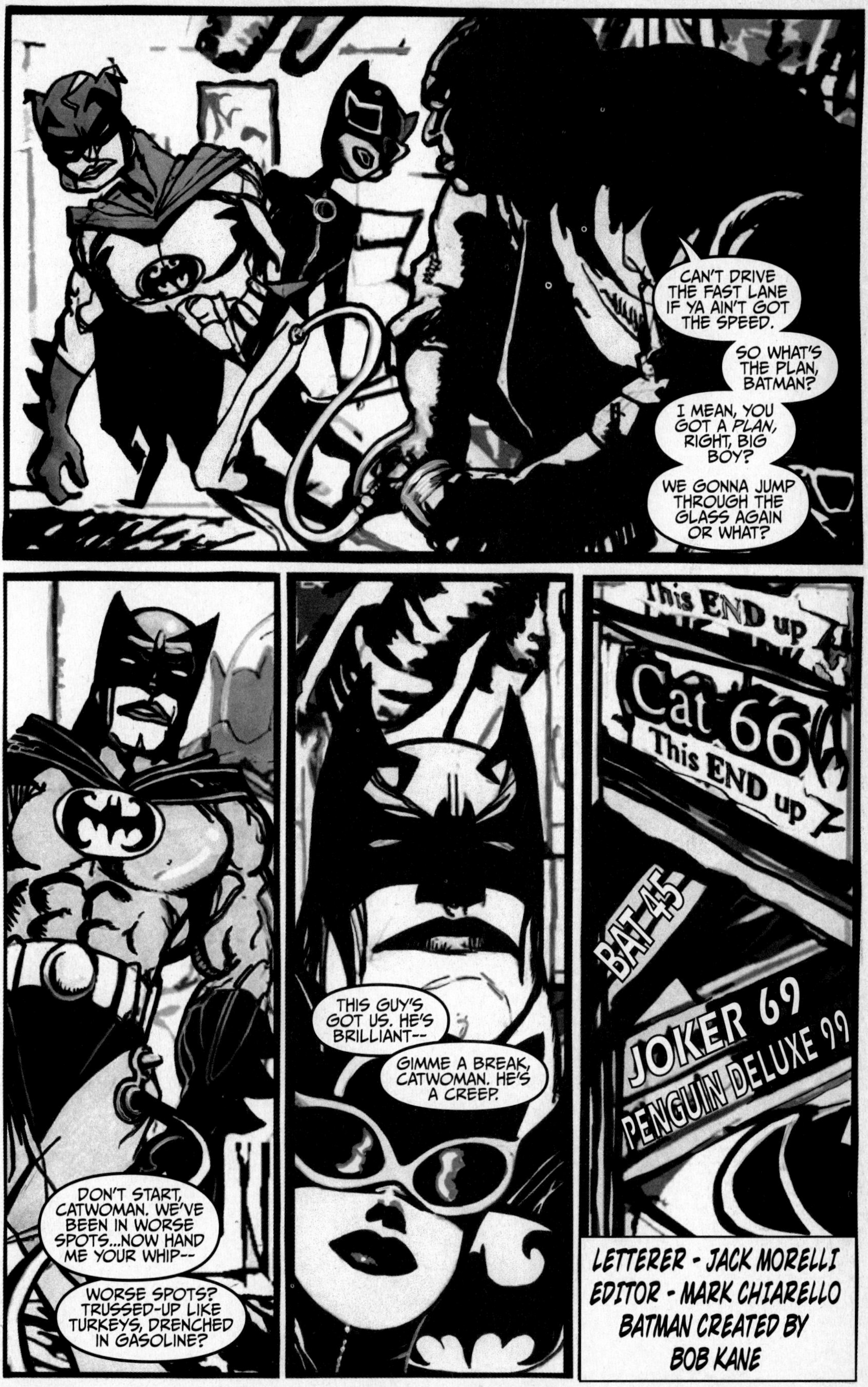
CAN'T DRIVE THE FAST LANE IF YA AIN'T GOT THE SPEED.
SO WHAT'S THE PLAN, BATMAN?
I MEAN, YOU GOT A *PLAN*, RIGHT, BIG BOY?
WE GONNA JUMP THROUGH THE GLASS AGAIN OR WHAT?
DON'T START, CATWOMAN. WE'VE BEEN IN WORSE SPOTS...NOW HAND ME YOUR WHIP--
WORSE SPOTS? TRUSSED-UP LIKE TURKEYS, DRENCHED IN GASOLINE?
THIS GUY'S GOT US. HE'S BRILLIANT--
GIMME A BREAK, CATWOMAN. HE'S A CREEP.
This END up
Cat 66
This END up
BAT 45
JOKER 69
PENGUIN DELUXE 99
LETTERER - JACK MORELLI
EDITOR - MARK CHIARELLO
BATMAN CREATED BY
BOB KANE

STORY BY ANN NOCENTI ART BY JOHN BOLTON

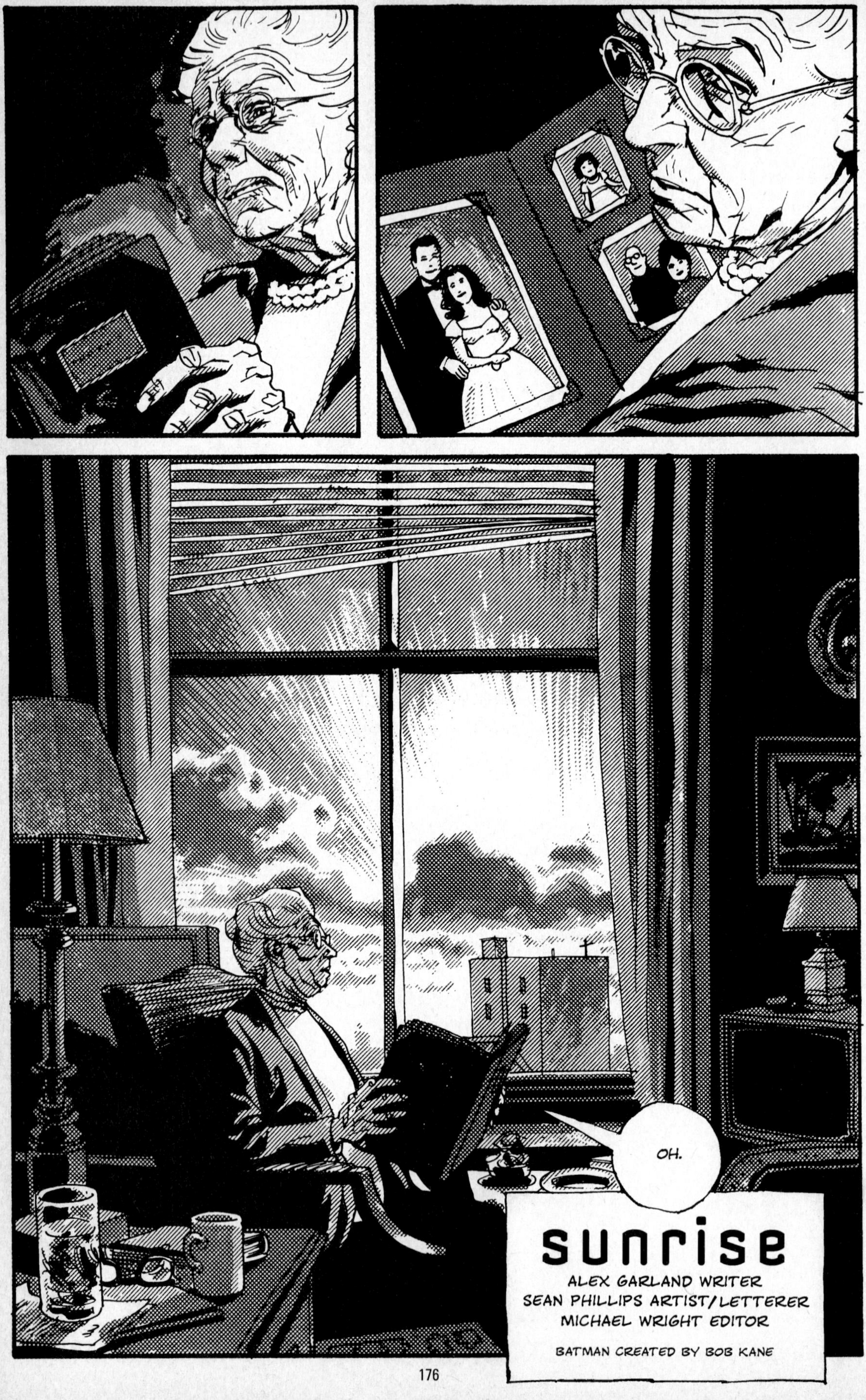
OH.
sunrise
ALEX GARLAND WRITER
SEAN PHILLIPS ARTIST/LETTERER
MICHAEL WRIGHT EDITOR
BATMAN CREATED BY BOB KANE

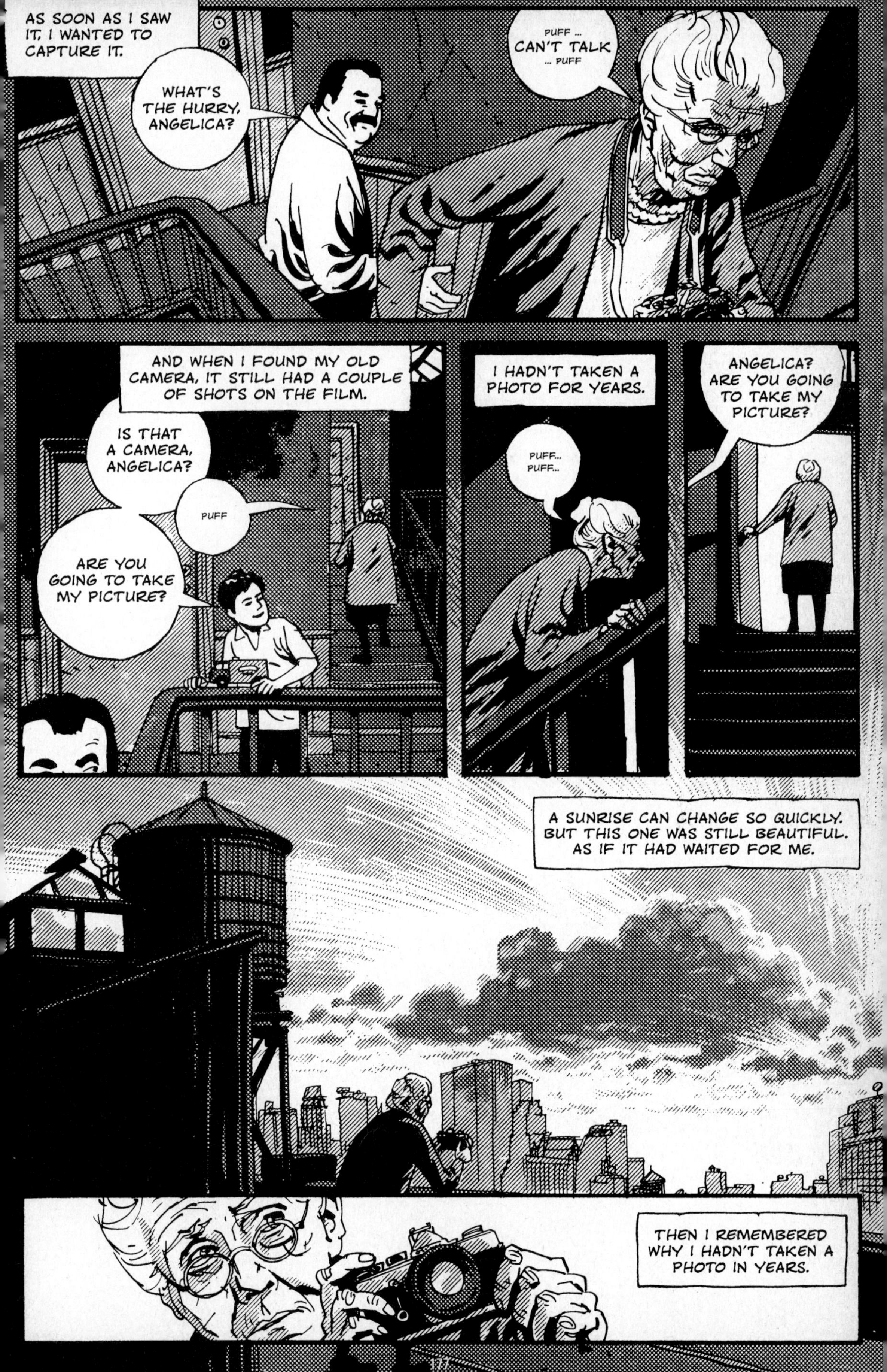
AS SOON AS I SAW IT, I WANTED TO CAPTURE IT.
WHAT'S THE HURRY, ANGELICA?
PUFF ... CAN'T TALK ... PUFF
AND WHEN I FOUND MY OLD CAMERA, IT STILL HAD A COUPLE OF SHOTS ON THE FILM.
IS THAT A CAMERA, ANGELICA?
PUFF
ARE YOU GOING TO TAKE MY PICTURE?
I HADN'T TAKEN A PHOTO FOR YEARS.
PUFF... PUFF...
ANGELICA? ARE YOU GOING TO TAKE MY PICTURE?
A SUNRISE CAN CHANGE SO QUICKLY. BUT THIS ONE WAS STILL BEAUTIFUL. AS IF IT HAD WAITED FOR ME.
THEN I REMEMBERED WHY I HADN'T TAKEN A PHOTO IN YEARS.

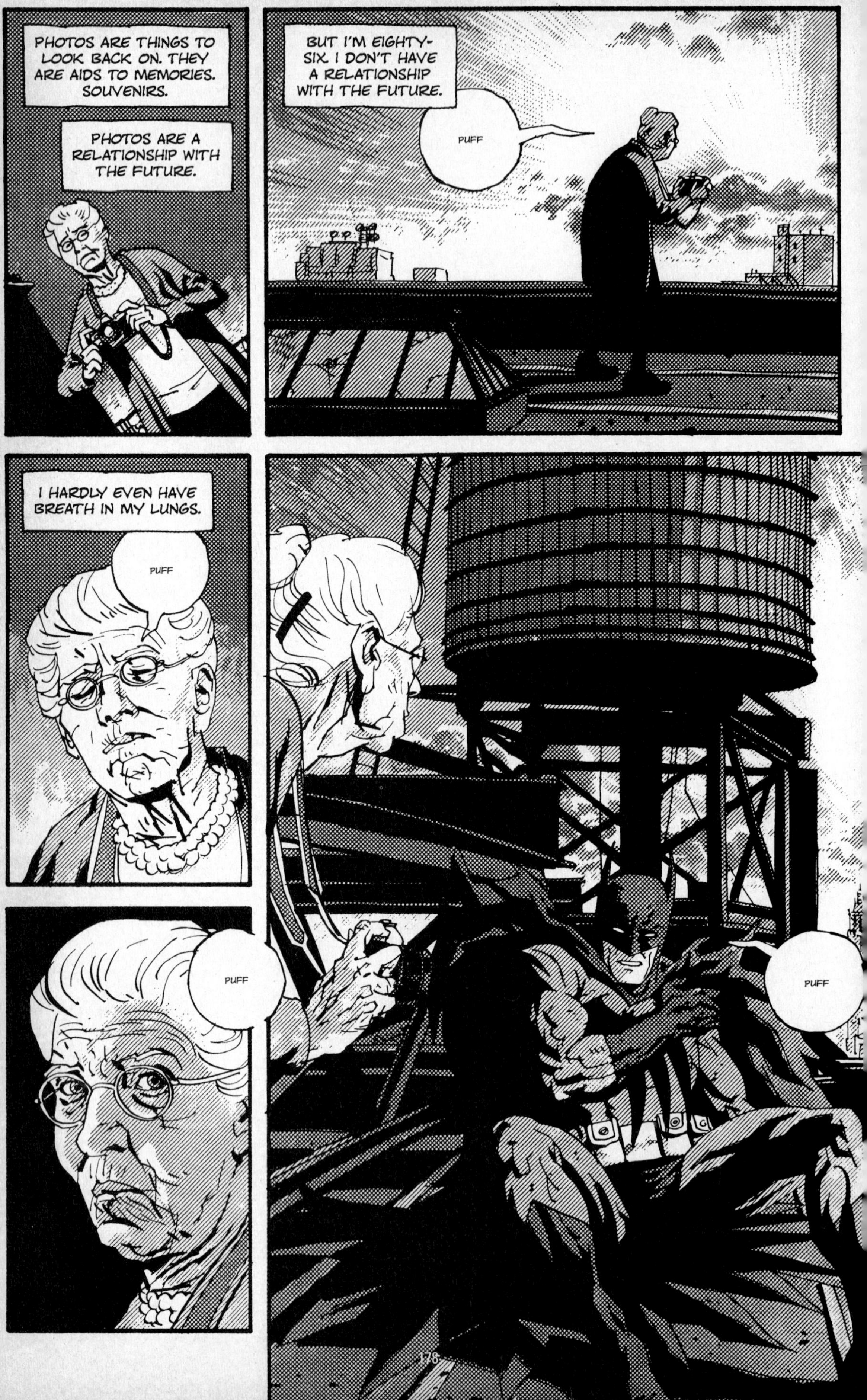
PHOTOS ARE THINGS TO LOOK BACK ON. THEY ARE AIDS TO MEMORIES. SOUVENIRS.
PHOTOS ARE A RELATIONSHIP WITH THE FUTURE.
BUT I'M EIGHTY-SIX. I DON'T HAVE A RELATIONSHIP WITH THE FUTURE.
PUFF
I HARDLY EVEN HAVE BREATH IN MY LUNGS.
PUFF
PUFF
PUFF

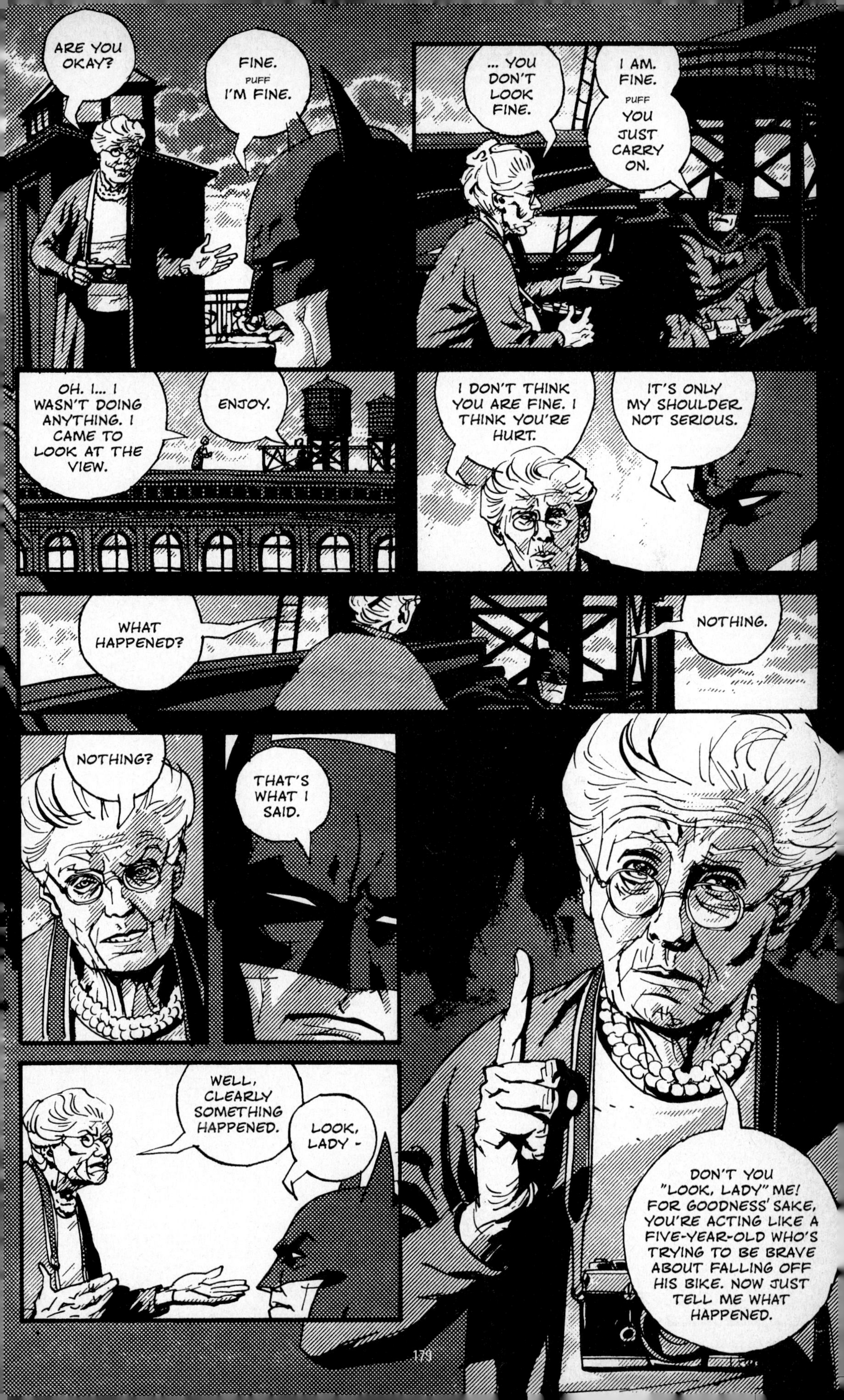
ARE YOU OKAY?
FINE. PUFF I'M FINE.
... YOU DON'T LOOK FINE.
I AM. FINE.
PUFF YOU JUST CARRY ON.
OH. I... I WASN'T DOING ANYTHING. I CAME TO LOOK AT THE VIEW.
ENJOY.
I DON'T THINK YOU ARE FINE. I THINK YOU'RE HURT.
IT'S ONLY MY SHOULDER NOT SERIOUS.
WHAT HAPPENED?
NOTHING.
NOTHING?
THAT'S WHAT I SAID.
WELL, CLEARLY SOMETHING HAPPENED.
LOOK, LADY -
DON'T YOU "LOOK, LADY" ME! FOR GOODNESS' SAKE, YOU'RE ACTING LIKE A FIVE-YEAR-OLD WHO'S TRYING TO BE BRAVE ABOUT FALLING OFF HIS BIKE. NOW JUST TELL ME WHAT HAPPENED.

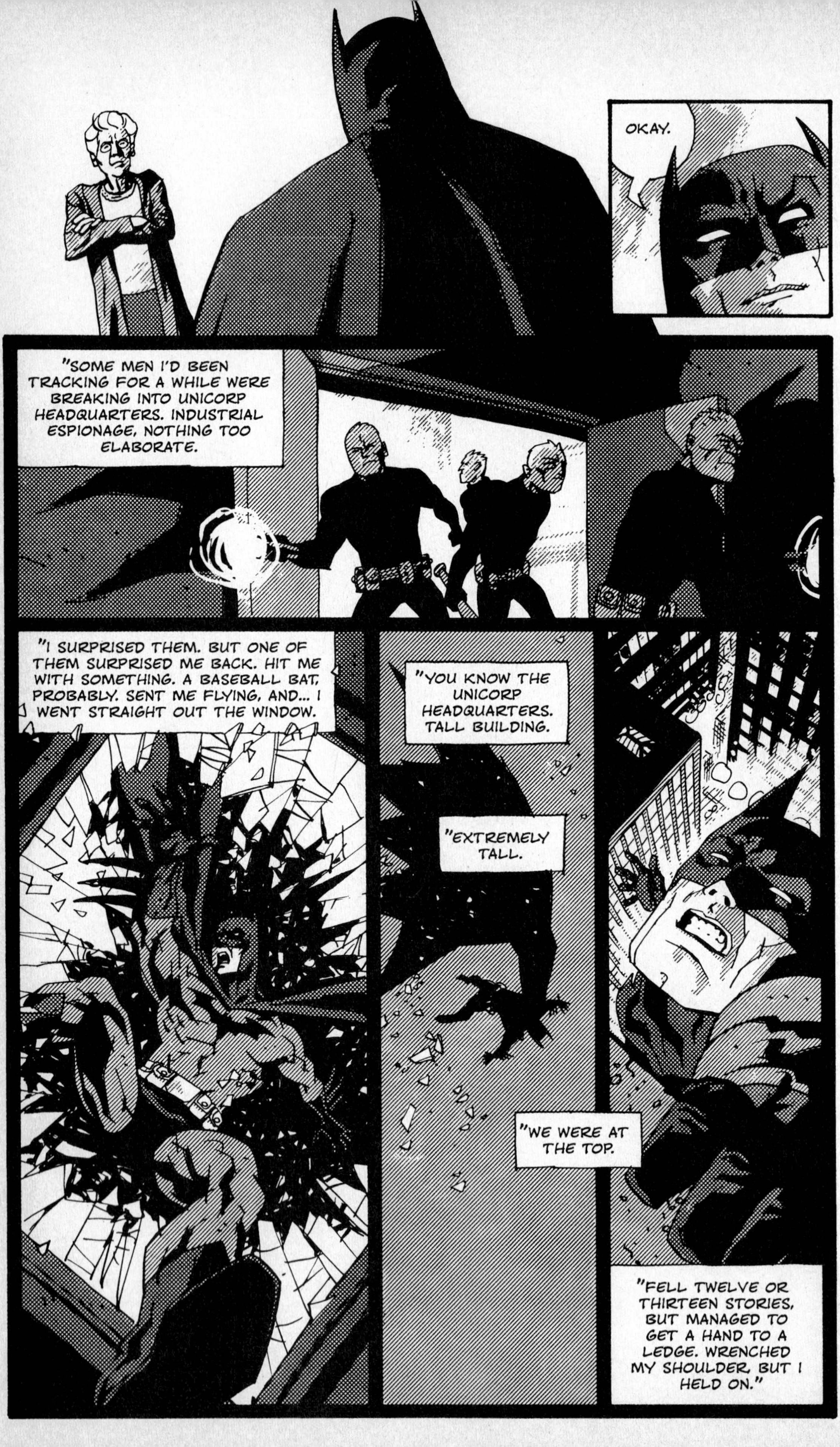
OKAY.
"SOME MEN I'D BEEN TRACKING FOR A WHILE WERE BREAKING INTO UNICORP HEADQUARTERS. INDUSTRIAL ESPIONAGE, NOTHING TOO ELABORATE.
"I SURPRISED THEM. BUT ONE OF THEM SURPRISED ME BACK. HIT ME WITH SOMETHING. A BASEBALL BAT, PROBABLY. SENT ME FLYING, AND... I WENT STRAIGHT OUT THE WINDOW.
"YOU KNOW THE UNICORP HEADQUARTERS. TALL BUILDING.
"EXTREMELY TALL.
"WE WERE AT THE TOP.
"FELL TWELVE OR THIRTEEN STORIES, BUT MANAGED TO GET A HAND TO A LEDGE. WRENCHED MY SHOULDER, BUT I HELD ON."

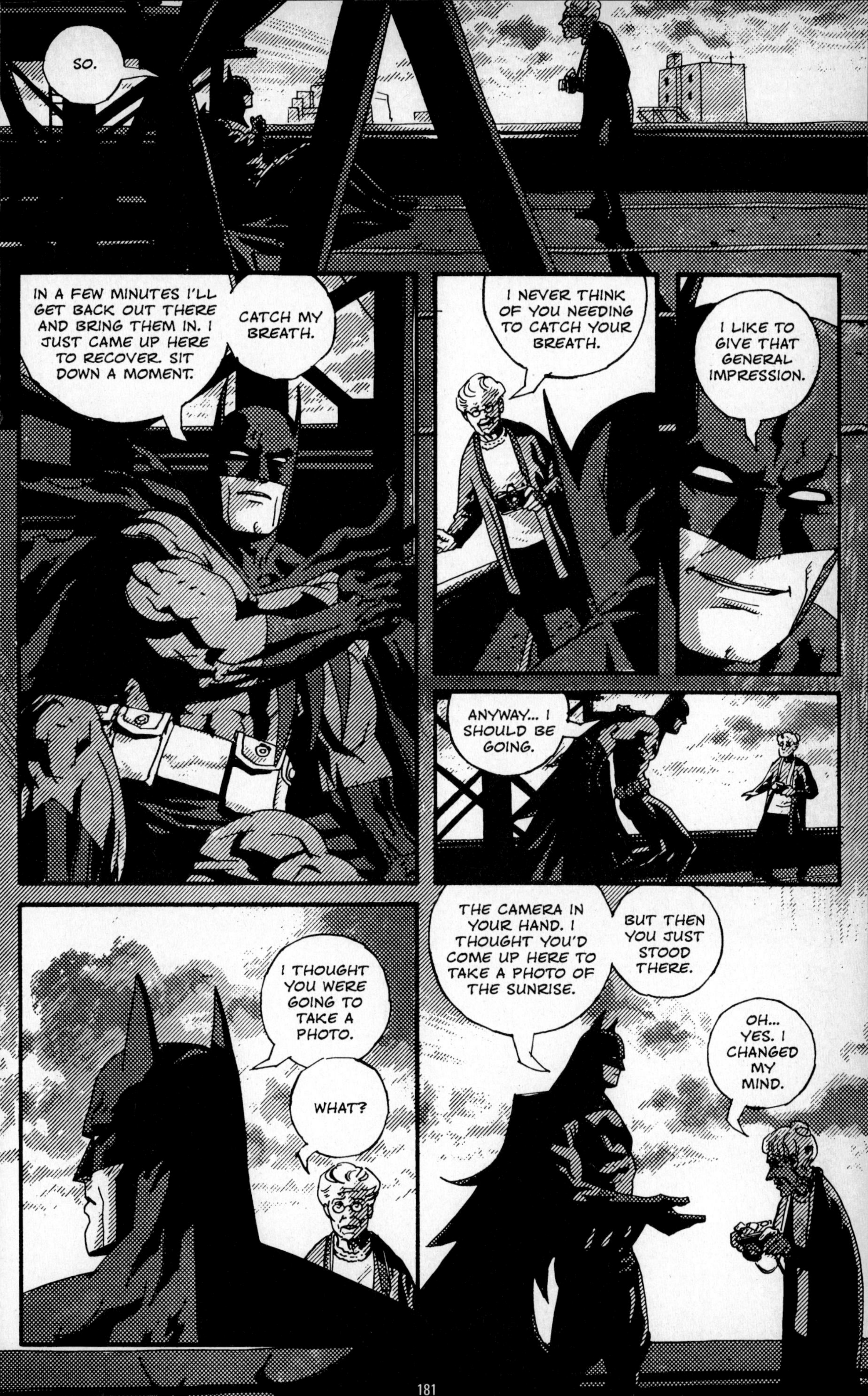
SO.
IN A FEW MINUTES I'LL GET BACK OUT THERE AND BRING THEM IN. I JUST CAME UP HERE TO RECOVER. SIT DOWN A MOMENT.
CATCH MY BREATH.
I NEVER THINK OF YOU NEEDING TO CATCH YOUR BREATH.
I LIKE TO GIVE THAT GENERAL IMPRESSION.
ANYWAY... I SHOULD BE GOING.
I THOUGHT YOU WERE GOING TO TAKE A PHOTO.
WHAT?
THE CAMERA IN YOUR HAND. I THOUGHT YOU'D COME UP HERE TO TAKE A PHOTO OF THE SUNRISE.
BUT THEN YOU JUST STOOD THERE.
OH... YES. I CHANGED MY MIND.

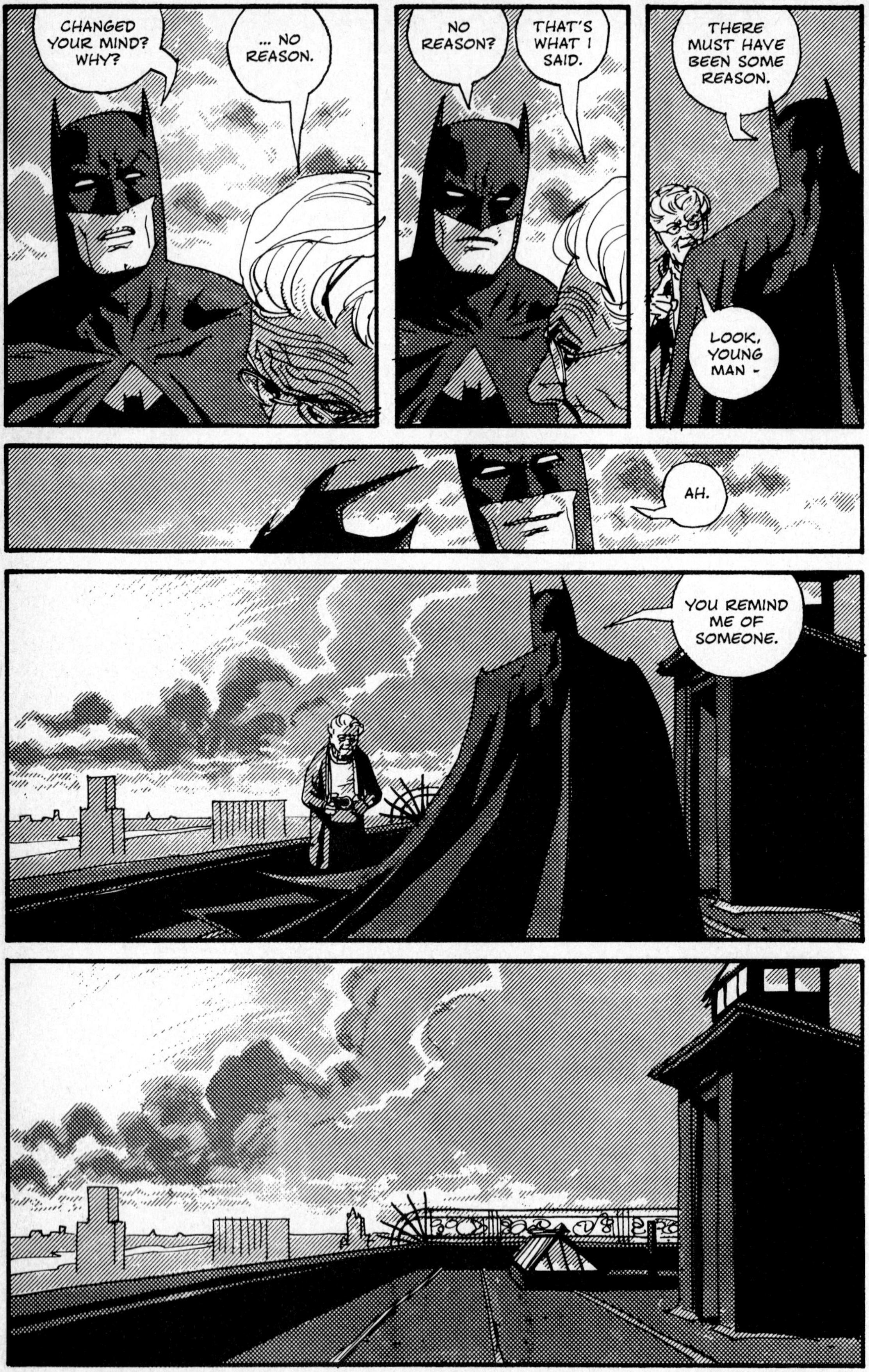
CHANGED YOUR MIND? WHY?
... NO REASON.
NO REASON?
THAT'S WHAT I SAID.
THERE MUST HAVE BEEN SOME REASON.
LOOK, YOUNG MAN -
AH.
YOU REMIND ME OF SOMEONE.

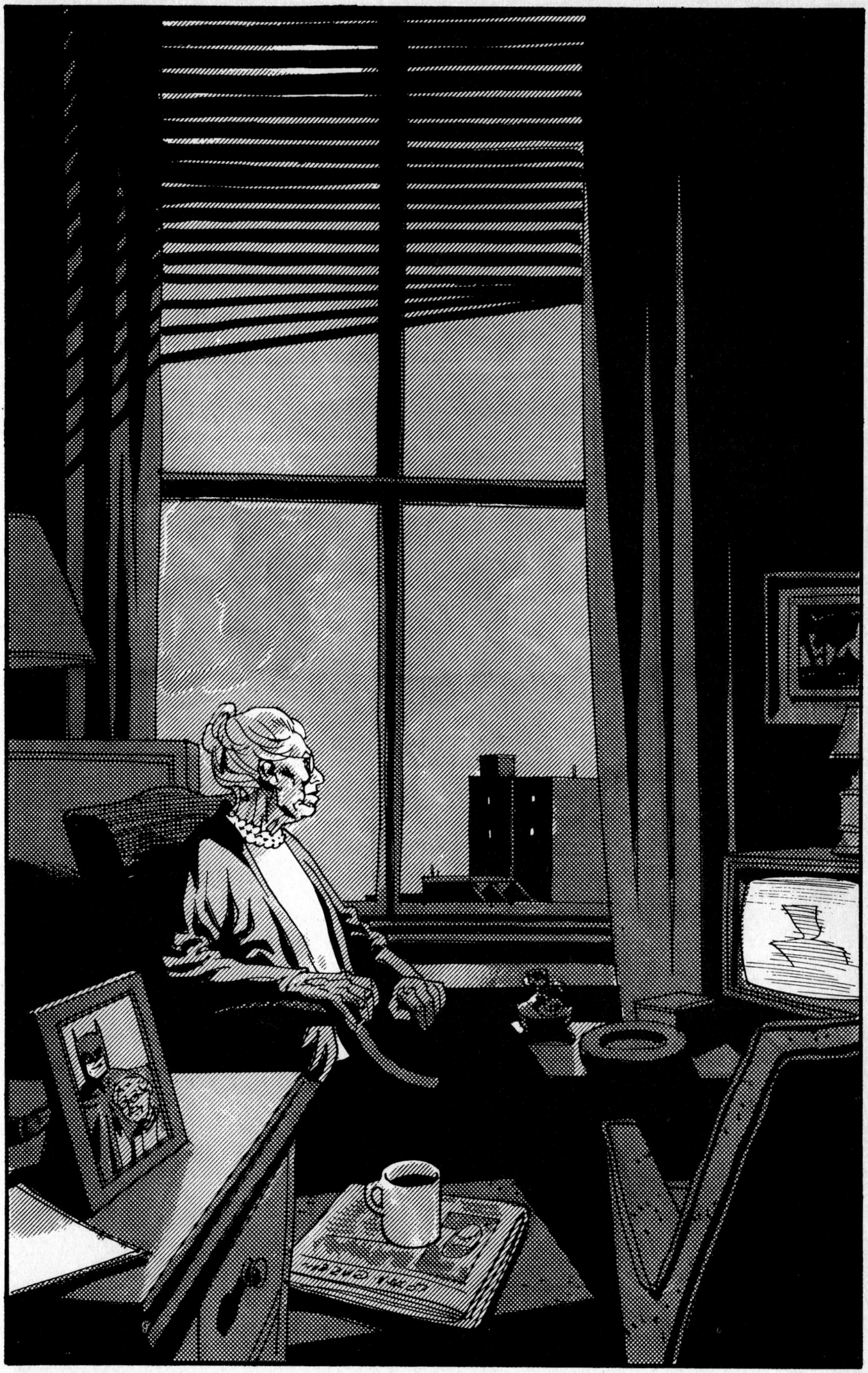

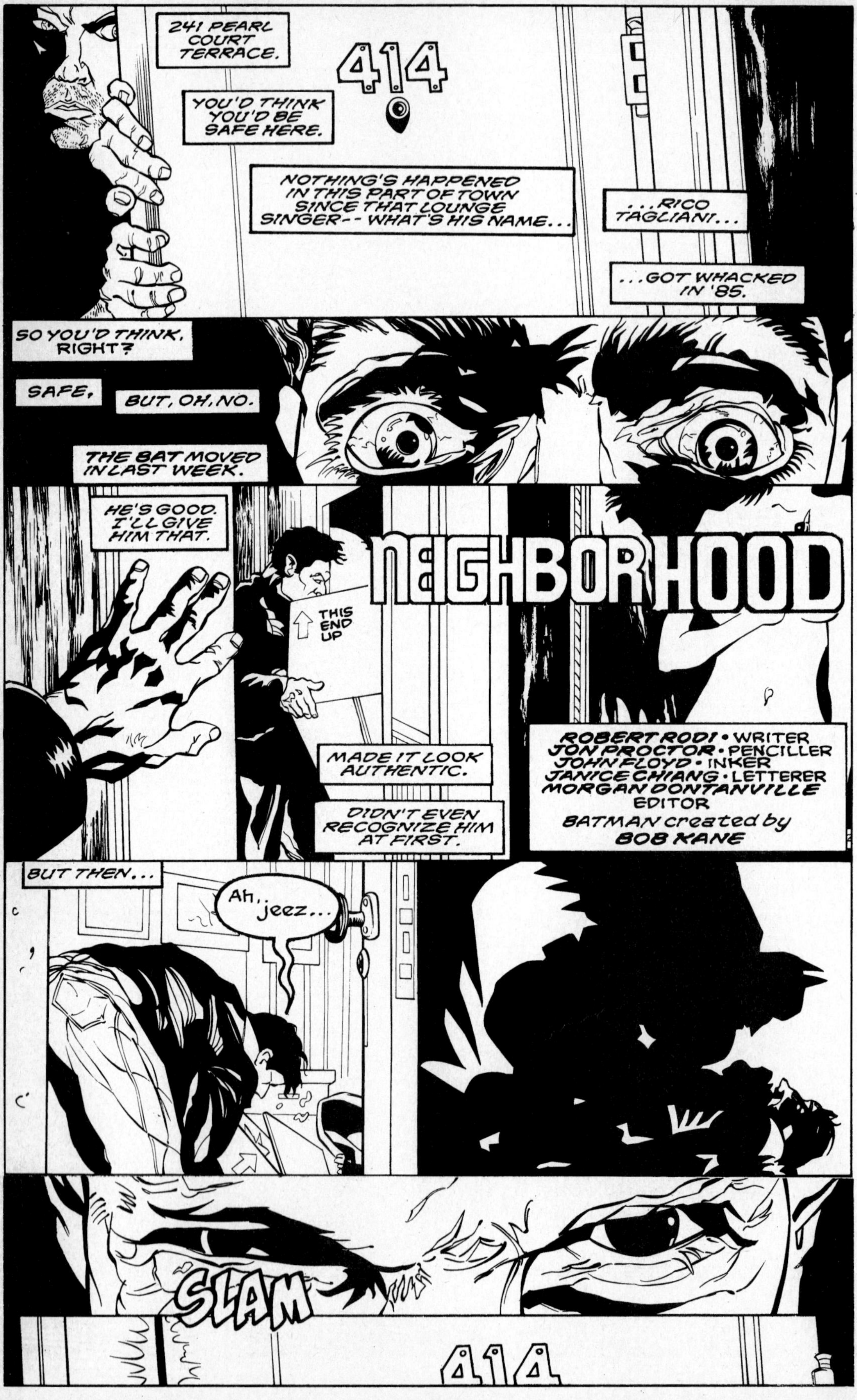
241 PEARL COURT TERRACE.
414
YOU'D THINK YOU'D BE SAFE HERE.
NOTHING'S HAPPENED IN THIS PART OF TOWN SINCE THAT LOUNGE SINGER-- WHAT'S HIS NAME...
...RICO TAGLIANI...
...GOT WHACKED IN '85.
SO YOU'D THINK, RIGHT?
SAFE,
BUT, OH, NO.
THE BAT MOVED IN LAST WEEK.
HE'S GOOD. I'LL GIVE HIM THAT.
NEIGHBORHOOD
THIS END UP
MADE IT LOOK AUTHENTIC.
DIDN'T EVEN RECOGNIZE HIM AT FIRST.
ROBERT RODI • WRITER
JON PROCTOR • PENCILLER
JOHN FLOYD • INKER
JANICE CHIANG • LETTERER
MORGAN DONTANVILLE EDITOR
BATMAN created by BOB KANE
BUT THEN...
Ah, jeez...
SLAM
414

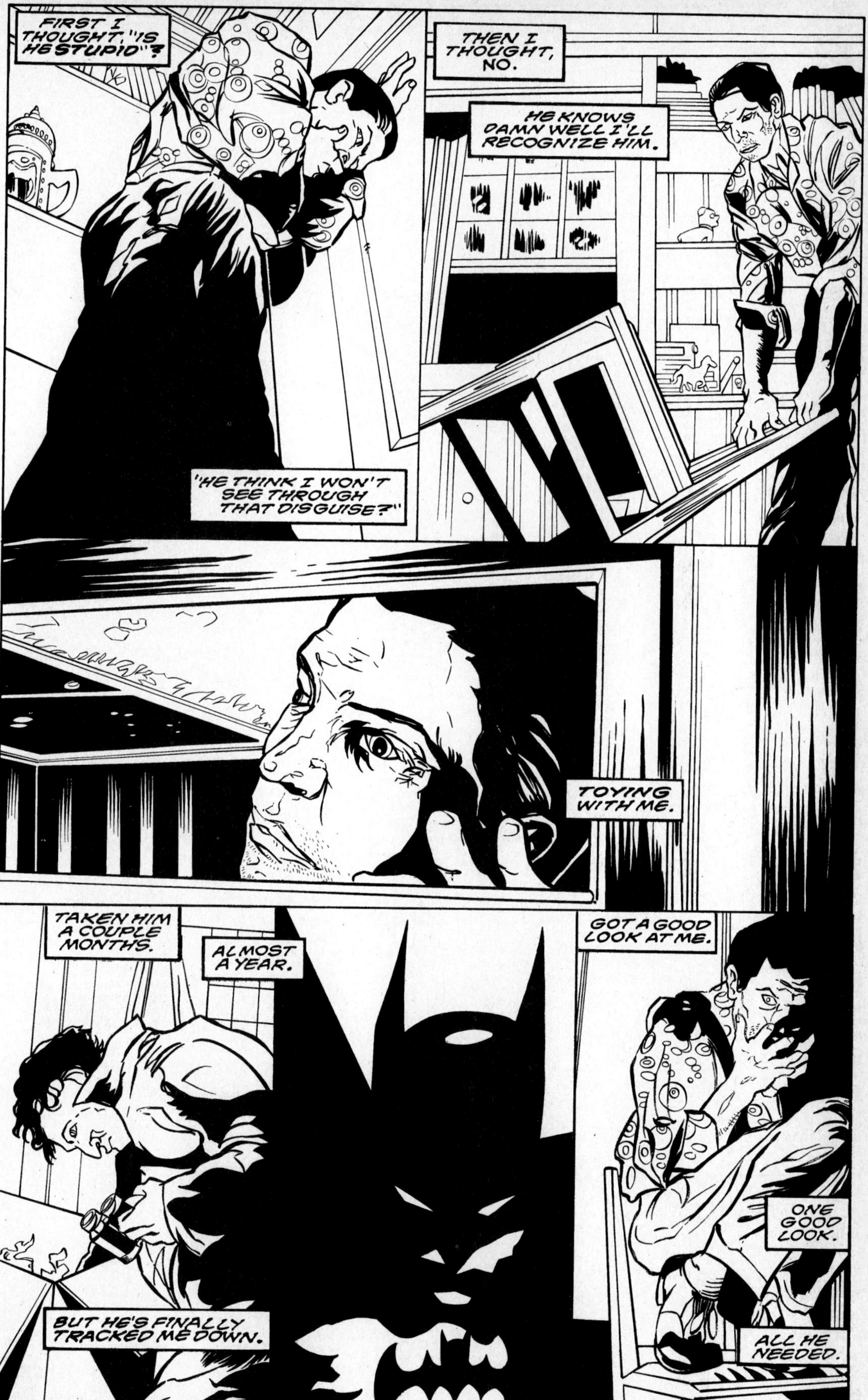

FIRST I THOUGHT, "IS HE STUPID"?
"HE THINK I WON'T SEE THROUGH THAT DISGUISE?"
THEN I THOUGHT, NO.
HE KNOWS DAMN WELL I'LL RECOGNIZE HIM.
TOYING WITH ME.
TAKEN HIM A COUPLE MONTHS.
ALMOST A YEAR.
BUT HE'S FINALLY TRACKED ME DOWN.
GOT A GOOD LOOK AT ME.
ONE GOOD LOOK.
ALL HE NEEDED.

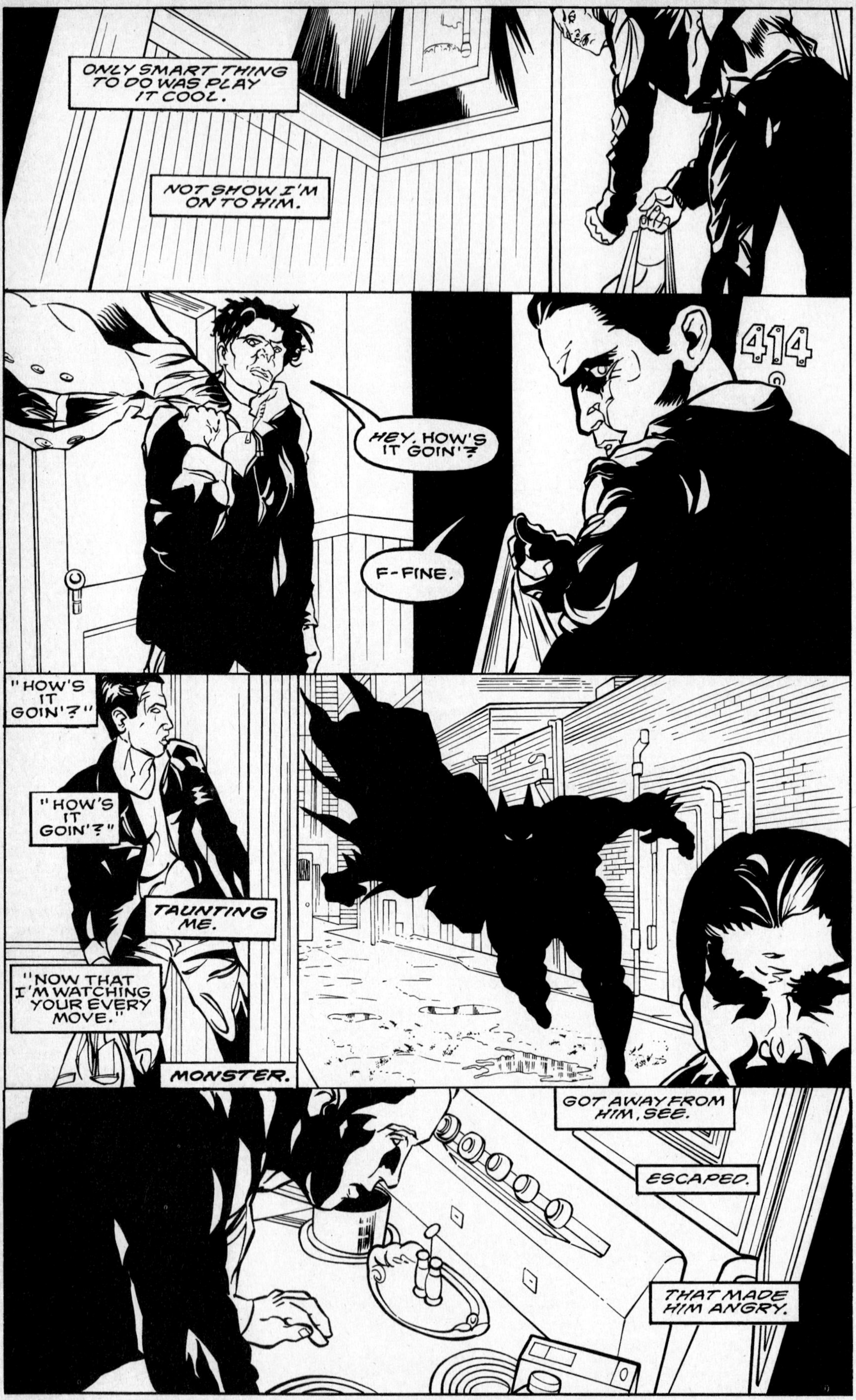
ONLY SMART THING TO DO WAS PLAY IT COOL.
NOT SHOW I'M ON TO HIM.
HEY. HOW'S IT GOIN'?
F-FINE.
"HOW'S IT GOIN'?"
"HOW'S IT GOIN'?"
TAUNTING ME.
"NOW THAT I'M WATCHING YOUR EVERY MOVE."
MONSTER.
414
GOT AWAY FROM HIM, SEE.
ESCAPED.
THAT MADE HIM ANGRY.

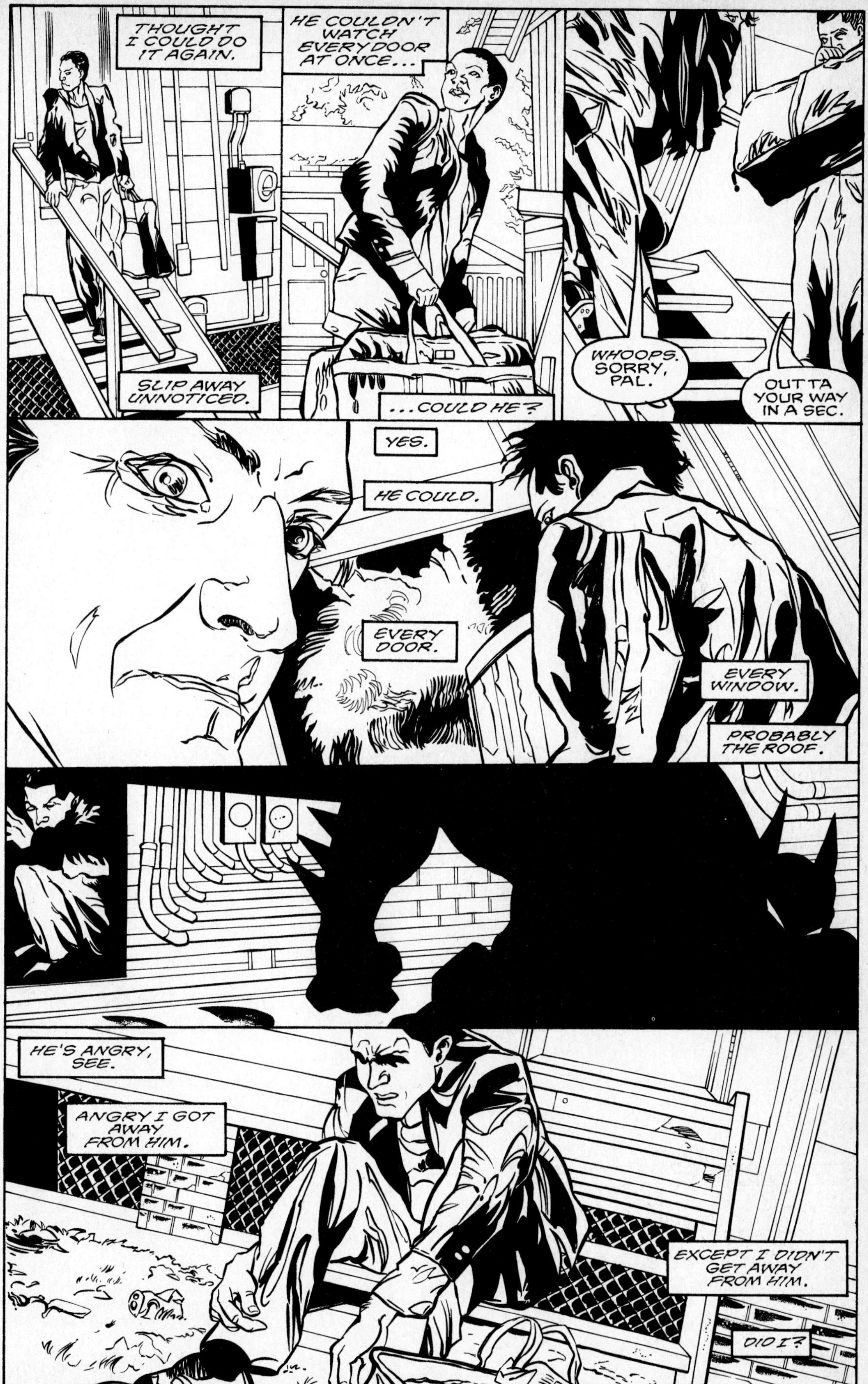
THOUGHT I COULD DO IT AGAIN.
SLIP AWAY UNNOTICED.
HE COULDN'T WATCH EVERY DOOR AT ONCE...
...COULD HE?
WHOOPS. SORRY, PAL.
OUTTA YOUR WAY IN A SEC.
YES.
HE COULD.
EVERY DOOR.
EVERY WINDOW.
PROBABLY THE ROOF.
HE'S ANGRY, SEE.
ANGRY I GOT AWAY FROM HIM.
EXCEPT I DIDN'T GET AWAY FROM HIM.
DID I?

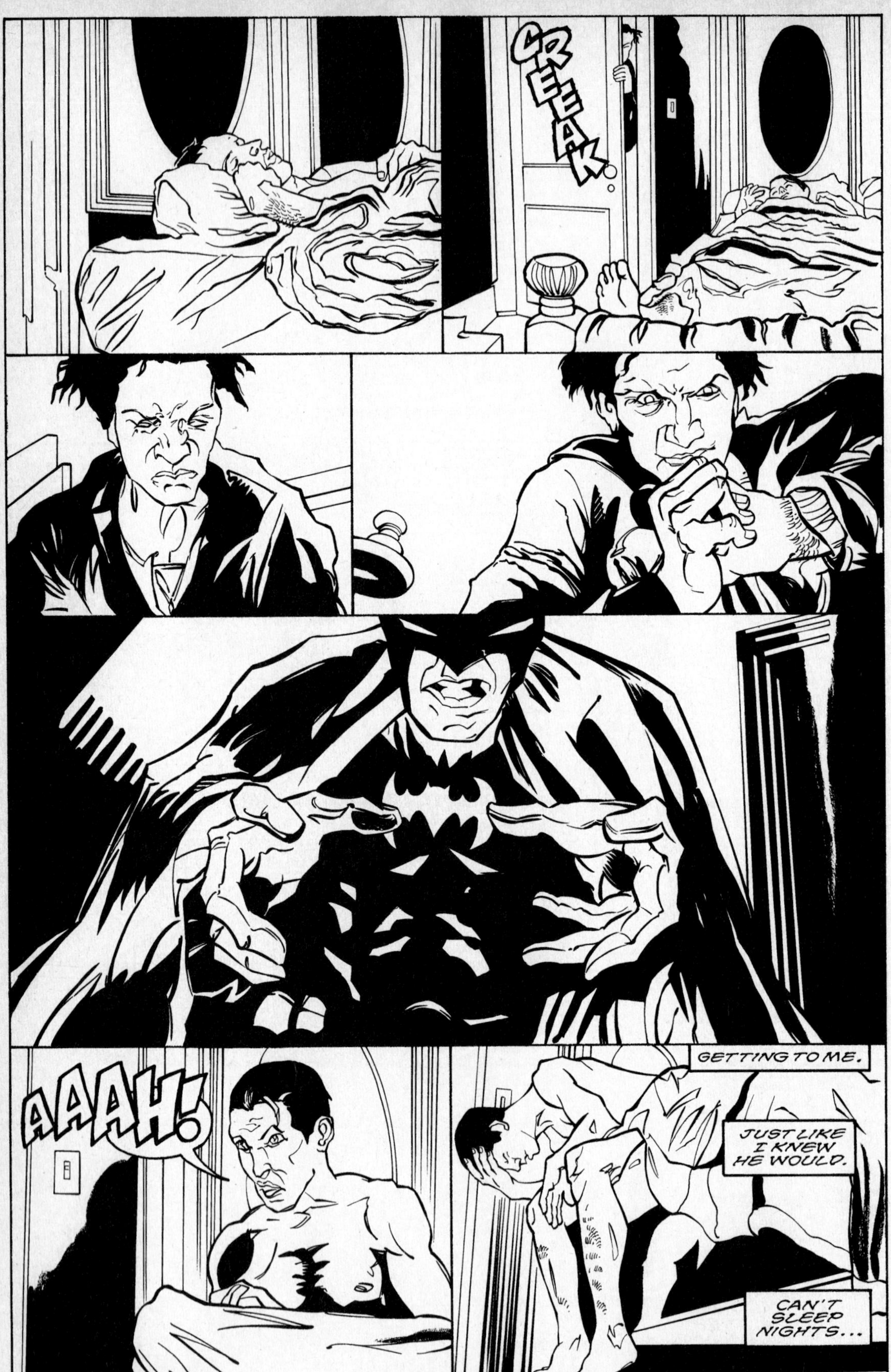
CREEAK
AAAH!
GETTING TO ME.
JUST LIKE I KNEW HE WOULD.
CAN'T SLEEP NIGHTS...

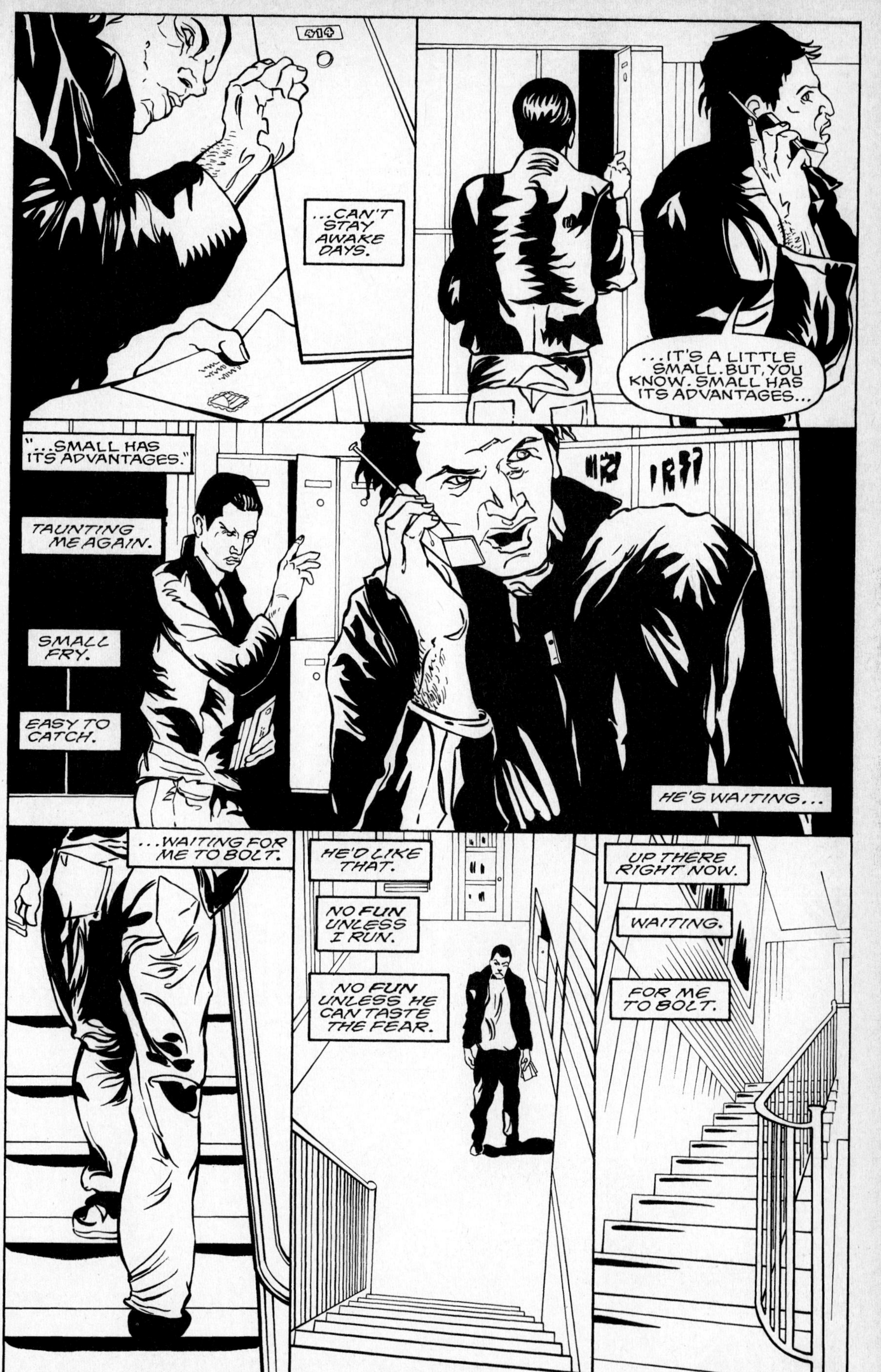
414
...CAN'T STAY AWAKE DAYS.
...IT'S A LITTLE SMALL. BUT, YOU KNOW. SMALL HAS ITS ADVANTAGES...
"...SMALL HAS ITS ADVANTAGES."
TAUNTING ME AGAIN.
SMALL FRY.
EASY TO CATCH.
HE'S WAITING...
...WAITING FOR ME TO BOLT.
HE'D LIKE THAT.
NO FUN UNLESS I RUN.
NO FUN UNLESS HE CAN TASTE THE FEAR.
UP THERE RIGHT NOW.
WAITING.
FOR ME TO BOLT.

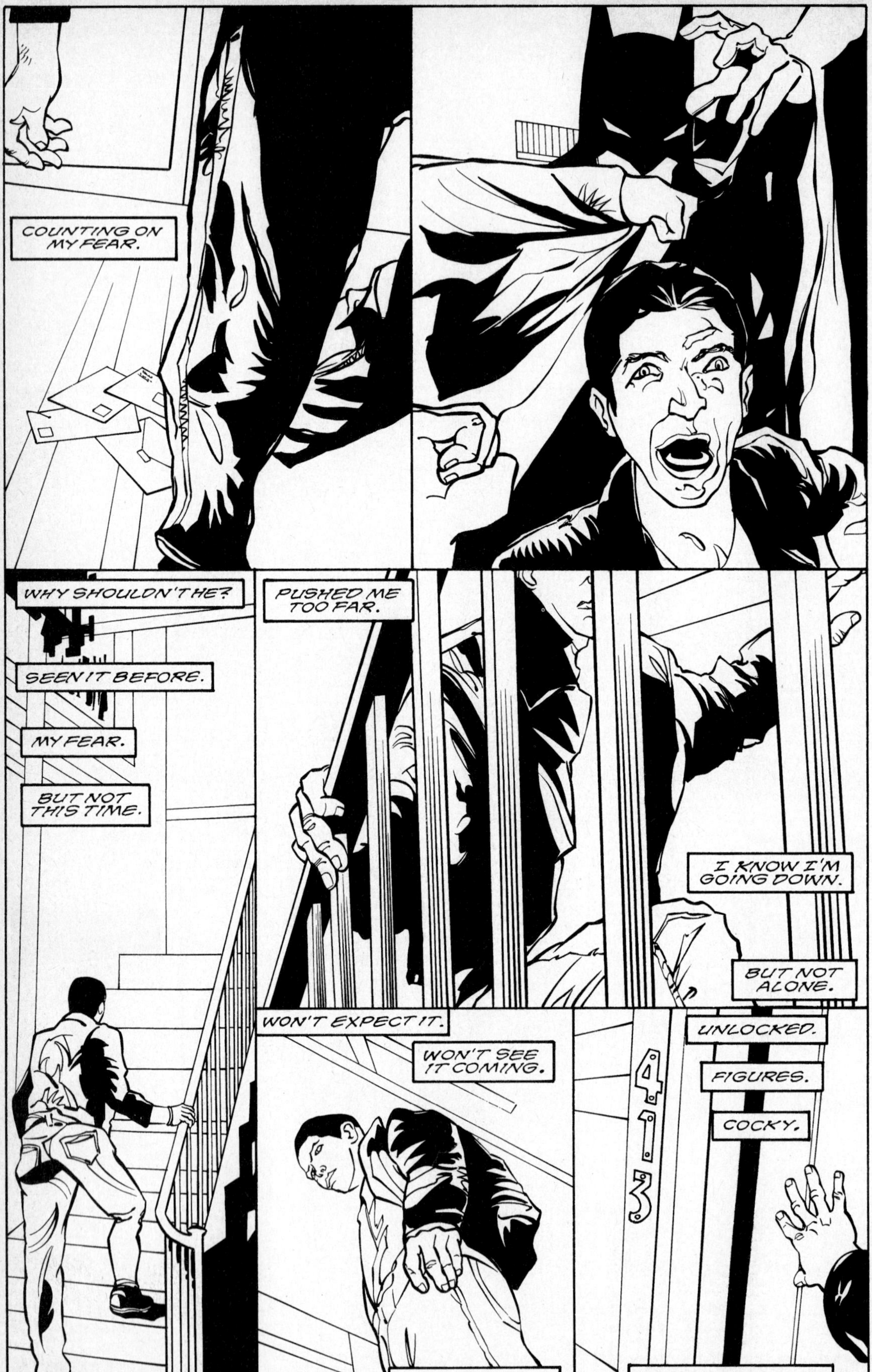
COUNTING ON MY FEAR.
WHY SHOULDN'T HE?
SEEN IT BEFORE.
MY FEAR.
BUT NOT THIS TIME.
PUSHED ME TOO FAR.
I KNOW I'M GOING DOWN.
BUT NOT ALONE.
WON'T EXPECT IT.
WON'T SEE IT COMING.
NOT FROM ME.
413
UNLOCKED.
FIGURES.
COCKY.
OVERCONFIDENT.

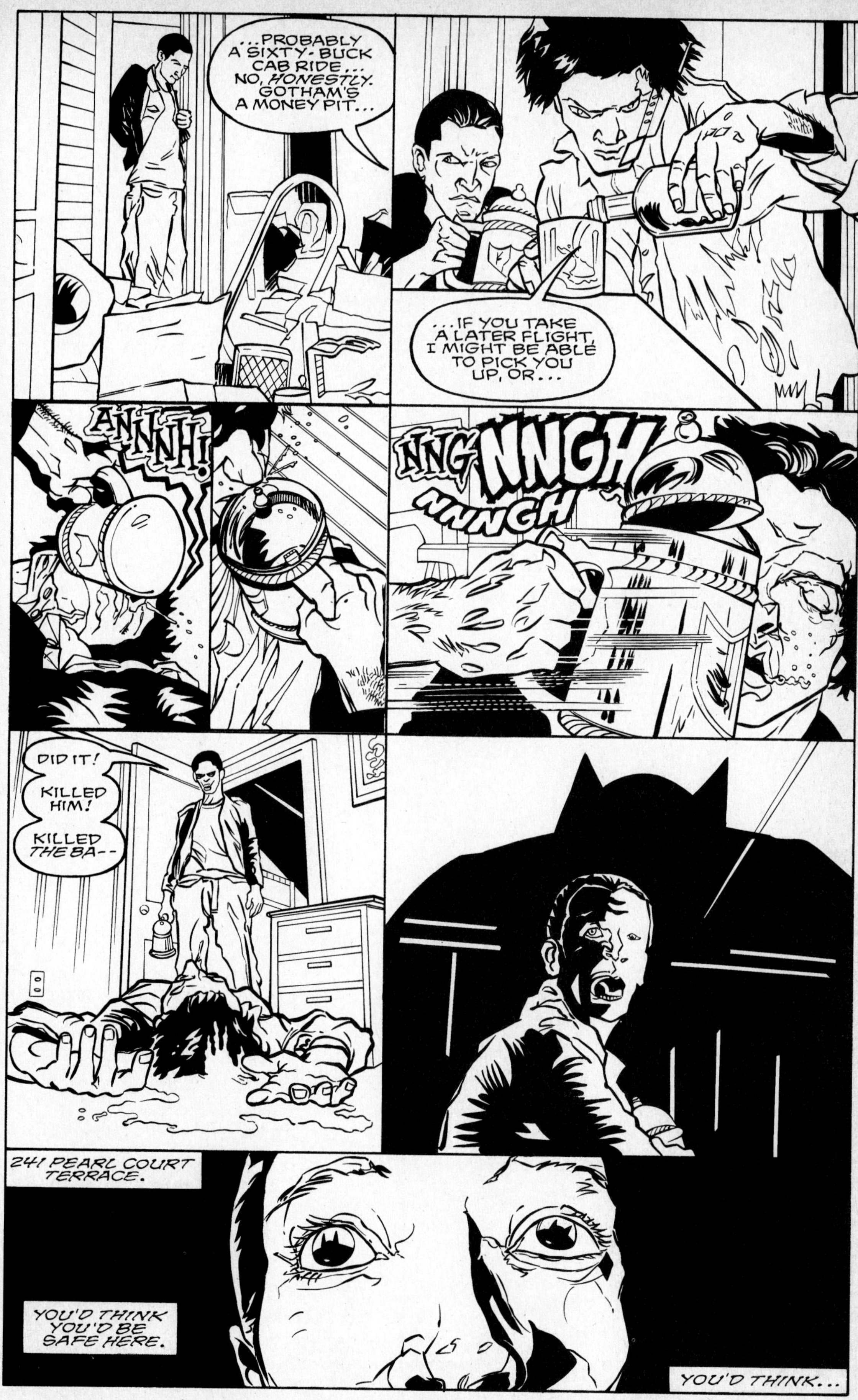
...PROBABLY A SIXTY-BUCK CAB RIDE... NO, HONESTLY. GOTHAM'S A MONEY PIT...
...IF YOU TAKE A LATER FLIGHT, I MIGHT BE ABLE TO PICK YOU UP, OR...
ANNNH!
NNG NNGH NNNGH
DID IT!
KILLED HIM!
KILLED THE BA--
241 PEARL COURT TERRACE.
YOU'D THINK YOU'D BE SAFE HERE.
YOU'D THINK...

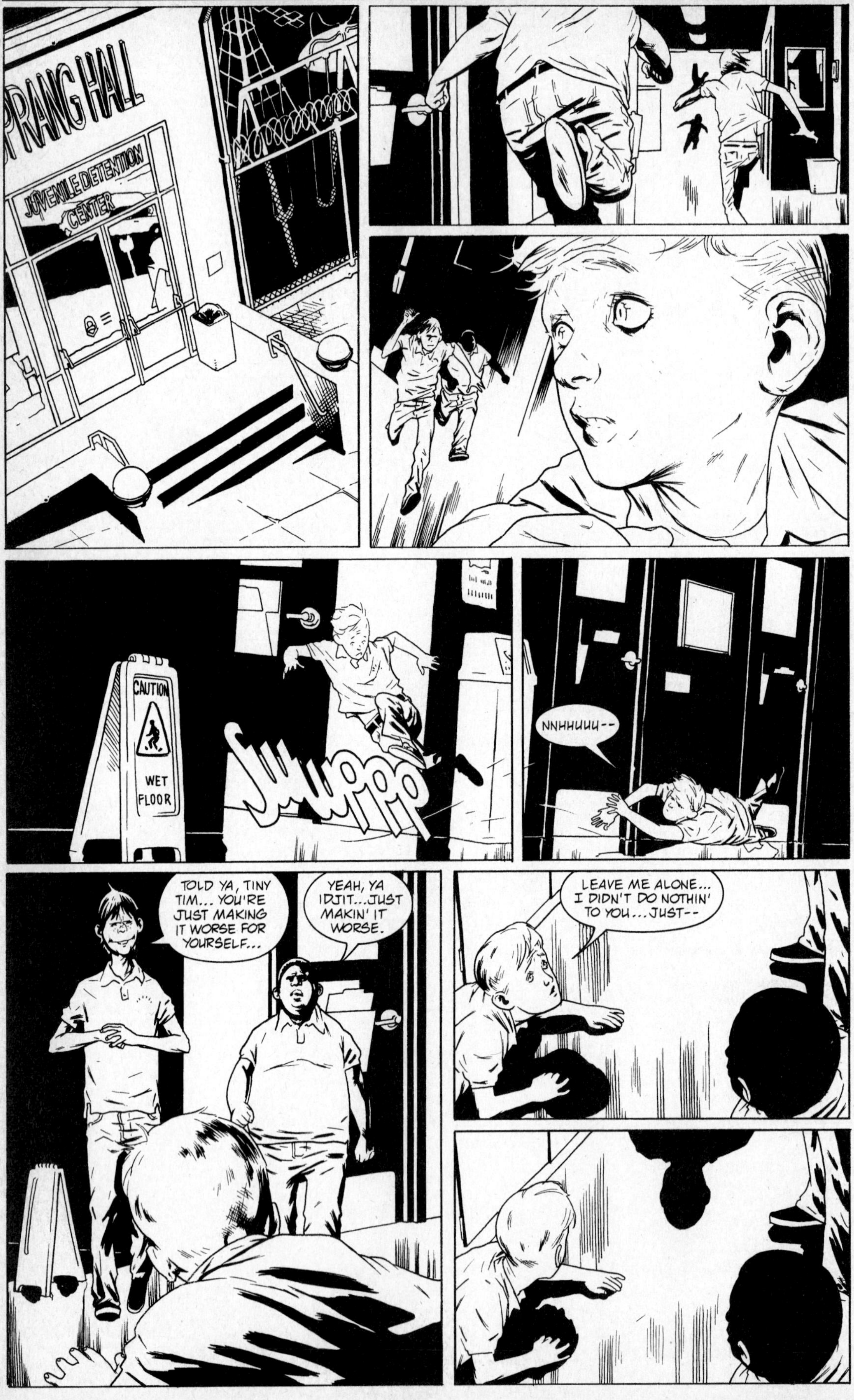
SPRANG HALL
JUVENILE DETENTION CENTER
CAUTION
WET FLOOR
SWUPPP
NNHHUUU--
TOLD YA, TINY TIM... YOU'RE JUST MAKING IT WORSE FOR YOURSELF...
YEAH, YA IDJIT...JUST MAKIN' IT WORSE.
LEAVE ME ALONE... I DIDN'T DO NOTHIN' TO YOU...JUST--

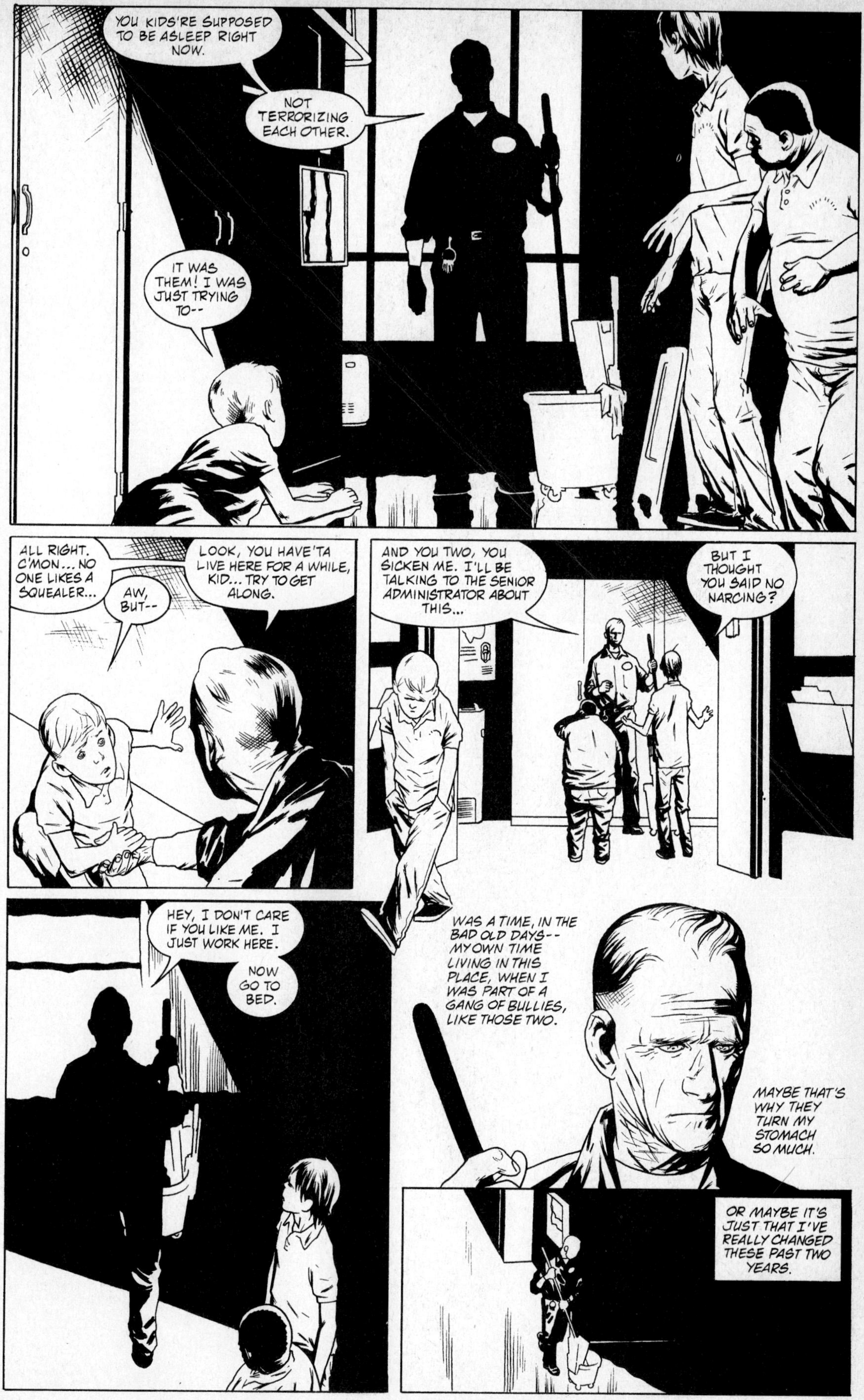

YOU KIDS'RE SUPPOSED TO BE ASLEEP RIGHT NOW.
NOT TERRORIZING EACH OTHER.
IT WAS THEM! I WAS JUST TRYING TO--
ALL RIGHT. C'MON... NO ONE LIKES A SQUEALER...
AW, BUT--
LOOK, YOU HAVE'TA LIVE HERE FOR A WHILE, KID... TRY TO GET ALONG.
AND YOU TWO, YOU SICKEN ME. I'LL BE TALKING TO THE SENIOR ADMINISTRATOR ABOUT THIS...
BUT I THOUGHT YOU SAID NO NARCING?
HEY, I DON'T CARE IF YOU LIKE ME. I JUST WORK HERE.
NOW GO TO BED.
WAS A TIME, IN THE BAD OLD DAYS-- MY OWN TIME LIVING IN THIS PLACE, WHEN I WAS PART OF A GANG OF BULLIES, LIKE THOSE TWO.
MAYBE THAT'S WHY THEY TURN MY STOMACH SO MUCH.
OR MAYBE IT'S JUST THAT I'VE REALLY CHANGED THESE PAST TWO YEARS.

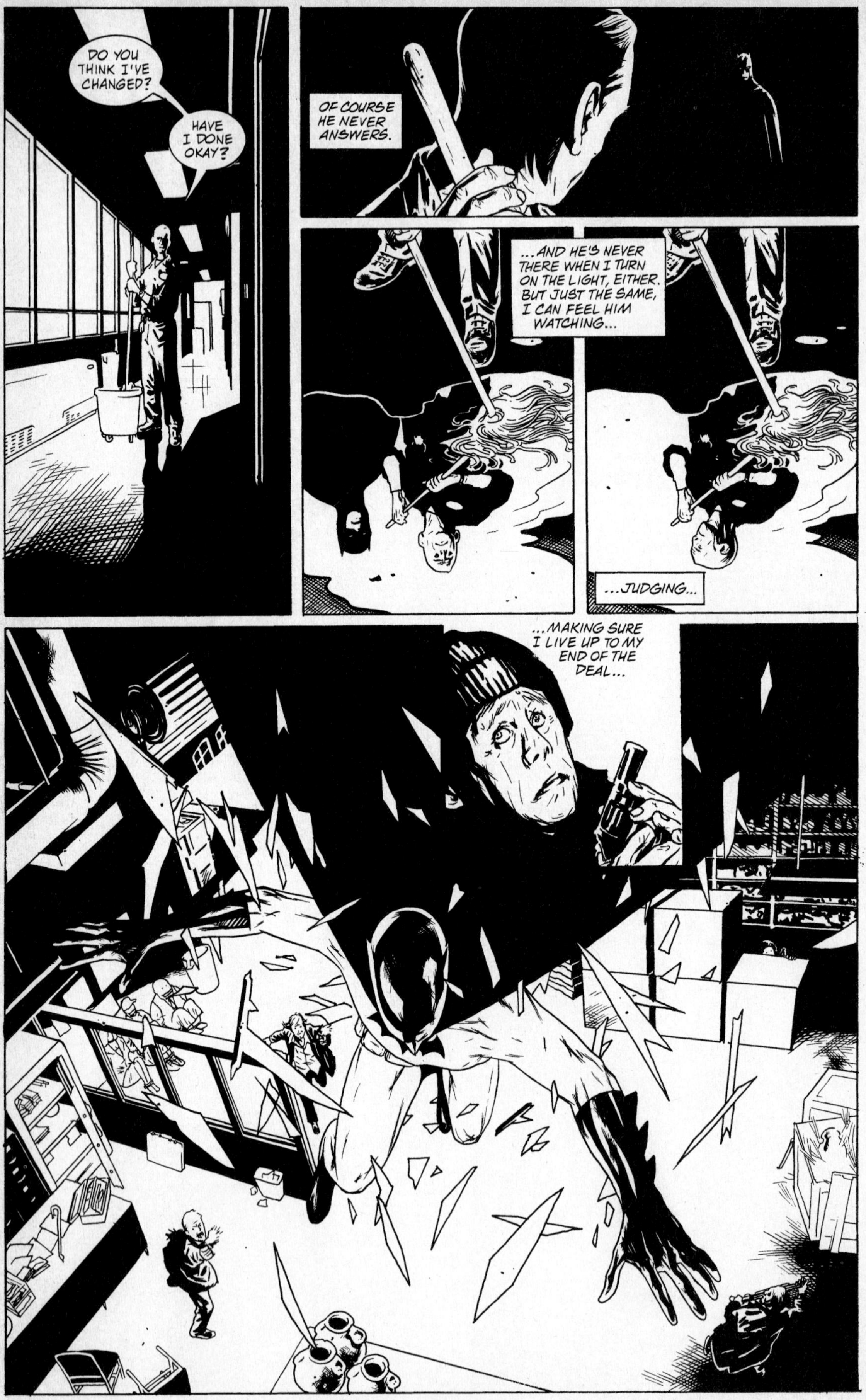
DO YOU THINK I'VE CHANGED?
HAVE I DONE OKAY?
OF COURSE HE NEVER ANSWERS.
...AND HE'S NEVER THERE WHEN I TURN ON THE LIGHT, EITHER. BUT JUST THE SAME, I CAN FEEL HIM WATCHING...
...JUDGING...
...MAKING SURE I LIVE UP TO MY END OF THE DEAL...

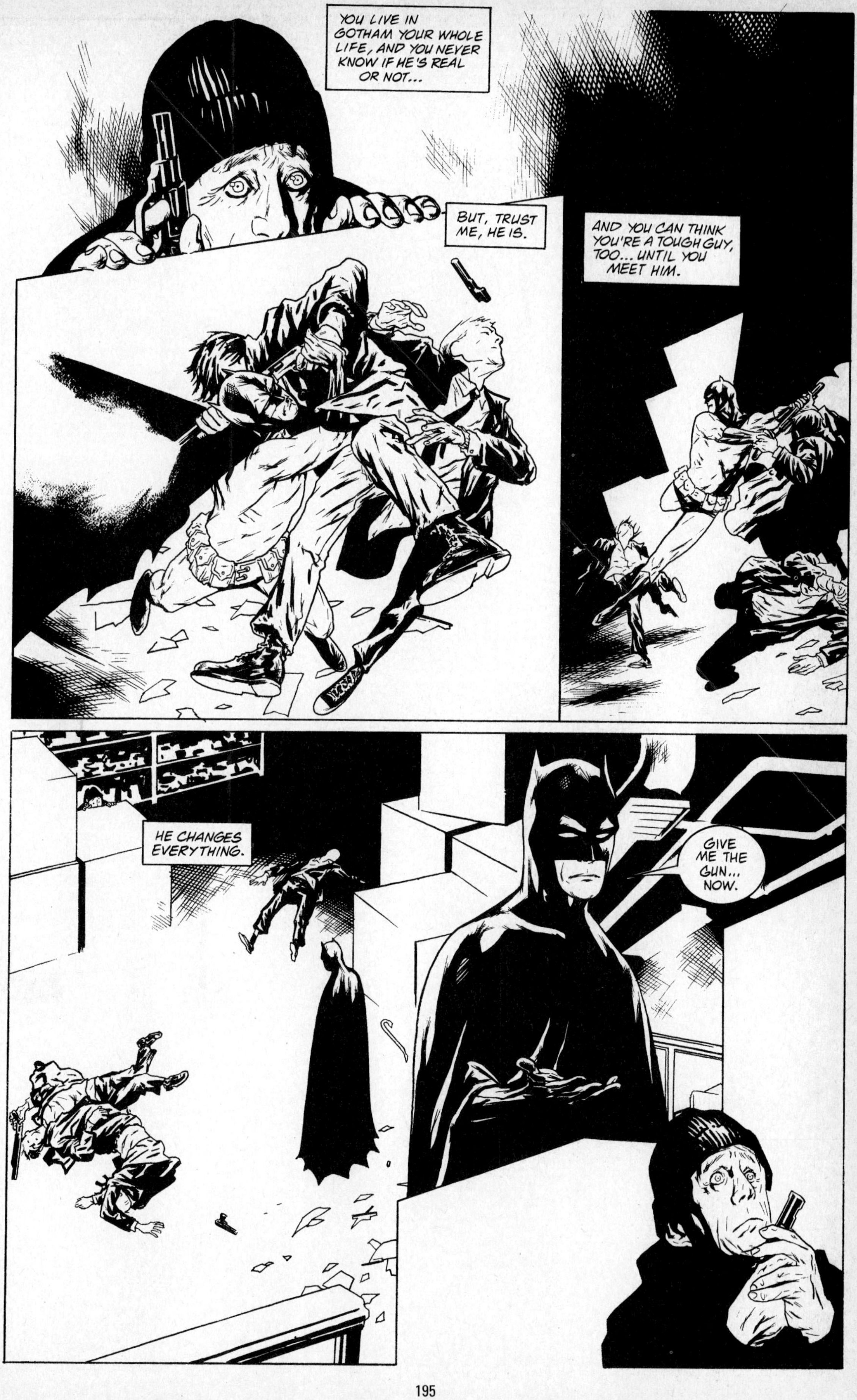
YOU LIVE IN GOTHAM YOUR WHOLE LIFE, AND YOU NEVER KNOW IF HE'S REAL OR NOT...
BUT, TRUST ME, HE IS.
AND YOU CAN THINK YOU'RE A TOUGH GUY, TOO... UNTIL YOU MEET HIM.
HE CHANGES EVERYTHING.
GIVE ME THE GUN... NOW.

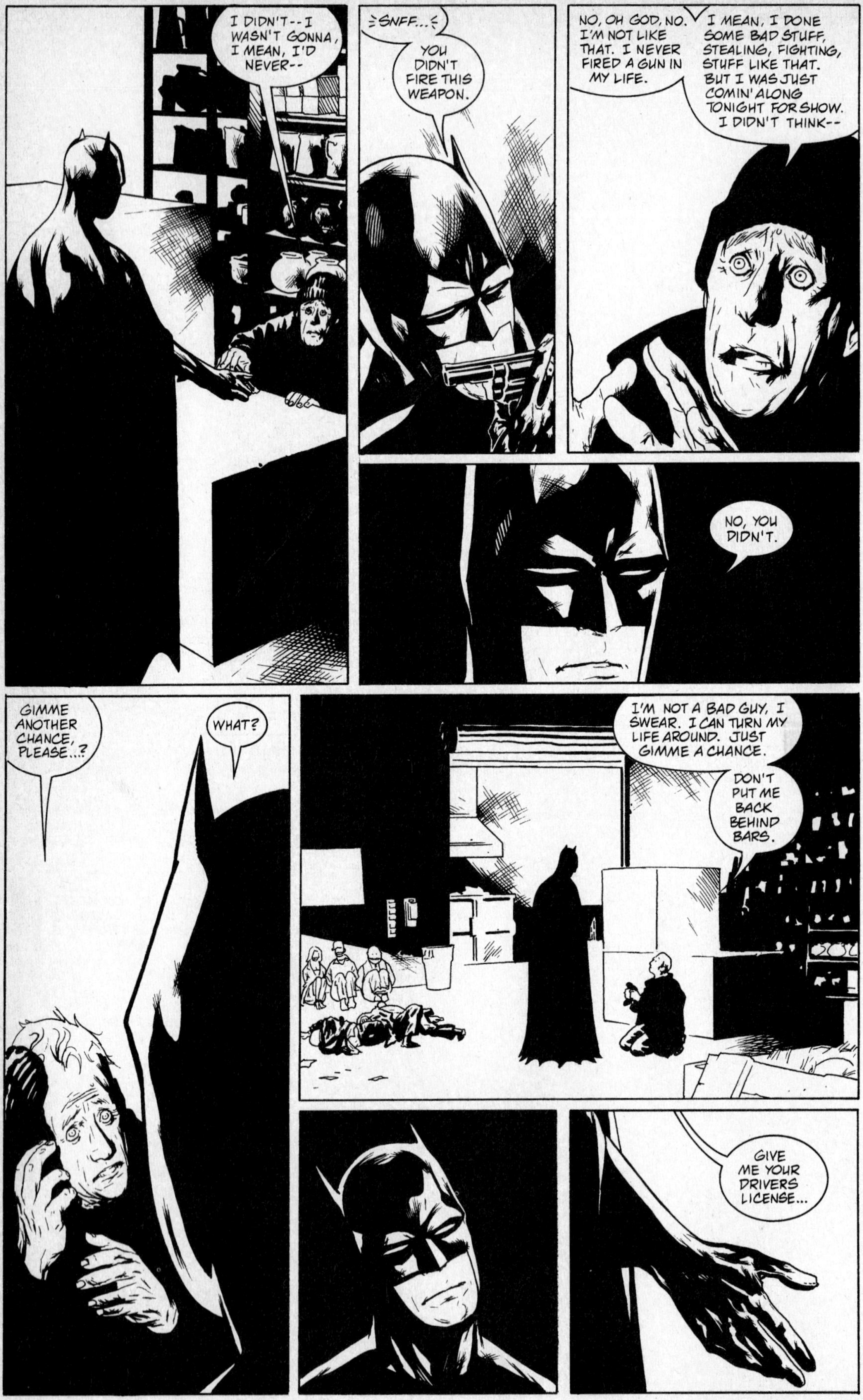
I DIDN'T--I WASN'T GONNA, I MEAN, I'D NEVER--
SNFF...
YOU DIDN'T FIRE THIS WEAPON.
NO, OH GOD, NO. I'M NOT LIKE THAT. I NEVER FIRED A GUN IN MY LIFE.
I MEAN, I DONE SOME BAD STUFF, STEALING, FIGHTING, STUFF LIKE THAT. BUT I WAS JUST COMIN' ALONG TONIGHT FOR SHOW. I DIDN'T THINK--
NO, YOU DIDN'T.
GIMME ANOTHER CHANCE, PLEASE...?
WHAT?
I'M NOT A BAD GUY, I SWEAR. I CAN TURN MY LIFE AROUND. JUST GIMME A CHANCE.
DON'T PUT ME BACK BEHIND BARS.
GIVE ME YOUR DRIVERS LICENSE...

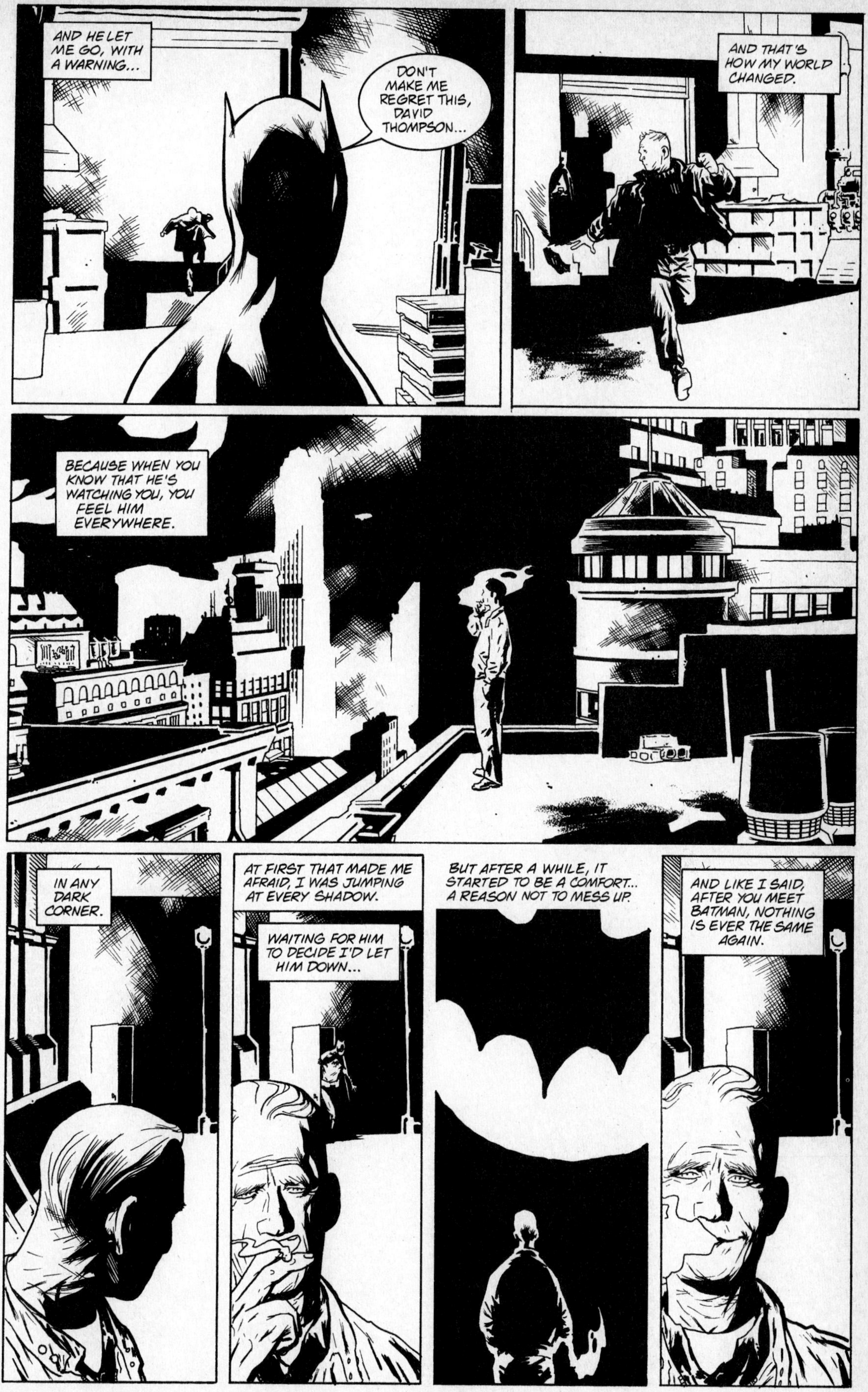
AND HE LET ME GO, WITH A WARNING...
DON'T MAKE ME REGRET THIS, DAVID THOMPSON...
AND THAT'S HOW MY WORLD CHANGED.
BECAUSE WHEN YOU KNOW THAT HE'S WATCHING YOU, YOU FEEL HIM EVERYWHERE.
IN ANY DARK CORNER.
AT FIRST THAT MADE ME AFRAID, I WAS JUMPING AT EVERY SHADOW.
WAITING FOR HIM TO DECIDE I'D LET HIM DOWN...
BUT AFTER A WHILE, IT STARTED TO BE A COMFORT... A REASON NOT TO MESS UP.
AND LIKE I SAID, AFTER YOU MEET BATMAN, NOTHING IS EVER THE SAME AGAIN.

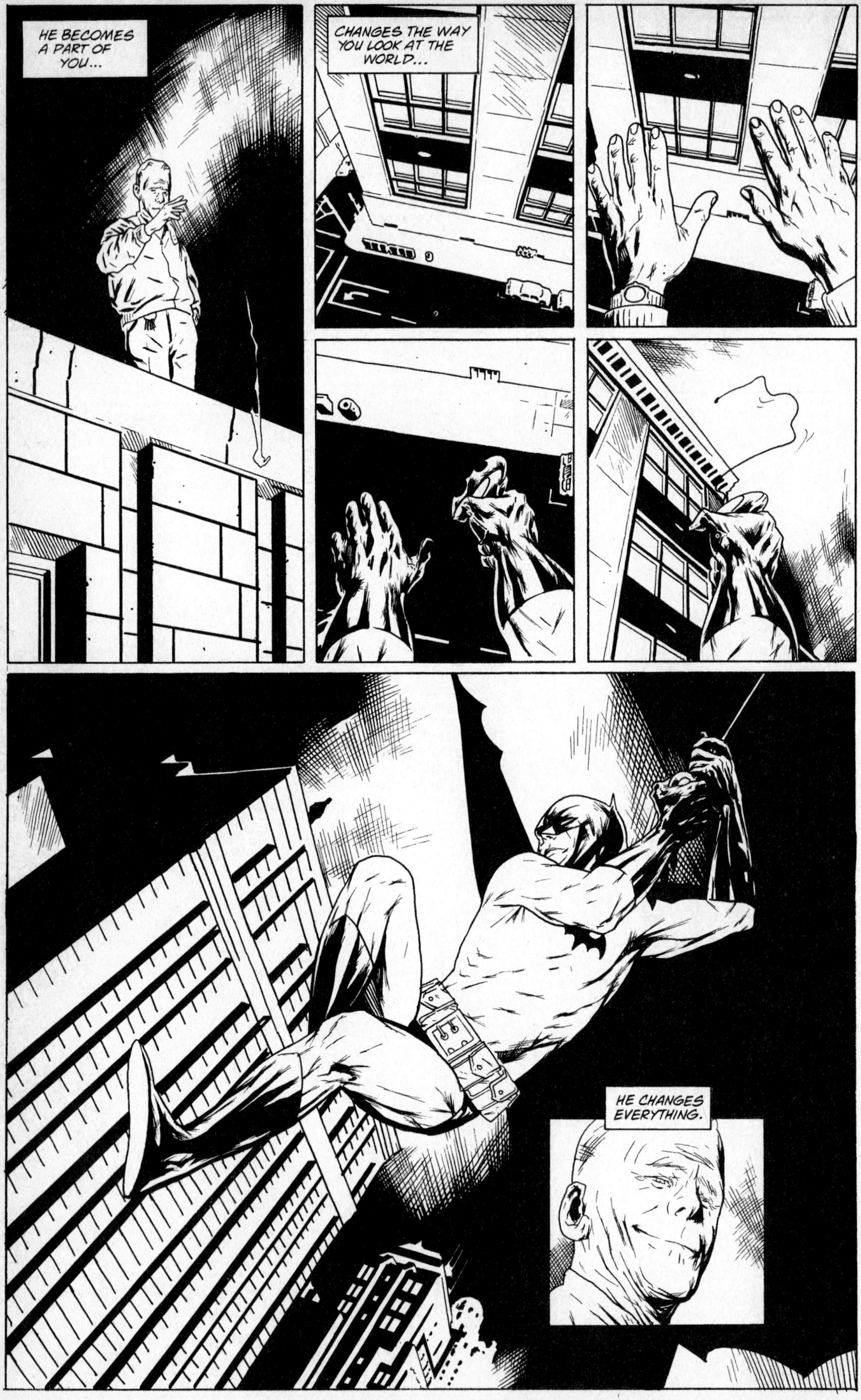
HE BECOMES A PART OF YOU...
CHANGES THE WAY YOU LOOK AT THE WORLD...
HE CHANGES EVERYTHING.

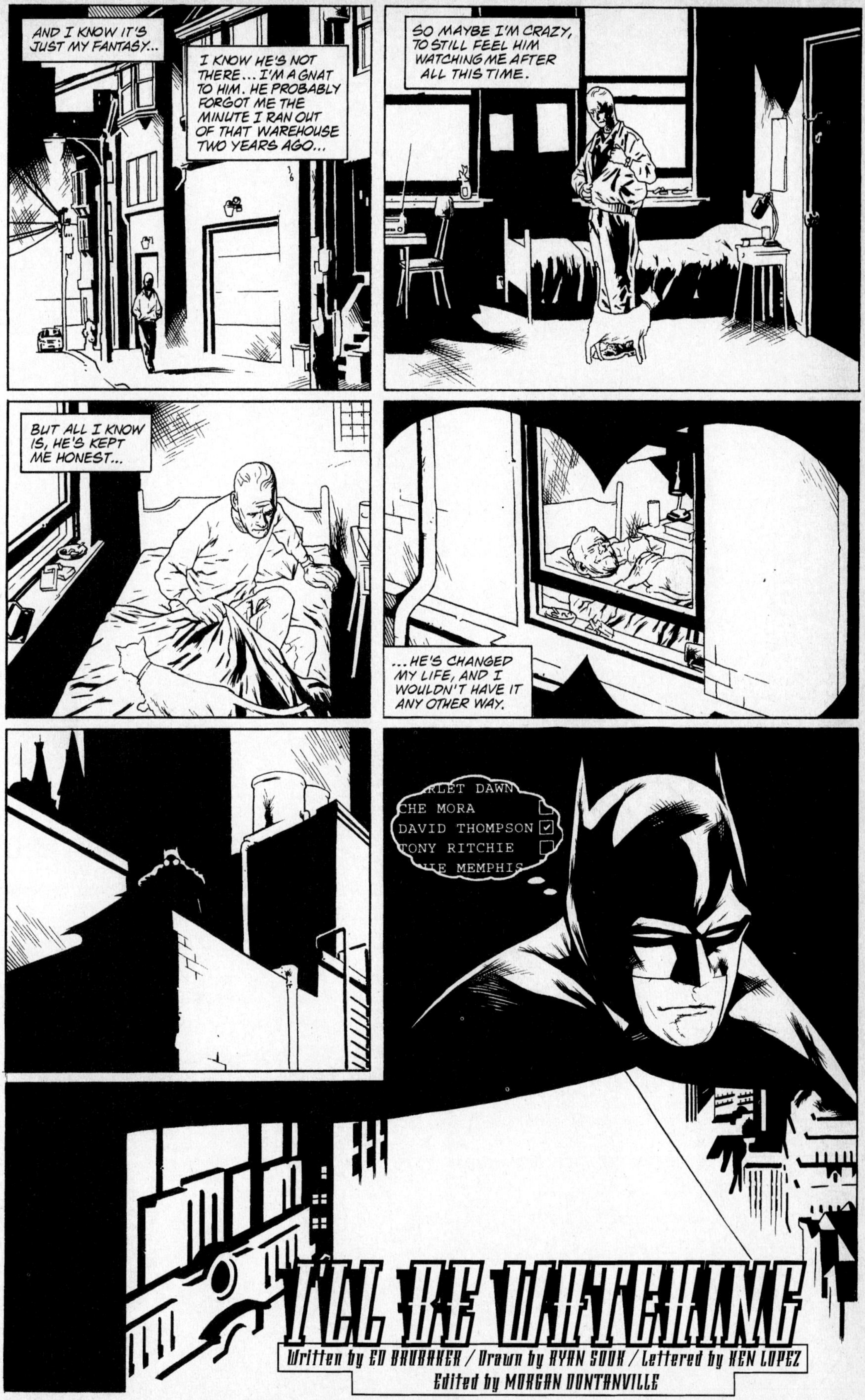
AND I KNOW IT'S JUST MY FANTASY...
I KNOW HE'S NOT THERE... I'M A GNAT TO HIM. HE PROBABLY FORGOT ME THE MINUTE I RAN OUT OF THAT WAREHOUSE TWO YEARS AGO...
SO MAYBE I'M CRAZY, TO STILL FEEL HIM WATCHING ME AFTER ALL THIS TIME.
BUT ALL I KNOW IS, HE'S KEPT ME HONEST...
...HE'S CHANGED MY LIFE, AND I WOULDN'T HAVE IT ANY OTHER WAY.
CHE MORA
DAVID THOMPSON
TONY RITCHIE
I'LL BE WATCHING
Written by ED BRUBAKER / Drawn by RYAN SOOK / Lettered by KEN LOPEZ
Edited by MORGAN DONTANVILLE

# GARGOYLES OF GOTHAM

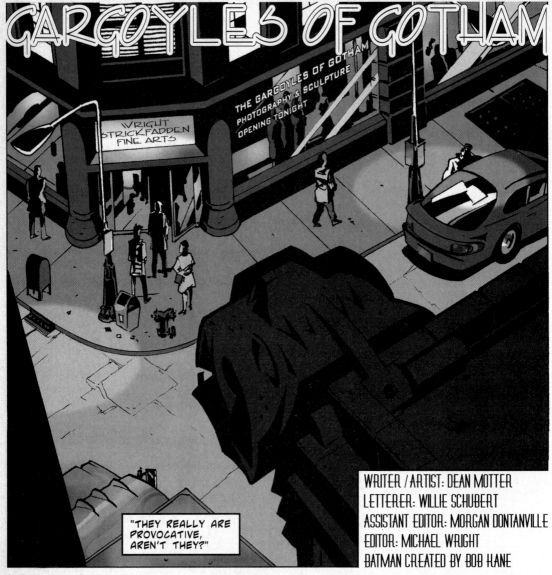

WRIGHT STRICKFADDEN FINE ARTS

THE GARGOYLES OF GOTHAM
PHOTOGRAPHY & SCULPTURE
OPENING TONIGHT

WRITER / ARTIST: DEAN MOTTER
LETTERER: WILLIE SCHUBERT
ASSISTANT EDITOR: MORGAN DONTANVILLE
EDITOR: MICHAEL WRIGHT
BATMAN CREATED BY BOB KANE

"THEY REALLY ARE PROVOCATIVE, AREN'T THEY?"

TO SOME OF US. BUT AREN'T THEY A BIT--LITERAL FOR YOUR CLIENTELE? ALMOST-- COMMERCIAL.

OUCH. WHY ARE YOU SO *MEAN* TO ME, BRUCE?

PHILLIP, BE AN ANGEL AND GET ME A SODA.

I ALWAYS THOUGHT YOU *LIKED* IT THAT WAY, J.D.

SEE ANYTHING YOU LIKE?

SOME FAMILIAR FACES. SPEAKING OF WHICH, HAVEN'T WE MET?

YOU HAVE A GOOD MEMORY, MISTER WAYNE. NEW YEAR'S EVE PARTY. MY LOFT ABOUT SIX YEARS AGO. GEORGINA GERSTNER.

THESE ARE *YOUR* PHOTOGRAPHS.

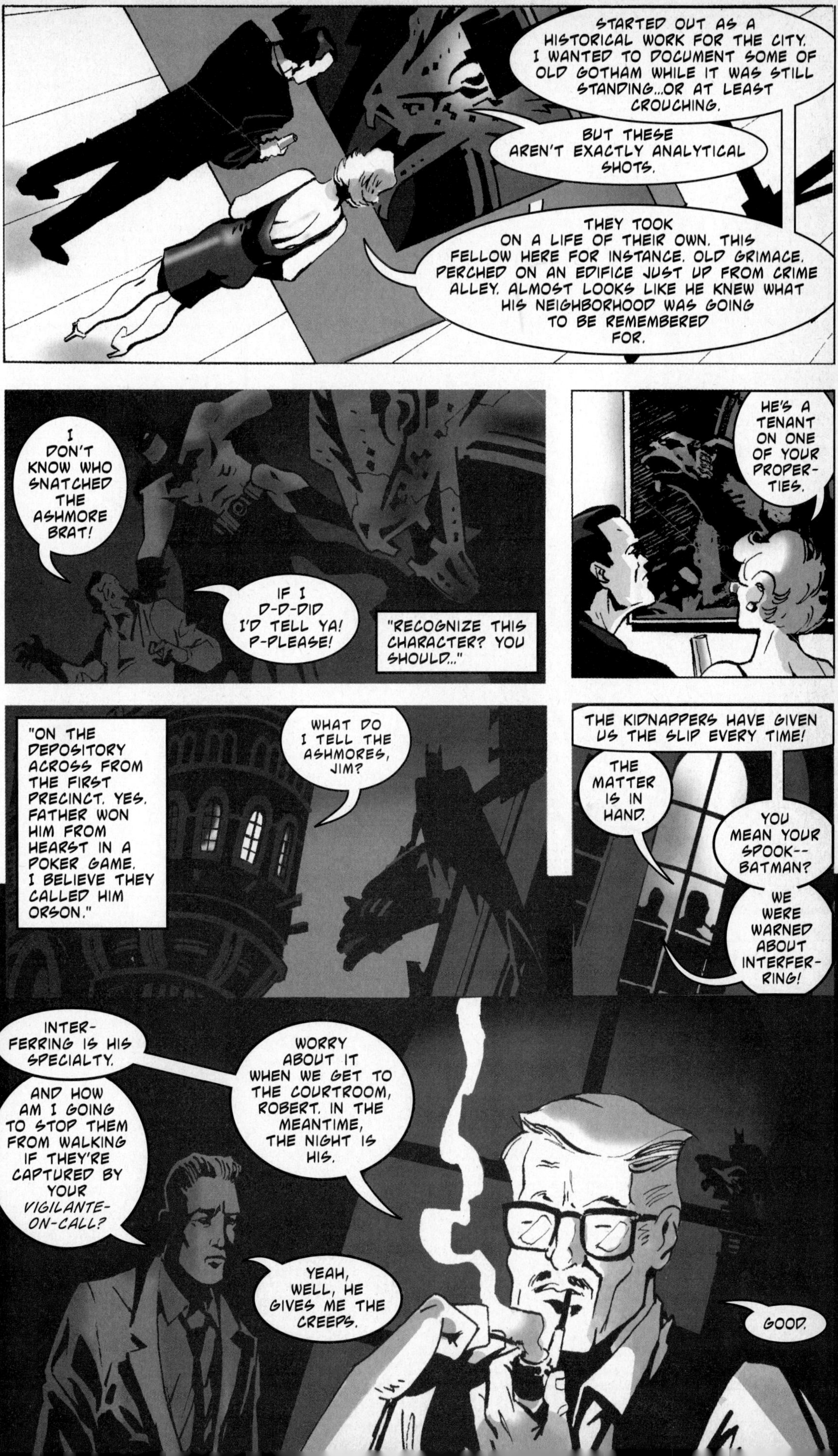
STARTED OUT AS A HISTORICAL WORK FOR THE CITY. I WANTED TO DOCUMENT SOME OF OLD GOTHAM WHILE IT WAS STILL STANDING...OR AT LEAST CROUCHING.
BUT THESE AREN'T EXACTLY ANALYTICAL SHOTS.
THEY TOOK ON A LIFE OF THEIR OWN. THIS FELLOW HERE FOR INSTANCE. OLD GRIMACE. PERCHED ON AN EDIFICE JUST UP FROM CRIME ALLEY. ALMOST LOOKS LIKE HE KNEW WHAT HIS NEIGHBORHOOD WAS GOING TO BE REMEMBERED FOR.
I DON'T KNOW WHO SNATCHED THE ASHMORE BRAT!
IF I D-D-DID I'D TELL YA! P-PLEASE!
"RECOGNIZE THIS CHARACTER? YOU SHOULD..."
HE'S A TENANT ON ONE OF YOUR PROPERTIES.
"ON THE DEPOSITORY ACROSS FROM THE FIRST PRECINCT. YES. FATHER WON HIM FROM HEARST IN A POKER GAME. I BELIEVE THEY CALLED HIM ORSON."
WHAT DO I TELL THE ASHMORES, JIM?
THE KIDNAPPERS HAVE GIVEN US THE SLIP EVERY TIME!
THE MATTER IS IN HAND.
YOU MEAN YOUR SPOOK--BATMAN?
WE WERE WARNED ABOUT INTERFERRING!
INTERFERRING IS HIS SPECIALTY.
AND HOW AM I GOING TO STOP THEM FROM WALKING IF THEY'RE CAPTURED BY YOUR *VIGILANTE-ON-CALL?*
WORRY ABOUT IT WHEN WE GET TO THE COURTROOM, ROBERT. IN THE MEANTIME, THE NIGHT IS HIS.
YEAH, WELL, HE GIVES ME THE CREEPS.
GOOD.

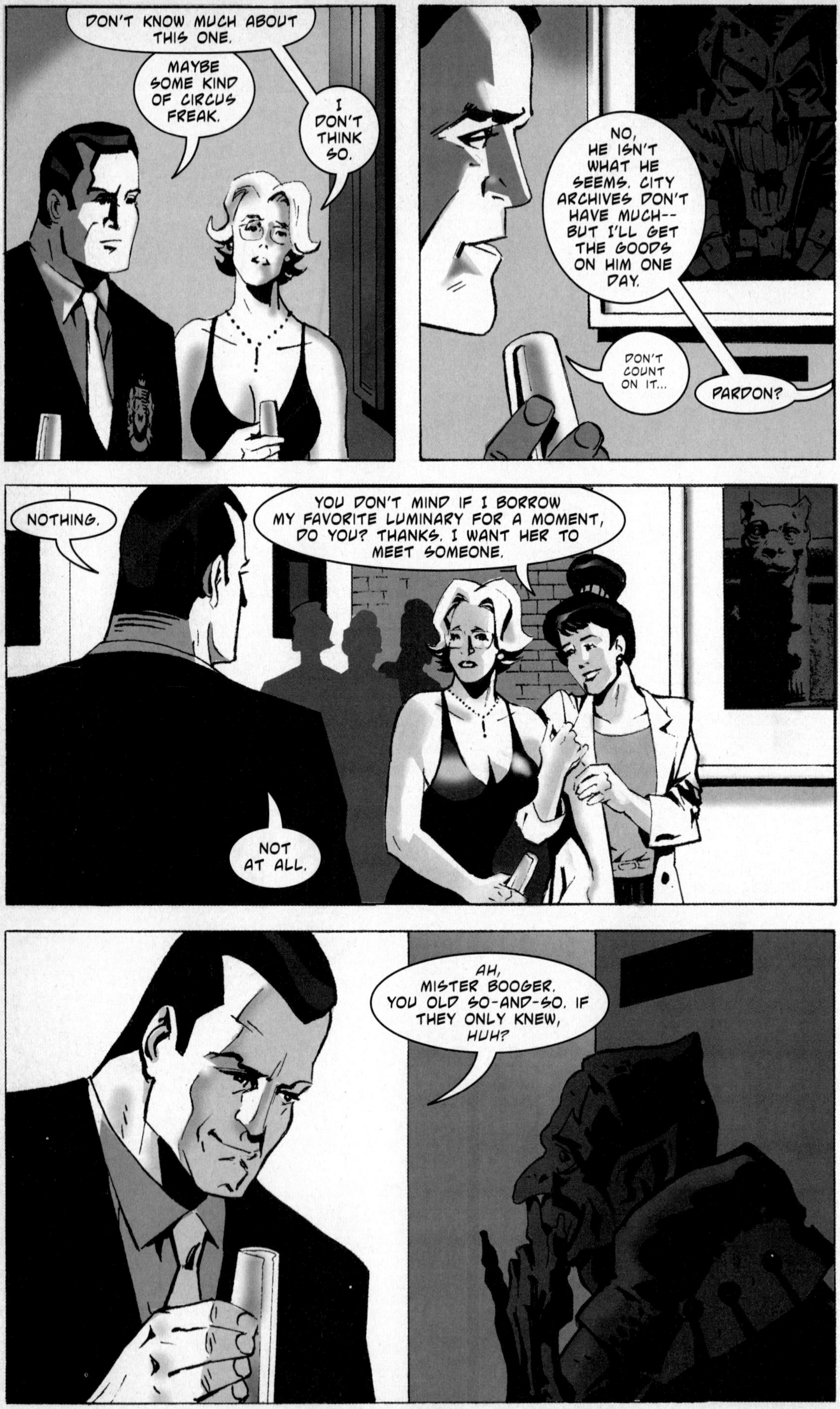
DON'T KNOW MUCH ABOUT THIS ONE.
MAYBE SOME KIND OF CIRCUS FREAK.
I DON'T THINK SO.
NO, HE ISN'T WHAT HE SEEMS. CITY ARCHIVES DON'T HAVE MUCH-- BUT I'LL GET THE GOODS ON HIM ONE DAY.
DON'T COUNT ON IT...
PARDON?
NOTHING.
YOU DON'T MIND IF I BORROW MY FAVORITE LUMINARY FOR A MOMENT, DO YOU? THANKS. I WANT HER TO MEET SOMEONE.
NOT AT ALL.
AH, MISTER BOOGER. YOU OLD SO-AND-SO. IF THEY ONLY KNEW, HUH?

IF YOU WANT TO SEE THE ASHMORE KID AGAIN-
LEAVE
TO THE
NO FUNNY
NO MARKED
REPLY

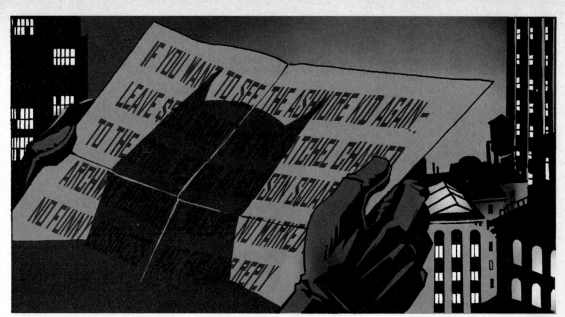

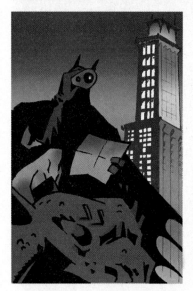

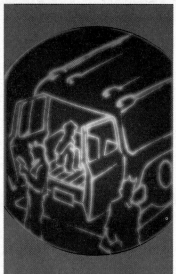

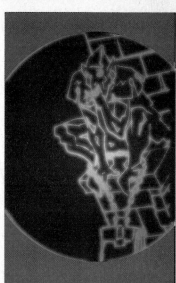

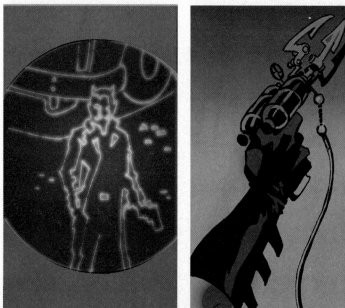

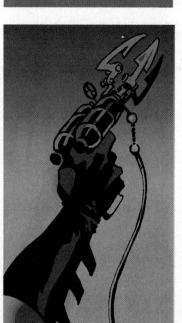

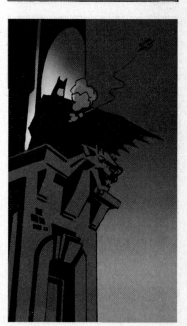

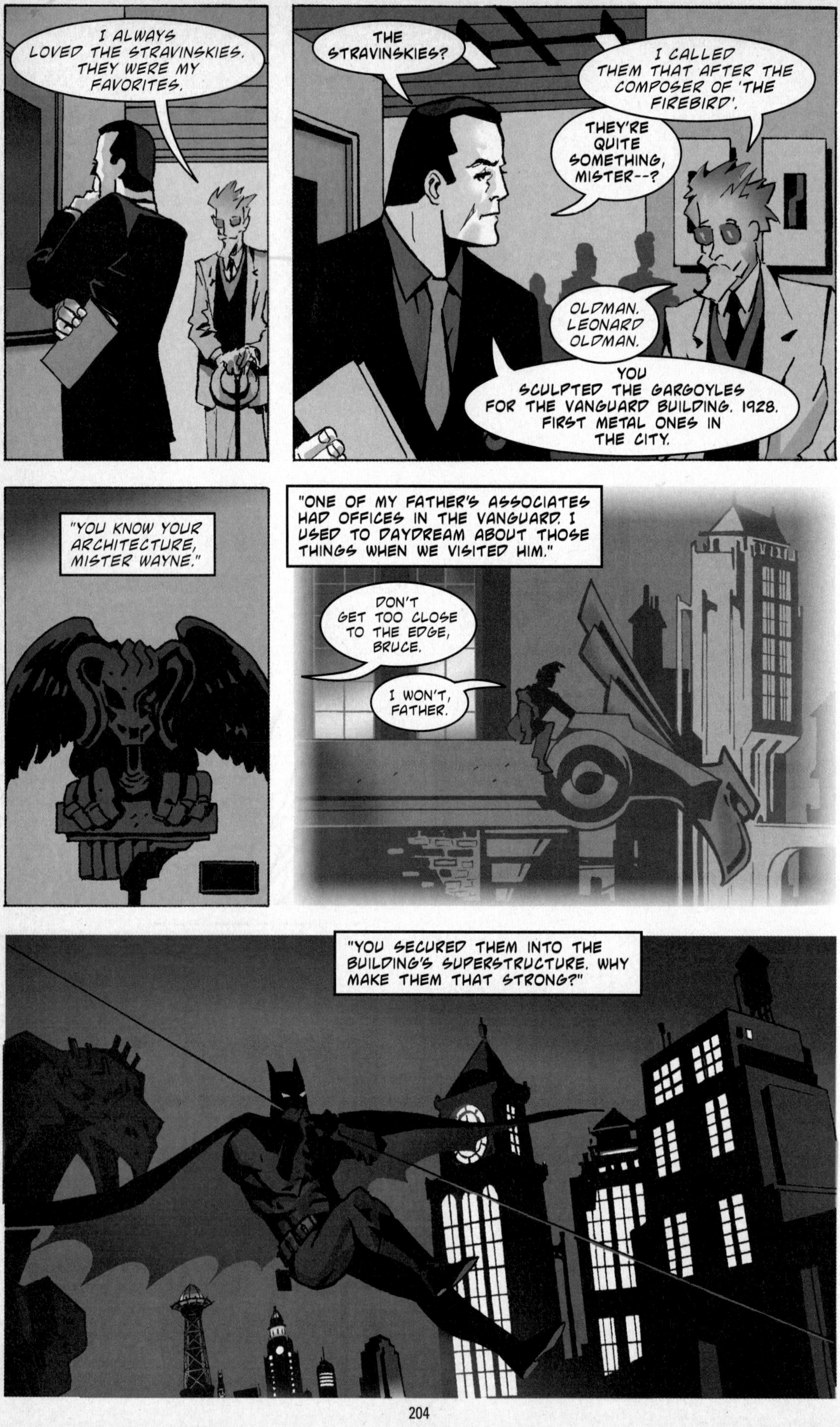
I ALWAYS LOVED THE STRAVINSKIES. THEY WERE MY FAVORITES.
THE STRAVINSKIES?
I CALLED THEM THAT AFTER THE COMPOSER OF 'THE FIREBIRD'.
THEY'RE QUITE SOMETHING, MISTER--?
OLDMAN. LEONARD OLDMAN.
YOU SCULPTED THE GARGOYLES FOR THE VANGUARD BUILDING. 1928. FIRST METAL ONES IN THE CITY.
"YOU KNOW YOUR ARCHITECTURE, MISTER WAYNE."
"ONE OF MY FATHER'S ASSOCIATES HAD OFFICES IN THE VANGUARD. I USED TO DAYDREAM ABOUT THOSE THINGS WHEN WE VISITED HIM."
DON'T GET TOO CLOSE TO THE EDGE, BRUCE.
I WON'T, FATHER.
"YOU SECURED THEM INTO THE BUILDING'S SUPERSTRUCTURE. WHY MAKE THEM THAT STRONG?"

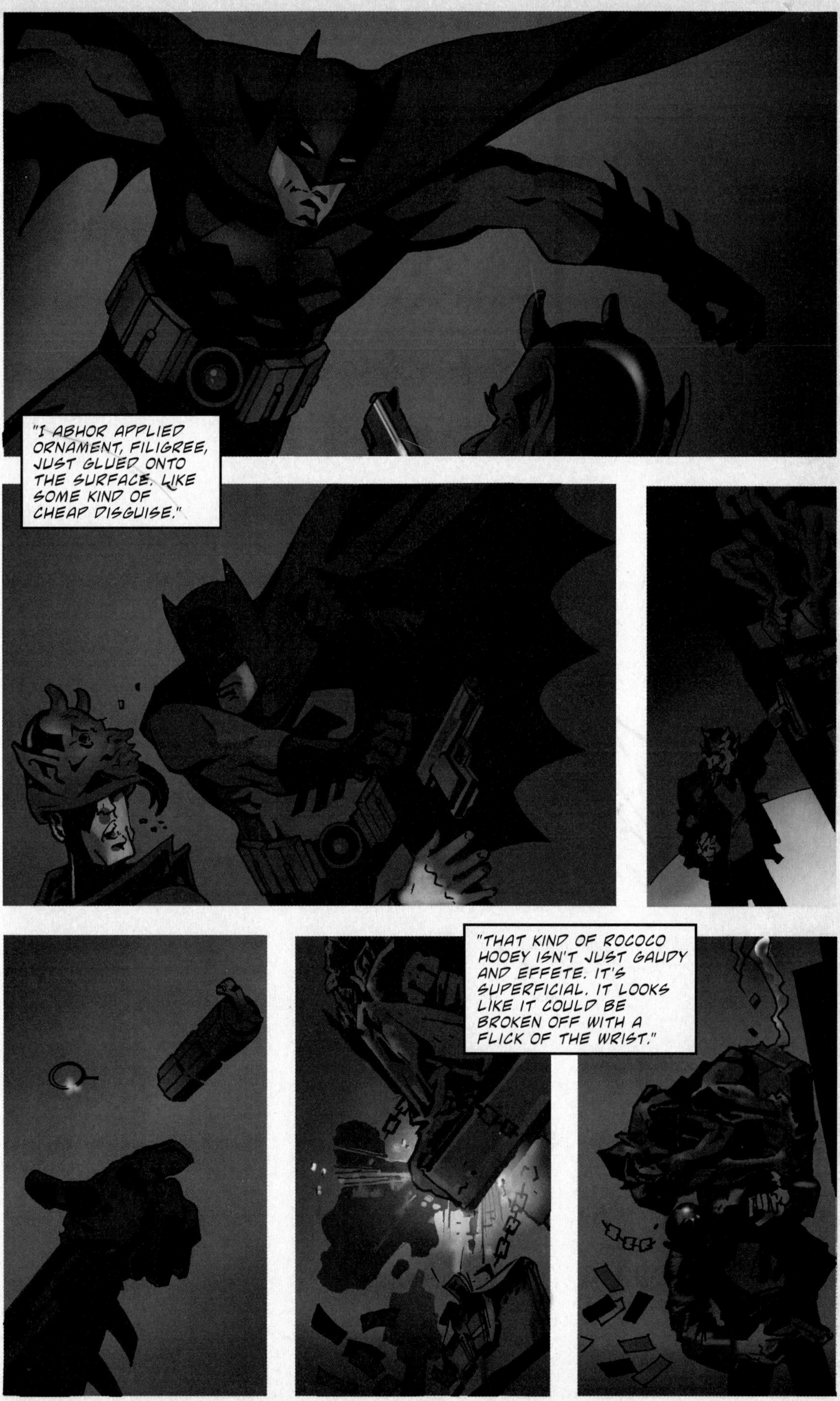
"I ABHOR APPLIED ORNAMENT, FILIGREE, JUST GLUED ONTO THE SURFACE. LIKE SOME KIND OF CHEAP DISGUISE."
"THAT KIND OF ROCOCO HOOEY ISN'T JUST GAUDY AND EFFETE. IT'S SUPERFICIAL. IT LOOKS LIKE IT COULD BE BROKEN OFF WITH A FLICK OF THE WRIST."

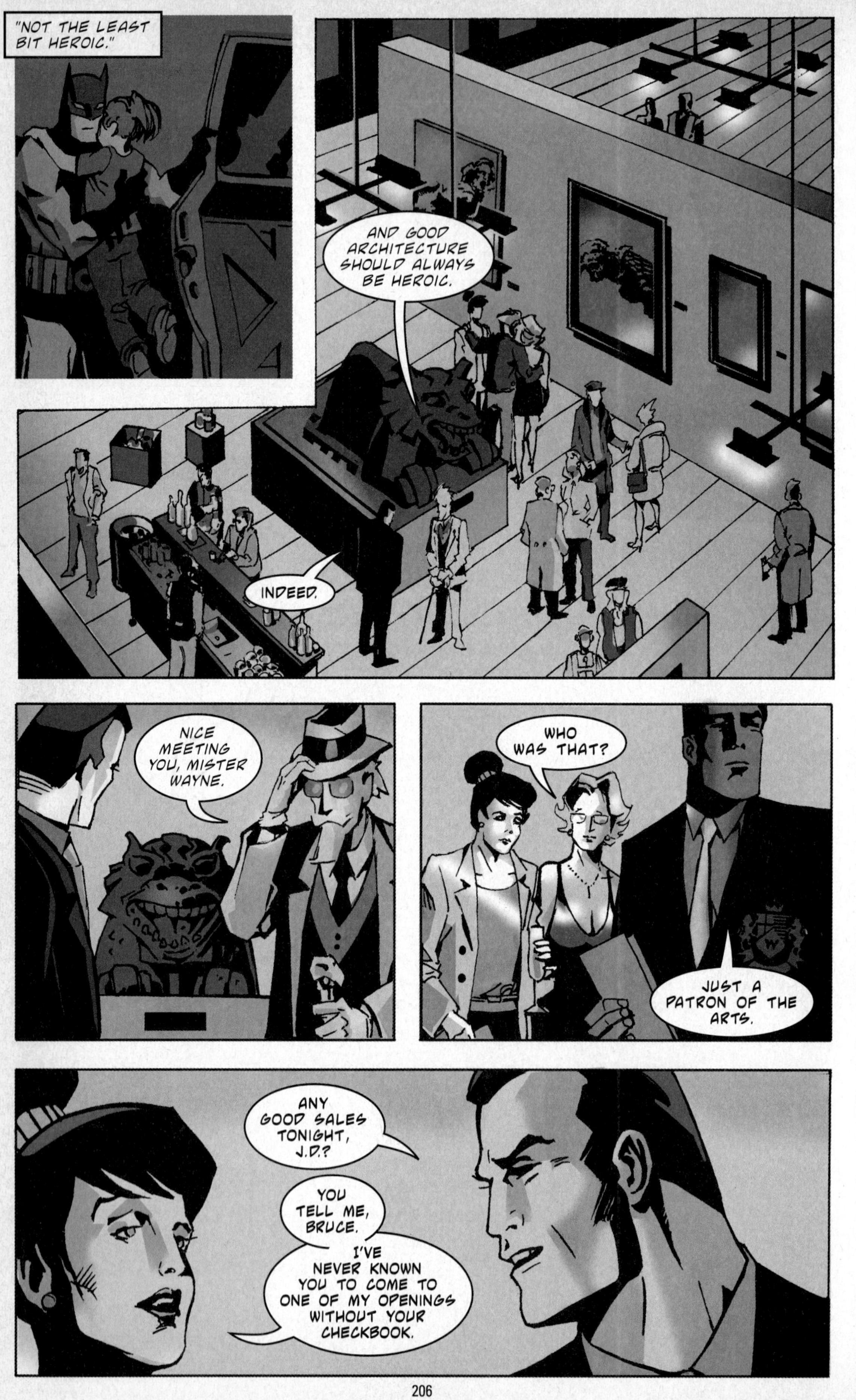
"NOT THE LEAST BIT HEROIC."
AND GOOD ARCHITECTURE SHOULD ALWAYS BE HEROIC.
INDEED.
NICE MEETING YOU, MISTER WAYNE.
WHO WAS THAT?
JUST A PATRON OF THE ARTS.
ANY GOOD SALES TONIGHT, J.D.?
YOU TELL ME, BRUCE.
I'VE NEVER KNOWN YOU TO COME TO ONE OF MY OPENINGS WITHOUT YOUR CHECKBOOK.

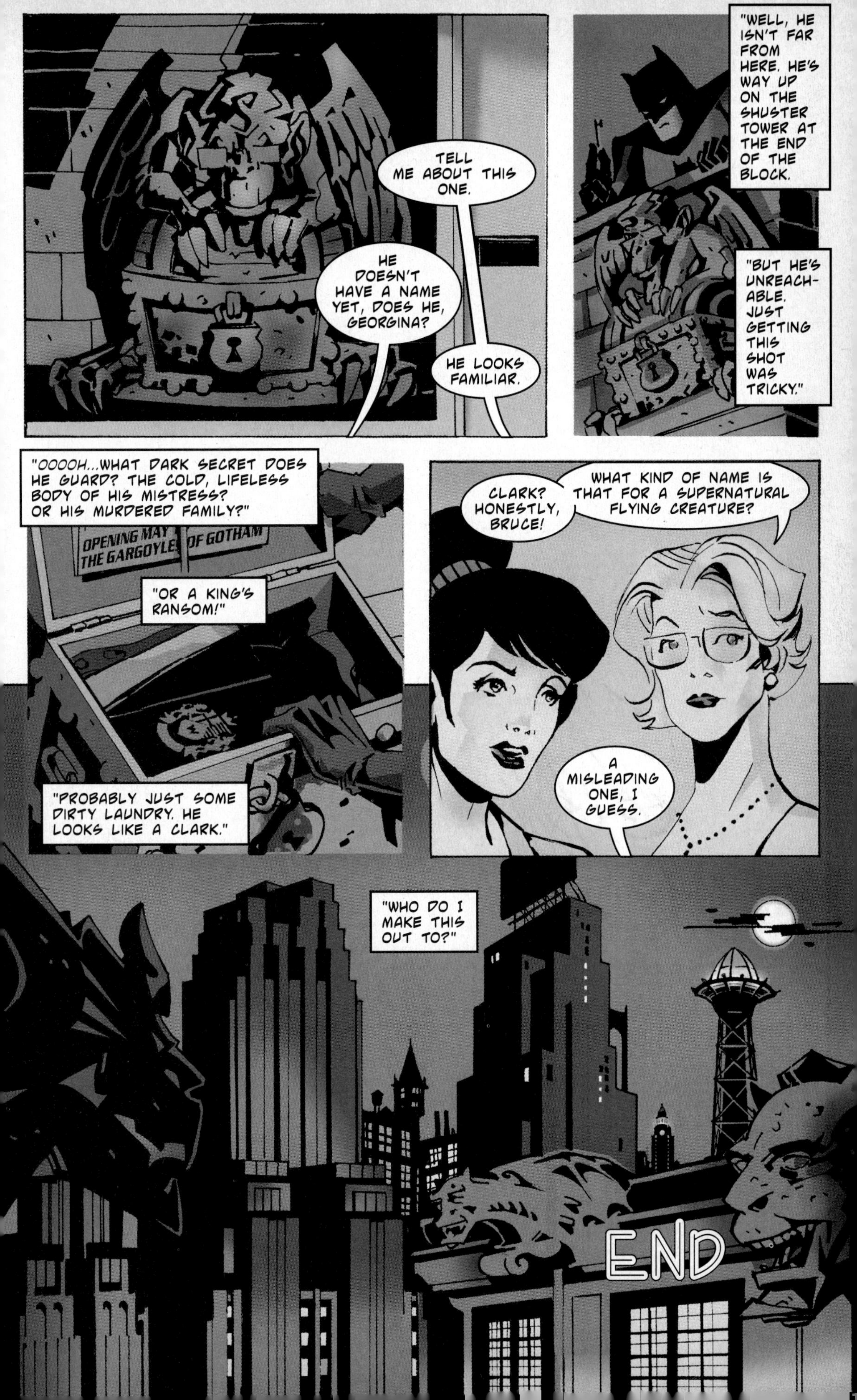
TELL ME ABOUT THIS ONE.
HE DOESN'T HAVE A NAME YET, DOES HE, GEORGINA?
HE LOOKS FAMILIAR.
"WELL, HE ISN'T FAR FROM HERE. HE'S WAY UP ON THE SHUSTER TOWER AT THE END OF THE BLOCK.
"BUT HE'S UNREACH-ABLE. JUST GETTING THIS SHOT WAS TRICKY."
"OOOOH...WHAT DARK SECRET DOES HE GUARD? THE COLD, LIFELESS BODY OF HIS MISTRESS? OR HIS MURDERED FAMILY?"
OPENING MAY THE GARGOYLES OF GOTHAM
"OR A KING'S RANSOM!"
"PROBABLY JUST SOME DIRTY LAUNDRY. HE LOOKS LIKE A CLARK."
CLARK? HONESTLY, BRUCE!
WHAT KIND OF NAME IS THAT FOR A SUPERNATURAL FLYING CREATURE?
A MISLEADING ONE, I GUESS.
"WHO DO I MAKE THIS OUT TO?"
END

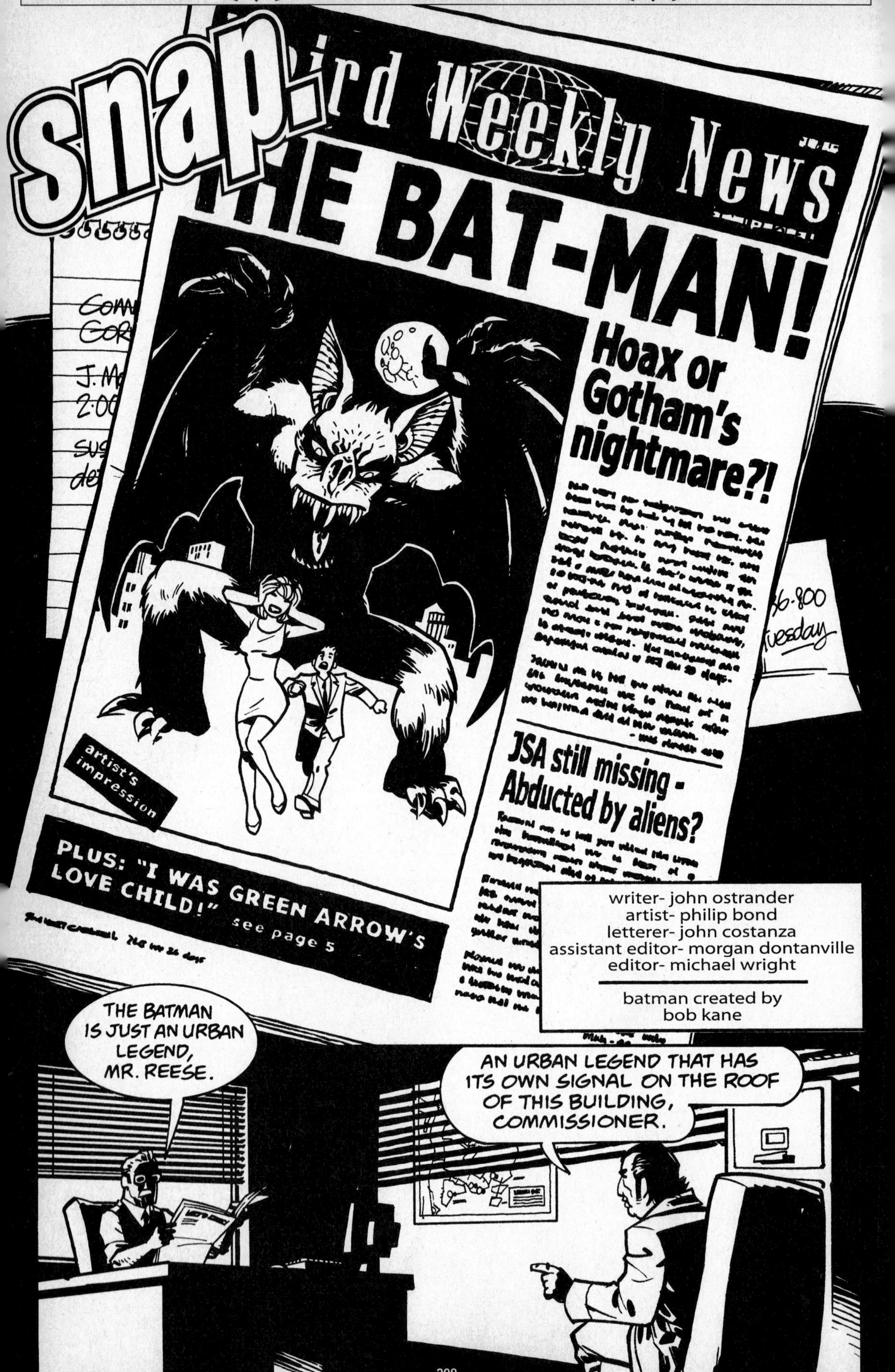
snap:
ird Weekly News
THE BAT-MAN!
Hoax or Gotham's nightmare?!
JSA still missing - Abducted by aliens?
artist's impression
PLUS: "I WAS GREEN ARROW'S LOVE CHILD!" see page 5
writer- john ostrander
artist- philip bond
letterer- john costanza
assistant editor- morgan dontanville
editor- michael wright
batman created by
bob kane
Tuesday
THE BATMAN IS JUST AN URBAN LEGEND, MR. REESE.
AN URBAN LEGEND THAT HAS ITS OWN SIGNAL ON THE ROOF OF THIS BUILDING, COMMISSIONER.

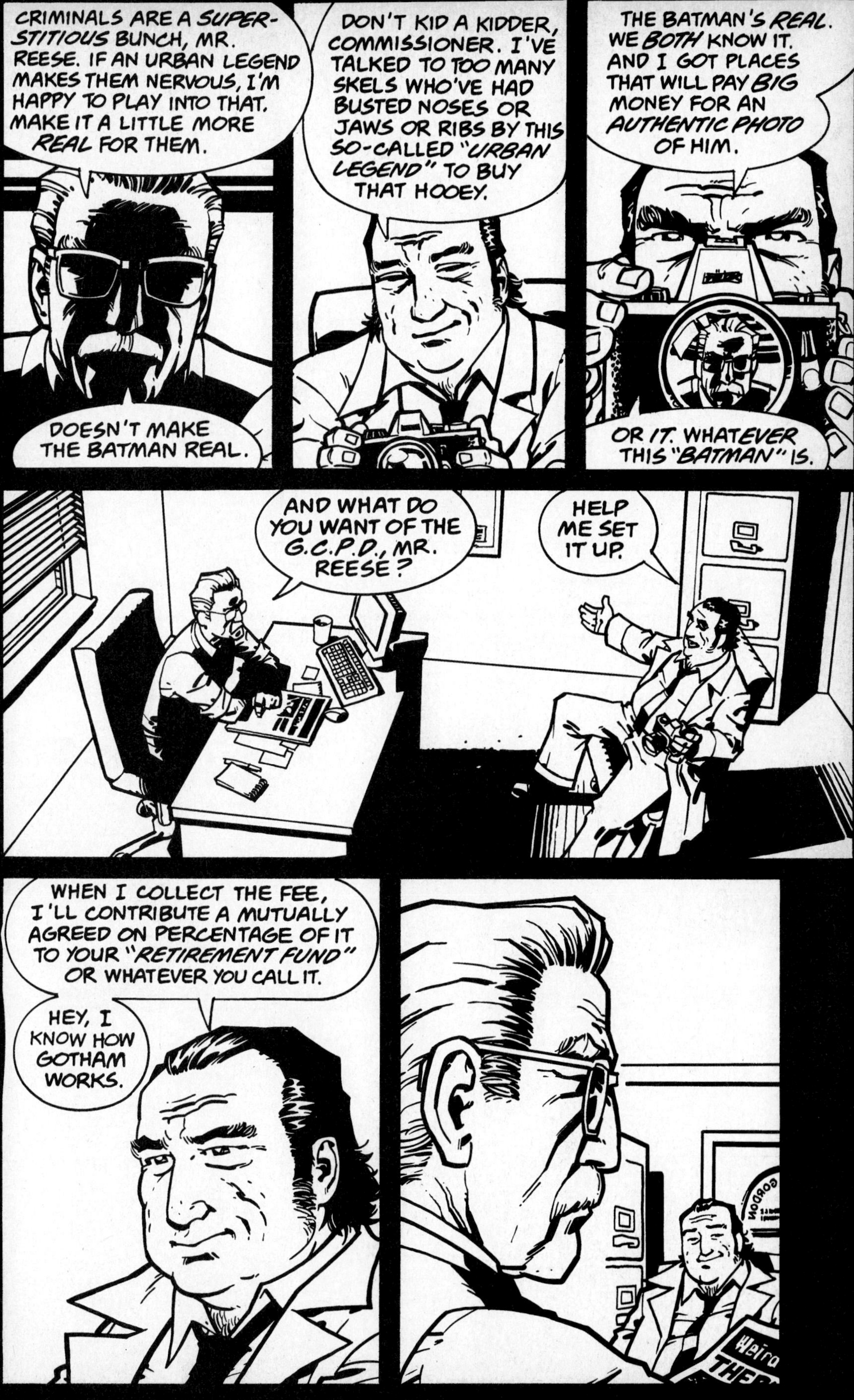
CRIMINALS ARE A SUPERSTITIOUS BUNCH, MR. REESE. IF AN URBAN LEGEND MAKES THEM NERVOUS, I'M HAPPY TO PLAY INTO THAT. MAKE IT A LITTLE MORE REAL FOR THEM.
DOESN'T MAKE THE BATMAN REAL.
DON'T KID A KIDDER, COMMISSIONER. I'VE TALKED TO TOO MANY SKELS WHO'VE HAD BUSTED NOSES OR JAWS OR RIBS BY THIS SO-CALLED "URBAN LEGEND" TO BUY THAT HOOEY.
THE BATMAN'S REAL. WE BOTH KNOW IT. AND I GOT PLACES THAT WILL PAY BIG MONEY FOR AN AUTHENTIC PHOTO OF HIM.
OR IT. WHATEVER THIS "BATMAN" IS.
AND WHAT DO YOU WANT OF THE G.C.P.D., MR. REESE?
HELP ME SET IT UP.
WHEN I COLLECT THE FEE, I'LL CONTRIBUTE A MUTUALLY AGREED ON PERCENTAGE OF IT TO YOUR "RETIREMENT FUND" OR WHATEVER YOU CALL IT.
HEY, I KNOW HOW GOTHAM WORKS.

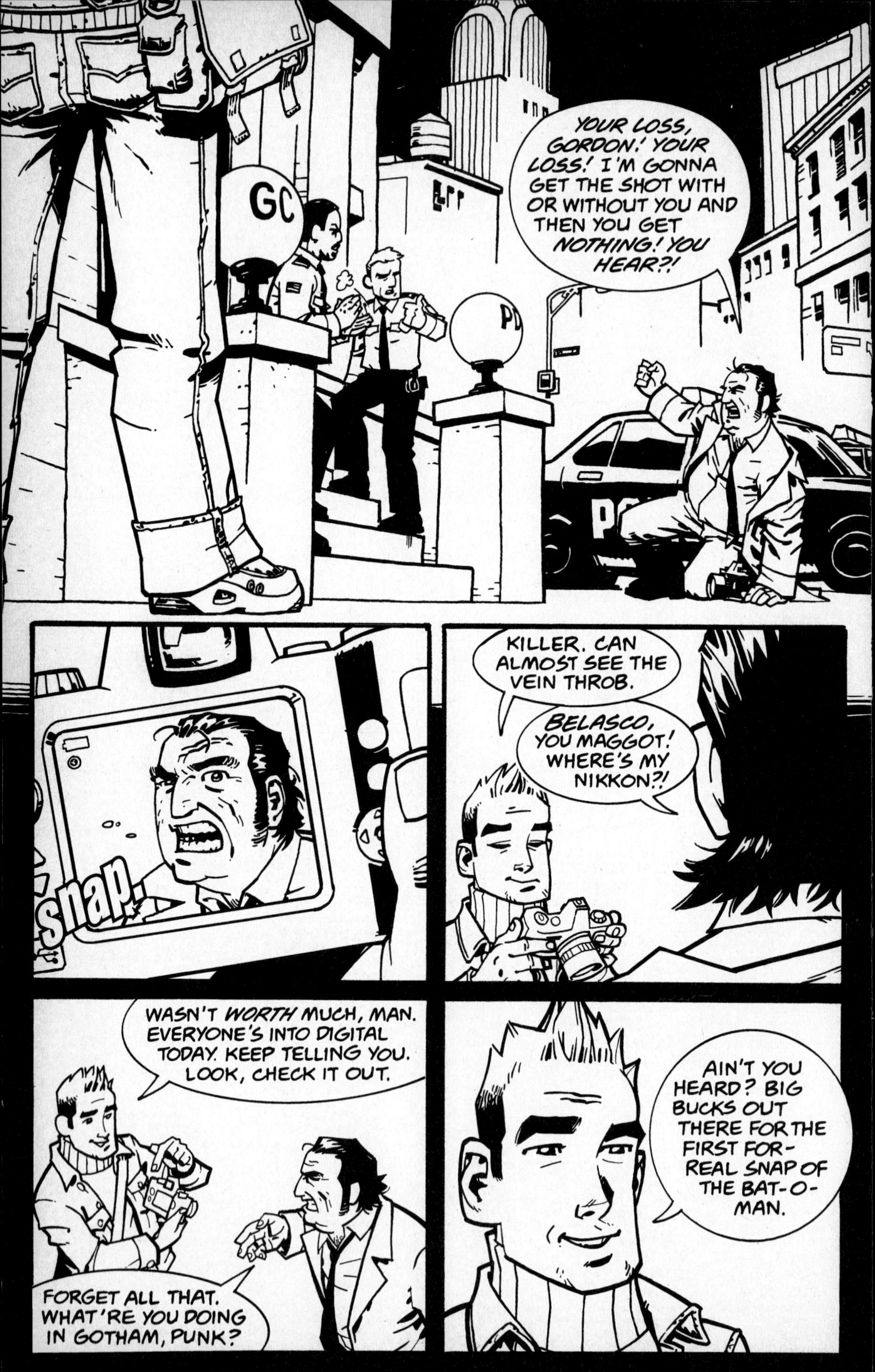
GC
PD
YOUR LOSS, GORDON! YOUR LOSS! I'M GONNA GET THE SHOT WITH OR WITHOUT YOU AND THEN YOU GET NOTHING! YOU HEAR?!
SNAP.
KILLER. CAN ALMOST SEE THE VEIN THROB.
BELASCO, YOU MAGGOT! WHERE'S MY NIKKON?!
WASN'T WORTH MUCH, MAN. EVERYONE'S INTO DIGITAL TODAY. KEEP TELLING YOU. LOOK, CHECK IT OUT.
FORGET ALL THAT. WHAT'RE YOU DOING IN GOTHAM, PUNK?
AIN'T YOU HEARD? BIG BUCKS OUT THERE FOR THE FIRST FOR-REAL SNAP OF THE BAT-O-MAN.

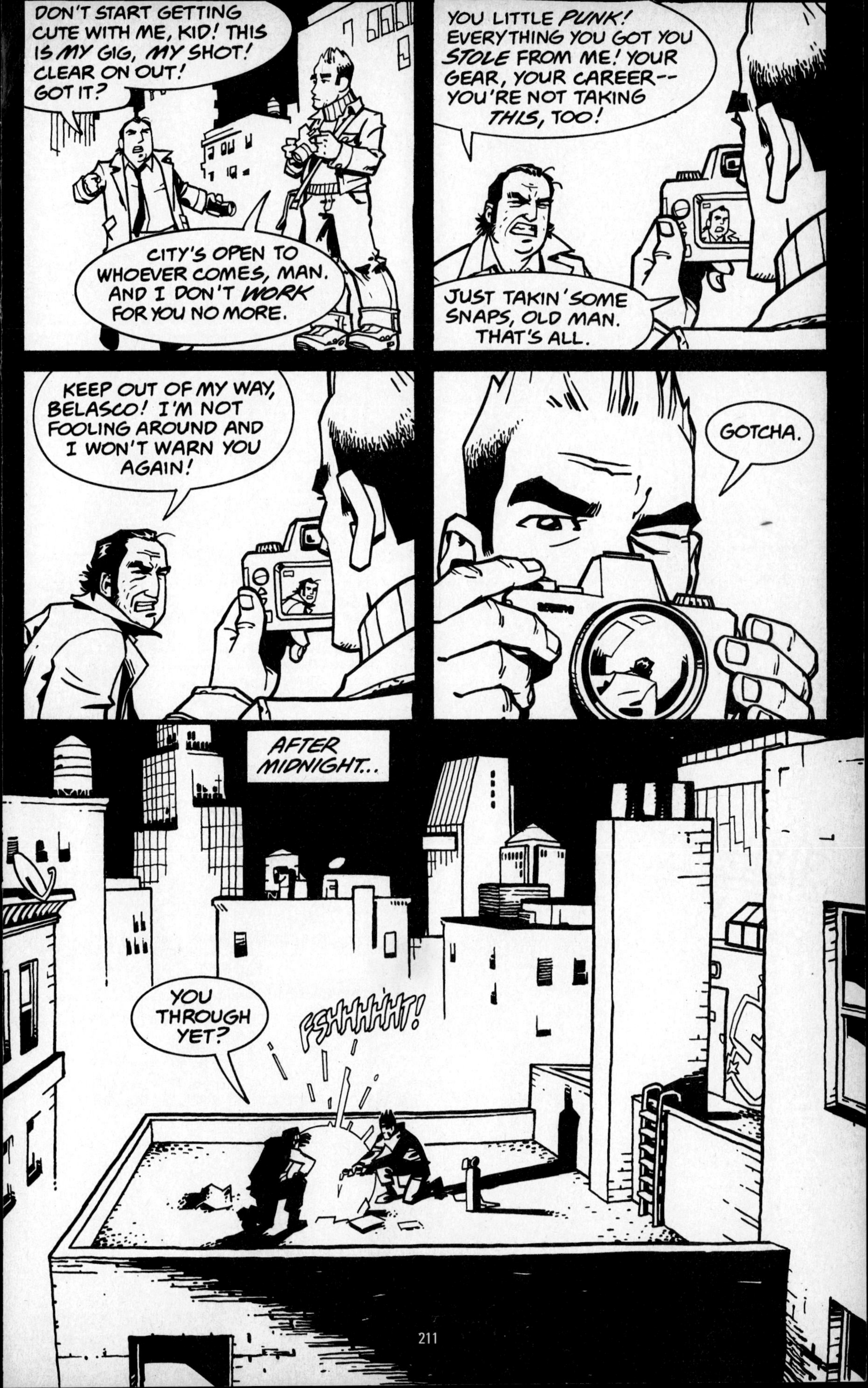
DON'T START GETTING CUTE WITH ME, KID! THIS IS MY GIG, MY SHOT! CLEAR ON OUT! GOT IT?
CITY'S OPEN TO WHOEVER COMES, MAN. AND I DON'T WORK FOR YOU NO MORE.
YOU LITTLE PUNK! EVERYTHING YOU GOT YOU STOLE FROM ME! YOUR GEAR, YOUR CAREER-- YOU'RE NOT TAKING THIS, TOO!
JUST TAKIN' SOME SNAPS, OLD MAN. THAT'S ALL.
KEEP OUT OF MY WAY, BELASCO! I'M NOT FOOLING AROUND AND I WON'T WARN YOU AGAIN!
GOTCHA.
AFTER MIDNIGHT...
YOU THROUGH YET?
FSHHHHHT!

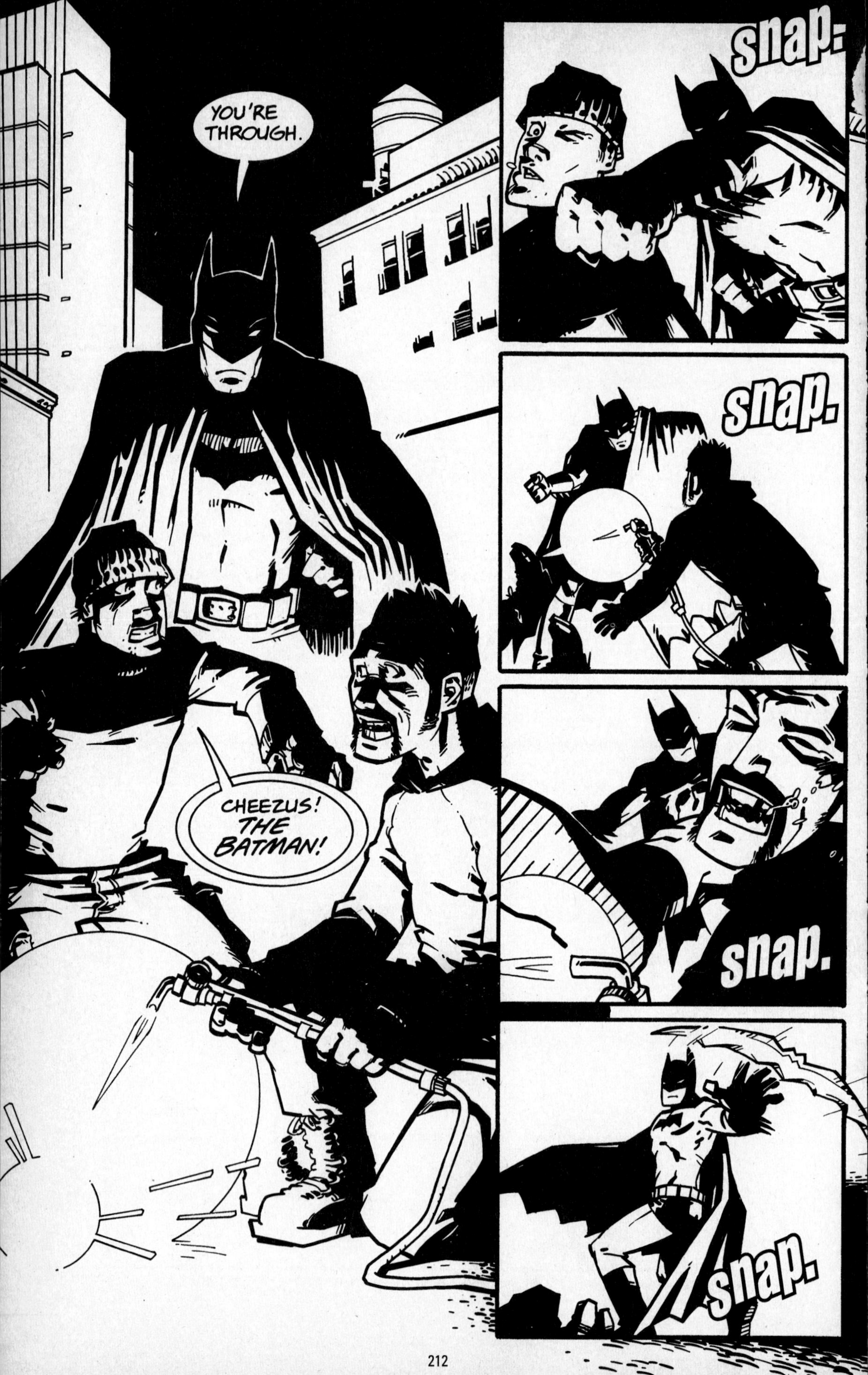
YOU'RE THROUGH.
CHEEZUS! THE BATMAN!
snap.
snap.
snap.
snap.

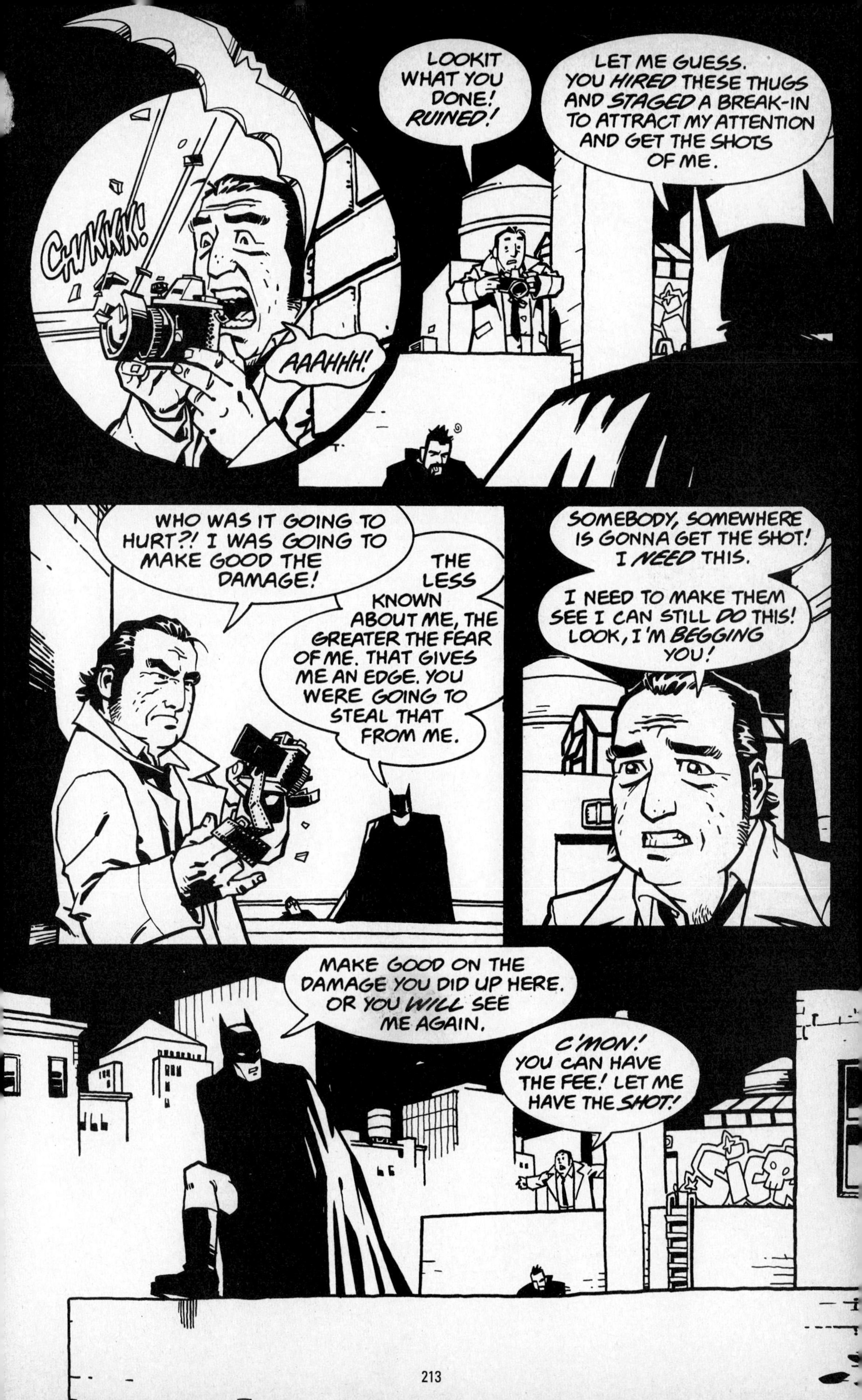
CHKKKK!
AAAHHH!
LOOKIT WHAT YOU DONE! RUINED!
LET ME GUESS. YOU HIRED THESE THUGS AND STAGED A BREAK-IN TO ATTRACT MY ATTENTION AND GET THE SHOTS OF ME.
WHO WAS IT GOING TO HURT?! I WAS GOING TO MAKE GOOD THE DAMAGE!
THE LESS KNOWN ABOUT ME, THE GREATER THE FEAR OF ME. THAT GIVES ME AN EDGE. YOU WERE GOING TO STEAL THAT FROM ME.
SOMEBODY, SOMEWHERE IS GONNA GET THE SHOT! I NEED THIS.
I NEED TO MAKE THEM SEE I CAN STILL DO THIS! LOOK, I'M BEGGING YOU!
MAKE GOOD ON THE DAMAGE YOU DID UP HERE. OR YOU WILL SEE ME AGAIN.
C'MON! YOU CAN HAVE THE FEE! LET ME HAVE THE SHOT!

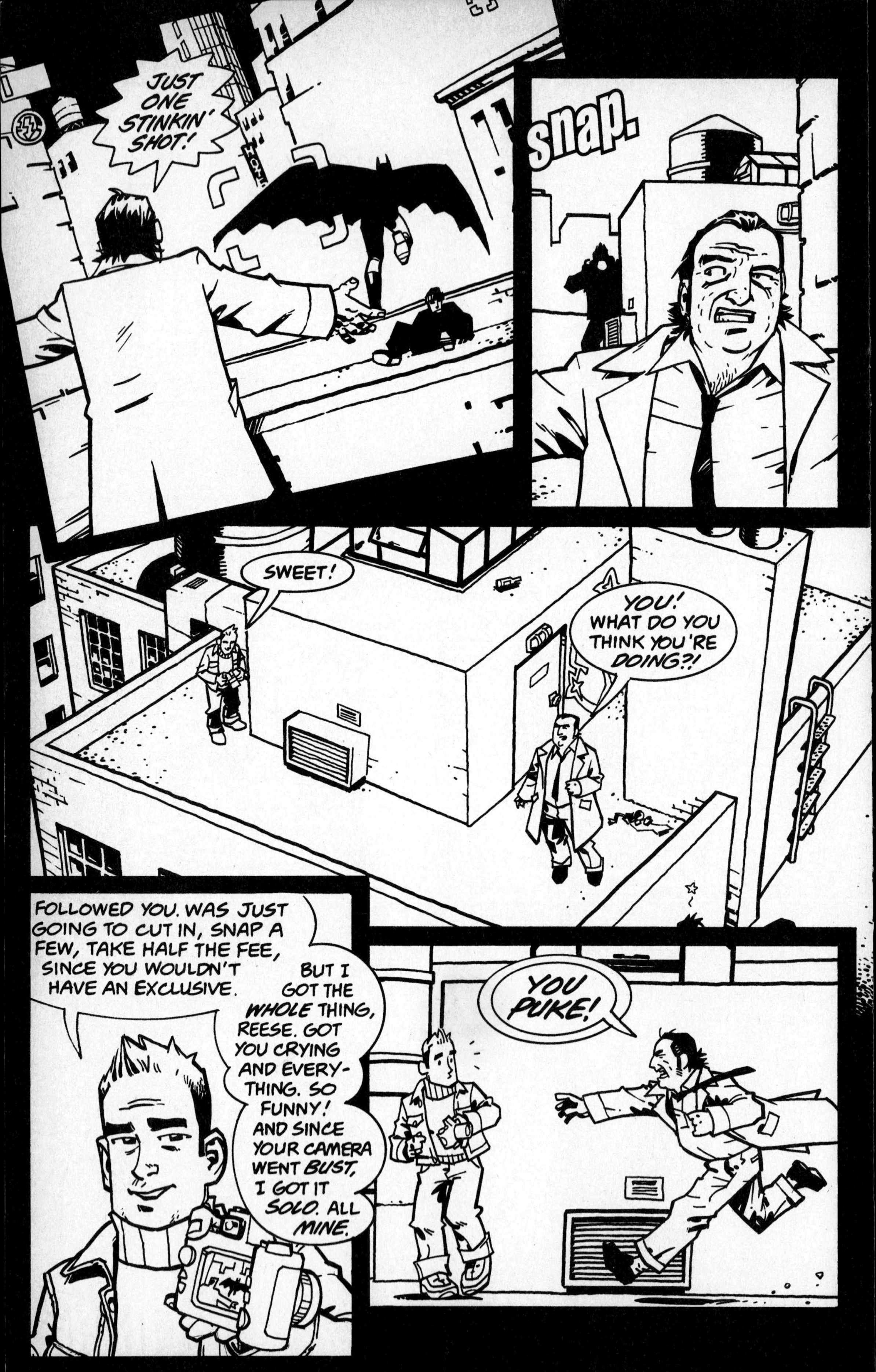
JUST ONE STINKIN' SHOT!
snap.
SWEET!
YOU! WHAT DO YOU THINK YOU'RE DOING?!
FOLLOWED YOU. WAS JUST GOING TO CUT IN, SNAP A FEW, TAKE HALF THE FEE, SINCE YOU WOULDN'T HAVE AN EXCLUSIVE.
BUT I GOT THE WHOLE THING, REESE. GOT YOU CRYING AND EVERY-THING. SO FUNNY! AND SINCE YOUR CAMERA WENT BUST, I GOT IT SOLO. ALL MINE.
YOU PUKE!

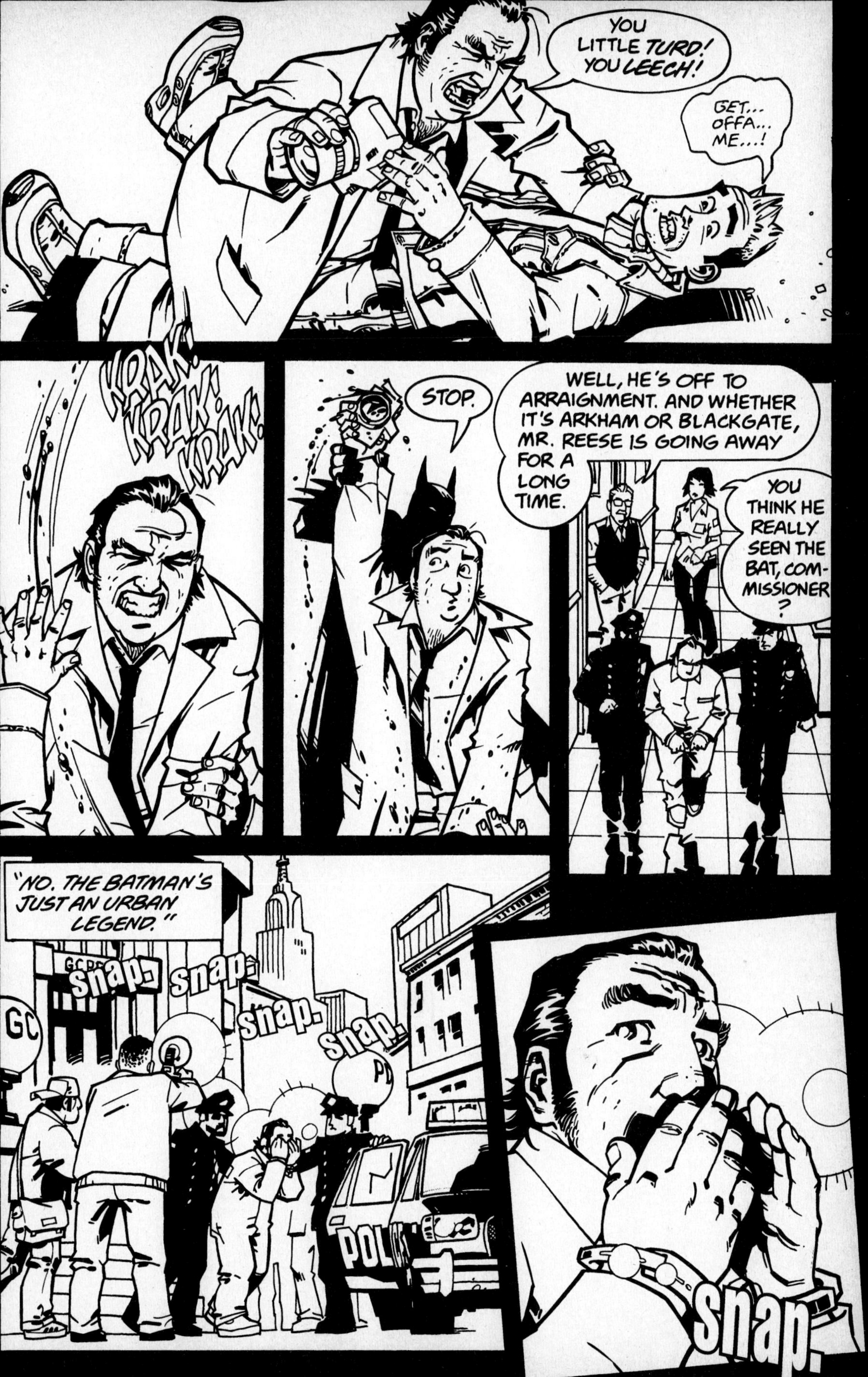
YOU LITTLE TURD! YOU LEECH!
GET... OFFA... ME...!
KRAK! KRAK! KRAK!
STOP.
WELL, HE'S OFF TO ARRAIGNMENT. AND WHETHER IT'S ARKHAM OR BLACKGATE, MR. REESE IS GOING AWAY FOR A LONG TIME.
YOU THINK HE REALLY SEEN THE BAT, COMMISSIONER?
"NO. THE BATMAN'S JUST AN URBAN LEGEND."
snap. snap. snap. snap.
POL
snap.

BATMAN

BLACK and WHITE

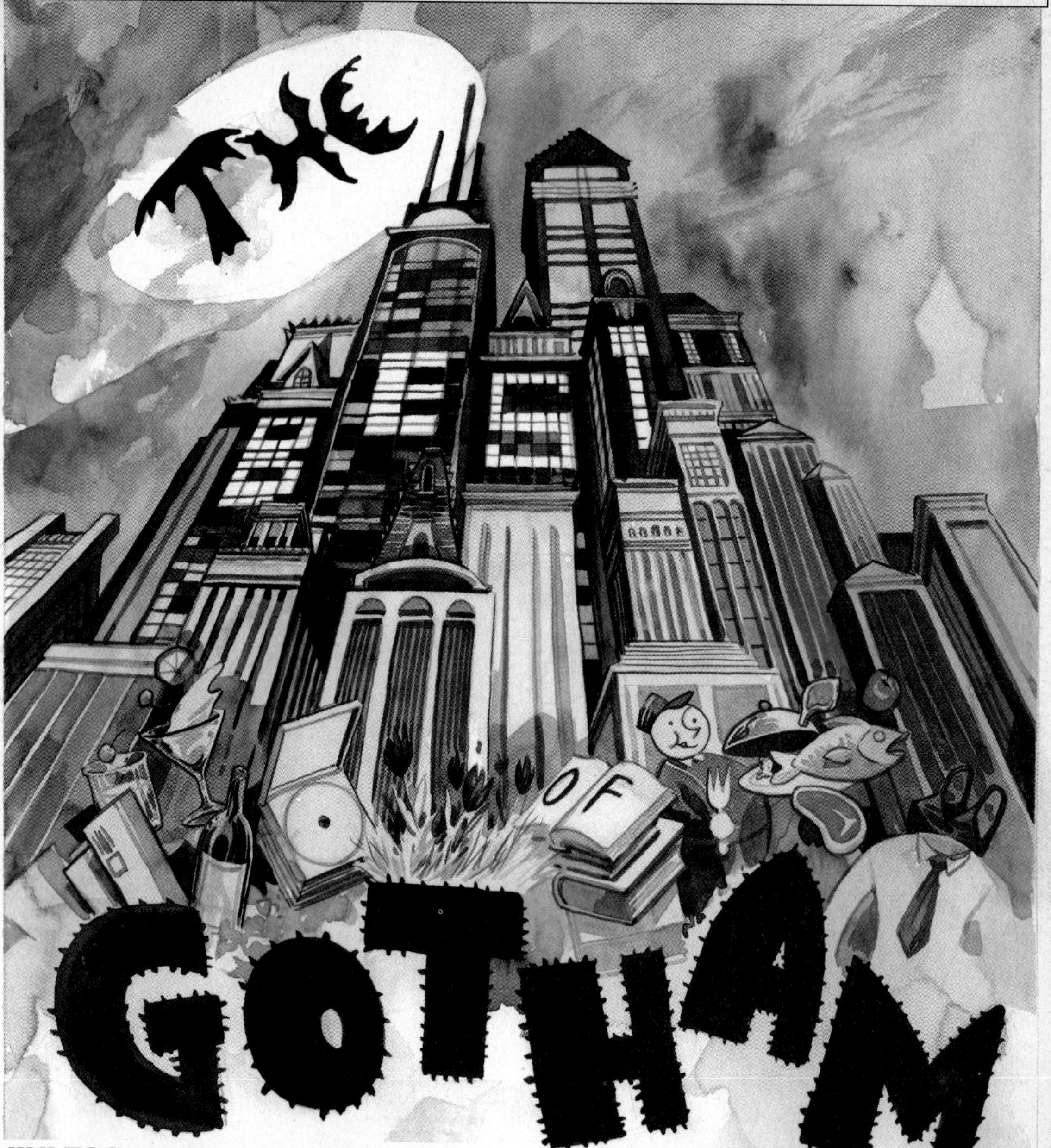
OF
GOTHAM

**UNLESS** you've been living under a rock, you're probably aware that Gotham City hasn't always had the most stellar of reputations. Sure, Gotham has the commerce and bustle of other grand coastal cities, but crime and violence forever tarnished the shine of her name. Overshadowed by Metropolis and Central City, Gotham has struggled to overcome the stigma of Crime Alley and the menace of Arkham Asylum.

But the low rents in Crime Alley made it attractive to the artistic community who were quick to take advantage of the warehouse space and turn the grittiest of warehouses into the hippest of art gallery districts. Cozy coffeehouses soon followed, and the local mom-and-pop diner overflowed with starving (literally) artists. Urban pioneers restored rowhouses, and rooftop gardens abound where pigeons formerly feared to tread.

In recent years, however, developers have gobbled up real estate at breakneck speed, and gleaming "loftominiums" are available at upwards of half a million dollars. The mom-and-pop diners and taquerias now rub elbows with the trendiest of restaurants, and the local watering holes overflow with the martini and Bellini crowd.

More recently, Hollywood's love affair with crime drama has made Gotham the number one locale for budget-conscious moviemakers who want New York aesthetics at affordable prices, and celebrities who fell in love with Gotham while filming have snapped up the luxurious penthouses that occupy the former hideouts of Gotham's super criminals.

So where can you go to see and be seen, taste the creations of the hottest new chefs and quench your thirst with the drink of the moment? Our BEST OF GOTHAM index spotlights the newest delights and charms that will make Metropolis and Central City green with envy.

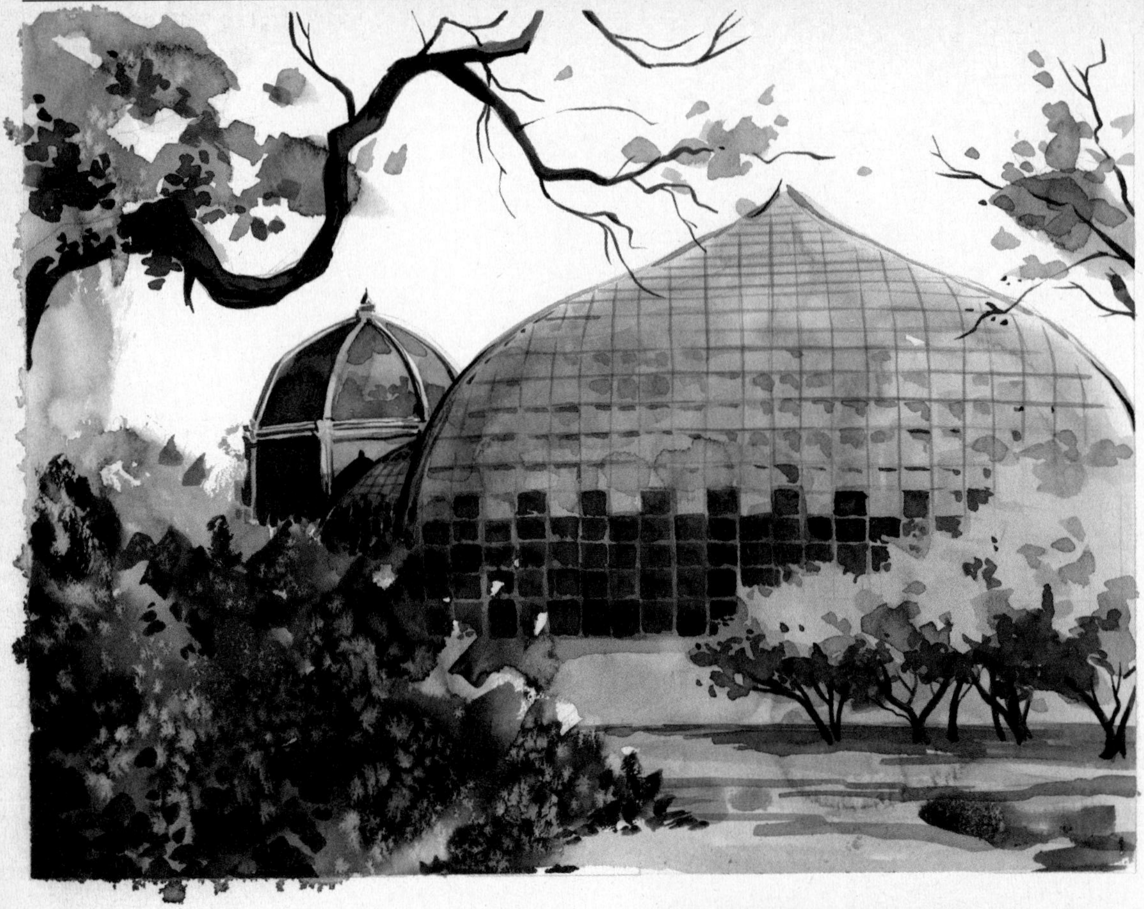

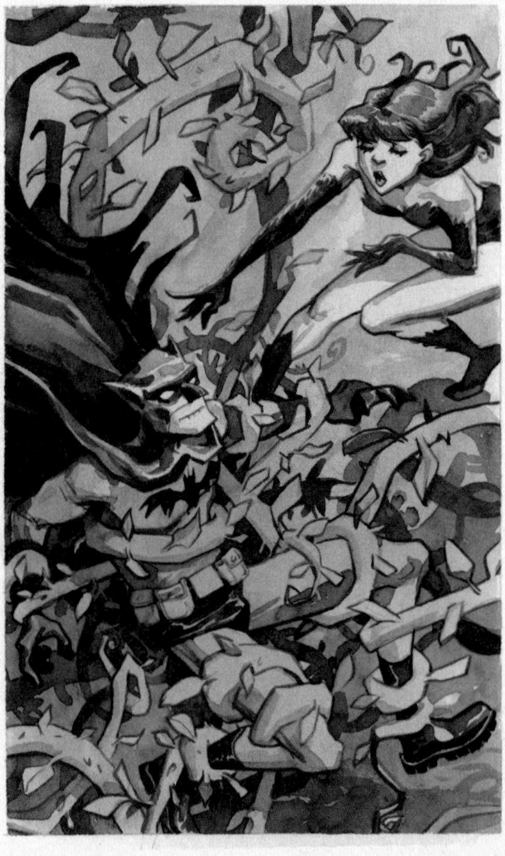

**AFTER** months of renovation, the Gotham Conservatory is once again home to a thriving variety of lush botanicals. Thanks to the generosity of cultural benefactor Bruce Wayne, 300,000 new panes of glass were replaced and thousands of exotic plants replanted after last winter's battle between The Batman and eco-terrorist Poison Ivy. Security cameras recorded a portion of the conflict (left) before structural damage sustained during the fight caused the roof to collapse. 28 Wayne Memorial Park Circle.

OPEN Monday through Friday 9 to 5, Saturday and Sunday 9 to 6. Admission $6 for adults, $3 for seniors and students, children under 12 free.

Through June: see a computer-generated animation of the battle that caused the renovation of the conservatory and step-by-step reconstruction of the Rainforest Room and Desert Oasis.

Through March: Island Paradise — sip cocktails and dance to Caribbean fusion music with the scent of night-blooming jasmine heavy in the air, as the Conservatory brings you the best of the tropics even in the dead of winter. Tuesday evenings 8 to 10 PM.

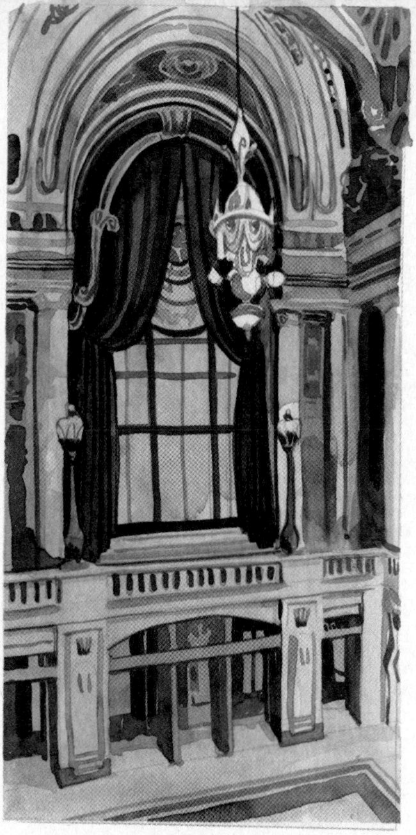

**INTERIOR OF A GRAND OLDE-TYME THEATRE:** Visiting the Hamilton St. Theatre at Christmas for the holiday staples *"A Christmas Carol"* or *"The Nutcracker"* has long been a standing tradition in Gotham's theater history, but due to the ravages of age never had the patronage it deserved during the rest of the year, until now. Local pop diva La-La-La has made the restoration of this venerable hall her pet project. Conservators spent over a year removing decades of dirt, grime and air pollution from the resplendent frescoes that adorn the acoustic ceilings. Since the cleanup, avant-garde productions such as *The Naked Truth, Spider and Fly,* and the hit musical *I'm In Love With Batman* (below) are giving Broadway a run for its money.

Classical concerts share stage time with edgy rock bands during the Gotham Music Festival here. Call 555-2821 for event schedule.

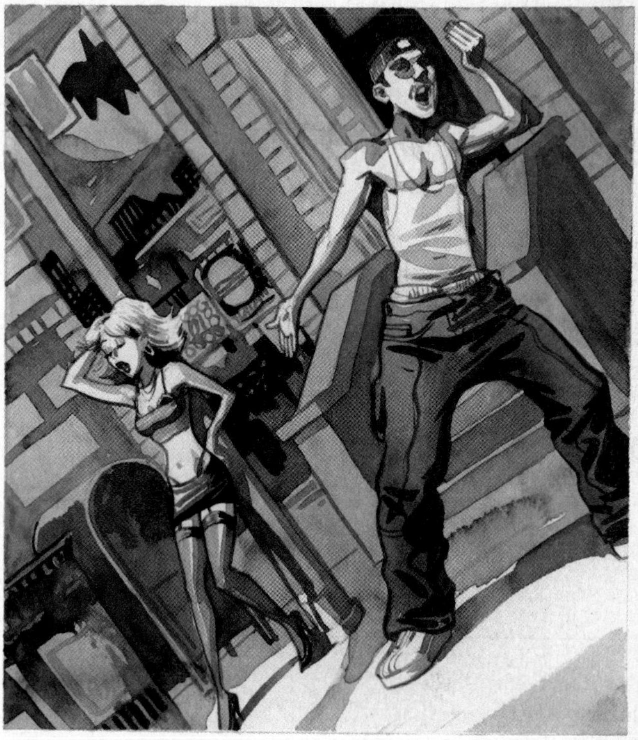

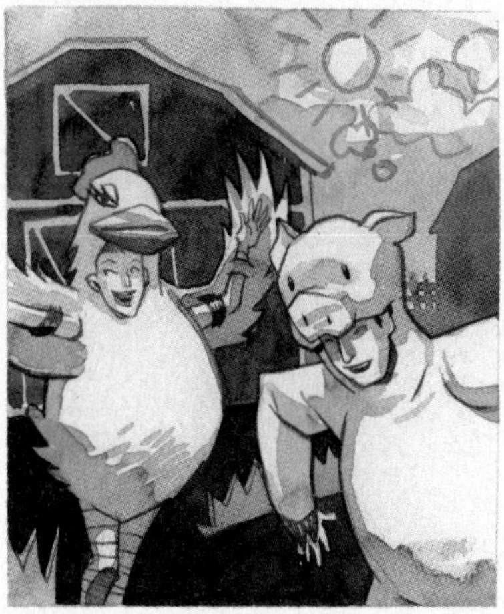

**BEST CHILDREN'S THEATER:** Mother May I? Productions presents *"BOO! The Barn is Haunted"* based on the book of the same name. This colorful tale of the food chain explains the facts of farm life with subversive song and dance. 7612 N. Greenwood Avenue (storefront). Call 555-play (7529).

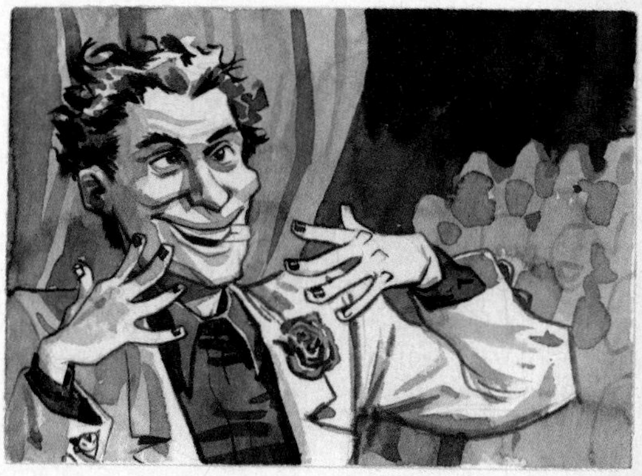

**BEST IMPROV:** *Improvalicious,* 1060 North Front St. This improv comedy troupe finally has a permanent space, so let the laffs begin! The engaging wit of Gotham's premiere comedy troupe is matched only by their ribald nonsense humor! Their new revue *"The Joker's On You!"* combines the best of both. Funnyman Garry Blatt's impersonation of the Clown Prince of Crime surpasses last year's performance in *"Riddler on the Roof!"* And who thought that was possible? Friday through Saturday 8 and 10:30 PM, Sunday 4 and 8 PM. Call 555-3991.

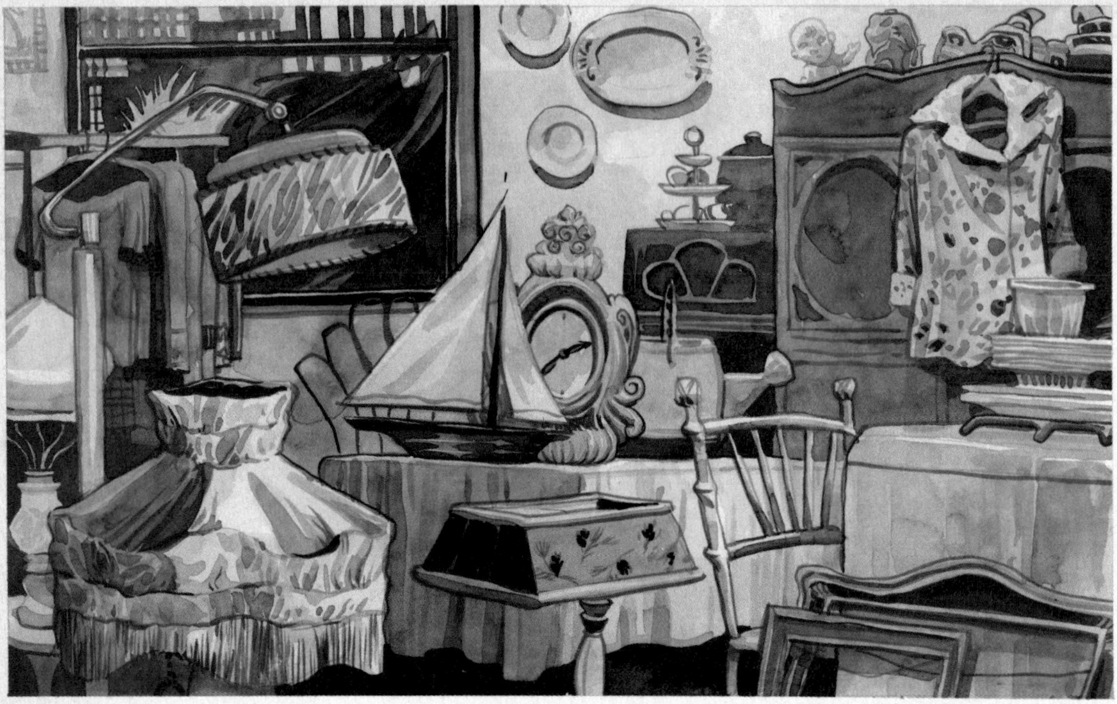

BEST THRIFT SHOPPING: *Kitschy Kat Clothing and Accessories.* Furniture and fun fill this 4,000-square-foot space with nostalgic charm. Unusual lamps, funhouse mirrors and distinct barware are sure to bring a unique touch to any home. 33 Robinson St., open every day 11 to 5.

BEST ONE-OF-A-KIND CLOTHING: *Costume.* Tucked away above a noodle shop, designer Susie Mai's showroom and workspace is a haven for those who crave a truly original wardrobe. All of her clothing is crafted from the confiscated costuming of Gotham's incarcerated villains. Needless to say her collections of clothing have a "cult" following, and this store has become one of Gotham's chic shopping destinations. 144 Sprang Galleria, Upper Level, entrance through Tung Sing Chinese Food. Open weekdays 11 to 8 by appointment, weekends 10 to 9. All major cards accepted, no checks. $$$

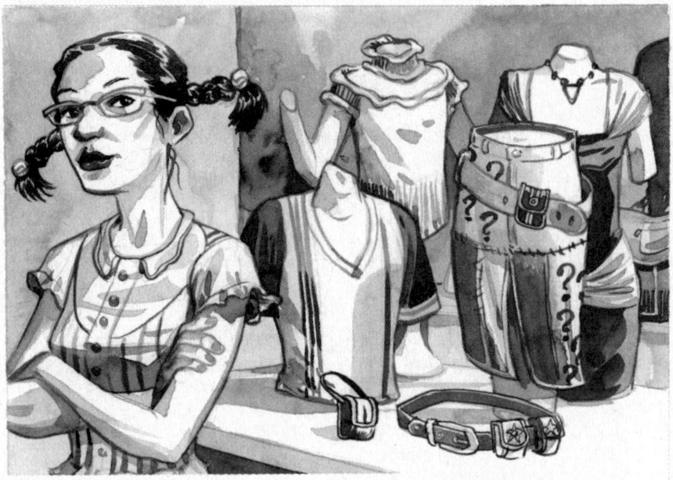

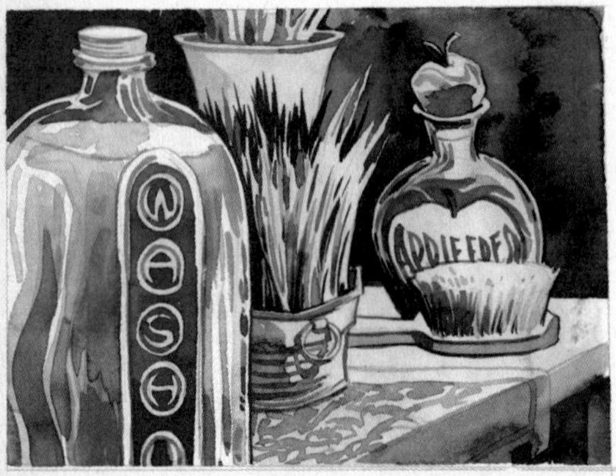
WASH

BEST BATH AND BEAUTY PRODUCTS: *Wash Your Mouth Out!* 82 West California Avenue. Coconut Oil, Oatmeal, Avocado, Honey, Cranberry, Basil, Lime...no, it's not your shopping list — it's just some of the all-natural ingredients used to make the luscious soaps and body products at the city's newest specialty shop. Andre Yu is often seen stocking up on the Avocado Moisturizer that keeps her looking so great on the evening news. Open 10 to 5 weekdays, 10 to 9 weekends. All major credit cards welcome. Call 555-2001 for free catalog and mail order service.

**NEED A BIT TO EAT** after all that shopping? Hungry after club-hopping? Here are the newest spots in Gotham to wine and dine.

*FORK* This upscale eatery offers earthy home-style fare with a twist, like turkey meatloaf with spicy tomato chutney and roasted garlic with thyme mashed potatoes. Freeform spinach lasagna with pesto tofu filling is hearty and tasty enough to fool any carnivore, and the four-cheese baked macaroni and cheese is impossible to resist. There's chocolate

*Former Commissioner James Gordon at the grand opening of COP SHOP*

mousse tart with fresh cream and berries, lemon cloud cake with coconut icing and creme brulee of the day, so leave room for dessert. Hey — pass me my fork, I'm hungry! 342 Market St. (555-3675) Dinner Mon-Sun 5PM-12AM, Sun Brunch 11AM-3PM. Average entree $20 and under.

*COP SHOP* Finally a place that puts *Mmm, Good! Donuts* to shame. This law-enforcement-themed diner benefits from police traffic (it's just down the street from the 83rd St. Precinct) and cop kitsch, with over 150 items of police memorabilia on the walls. Diners waiting for a table spend time in the "clink" — a former holding cell bought at police auction. Your photo is taken when you arrive and you know your table's ready when your "mug shot" is posted on "Gotham's Most Wanted" list. The theme continues throughout — the chairs have real billy clubs as legs, and orders are written on witness statements that you can take home as souvenirs. Criminals and civilians alike will enjoy their smoked pastrami sandwiches with waffle fries and dill slaw, bacon and egg breakfast sandwich, or the chili (all the way) served to them on a prison-issue tray. A selection of twenty kinds of donuts with coffee is available for dessert (or to go if you're on call). If only time in the Big House was as enjoyable as a trip to the Cop Shop. 163 83rd St. (555-9111) Breakfast, Lunch, Dinner. Open 6AM-9PM, carry-out window 24 hours. Entrees $6-12.

*COPPER BLUE* Chef Michael Tsonton has brought his incredible cuisine to Gotham and we thank him for it. Gotham's elite can be seen lining up to sample the fresh day-boat scallops with curry-cauliflower puree, or the best-ever braised short ribs with Chinese greens. Fresh organic vegetables abound, and the seasonal creations keep you coming back for more. The "Soup of Yesterday" is a Tsonton delight that has followed him wherever he hangs his chef's toque. And he's right — the roasted tomato cream soup with blue croutons is always better the next day. Don't be afraid to bring the kids. The children's menu is available until 7:30 PM. 5914 N. Fairfield (555-9866) Dinner Tues-Sun 5:30-11 PM. Average entree $22 and up.

*PIE HOLE* We still love *Luigi's Pizza* and give it an honorable mention, but this tiny joint (seats 12) in Gotham's Little Italy has the best slices we've had in ages. And yes, you can get whole pies. The cracker-thin crust and smooth, rich sauce never overpower the toppings. Try the sausage pizza with "Aunt Lou's dark sauce" for a one-of-a-kind treat, or mix and match from a variety of toppings. Just don't take too long to order...owner/operator sisters Lou and Lindy Abbinanti's patience runs thin. Order up and shut your pie hole! 312 Hudson St. (555-0694) No Res., Lunch and Dinner 11:30AM-3:30PM and 5-10PM. No delivery.

GOTHAM'S BAR SCENE has been growing more playful in recent years. This spread of *THE ICEBERG LOUNGE* holds some of our favorite picks in the ever-changing world of late-night drinks, dancing and diversions.

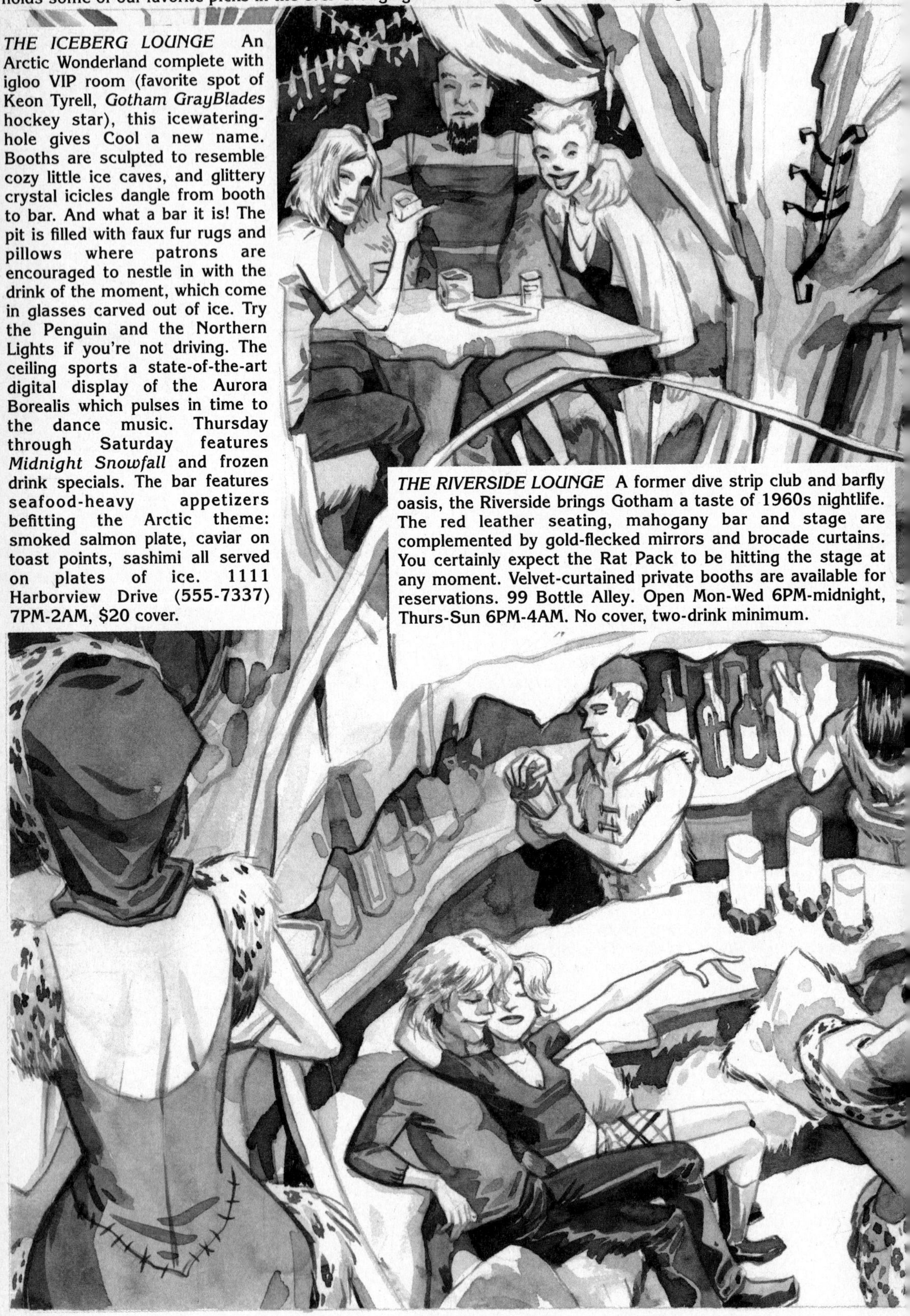

*THE ICEBERG LOUNGE* An Arctic Wonderland complete with igloo VIP room (favorite spot of Keon Tyrell, *Gotham GrayBlades* hockey star), this icewatering-hole gives Cool a new name. Booths are sculpted to resemble cozy little ice caves, and glittery crystal icicles dangle from booth to bar. And what a bar it is! The pit is filled with faux fur rugs and pillows where patrons are encouraged to nestle in with the drink of the moment, which come in glasses carved out of ice. Try the Penguin and the Northern Lights if you're not driving. The ceiling sports a state-of-the-art digital display of the Aurora Borealis which pulses in time to the dance music. Thursday through Saturday features *Midnight Snowfall* and frozen drink specials. The bar features seafood-heavy appetizers befitting the Arctic theme: smoked salmon plate, caviar on toast points, sashimi all served on plates of ice. 1111 Harborview Drive (555-7337) 7PM-2AM, $20 cover.

*THE RIVERSIDE LOUNGE* A former dive strip club and barfly oasis, the Riverside brings Gotham a taste of 1960s nightlife. The red leather seating, mahogany bar and stage are complemented by gold-flecked mirrors and brocade curtains. You certainly expect the Rat Pack to be hitting the stage at any moment. Velvet-curtained private booths are available for reservations. 99 Bottle Alley. Open Mon-Wed 6PM-midnight, Thurs-Sun 6PM-4AM. No cover, two-drink minimum.

*MY ALIBI* Where can you go to slug back a few refreshing beverages after a day of crime? Well, it used to be here. But it always seemed The Batman would show up to interrogate some stool pigeon, bust some tables or some heads, and be on his way. A few dozen busted heads later and the local crime element finally got the picture, no longer spending its hard-stolen money at this bar. Fortunately for the owners, the after-hours crowd took a shine to this dark, dingy watering hole and the former tattooed, pierced, leather-clad patrons were soon replaced by new tattooed, pierced, leather-clad patrons. No fancy drinks here, just smoke, pool and cigarettes. 80 Berkshire Place, 7AM-4AM 7 days a week.

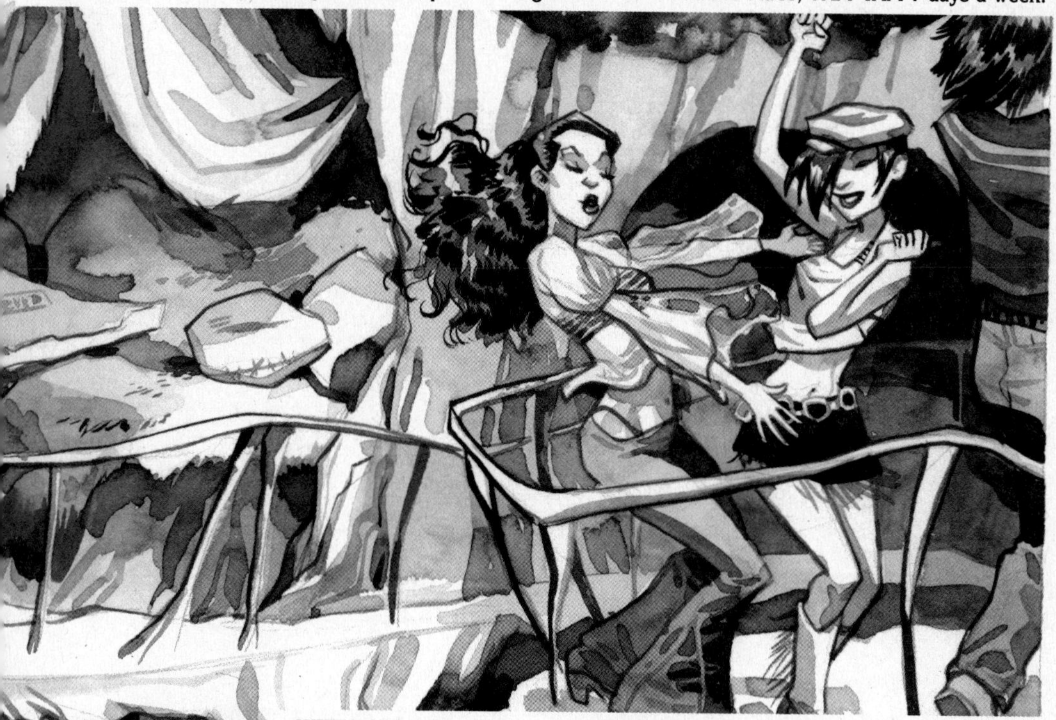

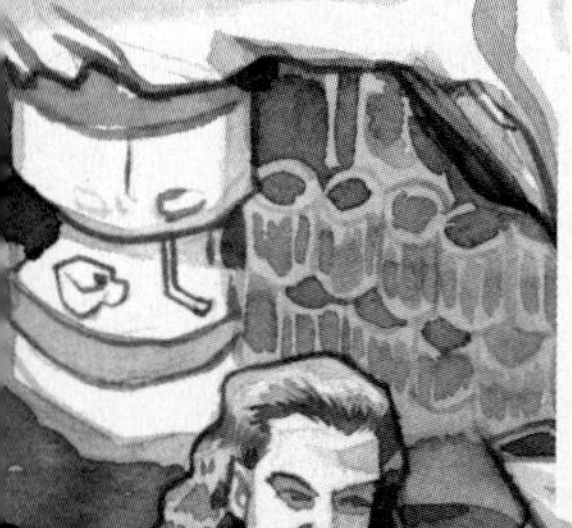

*KITTY CITY* The girls who run this bar pay homage to the underworld figure Catwoman, from the Kit-Kat google-eye clock to the cat-o'-nine-tails over the bar. House specialties include the Frosty White Tiger, the Blue Russian and the Kittini. Non-drinkers can choose from the "de-clawed" menu which features fruity, fizzy concoctions tasty enough to satisfy the finickiest of tomcats. Bar snax arrive at the table in pet dishes, but not to worry — even though the drinks are large enough to fill a bowl, they're served in funky cat-print glasses. Neon pawprints point the way to the litter box when the need to powder one's whiskers arises. 14 Fish St., Mon-Wed 3-11PM, Thurs-Sun 3PM-2AM, $5 cover.

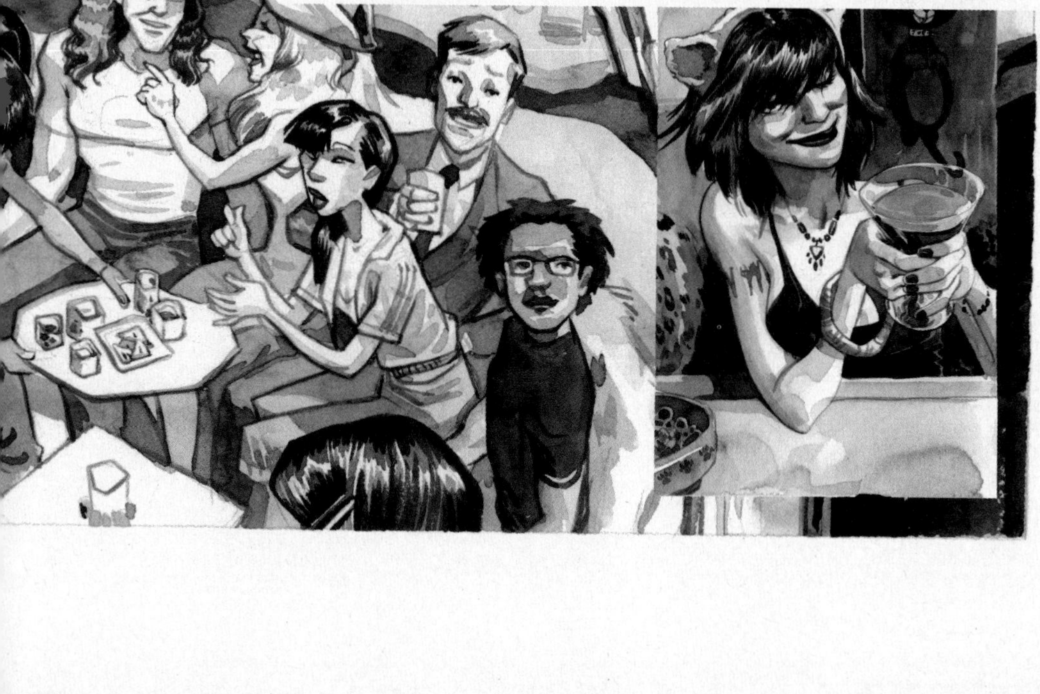

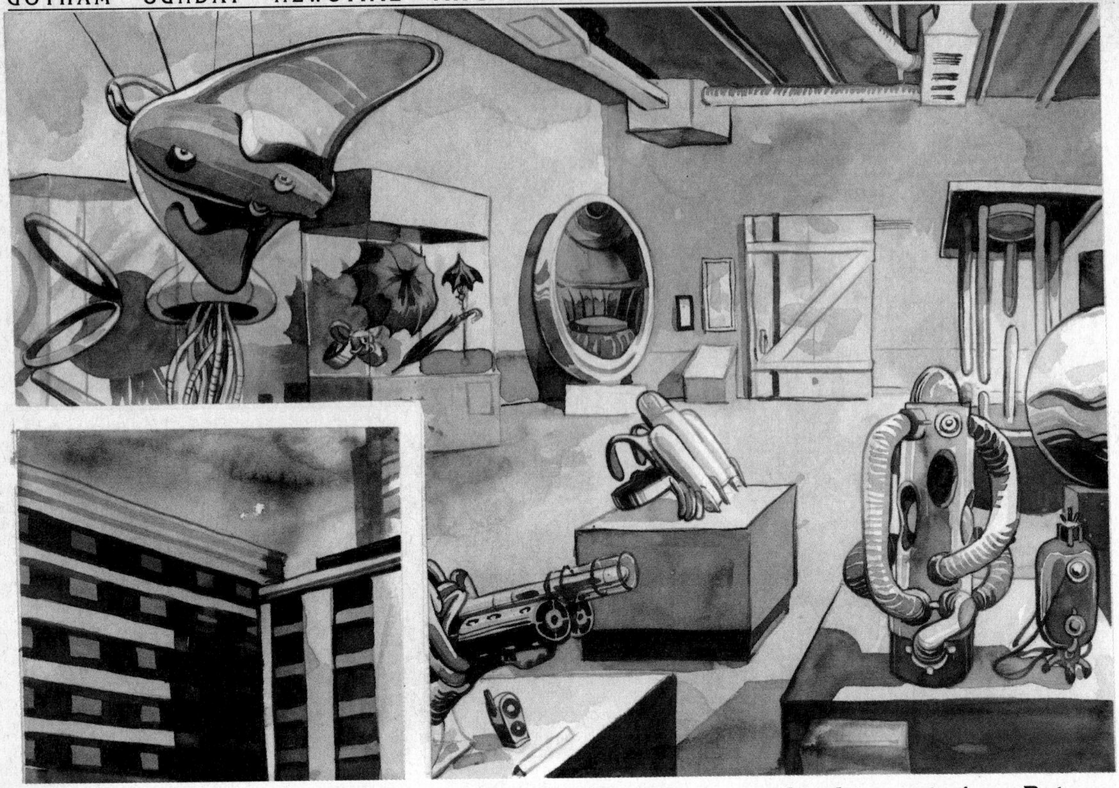

*Museum pick: the not-so-secret "HIDEOUT," brought to you by the mysterious Batman*

**BEST MUSEUM: *HIDEOUT*** Although nearly all major cities have their share of super-crime, Gotham seems to attract some of the biggest and the baddest. Fortunately, thanks to The Batman, Gotham's Dark Knight Detective, the most notorious are safely tucked away in Arkham Asylum. But what happens to all of their nefarious (but cool-looking) equipment? Safely deactivated by S.T.A.R. Labs technicians, you can get an up-close and personal look at these strange and ominous objects at Gotham's newest museum/art gallery located in the revitalized warehouse district. Sponsored by the Martha Wayne Outreach program, a philanthropic division of Wayne Industries. All proceeds from HIDEOUT will be donated to the Crime Prevention Association. 222 Fulton Market (555-4283) Wed-Sun 11AM-5PM, Admission $6 adults, $3 seniors & kids under 6.

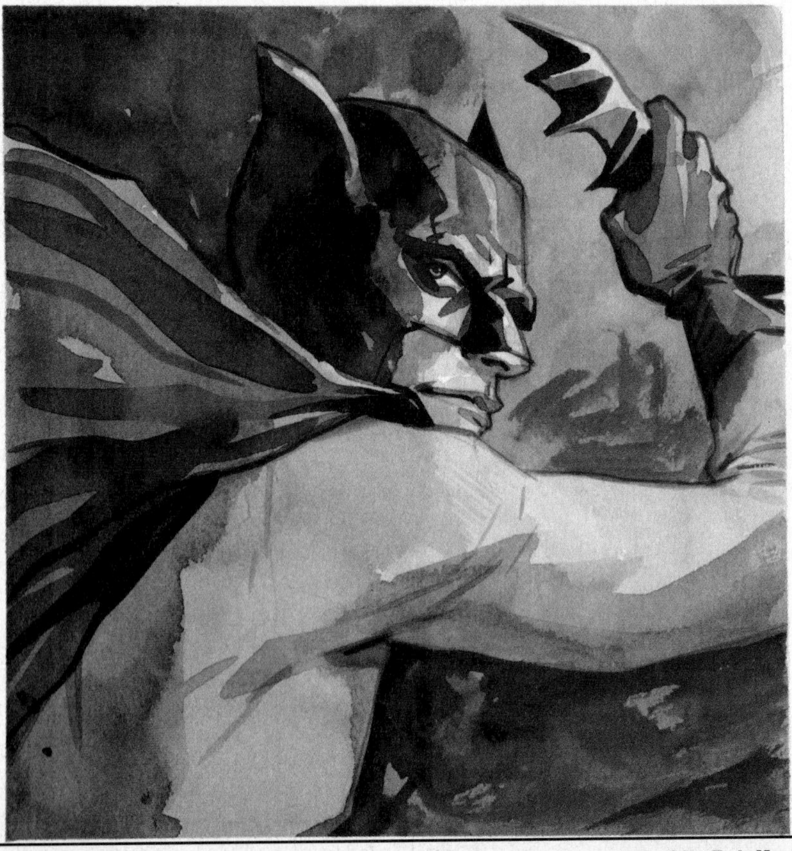

Story & Photos by Jill Thompson, type design by Todd Klein. Lysa Hawkins, editor. Batman created by Bob Kane.

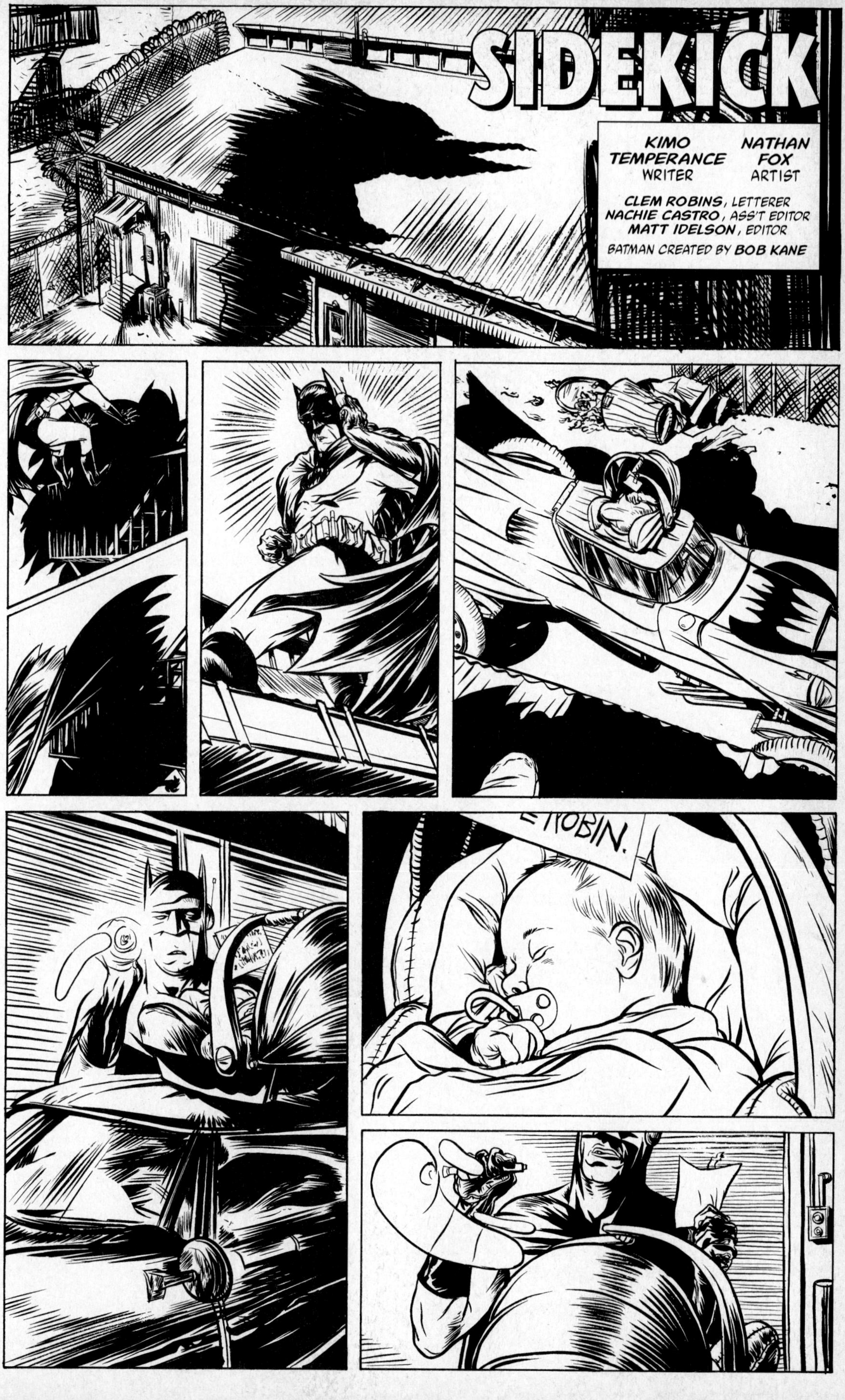
SIDEKICK
KIMO TEMPERANCE
WRITER
NATHAN FOX
ARTIST
CLEM ROBINS, LETTERER
NACHIE CASTRO, ASS'T EDITOR
MATT IDELSON, EDITOR
BATMAN CREATED BY BOB KANE
ROBIN.

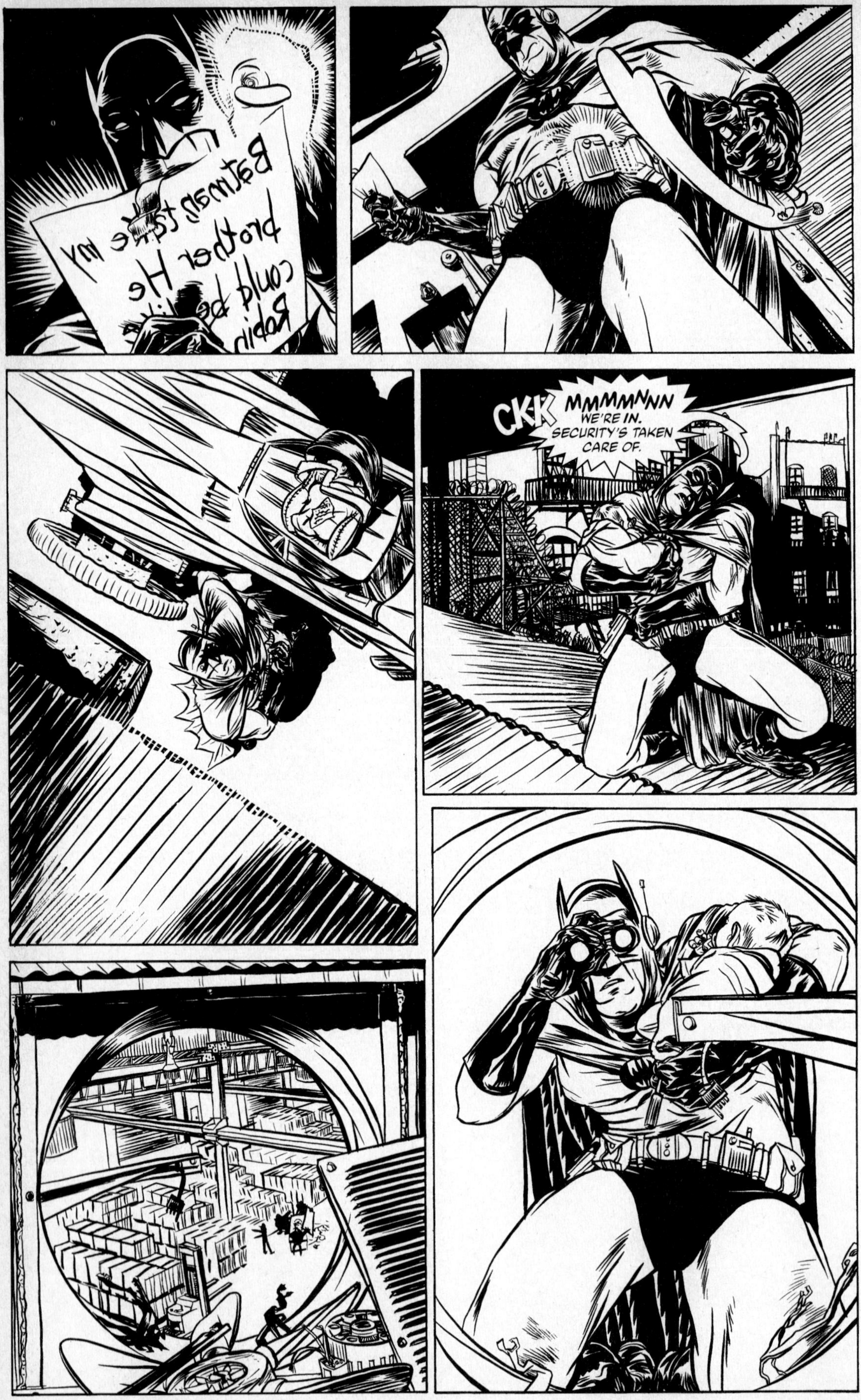
CK-K
MMMMNNN
WE'RE IN. SECURITY'S TAKEN CARE OF.

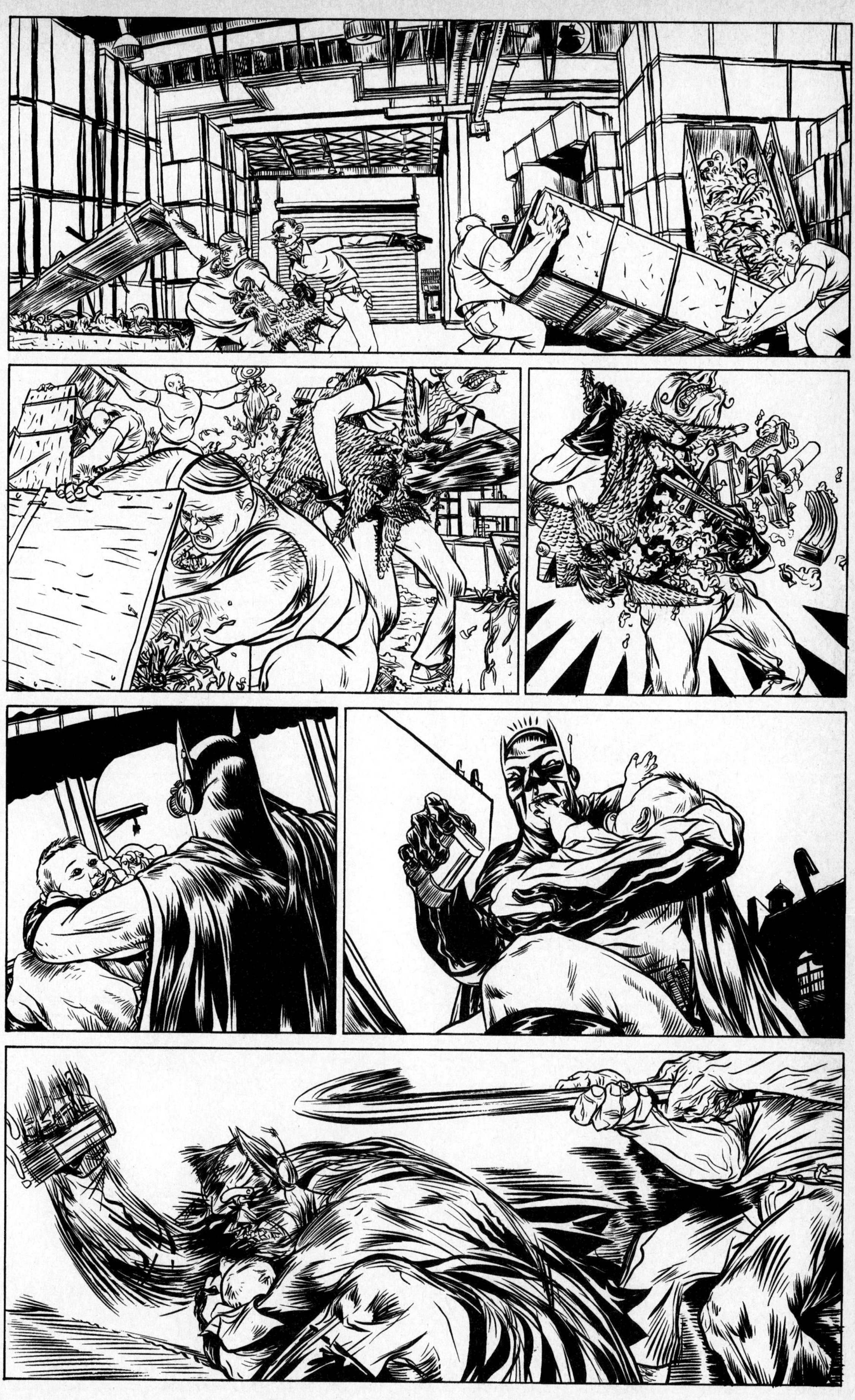

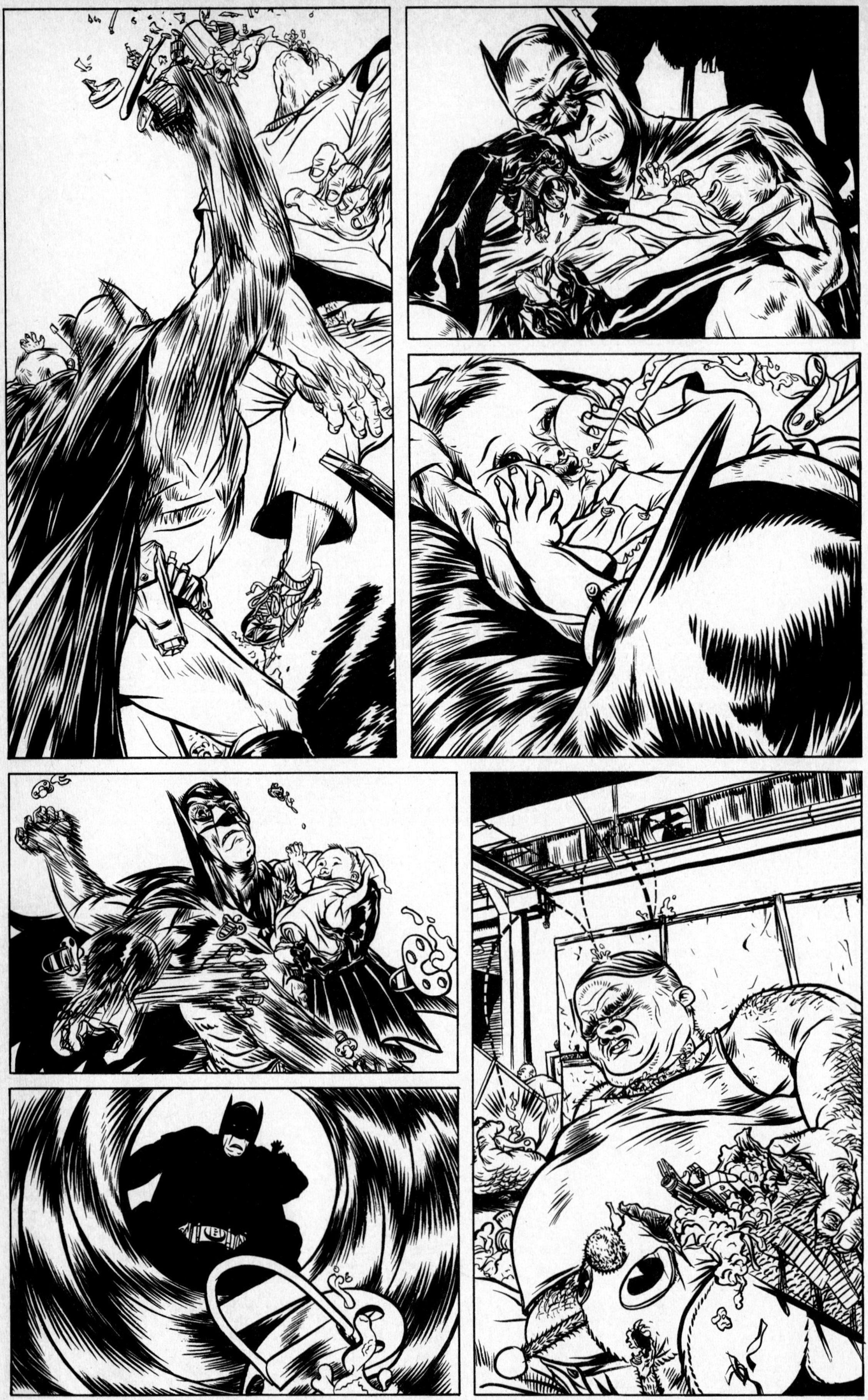

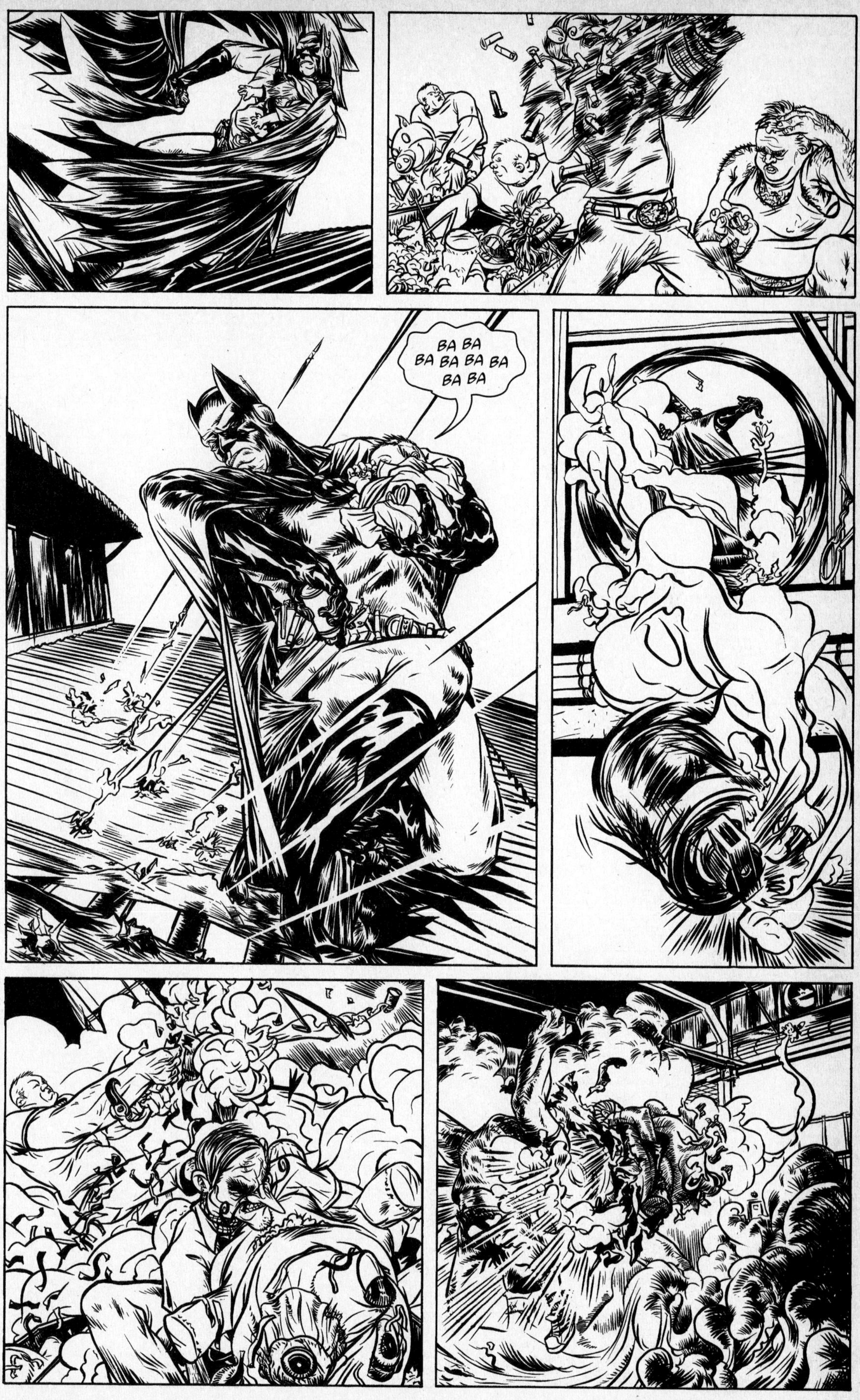
BA BA
BA BA BA BA
BA BA

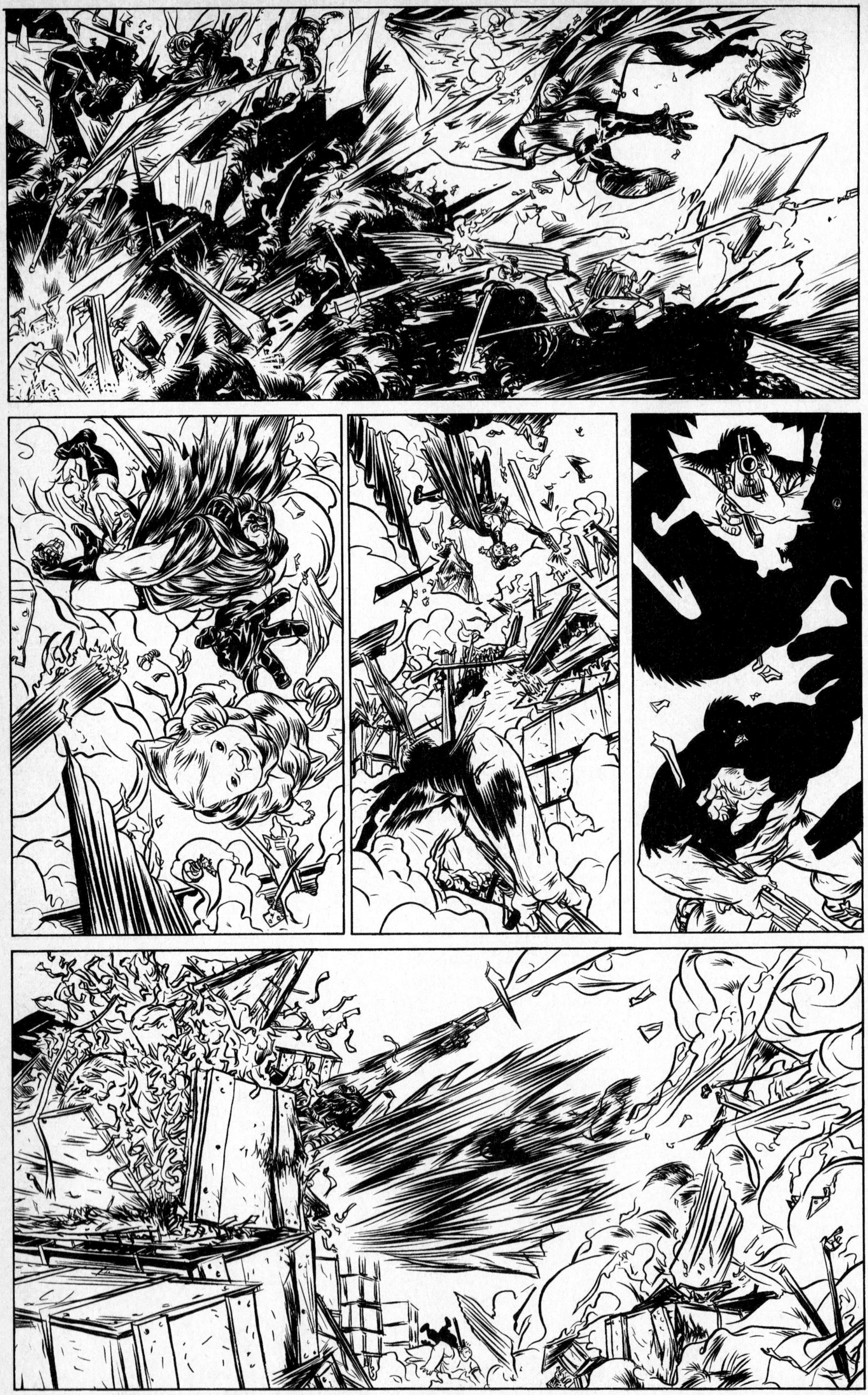

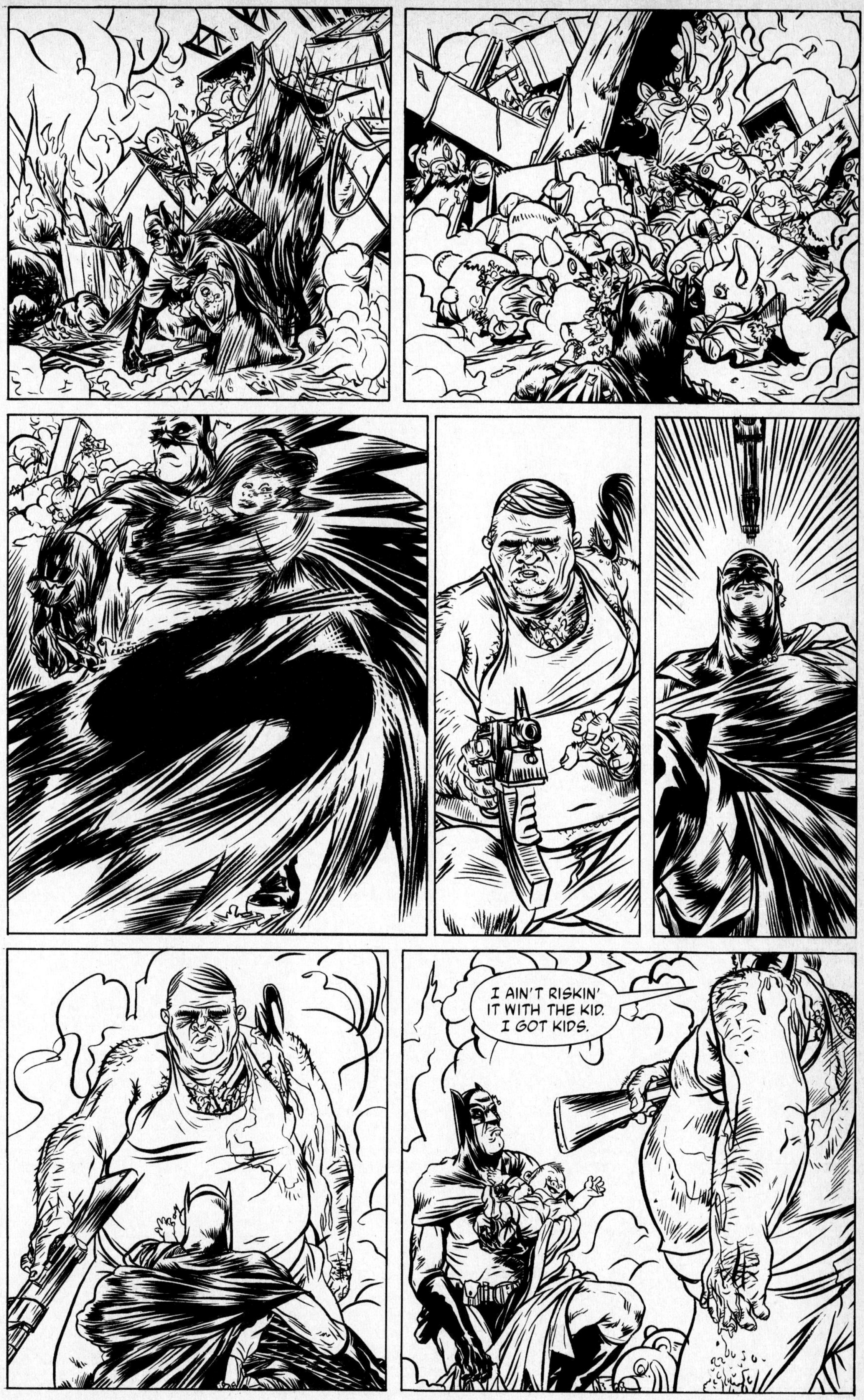
I AIN'T RISKIN' IT WITH THE KID. I GOT KIDS.

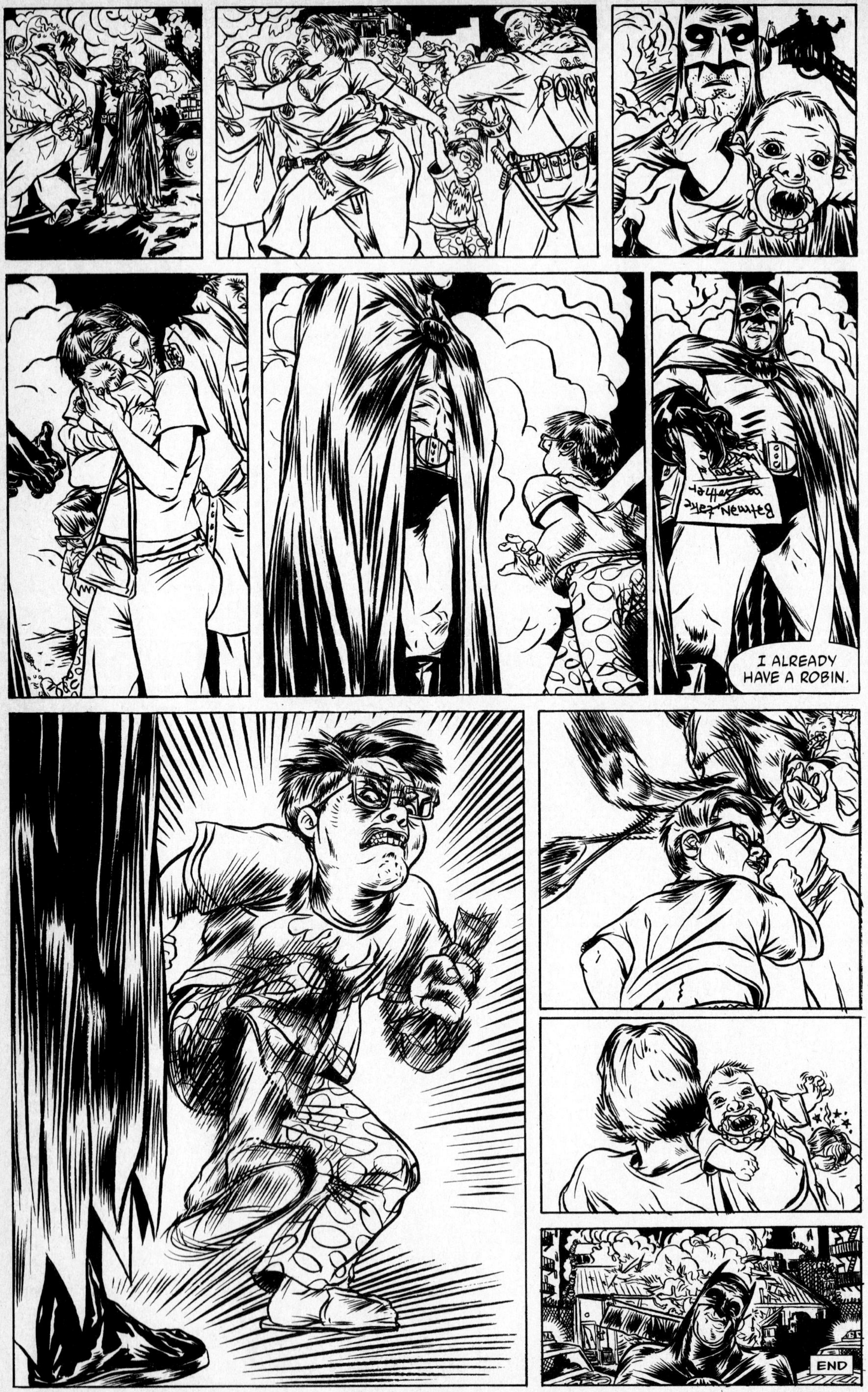
I ALREADY HAVE A ROBIN.
END

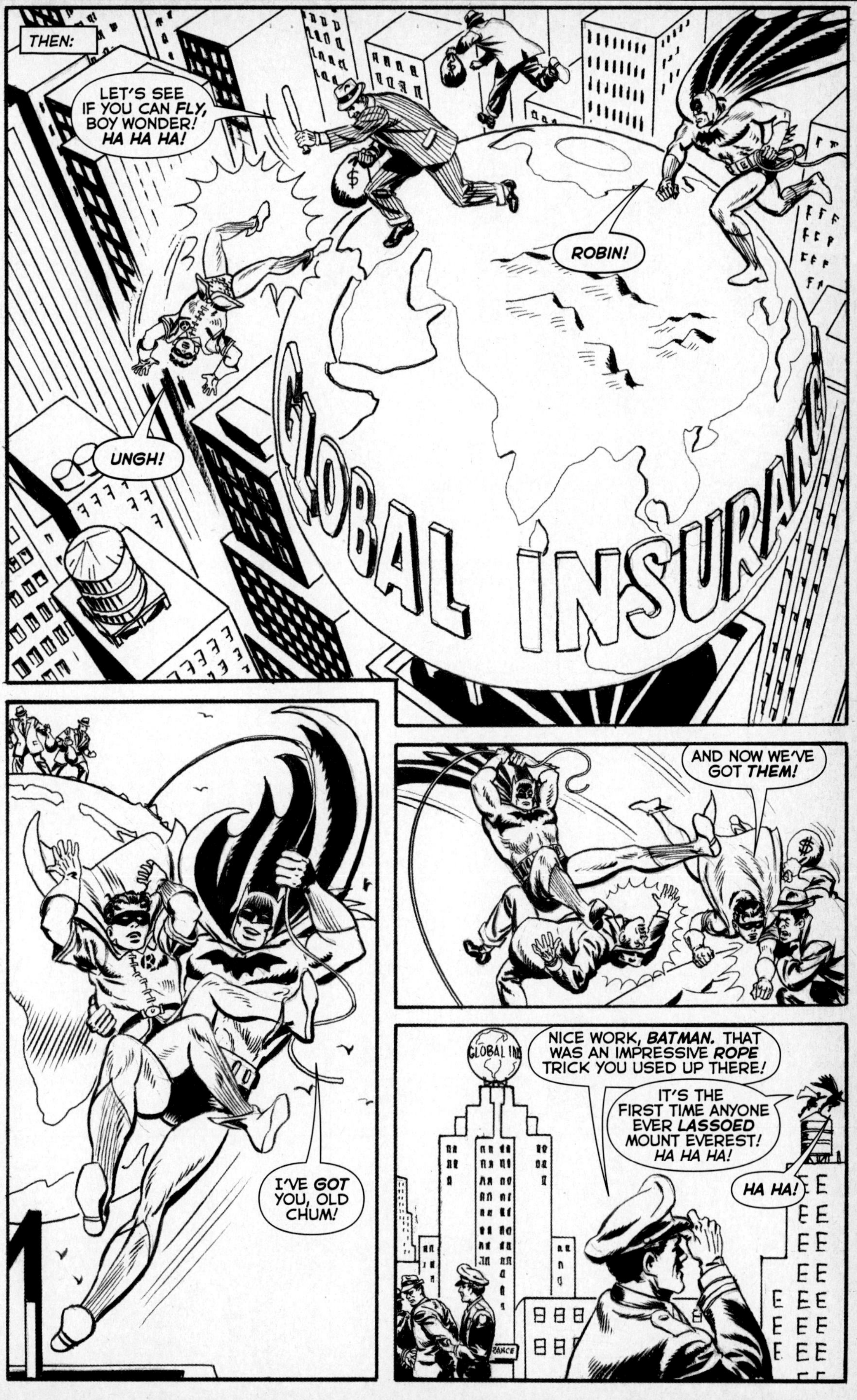
THEN:
LET'S SEE IF YOU CAN FLY, BOY WONDER! HA HA HA!
ROBIN!
UNGH!
GLOBAL INSURAN
I'VE GOT YOU, OLD CHUM!
AND NOW WE'VE GOT THEM!
NICE WORK, BATMAN. THAT WAS AN IMPRESSIVE ROPE TRICK YOU USED UP THERE!
IT'S THE FIRST TIME ANYONE EVER LASSOED MOUNT EVEREST! HA HA HA!
HA HA!

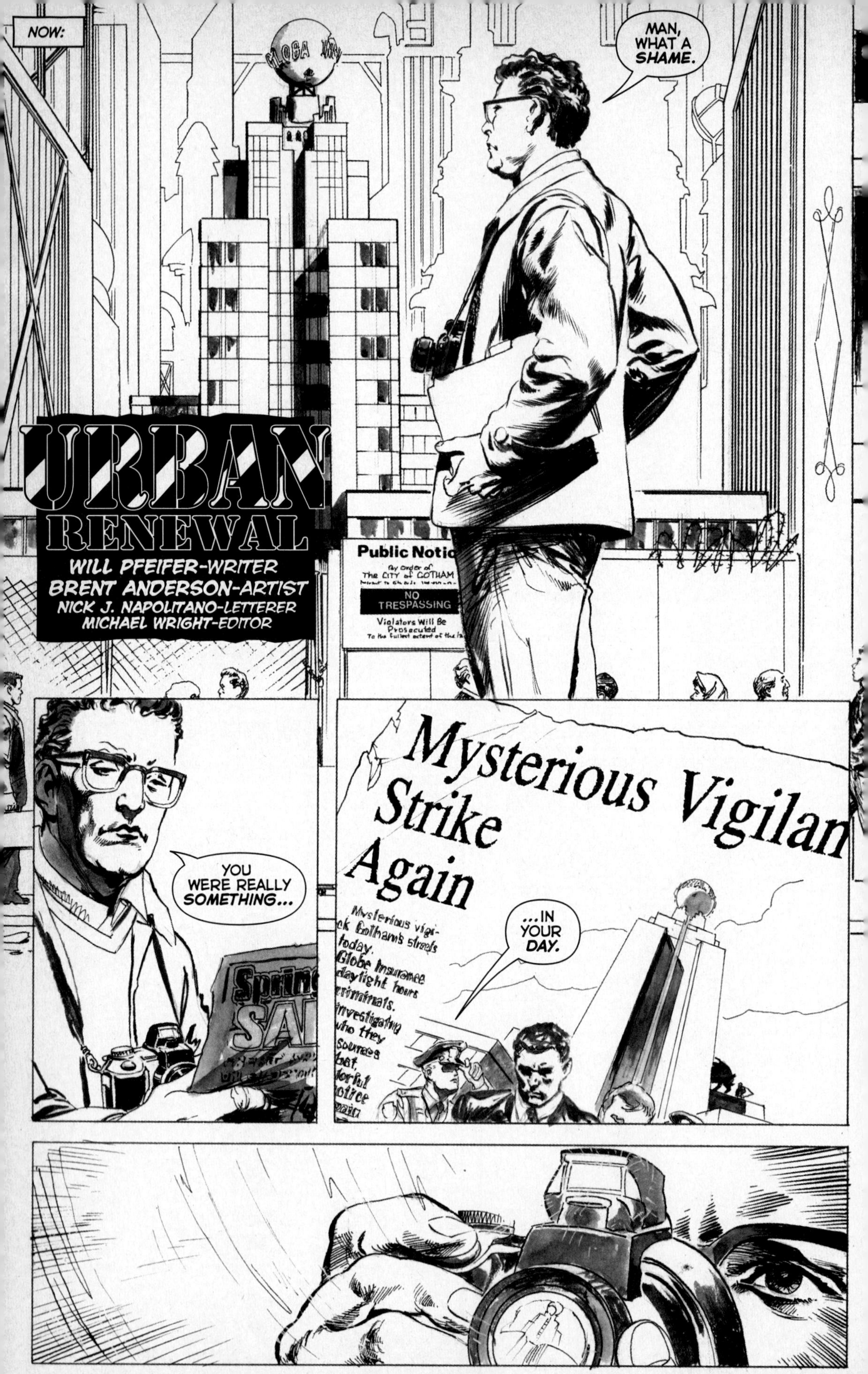
NOW:
MAN, WHAT A SHAME.
URBAN RENEWAL
WILL PFEIFER-WRITER
BRENT ANDERSON-ARTIST
NICK J. NAPOLITANO-LETTERER
MICHAEL WRIGHT-EDITOR
Public Notic
By Order of The CITY of GOTHAM
NO TRESPASSING
Violators Will Be Prosecuted
YOU WERE REALLY SOMETHING...
Mysterious Vigilan
Strike Again
...IN YOUR DAY.

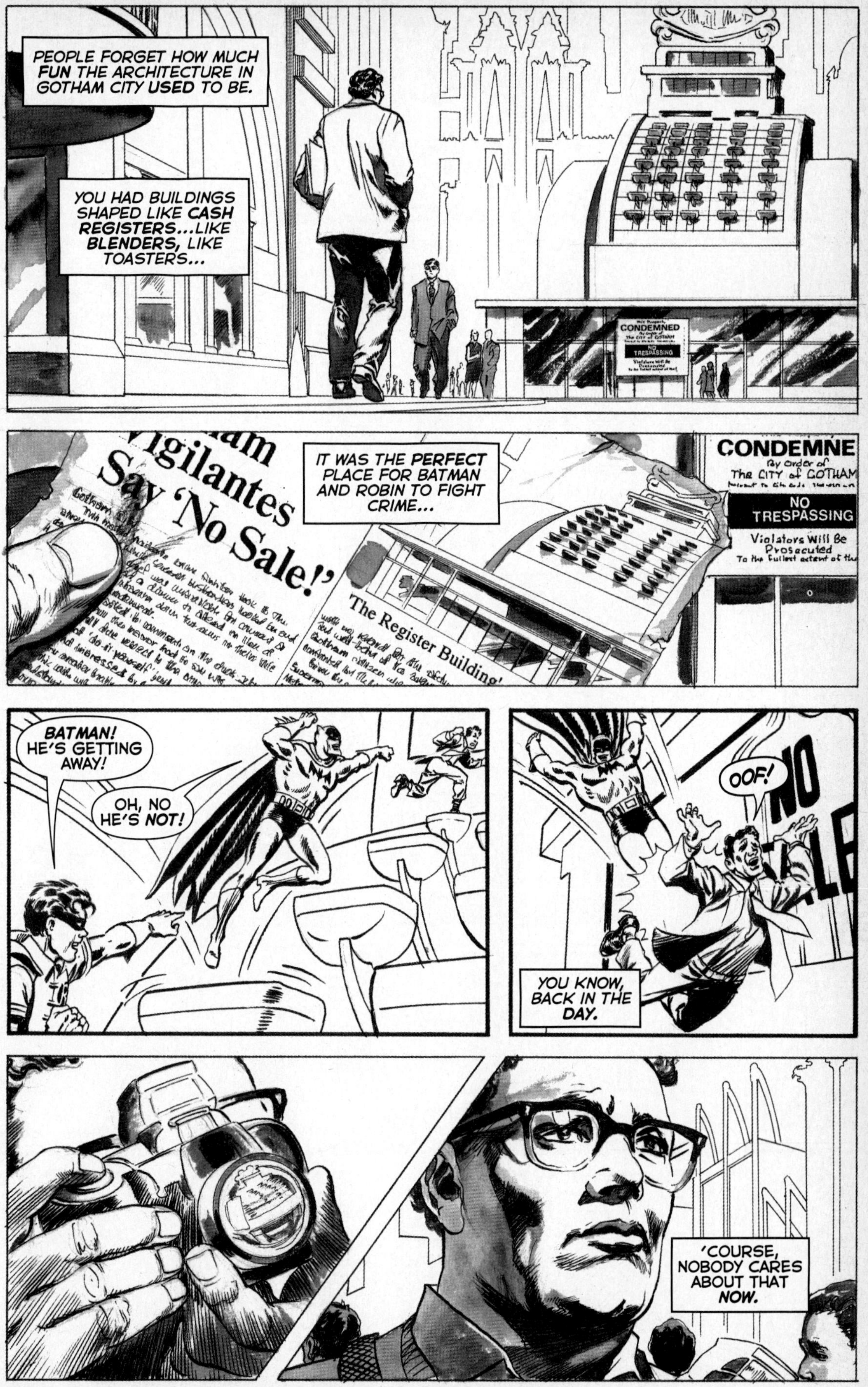

PEOPLE FORGET HOW MUCH FUN THE ARCHITECTURE IN GOTHAM CITY USED TO BE.
YOU HAD BUILDINGS SHAPED LIKE CASH REGISTERS...LIKE BLENDERS, LIKE TOASTERS...
CONDEMNED
NO TRESPASSING
Vigilantes Say 'No Sale!'
The Register Building
IT WAS THE PERFECT PLACE FOR BATMAN AND ROBIN TO FIGHT CRIME...
CONDEMNE
By Order of
The CITY of GOTHAM
NO TRESPASSING
Violators Will Be Prosecuted
To the fullest extent of the
BATMAN! HE'S GETTING AWAY!
OH, NO HE'S NOT!
OOF!
YOU KNOW, BACK IN THE DAY.
'COURSE, NOBODY CARES ABOUT THAT NOW.

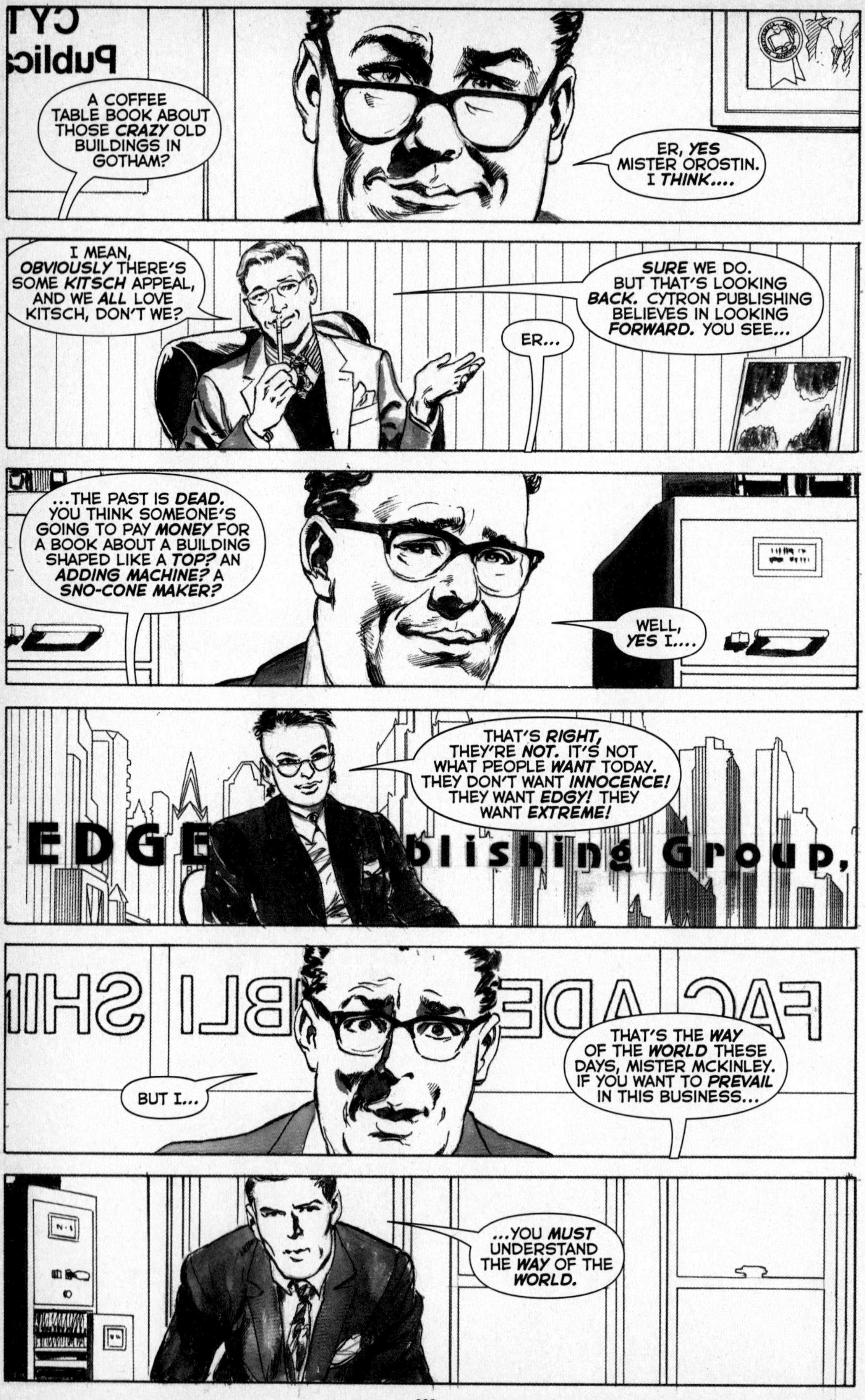
A COFFEE TABLE BOOK ABOUT THOSE CRAZY OLD BUILDINGS IN GOTHAM?
ER, YES MISTER OROSTIN. I THINK....
I MEAN, OBVIOUSLY THERE'S SOME KITSCH APPEAL, AND WE ALL LOVE KITSCH, DON'T WE?
ER...
SURE WE DO. BUT THAT'S LOOKING BACK. CYTRON PUBLISHING BELIEVES IN LOOKING FORWARD. YOU SEE...
...THE PAST IS DEAD. YOU THINK SOMEONE'S GOING TO PAY MONEY FOR A BOOK ABOUT A BUILDING SHAPED LIKE A TOP? AN ADDING MACHINE? A SNO-CONE MAKER?
WELL, YES I....
THAT'S RIGHT, THEY'RE NOT. IT'S NOT WHAT PEOPLE WANT TODAY. THEY DON'T WANT INNOCENCE! THEY WANT EDGY! THEY WANT EXTREME!
EDGE
blishing Group,
BUT I...
THAT'S THE WAY OF THE WORLD THESE DAYS, MISTER MCKINLEY. IF YOU WANT TO PREVAIL IN THIS BUSINESS...
...YOU MUST UNDERSTAND THE WAY OF THE WORLD.

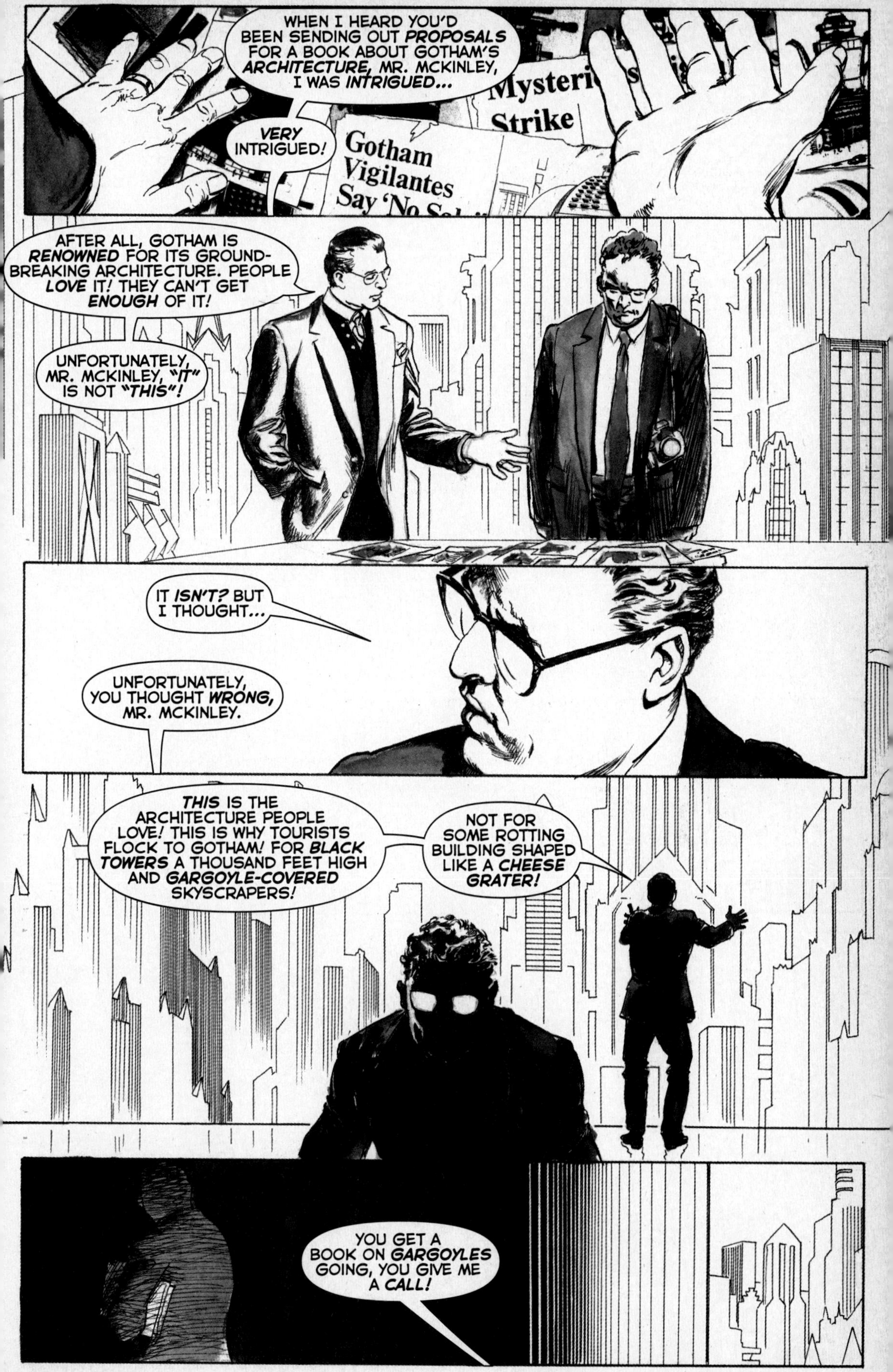
WHEN I HEARD YOU'D BEEN SENDING OUT PROPOSALS FOR A BOOK ABOUT GOTHAM'S ARCHITECTURE, MR. MCKINLEY, I WAS INTRIGUED...
VERY INTRIGUED!
Strike
Gotham Vigilantes
AFTER ALL, GOTHAM IS RENOWNED FOR ITS GROUND-BREAKING ARCHITECTURE. PEOPLE LOVE IT! THEY CAN'T GET ENOUGH OF IT!
UNFORTUNATELY, MR. MCKINLEY, "IT" IS NOT "THIS"!
IT ISN'T? BUT I THOUGHT...
UNFORTUNATELY, YOU THOUGHT WRONG, MR. MCKINLEY.
THIS IS THE ARCHITECTURE PEOPLE LOVE! THIS IS WHY TOURISTS FLOCK TO GOTHAM! FOR BLACK TOWERS A THOUSAND FEET HIGH AND GARGOYLE-COVERED SKYSCRAPERS!
NOT FOR SOME ROTTING BUILDING SHAPED LIKE A CHEESE GRATER!
YOU GET A BOOK ON GARGOYLES GOING, YOU GIVE ME A CALL!

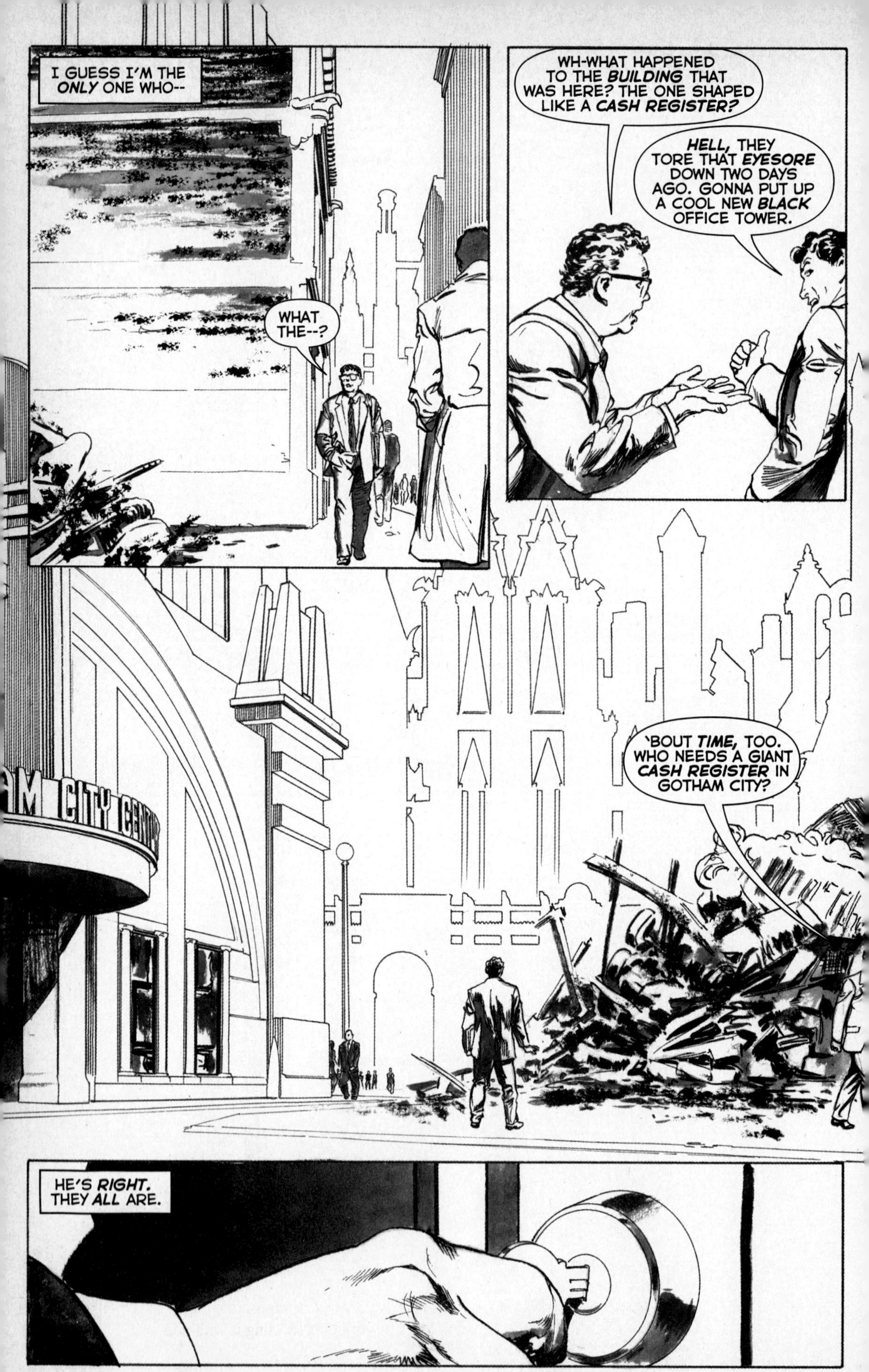
I GUESS I'M THE ONLY ONE WHO--
WHAT THE--?
WH-WHAT HAPPENED TO THE BUILDING THAT WAS HERE? THE ONE SHAPED LIKE A CASH REGISTER?
HELL, THEY TORE THAT EYESORE DOWN TWO DAYS AGO. GONNA PUT UP A COOL NEW BLACK OFFICE TOWER.
'BOUT TIME, TOO. WHO NEEDS A GIANT CASH REGISTER IN GOTHAM CITY?
HE'S RIGHT. THEY ALL ARE.

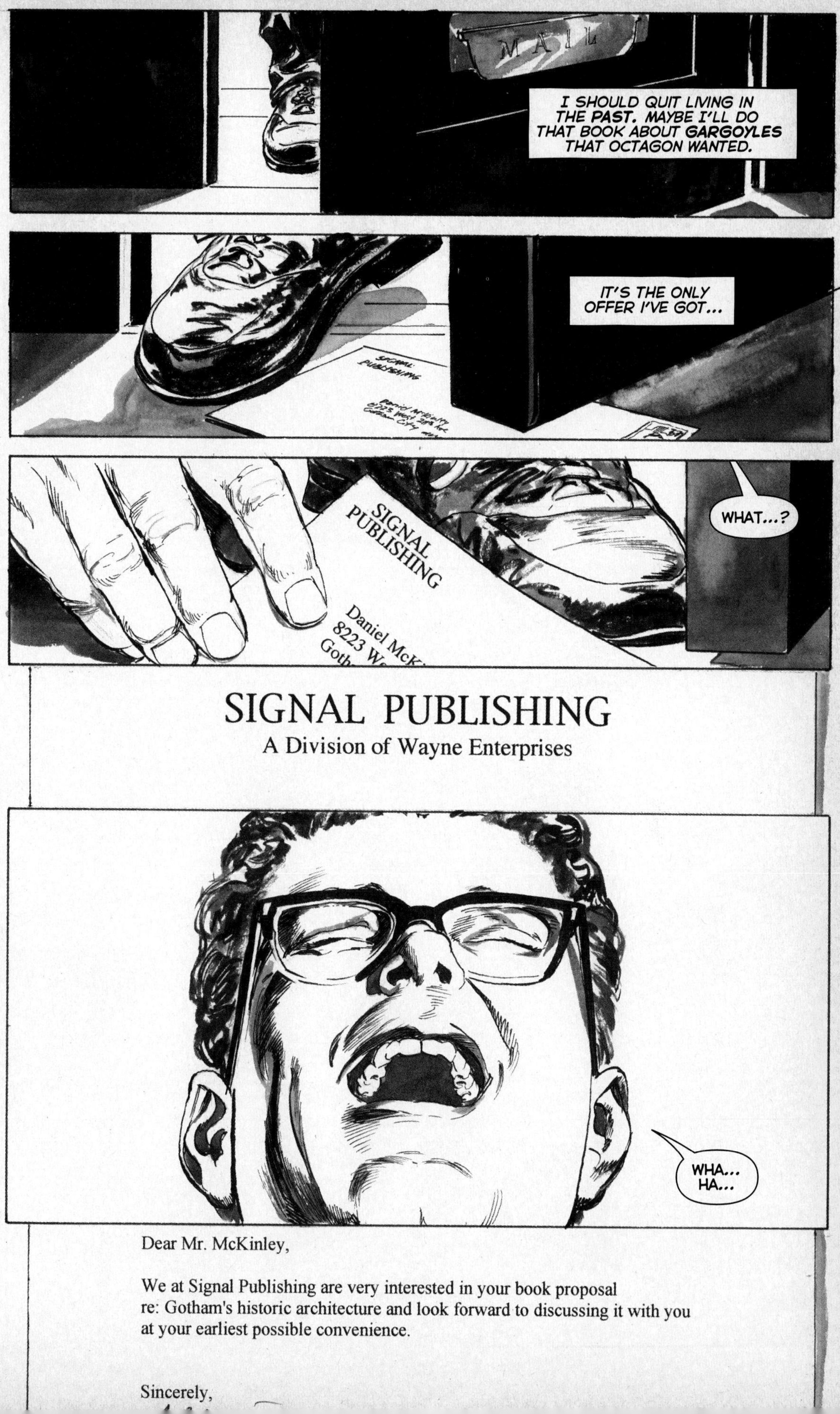
I SHOULD QUIT LIVING IN THE PAST. MAYBE I'LL DO THAT BOOK ABOUT GARGOYLES THAT OCTAGON WANTED.
MAIL
IT'S THE ONLY OFFER I'VE GOT...
SIGNAL PUBLISHING
WHAT...?
SIGNAL PUBLISHING
A Division of Wayne Enterprises
WHA... HA...
Dear Mr. McKinley,
We at Signal Publishing are very interested in your book proposal re: Gotham's historic architecture and look forward to discussing it with you at your earliest possible convenience.
Sincerely,

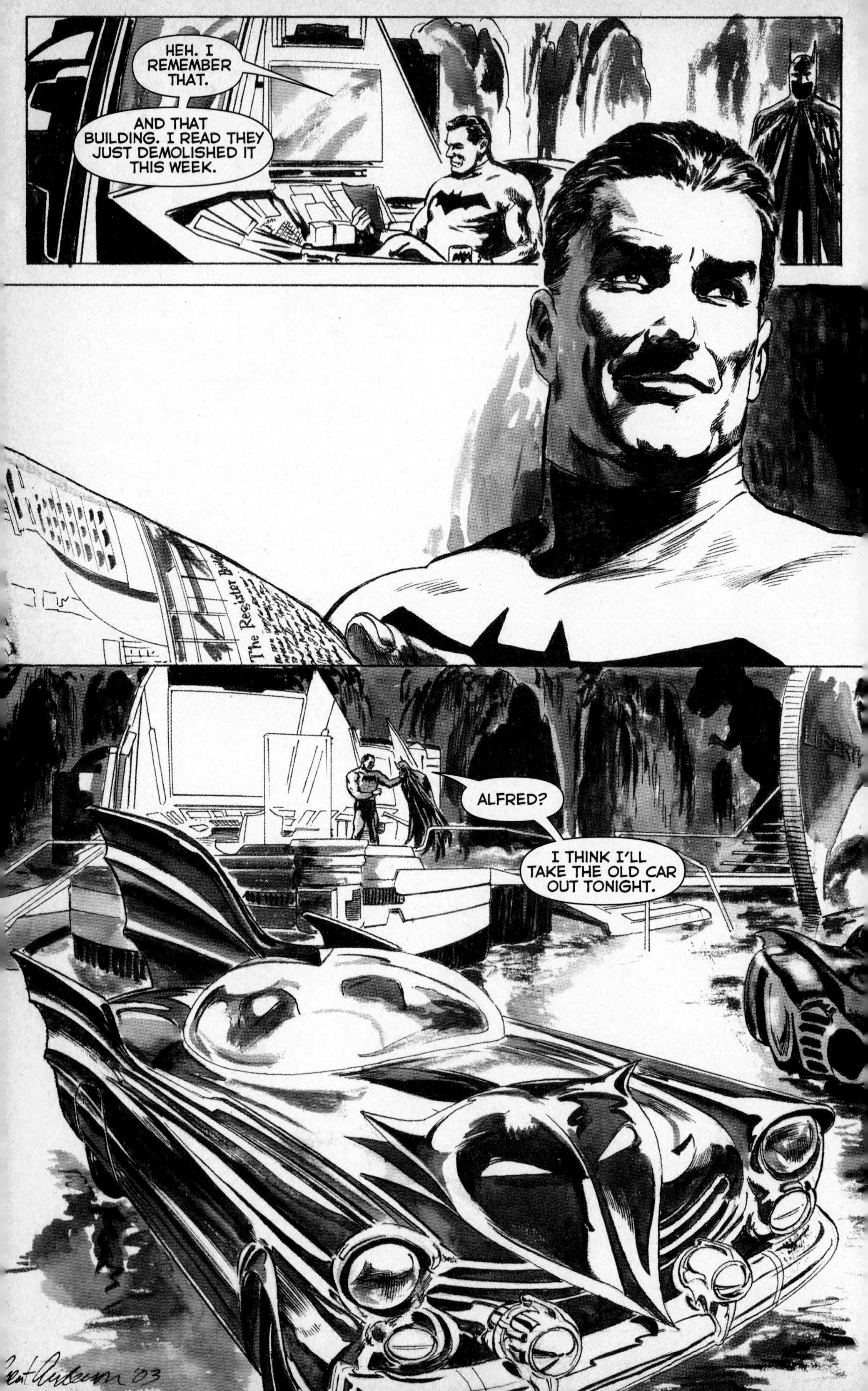
HEH. I REMEMBER THAT.
AND THAT BUILDING. I READ THEY JUST DEMOLISHED IT THIS WEEK.
ALFRED?
I THINK I'LL TAKE THE OLD CAR OUT TONIGHT.

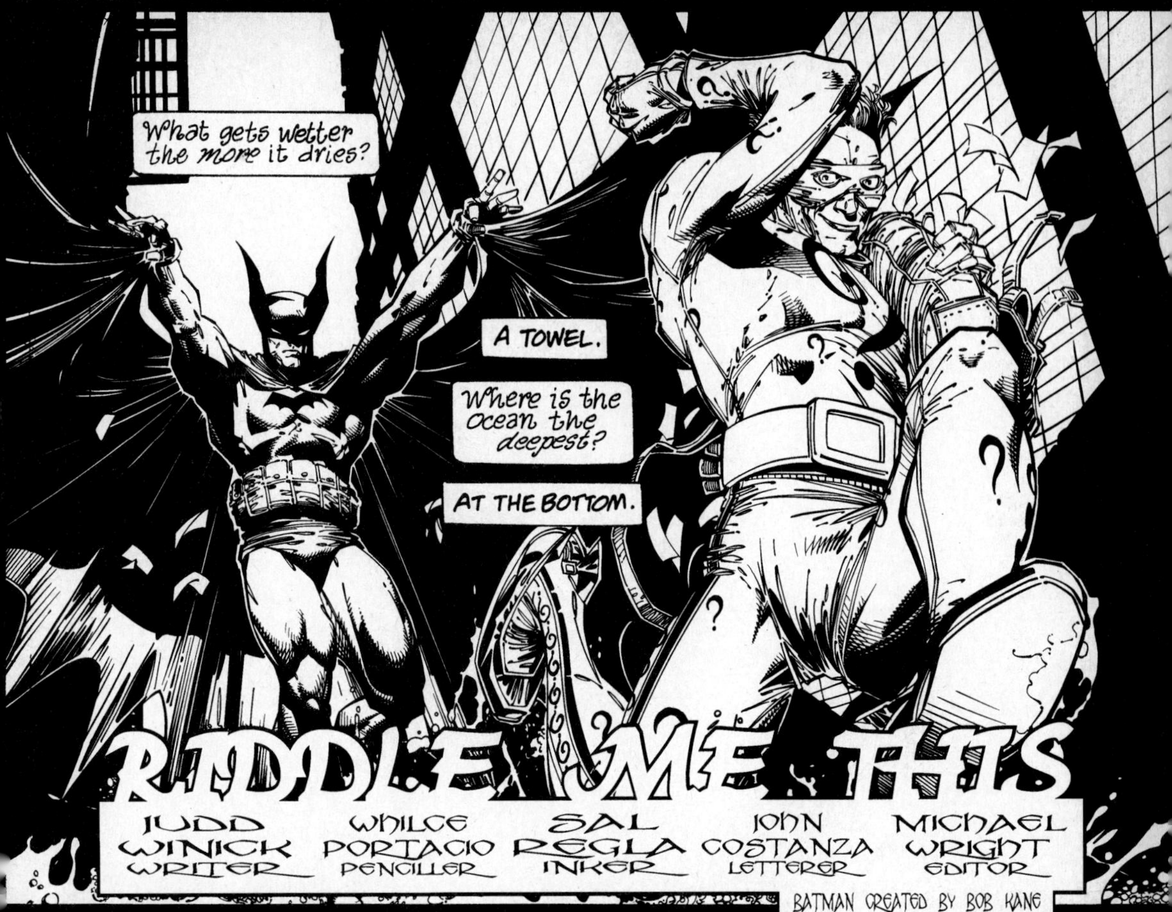
What gets wetter the more it dries?
A TOWEL.
Where is the ocean the deepest?
AT THE BOTTOM.
RIDDLE ME THIS
JUDD WINICK WRITER
WHILCE PORTACIO PENCILLER
SAL REGLA INKER
JOHN COSTANZA LETTERER
MICHAEL WRIGHT EDITOR
BATMAN CREATED BY BOB KANE

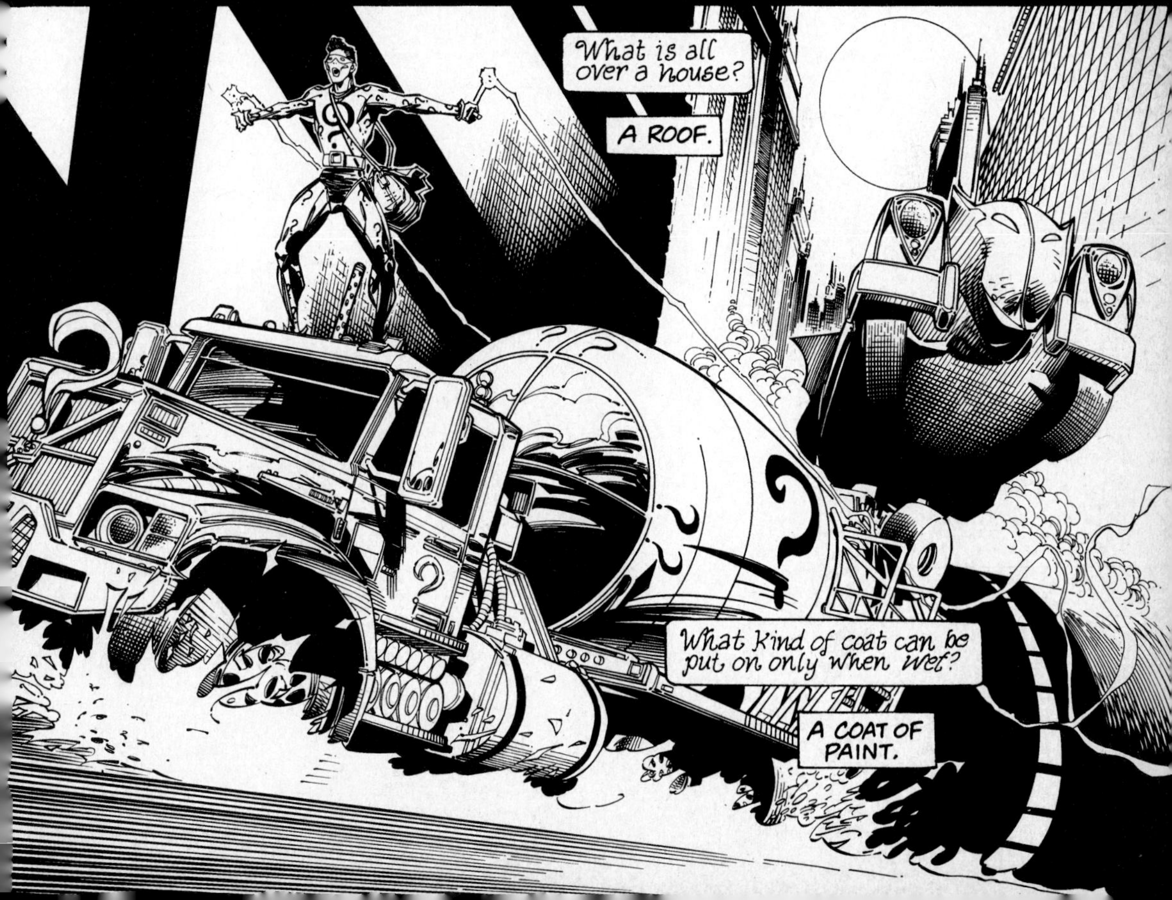
What is all over a house?
A ROOF.
What kind of coat can be put on only when wet?
A COAT OF PAINT.

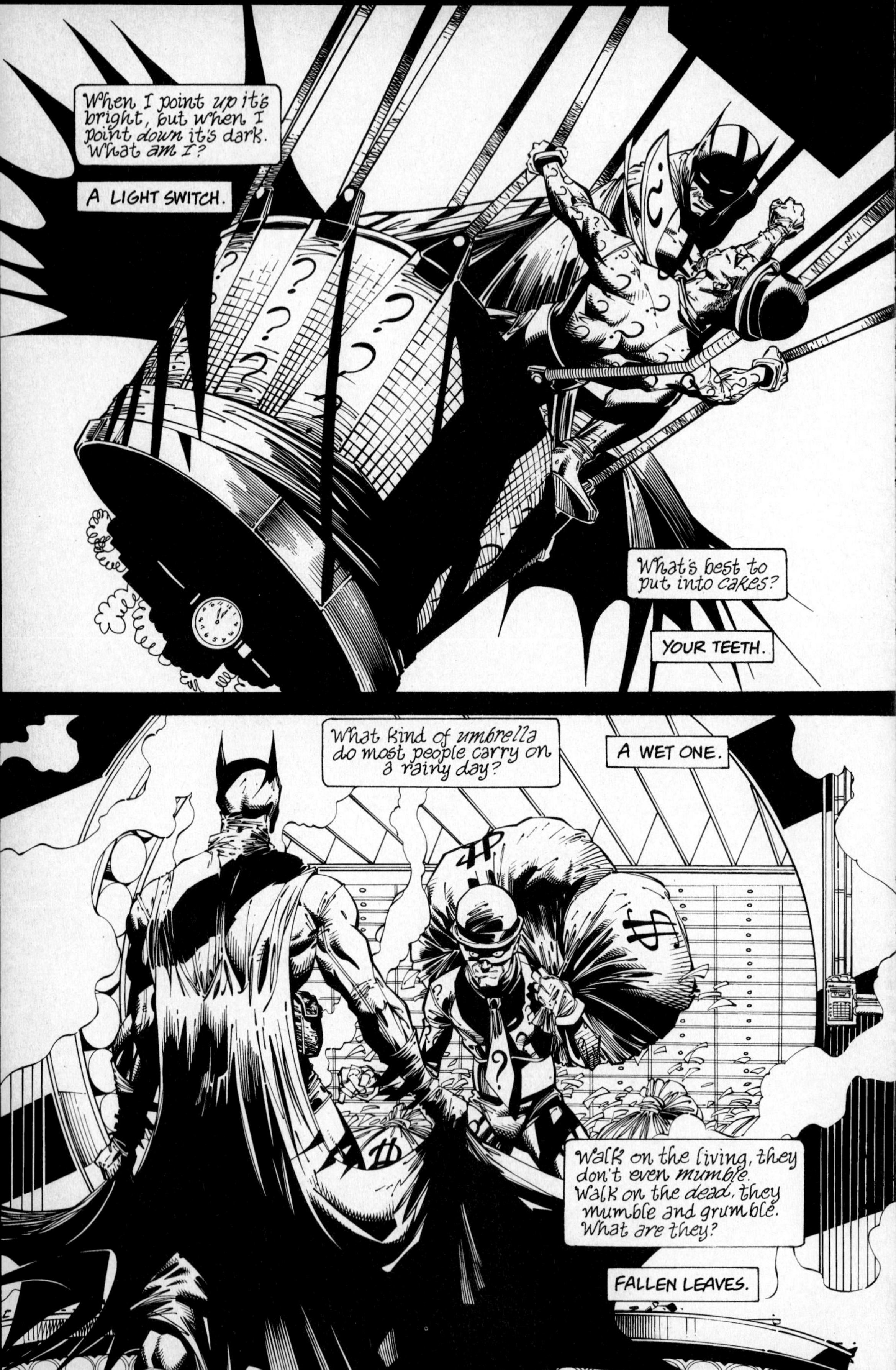
When I point up it's bright, but when I point down it's dark. What am I?
A LIGHT SWITCH.
What's best to put into cakes?
YOUR TEETH.
What kind of umbrella do most people carry on a rainy day?
A WET ONE.
Walk on the living, they don't even mumble. Walk on the dead, they mumble and grumble. What are they?
FALLEN LEAVES.

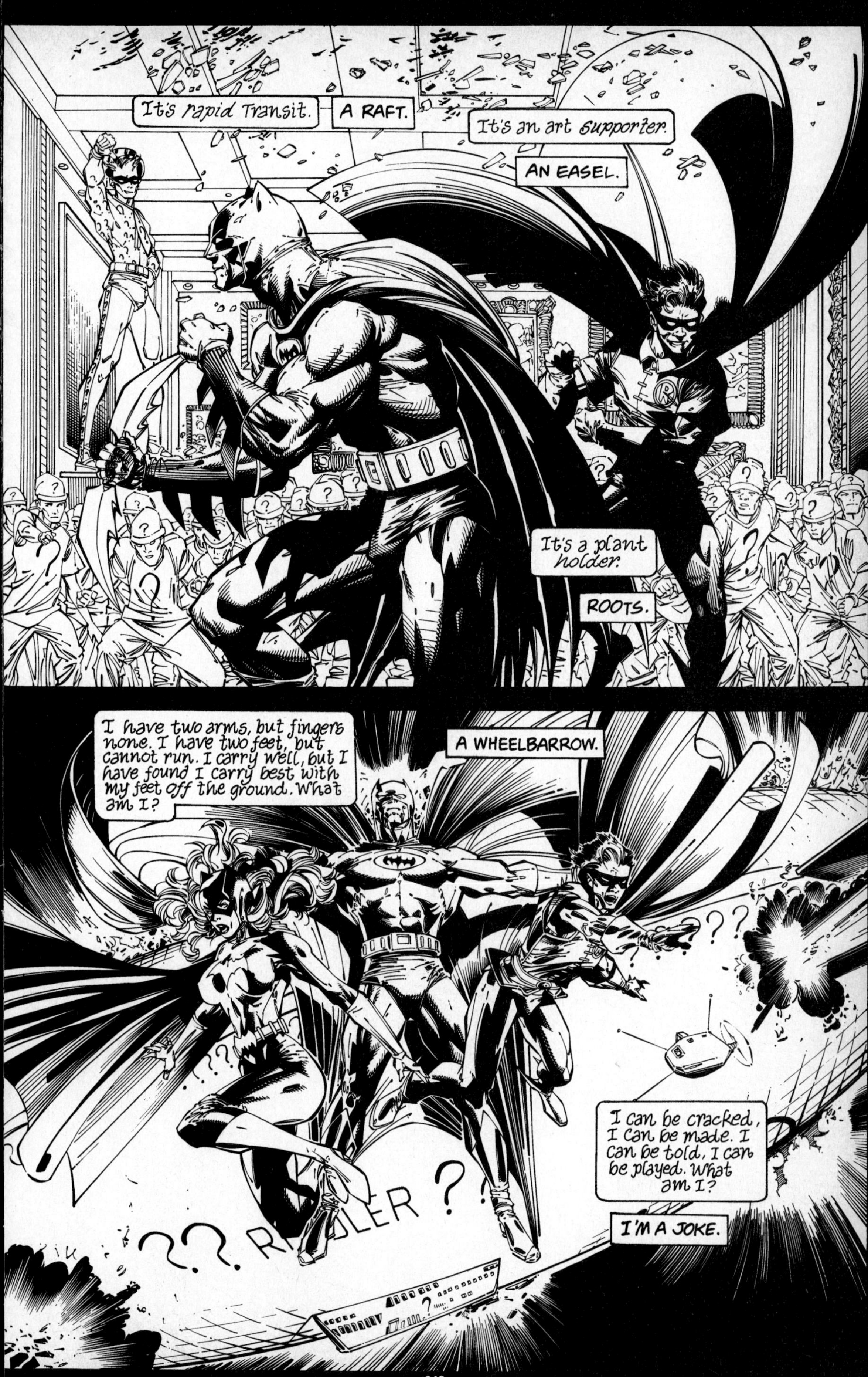
It's rapid Transit.
A RAFT.
It's an art supporter.
AN EASEL.
It's a plant holder.
ROOTS.
I have two arms, but fingers none. I have two feet, but cannot run. I carry well, but I have found I carry best with my feet off the ground. What am I?
A WHEELBARROW.
I can be cracked, I can be made. I can be told, I can be played. What am I?
I'M A JOKE.

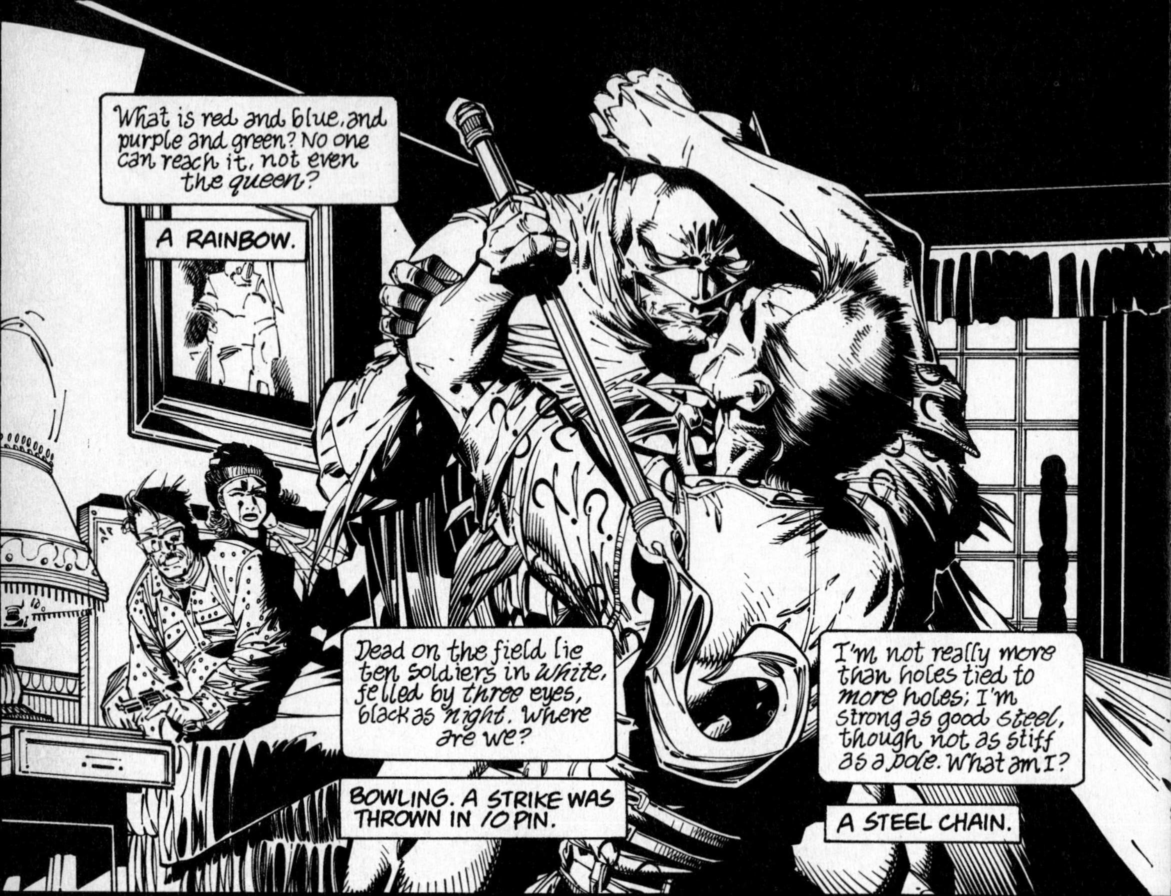
What is red and blue, and purple and green? No one can reach it, not even the queen?
A RAINBOW.
Dead on the field lie ten soldiers in white, felled by three eyes, black as night. Where are we?
BOWLING. A STRIKE WAS THROWN IN 10 PIN.
I'm not really more than holes tied to more holes; I'm strong as good steel, though not as stiff as a pole. What am I?
A STEEL CHAIN.

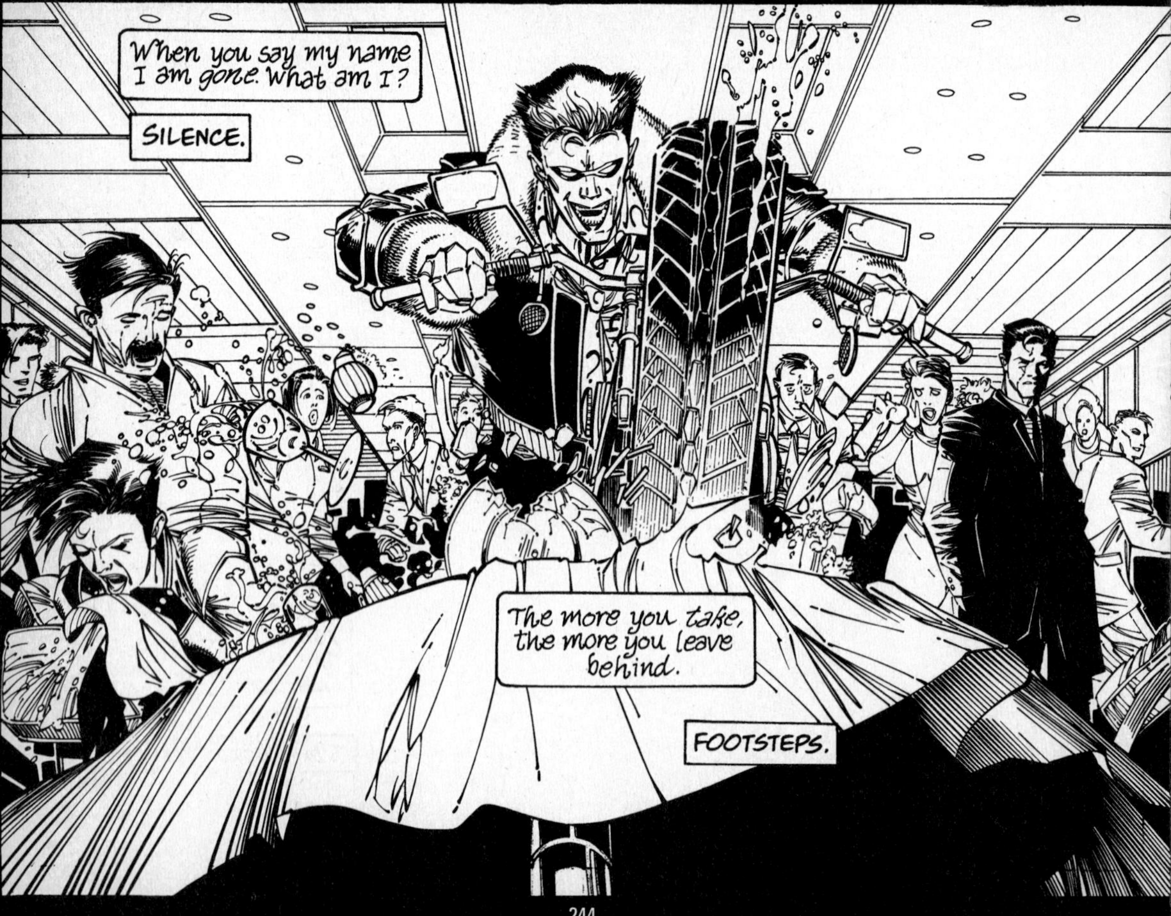
When you say my name I am gone. What am I?
SILENCE.
The more you take, the more you leave behind.
FOOTSTEPS.

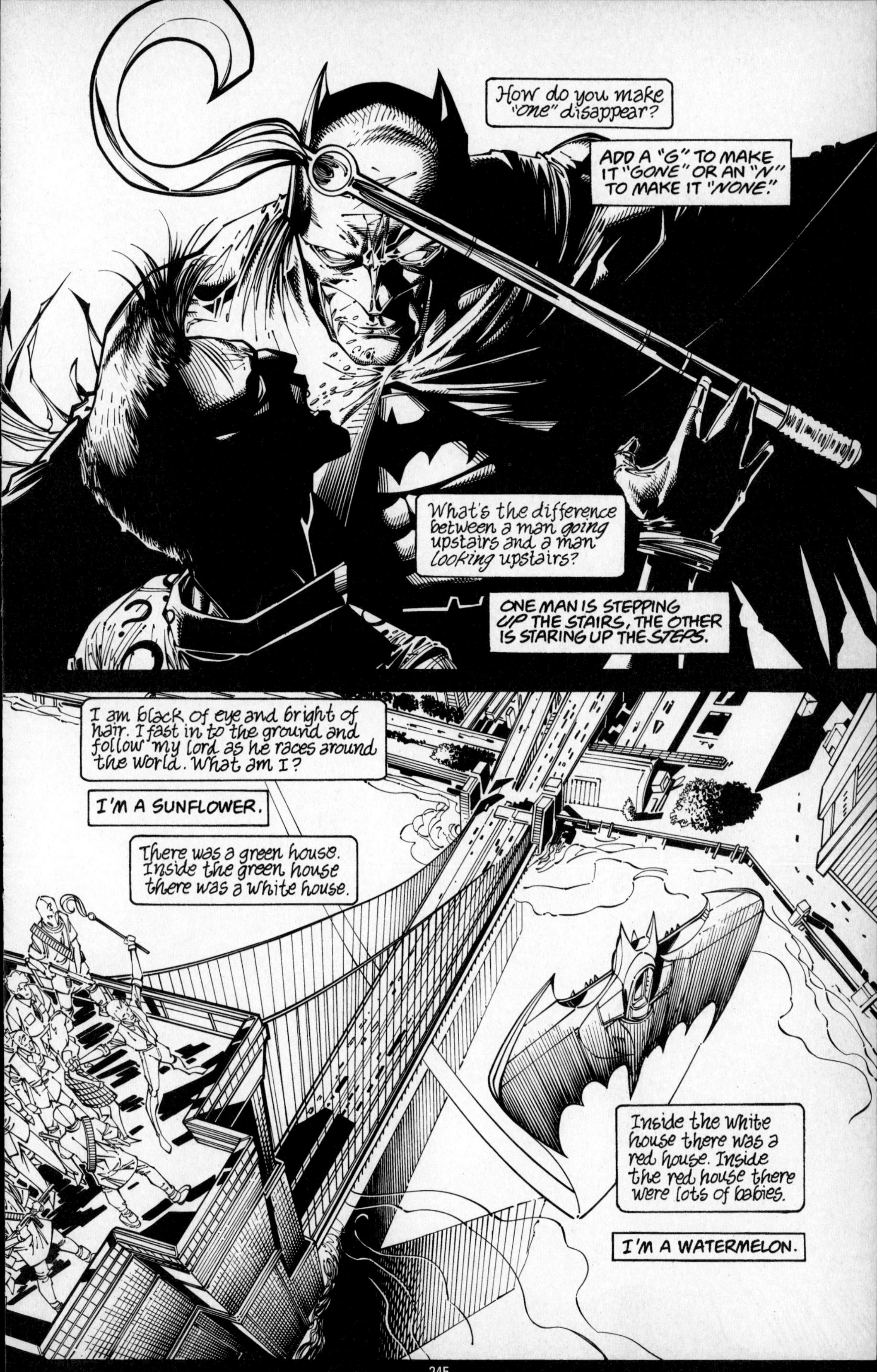

How do you make "one" disappear?
ADD A "G" TO MAKE IT "GONE" OR AN "N" TO MAKE IT "NONE."
What's the difference between a man going upstairs and a man looking upstairs?
ONE MAN IS STEPPING UP THE STAIRS, THE OTHER IS STARING UP THE STEPS.
I am black of eye and bright of hair. I fast in to the ground and follow my lord as he races around the world. What am I?
I'M A SUNFLOWER.
There was a green house. Inside the green house there was a white house.
Inside the white house there was a red house. Inside the red house there were lots of babies.
I'M A WATERMELON.

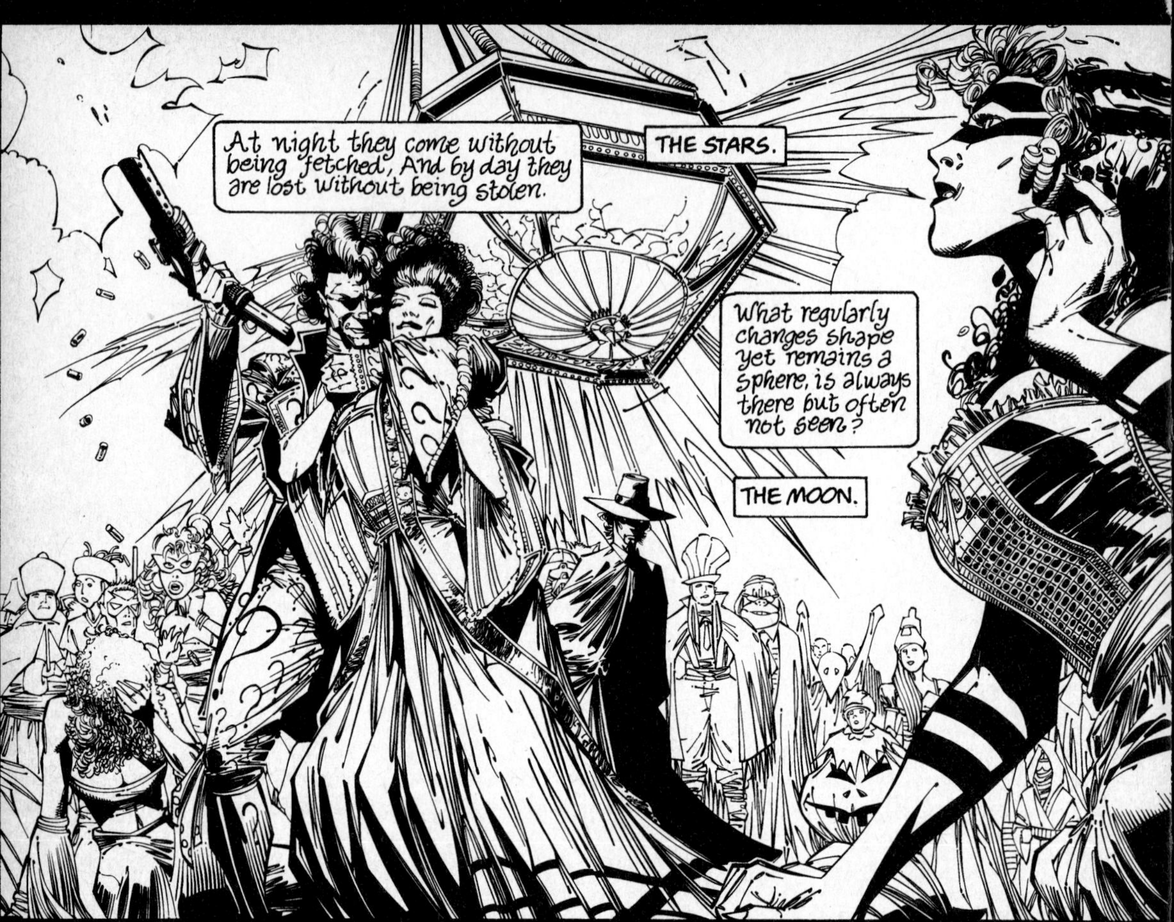
At night they come without being fetched, And by day they are lost without being stolen.
THE STARS.
What regularly changes shape yet remains a sphere, is always there but often not seen?
THE MOON.

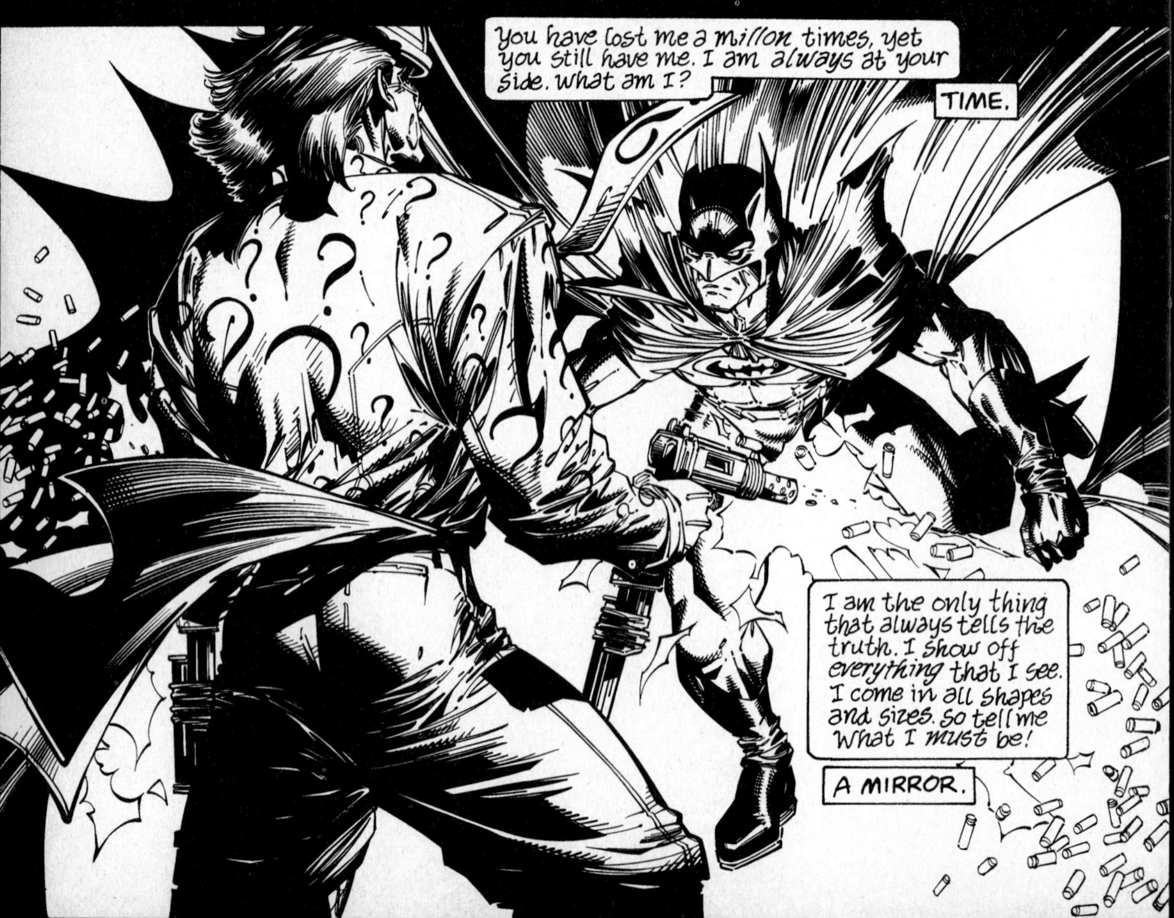
You have lost me a millon times, yet you still have me. I am always at your side. What am I?
TIME.
I am the only thing that always tells the truth. I show off everything that I see. I come in all shapes and sizes. So tell me what I must be!
A MIRROR.

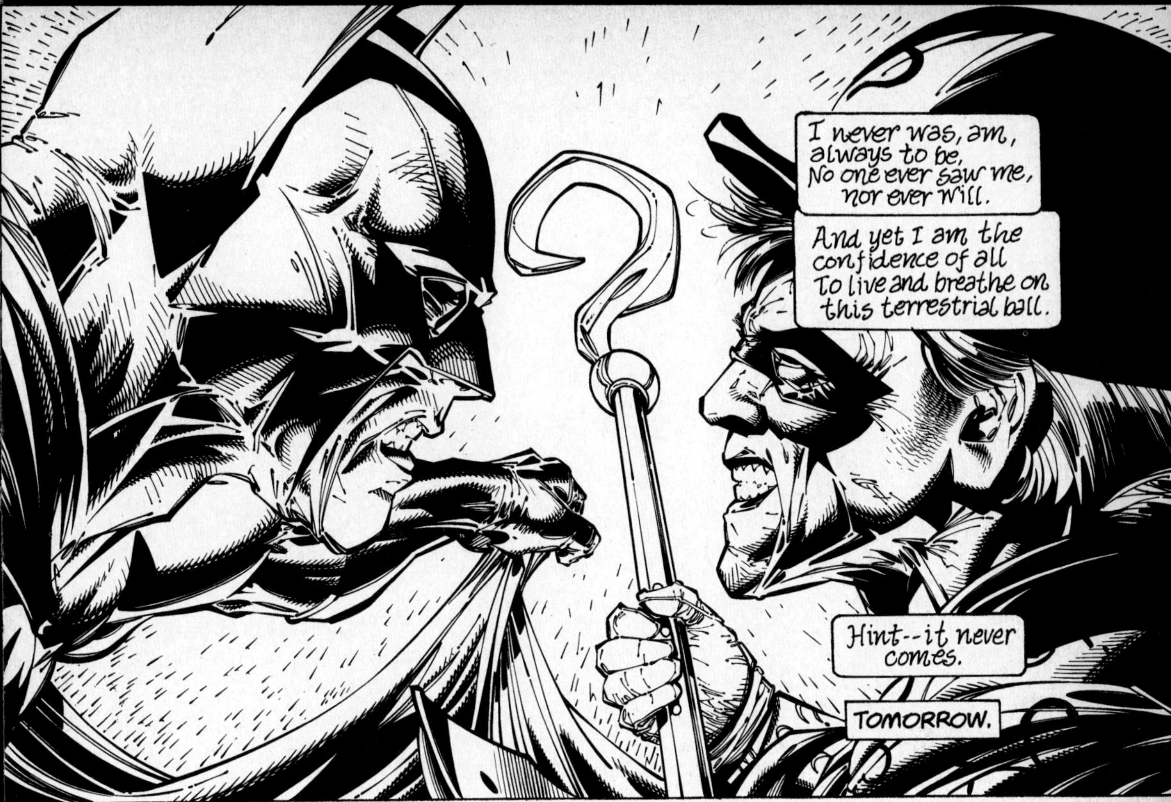
I never was, am, always to be, No one ever saw me, nor ever will.
And yet I am the confidence of all To live and breathe on this terrestrial ball.
Hint--it never comes.
TOMORROW.

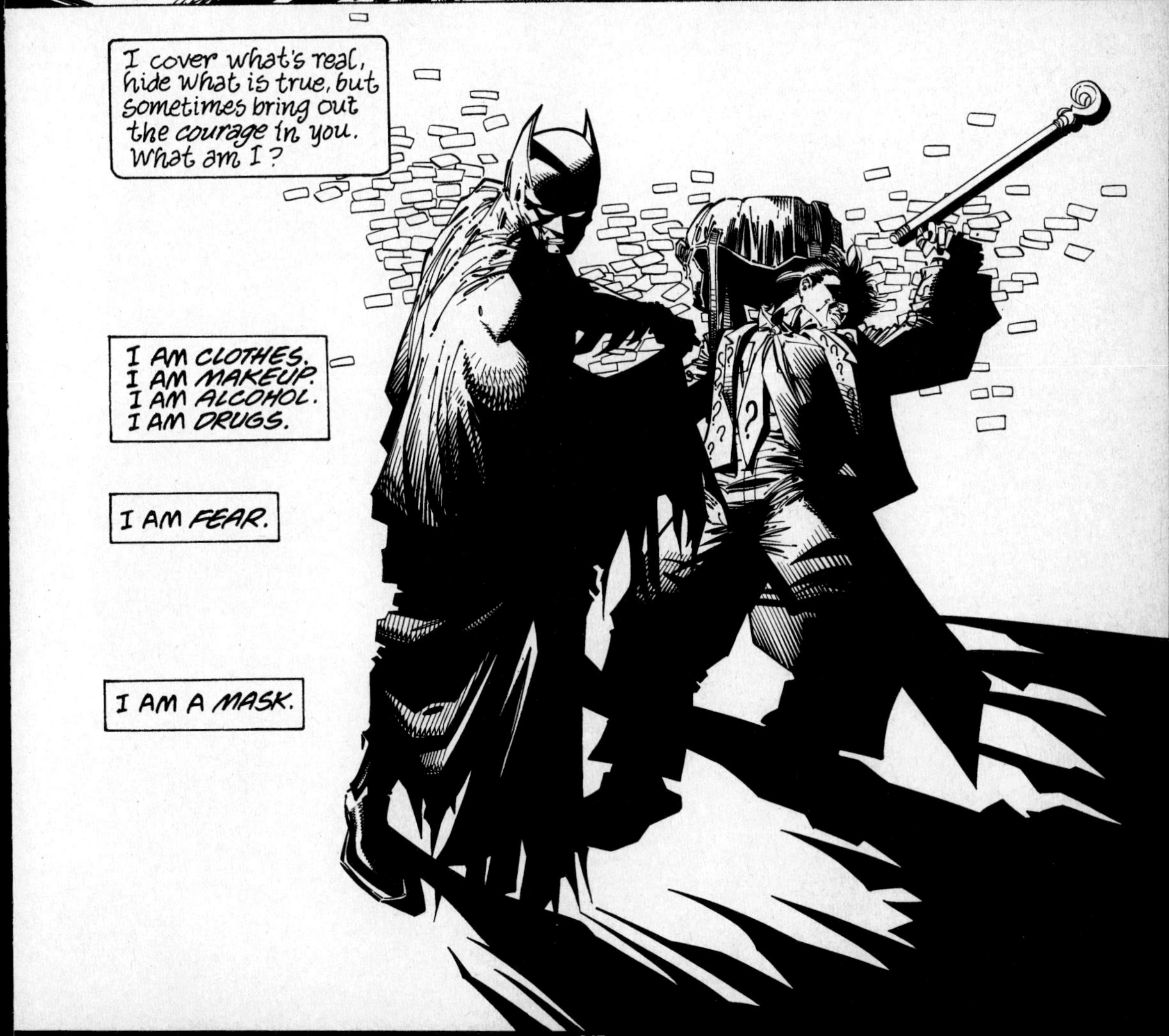
I cover what's real, hide what is true, but sometimes bring out the courage in you. What am I?
I AM CLOTHES. I AM MAKEUP. I AM ALCOHOL. I AM DRUGS.
I AM FEAR.
I AM A MASK.

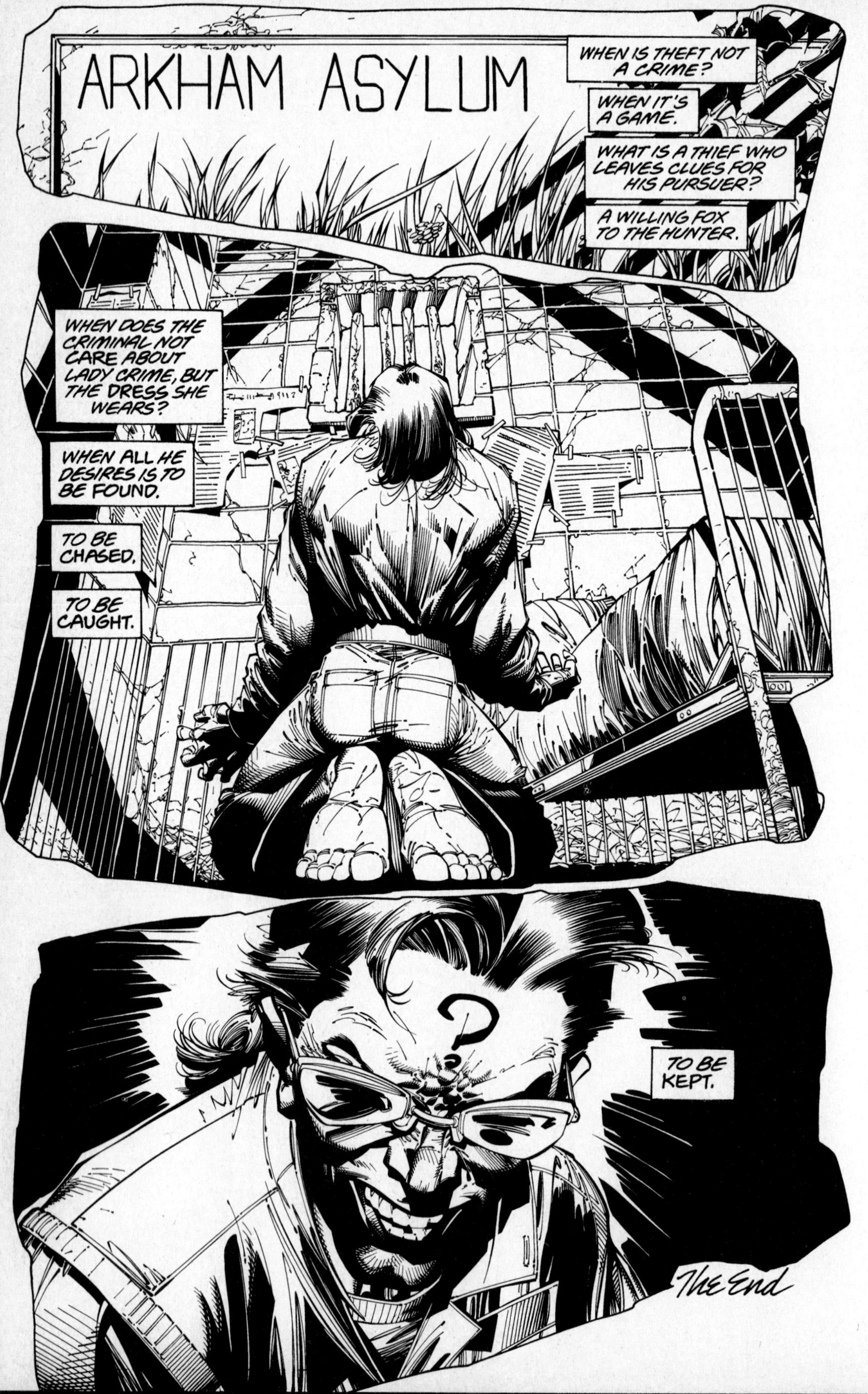
ARKHAM ASYLUM
WHEN IS THEFT NOT A CRIME?
WHEN IT'S A GAME.
WHAT IS A THIEF WHO LEAVES CLUES FOR HIS PURSUER?
A WILLING FOX TO THE HUNTER.
WHEN DOES THE CRIMINAL NOT CARE ABOUT LADY CRIME, BUT THE DRESS SHE WEARS?
WHEN ALL HE DESIRES IS TO BE FOUND.
TO BE CHASED.
TO BE CAUGHT.
TO BE KEPT.
The End

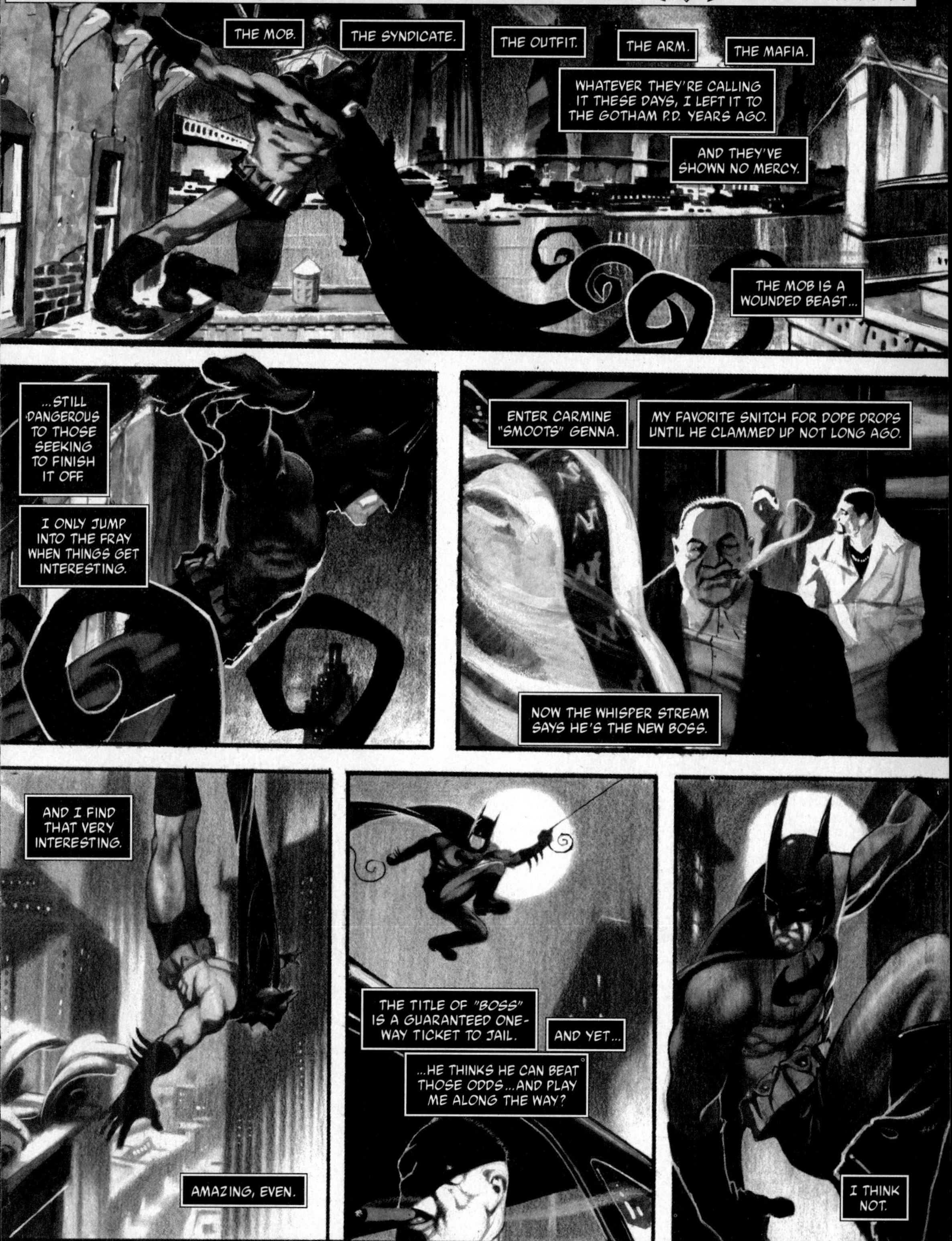
THE MOB.
THE SYNDICATE.
THE OUTFIT.
THE ARM.
THE MAFIA.
WHATEVER THEY'RE CALLING IT THESE DAYS, I LEFT IT TO THE GOTHAM P.D. YEARS AGO.
AND THEY'VE SHOWN NO MERCY.
THE MOB IS A WOUNDED BEAST...
...STILL DANGEROUS TO THOSE SEEKING TO FINISH IT OFF.
I ONLY JUMP INTO THE FRAY WHEN THINGS GET INTERESTING.
ENTER CARMINE "SMOOTS" GENNA.
MY FAVORITE SNITCH FOR DOPE DROPS UNTIL HE CLAMMED UP NOT LONG AGO.
NOW THE WHISPER STREAM SAYS HE'S THE NEW BOSS.
AND I FIND THAT VERY INTERESTING.
AMAZING, EVEN.
THE TITLE OF "BOSS" IS A GUARANTEED ONE-WAY TICKET TO JAIL.
AND YET...
...HE THINKS HE CAN BEAT THOSE ODDS...AND PLAY ME ALONG THE WAY?
I THINK NOT.

# THE MOB IS DEAD LONG LIVE THE MOB

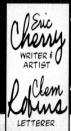

Eric Cherry WRITER & ARTIST

Clem Robins LETTERER

Michael Wright EDITOR

BATMAN CREATED BY Bob Kane

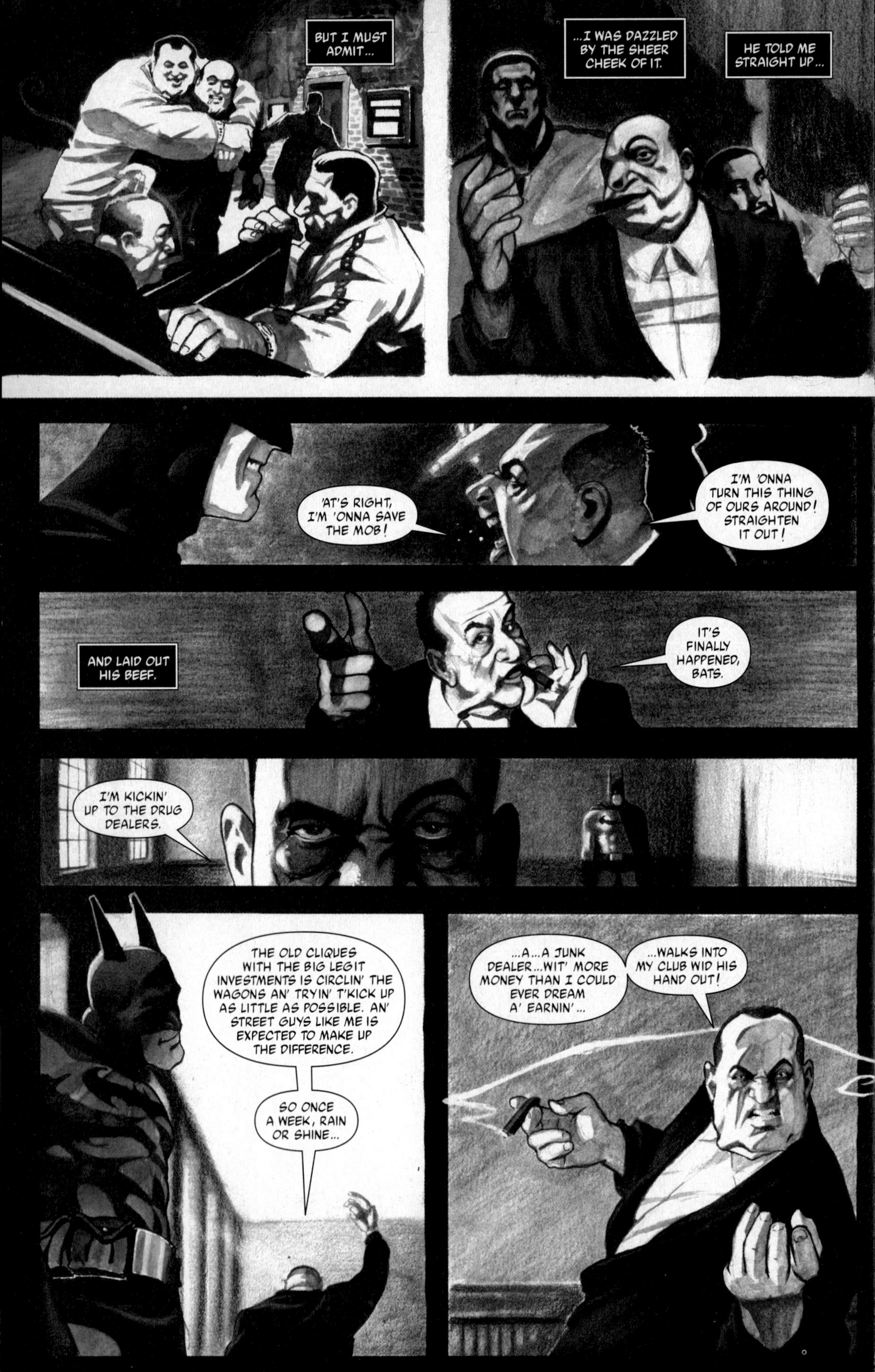
BUT I MUST ADMIT...
...I WAS DAZZLED BY THE SHEER CHEEK OF IT.
HE TOLD ME STRAIGHT UP...
'AT'S RIGHT, I'M 'ONNA SAVE THE MOB!
I'M 'ONNA TURN THIS THING OF OURS AROUND! STRAIGHTEN IT OUT!
AND LAID OUT HIS BEEF.
IT'S FINALLY HAPPENED, BATS.
I'M KICKIN' UP TO THE DRUG DEALERS.
THE OLD CLIQUES WITH THE BIG LEGIT INVESTMENTS IS CIRCLIN' THE WAGONS AN' TRYIN' T'KICK UP AS LITTLE AS POSSIBLE. AN' STREET GUYS LIKE ME IS EXPECTED TO MAKE UP THE DIFFERENCE.
SO ONCE A WEEK, RAIN OR SHINE...
...A...A JUNK DEALER...WIT' MORE MONEY THAN I COULD EVER DREAM A' EARNIN'...
...WALKS INTO MY CLUB WID HIS HAND OUT!

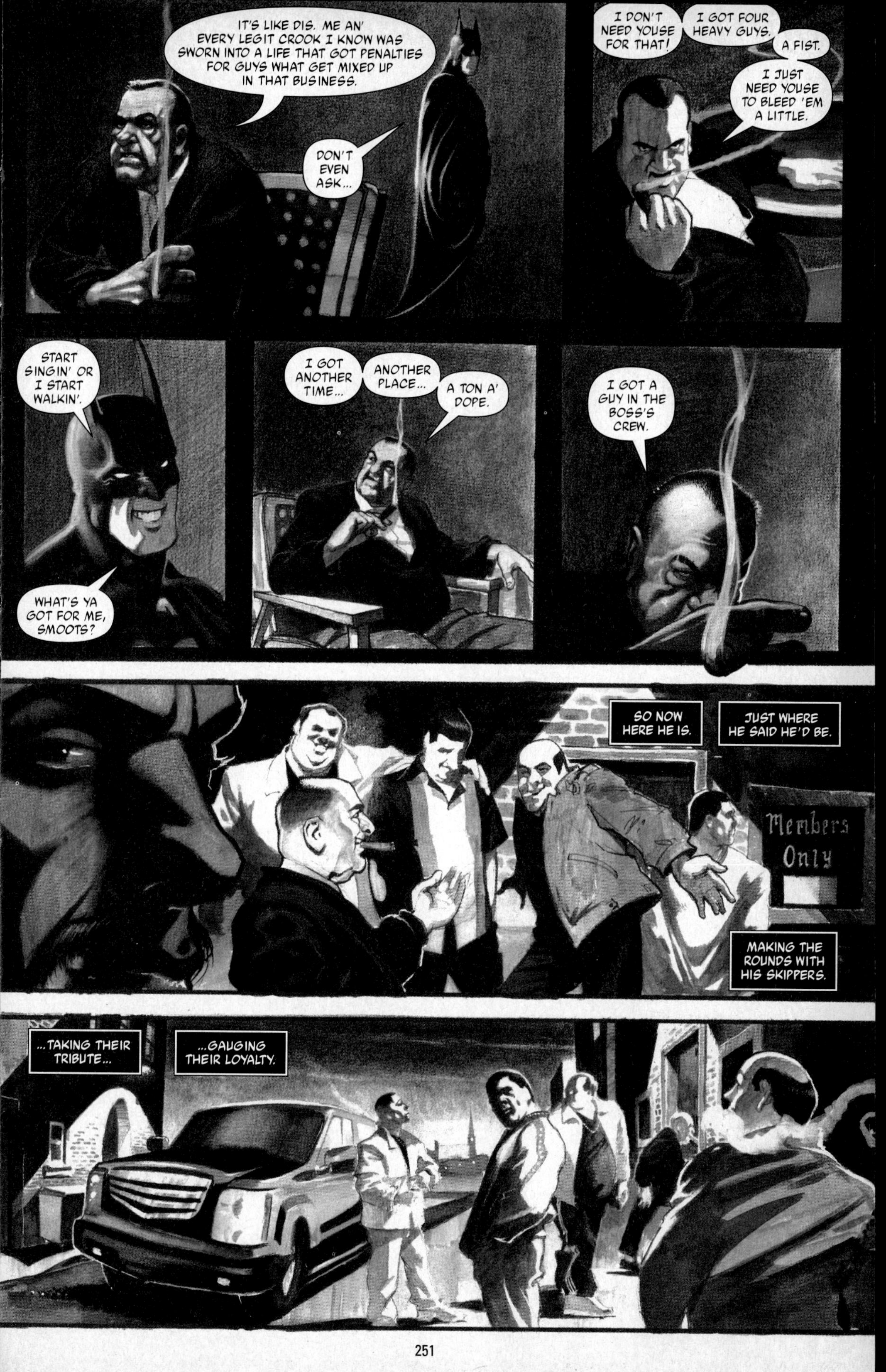
IT'S LIKE DIS. ME AN' EVERY LEGIT CROOK I KNOW WAS SWORN INTO A LIFE THAT GOT PENALTIES FOR GUYS WHAT GET MIXED UP IN THAT BUSINESS.
DON'T EVEN ASK...
I DON'T NEED YOUSE FOR THAT!
I GOT FOUR HEAVY GUYS.
A FIST.
I JUST NEED YOUSE TO BLEED 'EM A LITTLE.
START SINGIN' OR I START WALKIN'.
WHAT'S YA GOT FOR ME, SMOOTS?
I GOT ANOTHER TIME...
ANOTHER PLACE...
A TON A' DOPE.
I GOT A GUY IN THE BOSS'S CREW.
SO NOW HERE HE IS.
JUST WHERE HE SAID HE'D BE.
Members Only
MAKING THE ROUNDS WITH HIS SKIPPERS.
...TAKING THEIR TRIBUTE...
...GAUGING THEIR LOYALTY.

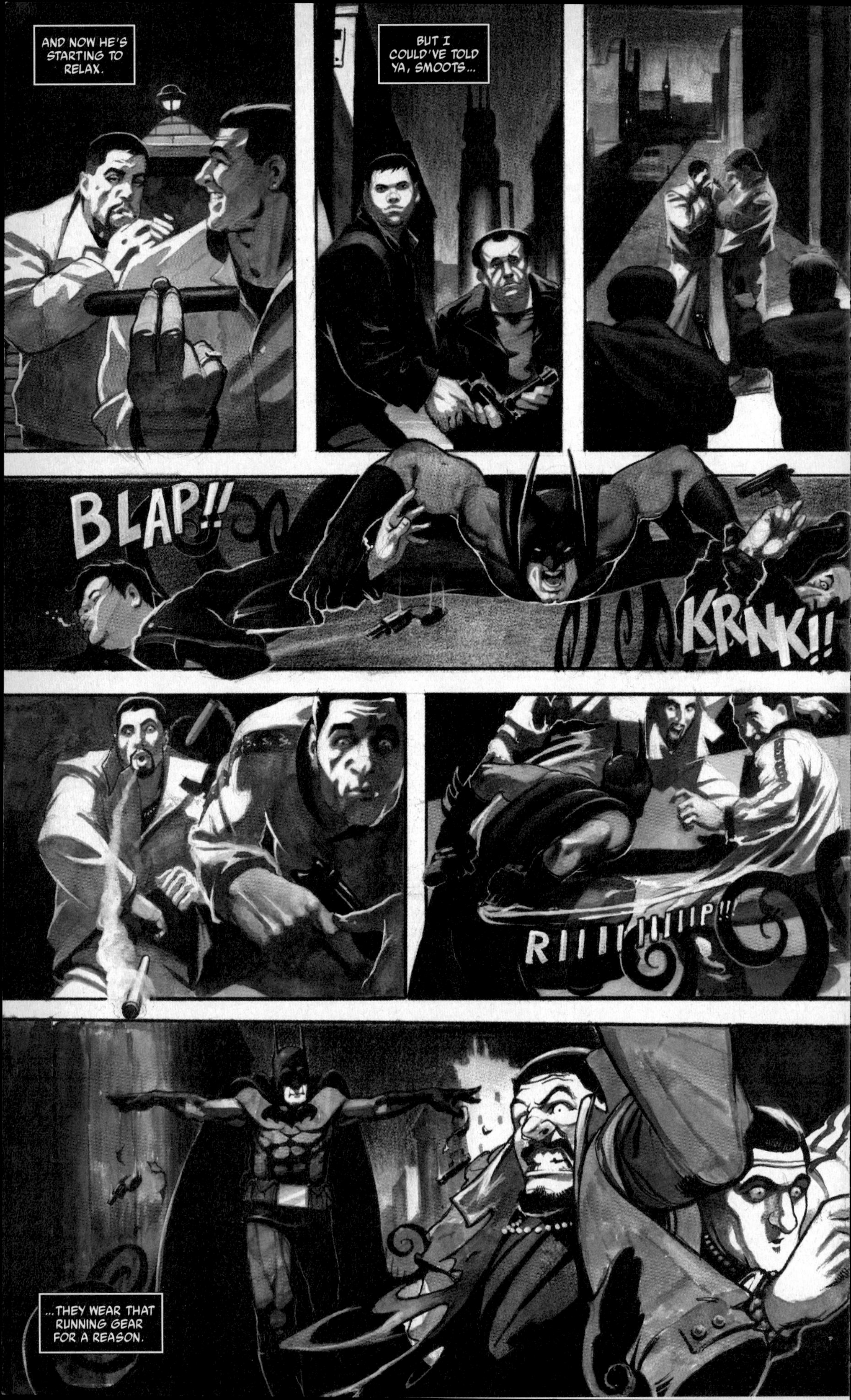

AND NOW HE'S STARTING TO RELAX.
BUT I COULD'VE TOLD YA, SMOOTS...
BLAP!!
KRNK!!
RIIIIIIIIIP!!
...THEY WEAR THAT RUNNING GEAR FOR A REASON.

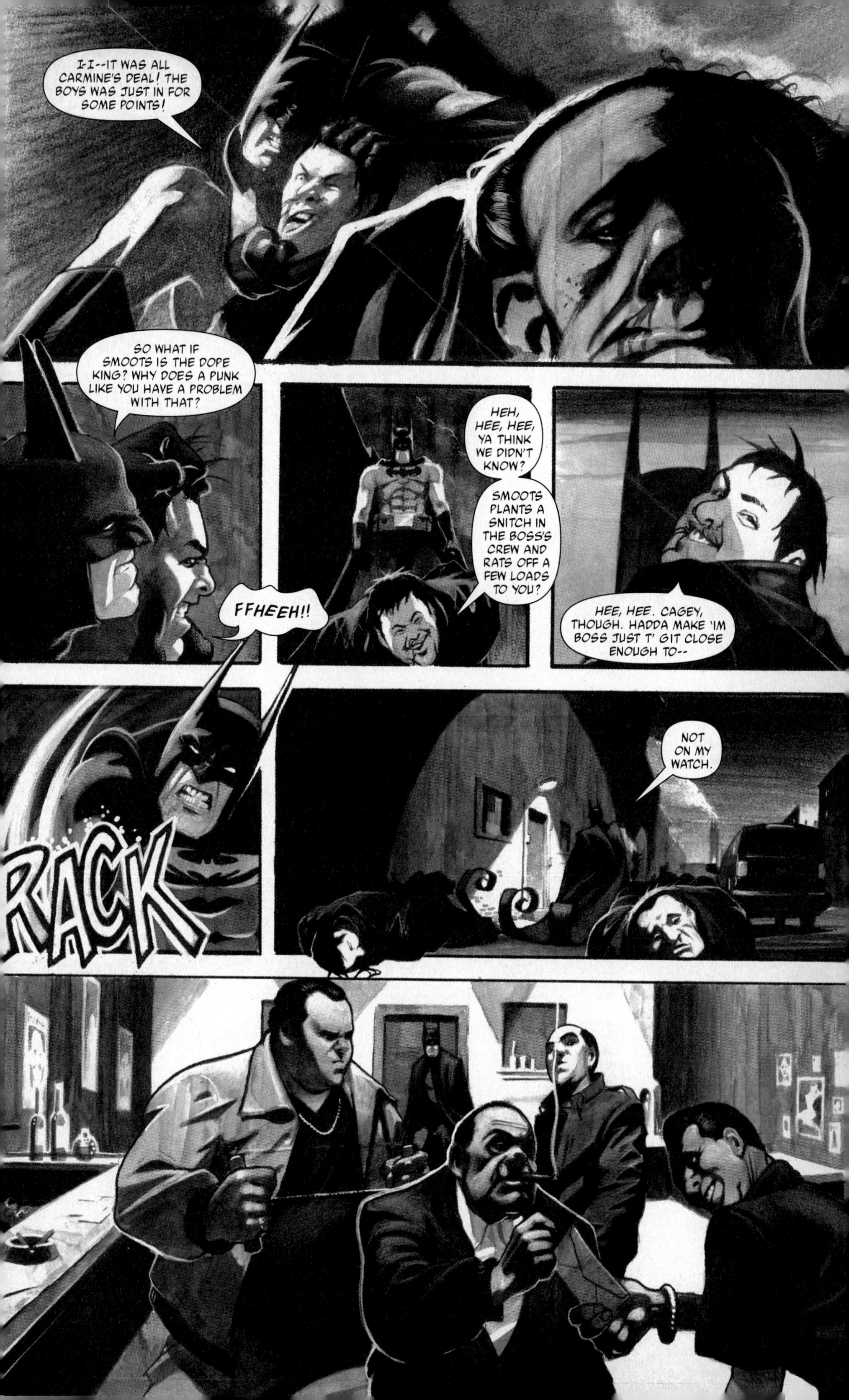
I-I--IT WAS ALL CARMINE'S DEAL! THE BOYS WAS JUST IN FOR SOME POINTS!
SO WHAT IF SMOOTS IS THE DOPE KING? WHY DOES A PUNK LIKE YOU HAVE A PROBLEM WITH THAT?
FFHEEH!!
HEH, HEE, HEE, YA THINK WE DIDN'T KNOW?
SMOOTS PLANTS A SNITCH IN THE BOSS'S CREW AND RATS OFF A FEW LOADS TO YOU?
HEE, HEE. CAGEY, THOUGH. HADDA MAKE 'IM BOSS JUST T' GIT CLOSE ENOUGH TO--
RACK
NOT ON MY WATCH.

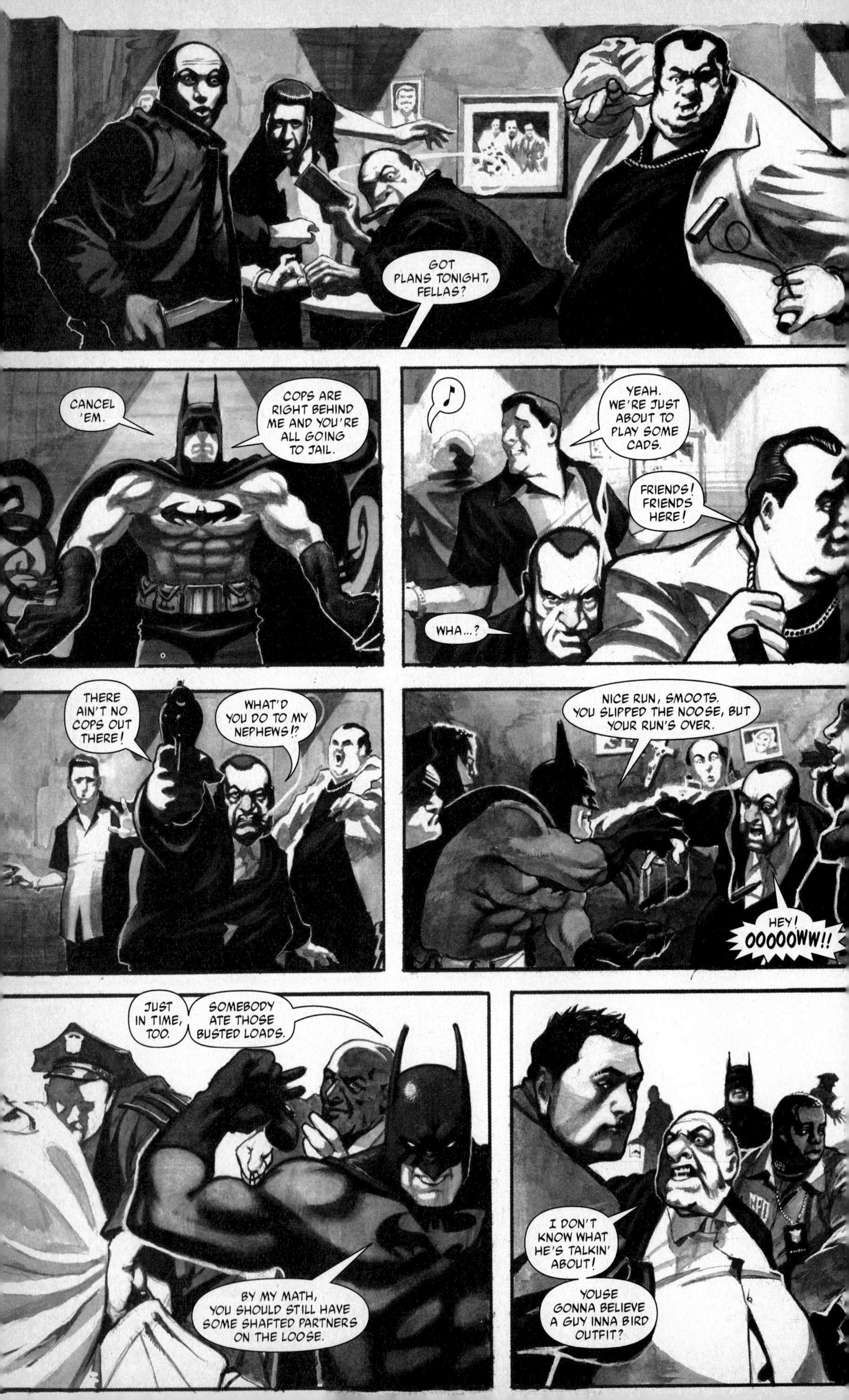
GOT PLANS TONIGHT, FELLAS?
CANCEL 'EM.
COPS ARE RIGHT BEHIND ME AND YOU'RE ALL GOING TO JAIL.
♪
YEAH. WE'RE JUST ABOUT TO PLAY SOME CADS.
FRIENDS! FRIENDS HERE!
WHA...?
THERE AIN'T NO COPS OUT THERE!
WHAT'D YOU DO TO MY NEPHEWS!?
NICE RUN, SMOOTS. YOU SLIPPED THE NOOSE, BUT YOUR RUN'S OVER.
HEY!
OOOOOWW!!
JUST IN TIME, TOO.
SOMEBODY ATE THOSE BUSTED LOADS.
BY MY MATH, YOU SHOULD STILL HAVE SOME SHAFTED PARTNERS ON THE LOOSE.
I DON'T KNOW WHAT HE'S TALKIN' ABOUT!
YOUSE GONNA BELIEVE A GUY INNA BIRD OUTFIT?

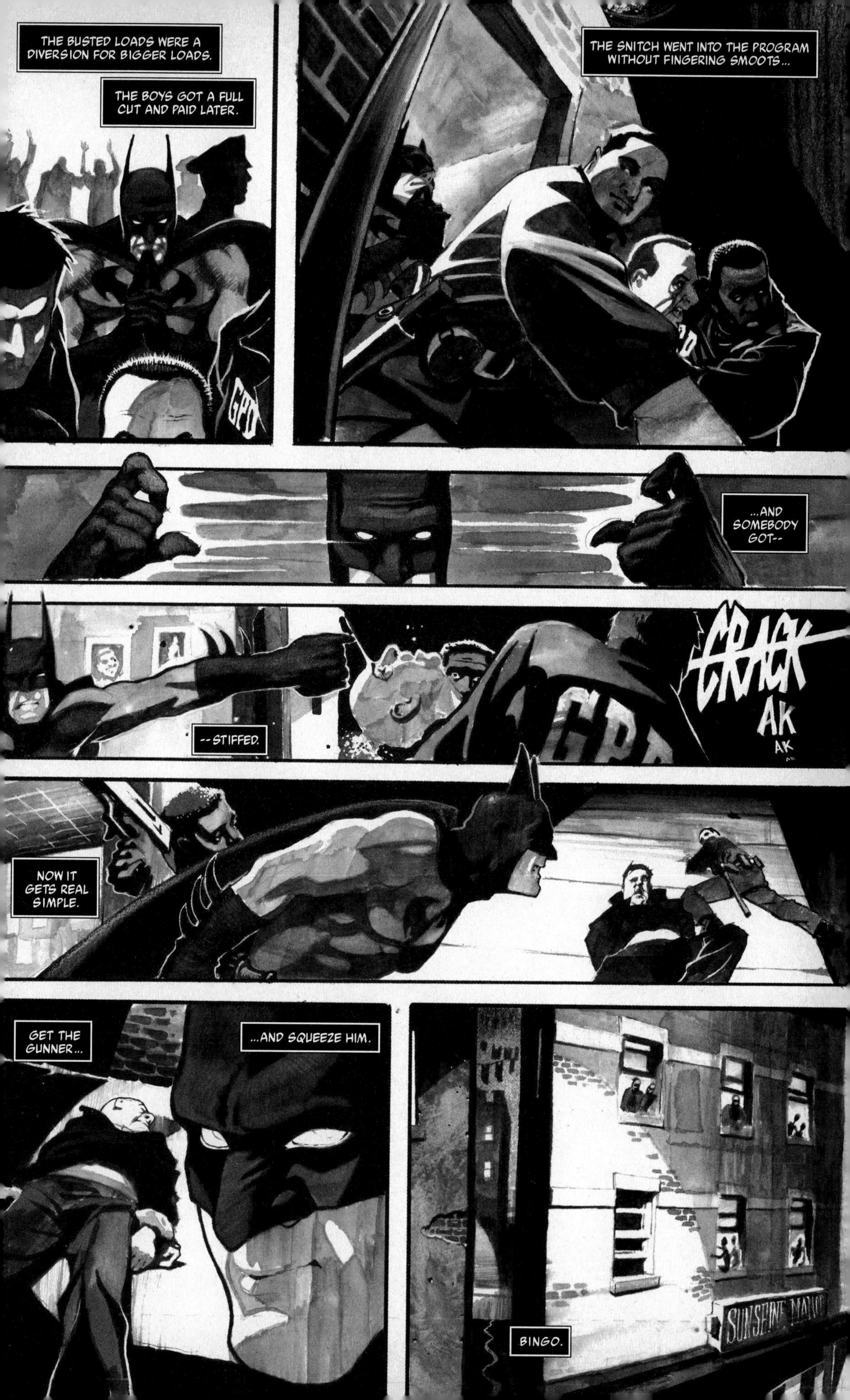
THE BUSTED LOADS WERE A DIVERSION FOR BIGGER LOADS.
THE BOYS GOT A FULL CUT AND PAID LATER.
GPD
THE SNITCH WENT INTO THE PROGRAM WITHOUT FINGERING SMOOTS...
...AND SOMEBODY GOT--
--STIFFED.
CRACK
AK
AK
NOW IT GETS REAL SIMPLE.
GET THE GUNNER...
...AND SQUEEZE HIM.
BINGO.

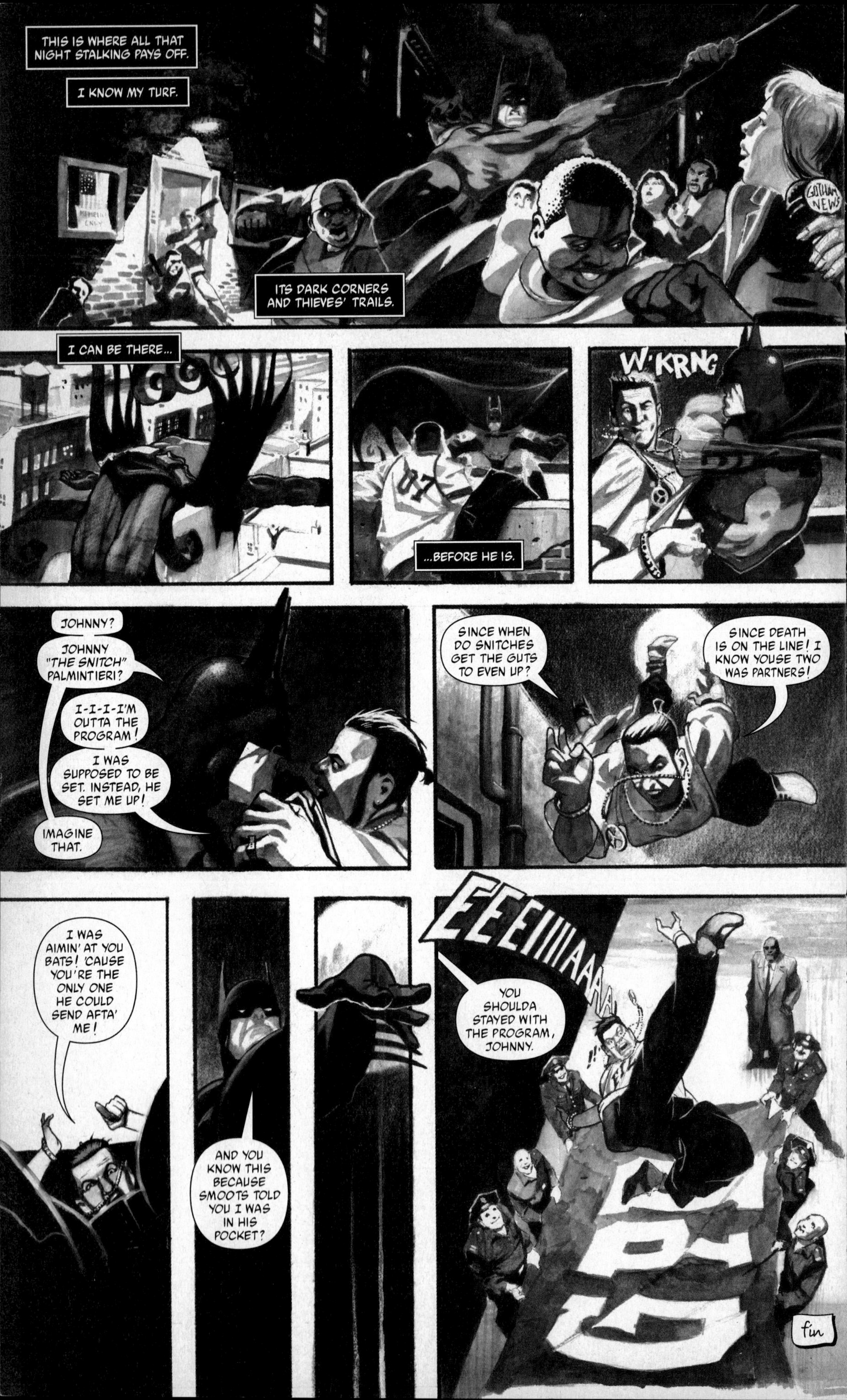

THIS IS WHERE ALL THAT NIGHT STALKING PAYS OFF.
I KNOW MY TURF.
GOTHAM NEWS
ITS DARK CORNERS AND THIEVES' TRAILS.
I CAN BE THERE...
...BEFORE HE IS.
W'KRNG
JOHNNY?
JOHNNY "THE SNITCH" PALMINTIERI?
I-I-I-I'M OUTTA THE PROGRAM!
I WAS SUPPOSED TO BE SET. INSTEAD, HE SET ME UP!
IMAGINE THAT.
SINCE WHEN DO SNITCHES GET THE GUTS TO EVEN UP?
SINCE DEATH IS ON THE LINE! I KNOW YOUSE TWO WAS PARTNERS!
I WAS AIMIN' AT YOU BATS! 'CAUSE YOU'RE THE ONLY ONE HE COULD SEND AFTA' ME!
AND YOU KNOW THIS BECAUSE SMOOTS TOLD YOU I WAS IN HIS POCKET?
EEEIIIIAAAA
YOU SHOULDA STAYED WITH THE PROGRAM, JOHNNY.
fin

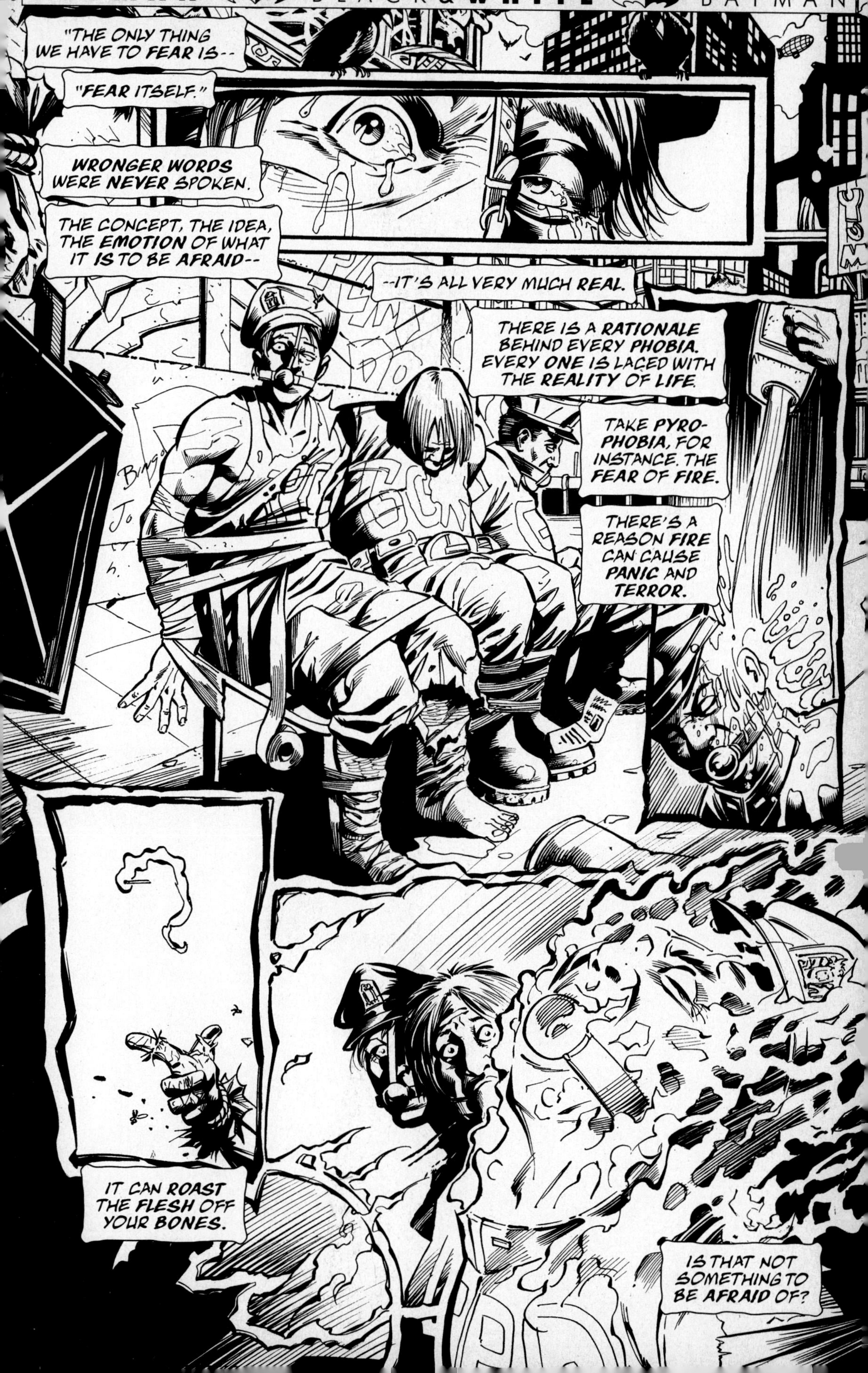
"THE ONLY THING WE HAVE TO FEAR IS--
"FEAR ITSELF."
WRONGER WORDS WERE NEVER SPOKEN.
THE CONCEPT, THE IDEA, THE EMOTION OF WHAT IT IS TO BE AFRAID--
--IT'S ALL VERY MUCH REAL.
THERE IS A RATIONALE BEHIND EVERY PHOBIA. EVERY ONE IS LACED WITH THE REALITY OF LIFE.
TAKE PYRO-PHOBIA, FOR INSTANCE. THE FEAR OF FIRE.
THERE'S A REASON FIRE CAN CAUSE PANIC AND TERROR.
IT CAN ROAST THE FLESH OFF YOUR BONES.
IS THAT NOT SOMETHING TO BE AFRAID OF?

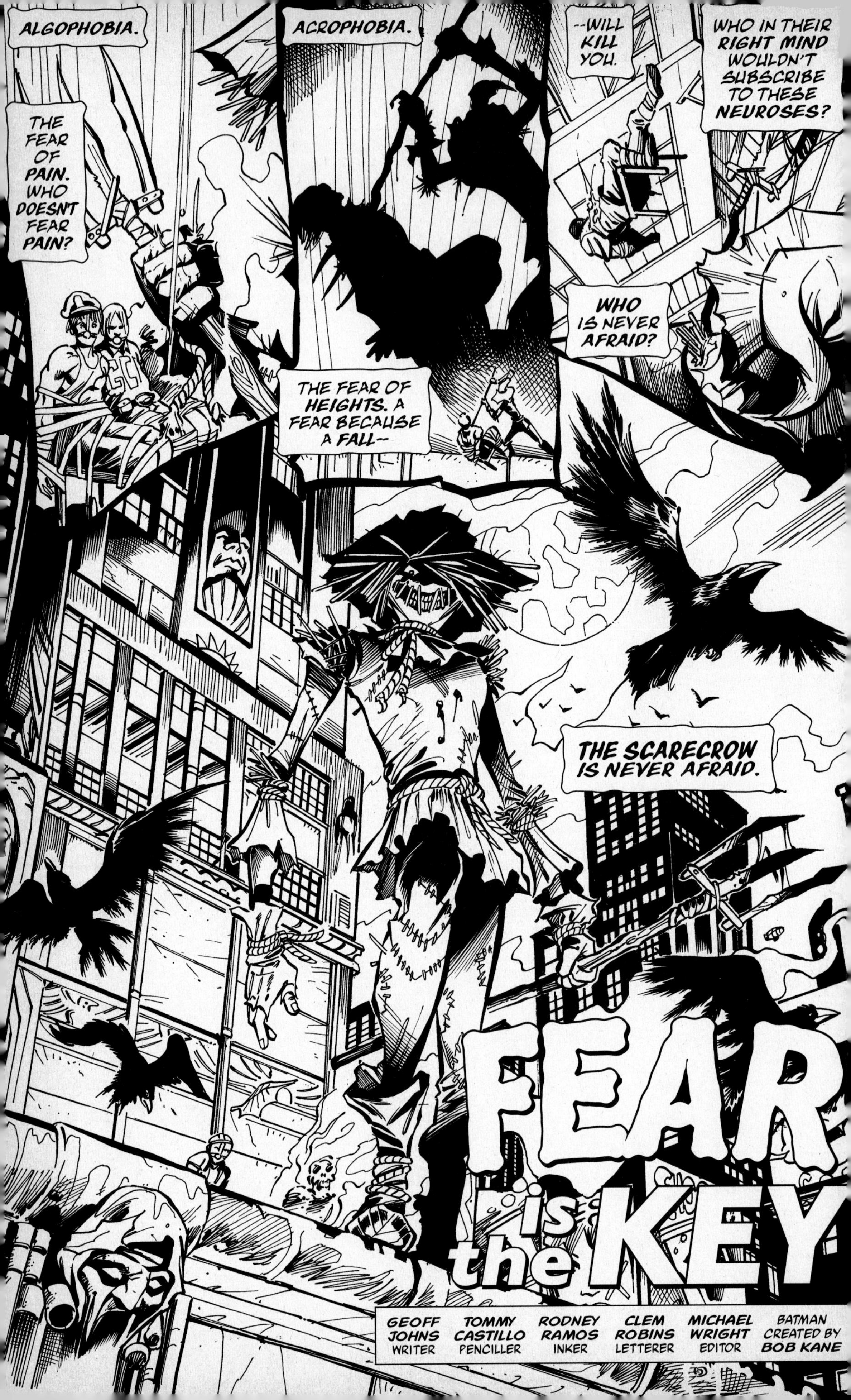
ALGOPHOBIA.
THE FEAR OF PAIN. WHO DOESN'T FEAR PAIN?
ACROPHOBIA.
THE FEAR OF HEIGHTS. A FEAR BECAUSE A FALL--
--WILL KILL YOU.
WHO IN THEIR RIGHT MIND WOULDN'T SUBSCRIBE TO THESE NEUROSES?
WHO IS NEVER AFRAID?
THE SCARECROW IS NEVER AFRAID.
FEAR is the KEY
GEOFF JOHNS WRITER
TOMMY CASTILLO PENCILLER
RODNEY RAMOS INKER
CLEM ROBINS LETTERER
MICHAEL WRIGHT EDITOR
BATMAN CREATED BY BOB KANE

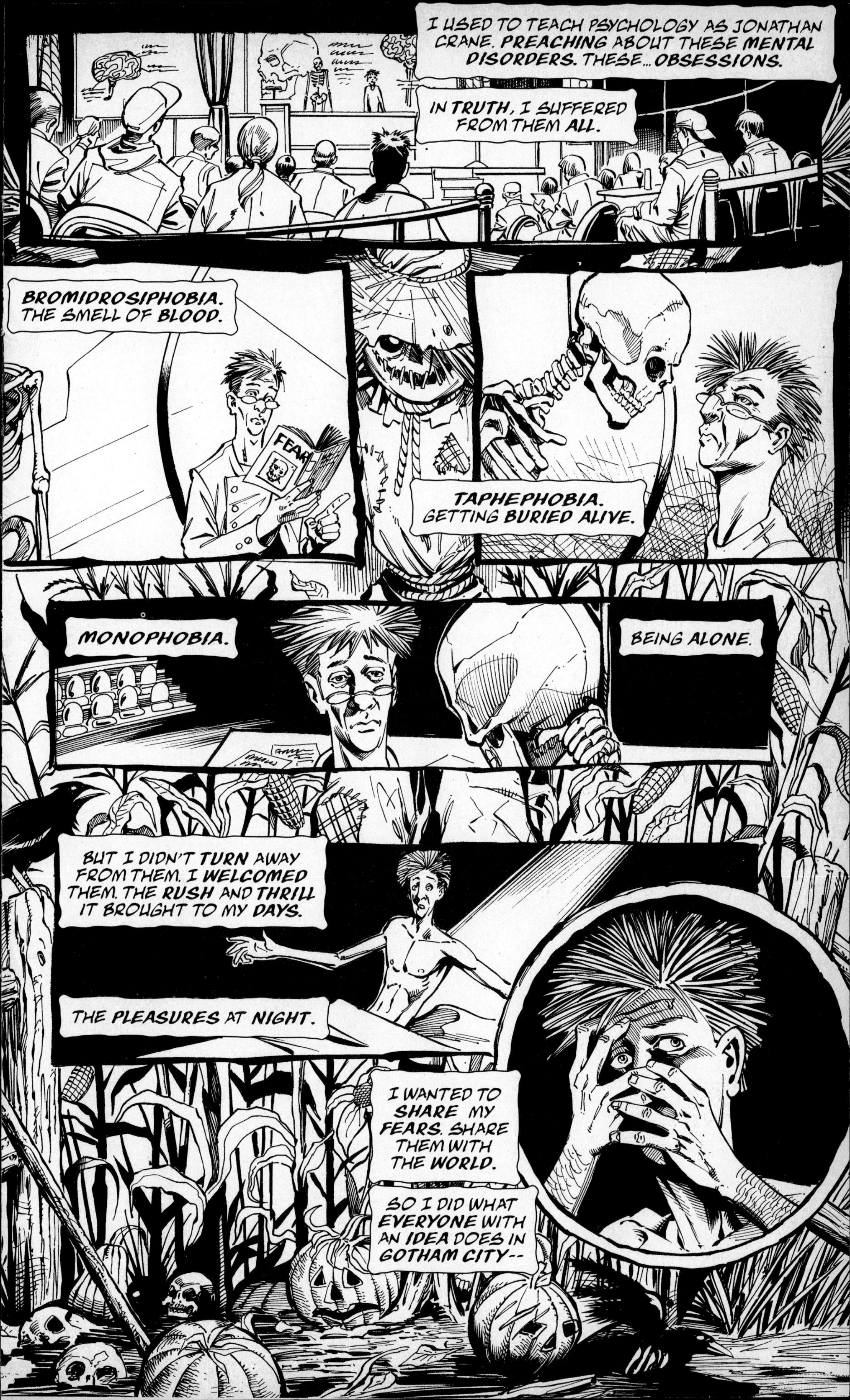
I USED TO TEACH PSYCHOLOGY AS JONATHAN CRANE. PREACHING ABOUT THESE MENTAL DISORDERS. THESE...OBSESSIONS.
IN TRUTH, I SUFFERED FROM THEM ALL.
BROMIDROSIPHOBIA. THE SMELL OF BLOOD.
FEAR
TAPHEPHOBIA. GETTING BURIED ALIVE.
MONOPHOBIA.
BEING ALONE.
BUT I DIDN'T TURN AWAY FROM THEM. I WELCOMED THEM. THE RUSH AND THRILL IT BROUGHT TO MY DAYS.
THE PLEASURES AT NIGHT.
I WANTED TO SHARE MY FEARS. SHARE THEM WITH THE WORLD.
SO I DID WHAT EVERYONE WITH AN IDEA DOES IN GOTHAM CITY--

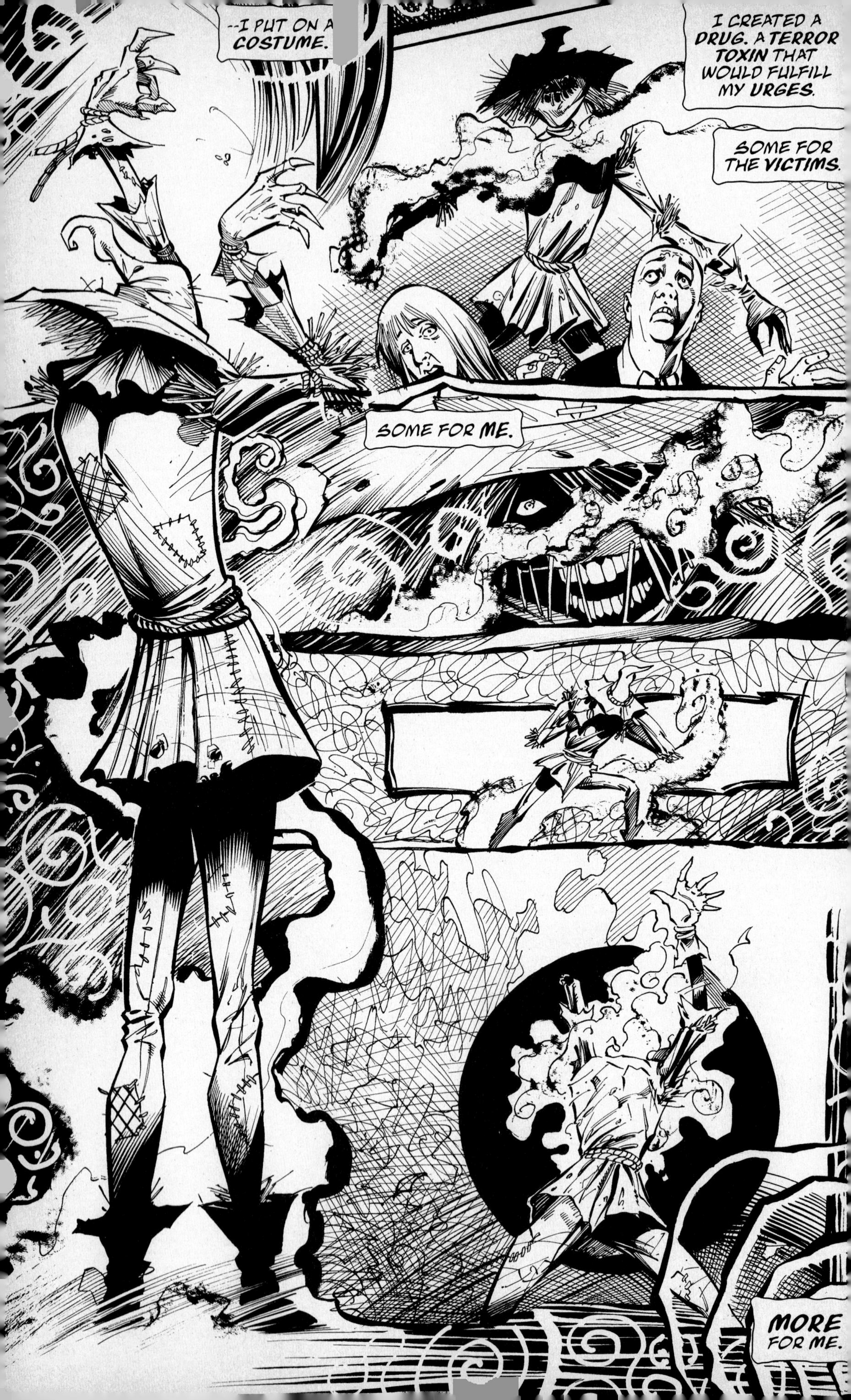
--I PUT ON A COSTUME.
I CREATED A DRUG. A TERROR TOXIN THAT WOULD FULFILL MY URGES.
SOME FOR THE VICTIMS.
SOME FOR ME.
MORE FOR ME.

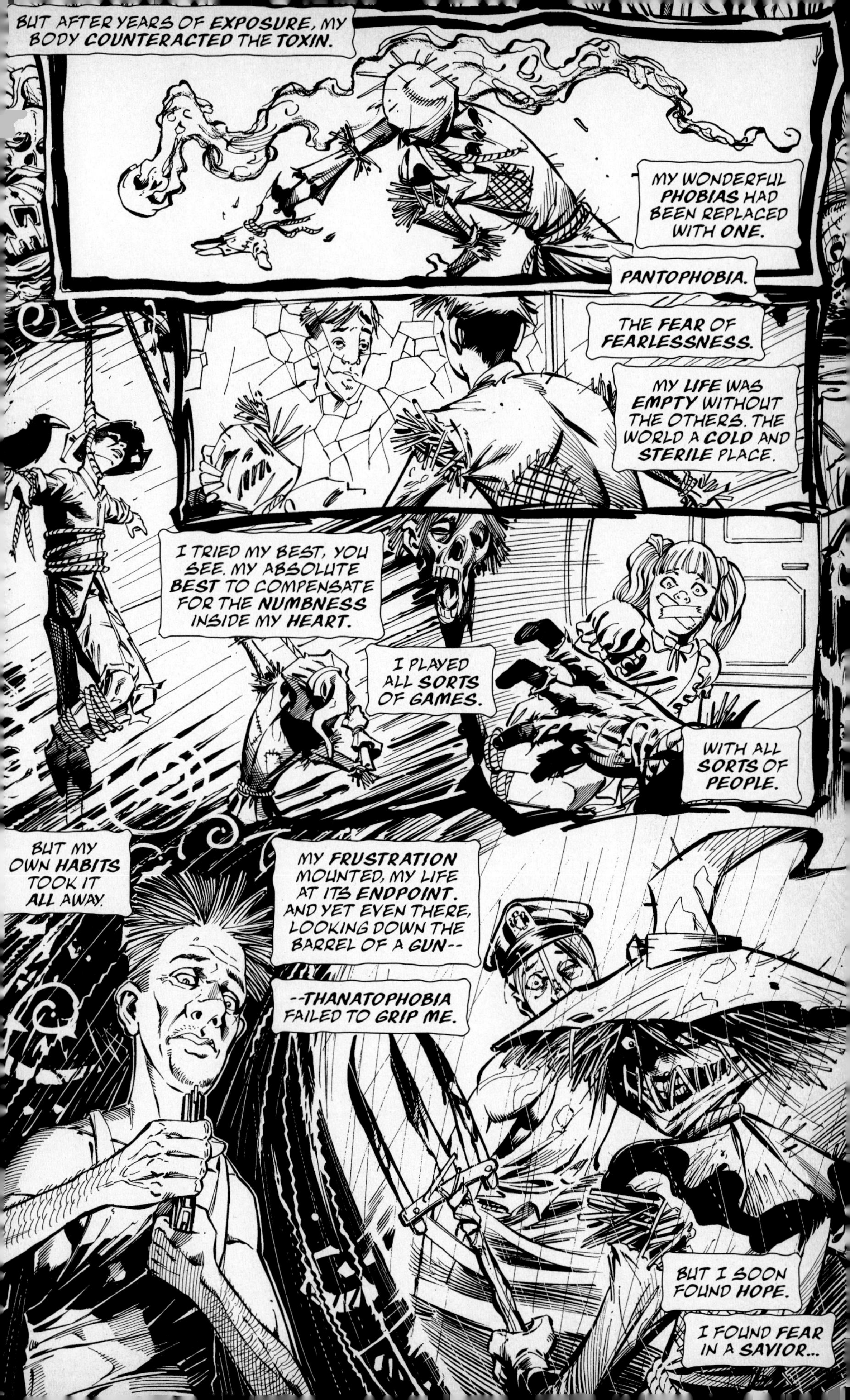
BUT AFTER YEARS OF EXPOSURE, MY BODY COUNTERACTED THE TOXIN.
MY WONDERFUL PHOBIAS HAD BEEN REPLACED WITH ONE.
PANTOPHOBIA.
THE FEAR OF FEARLESSNESS.
MY LIFE WAS EMPTY WITHOUT THE OTHERS. THE WORLD A COLD AND STERILE PLACE.
I TRIED MY BEST, YOU SEE. MY ABSOLUTE BEST TO COMPENSATE FOR THE NUMBNESS INSIDE MY HEART.
I PLAYED ALL SORTS OF GAMES.
WITH ALL SORTS OF PEOPLE.
BUT MY OWN HABITS TOOK IT ALL AWAY.
MY FRUSTRATION MOUNTED, MY LIFE AT ITS ENDPOINT. AND YET EVEN THERE, LOOKING DOWN THE BARREL OF A GUN--
--THANATOPHOBIA FAILED TO GRIP ME.
BUT I SOON FOUND HOPE.
I FOUND FEAR IN A SAVIOR...

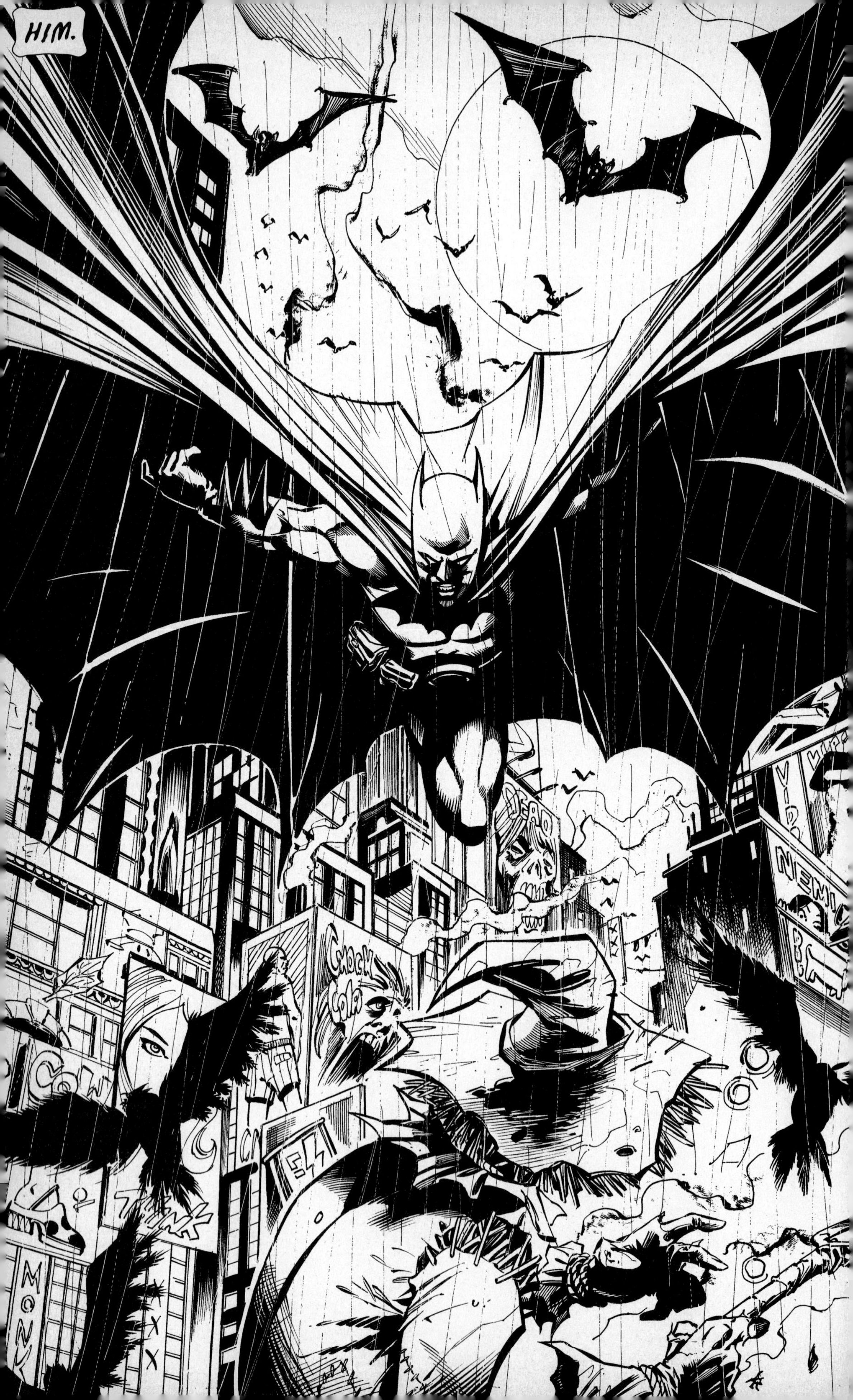
HIM.

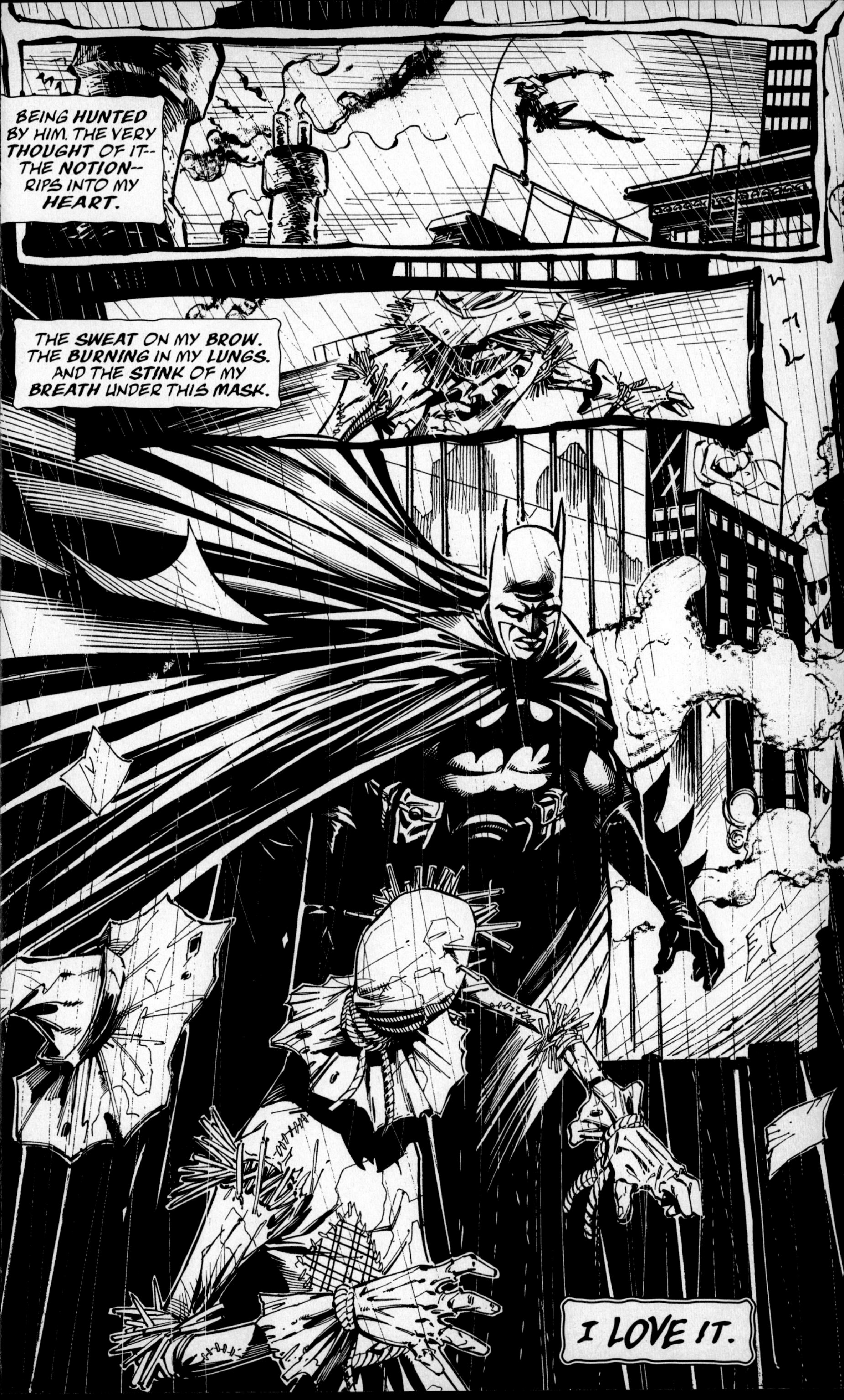
BEING HUNTED BY HIM. THE VERY THOUGHT OF IT-- THE NOTION-- RIPS INTO MY HEART.
THE SWEAT ON MY BROW. THE BURNING IN MY LUNGS. AND THE STINK OF MY BREATH UNDER THIS MASK.
I LOVE IT.

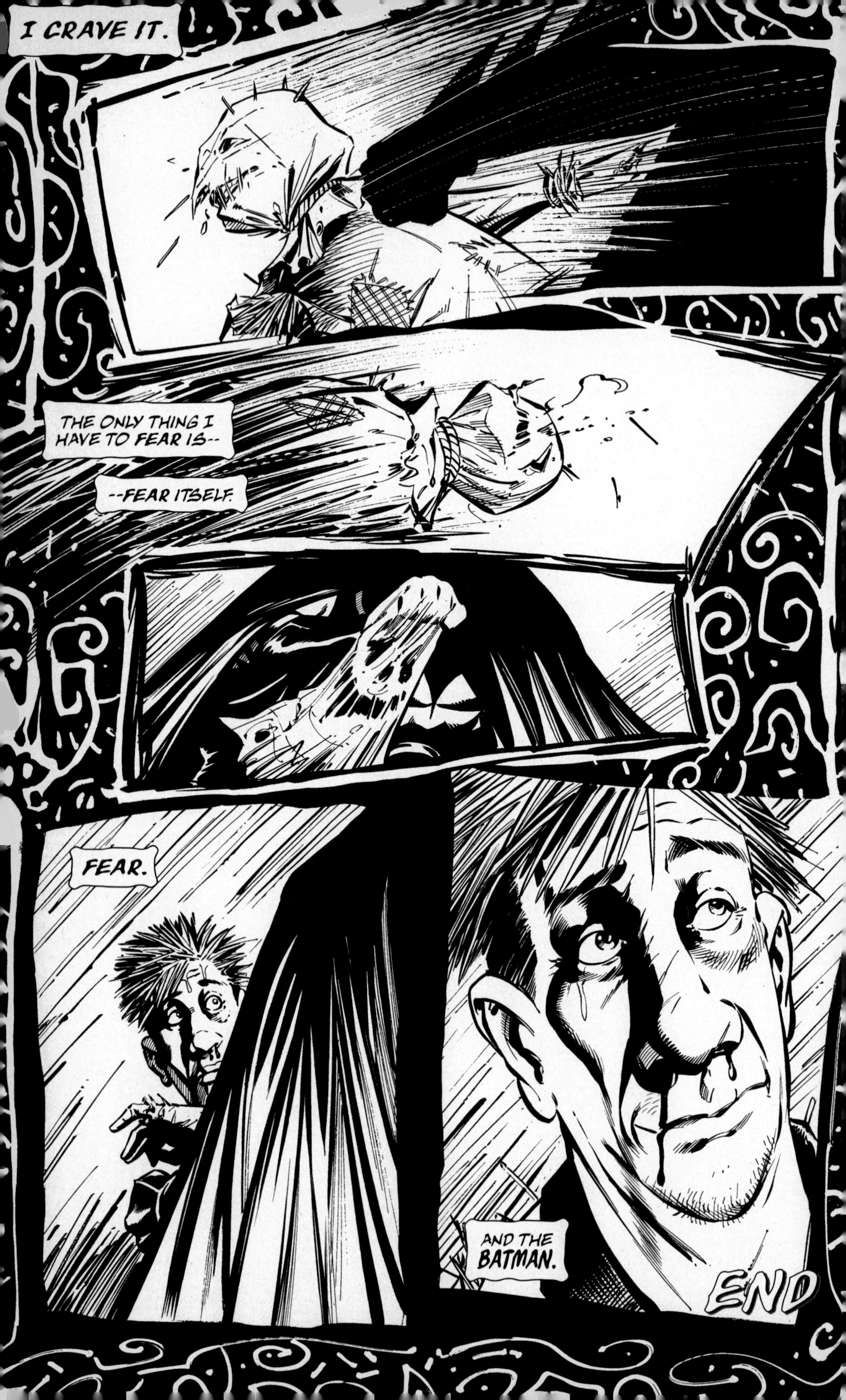
I CRAVE IT.
THE ONLY THING I HAVE TO FEAR IS--
--FEAR ITSELF.
FEAR.
AND THE BATMAN.
END

# THE GASWORKS

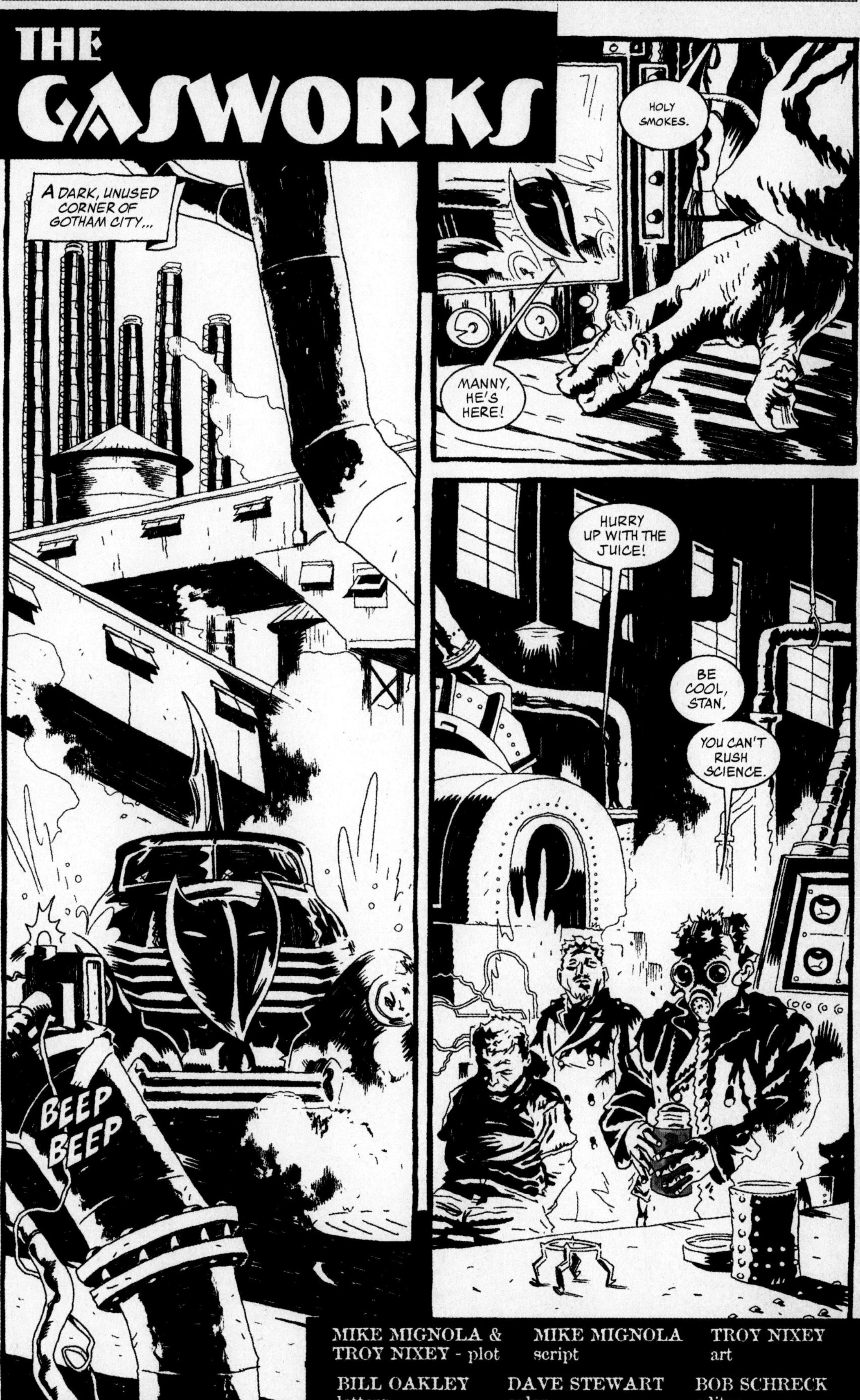
A DARK, UNUSED CORNER OF GOTHAM CITY...
BEEP BEEP
HOLY SMOKES.
MANNY, HE'S HERE!
HURRY UP WITH THE JUICE!
BE COOL, STAN.
YOU CAN'T RUSH SCIENCE.

MIKE MIGNOLA & TROY NIXEY - plot
MIKE MIGNOLA script
TROY NIXEY art
BILL OAKLEY letters
DAVE STEWART color
BOB SCHRECK editor

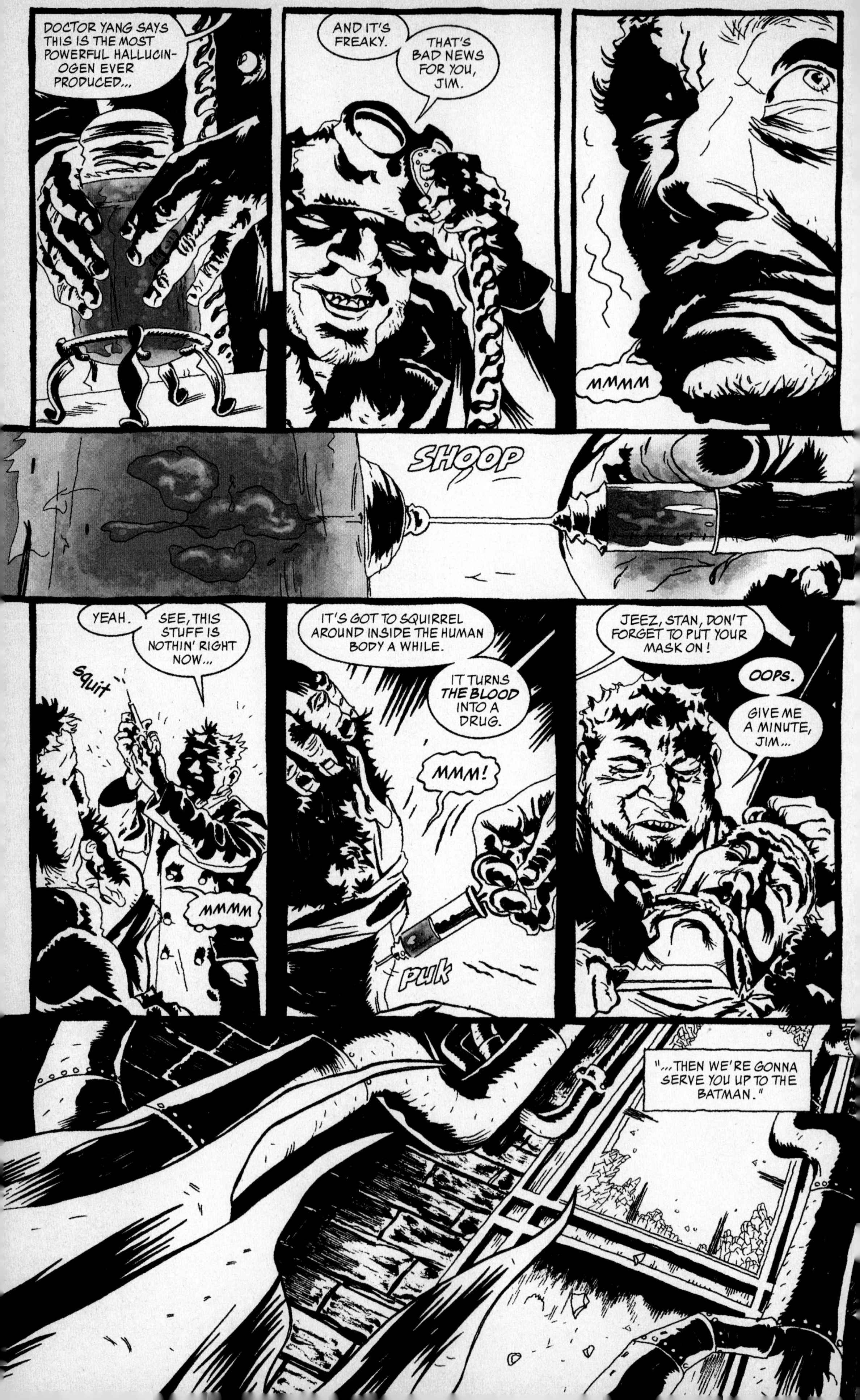
DOCTOR YANG SAYS THIS IS THE MOST POWERFUL HALLUCIN-OGEN EVER PRODUCED...
AND IT'S FREAKY.
THAT'S BAD NEWS FOR YOU, JIM.
MMMM
SHOOP
YEAH.
SEE, THIS STUFF IS NOTHIN' RIGHT NOW...
squit
MMMM
IT'S GOT TO SQUIRREL AROUND INSIDE THE HUMAN BODY A WHILE.
IT TURNS THE BLOOD INTO A DRUG.
MMM!
PUK
JEEZ, STAN, DON'T FORGET TO PUT YOUR MASK ON!
OOPS.
GIVE ME A MINUTE, JIM...
"...THEN WE'RE GONNA SERVE YOU UP TO THE BATMAN."

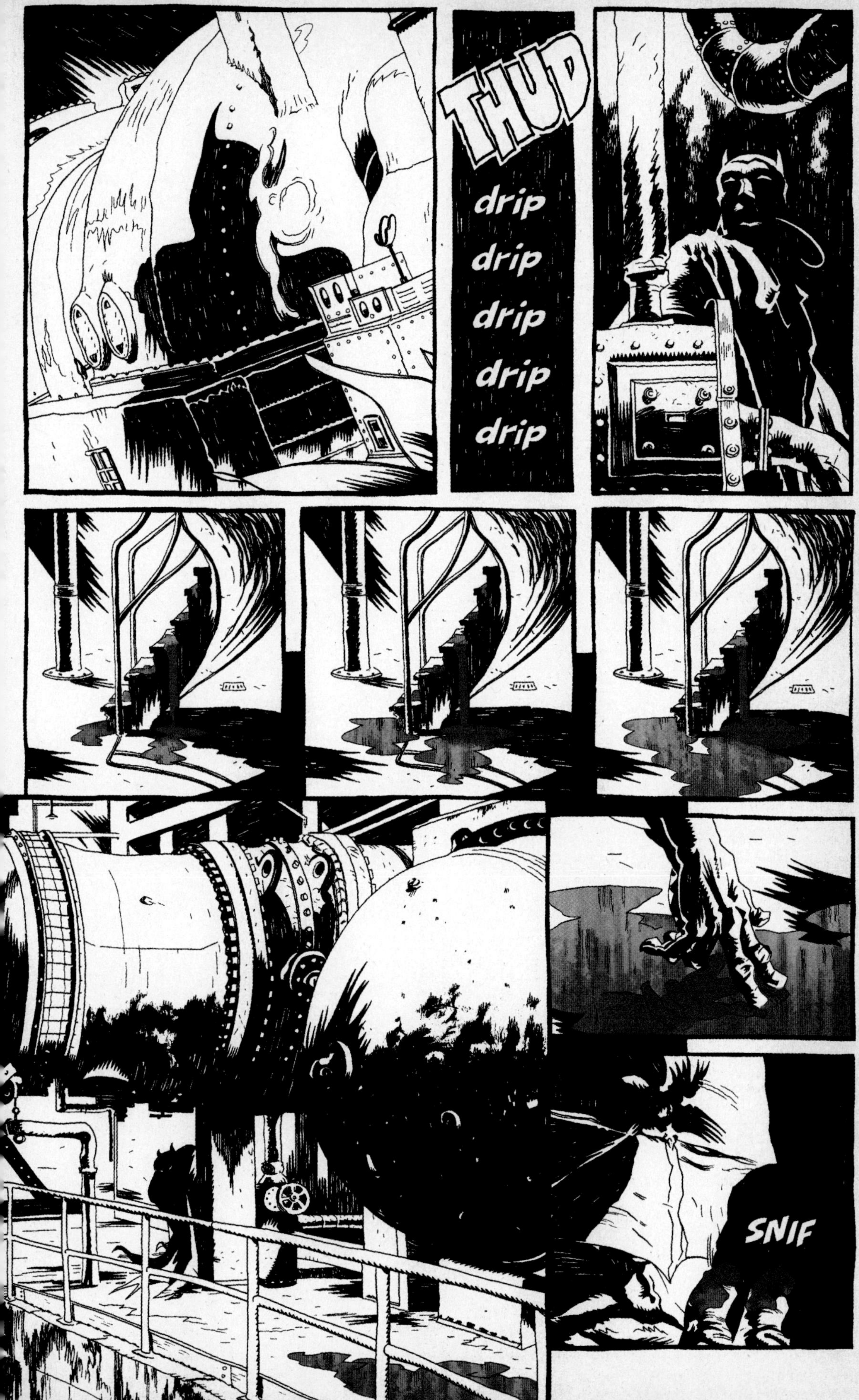
THUD
drip
drip
drip
drip
drip
SNIF

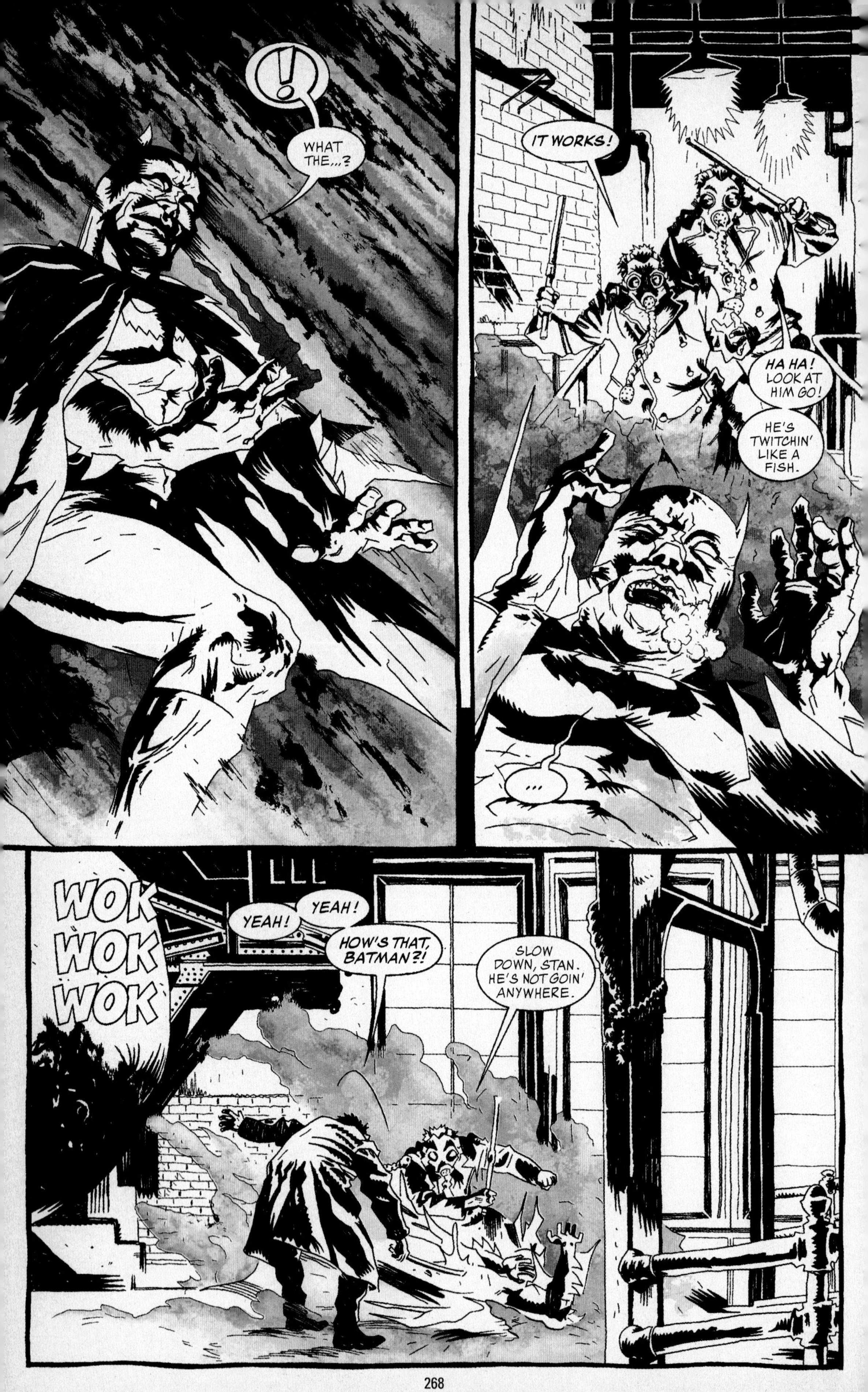
!
WHAT THE...?
IT WORKS!
HA HA! LOOK AT HIM GO!
HE'S TWITCHIN' LIKE A FISH.
...
WOK WOK WOK
YEAH!
YEAH!
HOW'S THAT, BATMAN?!
SLOW DOWN, STAN. HE'S NOT GOIN' ANYWHERE.

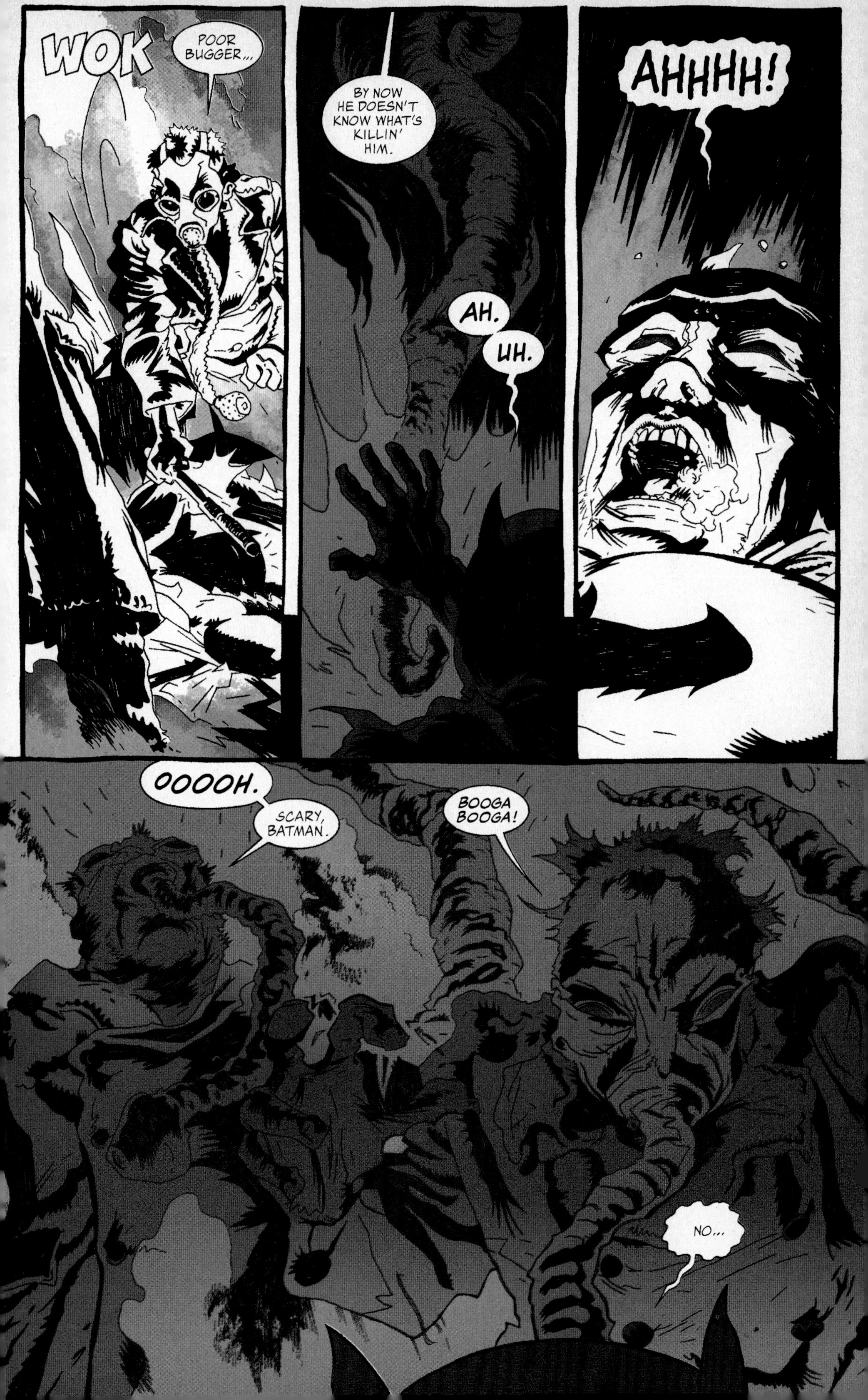
WOK
POOR BUGGER...
BY NOW HE DOESN'T KNOW WHAT'S KILLIN' HIM.
AH.
UH.
AHHHH!
OOOOH.
SCARY, BATMAN.
BOOGA BOOGA!
NO...

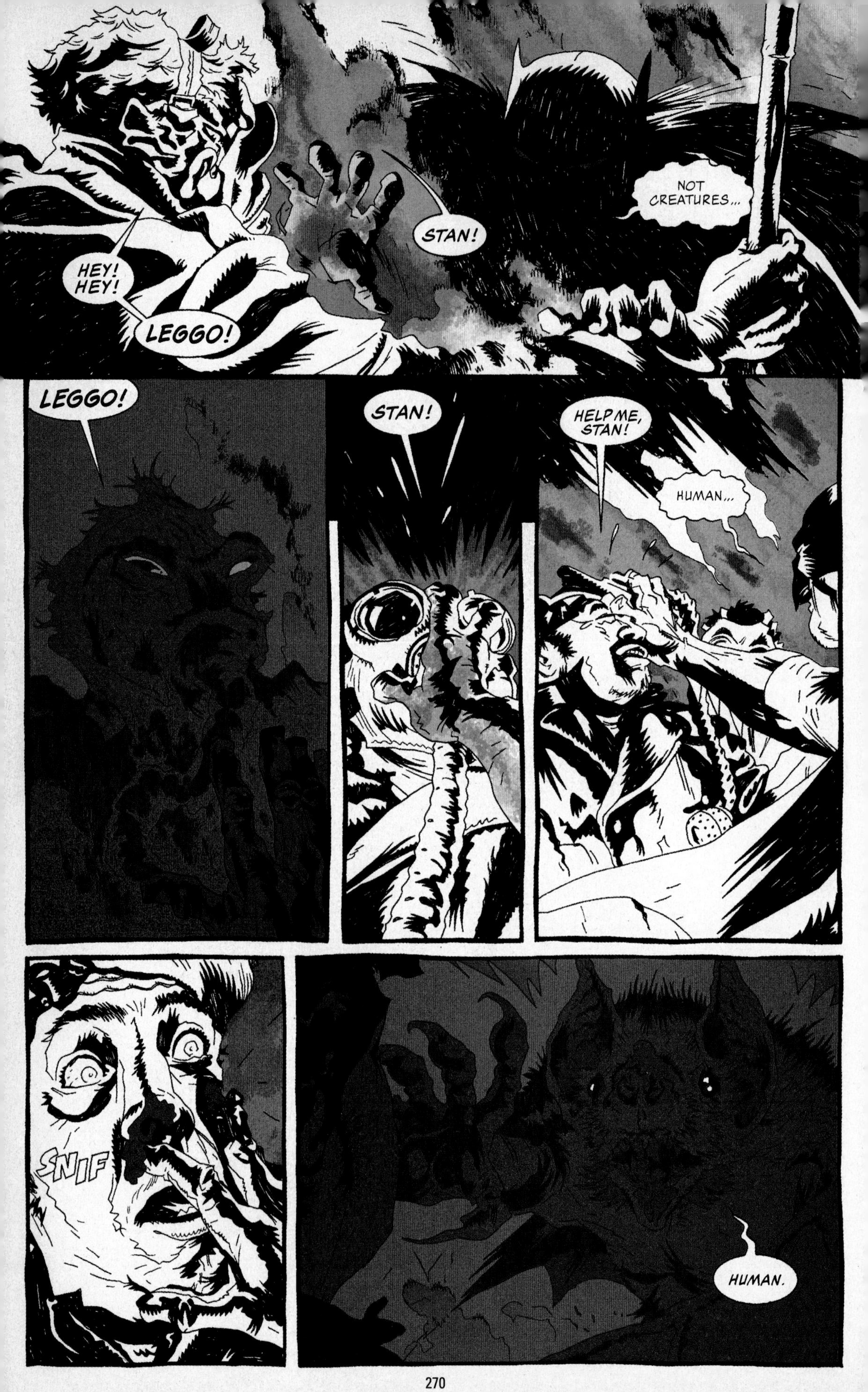
HEY! HEY!
LEGGO!
STAN!
NOT CREATURES...
LEGGO!
STAN!
HELP ME, STAN!
HUMAN...
SNIF
HUMAN.

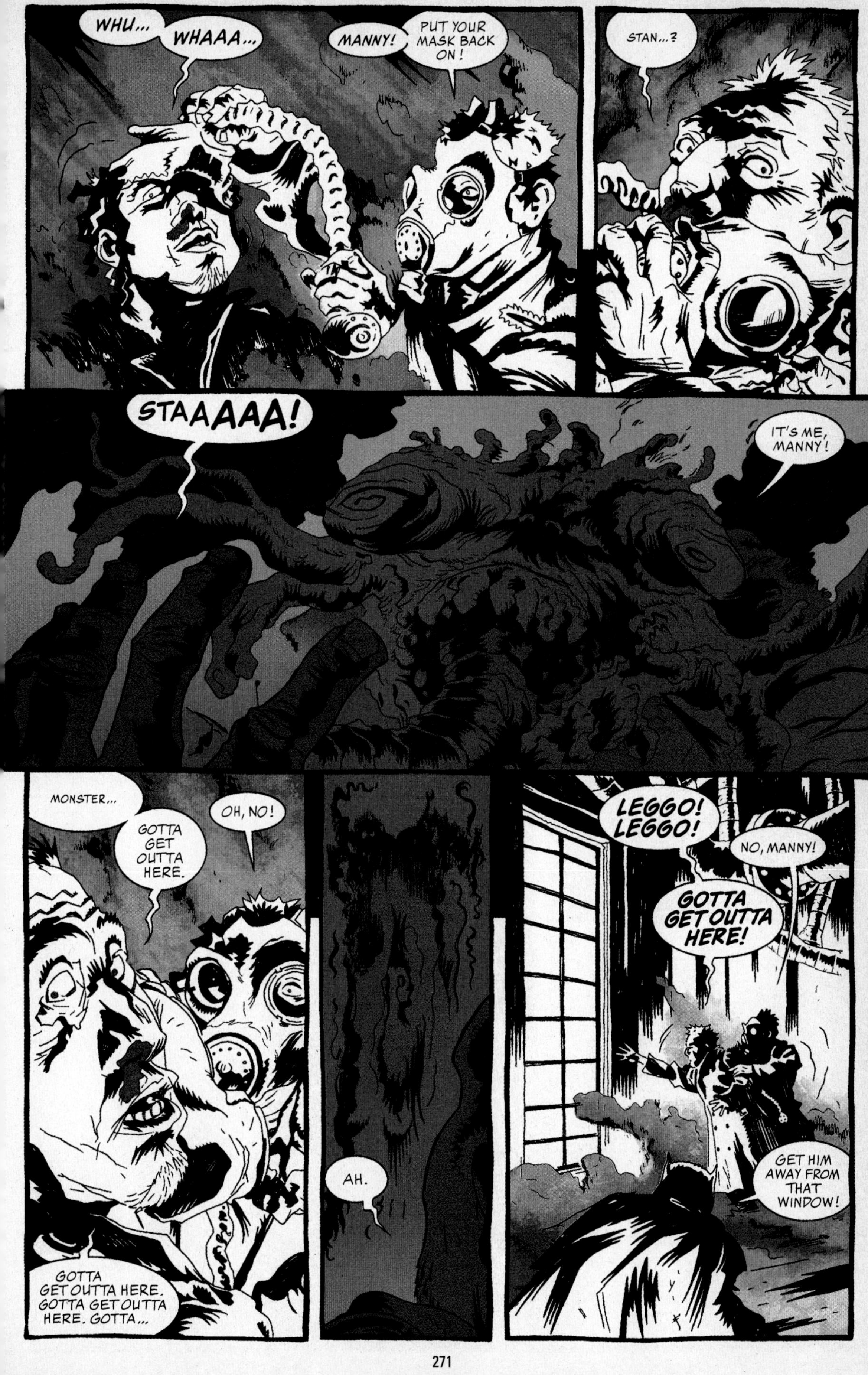

WHU...
WHAAA...
MANNY!
PUT YOUR MASK BACK ON!
STAN...?
STAAAAA!
IT'S ME, MANNY!
MONSTER...
GOTTA GET OUTTA HERE.
OH, NO!
GOTTA GET OUTTA HERE. GOTTA GET OUTTA HERE. GOTTA...
AH.
LEGGO! LEGGO!
NO, MANNY!
GOTTA GET OUTTA HERE!
GET HIM AWAY FROM THAT WINDOW!

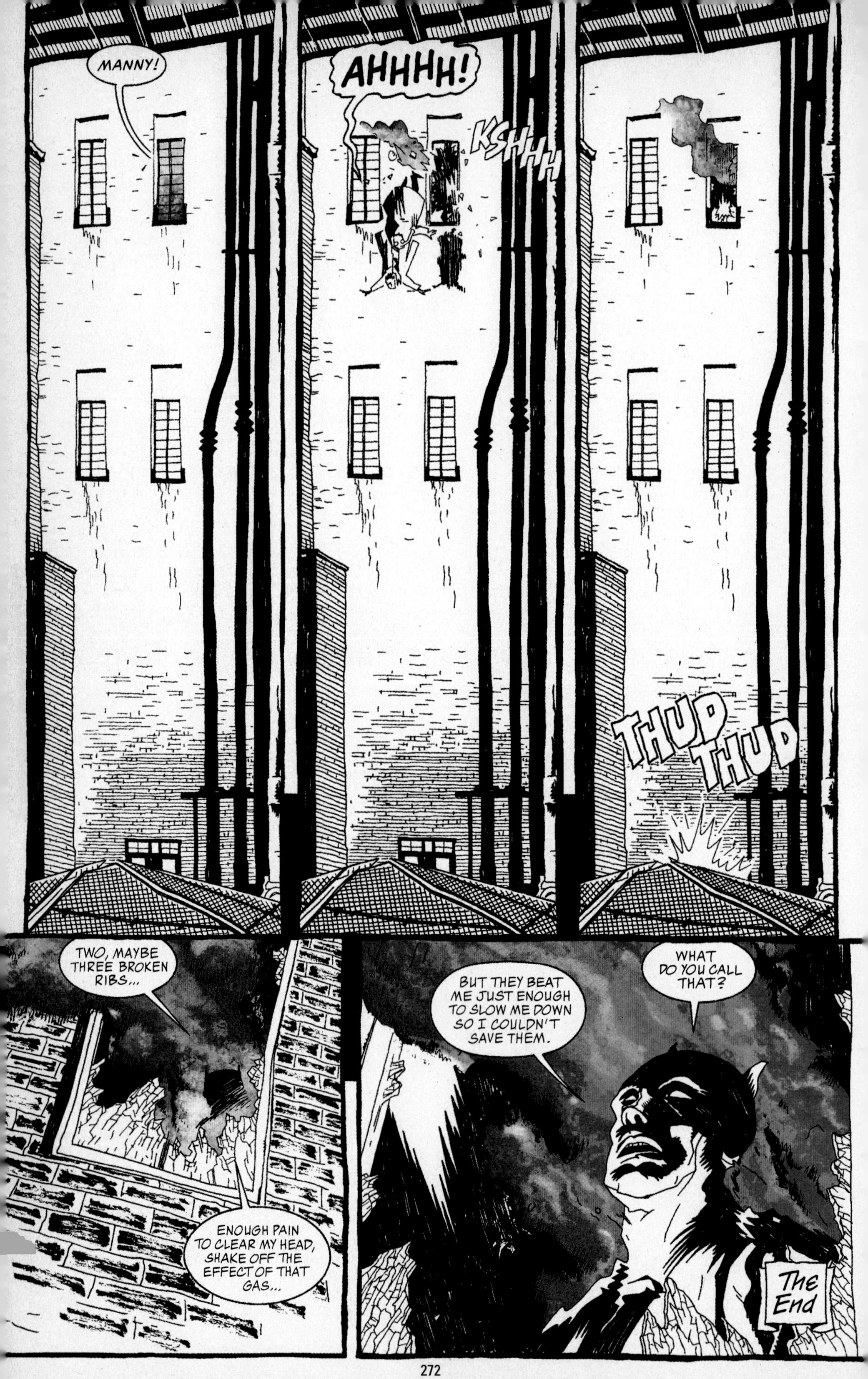
MANNY!
AHHHH!
KSHHHH
THUD THUD
TWO, MAYBE THREE BROKEN RIBS...
ENOUGH PAIN TO CLEAR MY HEAD, SHAKE OFF THE EFFECT OF THAT GAS...
BUT THEY BEAT ME JUST ENOUGH TO SLOW ME DOWN SO I COULDN'T SAVE THEM.
WHAT DO YOU CALL THAT?
The End

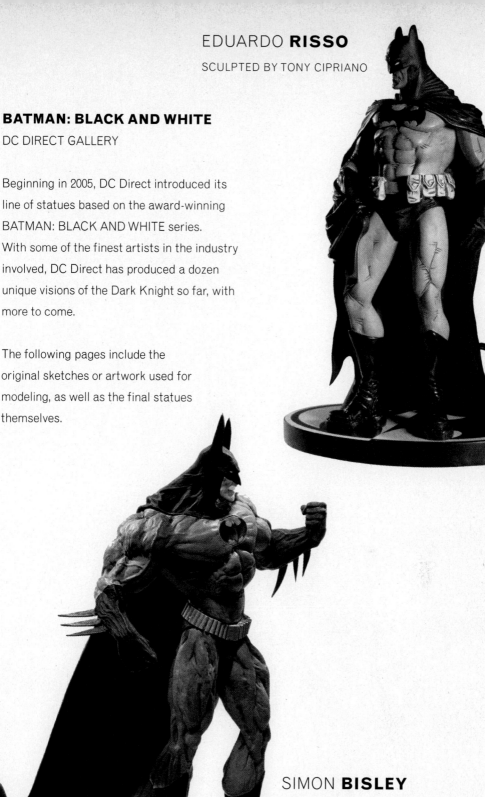

EDUARDO **RISSO**

SCULPTED BY TONY CIPRIANO

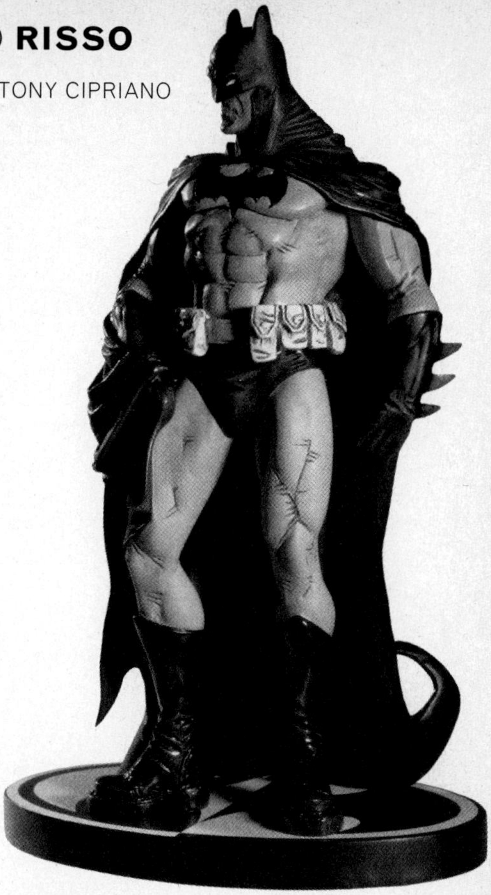

## BATMAN: BLACK AND WHITE

DC DIRECT GALLERY

Beginning in 2005, DC Direct introduced its line of statues based on the award-winning BATMAN: BLACK AND WHITE series. With some of the finest artists in the industry involved, DC Direct has produced a dozen unique visions of the Dark Knight so far, with more to come.

The following pages include the original sketches or artwork used for modeling, as well as the final statues themselves.

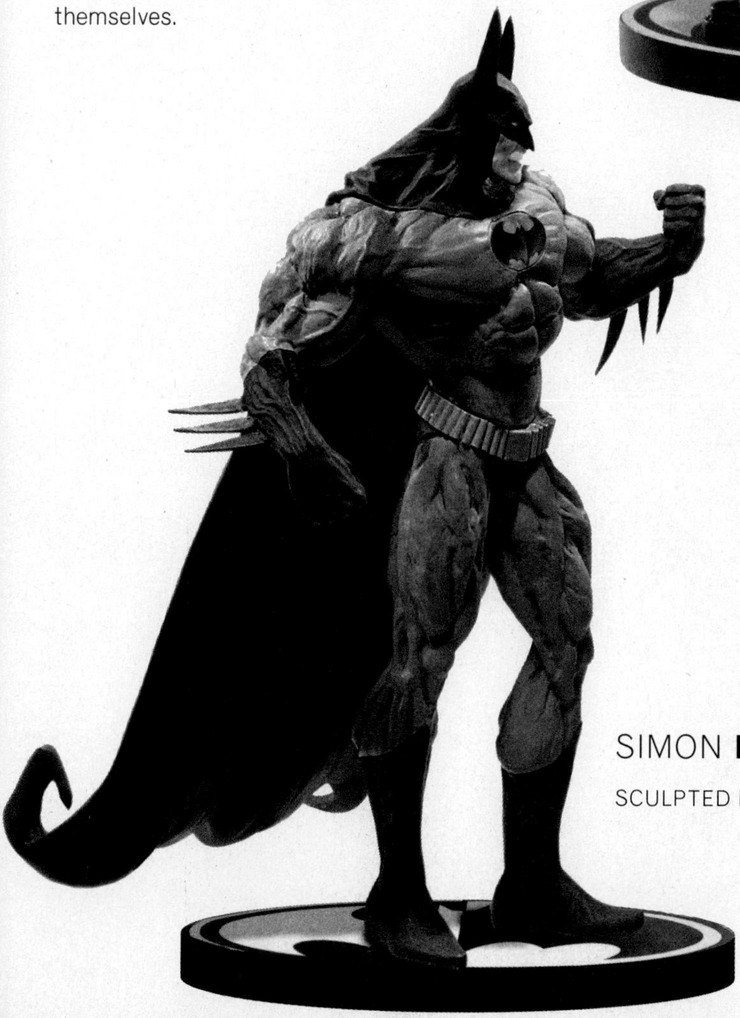

SIMON **BISLEY**

SCULPTED BY WILLIAM PAQUET

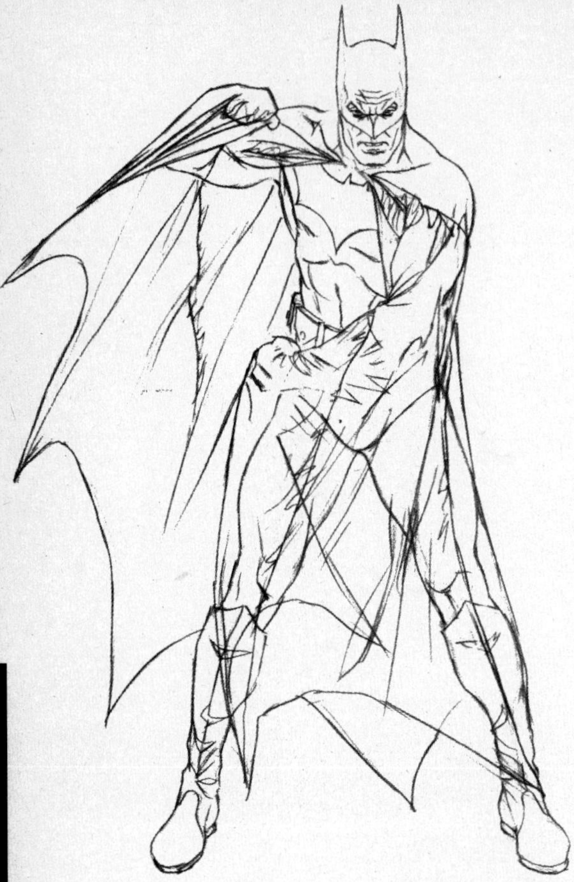

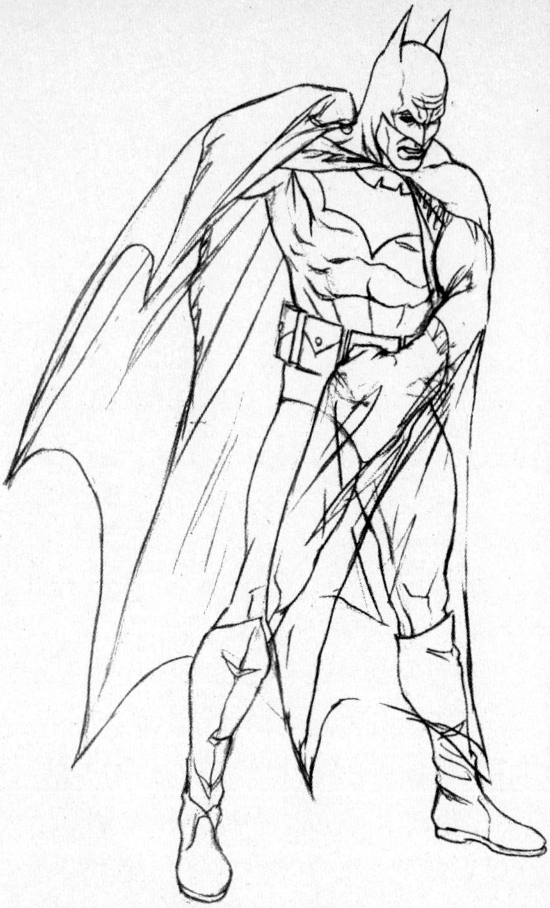

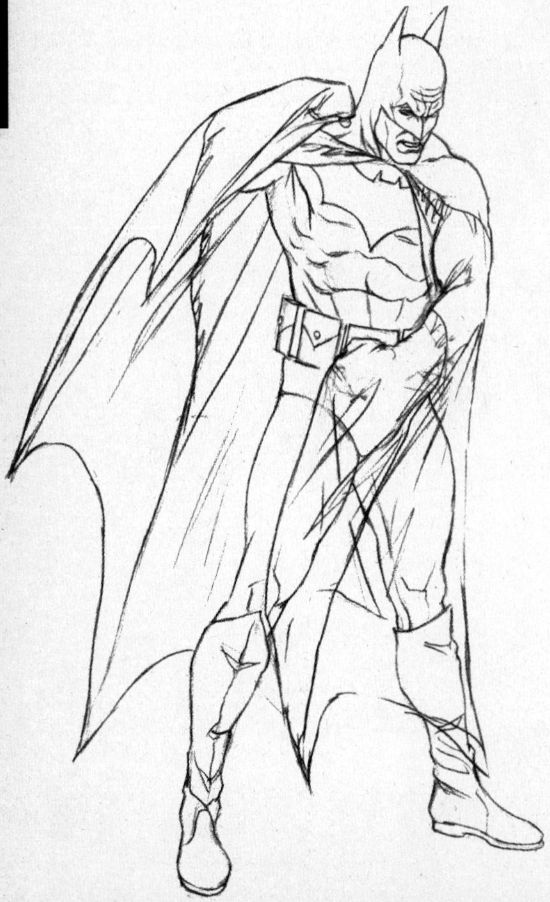

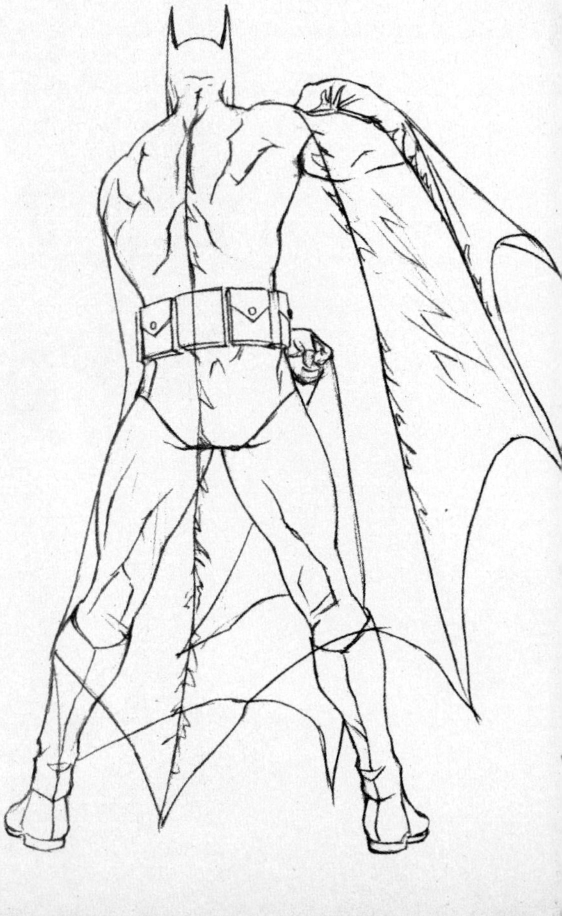

ALEX **ROSS**

SCULPTED BY KAREN PALINKO

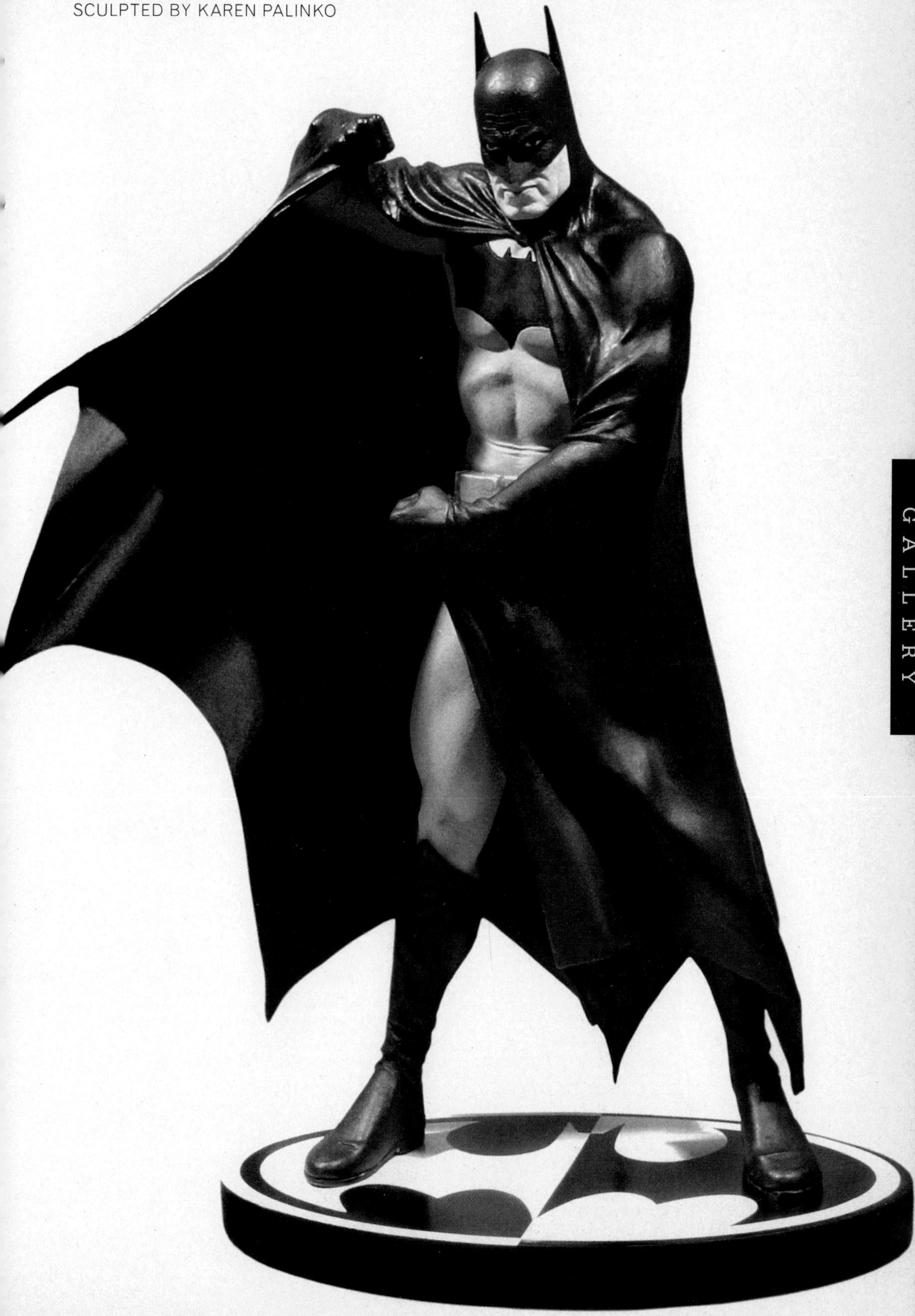

# MIKE **MIGNOLA**

SCULPTED BY JONATHAN MATTHEWS

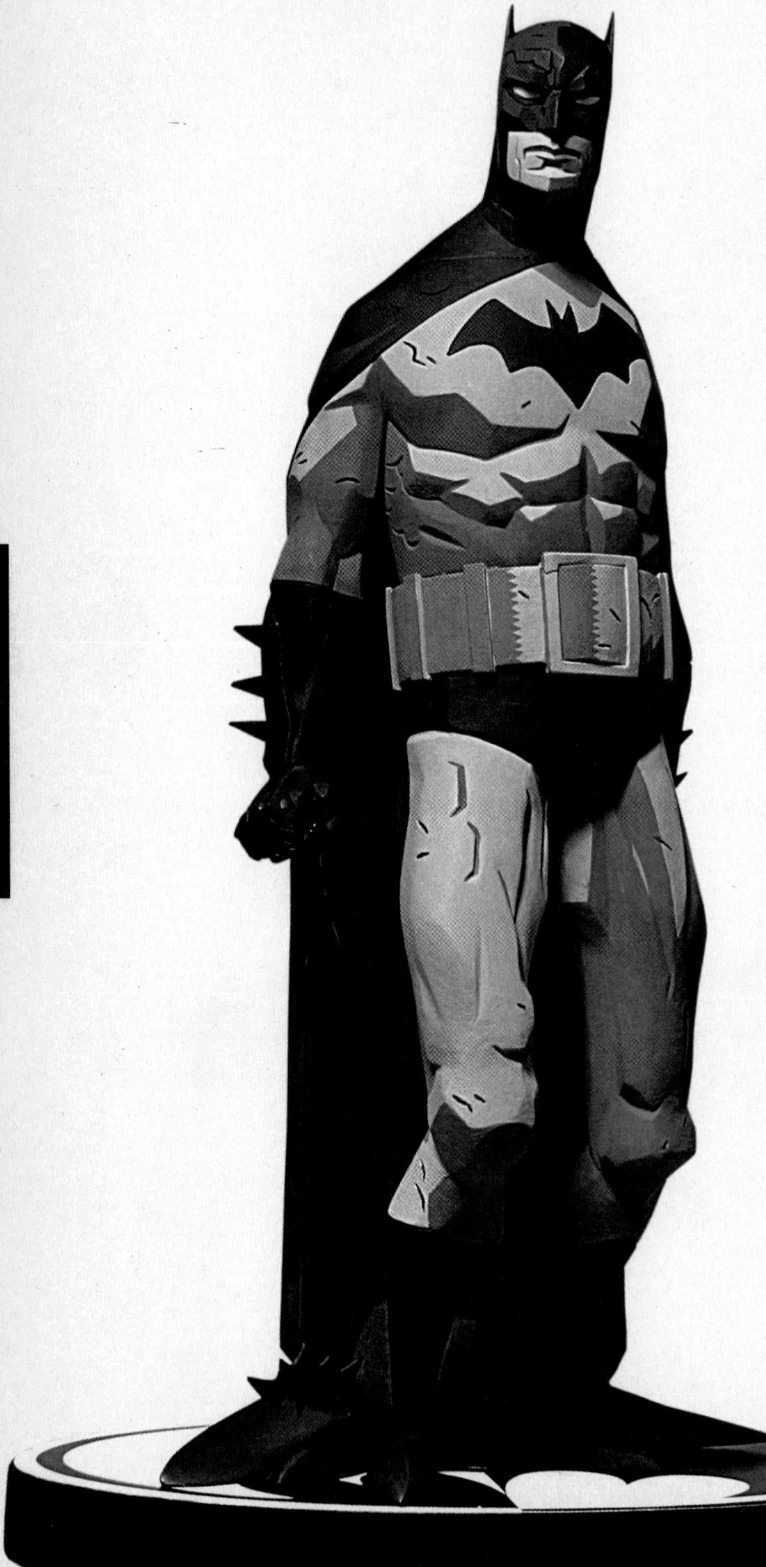

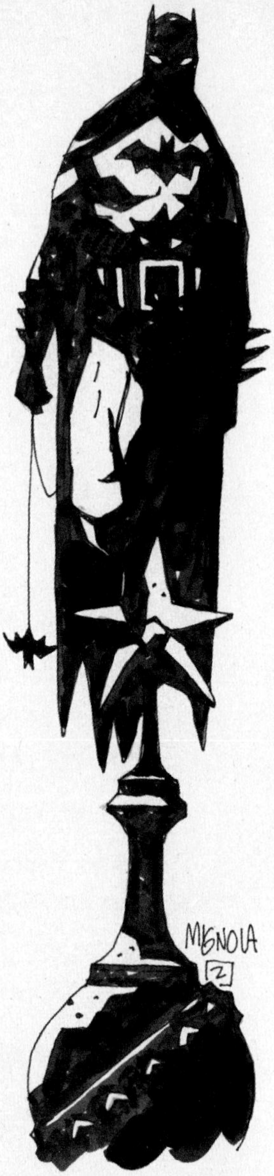

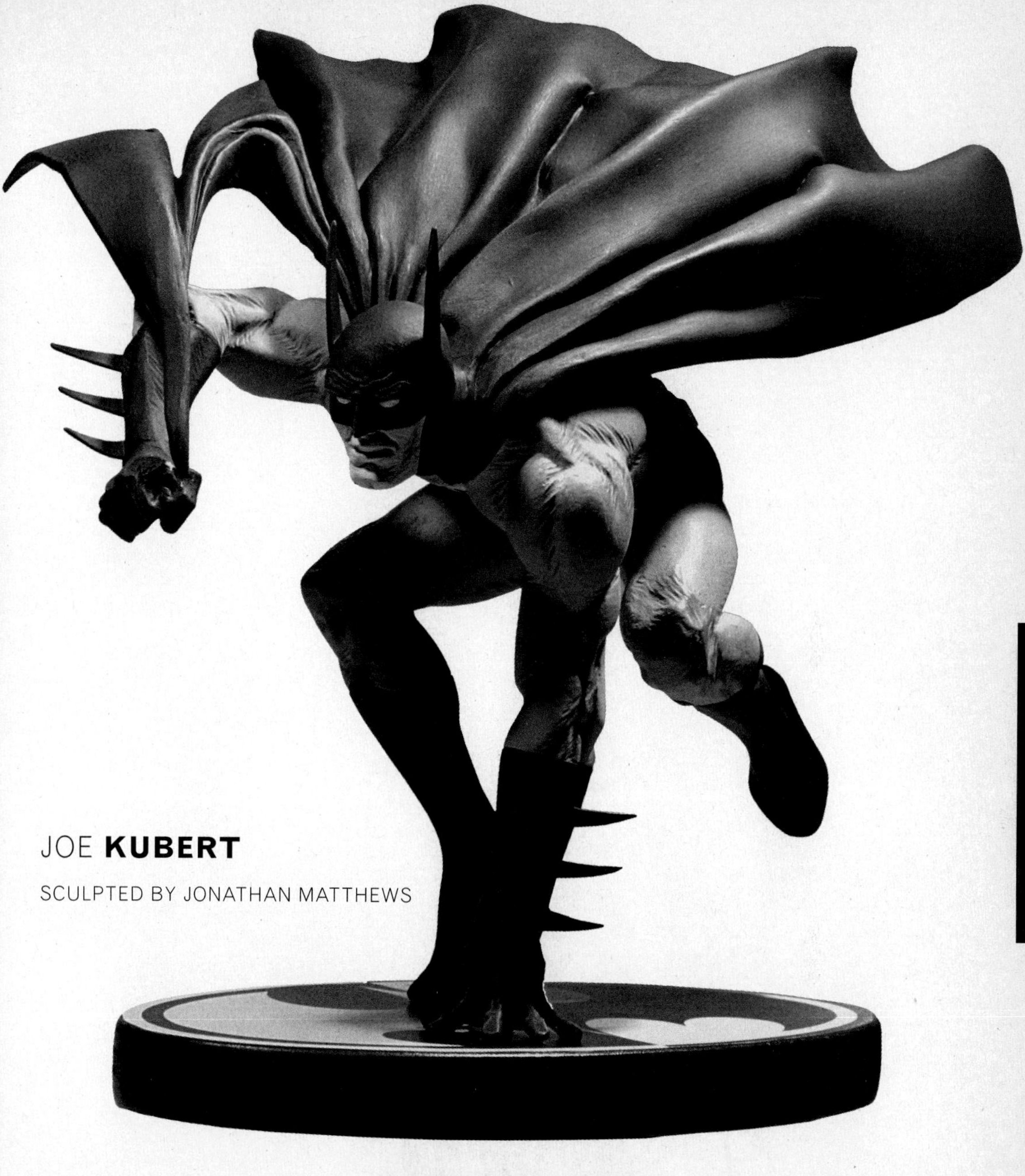

# JOE **KUBERT**

SCULPTED BY JONATHAN MATTHEWS

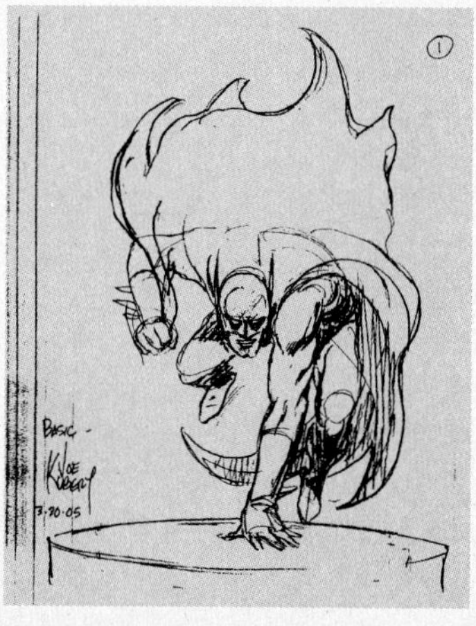
1
BASIC -
3.20.05

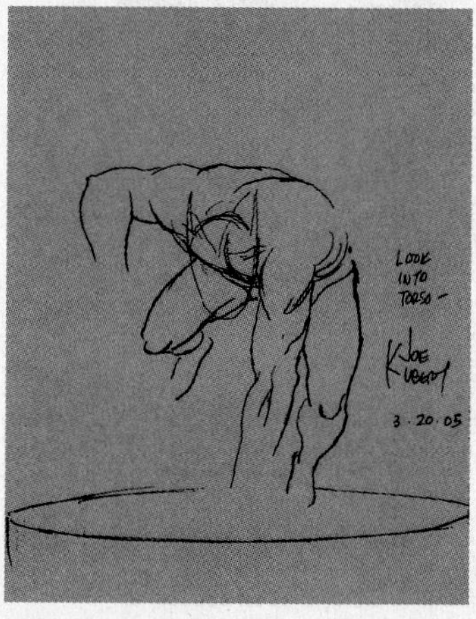
LOOK INTO TORSO -
3.20.05

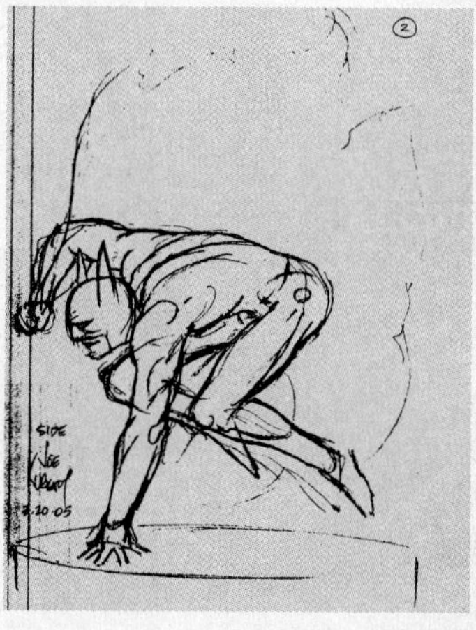
2
SIDE
3.20.05

## PAUL **POPE**

SCULPTED BY JEAN ST. JEAN

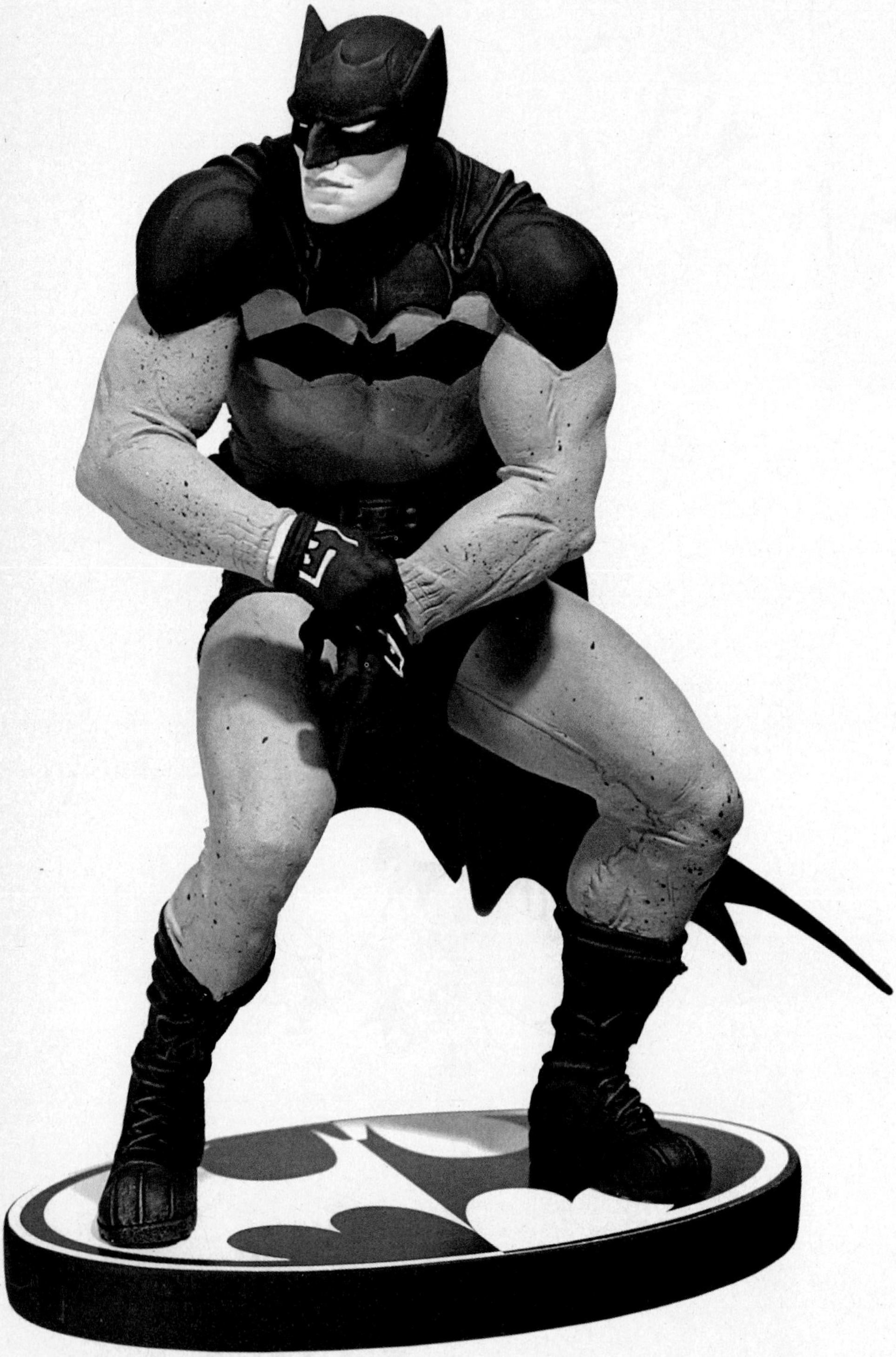

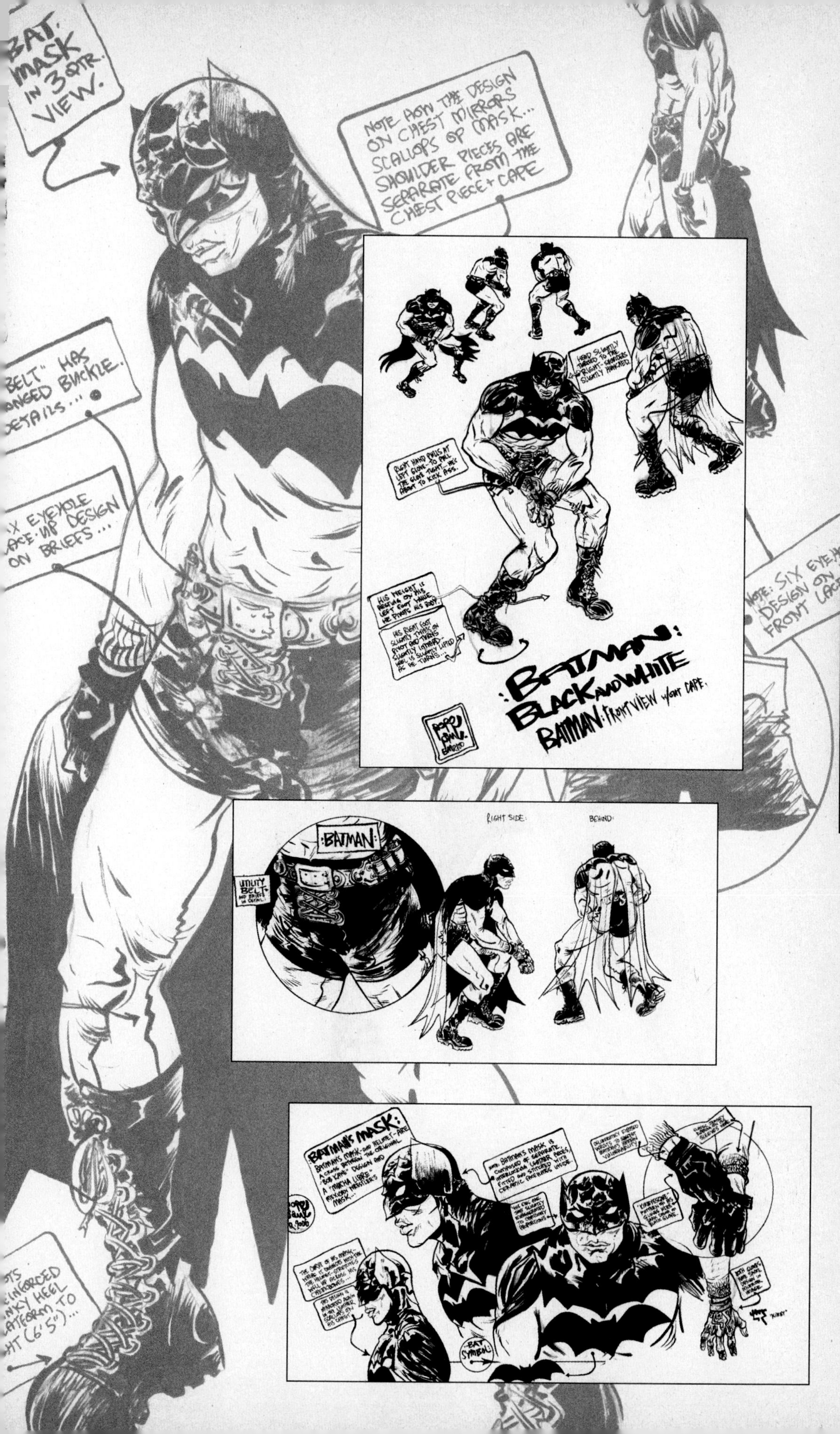
BAT MASK IN 3 QTR. VIEW.
NOTE HOW THE DESIGN ON CHEST MIRRORS SCALLOPS OF MASK... SHOULDER PIECES ARE SEPARATE FROM THE CHEST PIECE + CAPE
HEAD SLIGHTLY TURNED TO THE RIGHT - SHOULDERS SLIGHTLY HUNCHED.
RIGHT HAND PULLS AT LEFT GLOVE - TO PULL THE GLOVE TIGHT... HE'S ABOUT TO KICK ASS.
HIS WEIGHT IS RESTING ON HIS LEFT FOOT WHILE HE PIVOTS HIS BODY.
HIS RIGHT FOOT SLIGHTLY TWISTS ON PIVOT AND TURNS SLIGHTLY INWARD - HEEL IS SLIGHTLY LIFTED AS HE TURNS...
:BATMAN:
BLACK AND WHITE
BATMAN: FRONT VIEW W/OUT CAPE.
RIGHT SIDE:
BEHIND:
:BATMAN:
UTILITY BELT
BATMAN'S MASK:
BAT SYMBOL:
"KIRBY"

## BRIAN **BOLLAND**

SCULPTED BY JACK MATHEWS

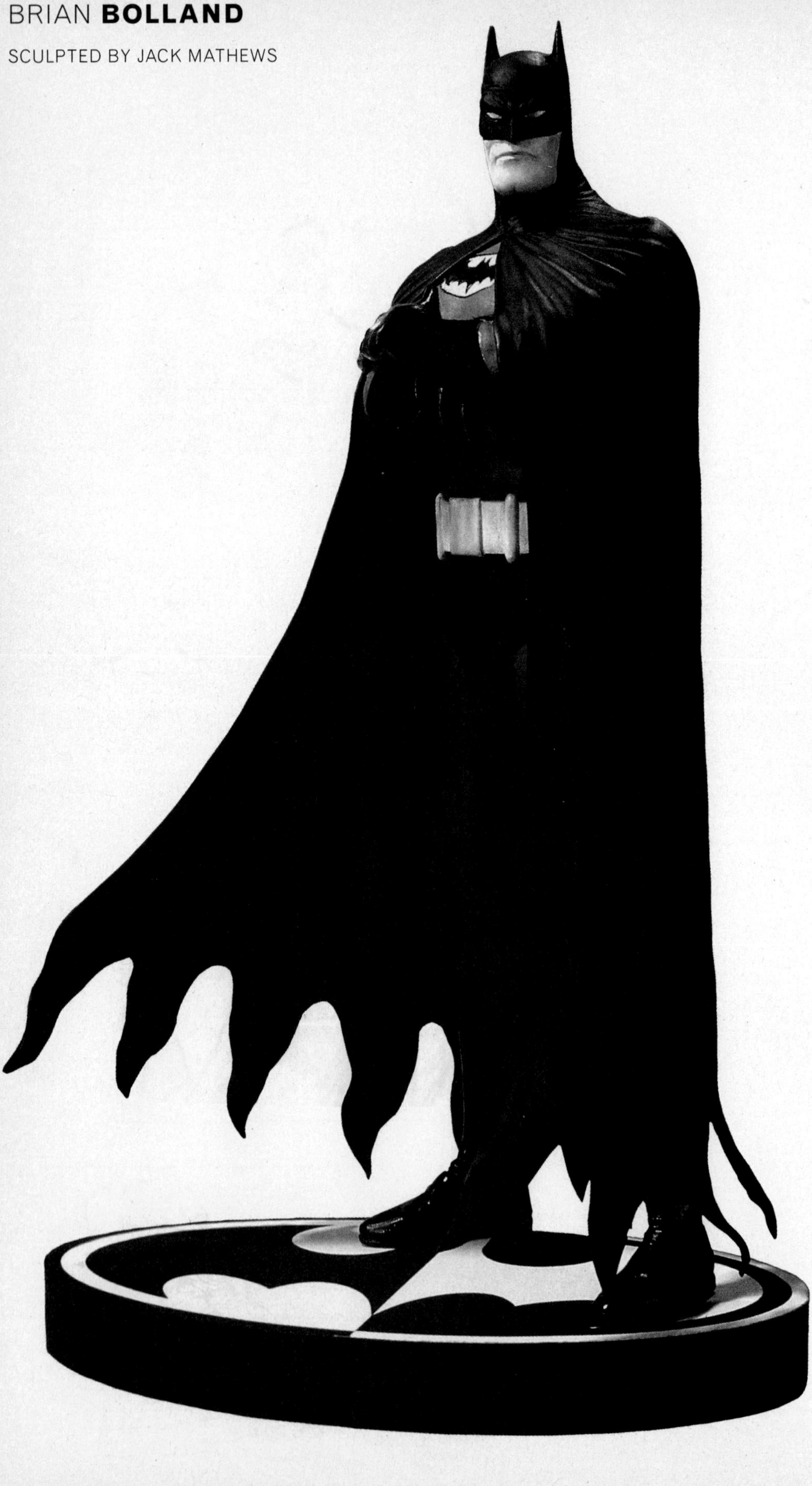

# TIM **SALE**

SCULPTED BY JONATHAN MATTHEWS

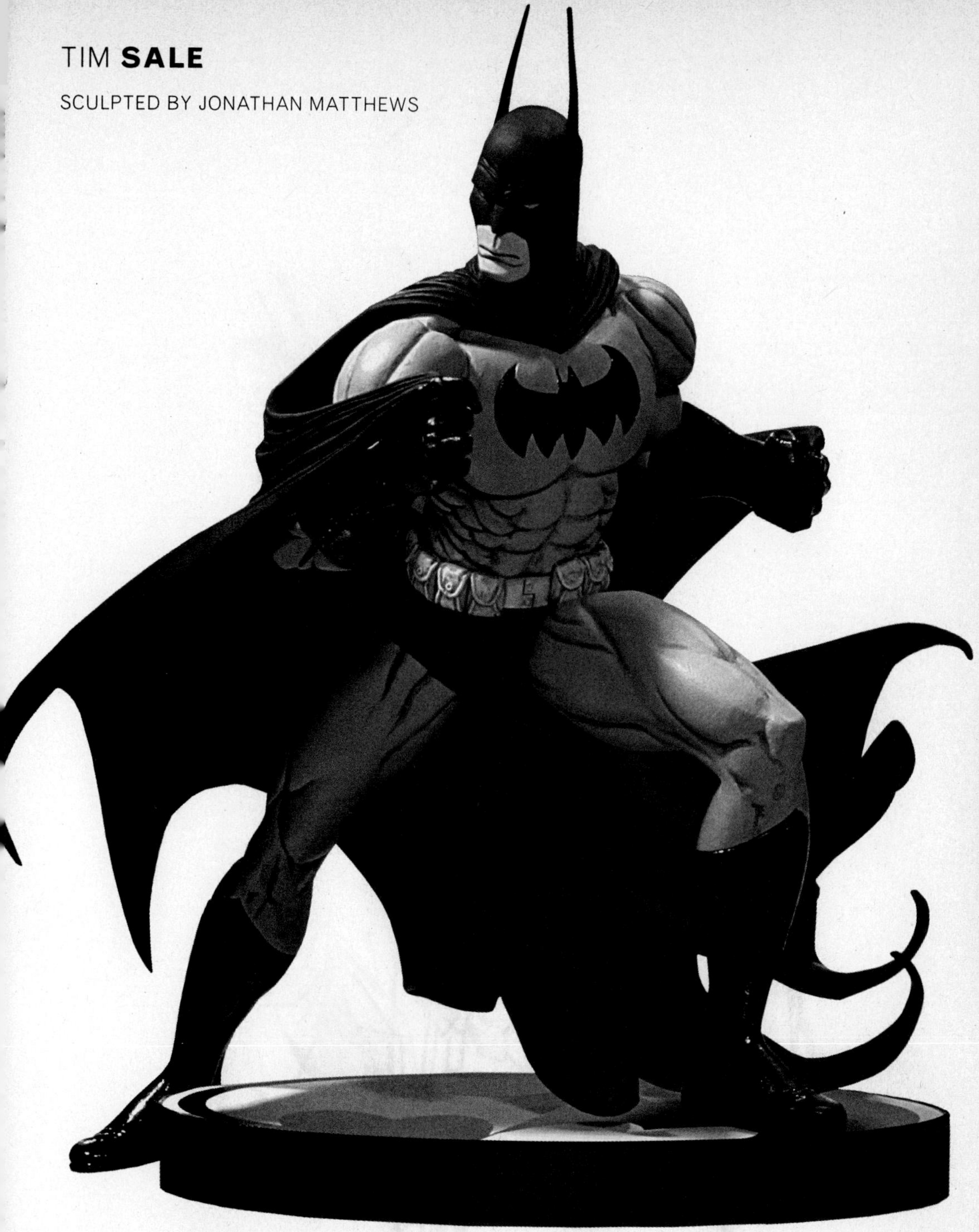

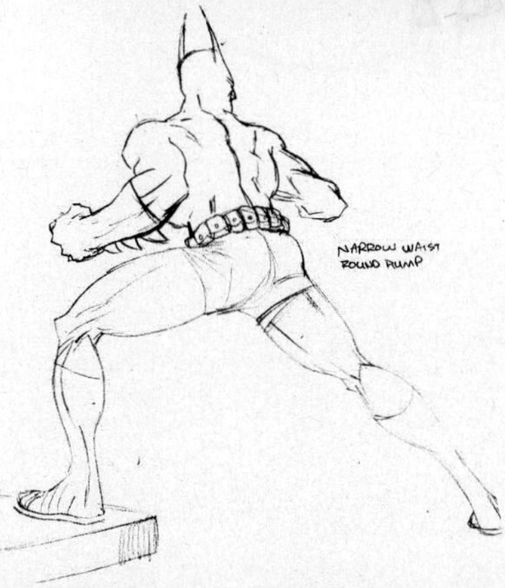
NARROW WAIST
ROUND RUMP

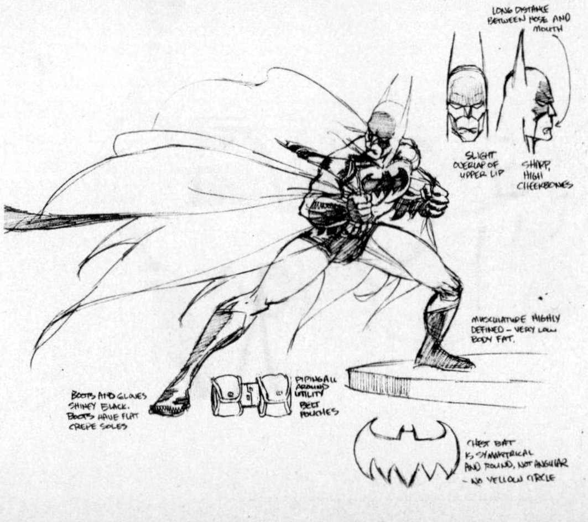
LONG DISTANCE BETWEEN NOSE AND MOUTH
SLIGHT OVERLAP OF UPPER LIP
SHARP, HIGH CHEEKBONES
MUSCULATURE HIGHLY DEFINED – VERY LOW BODY FAT.
BOOTS AND GLOVES SHINEY BLACK. BOOTS HAVE FLAT CREPE SOLES
PIPING ALL AROUND UTILITY BELT POUCHES
CHEST BAT IS SYMMETRICAL AND ROUND, NOT ANGULAR – NO YELLOW CIRCLE

## STEVE **RUDE**

SCULPTED BY JONATHAN MATTHEWS

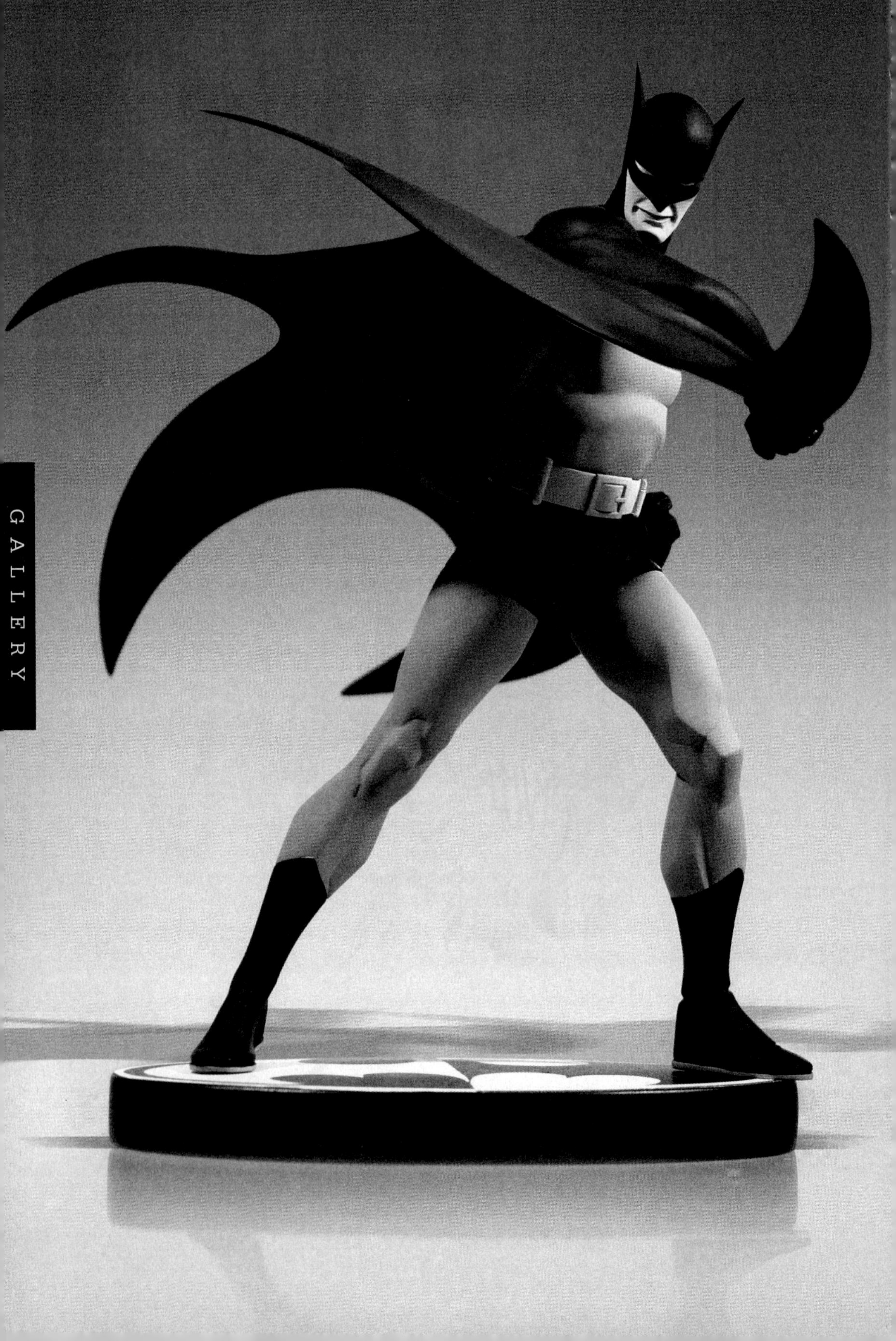

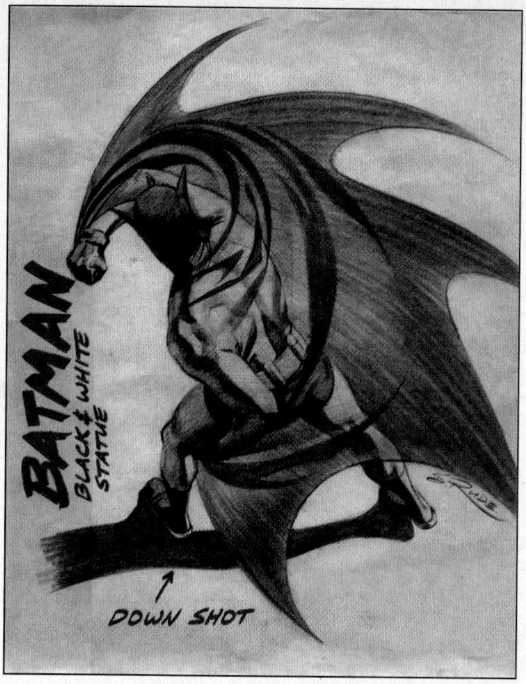
BATMAN
BLACK & WHITE STATUE
DOWN SHOT
S. RUDE

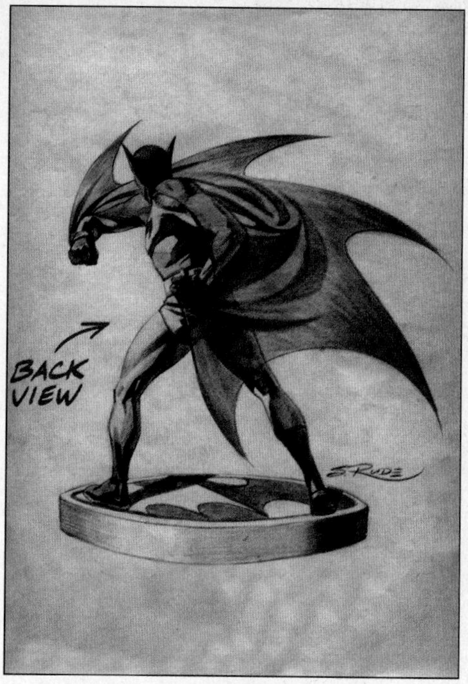
BACK VIEW
S. RUDE

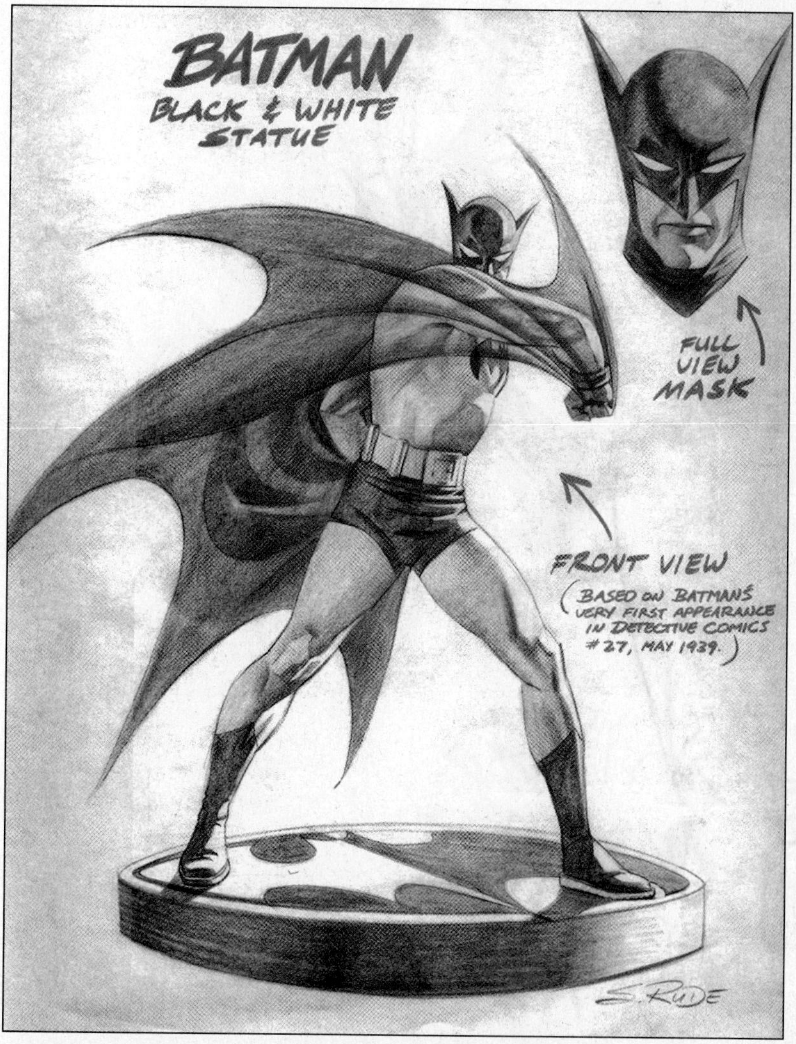
BATMAN
BLACK & WHITE STATUE
FULL VIEW MASK
FRONT VIEW
(BASED ON BATMAN'S VERY FIRST APPEARANCE IN DETECTIVE COMICS #27, MAY 1939.)
S. RUDE

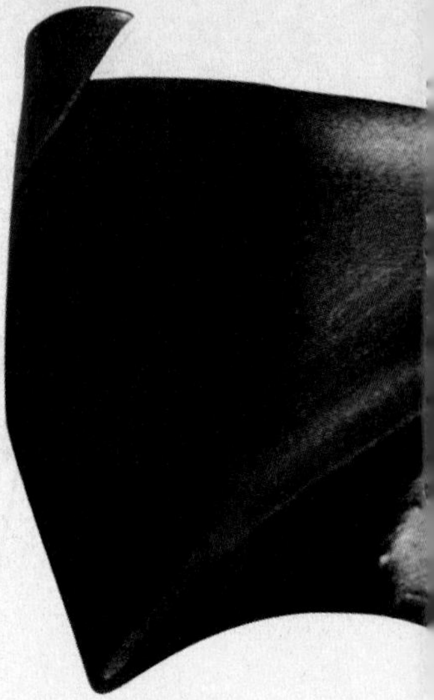

## JIM **LEE**

SCULPTED BY ERICK SOSA



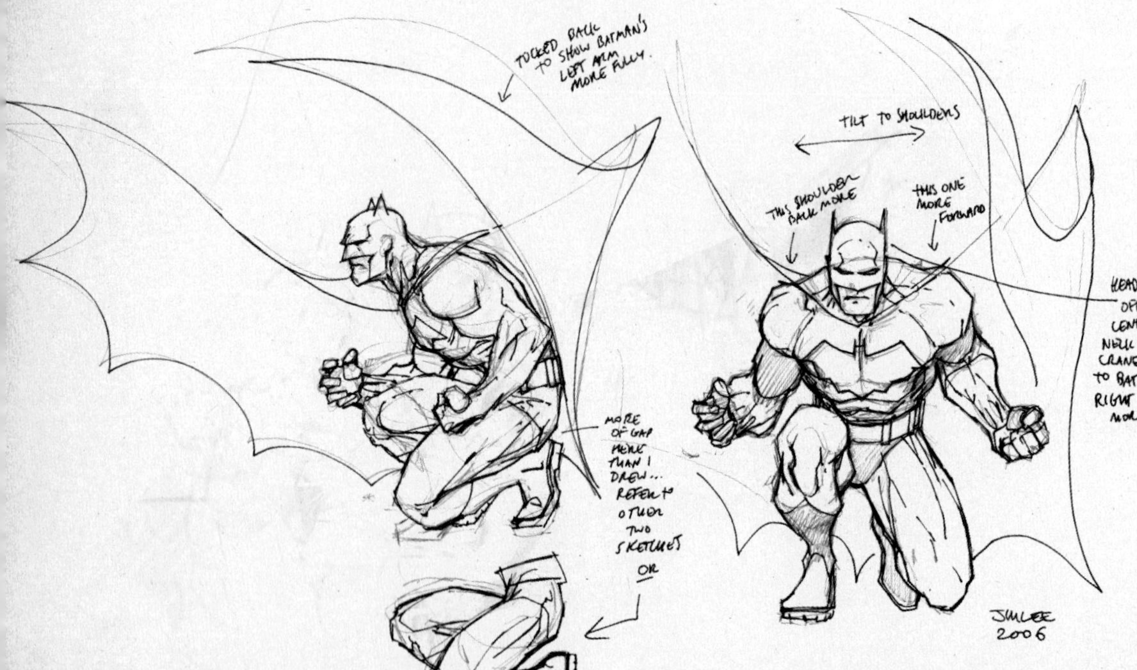
TUCKED BACK TO SHOW BATMAN'S LEFT ARM MORE FULLY.
TILT TO SHOULDERS
THIS SHOULDER BACK MORE
THIS ONE MORE FORWARD
HEAD OFF CENTER... NECK CRANED TO BATMAN'S RIGHT MORE.
MORE OF GAP HERE THAN I DREW... REFER TO OTHER TWO SKETCHES OR
JIM LEE 2006

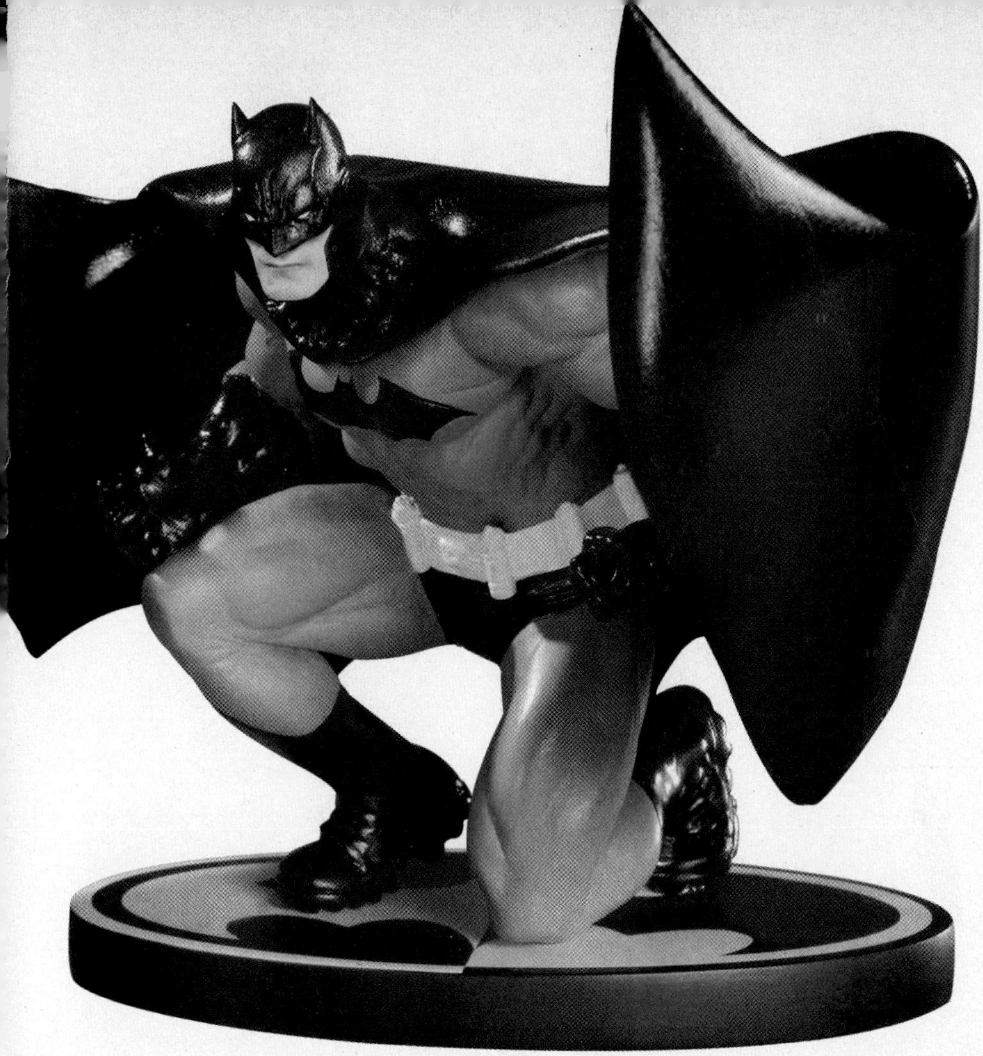

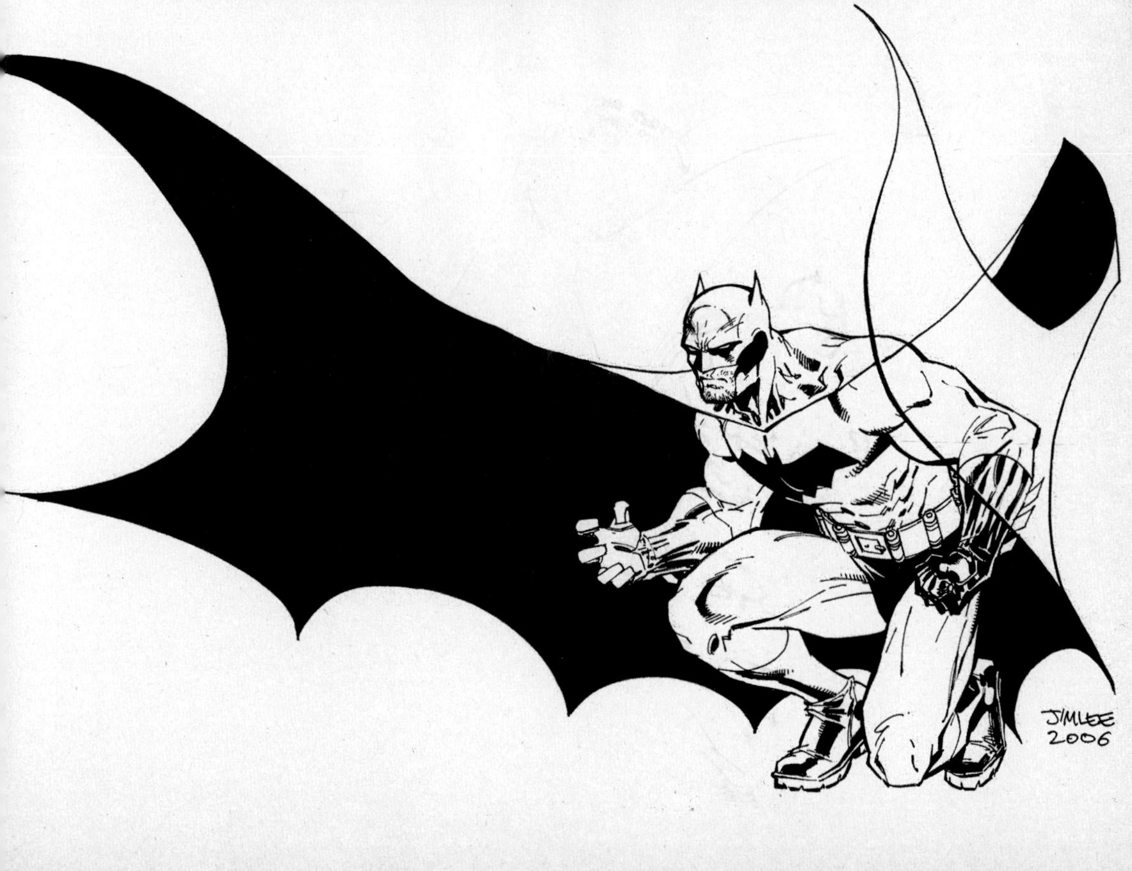
JIM LEE
2006

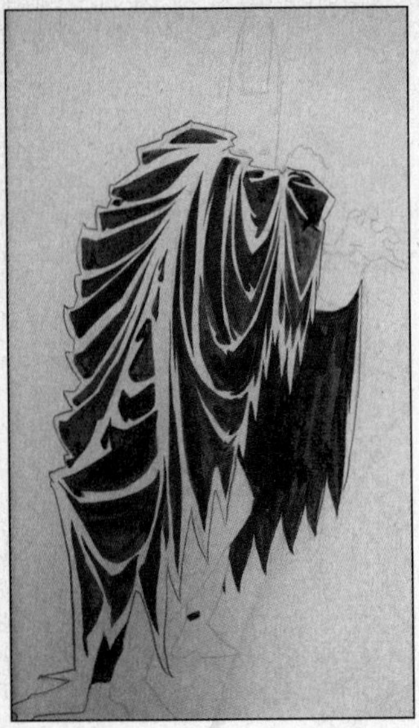

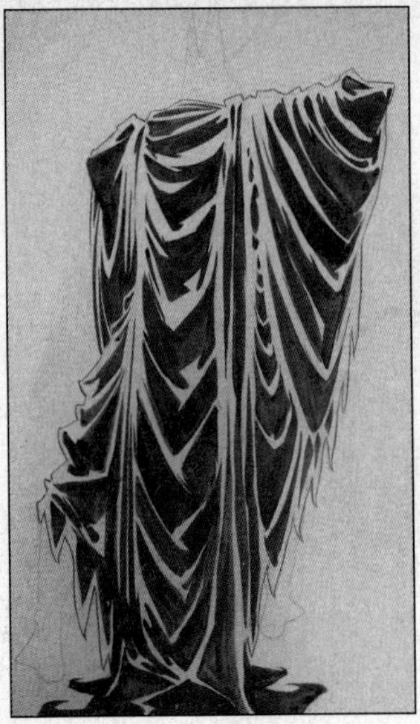

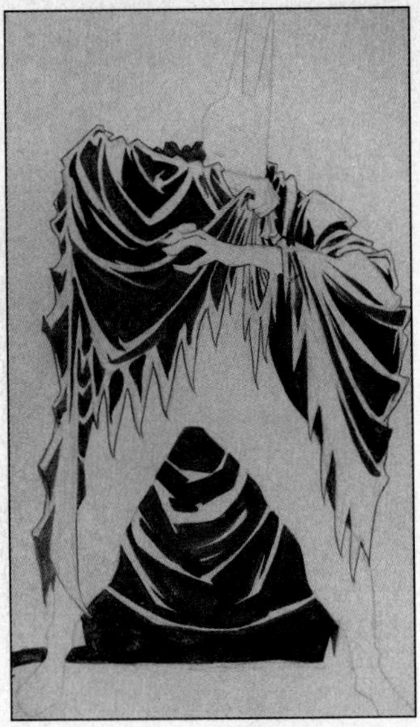

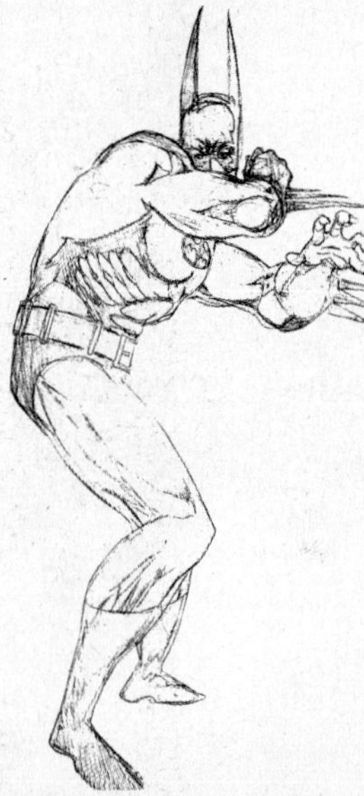

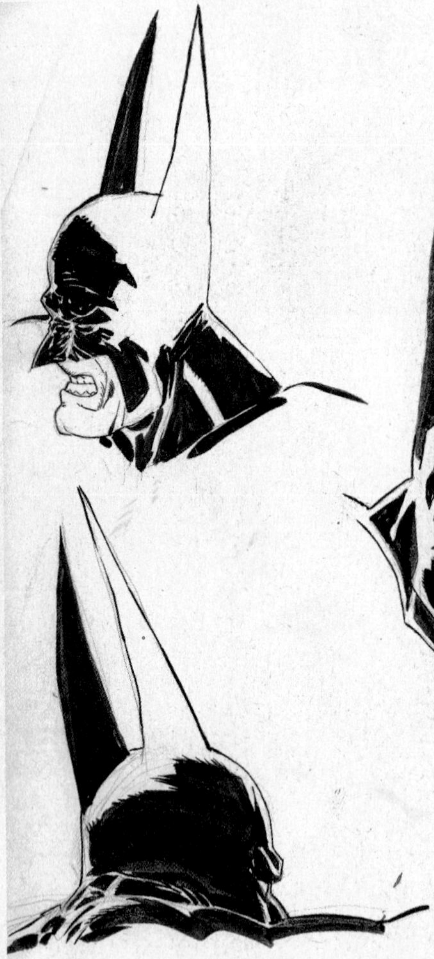

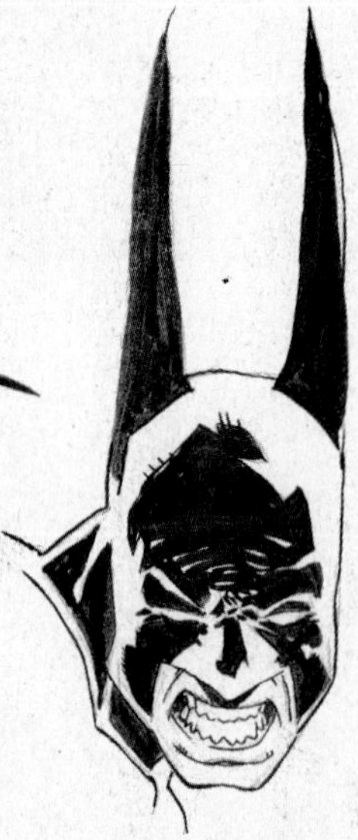

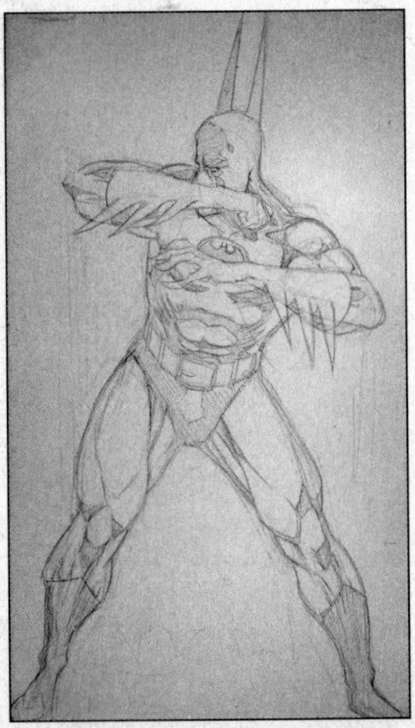

KELLY **JONES**

SCULPTED BY RAY VILLAFANE

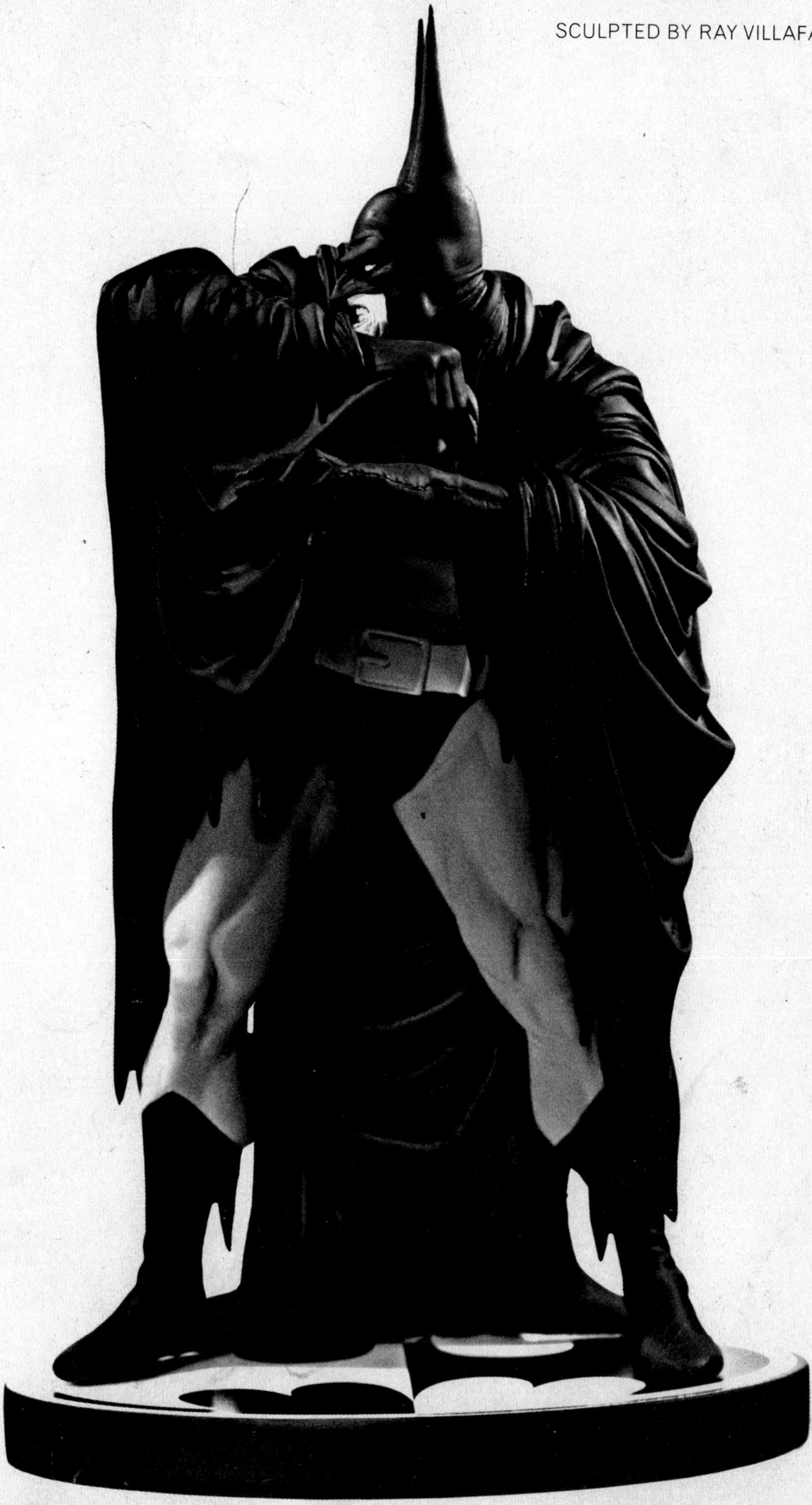

# MATT **WAGNER**

SCULPTED BY PAUL HARDING

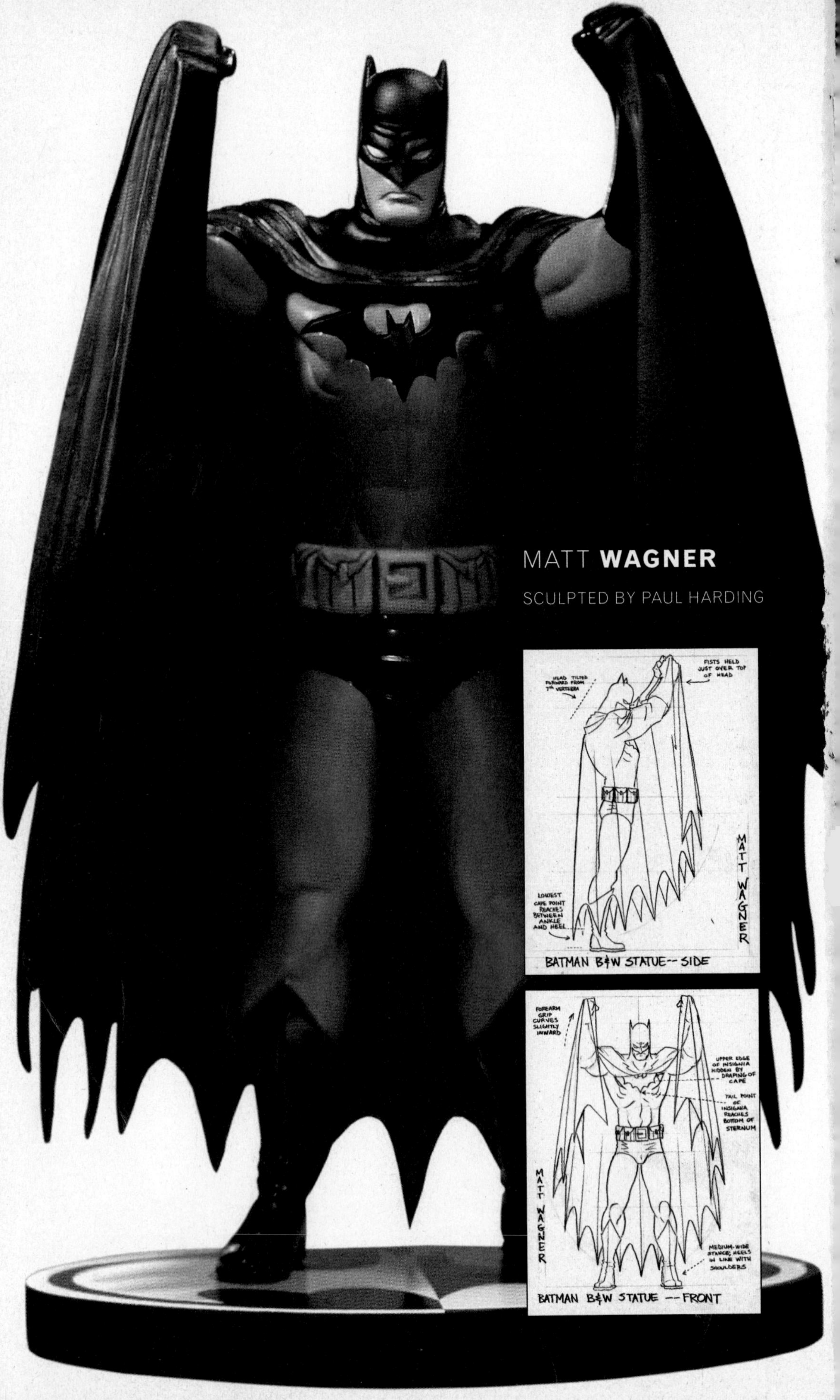
HEAD TILTED FORWARD FROM 7th VERTEBRA
FISTS HELD JUST OVER TOP OF HEAD
LOWEST CAPE POINT REACHES BETWEEN ANKLE AND HEEL
MATT WAGNER
BATMAN B&W STATUE-- SIDE
FOREARM GRIP CURVES SLIGHTLY INWARD
UPPER EDGE OF INSIGNIA HIDDEN BY DRAPING OF CAPE
TAIL POINT OF INSIGNIA REACHES BOTTOM OF STERNUM
MEDIUM-WIDE STANCE; HEELS IN LINE WITH SHOULDERS
MATT WAGNER
BATMAN B&W STATUE --FRONT